The Binding of Isaac, Religious Murders, & Kabbalah

Seeds of Jewish Extremism and Alienation?

LIPPMAN BODOFF

DEVORA
PUBLISHING
JERUSALEM ◆ NEW YORK

The Binding of Isaac, Religious Murders, and Kabbalah:
Seeds of Jewish Extremism and Alienation?

Published by DEVORA PUBLISHING COMPANY

Text Copyright © 2005 Lippman Bodoff
Editor: Elise Teitelbaum

Cover and Inside Design: David Yaphe

Cloth ISBN: 1-932687-52-1
Paper ISBN: 1-932687-53-X

Email: publisher@devorapublishing.com
Web Site: www.devorapublishing.com

Printed in Israel

Dedicated To The Memory Of

My Beloved Father
ABRAHAM BODOFF
(1901–1989)

אברהם שמחה בן יום טוב לפמן

My Beloved Mother
TYBEE BODOFF
(1904–1974)

טובה בת יעקב

My Beloved Brother
LIONEL BODOFF
(1934–1977)

אריה לייב בן אברהם שמחה

My Beloved Daughter
SARA HANNAH BODOFF
(1958–1970)

שרה חנה בת יום טוב לפמן

תהיינה נפשותיהם צרורות בצרור החיים
May their souls be bound in the Bond of Eternal Life

Acknowledgements

The author wishes to acknowledge the encouragement, in so many ways, of Chancellor Emanuel Rackman, of Bar-Ilan University, of my work and the need for its publication, and the assistance over many years of a number of persons, in the research and preparation of these articles: Yisrael Dubitsky, Reference and Public Services Librarian of The Jewish Theological Seminary of America, for his research and copying assistance; Professor Joseph Dan, for his advice and suggestions, especially on the history of Jewish mysticism and martyrdom; Professor Jose Faur, for his willingness to share with me his ideas and numerous articles relevant to my work on Jewish mysticism and related subjects, and to spend numerous hours with me discussing these subjects with me; Professor Haym Soloveitchik, for sharing his ideas with me on medieval Jewish martyrdoms, and his respectful consideration of my own, often differing ideas; the many rabbinic and academic scholars, and my many friends, for their continuing encouragement of my work despite being on my unsolicited "mailing list;" Maxine Gottlieb, for her invaluable and patient typing expertise and output despite my numerous draft changes and impossible handwriting; for the same yeoman work by Julie Weissman (aka "The Final Word"); Elise Teitelbaum, for her patient, incisive and insightful editing of my manuscript; David Yaphe for his final book design to ensure that the book would be attractive and easily readable for all; the continuing advice and encouragement of Rabbi Alan Yuter; the advice and encouragement of Rabbi Jordan Yasgur on my paper on innovation in Jewish liturgical music; the inspiring scholarly graduate courses I was privileged to take with Professors Gershon Shaked, David Roskies, David Ruderman, Joseph Hacker, Joseph Kaplan, Shaye J. D. Cohen, Benjamin Gampel; Yosef Hayim Yerushalmi, and Michael Stanislawski; my good friend and advisor, Professor Ari Zivotofsky; my "cousin-in-law," Jeffrey Green, for being such a wise, willing, and creative listener to so many of my ideas during my annual trips to Israel; Henry Siegman, who, as Executive Director of the American Jewish Congress, gave me the opportunity of a lifetime to serve as Assistant and later Associate Editor of the Congress' scholarly journal, *Judaism,* and to work with so many eminent scholars in that capacity; my beloved wife, Meri, for her daily encouragement, frequent — and always sound — advice, and for undertaking the difficult and always fruitful effort of proofreading so much of my work; and the many others who I undoubtedly have omitted who may wish to share in some way in my good fortune for the privilege accorded to me by Devora Publishing in publishing my work.

Permissions

The articles in this book are updated and revised versions of articles published originally in the journals listed below, and, to the extent required, are published here with the permission of the publications in which they originally appeared. They are listed chronologically, by journal.

—— 1 ——

"Was Yehudah Halevi Racist?" (1989);

"I.B. Singer and His Predecessors" (1990);

"*Letters to Felice* — Kafka's Quest for Jewish Identity" (1991);

"The Real Test of the *Akedah:* Blind Obedience versus Moral Choice" (1993); and

"Kabbalistic Feminism in Agnon's *Betrothed*" (1993)
    Published in *Judaism* by the American Jewish Congress
    (1989–1993)

—— 2 ——

"Secular Humanism and Creation Science in the Public Schools," published in *The Jewish Spectator* (1989)

—— 3 ——

"God Tests Abraham — Abraham Tests God," published in *Bible Review* (1993) and in the book *Abraham and Family** (2000) by the Biblical Archeology Society

*Published under the title "Who's Testing Whom: Was Abraham Really Ready to Kill His Son?"

—— 4 ——

Der Nister's "Under a Fence," *Yiddish* (1991)

—— 5 ——

"Music for Jewish Liturgy: Art for Whose Sake?" and "A Song in Every Psalm" (a review), published in *The Journal of Synagogue Music* (1987)

—— 6 ——

"Firing off a Jewish Canon," Review Essay of Ruth Wisse, *The Modern Jewish Canon,* reprinted from *Shofar* (Fall 2001), by permission of University of Nebraska Press. © 2001 by the University of Nebraska Press.

—— 7 ——

"Jewish Mysticism: Medieval Roots, Contemporary Dangers and Prospective Challenges," published in the *Edah Journal*, 3:1, Tevet 5763 (2003).

—— 8 ——

"The Tragedy of Jephthah," reprinted from *The Jewish Bible Quarterly* (2000), P.O.B. 29002, Jerusalem, Israel www. jewishbible.org.

—— 9 ——

"Fear and Awe: May Man Bring Song to Prayer?" *Tradition* (1987), and "Innovation in Jewish Music" *Tradition* (1988), with thanks to the Editors of *Tradition* and the Rabbinical Council of America for their permission to reprint these articles.

—— 10 ——

"The Promise of Canaan to Abraham's Seed," *Midstream* (1997)

"The Court Jew in the Modern World," *Midstream* (1997)

"Religious Murders: Weeds in the Garden of Jewish Tradition?" *Midstream* (1998)

"Science and Religion: Still Separate Worlds?" *Midstream* (1998)

"The Message of the Prophet Elisha" *Midstream* (1999)

"Rabbi Meir and His Wife, Beruriah — 'Till Death Do Us Part,'" *Midstream* (1999)

"The Binding of Isaac: Religious Paradoxes, Permutations and Problems," *Midstream* (2001)

"Challenging Lubavitch's New Messianic Claims," Review Essay of David Berger's *The Rebbe, The Messiah, and the Scandal of Orthodox Indifference, Midstream* (2001)

"Thoughts on Reading the *Akedah* Again," *Midstream* (2002)

"Hellenism vs. Hebraism on the Inevitability of Tragedy: Studying the Cain and Joseph Stories," *Midstream* (2002).

"The Tower of Babel: From Destruction to Dispersion," *Midstream* (2003)

"Genesis 9:12–17: 'Look to the Rainbow' — So Why Did the Sages Say 'Don't Look?'" *Midstream* (2003).

"Preparing for the *Akedah*: The Strange Case of the Two Missing Witnesses," *Midstream* (2005).

—— 11 ——

"Ezekiel 20:25–26 — Did God Ever Command the Sacrifice of Israel's Firstborn Sons?" *B.D.D.* (2000)

Table of Contents

Chapter 4: Mysticism

Chapter 5: Literature

Chapter 6: Science

Chapter 7: Music

General Introduction

The overall theme of this book is a simple proposition. Judaism was transformed in the last millennium. The Jewish people, sovereign in its own land, had the ability and incentive to produce a democratic,[1] rationalistic, creative, and productive culture. It did so until the destruction of the Second Temple by the Romans in 70 C.E., the failed Bar Kokhba rebellion of 132 C.E. and, in the 4th century, the victory of Christianity as the official religion of the Roman Empire and the claimed successor to Judaism in the world, from the Middle East to the Atlantic Ocean.

Thereafter, Jews spread throughout Europe, and the rabbinic elite that remained in the Middle East created — in the *Mishnah*, the *Gemarah* and Gaonic codifications and responsa — a portable Judaism based on the synagogue instead of the Temple, and a detailed legal system which was developed in Babylonia (up to the end of the 11th century) and in Palestine (up to the 4th century) to permit Jews to preserve their religious life in whatever land they resided.

At the end of the 11th century Pope Urban II galvanized the growing power and militancy of Christian Europe to undo the Moslem capture of Jerusalem. The unruly, uncontrolled armies of the First Crusade that resulted vented their conversionist emotions first on the Jews they encountered in 1096 in Germany, where the Crusaders went on a rampage against the Jewish population of the Rhineland. The Jews, relying strongly on the tradition that Abraham eagerly bound Isaac on the altar for sacrificial slaughter at God's command, asserted their continuing worth as God's chosen people by killing their children and themselves. Their goal was a final Divine vengeance on their enemies and an end to history, in which God, for some reason, had chosen to give worldly victory to Christianity over Judaism and Islam. This is the way the Chronicles of the martyrdoms, written from c. 1100 to 1200, after the Crusaders conquered Jerusalem, depicted the state of mind of the martyrs.

I believe we can trace the beginning of the acceptance, when proposed by pious Jews, of "strange fires" in Jewish practices, to the 12th and 13th century Talmudic commentators, the *Tosafist* sages, who failed to criticize the suicides and murders — despite their being contrary even to the *Tosafists'* expanded doctrine of permitted martyrdom — on the apparent ground that pious German Jews could do no wrong. This paved the way, I believe, for the ease and speed with which the "strange fires" of kabbalah merged with the legitimate ideas, practices and traditions of medieval Judaism, and preeminently so within three centuries.

The combination, in succeeding centuries, of exile, apparent historical religious defeat, continued increase in Christian power, persecutions, and pressures to convert — spearheaded during the 13th century by the zeal and animosity of the Franciscan and Dominican friars — caused Jewry to turn inward. Stimulated by the emergence of kabbalah, it withdrew from the Gentile world, concentrated on its own holiness, and became ascetic and mystical in its worldview and culture. Instead of bringing Heaven into the world, it sought to bring its world to Heaven by ecstatic rites of mystical union (*unio mystica*), theurgy, and an obsessive desire to see, understand, and describe God and the Divine processes and powers.

There ensued a battle between those who followed the rational, philosophic system of Maimonides and the new kabbalists who, during the 13th century, organized a strong rabbinic opposition to the Maimonideans. The "Maimonidean Controversy" lasted on and off about 100 years. Gradually, however, with the decline of Moslem rule in Europe, Christian ascendancy to political and religious power there, and expulsion of the Jews from Spain in 1492, the resulting trauma caused a retreat of Maimonidean rationalism. By the end of the 16th century, the mystical kabbalistic system of Isaac Luria, its ideas and practices, gained ascendancy among European Jewry as the touchstone of Jewish piety and thought. Jewish history was now seen in mythical rather than historical terms.[2]

By this time, the individualist Protestant Revolution overthrew the hierarchical Catholic European hegemony, and the medieval Christian world began to make major strides in science, medicine, astronomy, and other areas of scientific and technological progress, including instruments of measurement that made these advances possible.

Before civic emancipation came to European Jewry in the late 18th and 19th centuries, Jews had no option but to adhere to rabbinic rule of the Jewish community. Its religious rigidities and mystical rites, its magic and superstitious practices, its narrow interests and pilpul-driven religious studies could not help but produce internal pressures for reform. The Jewish Enlightenment movement (*haskalah*) sought to introduce, in modest ways, elements of modernity into the Jewish outlook and its educational and religious practices. The backlash from a newly united front of kabbalistic Hasidism and their erstwhile opponents, the Mitnagdim, helped thwart any significant success of the *haskalah*. But with the Jewish Emancipation, Jews gained new options — to leave the Jewish community entirely, or to adopt major religious reforms far beyond those contemplated by the *haskalah*. What was once simply a single Jewish community now splintered into Orthodox, ultra- (or *haredi*) Orthodox, Reform, Conservative, and, more recently, Modern Orthodox.

From a cultural standpoint, this period witnessed a new historiography by such pioneers as Heinrich Graetz and Simon Dubnov. A new, history-oriented literature documented the competing pulls on rationalist Jews to find a Jewish identity that could simultaneously embrace the exploding cultural advances in the Christian world and gain acceptance as Jews by a still hostile Gentile world.

Perhaps the first to experience this challenging opportunity were

13

the pre-Emancipation "Court Jews," who tried to serve Christian nobility while remaining loyal to the Jewish community subservient to that nobility. Formal Jewish emancipation simply broadened this opportunity and the struggle for a more comprehensive Jewish identity to millions more Jews who now had the right to be Jewish (or not) and to more fully participate in new world developments in economics, politics, and science. Throughout this pre-modern and early modern period, the ultra-Orthodox Hasidic and kabbalah-influenced Orthodox continued to oppose efforts by Orthodox rabbis and groups who sought to find a way to accommodate valuable elements of modernity with Jewish law. The essence of the Maimonidean struggle between rationalism and mysticism in Judaism inevitably continued during this period.

That struggle continues to this day. But the post-Holocaust rise of Orthodoxy in Israel and the United States has created new divisions. The *haredi* continue to look askance at engagement with the Gentile world and its activities, and even engagement with those in the Jewish world who do not adhere to the traditional, narrow focus of study and activity that has prevailed since the end of the 16th century. The world of what is now called *madda*, or — in Talmudic parlance — *hokhmah*, is considered by the *haredi* (including Hasidic sects) as at best a distraction and at worst a temptation to a watered down or abandoned religious life. The recent Modern Orthodox movement favors study, holiness in religious observance, and openness to participation in human ethical, moral and material progress.

Madda, hokhmah, or wisdom, which may be found among all the nations, to which Jewry should contribute, and from which it can benefit, uses a different methodology or approach to its subject compared to holiness. *Madda* is based on empirical evidence, and seeks improvement through change in the interests of human progress. Holiness is based on the notion of unchanging truths and tradition as the basis of religious piety, practice and purity of thought, in relationships with man and God. The tension between *madda* and holiness can produce dangerous friction or beneficial creativity.

Those wary of the effects of friction — who approach the fact of these two approaches to two different areas of knowledge with fear — will seek to abandon one or the other in order to protect the area they consider primary. Classical Judaism was open to both. Current Orthodoxy, except for the Modern Orthodox, sees no need for both approaches and is not prepared to risk the effects of friction for any benefit. Moreover, they have fought attempts by other Orthodox Jews to incorporate the view of Classical Judaism that a complete religious life includes Torah and *hokhmah*.[3] The classical prophetic message for Jewish behavior in exile — which would seem to apply also to Israel among the nations today — was pronounced by Jeremiah at the time of Israel's First Exile (c. 586 B.C.E.):

> Thus said the Lord of Hosts, the God of Israel, to the whole community which I exiled from Jerusalem to Babylon: Build houses and live in them, plant gardens and eat their fruit. Take wives and beget sons and daughters; take wives for your sons and give your daughters to husbands, that they may bear sons and daughters. Multiply there; do not [let your numbers] decrease, and seek the welfare of the [place] to which I have exiled you, and pray to the Lord in its behalf (Jer. 29:4–7).[4]

"Seeking the welfare" of non-Jews clearly involves activities of *hokhmah*. The world historian William H. McNeill has concluded that Western Europe's inheritance from Judaism, Christianity and Greco-Roman culture was the engine that created Western Civilization.

> This inheritance was shot through with contrariety. Europeans confronted unresolved and irresolvable tensions between the primacy of the territorial state as the "natural" unit of human society and the claim of the Church [i.e., religion] to govern human souls;

tensions between faith and reason, each claiming to be the preeminent path to truth; tensions between naturalism and metaphysical symbolism. [These] polar antitheses were built into the very fundament of European society and have never been either escaped or permanently resolved.

Coming late to the scene, and inheriting such incompatibles, the high civilization of the Far West has not yet come to rest but has revolutionized itself three times over. No other civilized society has ever approached such restless instability, nor exerted such drastic influence upon its followers all round the world. In this lies the true uniqueness of Western civilization.[5]

These kinds of tensions — since the radical break with Jewish tradition and the rise of Jewish mysticism in the centuries since 1096, after the martyrdoms of the First Crusade — have remained a continuing source of extremism and gridlock, instead of creativity, in Jewish history for the last thousand years, except for certain, relatively short periods of generally peaceful autonomy. The primary cause was that the national-political element of Judaism, in the form of its own territory and state, has been absent for virtually that entire period — in contrast to the national-political element of Christianity in Europe, where church and national power, religion and reason, have battled and had to compromise on more even terms. In the last century and in Israel today — indeed, since 1948 and even earlier with the development of the *yishuv* — we have seen major strides in the development of *madda*, and an outpouring of Jewish creativity. But the heritage of Jewish insularity is heavy and has created a serious impediment to the national state serving as a strong balance to religious interests and ideas. There is some tolerance, but certainly not the mutual appreciation and cultural symbiosis such as the Jews enjoyed in "Golden Age" Spain, unique in Jewish *galut* experience.

Most of the articles in this collection are devoted to attempts by Jews in every place and time to find an identity and a mission, in a changing world, that can embrace wisdom as well as holiness, nationhood and religion, in all their required and beneficial aspects. This struggle has been made more difficult by the preeminent power and influence in Jewish life of those religious elements described by McNeill that relate to holiness, but only weakly, if at all, to wisdom.

If Jews and Judaism are to survive and thrive, be a light unto the nations, and live in a way that sanctifies God's name, I believe they must accept the tensions that contribute to Jewish creativity — confident that, with new opportunity to live in their own state, they will harness those tensions seeking wisdom and holiness to achieve a new creativity in all aspects of *hokhmah,* while retaining a guiding, proud, Jewish religious identity.

Despite the language in some articles that are directed at the emerging "Modern Orthodox" movement, I believe this book will be of interest to all Jews, as well as non-Jews, who are interested in Judaism and Jewry as a religion, a culture, and a nationality.

The essays in this book touch upon major points of this historical highway traversed by Judaism over the last two thousand years. The *Akedah,* as the "Binding of Isaac" is known in Hebrew, as it was intended to condemn religious sacrifice, and as it was transformed primarily to explain and justify the trials and travails of Jews after the destruction of the Temple, is the subject of Chapter 1.[6]

Chapter 2, "Exegesis," provides examples of the still relevant Biblical stories that can and should serve as a unifying cultural element for all Jews, religious and secular. Unfortunately, it seems to be the case that our "best and brightest" students generally receive little education in the Jewish Bible, consisting of the Torah, or Pentateuch, the Prophets and the "Writings" (generally described with the Hebrew acronym *Tanakh*); they move quickly to either Talmudic or secular studies.

Chapter 3, "Jewish History," discusses the dangerous precedents set for Jews by misreading the *Akedah* as a portrait of Abraham eager to kill Isaac at God's command — despite God's earlier universal command to humanity in the Noahide Laws against human sacrifice or other murders — and the misapplication of that misreading at Masada, and again during the First Crusade. Chapter 3 also introduces the early modern tension experienced by the Court Jews, between being Jewish and engaging with the non-Jewish world. Finally it introduces the idea that Jewish destiny, even God's promises to permanently return the Jewish people to their land, can be forfeited, at least for long periods of time, by Jewry's quietism, its failure to pursue an active program of nationalism — looking toward a Jewish return to its own land and political sovereignty — and to make its case to the world for a role in history by achievements that advance world moral, political and material progress.

Chapter 4 is the pivot of this book, as it describes in detail how Judaism developed from its rational, cultural, classical interest in every aspect of God's creation and human activity to its current, largely insular, rigid and kabbalistically oriented Orthodoxy, in which holiness, religious greatness and political wisdom — and even Divine miracles and magic — are claimed by certain sages and ascribed to them by their followers,[7] thereby relieving the latter of their responsibility, as in Classical Judaism, to become involved in the legal and ethical texts of Judaism and the worthwhile knowledge of the Gentile world. In brief, Orthodoxy today is mystical in outlook, with little interest in *hokhmah*, general knowledge and wisdom, even as to Jewish nationalism in its land. From this standpoint, only the Modern Orthodox can be considered as carrying on the Classical Biblical and Rabbinic Judaism of the first millennium.

Perhaps an outstanding illustration of this gulf within Orthodoxy today is the Hasidic-kabbalistic view ascribing messianic and even (by some) Divine attributes to the recently-deceased Lubavitcher Rebbe. David Berger is perhaps the only Orthodox scholar to protest this development and to draw attention to the lack of any significant support for his concerns, even by the Orthodox community — which, as shown above, is not surprising.[8]

Chapter 5 discusses how Jewish literature arose as a modern reaction to the challenge of the European Enlightenment and Jewish Emancipation in the 18th to 19th centuries. It seeks to describe the difficulty of developing a Jewish identity — in exile and even in the Land of Israel — that embraces Jewish religion and world wisdom, especially in anti-religious or anti-Semitic environments. This literature also sought to describe how important it is for Jews to take the first step in addressing the concerns of, hopefully, enlightened Gentiles who view Jews in their midst as potentially good, valuable and contributing citizens but (until recently) backward and uncreative.[9] A major exception here were the effective business contributions by Sephardi exiles (from Spain and Portugal) who settled in port cities like Amsterdam, London, Hamburg, and other similar locales.[10]

This new Jewish literature sought to encourage introduction of some modern elements into Jewish education, the wider use of Hebrew and other modern languages, and emphasized the importance of creativity in the sciences, social sciences and the humanities, not inconsistent with Jewish law. In many ways, it reflected the underlying problem faced by the 18th century Court Jew, trying to live in a traditional religious world and a modern secular world at the same time and do justice to both. Classical Judaism, Maimonidean Judaism, and Modern Orthodoxy all take the position that this is necessary and possible. The prevalent Orthodox position is that it is neither, and disciplines and studies designed to prove otherwise are a waste of time, a distraction from sacred study, and a temptation to abandon Judaism altogether.

Chapter 6 discusses the current debate between religious and secular viewpoints, within the Judeo-Christian ambit, on the proper relationship between "Church" (religion) and State, and between scientific and religious beliefs. Secular Jews strongly believe that there must be separation in both areas: between Church and State, and between religion and science. Orthodox Jews are divided: *Haredi* Orthodox want financial support from the State, and no interference. Modern Orthodox favor some support and some standards in all government supported educational institutions. In the religion-science debate, secular Jews see a vast, unbridgeable, permanent gulf. *Haredi* Jews see the same gulf, but they do not accept scientific evidence that questions or impugns any traditional religious beliefs and ideas. Modern Orthodox are able to see convergence and consistency between science and religion. They posit that religion must be based on truth. So must science. Each must evolve as the other evolves in terms of their ideas, where possible, and their relationship to each other.

Unfortunately, as in the case of literature, most Jewish achievements in science have come from disaffected, alienated and secular Jews, and not from the religiously observant. Indeed, in the scientific field, it is primarily Christian scientists who have led the way in publicly demonstrating in recent years that the materialistic understandings of creation of the universe and the evolution of Earth's living creatures are scientifically flawed theories in light of the latest scientific evidence, and these majestic, awesome developments are more rationally explained by a purposeful guiding force. It is unfortunate, but not surprising, that religious Jews have not played a leading role in this new debate. It is also more likely to find non-religious Jewish organizations fighting recent trends in the public schools to treat materialist "explanations" of creation and evolution as theories, not proven facts. This hardly is conducive to better relationships, at the important personal and local level, between Jews and their Gentile neighbors, especially when Jews seek their favor and support on other issues. Worse, it is simply unseemly for non-scientists to take a Jewish position on scientific subjects on which scientific debates are now in progress.

Chapter 7 deals with Jewish music, primarily liturgical. Here we find a pattern of battles between rabbis and lay religious scholars, on the one hand, and those musically endowed to lead prayer services, on the other. The issue has been drawn not only over length of service, excessive liturgical repetitions and musical embellishments, but also with regard to innovations in the chants and melodies used. Here, too, we find what

I believe is a conflict between current, prevailing Orthodox views, and Jewish history. The prevailing view is that fixed traditions must not be breached. In fact, the existing chant modes were all, at one time, innovations based on the music of other peoples in various geographic areas. Indeed, it is hard to believe that the Levites, the original preceptors of the liturgy in Temple times, did not engage in the composition of new chants and melodies for the Israelites, because the first chants and melodies, so far as we know, were also composed and, logically, this did not justify any view that no further development should be allowed. In fact, new music was composed by some of the Talmudic Sages.

I wish to conclude by commenting on the message of the structure of this book. The *Akedah* (Binding of Isaac) chapter, the Exegesis chapter and the Mysticism chapter tell how classical Judaism, designed to guide Jews in every facet of an active, and interactive, life in this world, was transformed by the exilic oppression under a powerful and hostile European Christianity into an insular, withdrawn, ascetic, ecstatic, magical and mystical culture.

As a result, and as is reflected by what is contained and not contained in the succeeding chapters involving Jewish history, literature (nonsacred), science, and music, not much happened in Jewry in these areas until the European Enlightenment and Jewish Emancipation.[11] Virtually no writing of history took place, despite Moses's injunction to the Israelites to remember the past and learn from it (*Deut* 32:7), and despite the message of the stories in the Torah that people and peoples can learn from the past, correct what they have done wrong, redeem themselves, and progress in all ways in their lives toward a better future each day. The Talmud is based on just such an idea: How to live, to treat family, friends, enemies, strangers, and nature, and move forward. Exile will not last forever — God promised that — but it probably will not end tomorrow. Here is a formula for life, and follow it, say the Sages, along with Jeremiah's injunction (Jer. 29:4–7) to seek the welfare of the people where your exilic wanderings may take you.

There is little writing of history (historiography) because exilic Jewry starts out by living in relative peace with uninterested if not uncaring neighbors, followed by a second millennium of living under the hate, hostility, and religious power of a supremacist, conversionist religion, and a cycle of catastrophes which — notwithstanding the opinion of the eminent historian, Salo Baron, that Jewish history was less lachrymose than most thought[12] — left indelible memories of fear and unbearable vulnerability between catastrophes, small and large, that seemed to have no reason to end.

This history of Jewish history writing, or historiography, is therefore very brief, and covered succinctly in a brilliant, short book, *Zakhor*, by the historian Yosef Hayim Yerushalmi, must reading for every Jew, religious or secular. There was Josephus's historical writings; the anonymous 10th century rewrite of that history in *Yosippon*; some histories of Jewish halakhic development; and, for a brief moment, especially during the 16th century, primarily by Jewish scholars influenced by Sephardi culture, under the cloud of the 1492 expulsion and the light of the Italian Renaissance, which ends as abruptly as it begins. The writing of real history in the modern sense of the term is not resumed again for some two centuries, as part of the Jewish Enlightenment and Emancipation.[13]

We find the same situation in (fiction) literature. Besides rabbinic parables, and a few important memoirs (which are not fiction!), we don't find Jewish fiction until the *haskalah*, the 18th century Jewish Enlightenment, burst forth with fictional satire, irony, and similarly disguised and not so disguised criticism of Jewish culture in its superstitious insularness, and lack of a comprehensive education even in Jewish areas, like the Hebrew language, Jewish history, not to mention the sciences, or even music — which was largely uncomposed folk melodies and styles with little regard for creative, aesthetic, meaningful artistry for the liturgy of the Sabbath and holidays.

Very few were trained in these cultural disciplines. There is the poverty of a cloistered, text-focused life; narrow, brief education; and no accumulation of resources on a family, community or national or multi-national level that the "best and the brightest" of Jewish youth — in the rapidly exploding Ashkenazi population of the last four centuries — could rely upon for financial support, and which could provide them the pride and energy to pursue the explosion of knowledge with their individual interests and talents.[14]

As for science, Kabbalistic Jews do not do science; they have no time for it, no interest in it, and no room in their theology or theosophy to study anything but magical and mystical rites and mystical ideas that inoculate them from even considering scientific knowledge produced by others, much less using their minds to help their own people and their national and world community.

In contrast, there is richness in Classical Judaism, a love of life, and a continuing religious interest in making it better, morally and materi-ally, for all, that gradually disappears from the 13th to the end of the 16th century — just when ideas and inventions, science, and medicine, lit-erature and music, begin to explode in the non-Jewish European and American worlds.[15] We were hurt too much, perhaps; I would say very much, enough to explain the cocoon-like response of mysticism — but not enough to explain why the Talmudic Sages responded so differently, so actively, creatively, courageously, to their catastrophe. They not only didn't kill their families and themselves to avoid the temptations and pres-sures of joining their new rulers, political and religious. They created a for-mula for continued life, engagement with the world, and creativity. Rabbi Shimon bar Yohai may have looked down on Roman bridge-building proclivities. But the Talmud in reporting the story sounds impressed, as if to say — if we rely only on the Romans to build our bridges, what kind of a nation are we, or can we be?[16] There is *hokhmah* among the nations that is worthy of our emulation, to use it and to contribute to it.

And thus, we return to where we started, with the history of the *Akedah*, which portends, in its transformed form, the elevation of the glory of self-sacrifice, suicide and murder, rather than the exercise of our moral strength and resistance to calls to do wrong from any source, or to limit our interests and efforts, no matter how holy or respectable. As we know from *Genesis*, the first book of the Bible, Abraham responded to every apparent injustice to which he became privy, with protest, action, and, at least, silent prayer.[17] Then we move to the creative insights of Biblical exegesis, interpretation and commentary. Then we move to tragedy — *galut*, exile, and the sudden, explosive power of the religious revolution of Christianity, that treats Jews not as necessary witnesses to Christian authenticity, but as an evil, stubborn threat to Christianity's mission of world conversion and religious hegemony, and the centuries-long, problematic Jewish response to this unfortunate history. It is time to reconsider some of these responses. That is the issue I have tried to raise.

The book ends on a note of hope, not despair, because in studying our history — what we were, what we became, and what we are, lies the possibility of understanding and rebirth — even, perhaps, redemption.[18]

NOTES

1 *Tolerance, Dissent, and Democracy*, Moshe Sokol, ed. (Northvale, N.J.: Jason Aronson, Inc., 2002).

2 Yosef Hayim Yerushalmi, *Zakhor* (Seattle: University of Washington Press, 1982), pp. 73-5.

3 See generally, *Judaism's Encounter With Other Cultures*, Jacob J. Schacter, ed. (Northvale, New Jersey: Jason Aronson, Inc., 1997), and *Engaging Modernity*, Moshe Z. Sokol, ed. (Northvale, New Jersey: Jason Aronson Inc. 1997), esp. pp. 3-56.

4 See *The Prophets* (Phila: Jewish Publication Society, 1978); a similar meaning is provided in *Jeremiah* (Jerusalem: Mossad Harav Kook, 1983) (Hebrew), "work for the peace of the city and its welfare" (my translation), citing *Deut.* 23: 7 for similar usage.

5 Quotations are from *The Rise of the West* (Chicago: University of Chicago Press, 1962), Chapter IX, Section C and Section F, Part 1, Introductory.

6 Ibid, pp. 38-9.

7 See, e.g., Lawrence Kaplan, "*Daas Torah*: A Modern Conception of Rabbinic Authority," *Rabbinic Authority and Personal Autonomy*, Moshe Z. Sokol, ed. (Northvale, N.J.: Jason Aronson Inc., 1992), pp. 1-60; Moshe Idel, *Hasidism* (Albany: State University of New York Press, 1995), chapters 4-6.

As mentioned earlier in this Introduction, manifestation of a special regard for the problematic actions of the pious and learned occurred with the suicides and murders committed by the 1096 martyrs during the First Crusade. An important purpose of this chapter is to set the record straight on what I believe is a major error of this type by a number of Jewish historians who have sought to *justify* those acts and their assumed approval by later sages, the *Tosafists*, and not just explain them as caused by extreme mental duress — an explanation I could accept, if it were offered. But these new justifications were not even offered by the *Tosafists* when they approved martyrdoms by suicide, *but solely when based on fear of torture leading to conversion*; see, e.g., B.A.Z. 18a; and Haym Soloveitchik, "Halakhah, Hermeneutics, and Martyrdom," Part I, *JQR* (Winter 2004): 79, n. 6., and *passim*, and Part II of that article, *JQR* (Winter 2004): 79, n. 72 and *passim*. Moreover, I still do not understand on what basis these historians (including Soloveitchik) believe that the *Tosafists* approved the 1096 martyrdoms when, in fact, their radical new definition of permitted martyrdom by suicide (not murder) did not apply to the only evidence we are aware of that the *Tosafists* had before them — the Chronicles of the 1096 martyrdoms. They were written just a few decades later by Rhineland Jews who were presumably eager to present the best case they could as to the events and their justifications in the minds of the martyrs, which were based on zeal, not fear.

8   David Berger, *The Rebbe, The Messiah, and the Scandal of Orthodox Indifference* (London: The Littman Library of Jewish Civilization, 2001).

9   See, e.g., Ruth R. Wisse, *The Modern Jewish Canon* (New York: The Free Press, 2000); and Gershon Shaked, *The Shadows Within* (Philadelphia: Jewish Publication Society, 1987).

10 *Port Jews*, David Cesarini, ed. (Portland, Or.: Frank Cass, 2002). The struggle of Orthodox women in this area is discussed in Steven G. Kellman, "Storytelling as Both Sacred and Sacrilegious," *Forward*, February 18, 2005, p. 8.

11 The Mysticism chapter describes how Lurianic kabbalah became preeminent in Jewish piety and thought by the end of the 16th century; Yerushalmi, *Zakhor*, pp. 73-4. From that point on, until the Enlightenment and Jewish Emancipation in the 18th and 19th centuries, Judaism generally looked inward, with little engagement with the outside world. The contrast between that period and what followed is illustrated by comparing the scope of the papers in *Jewish Thought in the Sixteenth Century*, Bernard Dov Cooperman, ed. (Cambridge: University of Harvard Press, 1983) and *Jewish Thought in the Seventeenth Century*, Isadore Twersky and Bernard Septimus, eds. (Cambridge: Harvard University Press, 1987). Manasseh ben Israel, of Amsterdam, in the latter half of the 17th century, writing under the influence of Sephardi culture, did major work in engaging in practical messianic activity with the Gentile world to help collect Jews from far flung inhospitable, exilic locations, leading, *inter alia*, to the readmission by Cromwell of Jews to England on an informal basis; H. H. Ben-Sasson, "The Middle Ages," *A History of the Jewish People* (Cambridge: Harvard University Press, 1976), pp. 653-4. The 17th century also witnessed renewed massacres of the Jews in Eastern Poland, and the messianic eruption of the Sabbatean movement led by Shabbetai Zvi, which was, as Scholem describes it, directly influenced by Lurianic kabbalah, especially when Shabbetai Zvi's apostasy was defended as a necessary engagement with the *klippot*, the material vessels that were the locus of the remnant of evil that resulted from the Divine process of Creation; see, e.g., Ben-Sasson, ibid., pp. 701-7.

12 Yerushalmi, *Zakhor*, p. 132, n. 31.

13 Ibid, *passim*.

14 The Council of Four Lands (1580-1764) was largely a forum for Jews in the com-

munities of Eastern Europe to consider and decide judicial and legislative matters of common concern including the collection of taxes for the support of *yeshivot* and their students, and other community needs; Ben-Sasson, "The Medieval Period," p. 62-83.

15 Daniel J. Boorstin, *The Discoverers* (New York: Random House, 1983), p. 10, and *passim*.

16 B. *Shabb.* 33b.

17 B. *Ta'anit* 15a, and J. *Ta'anit* 2:4 and commentaries thereon.

18 As this book is going to press, I have become acquainted with a major defense of the importance of the study of general culture as a "civilizing and ennobling" force in Judaism by one of the leading figures in Modern Orthodox circles, Rav Aharon Lichtenstein, in the just published collection of his English language essays, *Leaves of Faith: The World of Jewish Learning* and *Leaves of Faith: The World of Jewish Living*, 2 vols. (Jersey City, New Jersey: KTAV Publishing House, 2003-4); see also David Singer's review, "For Torah and Culture," *First Things* (May 2005): 27-32.

1

The Binding of Isaac
(in Hebrew, *the Akedah,* or "The Binding")

It is not surprising, in the face of two thousand years of persecution and oppression — political, religious, economic, and social — that Jews have seen the *Akedah* as a kind of Divine sign or justification for voluntarily or involuntarily, but proudly and even joyously, accepting suffering as a badge of chosenness, a reason to passively let what was seen as God's will prevail.

In the last 50 years, however, especially since the establishment of the State of Israel, Jews have the right, and good reason, to examine this aspect of their tradition in light of the evident possibility that what seemed to be God's will — the continuing persecution and even destruction of Jews — may not be God's will at all. It is in this spirit that, about 20 years ago, I began to think about the *Akedah* differently. Numerous articles have been written on the *Akedah*. The need is plain. The text in *Genesis* 22 leaves the moral mind deeply troubled.

Clearly, Abraham had a strong sense of morality, of justice, of the sanctity of human life, long before the *Akedah*. Abraham was surely aware of the tradition, embodying the Divine Noahide Laws, against killing innocents. Abraham expected that the God who represented these values, whom he accepted as his God, would avoid or prevent the killing of innocents — as He earlier had assured Abraham he would before the destruction of Sodom and the banishment of Hagar and Ishmael. So how do we begin to explain, or conceive of, an Abraham at the *Akedah* rushing off, without doubt or question, to obey a Divine command to sacrifice Isaac?

The essays in this chapter represent the development of my thinking on this question. Each essay either adds to the reasoning of my approach, or adds nuance to that approach, and — in one case in particular — adds an argument that I believe is conclusive for my theory: from the Talmud, which indicates that Abraham silently prayed to God that Isaac be saved.[1] But wouldn't such a prayer mean that Abraham failed the test as traditionally interpreted — a test requiring unquestioning faith that he correctly understood and was required to carry out God's will? Unless, of course, we accept that the test was a different one: requiring Abraham to go forward with what he understood was asked of him — *with faith that the just and righteous God would answer his prayer* — and that it was Abraham's responsibility to do everything he could in the meantime — in this case, to pray for God's intervention — to prevent a terrible injustice from occurring. This chapter represents my attempt to make the case for what I believe was the original intent, and what should be viewed as the current and proper understanding, of the Binding of Isaac.

....

NOTE

1 I have not seen this point made in any other discussion of the *Akedah*. For this contribution, I am grateful to Rabbi Dr. Ari Zivotofsky of Bar-Ilan University, a good friend — he and his family — of me and my family, for many years.

The Real Test of the *Akedah*:
Blind Obedience Versus Moral Choice

I

Genesis 22:1–19 recounts the story of the binding of Isaac, known as the *Akedah*. The traditional interpretation is that God tested, *nisah* (Gen. 22:1), Abraham by commanding him to slaughter his beloved son, Isaac, on Mount Moriah. Abraham was about to sacrifice the boy on the altar when an angel called out to him to stop, "because now I see that you are a God-fearing person and you would not withhold your son ... from Me" (Gen. 22:12). Thereupon, Abraham looked about and saw a ram, which he sacrificed in Isaac's place, calling the place "where God will be seen." A second angelic voice then swears in God's name to bless Abraham by multiplying his seed (22:17).[1]

In the traditional understanding of this story, God never intended for Abraham to slaughter Isaac, because it was wrong — as we know from the end of the story when Abraham is told to desist. Abraham, on the other hand, out of fear of God, was willing to violate God's moral law against murder,[2] to which Abraham was committed, as we know by virtue of the earlier discussion between Abraham and God about the immorality of killing even ten innocent or righteous people who might live in Sodom and Gomorrah: "*Hashofet kol ha'arez lo ya'asseh mishpat?*" "Will the Ruler of the universe not do justice?" (Gen. 18:25).

The message of the end of the *Akedah* is quite plainly that God does not want even his God-fearing adherents to go so far as to murder in God's name or even at God's command. Implicitly, we are being told, God will never ask for this proof of loyalty or fear of God again. He asked it only of Abraham, the first Jew, the first forefather of the Jewish people, to demonstrate Abraham's boundless fear of God. How far Jews must be willing to go in demonstrating their faith is not to be learned from the *Akedah* but from specific rules promulgated by our Sages over the centuries in interpreting the Torah.[3] Clearly, Abraham is to be emulated for his fear of God, but not for the lengths to which he was willing to go to prove it. (In fact, some later traditions and uses of the *Akedah* "lesson" may be problematic in their zealotry.)[4]

II

Because Abraham is praised for being prepared to do what we may not do, and because God, the source of all morality, asked Abraham to do what no moral person before or since should ever contemplate, and expected Abraham to obey, the *Akedah* has remained one of the most difficult texts in *Tanakh* to understand, justify and transmit to new generations.

In the spirit of *shiv'im panim la-Torah* (the Torah has seventy, i.e., many facets), I would like to suggest the possible existence of a remarkable, coded, counter-message in the *Akedah*, that exists in parallel with the traditional meaning of the text — which has always been accepted but never fully understood. Specifically, I propose, first, that God was testing Abraham's willingness to refuse to commit murder even when commanded by God to do so; second, that Abraham went along with that command with faith that — in the end — he would not be required to do so, and not with the zealous intent to consummate Isaac's murder, although he was prepared, in the end, to resist the command to kill his son if he had to; and third, that Abraham was rewarded for his moral stance, and his faith that God really does not need or want child sacrifice, or any violations of His moral law, to prove man's love or fear of God.

This view of the *Akedah* is consistent with fundamentals of Jewish law and philosophy.

For example, we do not pay attention to heavenly voices or signs on matters of Jewish law;[5] murder is one of the three sins which one should refrain from committing even at the cost of one's own life;[6] the inquiry concerning a false prophet is not simply whether God has spoken to him or her, but whether the prophet commands the violation of Jewish law;[7] and worthy ends never justify anti-halakhic means except when the halakhah itself — through the rule of *hora'at sha-ah* — gives the Sages (and prophets) the authority temporarily to set aside a law when special circumstances threaten the halakhah.[8] Finally, we are supposed to emulate God in our actions, *ma hu, af ata;*[9] thus, "Just as God is compassionate, so you — man — must be compassionate." Similarly, we must emulate our forefathers: "*Ma'asse avot, siman le-banim.*" Yet, one of the quintessential statements of the traditional view of Abraham's greatness at the *Akedah* is found in the *Zikhronot* section of the *musaf* service on *Rosh Hashanah,* where he is described as having "*suppressed* his compassion to do Thy will ...!"[10] (emphasis added). Is this what we should learn?

Some of the more novel interpretations or homiletics of the *Akedah* exacerbate the problematic nature of its traditional interpretation. Ramban and Rashi tell us how morally difficult God made it for Abraham by emphasizing the details of the command.[11] Saadia tells us that the moral of the story is that Jews should be ready to sacrifice their lives for the sanctification of God's name, seemingly overlooking the fact that the traditional interpretation of the *Akedah* requires murder, not to sanctify God's name in the accepted sense of adhering to God's commandments, but in the sense of violating those commandments, including the fundamental precept of "be killed rather than kill another without proper cause."[12] Rambam says that God knew that Abraham would pass the test,[13] which is consistent with Rambam's view of a philosophic, all-knowing God; but this confidence, shared by the Ramban,[14] does nothing to eliminate the problem of Abraham being tested based on his willingness, through faith and fear, to commit one of the three most heinous crimes in Jewish law. Franz Rosenzweig says[15] that we and Abraham cannot and could not understand God's true purpose. Perhaps; but are we to understand that we must suspend our moral judgment when a holy person or a Divine voice, or a prophet says: "Violate the halakhah?" That may be Rosenzweig's Judaism but it is hardly authentic (see Part III). There is an interpretation of the text that says that Abraham misunderstood God, who never intended a real sacrifice.[16] Then what did God intend, and how does Abraham's willingness to slaughter Isaac make Abraham great? There is another interpretation[17] that says that killing one's child was not known to be clearly wrong in Abraham's time, which is strange, given Abraham's concern about killing the righteous in the earlier story of Sodom and Gomorrah. And, if killing was not known to be wrong, in what sense was the Akedah the ultimate test of Abraham's faith? Elie Wiesel suggests that God was perhaps wrong for asking, and Abraham for agreeing — which does nothing to make the text Jewishly palatable; quite the contrary. For one eminent world historian, the Akedah makes "perfect sense" because Abraham's "covenant with God was of such transcendent enormity that it demanded [of Abraham] something more [than animal sacrifice]: a sacrifice of the best loved in the fullest sense ...."[18] But transcendence should involve greater morality, not the greatest immorality.

In my midrashic view of the Akedah, it is a morality tale of Abraham's staunch defense of God's moral law against any temptation — even God's command — to violate it. It established Judaism's unique insight, among ancient religions, cults and cultures, about the dangers of having human beings submit to the orders of individuals who claimed unique access to the wishes of "the gods," or of any God, and who might be forced, through ignorance and fear, to submit to a cultic elite that, by its unique power and authority, could reign unchecked in human affairs and make man a moral slave. Judaism, alone, sought to make man morally free, and, to do so, it had to eliminate societal arrangements in which the majority were forced to accept the word of the few, as revealed only to them, as expressing God's wish, without any limitations or constraints to assure their authenticity and consistency with God's moral design of the world.

The corrective was a religion based on a covenant between God and all of the people, in a revealed text to which all had access and which all could master, and the stipulation (with rare exceptions, discussed in Part III) that no one, claiming to hear God's message directly and privately, could require anyone in the covenantal community to violate the text, as understood by the judges and sages of the people with the authority to interpret and apply that covenantal text. God's word was revealed and written. Its interpretation, by a holy, learned, covenantal community and its leaders, could be oral, but also had to be open. This jurispruden- tial structure assured that no person or elite could misguide the people down paths of immorality in the name of a supernatural power. (It may be significant if, as some believe, the invention of the alphabet [i.e., the original, Semitic one] occurred in Canaan circa the 18th century B.C.E., during Abraham's era, which broke the monopoly on knowledge previ- ously enjoyed by society's ruling elites, allowing literacy to spread to ordi- nary people). Thus, the Bible literally, and openly, commands parents to kill a "rebellious son," but that text has been so hedged about by publicly discussed and developed rabbinic exegesis, that the Talmud categorically states that, in juridical law, such a "rebellious son" never was found to exist.[19] One can imagine the much different results if such a law arose in a religion based on God's private revelations to a holy person.

III

Before examining the *Akedah* text to see if it supports the hidden mi- drashic interpretation that I propose, we need to answer two questions: first, is the traditional view of the Akedah any different from accepting, as God's will, a volcano that kills 10,000 people, including many who, in any halakhic sense, do not deserve to die? Second, aren't true prophets bound to agree to any Divine commands, and aren't all Jews bound to accept such prophetic messages? Aren't all such prophecies, per se, moral and consistent with Torah law?

Both questions can be answered simultaneously. Natural or miraculous acts of God should, indeed, be accepted as God's will without undermining a Jew's faith (Job 40:8), as difficult as this may be because of the event's personal impact or enormity.[20] We accept the acts of the *Dayan Emet* (the Judge of Truth) in this world, when humans are not asked to participate or evaluate God's actions; no halakhic issues are thereby involved. However, when humans are involved, the halakhah takes over, and man must exercise moral responsibility. The traditional view of the *Akedah* raises halakhic difficulties.

There are two issues to be distinguished. The first is: may a prophet object if he is told by God to do something, or told about God's plan to do something, that seems to be inconsistent with God's justice or compassion? The second is: what should Jews, including the prophet, do if instructed in God's name to participate in a violation of God's law?

In the first case, we have a number of examples. Abraham was told about God's plan to destroy Sodom, and objected, in contrast to Noah, whom our Sages criticize for not speaking up when God announced His plan to destroy the world by the Flood. Moses was told about God's plan to destroy the Jewish people and start a new nation from Moses' progeny, after the sin of the Golden Calf, and he is praised by our Sages because he objected. In Jewish tradition, a prophet's conscientious objection to a Divine plan or order is praise-worthy; it is not rare to find prophets who resist their Divine appointment and task. Jonah, who did more than question, but sought to escape his appointment even if he could not persuade God to relieve him of it, is considered a *kovesh et nevi'ato*, one who suppresses his prophecy, and is, thereby, subject to Divine punishment.[21] Therefore, we cannot justify Abraham's refusal to at least protest God's command that he kill Isaac on the grounds that prophets must silently obey whenever commanded or consulted by God. The opposite is true when God's justice or compassion are in issue. Moreover, as we shall see, even a true prophet may sometimes have to question the authenticity of his vision.[22]

Jewish law is similar in the second case. A Jew is generally not required to obey what appear to be Divine commands to violate the law. There are certainly cases, consistent with Jewish law, where Jews were required to obey Divine commands, through prophets, to cause enemies of Israel to be killed, as in the case of Samuel and Saul regarding Agag.[23] But the Talmud states that a command by a prophet in God's name to uproot God's law should not be obeyed. This raises questions about Abraham's and Isaac's willingness to participate in the *Akedah*.[24] Rambam — based on the distinction made between "uprooting" and "suspending" the law, and the opinion of R. Abahu,[25] summarizing the Talmud's discussion — asserts that there is a *hora'at sha-ah* exception for true prophets who order the violation of God's law in God's name in special, temporary cases, which Jews should obey unless ordered to commit idolatry.[26] Radbaz, three centuries after Rambam, still displays perplexity over whether we should obey a prophet who orders a violation of God's law involving relations between persons (e.g., murder); he concludes that a prophet should be obeyed even if he orders a violation of the Torah if his purpose is to protect the Torah, in those special circumstances where following the requirements of Torah law would lead to the undermining of Torah itself.[27] The paradigm is Elijah at Mt. Carmel, where — to uproot idolatry — he brought sacrifices outside of the Temple, contrary to Jewish law, to demonstrate to the people that God was supreme over the various idols which so many Israelites continued to worship.

In light of this discussion, the *Akedah* is plainly not a case of violating the law to save the law, as required by *hora'at sha'ah*. (Indeed, if it were deemed such a case, it would represent an act of extreme practicality rather than an act of supreme faith!). Therefore, the traditional interpretation of the *Akedah* assumes that Abraham (and Isaac) acted contrary to the halakhah, which prohibits murder, the obedience of prophets to heavenly commands to commit murder, and the compliance of others with prophetic transmissions of such commands.

Abraham was not ignorant of God's prohibition against murder, known since God's response to Cain's murder of Abel (*Gen.* 4:8–12) and the Divine Noahide laws (*Gen.* 9:1–17; *Ex. R.* 27:9). Recall Abraham's challenge to God for planning to destroy Sodom if any righteous persons lived there, and God's praise of Abraham after his death for his complete obedience to God's "commandments, statutes and laws" (*Gen.* 26:5). Thus, if he was not familiar with the law of *hora'at sha'ah*, there was no halakhic basis for killing Isaac, even by Divine command. If he was familiar with it, he knew the limited exception to the Divine law against murder that it provides. I believe that it is far more likely that he was fully familiar with the law (B. *Yoma* 28b), not only because of the sweeping character of God's praise of Abraham noted above, but because the purpose of the limited scope of *hora'at sha'ah* is to protect the Jewish people and Jewish law from the imagined or improperly understood messages of true prophets, and the falsified messages of false ones. (For this reason, even true prophets cannot prophetically add to Jewish law.)[28] Surely Abraham — who first found God and became the first prophet of the Jewish people — was sensitive to these common sense concerns, which are so essential to protecting God's moral law and which, ultimately, were formally incorporated in the halakhah. This was Abraham's tenth and final test, and we should embrace the chance to know that he passed it.

To sum up, there is no doctrine or belief in Judaism that whatever God tells a prophet to do, or instruct others to do, even if it requires a violation of God's law, must be obeyed without any prior discussion or objection, and we adhere to a Divine command to commit such a violation only in situations of *hora'at sha'ah*, i.e., when necessary to protect the Torah, or the Jewish people (*Esther R.* 4:16). But if the *Akedah* is not a case of *hora'at sha'ah*, and if the halakhah did not prevent Abraham from challenging God's command to violate Divine moral law, how can we interpret the *Akedah* in a way that is consistent with Jewish law? What does the *Akedah* teach us?

IV

I believe that there is a coded counter-message in the *Akedah*, which provides a simultaneous and necessary conceptual theological balance to the awesome mystery and the daunting problematics of the traditional interpretation. On the one hand, God was testing Abraham to see if he would remain loyal to God's revealed moral law even if ordered to abandon it. We know this because an earlier text expressly says that God wanted Abraham always to do what is "just and right" and to teach his children to follow this Divine path (*Gen.* 18:19). On the other hand, Abraham never intended to kill Isaac, and was terribly concerned at the fact that God had commanded him to do so. Abraham was testing the Almighty, as it were, as to what kind of covenant and religion he, Abraham, was being asked to join. Was it one that required man to follow heavenly voices to any length, even to immorality? Or was God, Himself, subject to the requirements of justice and righteousness, as Divinely defined and known, as Abraham had already indicated in his debate with God about the proposed destruction of Sodom and Gemorrah.[29]

After all, it was Abraham who found God, not the other way around,[30] and it is not surprising that he had certain moral expectations — and perhaps even requirements — of the all-powerful God of the ordered universe, Whose tradition he had received and studied, and in Whose Name he was about to establish a new, world religion.

In testing God, as it were, Abraham was, ultimately, testing himself. "I have found God," he seems to be saying, "and my tradition and experience have revealed Him and made Him known to me as an all-powerful, all-knowing, just and compassionate God. But I need to be sure that this is the God to which I truly wish to dedicate myself and my progeny and my followers for all time. If the God I have found demands the same kind of immorality that I saw in my father's pagan society, I must be mistaken. I must look further. To obey such a God is not a moral advance at all." To paraphrase our Sages, "Better observance without God than God without observance."[31]

37

It may be asked why Abraham did not challenge God at the outset, when first commanded to sacrifice Isaac, as he did when he learned of God's determination to wipe out Sodom and Gemorrah. Indeed, challenge is necessary when it is God who is preparing to do something, as with Sodom, and makes man complicit with or privy to what He is about to do. However, whenever one is asked to do something wrong by someone else — in the case of the *Akedah*, Abraham by God — there is an alternative strategy: stalling for time, whose exemplar (apart from Abraham) is Aaron in dealing with the Israelite demand for a Divine incarnation to worship (the golden calf).[32] As everyone familiar with the practice of a bureaucracy knows, those who seek simultaneously to obey their superiors — whom they admire, respect and sometimes fear — and give their superiors a chance to change their minds about what seems to be an unwise or immoral idea, rarely challenge the idea head on. They stretch things out, find problems at various steps on the way, move papers from one office to another, consult experts and conduct meetings to consider the various aspects. There are two things that they don't do: they don't tell their boss that his or her proposal is a bad idea — if they have reason to hope that the boss will decide that way, eventually; and they don't agree that the boss's proposal is a good idea and rush off intending to obey it — if they think that the idea is bad. The strategic objective is to keep faith with one's conscience, give the boss a chance to make the smart or moral decision in the long run, and make the bureaucracy look good — obedient — throughout. Similar behavior may be predicted among loved ones.

The matter may be compared to a father who asks his son to violate the Sabbath in some way. The child does not know whether the father is testing his obedience to the law — which requires him to resist his father and observe the *Shabbat* commandments[33] — or is testing the child's love (and fear) of the parent. The child can protest immediately, perhaps thereby showing disrespect and causing the parent anguish, or the child can make the necessary preparations to do what the parent has requested, seeming to go along with it, in the hope or expectation that the child's knowledge and obedience of the law is being tested, not its parental obedience, thus saving the need to object to the very end, when the actual consummation of the act that will violate the Sabbath is to occur, but confident that the parent will never let the child take the last step.[34]

Which approach is the more praiseworthy? The Bible gives the child the right to defy its parent, but never tells us how. Clearly, the more respectful, less insulting way, which also preserves the paramount nature of the Sabbath, is to stall, and give the parent the time and the opportunity to countermand the improper order.[35]

As we shall see, this is precisely what the texts tells us that Abraham did.[36] He did not rush — he stalled! He broke up the task that he was given into numerous tasks, or steps, and at each one he stopped, waiting to see whether "the Boss" had reconsidered. It was never Abraham's intention to kill his son, and God never indicated whether He wanted Abraham to kill Isaac, or if He wanted Abraham to refuse to do so. Given Abraham's moral purity, we may reasonably conclude that if, at the very end, God had not rescinded His command for Isaac's death, Abraham would have rejected the command, chosen the moral course of not committing murder, and saved his son — and then been forced to re-examine the prospects of his new religion, and the belief and faith on which it rested. Abraham was waiting for God to say: "Don't do it." Moreover, as we shall see, there is good reason to believe that God was waiting for Abraham to say: "I can't do it; it is contrary to Your moral law."[37]

The text can be interpreted to show Abraham stalling. It does not show Abraham leaping from receipt of God's command to his execution of it. Indeed, Abraham never agrees to accept it and perform it.[38] Instead, the text describes Abraham going through a series of separate steps: first he gets up, then he dresses his animals, then he gets his retinue in order, then he gets the rope, and the wood, and then he sets off, and then he sees Mount Moriah, and then he gets off the animal, and then he instructs his retinue to wait, and then he and Isaac walk (*vayelkhu*), but don't run,

39

toward Moriah, and then there is a conversation, and then the various distinct preparations of the altar, and then he stretches out his arm, and then, finally, he takes the knife, and then he raises his arm. Does this plodding, clearly unnecessarily detailed sequence of steps connote a man rushing off to do God's bidding? Hardly.

The point of the text is quite clear. At each step Abraham was waiting for God to evidence a change of mind, to withdraw His command; when that was not forthcoming, Abraham took the next step, and put the Almighty to the next test — as it were — always showing obedience, always giving God the opportunity to make the moral statement that God does not want man to murder or to commit other immoral acts in God's name. And, at the very end, when Abraham took the last step before he would have been forced by his conscience to stop and challenge God's command, the angelic order to stop finally came.

The traditional view that, until ordered to desist, Abraham intended to kill Isaac as God commanded, thus meriting great reward, is not held unreservedly in the Midrash. Thus, as noted above, some commentators observe that Abraham misunderstood God's command; others, that Abraham and Isaac had doubts, and were tempted to disobey it.[39] Moreover, if the command was ambiguous, wherein lies the test and Abraham's merit in his willingness to kill Isaac? For, if that is not clearly what God commanded, there is plainly nothing praiseworthy in Abraham's willingness to do such a thing. Under such circumstances it would be, at best, misguided zeal. The midrash that interprets Abraham's promise to his retinue, in *Gen.* 22:5, that "we [Isaac and I] will pray and [we] will return to you" as indicating that Abraham then knew, through a spirit of prophecy, that he would not have to kill Isaac, further supports the view that, at least from that point, Abraham had no such intention.[40]

Those who argue that Abraham intended to kill Isaac before being stopped, cannot prove it from the *Akedah*, because Abraham never agreed to kill his son, and never had to. Had he done so, and said "I still believe in God," we would have had proof. We would also have had a religion to which few and, perhaps, none of us could subscribe, because such a religion would never have endured. Those who argue that Abraham met the test, by virtue of his intent up to the last moment to kill Isaac, argue that God knew what was in Abraham's heart, that God gave Abraham a chance, through all the steps enumerated in the story, to change his mind, but Abraham was willing to obey to the very end.[41] Therefore, God — knowing this — could suspend the order to kill Isaac and, thereby, prevent what would have been an unjustified murder at the last moment. Unfortunately, this approach simply mires us even further in an interpretation of the *Akedah* in which God expects his followers to obey His commands whenever they believe that is what God wants — even if the command is for man to perform, without halakhic justification, an unequivocally immoral act, one that is totally contrary to fundamental Jewish law.[42]

But how shall we interpret the statement at *Gen.* 22:12: "For now I know that you fear God, since you have not withheld your son, your favored one, from me." One answer is that God did not know what Abraham would have done had the heavenly voice not called out to him to stop; all He knew was what Abraham had done up to then. We each have moral free will, and Judaism does not require acceptance of the idea that God knew in advance that Abraham would choose to slaughter his son. This philosophical problem has long been debated in Judaism. For Gersonides and Ibn Daud, for example, Abraham had free will to the very end on whether or not to kill Isaac, and his decision could not be known — even by God — until he actually made it by bringing down the knife on his son's body.[43]

But, apart from this theological rationale, I believe that a close reading of the text permits a midrashic interpretation along the following lines: God was testing Abraham to see if he would remain faithful to His revealed moral law even when Divinely commanded to violate it, in order fully and finally to expunge the belief and practice of child sacrifice, or any murder, (ostensibly) in God's name or for God's benefit. Abraham

41

never intended to kill Isaac but was determined to stall, with faith in God's morality and a determination to uphold it. God was waiting for Abraham to say, "I won't do it," and Abraham was waiting for God to say, "Stop, don't do it, I didn't mean it." The command for Abraham to desist comes. However, while the original command to kill Isaac came from God, the command that he spare him, because "now I know that you did not intend to withhold your son ... from Me," is not made by God but by an angel of God.[44] I submit that this change is crucial to a full, deep understanding of what occurred because, in Jewish belief, angels, unlike God, can have no foreknowledge of man's moral choices.[45] The text, therefore, could not attribute to God the knowledge of Abraham's intent to kill Isaac and, therefore, did not do so, because God, who *does* know what is in man's heart, knew that Abraham had no such intention!

Actually, there are two reasons why we are not required to credit the angelic statements (*Gen.* 22:12 and 16) that Abraham intended to kill Isaac. First, angels are not competent to know the intentions of human beings. They are purely mechanical in their perceptions; seeing (and hearing), for them, is believing. They unquestionably obey commands, and mechanically can observe acts of obedience or disobedience to commands. No angelic *Sanhedrin* would disobey Divine messages about the halakhah, as our Sages did.[46] They can also make prophecies and promises in God's name, as commanded. But they do not understand what is in the human heart. Only God is a *bohen kelayot valev*, one who understands what is in the innermost part of man's heart and the secret recesses of his mind.[47] What angels see is what they know, or can reason about, and all they could see was Abraham seemingly executing God's command, step by step.[48] Second, angels are never given more than one task at a time.[49] In this case, the first angel's task was to order Abraham to stop, and not take the final step that would consummate the slaughter of Isaac. The task of the second angel (necessarily a second angel because of the second task involved) was to promise Abraham that God would multiply his seed. Thus, the added statement that each angel made that

Abraham intended to kill Isaac (to justify, first, the order to desist, and, second, the promise of God's blessing), was also defective because, in each case, this observation went beyond the task that the angel was empowered by God to perform.

The incapacity of angels to know that is in the human heart may be deduced in a number of ways:[50]

1. To God, and not to angels, is universally attributed the power of knowing man's heart and mind. This is particularly evident in the liturgy. There is, also, the text in *Genesis* in which God turns to the angels and asserts that He (not they) knows or understands Abraham's intentions: *Ki yedativ et asher yezaveh* ("Because I know that he will command...." (*Gen.* 18:19).[51]

2. Man's understanding is equated to that of the angels. If angels could know the secrets of man's heart and mind, then — under this equation — man would have that power as well, which is clearly not the case. Indeed, the Bible chastises any belief in such human powers.[52]

3. Angels insist on strict observance of God's commands, having the quality of justice but not of compassion. This is because angels have no evil inclination, so that they cannot empathize with a person's moral dilemmas and wrong moral choices.[53]

4. The angels opposed man's creation, and oppose his repentance from sin.[54] Repentance requires an internalized resolution to abandon forever the sin that was committed. Angels, being pure goodness and lacking a bad inclination, manifestly cannot know whether or not a sincere "return" has taken place.[55]

5. The Sages say that God's power to know man's heart means both parts of man's heart: one consists of the good inclination and the other of the bad inclination. It is logically impossible that angels, who have only the good inclination, can know man's heart, which consists of both.[56]

6. Angels understand only Hebrew, *lashon ha'kodesh* (the "holy tongue"). But, if they can understand what man intends, what is in man's heart and mind, why can't they understand man's prayers in any language?[57]

The use of an angel to rescind God's command makes two important points. First, it tells us, or confirms for us, that Abraham never intended to kill Isaac, which is why God could not say that Abraham did so intend. Second, it draws a dramatic contrast between Abraham, representing a paradigm for mankind, and angels. For the angels, the test of the *Akedah* was the test that angels pass every day — to give God mechanical, un-questioning, obedience. This is one meaning of the legends of Satan and the angels — each, perhaps, with different motives — asking God to test Abraham with the *Akedah*.[58] The angels wanted to see if Abraham would unquestioningly obey God's commands, which would make Abraham as one of them; for them, God's command — once given — had to be obeyed, and Abraham — as far as he was allowed to go — passed this test, as far as they could see. Thus, the twin angelic observations: "and you did not withhold your son, your only son" (*Gen.* 22:12 and 16).

But the Almighty had a completely different test in mind — a test that would make sure that Abraham would not unquestioningly obey commands — even Heavenly commands — to commit immoral acts. In Jewish thought, man is not intended to be like the angels, but to exercise his free will to obey God's revealed moral law, indeed, all of God's re-vealed law, as interpreted by an educated, morally sensitized, pious, reli-gious community. What God did not want, and does not want, is human beings who are prepared to commit acts which they know to be immoral just because a holy man has received a private communication from on high. The religion that Abraham and God agreed to at Moriah is the re-ligion of a revealed God, a God who is revealed to all, and not privately, and Whose Law is similarly revealed, as Yehuda Halevi understood,[59] in a written text, publicly available for scrutiny, study and acceptance by all, and subject to subsequent interpretation and application — not on the basis of private, esoteric orders to a select few from Heaven, but the understanding of a religious community based on continuing study and piety.

There is one last textual problem to solve. In *Gen.* 22:15–18 we read the second angelic observation of Abraham's intent:

> 15. And the angel of the Lord called to Abraham a second time from heaven,
>
> 16. And said: *"By Myself have I sworn, says the Lord, that, because you have done this thing, and have not withheld your son,* your only son,
>
> 17. That I will indeed bless you and I will indeed multiply your progeny ...
>
> 18 ... Because you listened to My voice." [emphasis added]

Isn't it clearly God, and not an angel, saying here that Abraham intended to kill Isaac? I believe that the text can be read, midrashically, otherwise. The words, "By Myself have I sworn, says the Lord," at the beginning of verse 16, relate to the blessings in verses 17–18; God swears, as it were, that He will greatly multiply Abraham's seed. The concept of God swearing has no relevance to the intervening statement at the end of verse 16, "that because you ... Have not withheld your son ...." This is not a fact about which one swears. I suggest, therefore, that it is an angelic interpolation (see verse 15). Significantly, the angel here mechanically repeats the same observation about Abraham's intent to kill Isaac that was mechanically made by the first angel, without invoking the authority of God, when ordering Abraham not to harm Isaac (verse 12).

A stronger reason for considering the second statement, "because you have not withheld your son," as an angelic interpolation, and not as God's view of Abraham's intent, is redundancy. That statement is offered (*Gen.* 22:16) as the reason for God's blessing of Abraham (*Gen.* 22:17), but the same reason seems to be offered again immediately after the blessing (22:18): *"eykev ...,"* "because you listened to My voice." But the Torah is never superfluous; therefore, a different reason is evidently intended by the *eykev* formula, representing the Divine and not the angelic view — namely, "because you never intended to violate My moral law." Further support for this view can be ascertained from *Gen.* 26:5, where

God repeats, for Isaac, His earlier blessing to Abraham to multiply his seed, using exactly the same reason, exactly the same verbal formula, as is used at the *Akedah* after His blessing of Abraham: "*eykev ...*" — "because Abraham listened to My voice." However, to Isaac, God explains the meaning of the *eykev* formula: "and he [Abraham] kept My safeguards, My commandments, My statutes and My laws." The commentators generally agree that this statement includes such basic commandments as the prohibition against murder, etc., which would be plainly violated by the slaughter of Isaac. Although some believe that 26:5 includes a reference to the *Akedah*, the *Targum Onkelos*, the authoritative, Aramaic translation of the Torah, interprets this text as referring to Abraham's obedience to God's moral and other commandments, and the rabbinic "fences" surrounding them, and not to Abraham's intent to disobey them by killing Isaac.[60]

Moreover, if the highpoint of the *Akedah* was Abraham's willingness, even eagerness, to kill Isaac, his announcement that on this "mountain of God" his descendants would in the future build a temple to worship Abraham's commanding God (22:14) (as commentators, e.g., The *Targum* and Rashi, understand this verse) would have come when he was about to kill Isaac. Instead, it comes after he is told to spare Isaac — suggesting that it was only then that Abraham accepted the charge to become the father of the nation that would spread God's Name and word throughout the world — a God Who now revealed and proclaimed Himself as a God of compassion and morality, Who did not require or desire of His faithful total moral surrender and intellectual submission as proof of their loyalty and faith, but wished them to do what is "just and right" (*Gen.* 18:19).

When we read, and listen, to the end of the *Akedah* text, we should hear two voices, God's and that of the angels. God's voice is saying, "Stop, I promise to reward you for being staunch in observing my commandments, including the commandment not to kill — you passed the test; I wanted to be sure you were not an immoral, mechanical, "Yes man;" and the other voice, that of the angels, who would know about Abraham only what they saw, because they are, in their nature, without ability to know what is in the human heart and mind. Thus, they were applauding Abraham for having the very opposite intention from that for which God was rewarding him, because that is what they would have done in Abraham's place had they been similarly ordered and tested.

V

Even if we assume that it was God speaking through the angels on both occasions, there is another, simpler interpretation of the *Akedah* that rejects any intention by Abraham to kill Isaac, but accepts Abraham's actions, as far as they went, as reflecting his faith in God — specifically, faith in a God who does not want human sacrifice or murder of any kind, and Who would rescind His command rather than permit such an act even when it was Divinely commanded. Abraham's faith was in a God of justice, righteousness and compassion,[61] Who wants man to wage his mightiest struggle to the end that God's revealed moral law is made manifest in the world that God created. "Because you have done this thing, and did not withhold your son" (*Gen.* 22:18) does not say that Abraham intended to kill Isaac if God did not countermand His awesome command at the last moment. It says only that "you were willing to endure the confused agony of going ahead and acting in obedience to My command, to the very point of killing Isaac — with faith that I would never allow that to happen."[62] We may understand this as the same kind of faith as that which the children of Israel had when they plunged into the waters of the Red Sea at God's command — not the serene faith that God wanted them to kill themselves and their families by drowning, and their zealous intention of doing so, but the confident faith that God would, somehow, save them and keep His redemptive promises to them. Such a faith demonstrated, as did Abraham's, that God is, indeed, a God of justice and righteousness and not a God who tests the faith of His followers by testing their willingness to kill themselves or their loved ones just because God asks it.

47

Abraham could have protested God's command to kill Isaac then and there, when God commanded it, and passed the test that God had in mind, of being staunch in his defense and observance of God's commandments — even at the risk of challenging God's commands. Indeed, out of compassion and love for his wife, Sarah, and his son, Isaac, Abraham surely felt the almost irresistible compulsion to speak out against God's command right away, and, in that way — knowing God's answer — sparing them the agony of seeing Abraham go forward in obedience to God's command — an agony that would cause Sarah's death and Isaac's alienation from him forever after.[63] Yet, Abraham refused this course. His faith in God's justice and righteousness allowed him to pursue an even nobler course. He did not want God's moral law against murder to be affirmed merely as a Divine response to a human plea, as occurred at Sodom, nor to be proclaimed merely as a response to human arguments about God's mercy, God's promises,[64] what the other nations will think, or even about God's justice and righteousness. To achieve this, Abraham had to have an enduring, unshakable faith in God's justice and righteousness, a faith that allowed him to proceed with the *Akedah*, not with the steadfast, zealous intent to kill Isaac, but with the steadfast, serene faith that God, without the need for human pleas, would ultimately pronounce for all, and for all time, the prohibition against murder — even for God's glory and in God's name.

If I am right, it is possible to understand in a new way the strange formulation of the *Akedah* in the *Rosh Hashanah musaf* liturgy. There, at the end of the *Zikhronot* section, we recall how Abraham *"suppressed his compassion* to do God's will with a full heart," and we ask God: "Similarly (sic) *suppress your anger* at us, and deal compassionately with us" (emphasis added). But why should God have compassion on us, if Abraham *suppressed* his compassion for Isaac in his determination to kill him? I suggest that the text may mean, simply, that Abraham suppressed his compassion for Sarah and Isaac by going along with God's command despite the agony that he knew this would cause them, so that God could mani-

48

fest His abhorrence of murder without having to be pressed to do so by human pleas. Similarly (it is now possible to say), we ask God to *suppress* His anger and be compassionate with us, in the merit of Abraham who *suppressed* his feeling for his wife and child in order to demonstrate to the world his unshakable faith in God's justice and compassion.

In his determination not to kill Isaac, and his willingness to go forward with God's command until ordered to stop, Abraham passed the twin tests of the *Akedah*, the tests of the strongest moral courage, and the purest religious faith.[65]

....

NOTES

1   For Rambam's classic discussion, see *The Guide for the Perplexed*, M. Friedlander, tr. (New York: Dover, 1956), Part III, Ch. XXIV, pp. 306–7.

2   Abraham's courage at the *Akedah* was precisely his willingness to do what he recognized was the morally heinous act of murder — dating back to God's punishment of Cain; the punishment of the Flood for acts of violence (*Gen.* 6:13 and Ramban, *ad. loc.* in his *Commentary on the Torah*, C. Chavel ed. [N.Y.: Shilo, 1971]); and the Noahide prohibition against murder at *Gen.* 9:6. As Rabbi J.H. Hertz comments on *Gen.* 22:12: "All that God desired was proof of Abraham's willingness to obey his command, and the moral surrender had been complete" (*The Pentateuch and Haftorahs* [London: Soncino Press, 1938]). According to the Talmud (B. *Yoma* 28b, citing *Gen.* 26:5) and many commentators (e.g., Ramban on *Gen.* 26:5, Rashi on 26:5 and 32:5, Albo, *Ikkarim*, Bk. 3, Ch. 10), Abraham, Isaac and Jacob fulfilled the Torah before it was given at Sinai and, surely, the prohibition of murder. Some believe that Jewish tradition recognizes a morality independent of Torah; see n.12 and authorities cited in Michael Harris, "The Shared Moral Universe of God and Man: A Re-reading of the *Akedah*," *L'Eylah*, September, 1992: 15–19. Cf. Walter Wurzburger, "Breuer and Kant," *Tradition* (Winter, 1992): 72. In the Midrash, even Satan warns Abraham that he dare not obey God's command to kill Isaac, citing the Noahide laws applicable to all mankind long before the Ten Commandments (B. *Sanhedrin* 89b; *Gen. R.* 56:4; see other citations in Louis Ginzberg, *Legends of the Jews* [Philadelphia: Jewish Publication Society, 1968], Vol. I, pp. 272–4). Shlomo Riskin says, citing Ramban, that "from the very beginning of the world there lived in Canaan believers in the One God, who had maintained the traditions of Adam and Noah, and whose king — Shem, son of Noah — was priest of God on high" (See "Abram: Finishing His Father's Journey," *Jerusalem Post*, Week Ending November 7, 1992, p. 23).

3   The halakhah deals with Divine commands to prophets to violate the halakhah. Generally, the halakhah prohibits the violation of three commandments — murder, idolatry and incest — even if martyrdom results (Rambam, *Mishneh Torah, Yesodei ha-Torah*, V: 1–5), although this rule was modified by the Jewish people in extremis (see H. Soloveitchik, "Religious Law and Change," *AJS Review*, Vol. XII, No. 2 [Fall 1987]: 208–17).

4   Thus, there is a remarkable legend that Abraham completed the sacrifice, and that

Isaac was miraculously revived, although Ibn Ezra (on *Gen.* 22:19) rejects it. See B. *Ta'anit* 16a and *Tosafot, ad loc.*, and the penitential prayer of Isaac b. Reuben Barceloni (1043) (referring to the "Ashes of Isaac"), in *Selihot for the Whole Year*, p. 337. *Midrash Da'at Zekenim* 8a states that Abraham wished he could have been permitted to complete the slaughter of Isaac, lest his failure to do so reflect badly on his desire to obey God's command. The Midrash also notes that Abraham resisted the order not to kill Isaac because it came only from an angel, whereas the command to sacrifice Isaac came from God (Abarbanel on *Gen.* 22:15; *Tanhuma*, *Vayera* 23, *Tanhuma* [Buber, ed.], 46, 114 ff; and Ginzberg, *Legends*, Vol. I, p. 282). On whether Abraham actually did physically harm Isaac at the *Akedah* (and whether that tradition resulted from Christian influences), see Spiegel, pp. 3–8, 38, 43–59. See, also, Bruce Zuckerman, *Job the Silent* (Oxford Univ. Press, 1991), Ch. 2; *Pirke d'Rabbi Eliezer* 31; and *Midrash Ha-Gadol* on *Gen.* 22:19.

The traditional view of the *Akedah* influenced the willingness of Ashkenazi Jews, as discussed by H. Soloveitchik, *Op. Cit.*, to turn the Biblical prohibition against murder into an act that became recognized as a legitimate form of *kiddush ha-Shem*, when fathers killed their children and wives and then committed suicide rather than face forced baptism during the Crusades; it was "the paradigm and leitmotiv" of the chronicles of these events. See Y.H. Yerushalmi, *Zakhor* (Seattle: University of Washington Press, 1982), p. 38; see also Gerson D. Cohen, "Messianic Postures of Ashkenazim and Sephardim," *Studies in the Variety of Rabbinic Cultures* (Phila.: JPS, 1991), pp. 290–1, and notes 44–50; Shalom Spiegel, *The Last Trial*, Judah Goldin, tr. (N.Y.: Pantheon, 1967), ch. 3; the *piyyut* of Kalonymous B. Judah, *Amarti She'u Mini* (11th cent.), and the *piyyut* of Joseph of Chartres (12th cent.), *Elokim Be'alunu*, in *Kinot*, A. Rosenfeld, tr. and ann. (N.Y.: Judaica Press, 1979), pp. 140, 170; the *selihot* (penitential prayers) composed by Ephraim B. Isaac (12th century), Meir B. Isaac (11th century) and Benjamin B. Zerah (11th century), *Selihot for the Whole Year*, A. Rosenfeld, ann. and tr. (N.Y.: Judaica Press, 1978), pp. 204, 232, 320; David G. Roskies, *Against the Apocalypse* (Harvard Univ. Press, 1984), p. 46 (14th century *kiddush ha-Shem*). More recently, the *Akedah* has inspired the modern conception (beginning around the turn of the century) of *Daas Torah* as "an expression of the ethic of submission," which is "viewed in hasidic sources [from which it originated] as a reenactment of the *Akedah*, whereby the individual sacrifices his intellect on the altar of blind obedience to the words of the sages ...." See Lawrence Kaplan, "*Daas Torah*: A Modern Conception of Rabbinic Authority," *The Orthodox Forum — Rabbinic Authority and Personal Autonomy*, Moshe Z. Sokol, ed. (Northvale, N.J.: Jason Aronson, Inc. 1992), pp. 54–5.

5 See, e.g., B. *Baba Meziah* 59b; *Mishnah, Rosh Hashanah* 2:9; and the discussion in Eliezer Berkovits, *Not in Heaven: The Nature and Function of Halakha* (N.Y.: KTAV, 1983), Ch. 2, pp. 47–53.

6 See n. 3

7 See discussion in Part III, below.

8 See, e.g., B. *Yevamot* 90b (Tosafot); B. *Avodah Zarah* 24b; B. *Yoma* 69b; I *Samuel* 6:14, and *Nehemiah* 8:4. In brief, this is a halakhic doctrine (*hora'at sha-ah*) used by the Sages for situations of unique significance. Its applicability to prophets who are Divinely commanded to act or command others to act, contrary to God's law, is discussed in Part III.

9 B. *Sotah* 14a; see also Hertz's discussion of this principle at *Gen.*. 3:21, *Ex.* 33:19,

and *Lev.* 19:2. See, also, *Reflections of the Rav*, adapted from the lectures of Rabbi Joseph B. Soloveitchik by A.R. Besdin (Jerusalem: WZO, 1979), Ch. II, pp. 23–30.

10 The suppression concept is midrashic, and not uniform; in some forms Abraham suppresses his compassion for Isaac — in others, his urge to argue with God (Spiegel, pp. 88–97). The Talmud is relatively quiet about the *Akedah*, favorably noting Abraham's arising early the morning after the command, to start his journey to Moriah — as an example for the diligent in observing God's commands; and the credit that subsequent generations receive for Abraham's binding of Isaac, as if they had done so, (B. *Rosh Hashanah* 16a, *San.* 89b and *Pes.* 4a). Scholars differ as to when the concept of Abraham suppressing his compassion became part of the *musaf* text. Spiegel says (*ibid.*) that it was probably some time during the period of the *Amoraim* (Talmudic Sages between the 3rd and 6th centuries, C.E.). More recently, scholars believe that it was not part of a single, original integral text, but was added later (9th–11th centuries) by the Geonim as part of their battle against the Karaites. See, e.g., Leon J. Liebrich, "Aspects of the New Year Liturgy," *HUCA 34* (1963): 136–47; Naftali Widder, "Investigating Ancient Babylonian Practices," (Hebrew) *Tarbiz 37* (1967–8): 135; Daniel Goldschmidt, *Mahzor Le'Yamim Nora'im* (Prayer Book for the High Holidays), (N.Y.: Leo Baeck Institute, 1970) (Hebrew), Introduction, p. 29 and n.7; I.M. Elbogen, *The Historical Development of Prayer in Israel* (Tel Aviv: Dvir, 1972), p. 109; and Lawrence Hoffman, *The Canonization of the Synagogue Service* (South Bend: Notre Dame University Press, 1979), pp. 98–100. The current text of *Zikhronot*, including the *Akedah* material, is included in the 10th century *mahzor* of Saadia Gaon and in the liturgical compilation, *Seder of Amram Gaon*. The *Mahzor Vitry* (Nuremburg: Hurwitz, 1924) sheds no light on West European practice in the 12th century.

11 See Ramban, *Op cit.*, p. 276; Rashi, on *Gen.* 22:2.

12 Saadia gives ten reasons for the blowing of the shofar on *Rosh Hashanah*, the sixth being to remind us of the *Akedah*, to teach us that we, too, must be ready at all times to offer our lives for the sanctification of God's name. See *Emunot V'De'ot* (Leipzig, 1859). But Saadia also claims that basic morality exists even without revelation; David Hartman, *Maimonides: Torah and Philosophic Quest* (Phil.: Jewish Publication Society, 1976), pp. 238, 242; if so, shouldn't Abraham, in the name of basic morality, have at least questioned God's command?

13 *Guide for the Perplexed*, Part III, Ch. 24.

14 Chavel, *Ramban*, p. 275.

15 *Star of Redemption*, William W. Hallo, tr. (N.Y.: Holt, Reinhart and Winston, 1971), p. 266.

16 See *Gen. R.* 56:8; Rashi on *Gen.* 22:2; Hertz, *Op. cit.*, p. 74; Ibn Ezra on *Gen.* 22:1; Abarbanel on *Gen.* 22:2, 12.

17 *The Torah: A Modern Commentary*, G. Plaut, ed. and ann. (N.Y.: UAHC, 1981), p. 149, where the contradictory observations are made that the *Akedah* was a test of Abraham's faith, but Abraham could have considered the command "legitimate" in the "framework of his time and experience." "Otherwise," says Plaut, "he might have protested God's command with the kind of insistence he exhibited at Sodom and Gomorrah."

18 Elie Wiesel, *Messengers of God* (N.Y.: Random House, 1976), p. 108; Paul Johnson, *A History of the Jews* (N.Y.: Harper & Row, 1987), p. 18. Some strangely argue that sin redeems sin: viz., that the *Akedah* atones for Abraham's expulsion of Ishmael,

and that Abraham made a deal with God to kill Isaac then, in exchange for God's forgiveness of Israel's sins later; David Polish, "The Binding of Isaac," *JUDAISM* (1957): 17–21; Marvin Fox, "Kierkegaard and Rabbinic Judaism," *JUDAISM* (1953): 160–9; Louis Feldman, "Josephus: The *Akedah*," *Jewish Quarterly Review* (Jan. 1985): 238–40; and Ginzberg, *Legends,* Vol. I, p. 284.

19 *Deut.* 21:18–20 and Rashi *ad loc.*; B. *San.* 71a. As to the alphabet, see "Interview with Frank Moore Cross," *Bible Review* (December 1992): 18, 24. Isaac's birth, when Abraham was 100 years old, precedes the Exodus (circa 1225 B.C.E.) by four hundred years, thus placing Abraham's birth toward the end of the 18th century, B.C.E. Cf. I.J. Gelb, *A Study of Writing* (Univ. Of Chicago Press, 1963).

20 Even God's right to kill was challenged by Moses in his plea to God to enter Canaan: "You killed an Egyptian ... Who was smiting a Jew," God says. "I killed one Egyptian. Look how many You have killed," replies Moses. See Avraham Weiss, "Why is God So Unrelenting Toward Moses?" *Jewish World* (Long Island), July 19–25, 1991, p. 5; *Midrash P'tirat Moshe,* quoted by Nehamah Leibowitz, *Studies in Shemot,* Vol. I (WZO, 1976), at *Exodus* 2:12.

21 See 1 *Samuel* 16:1–2 (Radak cites other cases, *ad. loc.*, of prophets who objected to their mission); 1 *Kings* 19:7, 20:42; cf. 1 *Kings* 21. There were other prophets who objected to God's command for personal or other reasons. See *Jeremiah* 11:14, 15:1, 32:16–25; *Isaiah* 6:5–7; *Ezekiel* 21:5; *Amos* 7:1–6. As to *Jonah,* see B. *Sanhedrin* 89a–b, 90a.

22 See Rabbi Abraham Isaac Kook, *Orot Ha-Kodesh* 138 (p. 157), as supplemented in *Tarbiz* 59 (1990): 497, n.59. Moreover, there is a suggestion in Rambam that even a true prophet must be alert to the possibility that he has not actually or accurately heard or seen, or properly interpreted a "prophecy," just as a witness with proper qualifications, who must be believed, may — in fact — not be telling the truth (*Mishneh Torah, Hilkhot Yesodei ha-Torah*, Ch. 7).

23 1 *Samuel* 15; see also 1 *Kings* 20:42.

24 B. *Sanhedrin* 90a. B. *Sanhedrin* 89a–b mentions Isaac's obedience to Abraham in the context of discussing a prophet known to be true (*navi muhzak*); cf. n. 22.

25 B. *Sanhedrin*, 90a; see also *Yevamot* 90b.

26 *Mishneh Torah, Hilkhot Yesodei ha-Torah,* 9:3, citing B. *Sanhedrin* 90a, and *Deut.* 18:15; Rambam, *Commentary to the Mishnah,* Joseph Kafih, tr. (Jerusalem: Mossad Harav Kook, 1963–8), pp. 11–14.

27 *Responsa, #652;* see, also, *Encyclopedia Talmudit,* Vol. 8, *Hora'at Sha-ah;* Jonathan Sacks, "Creativity and Innovation in Halakhah," *The Orthodox Forum — Rabbinic Authority and Personal Autonomy,* Moshe Z. Sokol, ed. (Northvale, N.J.: Jason Aronson, Inc. 1992), p. 138.

28 See n.22; Rambam (la-Am, edition), *Commentary to the Mishnah,* Vol. 18, pp. 27–8; *Mishneh Torah, Yesodei ha-Torah* 9:4; *Sefer ha-Mizvot,* Root II; B. *Shab.* 104a, *Tem.* 16a, *Yoma* 80a; *Sifra* to *Lev.* 27:34; *Lev. R.* 1:14; *Ex. R.* 28:6, 42:8; *Deut. R., Nizavim* 8:6; M. *Eduyot* 8:7; J. *Ber.* 1:4; B. *B.M.* 59 a–b (even God cannot interfere with the ongoing process of rabbinic interpretation and application of the Torah). See, generally, Z.H. Chajes, *The Student's Guide Through the Talmud,* Jacob Schacter, tr. and ed. (N.Y.: Philipp Feldheim, Inc., 1960), p. 34; cf. p. 86 and B. *Suk.* 44 a–b; Elliot N. Dorff and Arthur Rosett, *A Living Tree* (Albany: SUNY, 1988), pp. 187–190; Louis Jacobs, *A Tree of Life* (N.Y.: Oxford University Press, 1984), ch. 5, esp. pp. 70–1; Urbach, *The Sages,* ch. 6; David Hartman, *Op.*

cit., pp. 108–119, 238–242.

29 Recall Abraham's direct challenge to God at Sodom regarding the death of innocents: "Will the Ruler of the entire world not do justice?" (*Gen.* 18:25).

30 *Mishneh Torah, Hilkhot Avodah Zarah* 1:1–3; *Guide to the Perplexed,* 1:36, 2:39, 3:29, 3:37. Rabbi J.B. Soloveitchik, quoting the Midrash, writes that "until Abraham arrived, God reigned only over the heavens...(*Sifri,* 313, *Ha'azinu*). It was Abraham who 'crowned' Him God on earth, the God of men .... (Rashi, *Gen.* 24:7; *Ber.* 59);" *Man of Faith in the Modern World, Reflections of the Rav,* Volume Two, adapted from the lectures of Rabbi Joseph B. Soloveitchik by Abraham R. Besdin (Hoboken, N.J.: KTAV, 1989), p. 50. Similarly, Yehudah Halevi in *The Kuzari* (N.Y.: Schocken, 1964), Part Four, para. 27 (p. 239), observes, through the Rabbi: "Perhaps this was Abraham's point of view when Divine power and unity dawned upon him *prior to the revelation accorded to him*" (emphasis added). See also Ginzberg, *Legends,* Vol. I, pp. 189–217 and Vol. V, p. 210.

31 *J. Hagigah* 1:7; Gerson Cohen, *Op. Cit.,* p. 73.

32 *Ex. R.* 37:2 and *Lev. R.* 10:3. What follows, which is what I call "the bureaucratic model" because it can be commonly found in that context, can be extended to a variety of other relationships (e.g., marriage), specifically when two persons feel respect, admiration or other positive feelings toward each other such that neither wants unnecessarily to rupture the relationship even when cherished goals or values are threatened. In consulting with Professor James S. Uleman of NYU, Faculty of Arts and Science, Graduate Program in Social-Personality Psychology, I was advised that there is some experimental work that supports my view, e.g., the famous Stanley Milgram (1974) experiments (pressure exerted on the tested individuals to subject others to increasing intensities of electric shock), reported in *Obedience to Authority: An Experimental View* (New York: Harper & Row, 1974), and the studies of Susan T. Fiske and Shelley E. Taylor, *Social Cognition* (Reading, PA: Adison-Welsley Publishing Co., 1984), pp. 106–111 (procrastination to gather information). During the Holocaust, certain Jewish community leaders turned some of their people over to the Nazis "in the hope of putting off death for as long as possible, for as many as possible," in hopes that the situation might change — pitting the view of Rabbi Avraham Duber Cahana Shapira of the Kovno ghetto (favoring such action) against Maimonides' medieval pronouncement. See Laurence Thomas, "Characterizing and Responding to Nazi Genocide: A Review Essay," *Modern Judaism* 11 (1991): 371–79, at 373; Berel Lang, *Act and Idea in the Nazi Genocide* (Univ. Of Chicago Press, 1990), pp. 68–76.

Professor Uleman, in a personal letter to the author, dated December 12, 1990, has stated that "procrastination for the purpose of information gathering" would be a predictable response if Abraham did not want to kill Isaac, and particularly if he was not sure whether this was actually being demanded of him.

33 See Rashi, and Hertz, *Op. cit.,* at *Lev.* 19:3; B. *Yeb.* 5b; *Sifra, Kedoshim* 10:87.

34 See Part V, where I show why Abraham chose to obey God's command and wait for God's order to stop, rather than protest and try to change God's mind by human pleas.

35 The strategy of stalling is one of three paradigmatic Jewish responses to the travails and tragedies of the Diaspora. Another response has been to accept, if not embrace, these events as God's plan of punishment or purification, or perhaps even an opportunity for *kiddush ha-Shem,* as Rabbi Akivah is said to have viewed his martyrdom at the hands of the Romans. But cf. Gershon Greenberg, "Myth and

Catastrophe in Simha Elberg's Religious Thought," *Tradition* 26 (Fall 1991): 45–6 (where the difference between the *Akedah* and anti-Semitism is recognized). The third response — epitomized by Zionists and Ghetto fighters — has been to fight back; Todd M. Endelman, "The Legitimatization of the Diaspora Experience in Recent Jewish Historiography," *Modern Judaism* (May, 1991): 195–210.

36 Cf. the aggadah that Abraham rushed to kill his son, e.g., Rashi and Hertz, *ibid.*, at *Gen.* 22:3, compounding the moral problem of the traditional interpretation.

37 Although the views expressed in this article were independently arrived at by the author, I wish to acknowledge the prior publication by Dr. Joel Wolowelsky of a brief note, in midrashic form, of the basic idea that Abraham never intended to kill Isaac, but waited for God to rescind His command ("Testing God — A Midrash on the Akedah," *Dor le Dor*, Vol. VIII, No. 2 [Winter 1979–80]: 98), and Rabbi Shlomo Riskin's suggestion that God was unhappy with Abraham for his eagerness to obey God's command to slaughter Isaac and, therefore, after the *Akedah*, God never spoke to Abraham again (*Baltimore Jewish Times*, Week Ending November 3, 1990, p. 52). Neil Gillman commented on the *Akedah* in a similar vein ("A Sabbath Week," *Jewish Week*, October 25–31, 1991).

Rabbi Samson Raphael Hirsch used the terms "twisted mind" and "raving madness" when the Reform scholar, Abraham Geiger, suggested that Abraham's greatness at the *Akedah* lay not in his willingness to slaughter Isaac, but in his will-ingness to desist from doing so at an angel's command. See his commentary in *The Pentateuch, Genesis*, Vol. I, second edition, Isaac Levy, tr. (Gateshead, England: Judaica Press, 1976), pp. 373–4. One is entitled to speculate how Hirsch would have responded to the views of Riskin, *et al.*, rather than to those of a leader of Reform, which was anathema for Hirsch.

38 Hertz expressly points this out (*op. cit.*, at *Gen.* 22:3).

39 See Rashi (citing R. Abba), and Hertz, *op. cit.*, on *Gen.* 22:2, 12; Abarbanel on 22:12; Ibn Ezra on 22:1; *Gen. R.* 56:8, 56:12; *The Midrash Says*, Moshe Weissman, ed. (Brooklyn, N.Y.: Benei Yakov, 1980), p. 200; *Pirke d'Rabbi Eliezer* 31; and Feldman "Josephus ...," *op. cit.*, p. 237.

40 See Hertz, *op. cit.*, at *Gen.* 22:5. Similarly, *Gen.* 22:8 where Abraham assures a concerned Isaac that God will provide a lamb for the sacrifice, which could also mean: "The God whom I worship will never let me kill you." Cf. Ibn Ezra on *Gen.* 27:18–19, who says that Abraham lied when he said, in 22:15, "we will return."

41 See, e.g., Chavel, *Ramban,* p. 278, commenting on *Gen.* 22:2.

42 Contrast the rabbis' praise of Abraham with their general condemnation of Jephthah for killing his daughter to fulfill a pre-battle vow, as well as the reli-gious leaders of the time for not finding a way out for him from his vow. *Midrash Tanhuma* (Jer. 19:5) tells of God's reaction to the "slaughter" of the daughter: "The Holy Spirit cried out: 'They have put their children to fire [clearly referring to more than just this incident]... Which I *never* commanded, *never* decreed, and which *never* came to My mind'" (emphasis added). See, also, Spiegel, *op. cit.* p. 79. As to all child sacrifices as a profanation of God's name, see *Lev.* 18:21, 20:2–5, 22; *Deut.* 12:30–31, 18:9–12; 2 *Kings* 3:27 ff., 16:3. The horror at killing one's child, even when God's law (of vows) seems to command it, is so great that some later commentators, e.g., Kimhi, Abarbanel, and — most recently — Steinsaltz, claim that Jephthah's daughter was not killed, but lived a cloistered life, as a virgin (Solomon Landers, "Did Jephthah Kill His Daughter?" *Bible Review* [August 1991]: 29–31, 42).

43 See Levi ben Gerson, *Sefer Milhamot Adonai*, III. 2, p. 126 ff; III, 4, p. 137 ff. See also J.D. Bleich, *With Perfect Faith* (N.Y.: KTAV, 1983), p. 417; and Julius Guttmann, *Philosophies of Judaism* (N.Y.: Schocken, 1973), pp. 243–4.

44 Ramban notes at *Gen.* 22:12 that there is significance in the fact that God ordered the slaughter of Isaac, but an angel ordered Abraham to desist (Chavel, *Ramban*, p. 279). Mysteriously, that explanation, promised to be provided at *Gen.* 48:16, is not there forthcoming. The Ramban does say earlier, at *Gen.* 18:1–10, that God often commanded by prophecy, but revoked the command by the word of an angel, although the Midrash claims that Abraham rejected the angelic order to desist because it lacked Divine authority (see n.4).

45 The bases for my conclusion that angels, in *fact*, do not have that power are discussed below; see text at notes 47–57.

46 See, e.g., *Ex. R.*, xviii, 5; R. Isaac of Corbeil, *Sefer Mizvot Katan*, sec. 53, and added citations in n. 49 below. See, also, the discussion in the text above, in connection with the citations in n.5. Disputes arose in the Sanhedrin, after the destruction of the Temple, concerning these two issues. The rabbi espousing the minority opinion sought to prove, through Heavenly signs, that his opinion was correct. In one case, even a Heavenly voice came to his support. The majority refused to change their view despite the Divine legitimation of the minority position.

47 In my research, I have found no instances, in classical Jewish texts, ascribing to angels the power to know what is in the hearts and minds of humans, but only angelic conclusions based on perceptions of human actions. Ascribing such power to God is found often, and such instances are well known. See, for example. The *Song of [God's] Unity* for Tuesday, said on *Rosh Hashanah*, the first two paragraphs of *Zikhronot* in the *musaf* service on that holiday, and the prayer just before *Al Het* which is said throughout *Yom Kippur* (*The Complete ArtScroll Mahzor for Rosh Hashanah*, Nosson Scherman, tr. [Brooklyn. N.Y.: Mesorah, 1985], pp. 146–7, 510–13; *The Complete ArtScroll Mahzor for Yom Kippur*, by the same publishers, pp. 92–3). See, also, *Proverbs* 20:27, *Chron.* 28:9, and *Jeremiah* 11:20. Abarbanel, in his commentary on the *Haggadah, Zevah Pesah*, comments on *Barukh ha-Makom* that only God knows what is in a person's mind and heart. See, also, *Gen.* 18:19 where God, speaking to the angels, emphasizes His special knowledge about Abraham's thoughts and intentions *(Targum, ad loc.* ["It is revealed before Me that Abraham will ...."]; Rashi, *ad loc.* [paraphrasing the *Targum*: "I know (what is) within him, that he (Abraham) will ...."]; Chavel, *Ramban*, pp. 240–42; *Exodus R.* 2:2).

48 B. *Hagigah* 16a equates the understanding *(da'at)* of humans with that of angels. Clearly, angels cannot know what is in the hearts and minds of people, since humans have no such power. The Abarbanel at *Gen.* 22:12 states that angels can reason from observed facts. But Abraham's obedience could have been a case of stalling, which would explain the angels' erroneous conclusion that Abraham intended to kill his son.

49 *Gen. R.* 50:2; Rashi on *Gen.* 18:2; B. *B.M.* 86b. However, Rabbi David Kimhi (Radak) adds that *angels can add or detract somewhat from their specific mission* (Chavel, *Ramban*, p. 257, n. 233). Radak's view is not an isolated one, but is based on — and, indeed, part of — the tradition that ascribes to angels certain abilities of feeling, action, and even initiative — complaining, reasoning, praising, criticizing, claiming reward (for the righteous; see, e.g., *Zechariah* 1:11) and punishment (for sinners) — *within the limitations of their essence*, which include goodness, total

obedience to God's commands, and the absence of the evil inclination. See, e.g., Rambam, *Guide*, pp. 162–3; *Sefer Yezirah*, Ch. 1, 7; B. *Hagigah* 16a; Abarbanel at *Gen.* 22:12; *Shir ha-Shirim R.* 1:8; Urbach, *The Sages*, pp. 174, 178, 181, 205–6, 221, 461. Thus, e.g., we see the angels complaining about man's creation, and about the giving of the Torah to Moses and Israel at Sinai; seeking justice for innocent Isaac on the altar (simultaneously praising Abraham for his obedience!); expressing joy at the deserved drowning of the Egyptians; and objecting to man's repentance. See, also, n. 54. While it is difficult for us, with a "modern" orientation and outlook, to understand the concept of angels, it is essential to distinguish between acts and statements of God and those of angels. Such distinctions are made in *Tanakh*, in the Midrash, and by our Sages and commentators, and we are, therefore, entitled to interpret *Tanakh* based on such distinctions.

50 Here I summarize the material in notes 47–48, and develop additional reasons from an analysis of angelic capabilities.

51 See n. 47.

52 B. *Hagigah* 16a. See, also, citations in Urbach, *The Sages*, p. 221, which state that man "sees" like the angels, presumably *external* rather than internal facts like thoughts and emotions (see n. 47).

53 R. Joseph Albo, *ikkarim* 2:28; *Yalkut Shimoni* 67; *Pirkei d'Rabbi Eliezer* 22; *Midrash Tehillim* 94:4; *Gen. R.* 48:11; *Shir ha-Shirim R.* 1:8; B. *Shabbat* 88b–89a; *The Torah Anthology* (TA) by Rabbi Y.B. Arguiti, Rabbi Aryeh Kaplan, tr., *Yalkut Me'am Lo'ez* 15 (N.Y.: Maznaim, 1984), pp. 220–3. See, also, S. Schechter, *Aspects of Rabbinic Theology* (N.Y.: Schocken, 1961), pp. 81, 82, 257, 285, and citations on p. 81, n. 2.

54 B. *Sota*, 33a; T.P. *Sanhedrin*, x, 2, p. 28c; *Lev. R.* xx, 3, p. 697; *Ruth R.* V, 14; *Deut. r.* ii, 4; *Midrash Tehillim* 94, 4; *Pesikta d'Rav Kahana* 24:11; see also Schechter, *Rabbinic Theology*, pp. 321–2, and citations on p. 322, n. 1; Urbach, *The Sages*, pp. 461, 753, 891. Consistently, the angels opposed the creation of man (*Gen. R.* 8:4–5; TA 15, p. 220; Urbach, *The Sages*, p. 206), and they opposed giving the Torah to man because humans could not always obey it (B. *Shabbat*, 89b; *Pesikta Rabbati*, 98a–b; *Ex. R.* 281; *Cant. R.* viii, 11). See, generally, David E. Fass, "How The Angels Do Serve," JUDAISM, vol. 40, no. 3 (Summer, 1991): 281–9.

55 Rabbi J.B. Soloveitchik has pointed out that repentance is fulfilled in two ways: by *kiyyum*, sincere abandonment and renunciation of sin, and commitment never to do the prohibited act (or neglect the doing of a positive commandment) in the future; and *ma'asseh*, the objective, physical act by which this intent is objectified (P. Peli [on J.B. Soloveitchik], *Al ha-Teshuvah* [Jerusalem: WZO, 1975] [Hebrew]; p. 40). There is an English translation by P. Peli, published in Jerusalem by Oroth, in 1975. I suggest that the angels oppose repentance because they cannot know or verify the internal aspects of its fulfillment in the human heart, and because — due to their own perfection — they inherently have no ability to feel compassion for man's moral struggle wth his evil inclination — because angels have no such inclination (or struggle) themselves. See, e.g., Rambam, *Guide*, Part 11, Ch. VII, pp. 162–3; and *Shir ha-Shirim R.* 1:8. Without understanding there can be no compassion, and without compassion there can be no forgiveness. This is evidently the root of angelic opposition both to man's creation and to the giving of the Torah to man.

56 *Num. R.* 22:9; *Midrash Tehillim* 14: 1; *Midrash Proverbs* 12. In kabbalah, the angels are said to consist of four heavenly elements: mercy, strength, beauty, and

dominion. *(Sefer Yezirah* 1:7; *Pardes Rimonim* 24:10). This is not necessarily inconsistent with the conclusion that angels cannot know what is in the human mind and heart, since the angelic element of mercy is not based on compassion but on justice. Thus, in *Tanhuma, Pirke d'Rabbi Eliezer, Midrash ha-Gadol* on *Gen.* 2:11–12, and Ginzberg, *Legends,* Vol. I, p. 281, they plead for Isaac, not out of compassion but because *the Akedah is* unjust to him (and to Abraham and Sarah, because of their merit and God's promises to them).

57 B. *Shabbat* 12b; *Shulhan Arukh, Yoreh De'ah, 335, 5* and *The Taz, ad loc.; Shulhan Arukh, Orah Hayyim, 101,* 4; B. *Sotah* 33a; cf. Abarbanel, *Zevah Pesah,* on *Ha Lahma Anya,* who states that angels understand all languages, citing B. *Sotah* 36b and *Pirkei d'Rabbi Eliezer,* 24.

58 See the three *midrashim* cited at the end of n. 56; also, Ginzberg, *Legends,* Vol. 1, pp. 272–3 and Vol. V, pp. 248–9. Angels cannot act morally independently because they have no evil inclination, only the good one, *yezer tov (Shir ha-Shirim Rabbah* 1:8; *Sefer Mizvot Katan* [1566], p. 81; Y. Culi, *The Torah Anthology: Me'am Loez [TA],* Vol. 3 [N.Y.: Maznaim, 1984], pp. 137–8). Cf. the Amoraic statement that the angels were envious of the Sanhedrin, cited in Urbach's *The Sages, pp.* 181, 205

59 See *The Kuzari,* Part 1. Arguably, the Noahide laws were not given by a private revelation but to all of Noah's family, validated by the publicly visible sign of the (first) rainbow, paralleling the "visible" thunder and lightning at Sinai *(Gen.* 9:1–17; *Ex.* 20:18). There have been post-Sinaitic "revelations" to individuals, e.g., many kabbalists, and the maggidic messages communicated through the lips of R. Joseph Karo; Moses Hayyim Luzzatto heard messages from the spirits of Biblical heroes; see his *Zohar Tinyana (The Second Zohar).* But Judaism rejects revelation as the source of post-Sinai legal decisions, or the addition, abrogation, suspension, or violation of halakhah, except for prophetic *hora'at sha-ah,* discussed above.

60 Similarly, B. *Yoma* 28b interprets *Gen.* 26:5 to mean that Abraham observed the written and oral law (See note 2). However, Rashi, Rashbam, and *Or Ha'hayyim* interpret "because Abraham listened to My voice" as referring to the trials of Abraham, including the *Akedah;* Ibn Ezra is uncertain. Ramban includes the *Akedah* trial under "My commandments," but also includes God's command that Abraham be *merciful* under My "statutes" (or My "ordinances"). Even if this text does refer to the *Akedah,* that would not tell us whether Abraham's merit there was obedience to God's voice or to His moral commandments.

61 *Gen. 18:19; Deut.* 12:31; 2 *Kings* 3:26–7; *Jer.* 7:31, 9.

62 B. *Rosh Hashanah* 16a's statement that blowing the ram's horn recalls for God, "for your benefit, the binding of Isaac ... And I shall account it for you as if you yourselves [future generations] bound yourselves up before Me," may be interpreted as reflecting this faith, and not a zealous desire by Abraham to kill his son.

63 Hayyim Nahman Bialik and Yehoshua Hana Ravnitzky, eds., *The Book of Legends,* William G. Braude, tr. (N.Y.: Schocken, 1992), pp. 40–41. Although Abraham and Isaac ascend Moriah together, the Torah emphasizes that Abraham "returned to his young men" alone *(Gen.* 22:19; *Midrash Hagadol* [Margulies edition], p. 360); they settle in different places and never meet or speak to each other again. See, also, Shlomo Riskin, "Love is Not Enough," *Jerusalem Post,* Week Ending November 21, 1992, p. 19, and Plaut, *op. cit., p.* 152. That Isaac did not receive the patriarchal blessing from his father, but only from God, who expressly predicated it on his father's devotion to God's law *(Gen.* 26:3–5; cf. *Gen.* 25:5 and

Rashi *ad loc.)*, which did not occur when Jacob received the blessing (27:28–9, 28:4), indicates that God intended finally to assure a traumatized and estranged Isaac that his father had never intended to kill him.

64 *The Book of Legends,* pp. 41–2. A key aspect of Abraham's test at the *Akedah* was the conflict between the command to kill Isaac, and God's earlier promise to Abraham that his seed would be perpetuated through Isaac. Actually, Abraham *did* plead, *indirectly*, but explicitly in the text, for Isaac to be saved, when he predicted to his retinue that God would cause a sheep to be seen and, thereby, serve as a Divine sign that it should be substituted for Isaac on the altar (*Gen.* 22:8 and 13). I don't recall seeing this interpretation elsewhere.

65 On whether Abraham had a duty to question the authenticity of what seemed like a Divine command to sacrifice Isaac, because of its problematic aspects, see Suzanne Last Stone, "Between Truth and Trust: The False Prophet As Self-Deceiver?" (2005), Fifth Annual Herbert Berman Memorial Lecture, Center for Jewish Studies, Queens College, City University of New York, October 29, 2003, for a comprehensive discussion of the different rabbinic views.

God Tests Abraham — Abraham Tests God

In Jewish tradition, the Torah has 70 — that is, many, inexhaustible — facets and interpretations. I would like to suggest a new one, of the *Akedah*, the binding of Isaac (*Genesis* 22), a story with as many facets as any in the Hebrew Bible.

In brief: God commands Abraham to slaughter his beloved son Isaac as a sacrifice to God. As Abraham is about to sacrifice the boy on the altar, an angel calls out to him to stop "because now I see that you are a God-fearing person and you would not withhold your son... from me" (*Genesis* 22:12).

In the traditional understanding of this story, God never intended Abraham to slaughter Isaac, because it was wrong — as we know from the beginning of the story, which speaks of God "testing" Abraham, and from the end of the story, when Abraham is told to desist. Abraham, on the other hand, out of fear of God, was willing to violate God's moral law in faithfulness to God's command. Abraham passed the test.

The message of the *Akedah* is quite plainly that God does not want even his most God-fearing adherents to go so far as to murder in his name or even at his command. Indeed, the angel orders Abraham "not to do anything to [the boy]." Implicitly, we are being told, God will never ask for this kind of proof of loyalty or fear of God again. He only asked it of Abraham, the first forefather of the Jewish people, to demonstrate Abraham's boundless fear of God.

Because Abraham is praised for being prepared to do what we may not do, and because God, the source of all morality, asked Abraham to do what no moral person before or since should ever contemplate, the *Akedah* has remained one of the most difficult texts to understand, justify and transmit to new generations.

I believe there is a counter message in the text that exists in parallel with its traditional meaning, a simultaneous and necessary conceptual theological balance to the awesome mystery and the daunting problems of the traditional interpretation.

I believe that God was testing Abraham to see if he would remain loyal to God's moral law, but Abraham — who could not know this — was simultaneously testing God to see what kind of covenant and religion he, Abraham, was being asked to join.

After all, it was Abraham who found God, not the other way around. According to the Midrash,[1] "Until Abraham arrived, God reigned only over the heavens."[2] It was Abraham who "crowned" Him God on earth, the God of man.[3] In these circumstances, Abraham not surprisingly had certain moral expectations — and perhaps even requirements — of the all-powerful God of the ordered universe, Whose tradition as a God Who abhorred violence and immorality he had received and studied, and in Whose name he was about to establish a new world religion.

In testing God, as it were, Abraham was, ultimately, testing himself. *I have found God,* he seems to be saying, *and my tradition and experience have revealed Him and made Him known to me as an all-powerful, all-knowing, just and compassionate God. But I need to be sure that this is the God to Whom I truly wish to dedicate myself and my progeny and my followers for all time. If the God I have found demands the same kind of immorality seen in my father's pagan society, I must be mistaken. I must look further. To obey such a God is not a moral advance at all.* To paraphrase our Sages: Better observance without God than God without observance.[4]

In short, Abraham wanted to see if God would stop him.

One may well ask, if this were the case, why Abraham didn't challenge God at the outset, when first commanded to sacrifice Isaac. Abraham had earlier done just that when God had told him his plan to destroy Sodom and Gomorrah (*Genesis* 18:20 — 32).[5] We cannot justify Abraham's refusal to at least protest God's command that he kill Isaac on the grounds that prophets must *silently* obey whenever consulted or commanded by God. The opposite is true when God's justice or compassion, and the morality of His commands, is at issue (see note 5).

There is an alternative strategy, however — stalling for time. I do not believe Abraham ever intended to kill Isaac. He was obviously terribly concerned that God had commanded him to do so. However, those who seek simultaneously to obey their superiors — whom they admire, respect and sometimes fear — *and* give their superiors a chance to change their minds about what seems to be an unwise or immoral idea, rarely challenge the idea head on. They stretch things out.

The matter may be compared to a father who asks his son to violate the Sabbath in some way. The child does not know whether his father is testing his obedience to the law — which requires him to resist his father and observe the Sabbath commandments — or whether his father is testing his love (and fear) of his parent. The child can protest immediately, perhaps thereby showing disrespect and causing the parent anguish, or the child can make the necessary preparations to do what the parent has requested, seeming to go along, hoping that when the actual time comes the parent will never let the child take the last step.

This is precisely what the texts tell us that Abraham did.[6] He did not rush — he stalled! He broke up the task that he was given into numerous tasks, or steps, and at each one he stopped and waited to see whether "the Boss" had reconsidered. It was never Abraham's intention to kill his son, and God never indicated whether he wanted Abraham to kill Isaac, or whether he wanted Abraham to refuse to do so. Given Abraham's moral purity, we may reasonably conclude that if, at the very end, God had not rescinded his command for Isaac's death, Abraham would have rejected the command, chosen the moral course to not commit murder and save his son — and then be forced to reexamine the prospects of his new religion, and the belief and faith on which it rested. Abraham was waiting for God to say: "Don't do it."

The text can be interpreted to show Abraham stalling. It does not show Abraham leaping from receipt of God's command to his execution of it. *Indeed, Abraham never agrees to accept this command and perform it.* Instead, the text describes Abraham going through a series of separate steps: First he gets up, then he dresses his animals, then he gets his retinue in order, then he cuts the firewood, and then he sets off, and then he sees Moriah, and then he instructs his retinue to wait, and then he takes the firewood and places it on Isaac's back, and then he takes "the fire and the knife," and then he and Isaac walk (*vayelkhu*) not run toward Moriah and then there is a conversation, and then he makes the various preparations of the altar, and then he ties Isaac onto the altar, and then he stretches out his arm and then, finally, he raises the knife above his son. Does this plodding, detailed sequence of steps connote a man rushing off to do God's bidding? — Hardly.

The point of the text is quite clear. At each step Abraham is waiting for God to evidence a change of mind, to withdraw His command. When that is not forthcoming, Abraham takes the next step, and puts the Almighty to the next test — as it were — always showing obedience, always *giving God the opportunity* to make the moral statement that God does not want man to murder or to commit other immoral acts in God's name. And, at the very end, when Abraham takes the last step before he would be forced by his conscience to stop and challenge God's command, the angelic order to stop finally comes.[7]

Those who argue that Abraham intended to kill Isaac before being stopped cannot prove it from the *Akedah*, because Abraham never agreed to kill his son, and never had to. Had he done so and said, "I still believe in God," we would have had proof. We would also have had a religion to which few, perhaps none of us, could subscribe, because such a religion would never have endured.[8]

62

When God says, "Because you have done this thing and have not withheld your son, your only son… I will indeed bless you and I will indeed multiply your progeny…." (*Genesis* 22:16 — 17), he means only that "You (Abraham) were willing to endure the confused agony of going ahead[9] and acting in seeming obedience to My [God's] command, to the very point of killing Isaac — with faith that I would never allow that to happen."[10]

This is the same kind of faith that the children of Israel demonstrated when they plunged into the waters of the Red Sea at God's command (*Exodus* 14:15–16) — *not the serene faith that God wanted them to kill themselves and their families by drowning, and the zealous intention of doing so, but the confident faith that God would, somehow, save them and keep his redemptive promises to them.* Such a faith demonstrates, as did Abraham's, that God is, indeed, a God of justice and righteousness and not a God Who tests the faith of His followers by testing their willingness to kill themselves or their loved ones just because God asks it.

Abraham did not want God's moral law against murder to be affirmed merely as a Divine response to a human plea — as occurred at Sodom — or to be proclaimed merely as a response to human arguments about God's mercy, justice and righteousness. To achieve this, Abraham needed an enduring, unshakable faith in God's justice and righteousness, a faith that allowed him to proceed with the *Akedah, not* with the steadfast, zealous intent to kill Isaac, but with the steadfast, serene faith that God, *without the need for human pleading*, would ultimately pronounce for all, and for all time, the prohibition against murder — even for God's glory and in God's name.

The *Akedah* is a morality tale of Abraham's staunch defense of God's moral law against any temptation — even God's command — to violate it. It establishes Judaism's unique insight among ancient religions, cults and cultures about the dangers of having human beings submit to the orders of individuals who claim unique access to the wishes of "the gods," or of any god.

The corrective is a religion based on a covenant between God and *all* of the people, in a revealed text to which *all* have access and which *all* can master. No person or elite can misguide the people down paths of immorality in the name of a supernatural power.

God was testing Abraham to see if he would remain faithful to His revealed moral law even when Divinely commanded to violate it, in order fully and finally to expunge the belief and practice of child sacrifice or any murder (ostensibly) in God's name or for God's benefit. Abraham never intended to kill Isaac but, with faith in God's morality, Abraham was waiting for God to say, "Stop, don't do it, I didn't mean it," just as God was waiting for Abraham to say, "I won't do it."

In his determination not to kill Isaac, and his willingness to go forward with God's command until ordered to stop, Abraham passed the twin tests of the *Akedah*, the tests of the strongest moral courage and the purest religious faith.[11]

....

NOTES

1 The Midrash is a genre of Rabbinic literature that includes homilies as well as commentaries on specific books of the Bible.

2 Joseph B. Soloveitchik in *Man and Faith in the Modern World, Reflections of the Rav*, adapted from the lectures of Rabbi Joseph B. Soloveitchik by Abraham R. Besdin (Hoboken, NJ: Ktav, 1989), vol. 2, p. 50, quoting *Sifri* 313, *Ha'azinu*.

3 Rashi, commentary on *Genesis* 24:7; Babylonian Talmud, *Berakhot* 59.

4 Jerusalem Talmud, *Hagigah* 1:7; Gerson Cohen, *Studies in the Variety of Rabbinic Cultures* (Philadelphia: Jewish Publication Society, 1991), p. 73.

5 This is in contrast to Noah, whom our Sages criticize for not speaking up when God announced his plan to destroy the world by the Flood. Moses, too, was told about God's plan to destroy the Jewish people and start a new nation from Moses's progeny, after the sin of the golden calf (*Exodus* 32:1 — 14), and he is praised by our Sages because he objected. In Jewish tradition, a prophet's conscientious objection to a Divine order is praiseworthy; in Jewish law, a prophet may only follow Divine commands to violate God's law if the purpose is to protect the law (See Responsum No. 652 of Radbaz, Rabbi David ibn Zimra of Egypt and Palestine, renowned 16th-century halakhic interpreter).

There is a basis in the Talmud for the view that Abraham was at least doubtful that God really intended for him to slaughter Isaac. The Sages tell us that even a prophet of truth — indeed, especially such a prophet — is required to question the reliability of what he or she perceives is a Divine message requiring problematic action. The reason: No two prophets hear God in the same way and, therefore, His message may not have been correctly and fully understood. See B.

San. 69a and Suzanne Last Stone, "Truth and Illusion," *Jewish Quarterly Review* (Winter 2004): 19-20.

6   Compare the *aggadah* (homiletic interpretation) that Abraham *rushed* to kill his son, e.g., Rashi and J.H. Hertz, *The Pentateuch and Haftorahs* (London: Soncino Press, 1938), at *Genesis* 22:3, compounding the moral problem of the traditional interpretation. Another example would be a boss asking his employee to "cook the books." The employee does not know whether the boss is testing the employee's respect for the law or his fear of his boss. On the issue of the morality of ends versus means — where Abraham was commanded to use immoral means (child sacrifice) for a moral end (show love and fear of God under extreme circumstances) — there is an interesting rabbinic dispute regarding Joseph's failure to contact his father, Jacob, and reassure him of his being alive, well and politically prospering, and his failure to reveal his identity to his brothers before tormenting them as Egypt's grand vizier. Nachmanides (13th century) defends Joseph: he believed he had a duty to God to make his Divine dreams, of his family acknowledging his rulership over them, come true. Rabbi Yitzhak Arama (15th century), disagrees; he contends that Joseph should have had faith that God would see to it that His promise to Joseph (prophesied to Joseph in his dreams), would be fulfilled — presumably, in a moral way. Joseph should not have relied on his own, immoral means to achieve that Divinely promised end. Rabbi Yehuda Gilad, a contemporary religious scholar, of Kibbutz Lavi in Israel, has written a *devar Torah* on Joseph's actions (e-mail — America Online, December 18, 2002), that supports Arama's (and my) view.

In Rabbi Gilad's view, it makes no sense for one to violate God's general will that we behave morally (see, e.g., the Noahide Laws and Tanakh, *passim*) in order to fulfill God's particular will here (Joseph's dream). Nehama Leibowitz [also says that Arama] was correct…Joseph…could have, and should have, chosen a moral course of action through which to [realize his dreams]…God's will [says Rav Gilad] for Joseph's destiny should have been brought about through moral channels… God's will has not been truly actualized if unfolded thorugh immoral means; see also *Artscroll Deuteronomy* on *Deut.* 18:20.

7   The Babylonian Talmud (*Ta'anit* 15a) records that on fast days called in response to community suffering, for example, a drought, the Israelites prayed: "May He Who answered Abraham on Mount Moriah answer [us]," a prayer that is still recited as part of the Yom Kippur liturgy. The Jerusalem Talmud (and commentary thereon) states that Abraham was [silently] praying for God to relieve him of the terrible command to kill his son (*Ta'anit* 2:4). While this tradition confirms that Abraham did not wish to kill Isaac, we must try to understand the text as it is written, in which Abraham apparently remained silent about Isaac until the end of the *Akedah*.

8   According to a midrash, Abraham's apparent obedience to God's command caused Sarah's death and Isaac's alienation from him forever after. Although Abraham and Isaac ascend Moriah together, the Torah emphasizes that Abraham "returned to his servants" alone (*Genesis* 22:19); Abraham and Isaac settled in different places and never spoke to each other again.

The *Malbim* (at *Gen.* 22:5, 13) says that Abraham did not want to sacrifice Isaac, and, even at the moment before he was told to stop, he was still undecided. The view that Abraham Tested God, "saying yes almost to the end," with "faith in God and His mercy," was offered by Elie Wiesel in *Messengers of God* (New York:

Pocket Books, 1977), pp. 104-107. The following quotes are noteworthy:

A double-edged test: God subjected Abraham to it, yet at the same time Abraham forced it on God. As though Abraham had said: I defy You, Lord. I shall submit to Your will, but let us see whether You shall go to the end...when the life of my son...is at stake.

All things considered, Abraham was perhaps wrong in obeying, or even in making believe that he was obeying.

9 There are hints in the text that Abraham never intended to kill Isaac. For example, Abraham brings along two young men on the trip, presumably to guard Isaac and him — but why take along potential witnesses to a killing, and why the need for them on a trip at God's command? Going up Moriah, Abraham tells them: "We [Isaac and I] will...return to you" (emphasis added). When Isaac asks Abraham, "Where is the lamb for the sacrifice?" Abraham answers, "God will find *for himself* the lamb" instead of "for us," — suggesting that Isaac was in no danger if the lamb was not found, *but God needed the lamb* in order to retain His only follower, and the founder of the world religion that would spread God's message of ethical monotheism. I also view this prediction as an indirect but explicit prayer that God save Isaac from sacrifice — an idea I have not encountered elsewhere.

10 Moreover, the Bible's use of angels, instead of God, to state that Abraham did not "[intend to] withhold" his son, actually suggests the opposite conclusion. In Jewish tradition (based on the story of Creation in *Genesis* and other Biblical and Talmudic sources), angels — in contrast to man, who is born with free will — are perfect in their essence, and therefore lack the capacity for, or understanding of, moral choice and intent. They can comprehend only human actions (see discussion by Rabbi Hayyim Hezekiah Medini [1833-1905], in his 18-volume quasi-Talmudic encyclopedia, *Sedei Hemed*). Thus, for example, the angels objected to the creation of man because he is subject to sin, and they cannot forgive a repentant sinner; they lack understanding of his temptation and later change of heart (see *Exodus* 23:21 and the authoritative medieval Biblical commentary of Rashi). The *Akedah*, therefore, is indirectly and subtly telling us that angels could *not* have known what Abraham intended to do; and is contrasting their *mechanical obedience* to God's will (evident by their believing and praising Abraham's apparent obedience to God's command to kill Isaac) with Abraham's silent *moral response* — which was to question and, if ultimately necessary, resist that terrible command.

11 Perhaps we might say that God was waiting to see if Abraham would go forward and submit, and "not withhold Isaac" (*Gen.* 22:12, 46), with faith and prayer that God would, in the end, save Isaac. The text does not say that Abraham was rewarded "because he was willing to sacrifice Isaac;" it only says what we (and the angels), definitely know — that Abraham did not withhold Isaac, implying — or permitting the implication, and meaning — that Abraham had faith that God would, in the end, intervene.

The Binding of Isaac: Religious Paradoxes, Permutations and Problems

I

I believe it can be shown that the deep structure of the impulse and act of child sacrifice has had a continuing and destructive impact on human religious activity from its inception to the present day. Further, I will argue that only a re-thinking of the concept can have any hope of reversing that destructive impact.

The original story in monotheistic religious texts embodying the ideal of child sacrifice is, of course, the Binding of Isaac (in Hebrew, the *Akedah* or *Akedat Yitzhak*), in which Abraham is commanded by God, as a test of Abraham's faith, to "raise up" Isaac, his cherished, first-born son (of his wife, Sarah), as a totally consumed burnt offering (*olah*) to God, at a place that God would show him.

In the story (*Genesis* 22), Abraham proceeds as instructed, without any words of agreement or disagreement or question as to this command, despite the fact that it conflicts with God's earlier promise to Abraham that his progeny would become a great nation *through Isaac* (*Genesis* 17:19) and, even more importantly, that it conflicts with God's much earlier, universal command to Noah, as part of the "Noahide Laws" (*Genesis* 9:6), prohibiting the killing of innocent human beings.

As Abraham raises his knife above Isaac in evident preparation to complete his task, a Divine voice commands him to stop and not to harm

67

Isaac in the slightest way, and this is followed by a Divine blessing given to Abraham because he "did not withhold" his son from God.

The moral message of the *Akedah* in Jewish tradition is that God does *not* desire human sacrifice in any form, and humanity is forbidden to consider it as a virtuous or pious practice (Jer. 19:5).[1] We know that the ideal of child sacrifice harkens back to pagan practices. Like so many other elements of the Jewish religion, the *Akedah* is a transformation of pagan values, specifically, the idea that the pagan gods of nature, embodying as they do projections of human emotions and desires, need to be assuaged and flattered, and — as a result — became recipients of the ultimate pacification by human beings, by the periodic sacrifice of their own kind.[2]

The *Akedah* takes that ideal and turns it on its head: such sacrifice is exactly and emphatically what God does *not* want, which in turn represents the *anti*-pagan idea that the one God, of Abraham and of all humanity, is *not* subject to understanding in terms of projections of human characteristics and concepts, and most emphatically is *not* a projection of human weaknesses and failings. On the contrary, the monotheistic idea of one God points directly to the idea that there are universal moral and ethical truths to which all humanity owes obedience and appreciation.

The *Akedah* transforms the pagan practice of human sacrifice into a moral test never meant to be fulfilled (Jer. 19:5); God uses the test — and here is a paradox — to announce for all time that human sacrifice, or any other form of arbitrary aggression against other human beings, all of whom are created in the image of God, is absolutely and eternally prohibited by the One God's moral law for mankind. The test, as most have since understood it, is to require Abraham to display a devotion to God in a form that is so extreme that it is unwanted by God. Again, the paradox. But there is no paradox in the underlying message. Having proved to mankind that humans are capable of excessive displays of love and loyalty even to God — indeed, opportunities for such excessive displays invite the false attribution of them as God's will — it remains for man to strive as far as he can to serve God and obey His moral law *without* such excesses because — and here we have another paradox — such actions are even more counter to God's will than disobeying a Divine call to perform them![3]

II

Christianity was born during a period of great social and political trauma and confusion. There were people looking for a Divine sign of redemption from poverty, persecution and religious and political divisions that precluded any sense that the Second Commonwealth of Israel — and, after its conquest by Rome in 70 C.E., the Israelite people — could survive its pressures and problems from within and without.

The new religious ideas of Christianity, which centered about the figure of the crucified Jesus as the Son of God, transformed the ideal of the sacrifice to God of the chosen son perceived in the *Akedah* into a paradigm[4] that explained why Christianity's chosen leader was despised, rejected and crucified. Why this awful paradox of God's chosen having to suffer? Why should this chosen of God be pushed himself to question God, of whom he is so beloved, supposedly asking, on the cross, "My God, my God, why hast thou forsaken me?" Isaac became the authentic religious paradigm that explained the paradox and turned it from a problem to a solution, a prophetic foreshadowing of Jesus' resurrection. In this transformed paradigm, Isaac became Jesus, and Abraham became God's agent. God wanted Jesus the way He wanted his other beloved, cherished son, Isaac. Never mind how that other story ended. The ideal of human sacrifice, the willingness to be sacrificed, of God's beloved, *is proof that he is God's beloved,*[5] and he is saved thereby.

This religious paradox serves, then, as balm, as the key to salvation of the oppressed and the confused. If you suffer, it is because God loves you, and He wants you near Him because of your devotion to Him, even unto sacrificial death, by which He saves you, if you believe in Him.

Clearly, Heaven is not only religious man's reward but religious man's goal. Strive to die for God and your death becomes proof — and here we get to one of the great problems with this paradox as a religious ideal — of your worthiness. Be happy in a sacrificial death, because that death is proof of your chosenness. But that religious paradox leaves no room for a life of striving to improve and correct life in *this* world. Yet, this is not surprising in an era when this life seemed to offer no future, much less present, opportunities for such achievement. So the paradox, born of hopelessness, creates the mystical impulse of escape and rebirth from an eternally inhospitable, i.e., evil world, for the spiritual purity of eternal life in Heaven.[6]

This idea is too powerful a potion for the suffering, helpless and hopeless masses to resist, even if it means death — indeed, *especially* if it means death, viewed as sacrificial death leading to escape and rebirth. It became too powerful for the Roman Empire to resist, when their power, without a moral code, resulted in degeneracy and decay.[7]

Within the space of just a few centuries, this mighty empire crumbled from within and without, and the powerless now assumed power. But their salvation was not built on a Divine moral and ritual legal code associated with the mission of humanity to engage in an active, creative and procreative life, but primarily on a sacrificial faith that mankind's redeemer had come. When it became clear that he had not come, they once more became powerless, forming the base of a new economic, social and political pyramid governed by a new regime of power; this time it was religious power that, in partnership with new, authoritarian political regimes, sought to provide the balm of hope and salvation through magic, miracles and mysticism, to replace the sensual gratifications of the pagan games and circuses of the past.[8]

And now a new paradox, laced with irony, appears as the new religious establishment sought to justify its having replaced Judaism with so little change in the real lives of the masses. The Jewish people, for whom the *Akedah* meant God's eternal moral command *against* persecuting innocents, created in God's image, were now displaced and became themselves the new suffering Jesus, despised, rejected, persecuted, and periodically even crucified, for rejecting the crucified Jesus, suffering at the hands of Jesus' Christian followers and worshippers what Jesus was understood to have suffered at the hands of the Jews, the progeny of the sacrificial Isaac who was the paradigm for Jesus' own deification — the paradox compounded.[9]

Now the twisted knot of the sacrificial ideal was given a new turn. For the suffering Jews sought to treat the *Akedah* as the once suffering Christians did, considering it, not as a message *against* innocent human sacrifice and suffering, but *as an explanation and an authentication of their persecution*, as a positive religious sign that the sacrifice and union with God of His persecuted, dying, beloved followers is what God wants of his cherished, chosen ones. In this new, twisted paradox, Jewish suffering becomes proof of God's love for them, it validates their continued loyalty to their God. Jews, suffering at the hands of Christianity, which initially transformed the idea of the *Akedah* from a message against sacrifice to a message embracing it, now transformed the *Akedah* for the Jews from an averted abomination into a completed, realized demonstration that God loves them, and they Him.[10]

So, for the Christian people, the suffering Jews replaced Jesus for centuries not by their equal holiness, but as the objects of a justified punishment, some form of Divine justice, by which the Jews must endure suffering, as Jesus did, for not accepting Jesus as their messiah. And the Jews embraced their new role: it explained their evident lot and role in history, as they looked back on the *Akedah* as forecasting their destiny, even as they, too, so often were forced to utter the precious paradox of their tormented lives: Our God, our God, why hast Thou forsaken us — we who are your Chosen People?"[11] Fortunately, Christianity and Christians have gone a long way, especially in recent years, toward rectifying their past attitudes towards Judaism and Jews. Indeed, there is now a recognized concept of a Judeo-Christian tradition, particularly in successful, democratic nations, of which both religions are proud.

The primary response of European Jewry to the paradox of persecution and chosenness over the years has been to embrace the paradigm of sacrifice in various ways. Thus, beginning with the First Crusade, and its radical shift in Christian attitude and behavior toward the Jews, we witness Jewish embrace of martyrdom, submissiveness, general hostility to Christian society and culture, and a desire to escape from the world that God created, through mysticism, including ecstatic ascents to heaven and union with God; theosophic speculations on the nature of the Divine pleroma as subject to characteristics and internal processes and sexual relationships that mirror human experience, including fragmentation and exile; and the theurgic restoration of Divine harmony, and human redemption thereby, by mystical efforts, including prayer and other ritualized mythical acts.[12]

Recent history — indeed, most of the last hundred years — has witnessed attacks against what came to be called, in the modern era, the Judeo-Christian civilization, launched by extremist ideologies without moral constraints. These attacks have reenacted the *Akedah* and the passion of Jesus as sacrificial paradigms of the necessary suffering of those whom God loves. Historically, we have seen once again murderous persecutors, e.g., Nazi Germany and Stalinist Russia, and currently, worldwide secular and religious terrorist networks, and mass suffering and submissive victims, as well as a courageous few willing to fight back, as occurred with European Jewry in the Holocaust.[13]

III

Is there a way to break these vicious circles and their paradoxes born of the sacrificial paradigm, to destroy the idea that there is some legitimacy, authenticity, or virtue in being either persecutor or persecuted?

I think there is, but it requires two intellectual breakthroughs, that must be led by men and women of scholarship, piety and wisdom, who must, in turn, persuade their religious communities.

The first breakthrough is being able to understand and persuasively demonstrate the self-defeating and the self-destructive results of wallowing in the role of persecutor or persecuted — whatever their presumed mythical, ancient justifications, which I will come to in a moment — because both of these roles, even the role of persecutor, cause weakness and, therefore, ultimate failure and rejection by the very masses who have supported these roles in the past. Historians should have no trouble proving from history that power corrupts and powerlessness corrodes.[14]

Second, religious scholars need to find and restore to primacy what I would argue is the original and authentic meaning and message of the *Akedah*, what it really should forever stand for in the hearts and minds of those who wish to be transformed by it.

The *Akedah* does *not* mean that God wants or accepts human sacrifice or self sacrifice that are not otherwise required by the ends of justice and righteousness, but performed solely to prove one's love of God or faith in Him. Abraham passed the test of the *Akedah* when he showed God that he was prepared to proceed as God commanded *with faith that the God of justice and righteousness in Whom he believed would never — and could never — let that sacrifice come to pass.*

I think we know this for two reasons. First, it cannot be that Abraham really was prepared to go through with the sacrifice, and that God was really prepared to accept it. That would make Abraham a pagan and the deity, to whom he was sacrificing his son, a pagan deity. There would have been no Jewish people, no prophetic ethical monotheism, and no Jewish history as we know it.

Second, the *Akedah* is never mentioned again in the Bible. If God intended to ask for human sacrifices, he surely would have done so again to make the point. Indeed, the prophets continually condemn the practice as evil (e.g., Jeremiah 19:5). Moreover, what *is* mentioned that is relevant to the issue, on many occasions, is God's command that Israel always remember the Exodus from Egypt, and that the Israelites must be compassionate because they were once slaves in Egypt. That message has two parts: first, when you are "on top" be kind and helpful to those who are weaker than you or subordinate to you; and second, when you are

73

"on bottom" remain hopeful that you can rise up some day.

Self-sacrifice is not how you prove your worth to God. Rather, stay the course, remember how God redeemed Israel from slavery and its sufferings in Egypt, and be careful whom you injure or exploit, lest you precipitate a new cycle of self-sacrifice.

It is in this context that I sometimes imagine God and Abraham in dialogue, a silent, parallel dialogue.

God: Does Abraham really intend to kill Isaac? Would he continue to believe in a God that would let him do that? How could he? What kind of a religion could he establish that was based on child sacrifice? How would he, or I, then be any different than the pagans from which I took him? Perhaps he has faith that I will stop this at the last minute. I hope so. I chose Abraham to father a nation that would bring Me to the world because he was righteous; why would he think I would want him to be different — or that I would be? Didn't I reveal to him My plan to destroy Sodom and Gemorah (*Genesis* 18:18–19) because of their evil ways because I knew that Abraham loves justice and charity, as I do? Why else would I confide in him that way?

Abraham: Does God really want this human sacrifice as proof of my belief and faith in Him? It is so contrary to all that I know about Him and the righteousness that has been His most consistent concern — going back to Cain, and His covenant with him; Noah and the Noahide laws; God's assurance to me that no harm would come to any righteous people at Sodom and Gomorrah; God's assurance to me that no harm would come to Hagar and my son, Ishmael, if I sent them away into the desert as Sarah demanded. I guess God could rescind His promise to me that my progeny would thrive through Isaac as a great nation — perhaps I did something wrong since then to warrant His changing His mind about that; I'm not perfect.[15] But what would the righteous of the world think of Him if He stood for human sacrifice? How could He demand more of any people than the practices of pagans, who sacrifice their children out of fear of the gods? But, if I'm right about Him, Isaac will live through

74

this. I've taught Isaac well, so I'm sure that Isaac knows this, too. God will reveal His true intentions, His true character, which is a God of justice and righteousness, Who demands righteousness of human beings toward one another. I need to have faith in that. I must pray to God not to let this sacrifice come to pass.[16] I'm sure He will hear me. I will go forward with that faith.

And Abraham was rewarded for that faith.

So, God says to us through the story of the *Akedah*, mankind must reject equally both of the paradigms that emerged from the *Akedah*, that is, the paradigms of the sacrificer and the sacrificed, of the persecutor and the persecuted — and the role of the powerful and intellectual observer who finds difficulty in knowing who is good and who is evil, who is eager to find good and evil in both sides, and reasons and explanations for every act, and can find no solution other than re-inventing the pagan-like sacrifice of innocents to make these problems go away.

The persecutor flees God for worldly power, but — without a moral core — degenerates and falls; the persecuted, who find in their persecution God's will, sooner or later lose their best progeny, who flee to mystical fantasy, or fruitless retributions.[17] And the "neutral" observer eventually will become a victim, too. There is no virtue or utility in any of them. They serve neither God nor mankind.

Classical Judaism — that is, Biblical and Rabbinic Judaism — was designed to assure spiritual and material strength and achievement, to find that path in which man flees neither God nor His creation, but embraces both, God's moral power and man's God-given creative power, because this path will result in the everlasting mutual courtship, embrace and love of the One with the other — without paradox, without role transformation, without value transvaluation, and without loss or alienation when troubles come.

No religion can survive if it disrespects either God or His creation, either man or God's moral law. Neither, I believe, can any society. It is time, I believe, to make these truths self-evident.

....

NOTES

1 B. *Ta'anit* 4a.

2 Jon D. Levenson, *The Death and Resurrection of the Beloved Son* (New Haven: Yale University Press, 1993), Preface and Chapters 1-6. It has been suggested that sacrifice of Jewish firstborn to God is implied by true faith throughout *Genesis*; ibid. But, I suggest that a more explicit and continuing message, throughout the Pentateuch, is contained in the repeated Divine command to Israel to obey God's commands as a reminder of the Israelite exodus from Egypt. Surely, this remembrance includes how God smote the Egyptian firstborn and saved the Israelite firstborn. God cherishes Israel's firstborn as he cherishes the people of Israel, in the Biblical metaphor, as God's firstborn. Thus, the furthest thing from His mind is that Jewish fathers should think of sacrificing their children — any of their children. To the extent that such a Freudian-based hostility between father and son may exist, the continuing emphasis in the Bible that we remember the Exodus, and its symbolic meaning of how God cherishes the lives of all Israel, together with the ultimate outcome of the *Akedah*, in which Isaac is spared, serve as a continuing antidote to any such hostility. As God assures Israel in *Exodus* 15:26, "...all the punishments that I placed upon the Egyptian people, I will not place upon you..." God does not want any more sacrificial "bindings" of children for sacrifice just to prove how zealously the parent submits to God's will.

3 A similar idea may be found in Abraham Isaac Kook's interpretation of the *Akedah*; see Jerome I. Gellman, *The Fear, The Trembling, and the Fire* (New York: University Press of America, 1994), pp. 112-16. An alternate view of the *Akedah* test, which I have proposed, is that God sought, and Abraham demonstrated, faith that God would *not* let the *Akedah* be completed; see, e.g., my article, "God Tests Abraham, Abraham Tests God," *Bible Review* (October, 1993):52. See also my discussion at the end of this article. Elie Wiesel has recently similarly noted that the *Akedah* was "a double test: Just as God tested Abraham, Abraham tested God: 'Let's see if you really want me to go ahead with it and kill my son...'Abraham is trying to obey God, but not to kill." See "Contrasting Insights of Biblical Giants," *Biblical Archaeology Review* (July-August, 2004):34.

4 Levenson, ...*Beloved Son*, *Op. cit.*, Chapters 15-16.

5 Ibid.; S. Giora Shoham, *Valhalla, Calvary & Auschwitz* (Cincinnati: Bowman & Cody, 1995), pp. 115-7, 168. See also, Daniel Boyarin, *Dying for God: Martyrdom and the Making of Christianity and Judaism* (Stanford: Stanford University Press, 1999), p. 122; Bruce Feiler, *Abraham* (New York: Harper Collins, 2002), pp. 93-101.

6 For a discussion of the psychological elements of Jewish mysticism, see generally, e.g., Mortimer Ostow, "Judaism and Psychoanalysis," and *idem.*, "The Jewish Response to Crisis," in *Judaism and Psychoanalysis*, Mortimer Ostow, ed. (New York: Ktav Publishing, 1982), pp. 1-44, 231-66.

7 Leonard R. Sillman, "Monotheism and the Sense of Reality," *Judaism and Psychoanalysis*, *Op. cit.*, pp. 283-305.

8 Ibid.; James Carroll, *Constantine's Sword* (New York: Houghton Mifflin, 2001).

9 Ibid.; Shoham, ...*Auschwitz*, *Op. cit.*, p. 272.

10 See, e.g., Shalom Spiegel, *The Last Trial* (Woodstock, Vt.: Jewish Lights, 1993); Robert Chazan, *European Jewry and the First Crusade* (Berkeley: University of California Press, 1987), pp. 127, 158-9, 163-5, and the appendices; Shoham, ...

Auschwitz, pp. 131-2, 169-70; Feiler, *Abraham*, pp. 93-101. Perhaps the lone exception to the midrashic history glorifying Abraham for his desire to sacrifice Isaac, is a little-known seventh century *piyyut* for *Shavuot* (Pentacost, which falls seven weeks after Passover). Composed about the time of the end of the Talmudic age, it tells of a complaint by the Torah to God, questioning Abraham's worthiness to receive the Torah for his progeny:

[But] can I be his [Abraham's] when he has no mercy

His [veritable] right eye was he [Isaac]

Yet he stretched out his hand cruelly to shed blood.

He should have pleaded for mercy [from God] and found it.

But [Abraham] showed no mercy.

Oh, if mercy [from God] had not been found...!

See Yosef Yahalom, *Poetry and Society in Jewish Galilee of Late Antiquity* (Tel Aviv: Kibbutz Ha-Me'uhad/Yad Yitzhak Ben-Zvi, 1999); see also, Peretz Rodman, "Squelching Your Sense of Justice and Decency," *Forward*, September 26, p. 17. The ending — with its striking negative form — implies that God would certainly have shown mercy and prevented Isaac's sacrifice, because for God to have allowed (required) Abraham to complete the sacrifice is unthinkable. I think this is self-evidently true, and further supports my view that Abraham surely came to the same conclusion, justifying his going forward in obedience to God's sacrificial command, *and* his prayer (see note 16), and faith that Isaac would, indeed, be saved.

11 In Judaism, the idea of "Chosen" does not mean for material benefits and privileges, but chosen to deliver and represent God's message of justice, righteousness and lovingkindness, "ethical monotheism."

12 See, e.g., Shmuel Shepkaru, "From Death to Afterlife: Martyrdom and its Recompense," *AJS Review* (1997): 1-44; Mortimer Ostow (see note 6); Nissim Rejwan, *Israel's Place in the Middle East* (Gainesville, Florida: University Press of Florida, 1998), Ch. 3; Shoham, ...*Auschwitz*, *Op. cit.*; p. 309 and *passim*; and David Rosenberg, *Dreams of Being Eaten Alive* (New York: Harmony Books, 2000). Cf. David Berger, "Judaism and General Culture in Medieval and Early Modern Times," *Judaism's Encounter With Other Cultures*, Jacob J. Schacter, ed. *(Northvale, N.J.:Jason Aronson, Inc., 1997), pp. 113-40*. See generally, e.g., Gershom Scholem, *Major Trends in Jewish Mysticism* (New York: Schocken, 1954); Joseph Dan, *Jewish Mysticism* (Northvale, N.J.: Jason Aronson, Inc., 1998); and Moshe Idel, *Kabbalah: New Perspectives* (New Haven: Yale University Press, 1988).

In the 19th century, Hegelians viewed Christianity with hostility, and blamed its alleged progenitor, Judaism, for Christianity's alleged evils, claiming that Jewish human sacrifice influenced Christian religious symbolism — which soon led to a wider rejection of Jews themselves; see Shmuel Ettinger, "The Modern Period," in H. H. Ben Sasson, ed., *A History of the Jewish People* (Cambridge: Harvard University Press, 1976), pp. 805-6.

13 Shoham, ...*Auschwitz*, pp. 179, 193, and *passim*. Maimonides prophetically wrote, eight centuries ago, that an ideology would arise that "will strive to kill his enemy [Judaism] and remain alive, and if he cannot achieve this, he will devise a scheme whereby both will be slain;" see "Epistle to Yemen," *Epistles of Maimonides*, Abraham Halkin, tr. and David Hartman, comm. (Philadelphia:

Jewish Publication Society, 1985), p. 98.

14 See, e.g., Shoham,...*Auschwitz*, *Op. cit.* Chapters 7, 10; and Sillman, "Monotheism...," *Op. cit.*, p. 299.

15 In Jewish tradition, God reserves the right to rescind a promise if its beneficiary subsequently acts so as to become undeserving of it. See *Artscroll Tanakh*, *Genesis* (Brooklyn, N.Y.: Mesorah Publications, 1977), Vol. IV, on *Gen.* 32:8.

16 In Jewish tradition, now memorialized in the High Holiday liturgy, Abraham silently prayed to God to save Isaac from the commanded sacrifice; see B. *Ta'anit*, 15a, J. *Ta'anit* 2:4, and rabbinic commentaries thereon.

17 See, e.g., Sillman, "Monotheism..., *Op. cit.*

Thoughts on Reading the *Akedah* Again

I

The *Akedah* has played such an important role in Jewish tradition and culture, history and liturgy, that one is impelled — even challenged — to continually re-think its meaning to be sure we have it right.[1]

Doing so, it occurred to me that the secret of this challenge is the paradox that the *Akedah* presents, that national salvation requires that a cherished son of God, as all of humanity is, must be sacrificed to God.[2] If cherished, why sacrificed; and if sacrificed, in what way cherished?

It then occurred to me that the real paradox of the story may not be in the *message* but in the *means necessary* to convey that message — a very *different* message — in a *text*. If, as I have maintained, the test was, "Will Abraham obey Me with faith that I, God of the universe, will not let the sacrifice of Isaac come to pass,"[3] and not "Will Abraham be willing to sacrifice Isaac at My Command," then I would argue — and here is the paradox — that it was necessary to portray Abraham *as going forward ready to perform the sacrifice!* This is so because, if the text instead said something like "And Abraham woke up the next morning (after being commanded to sacrifice Isaac) with faith that God would never, in the end, demand such a sacrifice, because this would not only violate His prior promise to Abraham to father a great nation through Isaac[4] but would run counter to everything that Abraham knew that God stands for, and demands of mankind — namely, justice, righteousness and lovingkindness" — then the text would be putting God on trial for the entire three-day trip to Mount Moriah. During that time, we would know how Abraham feels — this sacrifice cannot be right, cannot be moral, and cannot be what God really wants — but we would not know where God stands!

You see, once you introduce the readers, the receivers of the tradition in each generation, to Abraham's inner faith, the story falls apart. We know, Abraham knows, everybody knows what Abraham believes about this demanded sacrifice, but no one knows yet what God believes, except that He requested it. It's true that the text starts with "God tested Abraham," but what was the test? That Abraham would be ready to sacrifice Isaac, or that he would go forward with stalwart faith that the God of righteousness in Whom he had come to believe could not possibly let him complete such an act?

Moreover, there is another reason why it is inappropriate to tell the reader or listener, up front, about Abraham's faith that God will not let the sacrifice happen. Every human being has free will and is vulnerable morally, as Abraham showed on a number of occasions.[5] Therefore, until we know how strong his faith was about God's righteousness in this matter of sacrificing Isaac, that is, until the very last second before Abraham would have to slaughter or save his son, Isaac, we can't say for sure, and — as we have already shown — we certainly can't set the story up so that Abraham appears more righteous than God. So Abraham must be portrayed *until the very end* as silently proceeding as if prepared to sacrifice his son. And, at that very last moment, God's certain, eternal rejection of child sacrifice inevitably must, in the textual exposition, trump Abraham's faith that God would save Isaac. Divine rejection of human sacrifice must be the climax of the trial, and Abraham's faith must remain hidden in the text.

Well then, Abraham had faith, but he also knew that he had the human right, or opportunity, to back away at the last minute if God remained silent. "In the meantime, let me continue with the preparations, and give God a chance to prove His moral greatness beyond any other

80

power in the universe, and justify my faith in Him."

Finally, if the text told us that Abraham knew that God would not let the sacrifice occur, then God's later order to Abraham to desist would not only be anticlimactic, it would suggest that the desist order came *not* because God is against human sacrifice, but because God wanted to be nice to the one person in the world who believed in Him. He simply did his servant a favor.

For all these reasons there is no other way to write this story, or tell this story orally (try it!) but for Abraham to obey *and* keep silent, and for God to make the second great move in the story, by saying, "Stop." This makes it all come out right — now we have the benefit of God commanding against human sacrifice because that is what God really wants, and not because His cherished son, Abraham, wanted it out of fatherly love, which would have removed the moral force from that order when it came. And the story has a dramatic moral punch because the reader or listener of the tale does not know in advance that it will all turn out alright.

But, as against that, we have Abraham looking like a father, a righteous man, ready to kill his son just because God commanded it, without a word of protest, even though Abraham didn't want to or intend to do so.

So the paradox lies in the *means* required to tell that story, not its *message*. The paradox arises from the fact that to tell the story with a powerful, moral ending, Abraham, who had faith all along that all would come out right, is required to be silent for virtually the entire episode, until God makes His moral position known.

But that silence is no reason for us to interpret the story as God rewarding Abraham for wanting to kill Isaac because God asked for this, or as Abraham wanting to do so and deserving his Divine reward for that reason. An interpretation that God rewarded Abraham for his faith — which he, in fact, had — that God would make this all come out correctly, consistent with God's emphasis on the virtues of righteousness, justice and lovingkindness, makes perfect sense of the *Akedah*. The traditional view that God wanted Abraham to show he was ready to sacrifice Isaac, and that Abraham actually was ready to do so, does not. First, God never, in the Jewish Bible, commands a righteous man to act unjustly. Second, God never changes His mind about what is moral and what is not.[6] Third, we know from *Jeremiah* (19:5) that God considers child sacrifice an unmitigated, obscene injustice. Fourth, the injustice of child sacrifice is no less wrong because it is something that God wants; Abraham knew this from his earlier discussion with God about the injustice of God killing any righteous persons that might be found in Sodom (*Gen.* 18:15–33).

So there is ample basis to argue, and conclude, that Abraham had faith that God really did not want Isaac to be sacrificed, and would not let it happen.

One may ask, how strongly did Abraham believe that God would never let Isaac's sacrifice come to pass? We can't know for certain, of course, but consider: In *Jeremiah* 19:5, the prophet represents, with regard to child sacrifice, that this is something that no God-fearing person should even think that God would want or entertain, nor would He consider it as anything but the most obscene, evil act, something that "I never commanded, never decreed, and which never came to My mind." That is a very powerful statement, repeated three times, which the rabbis let us know[7] refers to three places in *Tanakh* which may otherwise suggest that God would favorably entertain a human sacrifice made to show one's love and submission to God. Those three places are the story of Mesha, king of Moab (2 *Kings* 3); Jephthah, one of Israel's judges before Saul was named the first king of Israel (*Judges* 11); and Abraham at the *Akedah* (*Genesis* 22).[8] So the obvious conclusion is: Abraham, with his knowledge of God's attributes of justice and righteousness, surely knew this of God, as Jeremiah did in chastising Israel about what was expected of all good Israelites concerning human sacrifice. If God's desire for child sacrifice should have been inconceivable to any ordinary Israelite, wouldn't it have been inconceivable to Abraham?

But one may ask, "If Abraham's faith was so great, where, then, is the test?" I have two related answers. First, faith is one thing and perfect faith is a little stronger, but even perfect faith is not perfect knowledge. The second answer is: the question assumes that men of faith by definition cannot be tested. But, in fact, they can, and they were. This can be seen from the text of *Genesis* itself. We know that Abraham faced 10 trials, each one a Divine test, designed to teach Abraham, and us, what God expects of us.[9] Clearly, Abraham — that giant of faith — could be tested. And more: The *Akedah* was the *final* trial.[10] The trial that immediately preceded it was much like the *Akedah*; Sarah demanded that Abraham send his concubine and their son, Ishmael, into the desert to certain death. Abraham considered this an immoral act, but agreed to Sarah's request when God personally assured him that mother and child would survive, and that Ishmael would father a great nation. How does the *Akedah* trial differ? In one respect: at the *Akedah*, Abraham was asked once again to send his son — this time, Isaac — to certain, Divinely commanded death, *but without any Divine assurance that all would come out alright*. Evidently, the text believes that asking Abraham to sacrifice his son without any guarantees that Isaac will live, and expecting Abraham to proceed without any such guarantees, is a new test, a more difficult test, than the Hagar-Ishmael test, no matter what Abraham presumably learned about God's righteousness even earlier at Sodom (where Abraham tested God's intentions to destroy all that city's inhabitants even if some righteous individuals lived there) and at the incident of Hagar and Ishmael. Evidently, faith at the *Akedah* was considered an achievement, something that can be tested, and *not* a paradox as is implied by the question, "If Abraham had faith where is the test?"[11] Even the most faithful can be tested. Even the most faithful are human, and may not pass every test of life.

Let me conclude with one more observation about what Abraham knew, and when he knew it — and, I may add, what we should know, and when we should have known it.

Suppose God let Abraham complete the sacrifice — say, to prove to the world that Abraham was willing to go that far, so powerful was his faith. Then what? Would Abraham have finished the job, and completed the sacrifice?

One answer, that I have heard from many to whom I have addressed this question, is: "That's an impossible question; God never would have allowed Abraham to complete the sacrifice" (I guess those responses are based on Jeremiah's chastisement of Israel, discussed above!). Well, if so, why can they figure this out, but resist the idea that Abraham could, too! And if he did figure it out, why might he not proceed as commanded, *with faith that his silent prayer that Isaac be saved would be answered*, and that his understanding, and ours, of how God's righteousness would play out in the end, based on the inconceivability of any other conclusion — recall that Jeremiah says God expects such understanding of *all* who believe in Him — would prove correct?

Another answer to my question might be: "Yes, it's possible that God might have let Abraham complete the sacrifice, and that Abraham would have done so; what's wrong with that?"[12] What's wrong with it is that such a scenario makes Abraham a pagan, sacrificing to a pagan god, just like the society of his father used to do before Abraham was commanded by God to leave that society (*Gen.* 12:1). If Abraham actually sacrificed Isaac, such an outcome — assuming it did not destroy the Jewish people in its womb — would have resulted in a completely different Judaism, a different Abraham, a different God, a different Torah, in which no Jeremiah, or any other prophet, could scold the people for engaging in child sacrifice — I could go on and on.

Judaism, to put it succinctly, would have been a religion suffused with child sacrifice, with no prophetic calls for its cessation possible or forthcoming. We would be morally at sea had *Genesis* 22 rewarded Abraham for killing Isaac. We would not exist today as a nation, much less as a religion. There would have been no chain of tradition from Abraham to Isaac to Jacob and on through Jewish history, a story of God courting and cajoling a difficult people to follow His ways of justice, righteousness and lovingkindness, to all, and a people vacillating from need of God, to rejection of God, to love of God, but always betrothed to God, and unable and unwilling to embrace any other God but the One who revealed Himself, in all His power and moral attributes, to Abraham, and Isaac, and their progeny.

These are the considerations that I believe must govern when asking whether God could have let Abraham complete the sacrifice. I believe they are self-evident, and I believe that they were self-evident to Abraham, the silent, suffering hero of the *Akedah* trial.

So Abraham passed this final test, demonstrating his faith in God's justice, righteousness, and lovingkindness, while inviting the eternal Divine prohibition against human sacrifice, for which the *Akedah* must always be remembered.[13]

....

NOTES

1 See, e.g., discussions in earlier articles of mine, e.g., "God Tests Abraham, Abraham Tests God," in this chapter. See also, "Contrasting Insights of Biblical Giants," *Biblical Archeology Review* (July/August 2004):34.

2 See, e.g., Jon D. Levenson, *The Death and Resurrection of the Beloved Son* (New Haven: Yale University Press, 1993), Preface and Chapters 1-6.

3 See note 1 above.

4 *Gen.* 21:12, 17:19-21; see also my article, "The Promise of Canaan to Abraham's Seed," in Chapter 3.

5 See Nachmanides, *Commentary on the Torah*, at *Gen.* 12:12-13.

6 Compare *Ezekiel* 20:25-6. See my article, "Ezekiel 20:25-6: Did God Ever Command The Sacrifice of Israel's Firstborn Sons?" in Chapter 2 .

7 See B. *Ta'anit* 4a.

8 See my articles on the *Akedah*, e.g., "God Tests Abraham…," in this chapter; The Tragedy of Jephthah," and "The Message of the Prophet Elisha," in Chapter 2. The only way for Abraham to respond to God's command, viewed as a test for both God and Abraham (see my article, "God Tests Abraham — Abraham Tests God," in this Chapter) is to pray *silently* for Isaac to be saved, as he did (see B. *Ta'anit* 15a and J. *Ta'anit* 2:4 and rabbinic commentary thereon, *ad loc.*), thereby forcing God to pronounce His moral law: "Do not [even] touch the boy!" as the climax of this event. Indeed, this pronouncement goes beyond Isaac; it bespeaks a universal prohibition against all child sacrifice to please or appease God; *Jeremiah* 19:5; B. *Ta'anit* 4a; Shlomo Riskin, "The Sacrifice of Yitzhak," *Jewish World* (Long Island, New York), November 1-7, 1996.

9 *ArtScroll Tanach Series*, *Genesis* (Brooklyn, N.Y.: Mesorah Publications, 1977-95), Vol. 1a, at *Gen.* 12:1.

10 *Ibid.*

11 See, e.g., Shubert Spero, "The *Akedah: Machloket L'Shem Shamayim*," *Jewish Bible Quarterly* (January 2000), and the response of Berel Dov Lerner, "The *Akedah*: *Machloket L'Shem Shamayim*," *JBQ* (April/June 2001).

12 See, e.g., Levenson, ...*the Beloved Son, Op.cit.*

13 From a psychoanalytical standpoint, Abraham's (silent) prayer to God to save Isaac (see my articles in this chapter:, "God Tests Abraham — Abraham Tests God," esp. note 5, and "The Binding of Isaac: Religious Paradoxes, Permutations and Problems," note 16, and Abraham's faith that this prayer would be answered *(see prior articles, passim)*, are particularly noteworthy as elements of his passing the test of the *Akedah*. He resisted his Oedipally-based, unconscious hostility to Isaac's desire for his mother, Sarah. Such a response would be a projection of Abraham's own natural, unconscious, similar feelings as a child towards his own mother. Abraham's moral strength, in this context, is especially noteworthy because the Midrash goes to some lengths to describe the close emotional and physical ties between Sarah and Isaac, which provided Abraham with an intensified, Divinely-sanctioned opportunity to act out this unconscious impulse to do away with his son — which Abraham successfully resisted. I am grateful to Dr. Robert Fiore, Ph.D., for this psychoanalytical insight. See also, Nicky Lachs, "Isaac: A Psychological Perspective," *Jewish Bible Quarterly* (October-December 2002):266-71.

Preparing for the *Akedah*: The Strange Case of the Two Missing Witnesses

I

For the past fifteen years, I have been writing extensively on the *Akedah*,[1] to develop an understanding of the text that deals with what I and many others have perceived as its baffling moral implications. In the back of my mind, throughout this period, there has been lurking the need to deal with the issue of how this event was intended to be transmitted in a believable way to Abraham's progeny. I think this issue itself needs some explanation, before going ahead with an approach to its resolution.

II

I start with the notion that seems consistent with the text in *Genesis*, in which Abraham does not tell Sarah about God's command that he leave home to sacrifice Isaac, which rabbinic commentators understand to mean that Abraham was afraid to tell Sarah about his trip — and much less its purpose.[2] Indeed, it is not clear from the text that he told her he would be away for about a week — the trip to Moriah took about half a week, apart from the climb to the top[3], perhaps hoping to have an explanation ready for her about what happened by the time he returned. It is likely that he himself was unaware what would eventually take place — particularly if my theory about Abraham's faith and prayer that Isaac would be saved is correct[4] — and he certainly had no time to think clearly and definitely about what to say to her in advance, given the need for him to begin to demonstrate his obedience to God's command,[5] and Sarah's likely response if her suspicions were aroused.

We know, for instance, that Isaac was Sarah's only child, her first and only-born son, whom she cherished and protected from any harm or improper influence, from his brother, Ishmael.[6] We also know that she did not believe even God when she received the Divine promise that she would give birth to a healthy son at the age of ninety years.[7] Indeed, I venture the thought that both she and Abraham failed the test of having faith that this Divine promise would come true, and that the *Akedah* was, at least for Abraham, a redemptive or "make-up" test, harder than the first: Having not believed the Divine promise of Isaac's birth, which did come true despite his (and Sarah's) refusal to believe it — would he believe, and how would he react to, a Divine command that promised, as it were, Isaac's death — at Abraham's own hand![8]

In any case, it is clear that Abraham, and we, had and have a right to assume that Sarah would never have allowed Abraham to go ahead with this last test; it would kill her before it would ever have a chance to kill Isaac.[9]

That means two things. First, Abraham could not tell Sarah what God had asked of him. Second, he could not tell her before the fact: God expected Abraham to go and not ask questions, nor be delayed by having to answer Sarah's questions. So he left early in the morning. Either he told her nothing, saving the story for his return, perhaps *without Isaac*, as discussed above, or — as some rabbinic commentary would have it — he told her that Isaac, now 37 years old, was being taken to study at the school of monotheism of Shem and Ever, now run by the High Priest of Jerusalem (then "Salem"), Malkhitzedek, identified by the Sages as Shem, Noah's praiseworthy son.[10]

III

We now come to the focal point of this paper. The text tells us[11] that

Abraham took "his two young men" with him, but then left them at the bottom of the mountain. Why mention them? Abraham was very wealthy, the trip was arduous, and we don't find any specific mention of Abraham being accompanied by servants or bodyguards in connection with any of his other trips during his life. Why here? Let's go further.

If we had to guess whom Abraham would take along in carrying out this Divine task, to somehow bear witness to Abraham's obedience, we would have to advance two names: Ishmael, Abraham's other beloved son, born through Hagar, his concubine, at Sarah's suggestion, while she was still barren;[12] and Eliezer, Abraham's trusted prime disciple and chief servant, his *factotum*, to whom he would later entrust the daunting task of finding a suitable wife for Isaac. This seems to be the accepted view of the commentators as to the identities of the "young men."[13]

But why take them along if Abraham intended to leave them behind when he and Isaac ascended Mount Moriah? Clearly, he did not want them to see what would happen there. Perhaps he did not want them to know, fearing that they would try and stop what they would perceive as the bizarre behavior of a very old man.[14] Did Abraham even know what would happen there? The traditional view is that he did, that he proceeded with eagerness to obey God's sacrificial command as soon as he was advised of God's wish that he sacrifice Isaac, and that he wanted to bring that sacrifice to prove his love and loyalty to God no matter what would be demanded of him.[15]

If that view is correct, what would be the best way to transmit that message to his progeny? To begin with, we must ask, "What progeny?" God's promise of Abraham fathering a nation was that this would take place *through Isaac*,[16] who was still unmarried and without children. So God had, by His request for Isaac's sacrifice, nullified this promise to Abraham. But the God of Abraham, as Abraham and we have understood Him, is One; *that* God does not change His mind. It is an article of Jewish faith, recited every day in the morning in the *Yigdal* prayer.[17] God does not change His mind nor abrogate His laws or commands.

Let us put aside these matters of Abraham's faith in God's sacrificial command, despite its problematic aspects, including the moral issues. If Ishmael and Eliezer would have been there to bear witness to Abraham's faith, culminating in the sacrifice of his own son to God, why wouldn't he have taken them to the top of Moriah to witness this great act of faith? If that is what would have occurred there, or — even assuming that Abraham still had some hope that it would not — why not enable them to testify to what they would have seen with their own eyes? Otherwise, if Abraham would come back without Isaac, they could imagine other scenarios, e.g., Isaac running away when he realized what was about to occur or Isaac being killed accidentally, perhaps by a fall or a wild beast.

It is possible to say, as some commentators do, that the Divine plan was for the *Akedah* to first become known to Israel and the world only as part of the revealed Torah at Mount Sinai, which was the way Abraham's act would become known *and* accepted as fact.[18] But this answer seems problematic. A more acceptable goal would be for the nation of Abraham (through whatever progeny it would emerge, even if Isaac were Divinely resurrected *after* his sacrifice!)[19] to know of their founding father's boundless faith and love of God tested at the *Akedah, and to know this as soon as possible, and not a few hundred years* later. As the crowning achievement of Abraham's faith, to which none could thereafter similarly aspire, it would be a theological foundation of the new religion that Abraham sought to bring into being for his progeny, and the monotheistic religion he sought to spread throughout the world. The sooner it would become known, the better.

On the other hand, suppose that — as I have suggested in my prior articles — Abraham was not sure that Isaac's sacrifice would be consummated at the top of Moriah. So he would take Isaac, and the wood for the sacrifice prepared *before* the journey,[20] and the material for the fire (commented on by Isaac on the way up).[21] If the two witnesses were there too, they would see Abraham build the altar with only Isaac but no animal present as the life to be sacrificed, and then — without hearing God's angelic command to Abraham to desist, audible only to him[22] — they would see Abraham turn from the bound Isaac, espy a ram, take the ram, unbind Isaac, and sacrifice the ram in his stead. What message would that give to the witnesses other than that Abraham started and attempted to sacrifice Isaac to God, and then, *for some unknown reason*, couldn't bring himself to do it? They would conclude that Abraham's love for Isaac had evidently outweighed whatever faith and love of God had driven him to consider sacrificing Isaac. With that scenario, and with that message to the two witnesses, it would be better if these two potential witnesses to a sublime act of courage never saw it in its incipient stage, than to see it attempted and fail, for an apparent lack of the necessary faith, loyalty and love of God on Abraham's part. Better that they return home, in such a case, without ascending Mount Moriah, to tell of how Abraham ascended Moriah with Isaac to bring a sacrifice to God. Assuming that Isaac was not privy to the *Akedah* conversations of God and Abraham, the only new information they would bring back would be the future holiness of Mount Moriah.[23] That would be part of the religious inheritance of Abraham's progeny. They already knew from Abraham's earlier debate with God at Sodom, and from the Noahide Laws, about the sanctity of human life. That would be fundamental to them throughout the period before Sinai. That would not change, and, for all they knew — until the Torah and the true *Akedah* story would become known — had never been endangered. The *Akedah* then would become an act of faith by Abraham, first revealed by God at Sinai, that there are certain acts obscene in God's eyes no matter how zealous — indeed, *because of* how *over* zealous — they are, morally and psychologically, as a humanly proffered proof of one's love of God and submission to Him. That kind of submission is too much for God to bear and too obscene for God to ask of humanity.[24] It runs counter to everything that God stands for, counter to the essence of Abraham's teaching of ethical monotheism, and counter to the revelation of Torah at Sinai.

Alternatively, Abraham (and Isaac, newly informed) might have told the two attendants what really happened. If so, God's message would have become part of Israel's tradition from that time, but the full story of what occurred would probably not have been believable to them, and its moral implications would have been too difficult to make such a disclosure by Abraham wise. It would have destroyed his credibility as a religious leader.

IV

The two witnesses came along to protect Abraham and Isaac, surely, but also to testify that they went up together, and came down together, without the wood and the fire, which were used to bring an animal sacrifice to God at a place that God had newly appointed and would later again appoint as His place for the Jewish nation to bring their required and authorized sacrifices to God. They were not there to bear witness to an act of human sacrifice that Abraham would never and could never complete. Taking these witnesses to the top would only have undermined the message of the *Akedah*, which was destined to be described in detail as part of the Divine revelation at Sinai, as it became later fully known in Scripture.

Abraham passed the ultimate, Divine test of his faith in God's justice and righteousness. He proceeded up the mountain with Isaac, with faith and prayer that the sacrifice of Isaac would not have to take place. In turn, God demonstrated to Abraham, and to all who would later learn about the *Akedah*, that this faith in God would always be justified, as played out in history over all times and lands. "Your throne rests upon equity and justice; love and truth serve thee," and "Your judgments [throughout history] are all just [true and consistent] all together."[25]

....

NOTES

1 "The Real Test of the *Akedah*: Blind Obedience Versus Moral Choice," *Judaism* (Winter 1993):71; "God Tests Abraham, Abraham Tests God," *Bible Review* (October 1993):53; "Who's Testing Whom? Was Abraham Really Ready to Kill His Son?," *Abraham & Family — New Insights into the Patriarchal Narratives*, Hershel Shanks, ed. (Washington, D.C.:*Biblical Archeology Society*, 2000), pp. 13-20; "The Binding of Isaac: Religious Paradoxes, Permutations and Problems," *Midstream* (November 2001): 25; "Thoughts on Reading the *Akedah* Again," *Midstream* (January 2002): 22.

2 Radak, *Yalkut Shimoni* and *Midrash ha-Gadol* on *Gen*. 22:2. Isaac, of course, was aware of the coming trip, but not its purpose, that he be sacrificed at God's command.

3 *Gen*. 22:4.

4 See note 1.

5 I suggest in "The Real Test..." (see note 1) that, while Abraham started out promptly, he proceeded deliberately, reflecting his unwillingness to rush to sacrifice his son. Compare the *Akedah* text with the language where Abraham shows real alacrity to carry out the Divine command of circumcision in *Gen*. 17:23-4. Thus, the modern commentator, *Malbim*, says on *Gen*. 22:5 (where Abraham orders his attendants on this journey, Ishmael, his son, and Eliezer, his chief servant and disciple, to stay behind while he and Isaac ascend Moriah), that Abraham spiritually rebelled against the command to slaughter Isaac, and was ashamed at the thought of performing this deed before them.

6 *Gen*. 21:9-12.

7 *Gen*. 17:15-19 (Ramban, Abarbanel, Hirsch and *Or ha-Hayyim*, *ad loc.*, and *Gen.*:10-15.

8 See note 7. At least one commentator suggests that the *Akedah* was a punishment for the peace treaty that Abraham signed with the Philistine king, Abimelekh, described in the text just before (actually, a few years before) the *Akedah*, in which Abraham granted him sovereignty over land that God had promised to Abraham. See Rashbam on *Gen*. 22:1.

9 The Midrash so interprets the story of Sarah's death immediately after the *Akedah*; Rashi at *Gen*. 23:1.

10 *Tanhuma Yashan, Midrash ha-Gadol, Sefer ha-Yashar*, and *Yalkut Shimoni* on *Gen*. 22:2; *Targum Yonatan, Me'am Lo'ez* on *Gen*. 22:19. On Isaac's age at the *Akedah*. see discussion in *ArtSroll Genesis* at *Gen*. 22:1.

11 *Gen*. 22:3

12 *Gen*. 16:1-4.

13 Rashi and *Pirkei D'Rabbi Eliezer* at *Gen*. 22:3, and see also *Gen*. 24:1-9.

14 Sforno at *Gen*. 22:5. Abraham was 137 years old at the *Akedah*; we know he was 100 at Isaac's birth, and it is generally reckoned that Isaac was 37 years old when he ascended Mt. Moriah. Sarah was 90 years old at Isaac's birth and 127 the year of the *Akedah* and of her death. See discussion in *ArtSroll Genesis* at *Gen.*22:1.

15 See, e.g. Rashi at *Gen*. 22:3; B. *Pes*. 4a; and Maimonides, *Guide for the Perplexed*, M. Friedlander, tr. (New York: Dover, 1956), p. 306. Not surprisingly, rabbinic commentaries not only accept Abraham as a willing, even eager sacrificer, but also agree that when Abraham told his two attendants that he *and* Isaac would

return to them, he did not mean it, but uttered an unwitting (sic) prophecy of what would occur; Rashi on *Gen.* 22:5. See also on this verse the commentaries of Albo and Maharsha. I find this a highly problematic understanding of the text, on two counts. First, the idea of Abraham lying, unwittingly or otherwise, is difficult. Second, I don't know what an "unwitting prophecy" is; I don't recognize it in Hebrew Scripture, where prophets are *aware* of a Divine message, and proceed, with full belief and intent about its content, to transmit it to its intended audience. Far more reasonable is the idea that Abraham knew, as a matter of faith in God, and of hope that his silent prayer for Isaac to be saved would be answered, `that he and his son would return from their ascent up Mount Moriah. The silent prayer is referred to in *B. Ta'anit* 15a and *J. Ta'anit* 2:4, and rabbinic commentary thereon. See also note 22.

16 *Gen.* 17:15-23, 21:12.

17 This idea is found in the seventh line of *Yigdal*. This song summarizes the thirteen principles of faith of Maimonides in his *Commentary on the Mishnah*, B. *Sanhedrin* 10.

18 See the commentary *Akedat Yitzhak* on *Gen.* 22:1.

19 See, e.g., Shalom Spiegel, *The Last Trial*, Judah Goldin, tr. and intr. (Woodstock, Vt.: Jewish Lights, 1993), pp. 33, 37-44.

20 *Gen.* 22:3

21 *Gen.* 22:7.

22 *Pirkei D'Rabbi Eliezer* and Hirsch indicate that only Abraham and Isaac could see God's cloud over the mountain. However, since Isaac did not hear God's original command, it is not likely that he heard God's voice ordering Abraham not to harm Isaac, at the climax of the *Akedah*. Nevertheless, it is likely that Abraham told Isaac what had happened, including his silent prayer and his faith in the ultimate outcome, so that this lesson would be transmitted through Isaac to what would become the people of Israel. It is hard to believe that Abraham would let Isaac go on believing that he intended to slaughter him. That intent is negated by the *mi she'anah* prayer in the Yom Kippur liturgy, in which Isaac, too, successfully prayed to be saved, discussed in B. *Ta'anit* 15a and J. *Ta'anit* 2:4, and the rabbinic commentary thereon.

23 See Rashi and Radak on *Gen.* 22:14.

24 *Jeremiah* 9:5-6; see also 7:31 and 32:35, and B. *Ta'anit* 4a.

25 *Psalms* 19:10 and 89:15.

2

Exegesis

This chapter consists of new interpretations, using modern ideas and experience, of difficult passages in sacred Jewish texts, principally in the Jewish Bible (Tanakh), consisting of the Pentateuch (The Five Books of Moses), the Prophets and the Writings. **"The Message of the Prophet Elisha"** contains not only an element (2 Kings 4:1–38) related to the *Akedah*, but also my view of the proper meaning (*p'shat*) of one of the most difficult passages in Tanakh (2 Kings 3:27).

In this passage we find the armies of the kings of Judah, Israel and Edom near an easy and complete triumph over Mesha, king of the rebelling kingdom of Moab, exactly as prophesied by the prophet Elisha (3:13–20). As a last resort, Mesha takes his eldest son and sacrifices him — some Sages say to the God of Israel, and some say to his own, pagan god — "whereupon there came a great wrath upon Israel" and they lift their siege of Mesha and return to their homes.

Who was angry at Israel? Why? And why is Mesha's human sacrifice of his innocent son seemingly rewarded? Is this story inconsistent with the message of the Binding of Isaac? With the help of modern history my essay answers, in a simple way, these questions. In addition to my analysis of this story, I demonstrate how the immediately following story (2 Kings

4) confirms my interpretation. Elisha and the kindly woman of Shunam, whose son — born to her in her old age — prematurely dies, protest to God and entreat Him, successfully, to restore the child to life.

Like the story of the Shunamite woman and Elisha, the essays on Jephthah, Ezekiel, Hellenism and Hebraism, the Rainbow, the Tower of Babel, and Rabbi Meir, look to a heroic humanity that struggles to achieve justice and righteousness because of — and sometimes in spite of — what may appear to be evidence of an unjust or indifferent God. This struggle reflects humanity's responsibility, since the covenant with Noah after the Flood, to do what is just and right.

Finally, it appears from these essays — sometimes explicitly, sometimes implicitly — that looking to unite with God as a solution to humanity's problems may be a misguided and even dangerous diversion of our Divinely gifted potential for broad creativity in the service of human progress.

In the **Jephthah** paper, I consider why a great judge and leader in Israel, after his conquest of Israel's enemies, experienced such an unfortunate end — he lost his daughter and died during a civil war between Israel's tribes. My answer, from traditional commentaries on Scripture, is: He was wrong to make an oath to kill whatever would be first to greet him, if he was victorious against Israel's enemies (the *Akedah* theme revisited). And he compounded this error when he stubbornly refused to ask others of greater halakhic expertise to consider whether such an immoral oath could be voided.

Had he done so, the religious authorities of the time — who, according to the Midrash, were too proud to go to Jephthah with this advice — would have told him that his religious zealotry to fulfill the Biblical command that "[oaths] that you utter you shall fulfill" did not apply, according to the Oral Law, to killing an innocent child or acting contrary to Jewish law. Moreover, while Jephthah was careful and diplomatic in first seeking a peaceful solution with Israel's enemies, he rushed into a civil war between Israeli tribes without ever giving diplomacy a chance.

Apparently, he failed to discern the power of speech — when it was a good thing in dealing with his enemies, and, when it was a bad thing, when he seemed to challenge God for His favor in battle, when he swore to kill what turned out to be his daughter. He was a warrior without wisdom.

So he died a slow, horrible death, by a disease akin to leprosy, the traditional punishment in Scripture for Jews who sin with words.

My **Ezekiel** paper discusses two of the most problematic and difficult sentences to understand in all of Scripture, *viz.* Chapter 20, verses 25–6. They seem to say that, at one time, earlier in Jewish history, God had given Israel commandments that were "not good," and go on to suggest that they involved child sacrifice! I argue that there was a precedent in *Leviticus* (*Lev.* 4:2, 4:13, 4:22, 4:27) for this odd, counter-intuitive sounding formulation, and that there were good reasons why Ezekiel was justified in using it here. Had he not done so, he could here be interpreted, as one eminent scholar has, as supporting the view that the *Akedah* was a serious test, in which God expected Abraham to be ready to sacrifice Isaac unquestioningly, and that Abraham believed that God really wanted this, and that he was obligated to obey, as would Jews in the future who might zealously perceive that they were being similarly tested. I explain why this view cannot stand up to scrutiny.

There are other stories in *Genesis*, e.g., about Cain, Noah, Abraham, Isaac, Jacob, Joseph and his brothers, that have been commented on by many Jewish scholars, and I have written about a few of the stories that I found of special interest. These commentaries generally raise questions about why the Jewish forefathers and mothers sometimes acted in objectionable ways. The commentators point out that the purpose of these stories, and of *Genesis* generally, is to show that even Jewry's great progenitor ancestors had human frailties like we, but they found the moral strength to overcome their mistakes, to redeem themselves through greater self-understanding, self-control, and religious strength. My emphasis is on demonstrating *the great Jewish innovation in its understanding of hu-*

man history, viz., that we can overcome adversity, weakness and error, and that the Greek view of history controlled by destiny is the wrong outlook. Rather, Jewish ideas of redemption and free will correctly describe humanity and its condition in history.

The **"Rainbow"** article asks the question: Why did the Sages say that Jews cannot look at the rainbow or other vessels of God's glory, whereas the text in *Genesis* encourages humanity to look at it, as a reminder of God's promise never to destroy the world again?

The answer I offer is that Noah's son Ham (and *his* son, Canaan) — by his terrible actions against a defenseless Noah after God displayed the first rainbow — showed that allowing man to get too close to God is dangerous for man. Paradoxically, it can arouse improper thoughts and actions, and an improper hubris about man's divinity, and even, in Jewish mystical thought, the lack of total goodness, and the existence of an independent evil element, in the Divinity, and the idea that evil cannot be overcome through normal human effort but only by magic and mystical rites. In a word, allowing too much human closeness to God arouses in man the tempting idea of acting outside of God's plan for man to perfect the world that God created, in favor of hopelessly seeking escape from it to join God in Heaven.

The Tower of Babel is another story about hubris and misguided attempts to control the free will of the masses. My paper on this episode asks: Why wasn't a universal culture for mankind a good idea? Why the Divine preference for different languages, cultures and ideas? Isn't this what modern liberal thought is against? Down with boundaries, with separation; we are all the same, and there is good in bad, and bad in good, and the idea of good *and* bad as two separate and identifiable things is wrong and immoral.

I answer these questions by showing how progress, *tikkun olam*, and the blessing, the opportunity, that comes from free will, can come only through the contrasts and cross-fertilization among different cultures. God didn't want all nations to be like Jews, or to become Jews, nor to become one universal national, political and cultural entity. You need to experience Egypt to appreciate individual and national freedom. You need all the experiences of history to learn which way lies true progress. All must share a common morality, but not cultural uniformity. As the Sages say, there is wisdom (*hokhmah*) in the other nations, but not [yet] holiness.

What could the great **Rabbi Meir**, Talmudic sage, have been thinking when he induced a disciple to seduce R. Meir's wife, Beruriah, renowned for her learning and character? The disciple was successful, and Beruriah committed suicide. Tradition has it that R. Meir was trying to prove to his wife that women, even his wife, are more "lightheaded" than men, an idea that seems to have been held by some of R. Meir's contemporaries. But this interpretation of the story seems problematic, both in the rabbi's ends *and* his means. I make a case for a different interpretation, based on Talmudic sources, as to what happened here and, in particular, what lesson R. Meir was trying to teach his wife — which was very far from feminine lightheadedness.

At one time, after their two children died while he was away, she tried to prove to him that there is no injustice in the world; all is God's will, even the death of their cherished children, and therefore there is no use grieving, challenging, protesting, or questioning, what occurs. R. Meir sought to disprove that idea by inducing her to sin, so she would *see that passive acceptance of evil as God's will is very dangerous and contrary to fundamentals of Jewish thought*. There are times when questioning, protest and anger at an apparent injustice are inevitable, and even necessary, as an exercise of a human's sense of injustice. But R. Meir's extreme method of educating his wife led to tragic consequences, and was bound to, if it succeeded in making its point. Even the most righteous among us can go too far in a good purpose, and their righteousness cannot transform a wrong action into a right one — a theme that can be found in a number of the articles of this book, and one well worth pondering when some religious leaders seek to direct political action in dangerous ways.

The Message of the Prophet Elisha

In this paper, I would like to offer a new view of a little known story in Chapter 3 of the second book of Kings, concerning Mesha, the pagan king of Moab (c. 9th century B.C.E.), and its connection to the well known story in the very next chapter, concerning the Israelite woman of Shunam. I believe they have much to tell us about the role of child sacrifice in Jewish tradition, and the broader question of whether we must passively accept injustice and the misfortune of innocents, their suffering and sacrifice, even when they are presented to us as God's Will.

The Mesha story (2 Kings 3) seems, at first reading, to contradict the traditionally accepted message of the *Akedah*, the "Binding of Isaac" (*Gen.* 22), that God rejects and abhors the Greek and pagan practice of child sacrifice.[1] Mesha, king of Moab, has rebelled against the kingdom of Israel. He is about to be easily defeated by the latter and his allies, the kings of Judah and Edom, as prophesied by the prophet Elisha, after a series of miracles that were forecast in that prophecy. In desperation, Mesha publicly sacrifices his son to the God of Israel atop the walls of the city where he is besieged, whereupon "a great anger comes over Israel;" it is not clear *who* becomes angry at Israel, or *why*, and the three kings lift the siege and return home.

The medieval commentators, not surprisingly, try to refute the apparent message of this story that God welcomes human sacrifice.[2] One commentator says that Mesha did not sacrifice his own son, but the son of the king of Edom, whom he had captured during the siege, causing the Edomites to become angry with Israel for causing the death of their king's son. This, presumably, breaks up the alliance and allows Mesha to "snatch victory from the jaws of defeat." Some commentators say that Mesha's act caused God to become angry at Israel for behaving similarly in the past, i.e., engaging in child sacrifice, violating God's prohibition of this pagan practice.[3] But all of the commentaries are subject to a fundamental objection: since Elisha had prophesied Israel's easy victory, how could Mesha prevail in the final battle against him?

The Mesha story seems so problematic that one scholar relies heavily on it to support his view that, despite the "happy ending" of the Binding of Isaac, Abraham's passive submission to the call to sacrifice his beloved firstborn to God remained a religious ideal in Judaism long afterward, as the ultimate demonstration of true faith in God. This ideal would, thus, provide continuity from Judaism to Christianity, based on a common pagan background of sacrificial theology.[4] Another scholar has argued that Abraham represents the Jewish ideal of "Sacrificial Man," accepting, even embracing, the opportunity for suffering and martyrdom, mystical self-annihilation and self-deprivation, and communion with the Divine realm, as evidence of love of God and submission to His Will.[5] Indeed, one midrash ties the two stories together; it portrays Mesha as seeking to emulate Abraham, but seeking to go Abraham "one better" as it were, by actually killing his own son, even without being asked.[6]

These views have not gone unopposed. One recent essay in the Orthodox scholarly journal, *Tradition*, flatly states that, insofar as the Binding of Isaac (*Akedah*) could be viewed as presenting Abraham with the choice of obeying God and killing Isaac, or disobeying God and not killing Isaac, Jewish law forbids human murder and Abraham would be forbidden from killing his son.[7] In a recent paper in *Midstream*, I have pointed out that the Talmudic Sages sought to define Abraham *not* as "sacrificial" but as a loving, life-embracing, personality who silently prayed to God that Isaac should not have to be sacrificed.[8] At the 1997 Conference of the Association for Jewish Studies, one scholar developed the theme that the *Akedah* did, indeed, reject the pagan ideal of child sacrifice; that Christianity re-adopted that idea, in a transformed way to be sure; that the Jews became a kind of sacrifice continually offered to God by their religious oppressors in human history; and that the Jews responded to this oppression by developing a transformed understanding of the *Akedah* that would explain their oppression in theological terms. Thus, they began to view the *Akedah* as a paradigm of their history, and a prophecy of their destiny, as sacrifices to God. Jewish suffering was seen not merely as a matter of helplessness, but evidence of Israel's purity, spirituality, nobility, even its chosenness, to be accepted, even embraced, as God's Will.[9]

Given the on-going debate in Jewish history and Jewish thought on the proper response to the suffering of innocents, I believe that the Mesha-Shunamite stories support resistance, and not passive acceptance and willing sacrifice, as the view of Jewish Scripture.

The key to the Mesha story is to view his bold, public act of sacrificing his son, before the shocked eyes of the Israelite armies, as an act of Churchillian defiance — as if to say, "You Israelites (and Judeans and Edomites) may think that this final battle will be easy, but it will not be; it will be the hardest, longest, bloodiest battle you have ever experienced. We will fight you in every street, in every alley, in every house, in every room, until the last man, woman and child dies in battle, if necessary; we will never surrender. And, as proof, in case you have any doubts about our determination on this matter, here — see what sacrifice I am prepared to make. I am prepared to kill my own son, as you can see, and I do it now. And every one of my people will follow me in sacrificing their most precious lives — their own, and their family's. We will never surrender."

At this juncture, a "great anger" did, indeed, come over the Israelites, not God's anger, but their *own* anger, born of frustration that the easy victory that had been prophesied for them by Elisha was evidently not to be. *Instead of faith in Elisha's prophecy of an easy victory, they were overcome with fear of death and defeat by Mesha's show of determination to fight to*

102

the end, and they and their allies, in anger and frustration, lifted their siege against Mesha, and returned to their homelands. Thus, Elisha's prophecy was forfeited, *not* because God accepted Mesha's sacrifice, but because the Israelites lacked the faith to accept God's promise of an easy victory, and act on it.[10]

Not only does the Elisha-Mesha story *not* prove that God welcomes and rewards child sacrifice, but the story of Elisha and the Shunamite woman that follows it is clearly designed in its plot, theme and language, to parallel the story of the binding of Isaac, and to convey thereby the common message of both, *that Man is neither required nor praised for passively accepting the sacrifice of children or other innocents to God as proof of his (or her) piety, faith or love of God. To the contrary; faced with the reality of injustice, of evil, of the suffering or misfortune of innocents, Man has a right, even a duty — and God expects of Man nothing less — to resist such reality, to "wrestle with God" as it were, in every feasible way, whether it be by the psychological resistance of "denial" or anger, the religious resistance of doubt, physical resistance against human evil and the indifferent malevolences of nature, or the spiritual resistance of prayer.*

God may not always accept our resistance, our protests, and our prayers, that our innocents be spared. But, while God's ultimate plans and decisions are not ours to fathom, God will always respect *our human* actions and attitudes with all their inherent limitations when they are governed by a desire for justice and righteousness, because this is the only compass that God has given to us to guide our response to the tragedies of life.

The story of Elisha and the Shunamite is easily summarized. After establishing Elisha's rapport with the common people, and the miracles he performed for them in times of need, we read of the kindness of the woman of Shunam to the prophet Elisha, as Abraham was known for his kindness to strangers who came his way. Elisha offers to do a kindness for her in return, and, in words that precisely follow the angelic promise to Abraham of the coming birth of Isaac, Elisha promises her a son exactly one year later. She doesn't believe him, for she and her husband are old (2 Kings 4:14, 16, 28), as Sarah and Abraham had not believed the Divine promise to them of a son, for the same reason (Gen. 17:17 and 18:12). As prophesied, she gives birth to a son one year later, as did Sarah, and the boy grows up, as did Isaac. One day, God "takes" her son, who dies suddenly, evidently as a result of a stroke, as God sought the life of Isaac in the Akedah. Protesting her son's death, and angry at the prophet, and at God, the Shunamite does not bury her son. Instead, she places her son's dead body on the bed which she had set aside so many times for Elisha's use when he passed through her village, as if to say: "This is the way God has repaid my kindness to His prophet." And now, standing between her son's death and burial, when Jewish law — with great psychological insight — accords the mourner significant freedom in religious observances, feelings, and beliefs,[11] she goes to find Elisha, and bitterly remonstrates with him about her son's death because, according to a midrash, Elisha had promised her earlier that her son would not die prematurely, before his parents, just as God had promised Abraham that Isaac would survive him and sire Abraham's progeny.

Now, if the sacrifice of a child to God is an act of piety, then Elisha's response to the distraught Shunamite should have clearly said so: "If Abraham (and Mesha) were rewarded for their sacrificial acts of faith, surely your piety will cause you to accept, even embrace, as a religious privilege, your son's sacrifice, by God's own hand, as a true act of faith." But Elisha's actual response to the grieving Shunamite mother could not be more different. The sense of his response, reflected more in his deeds than his words, is the following: "I did not know about this [death of your child]: God hid it from me. It is unjust. I do not accept what has happened.... I pray to you, O God, not to keep this child that You have so suddenly taken from its mother. I intend to resist Your decree, just as its mother is doing, even to cause you to reverse it, if that is possible, by every resource at my command, every rite and every ritual, every Divine miracle that I can summon. I beseech You to respond to my pain and my prayers, and the pain and prayers of this dead child's mother, as you answered and responded to Abraham's prayers on Mount Moriah that You save Isaac."[12]

The text now tells us of the rites, rituals and prayers of Elisha as he seeks of God the ultimate miracle, to reverse the Divine decree of death, and to restore the life of the Shunamite woman's dead son. Like Abraham's, none of the words of Elisha's prayers are provided to us. The texture of the text, as Elisha seeks to bring the child back to life, bespeaks a determination almost akin to a demand, a rightful, but bold demand.[13] And suddenly, abruptly, the text ends: "... the lad opened his eyes... He [Elisha] summoned her [the mother] and she came to him; he said, 'Pick up your son.' She came and fell at his feet and bowed down to the ground; and she picked up her son and left."

This story is perhaps the most extreme example in Scripture of successful resistance against an apparently unjust Divine decree. As such, it re-enforces similar responses by Abraham at Mount Moriah, praying that Isaac be spared from sacrifice; Moses in the desert, challenging God not to violate His covenant by destroying the Israelites on account of their worship of the Golden Calf, and to strike Moses's name from the Torah, if necessary; Aaron, the High Priest, refusing to perform part of his duties in the Tabernacle after his two sons were strangely consumed by a Divine fire; Job (in what some commentators say is a parable), who sought a Divine accounting for his suffering; and Jonah, the prophet (8th century B.C.E. disciple of Elisha) who sought to escape his Divine mission to urge the non-Israelite city-state of Ninveh to repent from its evil ways, because he was afraid that their repentance would lead to Israel's destruction.[14] While these protests were not as dramatic and successful as Elisha's on behalf of the Shunamite mother, they demonstrate that resistance to tragedy is not only acceptable before God, but is also *desired* by Him, because that response, not passivity, always has a chance of saving human life, and perpetuates in us the impulse for justice and righteousness that is our Divine mission in the world.[15]

....

NOTES

1 Jer. 7:31, 19:5, and 32:35; B. Ta'anit 4a. See also Shalom Spiegel, *The Last Trial* (Woodstock, VT: Jewish Lights, 1993 reprint), pp. 64, 73, 79-80, 116. There are only four cases in the *Tanakh* (comprising the Pentateuch, The Prophets and the Writings) where parents sacrifice their children: Jephthah, who sacrifices his daughter in fulfillment of a vow, and is condemned by Scripture (see Jeremiah citations above) and the rabbis (B. Ta'anit 4a) for doing so; Ahab and Menasseh, kings of Israel, who are explicitly condemned for doing so (2 Kings 16:3 and 21:6), and Mesha.

2 See, e.g., *Mikra'ot Gedolot*, A. J. Rosenberg, ed. (N.Y.: Judaism Press, 1980), *ad loc*. See also B. San. 39b and B. Ta'anit 4a, where the rabbis interpret Jeremiah (see n. 1) as condemning Mesha as well as Jephthah, without dealing with the difficulties of the Mesha text.

3 Cf. the strange Abarbanel on *Jer.* 7:31 based on a midrash on 2 *Kings* 3:27, that Israel's *enemies* were punished because of Mesha's obscene act.

4 Jon D. Levenson, *The Death and Resurrection of the Beloved Son* (New Haven: Yale Univ. Press, 1993), Preface, p. 198, Chapters One, Six and Twelve, and *passim*. Cf. text at note 9, below.

5 Yehudah Gellman, "And Sarah Died," *Tradition* (Fall, 1997):57-68. Gellman concedes that Abraham's alleged desire for Sacrifice must be balanced by Mercy, represented in Gellman's view by Abraham's wife, Sarah. However, in Jewish tradition, Mercy is balanced by *Justice*, not Sacrifice, much less Sacrificial Murder; see Spiegel, ...*Trial*, pp. 89, 92. Gellman correctly observes (p. 62) that Abraham, as Sacrificial Man, is father of "an entire spiritual orientation," embracing Jewish mysticism, as well as mystical ideals in Christianity, Islam, and in certain ways Hinduism and Buddhism. But this is precisely the philosophy that Classical Judaism rejected (see my article cited in note 8). If this is the way to justify mysticism, that aspect of Judaism becomes problematic at birth.

6 Spiegel, ...*Trial, Op. cit.*, pp. 78-80; B. San. 39b. It is difficult to understand in what way Spiegel believes that this midrash was designed to make the Sages *more* comfortable with the Mesha text. It may reflect their view that the ambiguity of Abraham's passive, silent obedience set a bad example for others later on, who used the *Akedah* as precedent for both passivity and violence; see my article (note 8), and Gershon Mamlak, "The Roots of 'Religious' Anti-Zionism," *Midstream* (May-June, 1998): 10-15; see also note 9.

7 Eugene Korn, "*Tselem Elokim* and the Dialectic of Jewish Morality," *Tradition* (Winter, 1997):5-30.

8 See B. Ta'anit 15a (and commentary of the *Ran*) and J. Ta'anit 2:4 (and commentaries of *Korban Ha'Edah* and *Pnai Moshe, ad loc.*); Lippman Bodoff, "Religious Murders: Weeds in the Garden of Jewish Tradition?" *Midstream* (January, 1998): 9-14; see also note 12. Because of its Talmudic source *and* halakhic context, this view of Abraham is embodied in the liturgy of our public fasts, including Yom Kippur. I believe it must be accepted as the most authoritative rabbinic view. Accordingly, references to Abraham's *desire*(!) to kill his son, in the morning service liturgy of certain prayer books, seem highly inappropriate.

I believe that the Sages sought to discredit the idea of Abraham as silent, "Sacrificial Man" by parody and irony in a midrash on which Gellman relies. In it, Abraham — previously silent — presses God to be allowed to slaughter, strangle or maim Isaac, *even after God has ordered him not to touch the boy*(!) — teaching us, I believe, to *avoid* such fanaticism that embraces the extremes of first submission and then violence — and, moreover, violence that is now contrary to God's express command to desist! A midrash that appears to praise Abraham for his silent submission at the *Akedah* (Spiegel, ...*Trial*, pp. 90-1), is really based on the idea that God and Israel must have faith in each other's righteousness. Abraham is described, after his ordeal, as urging God to speak up in Israel's defense, and to have compassion for it, when it transgresses in future years, just as Abraham *refused* to speak out against the injustice of God's command that he sacrifice Isaac, and *suppressed* his compassion for his son. Isn't this a blatant non-sequitur? Not really, provided we understand Abraham addressing God this way: "Just as I remained silent, *with faith in Your abiding righteousness* to save Isaac, so I ask You, in future times, to speak in Israel's defense, and have compassion for it, *with faith in Israel's abiding righteousness*, and the sincerity of its repentance.

9   Arnold J. Band, "Scholarship as Lamentation: Shalom Spiegel on The Binding of Isaac," *Jewish Social Studies*, n.s. (Fall 1998, Winter 1999):80-90. Sadly, Jews who have passively accepted oppression have sometimes turned to violence against other Jews, who were seen as apostates, contaminators, and traitors to the Jewish people. See, e.g., my paper, note 8; Todd Endelman, "Jewish Converts in Nineteenth Century Warsaw: A Quantitative Analysis," *Jewish Social Studies*, n.s. (Fall, 1997):34 (*eighteenth* century murders of Jewish apostates by family members); Meyer Balaban, *A History of the Liberal Synagogue of Lvov* (Lvov, 1937, in Polish) (nineteenth century murder of a Liberal rabbi and his daughter by a Hasidic Jew). I am indebted to Michael Stanislawski for this cite.

10 *Artscroll Genesis* (multi-volume edition), Vol. IV (Brooklyn, N.Y.: Mesorah Publications, 1979), at Gen. 32:8,11. See also Asher Wiser's similar view that the Israelites forfeited Elisha's prophecy because they could have stopped Mesha's child sacrifice but did not, and were Divinely struck by plague, in *Tanakh* (Tel Aviv: Dvir), at 2 Kings 3:27.

11 *Shulhan Arukh, Y.D.*, sec. 341, no. 1.

12 See n. 8. I believe that Abraham did not say "No" at the outset to God's command to sacrifice Isaac, because he wanted the rejection of child sacrifice to be forthcoming in the tradition and text of the *Akedah* as a *Divine* imperative, and not just as a Divine acquiescence to a *human* value tinged, as it would inevitably be seen to be, with "selfish" parental love.

    Shemaryahu Talmon notes that the story of the woman of Shunam (2 Kings 4:8-37) is not part of the Bible's barren wife stories, that are designed to show how sometimes Divine election of a child is the key to that child's later history. It is, therefore, appropriate to assign a different message to the Shunamite story, as I do; "Literary Motifs and Speculative Thought in the Hebrew Bible", *Hebrew University Studies in Literature and the Arts* (1988):157-65.

13 See, e.g, *The Torah Anthology: Me'Am Loez* (N.Y.:Moznaim, 1997), p. 51.

14 See *Ex.* 32:11-14, 32-5, and 34:1-10 (Moses' plea); *Lev.* 10:1-3, 16-20 (Aaron's refusal); Job, *passim*; and Jonah 1:1-3 (and commentaries of Rashi and *Malbim*, *ad loc.*).

15 Significantly, on public fast days during the year, the Torah reading includes Moses' plea, and the liturgy (*Mi she'anah*) makes reference to Abraham's prayer at Mount Moriah, pointing to the similarity of their responses. *Similarly, Ashkenazi tradition has paired the story of Elisha and the Shunamite as the haftorah of the Akedah reading every Fall season, signifying that neither God nor Israel wish the human*

sacrifice of children to prove love of, or obedience to, God. In the Sephardi tradition, the Shunamite story ends when she is about ready to leave her home to remonstrate with Elisha about her son's early death. Torah-haftorah connections are discussed in Yehuda Shaviv, [Connections] *Between the Haftorah and the Parashah* (Jerusalem: Reuben Mass, 2000) (Hebrew), pp. 24-7, reviewed in *Tradition* (Winter 2001):79-87.

As to the absence of a reference in *Genesis* 22 to Abraham praying, I believe that his predictions to Isaac that God would show them the sheep to be sacrificed (relieving Isaac's concern that *he* might be the intended sacrifice) constitutes, indirectly but clearly, a prayer to God to find an animal sacrifice to substitute for Isaac — certainly indicating Abraham's wish and expectation that this will be the final outcome of their awesome test. I have not seen this idea in my research for the *Akedah* over the years.

The Tragedy of Jephthah

The Hebrew Bible has remained fresh and relevant over the centuries, while the Oral Law interpreted, applied and expanded the written law of the Torah, and the Midrash explained, in ever new ways, Jewish theology and history, and Jewish ideas and values as embodied in the sacred texts.

An excellent illustration of this can be found in a comparison of the story of Jephthah in the text and its treatment in the Midrash. Jephthah, a "mighty man of valor," was called upon by the elders of Gilead[1] to defend Israel against the Ammonites. Jephthah tried to make peace with Ammon through diplomacy, and sent emissaries to plead Israel's cause, not once but twice. Each time, his peace overtures were rebuffed. Facing the need to do battle as a last resort, he swore an oath to God that, if he should be victorious, then *whatever . . . will emerge from the doors of my house . . . shall belong to God, and I shall offer it up as an* olah, *an elevation offering* [sacrifice] (*Jud.* 11:31).

To his chagrin, when he returned home from the battle the first to emerge from his house after his victory was his daughter, his only child. When he saw her, he tore his clothes and cried out: *"I have opened my mouth* [with an oath] *to God, and I cannot recant"* (v. 35). His daughter's response was to affirm her father's duty to make good on his vow, since he had returned victorious. She only requested a two-month respite in which she and her friends *"could go and wail upon the mountains and weep over my virginity"* (v. 37). He agreed, and two months later, upon her return, *he carried out the vow that he had vowed, and she never knew a man* (v. 39).

The rabbis of the Talmudic era clearly could not let this text go without clarifying comment: Jephthah was not permitted to sacrifice his daughter, nor could he obligate her to participate in such a sacrifice. Yet, from as much as appears in the text, the sacrifice was not condemned, and presumably found Divine acceptance. Indeed, at least one modern scholar cites Jephthah in support of the argument that sacrifice of the firstborn remained a religious ideal long after the binding of Isaac. While noting the later rabbinic criticism of Jephthah, he emphasizes that ". . . the Bible seems not to fault him."[2]

The Midrash[3] condemns everyone associated with this tragedy. First, Jephthah, who made such a heedless, open-ended vow; who carried out the vow though he was not obliged to, since it required him to perform a sinful act; who, out of pride, did not go to Phinehas, the High Priest, to have the vow annulled. Second, Phinehas, who, out of pride, did not go to Jephthah to annul the vow. Third, the sages of that time, who failed to annul the vow because they had forgotten the law. Fourth, the Israelites of the time who, knowing what was about to happen, made no effort to stop the sacrifice because they were ignorant of the law.

The midrashic treatment of Jephthah's daughter (which gives her the name Shielah[4]) is in five parts. At first, she encourages her father to go through with the sacrifice so they can emulate the model of Abraham and Isaac, the father "who offered his son as a burnt offering," and the son who "consented gladly, and the offerer and the offered were both full of joy [over the sacrifice]."[5]

The Midrash goes out of its way to insert a reference to Abraham, eagerly preparing to sacrifice Isaac on Mount Moriah, on at least two occasions when it is critical of others who choose to kill their children in ostensible conformance with God's will: in this case of Jephthah, and in the case of Mesha, King of Moab. Indeed, the Talmud cites Jeremiah for the view that God condemned child-sacrifice in these two instances and in the case of Abraham at the *Akedah*.[6] This suggests that, in their view, there is something wrong with any assumption that Abraham was willing and even eager to sacrifice his son, and in fact, the Talmud rejects this idea.[7]

The Midrash next portrays Shielah as grieving at having to die for no good reason. She was not the intended sacrifice of Jephthah but the mere victim of chance: such a sacrifice surely can have no religious significance. Indeed, "I fear, therefore, that I may not be an acceptable sacrifice."[8] Nevertheless, it seems that Abraham sacrificing Isaac continues to serve for her as a paradigm of piety, even though it is now unattainable.

In the third part of the midrashic treatment of Jephthah's daughter, God appears to her in a vision to disabuse her of the idea that her sacrifice by her father's hand could have any redeeming religious significance, condemning her father and the sages of his generation for failing to summon the wisdom and courage to nullify her father's vow and abort the sacrificial murder about to take place. Consolingly, however, God assures Shielah that He will accept her soul at her request, as an innocent victim, "and your death shall be precious before My face all the time."[9] For the Midrash, it appears, even a mystical dwelling with God's presence in heaven is but a *consolation* to an innocent victim, which cannot compare to avoiding the sacrifice of innocents to God, even as demonstrations of religious piety and conformance to God's will.

In the fourth part of the Midrash on Shielah, we read about her final thoughts and feelings as she wanders during the last two months of her life. She longs for the true joys to which she should aspire, not death and abiding with God, but the joys of life that she will be denied: a wreath of betrothal, a wedding, being outfitted in her wedding ornaments, scented with aromatic perfumes, and anointed with oils prepared just for her. She visualizes what she will experience instead: a grave as a bridal chamber, her garments eaten by moths and destroyed by worms.[10]

In the final part, she prays that she be killed by the beasts of the forest, clearly to prevent her father from carrying out his vow to sacrifice her, which she now realizes is a terrible obscenity.[11] But this prayer is not answered, and she goes to her death at her father's hand.

Is the midrashic condemnation of Jephthah completely without textual foundation? I do not think so. I believe that if we read carefully what the text of Judges tells us about Jephthah's remaining life after he sacrificed his daughter, we will find hints at his condemnation that are both awesome and enlightening.

Judges 12 tells of how Jephthah, previously so slow to go to war against Israel's foreign enemy, the Ammonites, rushes after his victory over them to initiate a civil war among the Israelites, in which Jephthah and his fellow Gileadites kill 40,000 from the tribe of Ephraim. It would appear that the sacrifice of just one innocent human, his own daughter, quickly hardened and desensitized Jephthah to the precipitate slaying of tens of thousands of his own people.

Soon thereafter, he died, and, the text tells us, he was buried in *cities of Gilead* (12:7). This odd reference to a number of cities, the Midrash tells us, is not a scribal error of some sort, but signifies that he died a horrible death — his limbs atrophied and fell off one by one from his body, and were buried separately where each loss of limb occurred, as required by Jewish law.[12] Of course, the text and the Midrash together are telling us of classic manifestations of leprosy, the Divine punishment throughout the Bible for moral transgressions committed through improper speech and its destructive consequences.[13]

There was a tragic arc to Jephthah's life. He moved first from an ability to overcome a troubled early home life,[14] to become the leader of the tribes of Gilead. He then demonstrated patience and diplomacy with their enemies in attempting to reach a peaceful resolution of their dispute. This is followed by the gradual dissolution of his moral character, as he moved from irresponsible speech to overly zealous, inhuman dedication to fulfill a heedless vow that should not have been made and could have been nullified or even ignored.[15] Finally, he rushed to kill tens of thousands of his fellow Israelites without making any attempt to reach a peaceful solution with them.

Jephthah's tragedy thus comes full circle; from rejection and expulsion from his home, land and family, that would not accept him because of his problematic lineage, to rejection and expulsion in death — a death in which, because of his strange, scattered burial, no part of his people or the land would have to acknowledge and accept him as their own.

A complex man, Jephthah had the opportunity to be a noble, pious, and wise savior and leader of his people. He ended as a tragic lesson for them, and all of us, to which not only Jephthah, but his family, the community, and its leaders all contributed.

....

NOTES

1 The region in Trans-Jordan settled by the Israelite tribes of Reuben, Gad and half the tribe of Menasseh (*Num.* 32; Josh. 22:9, 15). Quotations are from the *ArtScroll Tanakh*, Stone Edition (Brooklyn: Mesorah Publications, 1996).

2 Jon D. Levenson, *The Death and Resurrection of the Beloved Son* (New Haven: Yale University Press, 1993) p. 16.

3 The Midrash consists of the exegesis of Talmudic and other religious scholars of problematic language and silences in Scripture that seem inconsistent with Jewish tradition. It is found in the Talmud, in separate midrashic compilations and other literature which grew over a period of a 1,000 years. In this article, I have relied primarily on the material in Louis Ginzberg, *Legends of the Jews*, Vols. IV, pp. 43-47, VI, pp. 202-204 (Phila.: Jewish Publication Society, 1938-67). See also, Shalom Spiegel, "Introduction to Legends of the Bible by Louis Ginzberg," in *The Jewish Expression,* Judah Goldin, ed. (New Haven: Yale University Press, 1976) pp. 134-142.

4 She was so named by her father because she is the one who is demanded by God to be given to Him (from the Hebrew verb root שאל — *sha'ol*). The Midrash recounts, in *Genesis R.* 60:3; *Tanhuma Behukotai*, sec. 5; *Tanhuma B, Behukotai*, sec. 7, that God condemns her father's obstinate refusal to even attempt to avoid her sacrifice, using the triple-phrased condemnation by Jeremiah of child sacrifice: *which I never commanded, never decreed, and which never came to My mind* (*Jer.* 19:5-6).

5 Ginzberg, Vol. IV, p. 44.

6 Shalom Spiegel, *The Last Trial* (Woodstock, VT: Jewish Lights, 1967-93) pp. 78-9. The story of Mesha is in II Kings 3. See *B. Ta'anit* 4a, where the Talmud cites Jeremiah 19:5-6.

7 See *B. Ta'anit* 15a and *J. Ta'anit* 2:4 and the commentaries thereon in standard editions of the Talmud. See also, Radbaz (Rabbi David ibn Zimra), *Responsa*, No. 652 and my article, "The Message of the Prophet Elisha," *Midstream* (Feb./ March 1999) p. 10.

8 See reference in Note 5.

113

9 Ginzberg, Vol. IV, p. 45 and Vol. VI, pp. 203-204.

10 Ibid.

11 Ibid.

12 *Genesis R.* 60:3. See also Ginzberg, Vol. VI, p. 46. Although some translators amend the text by inserting "one of the" before "cities" rather than using the literal translation followed by Artscroll, the latter — which I follow (see Note 1) — is backed by the Midrash and most of the classical commentators; see, e.g., Abarbanel (on 11:10); *Me'am Lo'ez* (on 12:7), and others that could be cited. See also Ralbag (on 12:7) and *Metzudat David* (in *Mikra'ot Gedolot* on 12:7), who also agree that Jephthah's limbs were scattered among various cities in Gilead, but *after* his death to *honor* him for saving them from Ammon ! Radak (12:7) does not amend the text; he agrees with the Midrash but says that the "simple meaning" (*peshat*) is "in one of the cities". I don't see how one can accept his simple meaning without reading the text differently.

13 *Numbers* 12:10 and *Deuteronomy* 24:9.

14 Because his mother was a concubine, he was forced by his half-brothers to leave home and settle in a heathen district. This may explain his later willingness to engage in the heathen practice of child sacrifice. See Judges 11:1-3. See also Ginzberg, Vol. IV, p. 43, and Vol. VI, notes 106-107.

15 See discussion above. Similar cases of heedless vows to demonstrate righteousness are found in *Genesis* 31:25-35 and 44. The first, involving a rash oath by Jacob, had tragic consequences, resulting, according to the Midrash, in the death of his wife, Rachel, and the second, a similarly rash oath made by Joseph's brothers on the way home from Egypt, might well have had similar consequences, but for the sensible response of an Egyptian army leader. On Rachel's death, see *Artscroll Bereshis,* Vol. IV (Brooklyn, N.Y.: Mesorah Publications, 1979), pp. 1358-60.

Ezekiel 20:25–6:
Did God Ever Command the Sacrifice of Israel's Firstborn Sons?*

There is a text in *Ezekiel* that has long challenged scholars. It reads as follows:

> Moreover, I gave them laws that were not good, and rules by which they could not live: When they set aside every first issue of the womb, I defiled them by their very gifts — that I might render them desolate, that they might know that I am the Lord (20:25–6) (translation of the 1978 Jewish Publication Society edition of *The Prophets*).

The obvious questions arise: first, why would an eternal, just God, so portrayed in *Ezekiel* and throughout *Tanakh*, admit — even boast — that He had, at an earlier time, commanded Israel to perform deeds that are "not good," that is, that are evil, from a moral and ethical point of view,[1] in particular as they involved the sacrifice of Israel's firstborn children — for which it is now being punished. When did He so command Israel, through which prophets, and where is all this recorded — or is it only recorded by *Ezekiel* as a recollected event?

As the scholar Jon D. Levenson has noted, commentators have, from

*Published originally in B.D.D. 10, Winter 2000, Bar Ilan University Press, copyright: Bar-Ilan University, Ramat-Gan, Israel.

the very beginning, sought to explain away and eliminate the idea that God purposely, for any reason, commanded Jews to disobey His law, arguing, for example, that God did not command these evil acts but allowed Israel to be swayed by its own evil inclination. Another approach that has been taken is that the Divine command of laws "that were not good," which is, indeed, not otherwise recorded in *Tanakh*, refers to an era prior to the first exile, in which the hearts of the Israelites were "hardened" to commit this obscenity as a punishment for other acts of disobedience, as Pharaoh's heart was hardened against Israel as punishment for his prior evil acts. Among traditional commentators, the late medieval rabbi and Jewish leader, Isaac Abarbanel, provides a simple and, I believe, the most plausible interpretation of the *Ezekiel* text: that God had given to Israel — on a number of occasions in the Bible — the choice between obeying His commandments and disobeying them, characterized as a choice between life and death, blessing and curse. They are good or bad, as are their consequences, depending upon whether man chooses to obey them. Thus, concludes Abarbanel, because all the commandments come from God as choices, it is correct to say that "I also gave them laws that are not good." There is a much more recent, yet traditional, commentary, by Meir Ish Shalom, from about a century ago, that postulates that the "bad laws" given by God to Israel refer to laws to prevent or punish improper behavior. As examples, he cites the laws restricting Israelite enjoyment of many aspects of the sacrifices in the desert Tabernacle and the Jerusalem Temple, which are reserved for the priests, because only the latter did not participate in the sin of the Golden Calf, and laws restricting sacrifices to those Divinely-appointed sacrificial sites to discourage sacrifices to pagan gods elsewhere. He also cites the laws restricting the nazirite, whose vows of ascetic abstention from permitted pleasures are considered overly zealous, and the laws governing a soldier returning from battle, who is smitten by the beauty of a married woman brought back in captivity, and desires to sleep with her.[2]

But even if one can find an explanation or rationalization for Ezekiel's language, none of the commentators address the question of *why* Ezekiel chose to call God's commandments "bad!" In the concluding section of this paper, I will suggest an amplification of Abarbanel's and Ish Shalom's views, and a synthesis of their implied messages, that suggest an answer to this question.

While the exculpatory approaches referenced above seem desirable to maintain the coherence and unity of the Ezekiel text, some modern scholars, according to Moshe Greenberg, believe that God *did* change His command regarding sacrifice of the first born son. Thus, Jon D. Levenson asks, where else do we find that God *actually commanded* a sinner to do certain admittedly *sinful* acts *as part of God's law*? When God hardens the heart of a sinner, like Pharaoh, all that the world can see and know is that the sinner is at it again — no surprise there, and nothing to taint the Divinity with similar evil. Here, in *Ezekiel*, in contrast, God is said to have once commanded acts that are, simultaneously, part of God's law, *and evil*, i.e.,"laws that were not good." It is true that *Exodus* tells us that God hardened Pharaoh's heart, causing Pharaoh to continue to sin, so we know that what God did was purposely punitive, and not considered by God to be good behavior, but exactly the opposite. Nevertheless, as Levenson correctly points out, the Pharaoh text doesn't say that God "told" him to violate His "good" laws, or to obey a "bad" law. What Ezekiel *uniquely* says is that God gave the Israelites "bad laws," which *Ezekiel* is *now* renouncing. It would seem, concludes Levenson, that "there is no reason to think that [Ezekiel, God] regards the practice of the sacrifice of the firstborn as contrary to God's will in the time for which God ordained it." According to Levenson, what is now obscene and bad was once commanded by God, to humiliate Israel into submitting to God. Indeed, Levenson uses the *Ezekiel* text to support his view that sacrificing the firstborn was a religious ideal at the *Akedah*, and for a long time thereafter, although ritually transformed.[3]

Moshe Greenberg believes that the idea of some modern scholars that God changed a commandment from commanding sacrifice of the firstborn son to abhorring it — is "inherently improbable." Ezekiel is only condemning those who practiced the popular, rather than the normative, religion of Israel, who perhaps may even have believed, erroneously, that their human sacrifices were *Divinely* commanded. Thus, no such "bad" laws were ever commanded to Israel, although, in Greenberg's view, it may have been a popular idea to think that He did.[4]

Preliminarily, we should note that Ezekiel's odd formulation merely follows a similar one in *Leviticus* (4:2, 4:13, 4:22, 4:27), which speaks of a person performing a commandment of God that may not be performed," which literally, as with Ezekiel, speaks of violating a Divine prohibition as "performing a commandment." As to the Ezekiel context, the analysis is multi-faceted.

In Levenson's view, however, that is not what the *Ezekiel* text says. It says that "I [God] gave them bad laws." Moreover, if it was so popular, doesn't that suggest that they were, indeed, normative? Can't it be, as Levenson suggests, that there was an earlier commandment, punitive in intent or otherwise, which Ezekiel admits, but is now denouncing? In the remainder of this article I will attempt to explain: 1) why I think this "changed commandment" concept must be rejected; 2) why I think Abarbanel's view is historically and theologically the correct one; and 3) why Ezekiel may have chosen such a problematic way to present Abarbanel's idea of choice that is otherwise so clearly set forth in the Bible.

To begin, there are a number of reasons why the idea of God commanding Israel at an earlier time to engage in child sacrifice of any kind, for any reason, and later pronouncing that it is a law that is, or was, "not good," is untenable. The first has to do with Ezekiel's relationship with Jeremiah. Ezekiel was his disciple, colleague and, according to some authorities, his son (see note 5). Regarding child sacrifice, Jeremiah had asserted in God's name, with repetitive insistence, that it is a practice "which I did not decree, did not command, and which never entered My mind." Indeed, Jeremiah's multi-phrased denouncement of the practice, which, in turn, is repeated three times by Jeremiah, causes Levenson to comment that "the prophet doth protest too much."[5] Putting aside that cavalier comment on a matter of such obvious concern to Jeremiah, we must ask ourselves: Would Ezekiel, Jeremiah's son and disciple, and his successor as a true prophet of God, openly and boldly contradict Jeremiah so soon after his teacher had emphatically and repeatedly said that God *never* asked or thought of asking anyone to engage in child sacrifice as a show of obedience to God's will? Would Ezekiel in such circumstances tell Israel's elders, "O yes, He did command Israel to commit such heinous acts — indeed, God told me to tell you, 'And I also gave you laws that were not good... when you sacrificed every firstborn....'" This kind of impertinence and defiance of one's teacher, before the same Israelite nation that heard Jeremiah say just the opposite not long before, is something which I find impossible to accept.

Moreover, there is a major problem in the scenario which has God changing a commandment — in this case, from "Sacrifice your firstborn" to "I detest and abhor your sacrifices of your first born."[6] If God once commanded Israel to obey laws that are "not good," to punish them for prior transgressions, how is Israel to know whether such laws are punitive, thereby compounding their transgressions, or represent behavior that God really desires? If God once commanded Israel to obey His laws that only now, at a later time, they are told are "not good," how is Israel ever to know that it won't be punished later for its prior obedience? How can Ezekiel expect Israel's elders to accept such a defense of Divine justice?[7] Their response would be quick, simple, and understandable: "Why should we believe in, much less obey, such an inconsistent God, who changes His mind from time to time as to what is 'good' and what is 'bad,' what we should do and what we should not do, thereby exposing us to punishment *retroactively* for obeying Him?"

In brief, the notion that God ever commanded Israel to sacrifice its firstborn sons simply makes no sense in the context of the rest of *Ezekiel*, and the rest of *Tanakh*, at least as the redactors and canonizers of *Tanakh* as a unified text seek to portray God.[8] To gratuitously introduce the idea of an inconstant, inconsistent God, Who changes His mind about particular behavior from a Divine command to a prophetically denounced evil, is no way for Ezekiel, as a Divine spokesman, to obtain the repentance and renewed allegiance of the Israelite people to a just Divinity. Such a God leaves His people without a moral compass. On balance, therefore, the Greenberg view seems correct — that the idea of God changing his mind about a commandment is "inherently improbable," despite Levenson's reservations about the more traditional interpretations.

I believe that something more can be added to Abarbanel's understanding of what Ezekiel had in mind in 20:25–6. Recalling that the Book of *Deuteronomy* was found during the reign of King Josiah, after a long hiatus, not long before Ezekiel's text was written,[9] we should note the fundamental and new formulation of good and bad behavior that Moses presents there in behalf of God:

> Behold, I set before you this day a blessing and a curse: the blessing, if you shall obey the commandments of the Lord... which I command you this day; and the curse, if you shall not obey the commandments... And it shall come to pass, when the Lord... shall bring you into the land where you are going to possess it, that you shall set the blessing upon Mount Gerizim, and the curse upon Mount Ebal (*Deut.*11:26–9) (from the translation of J. H. Hertz in the 1938 edition of *The Pentateuch and Haftorahs*).

Briefly, evil in the world is part of God's plan for human free will. Good and bad behavior, blessing and curse, and the physical, tangible symbols of these choices in the form of Mount Gerizim and Mount Ebal, are simply two sides of one coin. While a similar idea is presented in *Leviticus* 26, where God presents Israel with the choice between obedience and reward versus disobedience and punishment, the covenant in *Deuteronomy* goes a step further in concretizing these choices in a physical way, in the embodiment of blessing and curse in two mountains, looming before the very eyes of the Children of Israel. God, as it were, has created the substance of *both* choices, good and bad, *and presented both choices, in all their physicality and their details, to humanity, here on earth.* Therefore, when man chooses incorrectly, when man sins, God is complicit, because He has not only provided the *choice*, he has also supplied the *details* of that sinful behavior. In the words of *Deuteronomy*, which provide the underlying blueprint for Ezekiel's moral instruction, "Behold, I set before you this day... a curse" (*Deut.* 11:26), and later, at the end of Moses' final instruction to Israel, even more dramatically (30:15):

> See, I have set before you this day life and good, death and evil, in that I command you this day to love the Lord..., to walk in His ways, and to keep His commandments and His statutes and His ordinances; then you shall live and multiply, and the Lord... shall bless you in the land where you are going to possess it. (Hertz translation).

This interpretation of *Ezekiel* 20:25–6 is consistent with the reason that *Ezekiel* offers in that very text for God giving Israel "laws that were not good" — i.e., "that I might render them desolate, that they might know that I am the Lord." The meaning is that just as Israel would learn that "I am the Lord" by choosing correctly and thereby experiencing the Divine blessings promised to it, so, too, would Israel learn that "I am the Lord" by choosing incorrectly, and thereby experiencing the curses, the exile and desolation that was Divinely promised to it. God, like any parent, proves His authority by making good on promises of reward for good behavior and promises of punishment for bad behavior.

If this interpretation of *Ezekiel* 20:25–6 is correct, there was no Divine change of mind about sacrificing the first born, nor could there be. God is eternal and constant. His values, His ways, are constant. His will is constant. The blessing and the curse, the same blessing and the same curse, are always there. There has been no normative change. There can be no

God, and no people to believe in Him, otherwise. What changes, from time to time are man's choices between life and death, good and bad, blessing and curse. That is always up to us.

Abarbanel's interpretation of Ezekiel, which builds on the *Deuteronomy* Covenant, is particularly apt when we consider the role of *Deuteronomy* in the prophet's background and heritage: Not only was Ezekiel the disciple and possible son of Jeremiah, but the latter was the son of Hilkiah, the priest, who discovered the Book of *Deuteronomy* during the reign of King Josiah.[10]

One may still reasonably ask why Ezekiel, in 20:25–6, chose such an oblique way to make his point to Israel's elders: that Israel had chosen to sin, therefore Israel was being punished. Why suggest, in the middle of a prolonged remonstration with Israel about how it had sinned and thereby brought about Divine punishment, that God, too, was implicated in Israel's disobedience of Divine Law, that, in some fashion, God facilitated Israel's decision to sin and may therefore be said, in some fashion, to have "given" Israel the command to do so? Why not just say, "Israel is being punished because it made the wrong choices?" Further, why should any of God's laws, even those that Ish Shalom says are to punish or prevent *bad* behavior, be described as "bad?"

I believe that we must first establish whether Ezekiel's prophecy is mystical or practical before we can understand the strange formulation of 20:25–6. Let us first recall the three boldest elements of Ezekiel's prophesy: the visions of the Divine throne and chariot; the dead bones coming to life; and the restored Temple and the Temple service in Jerusalem. Second, we know that the national remnant of Israel, the Southern Kingdom of Judea, was in shock at what was happening to them — defeat, and destruction of its nationhood, its capital and Temple, its armies, and their land, and its exile and perhaps even its dispersal and disappearance, like the fate that had evidently overtaken the Ten Tribes as such when they were defeated and exiled 150 years earlier. Israel was now demoralized, believing that God had terminated his special relationship with Israel and Jewish history, and doubtful about the very existence of God. In these circumstances, Ezekiel's visions were not mystical, escapist flights to the Divine world, including, as some commentators remark, his vision of the *Third* Temple (and not the Second Temple) at the end of history.[11] Rather, Ezekiel's visions were an attempt, speaking for God, to reassure the Jewish people that they had a future Divine destiny in this world; as if to say:

"God exists, despite your defeat at the hands of those who only believe in idols and pagan worship — I have seen God's glory. You shall be restored to a vibrant, living nationhood — I have seen your dead, dry bones rising to life. And the Temple and its sacred service that you saw destroyed before your eyes — that too, will be restored to a living, thriving reality — for I have seen the next Temple and the details of how its services shall be performed."

In this practical, this-world approach to Israel's future, Ezekiel was following the path of *Deuteronomy* and of his teacher, Jeremiah, who instructed the Israelites (*Jer.* 29:4–7) to "build homes and live in them, plant gardens and eat their fruit," build generations of families, "multiply there, do not decrease, and seek the welfare of the city to which I have exiled you, and pray to the Lord in its behalf, for in its prosperity you shall prosper." (translation of the 1978 edition of the Jewish Publication Society edition of *The Prophets*). This hardly sounds like a recipe for mystical escapism.

Whatever use others may have later made of *Ezekiel* as the source of a mystical life, he makes it clear in Chapter 18 (verses 5–9) that his message is an entirely different one, which has to do with how man should live in this world:

If a man is righteous and practices justice and righteousness: he does not partake [of idolatrous sacrifices] upon the mountains; does not lift his eyes to-

> wards the idols of the House of Israel; does not defile
> his neighbor's wife nor approach an impure woman;
> does not oppress any man; returns a collateral for a
> debt; does not rob and loot; gives his bread to the
> hungry and covers the naked with clothing; does not
> give [loans] with usury nor take interest; withholds
> his hand from corruption; executes true justice be-
> tween man and man; goes according to My decrees
> and observes My ordinances to practice truth, he is a
> righteous man; he shall surely live by the word of the
> Lord... (translation of *ArtScroll Tanakh*, 1996)

Israel is being punished, says Ezekiel throughout, not because it failed to visualize, understand or unite with God, but because it did not obey God's law. I believe this is the correct meaning, certainly the deeper meaning, of the famous statement found in *Deuteronomy* (29:28), which is so prominent in Ezekiel's prophecy for the historical reason noted above:

> The secret things belong to God, but the things
> that are revealed belong to us and to our children for-
> ever, that we may do all the words of this law.

God's essence and God's role in creating and governing the world are hidden; man's role in the affairs of individuals and nations is revealed — it is based on the exercise of human free will to obey or disobey God's laws. Ezekiel's visions, therefore, do not represent mystical flight from a world in which Israel has no future, but the very opposite: practical reassurance that Jewish history is not over, and Israel's future as a people, and as a religion, in this world, is assured. There will once again be a national and religious role for Israel, and even glory in its achievements in the eyes of the world. With this introduction, we can address the question that the elders undoubtedly asked after hearing Ezekiel's prophecy: "Why do you call *any* of God's laws 'bad'?" I suggest that Ezekiel might have responded in the following way:

Not everyone responds to catastrophe and crisis in the same way. Your brothers, the Ten Tribes, have responded over the past 150 years by uniting with the world, assimilating with other nations, and abandoning God and their people at a critical juncture of human freedom and Divine providence, which has allowed their disappearance to happen, at least for the time being.[12] But there is an opposite extreme and an equally wrong response to catastrophe and despair, that involves abandoning the world and seeking union with God. When this occurs, it assumes various forms of mysticism and spiritual escapism[13] such as that which I see beginning to occur throughout the world, from China and India westward to Mesopotamia.[14]

But this is not the way God designed the world. Evil in the world is part of God's plan of free will for humanity. The free will with which Israel, like mankind, has been blessed, involves not just triumphs and successes, but "bad laws" and decrees, in the sense of individuals and nations choosing conduct that God has described as "bad" that will cause death and curse instead of life and blessing. God's plan for Israel is *not* that you abandon the world when your free will choices and God's providence result in catastrophe and trauma, but that you continue to fight for righteousness, for obedience to God's laws that will contribute to life and blessing. Thus, the extreme response of despair and hopelessness, and abandoning the world to unite with God, in whatever forms that mystical, spiritual, impulse may take,[15] is not an escape *to* God, but an escape *from* God, and the world and its destiny, with man as His partner, as He has created it.

The course of life between the extremes of abandoning God and abandoning the world is to maintain your national and religious identity, maintain your loyalty to a transcendent, providential God, and yet relate to the other peoples of the world in ways that allow you to enrich, and be enriched by, them in the struggle of humanity to understand and control itself and nature, and secure the blessings of peace and spiritual and material progress, until the ultimate redemption.[16]

While this amplifies Abarbanel — who, significantly, was a man of the world as well as a great spiritual leader[17] — I believe that there is a parallel and complementary amplification that may be found in the commentary of Ish Shalom that should be integrated with it. Together they suggest Ezekiel's purpose and his message in the odd language he employed in 20:25–6.

I believe that the general message implied in Ish Shalom's commentary is that God's laws were designed not to prevent the enjoyment of life but to curb human excesses, whether they be the zeal of loving God or gods too much, or loving life too much; this includes the wish to see God and objectify Him in the form of a Golden Calf or any other form; or the zeal of withdrawing from the world by asceticism that is the nazirite's way of showing a love of God by self-imposed vows of abstention from enjoyment of permitted pleasures of life; or the excess of passion from a love of life that causes a soldier to desire to sleep with a female captive who has temporarily captured his fancy while he was away from his family and engaged in battle. Annihilation of the self and withdrawal from the world, no less than excessive love of the self and the embrace of worldly passions, are attempts to escape from God by nullifying His plan of Creation.

It is apparent, of course, that, in defining "bad" laws as those which prevent or punish bad conduct, Ish Shalom has embraced virtually the entire corpus of Biblical law. All of God's legislation was designed to curb the excess of our passions — both the physical and the spiritual ones — by laws that curb the impulses and desires of life, and thereby sanctify them with Divine blessing and approbation. Such curbs and limitations, while channeling man's joys and pleasures in embracing God and life in the material world, make man continually aware of the transcendent God Who has created the world that makes life and its enjoyment possible, yet disciplines us against those excesses that would be destructive of life, our own and the lives of others.

It is noteworthy the Ezekiel, in referring to those "bad laws" that restrict man's excesses, singles out one of the most heinous of ancient man's and Israel's well-intentioned excesses, the sacrifice of children to God, which — in its essence — is an attempt to give oneself to God and thereby abandon life to unite with Him.

Thus, whether we read *Ezekiel* through the lens of Abarbanel or that of Ish Shalom, the message is fundamentally the same, in the end: If it is here, in the world, in history, that Israel and all of mankind, with free will, has been placed by God; if it is here, in the world, in history, where correct choices, involving spiritual and material issues, must be made; if it is here, in the world, in history, that the blessing and the curse, life and death, have been placed before us, to be allotted to individuals and nations based on their freely willed actions and God's providential response to them — then it is here that man, and especially Israel, must focus his energies. For God clearly states at the conclusion of the *Deuteronomic* Covenant[18] that the covenant is not just with those standing before Him, about to cross into Canaan, but with their progeny who are not standing there, until the redemption.

Therefore, it is here, in this world, in history, that Israel — no matter what catastrophes may temporarily befall it — must stay the course, abandoning neither the other nations nor our nationhood, abandoning neither the material world nor God, indulging neither the excess of love of man nor love of God. We must make the right choices, and never lose hope when we suffer because we — or someone else — has not made those right choices; we must ultimately recognize that those "bad" laws are a manifestation of God's love of man and the way to achieve the blessing and life that freedom and free will can bring to the world, is to reject them; on that day God will be [recognized as] One, and His Name will be One.[19]

And so, Ezekiel, in ear-arresting form, gave Israel a crucial instruction in that strange statement in 20:25–6 — that the proper religious response to historical trauma lies not in obsession with the Divine realm, but is here, down below; its greatest challenges are choices presented by God that must be made in the material world, represented by Mount Ebal and Mount Gerizim in all their materiality and physicality. It is here that the daily battles for progress, *tikkun olam* — correction of the world's imperfections — and ultimate redemption, must be fought and won. Viewed in this light, Ezekiel was not only a prophet for his time, but for all time.

....
NOTES

1 See *Ezekiel* 20:3, where the elders ask the prophet why God is punishing them with suffering and impending exile.

2 See *The Anchor Bible*, Introduction and Commentary by Moshe Greenberg (Garden City; N.Y.: Doubleday & Company, 1983) on Ezekiel, especially his comments on 20:25-6 (future textual references to Greenberg are to this source); and Jon D. Levenson, *The Death and Resurrection of the Beloved Son: The Transformation of Child Sacrifice in Judaism and Christianity* (Philadelphia: Jewish Publication Society, 1988), pp. 5-9, who discuss various approaches that downplay or explain away this text. See, e.g., *Targum Jonathan* on *Ezek.20:25*; *Radak, ad loc.* (Israel subjugated by foreign nations that imposed evil decrees); *Malbim, ad loc.* (Israel determined that the commandment against child sacrifice was "not good," and not feasible as part of its national life); *Abarbanel, ad loc.*, who notes that in *Leviticus 26:46* the prior curses of that chapter are referred to as the "... laws that the Lord made between Him and the children of Israel at Mount Sinai...;" and Meir Ish Shalom, Comments on Chapter 20 of *Ezekiel, Ha Tziyun, "Kadimah"* (Wein: *Akdemisch Verein*, 1888), *ad loc.* (I am indebted to the referee, who reviewed this paper for BDD, for drawing my attention to this work. All views that are expressed in this paper are, of course, my own). The view that the possibility of choice is a Divine gift is discussed by Shlomo Riskin, citing the *Pri Zadik* and *Devarim Rabba* 4, in "The Mountain of Love," *The Jewish Week*, August 6, 1999.The same idea is expressed by Reuben Bulka, commenting on *Isaiah 45:7* that God makes peace and creates evil: "God created evil... means that God gave to each of us the precious gift of free choice;" see "Dear Rebbe," *The Jewish Spectator* (Fall, 1999):34.

3 Levenson, *Child Sacrifice...*, *op. cit.*, note 2, pp. 7-8 and *passim*. Levenson also argues (p. 4), *inter alia*, that *Ex. 22:28* reflects a requirement that Israel's firstborn sons belong to God in some sense beyond mere monetary redemption. But the distinction between *sacrificing* firstborn animals and *redeeming* firstborn sons, made earlier in *Exodus* (13:13, 15), and referred to by Levenson, is not easily dismissed, especially when the very next verse (13:16) permanently incorporates the *redemption* version in the parchment texts of the *tefillin*, Biblically prescribed to be worn forever after by Jews throughout the year. The two cubicles that comprise the *tefillin* are worn on the head and on the left arm (or the right arm, if the weaker); each contains parchment on which is inscribed the texts of *Exodus* 13:1-10, *Exodus* 13:11-16, *Deuteronomy* 6:4-9, and *Deuteronomy* 11:13-21; see, generally, Abraham Chill, *The Minhagim* (N.Y.: Sepher-Hermon Press, 1979), pp. 25-38.

4 *Anchor Bible, Ezekiel, op. cit.*, p. 369. See, e.g., S.L. Gordon's commentary on *Ezekiel* (Tel Aviv, 1956).

5 *Jeremiah* 7:31, 19:5, and 32:35; Levenson, *Child Sacrifice...*, *op. cit.*, note 2, p.4.

For various views of Ezekiel's relationship with Jeremiah, see Radak and Abarbanel and authorities cited there, on *Ezek.* 1:3; and *The Pentateuch and Haftorahs*, J.H. Hertz, ed. (London: Soncino Press, 1938), p.229. With regard to Jeremiah's repetitious condemnations, the Talmud notes (B. *Ta'anit* 4a) that Jeremiah had *three* traditions of child sacrifice in mind: The Binding of Isaac; Mesha, the Moabite king who sought God's favor in a war against Israel by sacrificing his firstborn son (II *Kings* 3); and Jephthah, who sacrificed his daughter to fulfill what he thought was an unavoidable oath, taken earlier, to sacrifice whatever first emerged from his house if God gave him victory over Israel's enemies (*Judges* 11). Levenson's approach to *Ezekiel* and *Jeremiah* seems to be adopted by Ziv Howard Adelman in his *A Cultural History of the Jews*, Part 3, "The *Akedah* and History: Child Sacrifice and Redemption," Jewish University in Cyberspace, Jewish Agency for Israel, Department for Jewish Education, URL http://www.jajz-ed.orig.il/juice/history/week three.html.

6   Levenson, *Child Sacrifice...*, *op. cit.*, note 2, p. 5. This view is restated by Levenson in "Abusing Abraham: Tradition, Religious Histories, and Modern Misinterpretations," *Judaism* (Summer, 1998):271.

7   See note 1.

8   On the redaction of *Tanakh* into a single text, see, e.g., Moshe Greenberg, "The Stabilization of the Text of the Hebrew Bible Reviewed in the Light of the Biblical Materials from the Judean Desert," *Journal of the American Oriental Society* 76 (1956):157-67; Shnayer Z. Leiman, *The Canonization of Hebrew Scripture: The Talmudic and Midrashic Evidence*, Transactions of the Academy of Arts and Sciences (Hamden, Ct.: Archon Books, 1976); *idem.*, "Inspiration and Canonicity: Reflections on the Formation of the Biblical Canon," *Jewish and Christian Self-Definition*, Volume 2, E.P. Sanders, ed., with A.I. Baumgarten and Alan Mendelson (Phila: Fortress Press, 1981), pp. 56-63; Shalom Spiegel," Introduction to Legends of the Bible," in *The Jewish Expression*, Judah Goldin, ed. (New Haven: Yale University Press, 1976), p. 135.

9   II Kings: 22-25; J. H. Hertz, ed., *The Pentateuch...*, *op. cit*, note 5, p. 937; A. Tadmor, "The Period of the First Temple, the Babylonian Exile and the Restoration," *A History of the Jewish People*, H. H. Ben-Sasson, ed. (Cambridge: Harvard University Press, 1976), pp. 148-63; *Ezekiel* (New York: Mesorah Publications, 1977), Vol. I, "Twilight of the Monarchy," pp. lxiv-lxv. On the important influence of *Deuteronomy* on Jeremiah, see Reuben Hammer, "Deserving the Land," *Jerusalem Post (In Jerusalem* insert), August 15, 2003, p. 9.

10   See II *Kings* 22; *Ezek.* 1:3, *Jer.* 1:1 and Radak and Abarbanel and authorities cited therein, *ad loc.*, and note 5, *supra;* See also B. *Meg.* 14b and Rashi *ad loc.*; and Steve Delamarter, "Thus Far the Words of Jeremiah,'" *Bible Review* (October, 1999):34 ff.

11   *Ezek.* 37:1-28, 43:10-27, 44:15-31 and ArtScroll's edition (1992) of *Chronicles* 34:22, p. 302. Israel's demoralization, brought on by the cognitive dissonance of its national catastrophe, is captured in the discussion between Ezekiel and 10 men, recorded in B. *San.* 105a. As noted in Hertz, ed., *The Pentateuch...*, *op.cit.*, note 5, p. 494, Ezekiel prophesied to an Israel that "was overwhelmed by doubt as to the existence of a Righteous Ruler of the Universe," and that "God's glory is bound up with the resurrection of Israel," i.e., its restoration as a people on its land. On the Third Temple, see ibid., p. 964. In general, there is no mysticism in *Tanakh*; see Gershom Scholem, *Kabbalah* (New York: Meridian Books, 1974) and

Julius Guttmann, *Philosophies of Judaism*, David W. Silverman, tr. (N.Y.:Schocken, 1973), Chapter 1, nor was it a significant aspect of Talmudic Judaism; ibid., Chapter 3; and Joseph Dan, *Jewish Mysticism* (Northvale, N.J.: Jason Aronson, Inc., 1998), Volume I, Chapter 2.

12 There is evidence, however, that refugee elements of the Ten Tribes (the Northern Kingdom) probably did return to, and merge with the Southern Kingdom of Judea; see Moshe Greenberg, *Anchor Bible, Ezekiel, supra*, Vol. 2 (1997), pp. 754-59; Farrel Bloch, "Are Most Jews B'nai-Judah,?," *Jewish Bible Quarterly* (July-September, 2004), pp. 158-61; and Abarbanel on *Ezek*. 37:16. See also *Jer*. 31:2-20, 50:17-20, B. *Meg*. 14b and B. *San*. 110 b, e.g, for contrasting Talmudic views on the issue of the merger of the two kingdoms. Their messianic ingathering and reunification are prophesied by *Ezekiel*, Chapter 37. The fate of the Ten Tribes is clearly a complex matter in the sources. For recent scholarship on the current whereabouts of remnants of the Twelve Tribes, see, e.g., Hillel Halkin, "Wandering Jews — and Their Genes" *Commentary* (September 2000): 54-61. On the joint role of human freedom and Divine providence in history — and the importance of science and the humanities as a complement to Torah to fulfill Israel's Divine role and destiny — see Aharon Lichtenstein, "Torah and General Culture: Confluence and Conflict," in *Judaism's Encounter with Other Cultures*, Jacob J. Schacter, ed. (Northvale, N.J.: Jason Aronson, Inc., 1997), pp. 217-292, esp. 236-242; and Guttmann, *Judaism, op.cit.*

13 On the general principle of Jewish mysticism in its various forms as escape from crises in the environment, see Mortimer Ostow, *Ultimate Intimacy — The Psychodynamics of Jewish Mysticism* (London: Karnoc Books, 1995), pp. 1-80, 129-41, and *passim; idem.*, Introduction in *Jewish Mystical Leaders and Leadership in the Thirteenth Century*, Moshe Idel and Mortimer Ostow, eds. (Northvale, N.J.:Jason Aronson, Inc., 1998); José Faur, *Homo Mysticus, A Guide to Maimonides' Guide for the Perplexed* (Syracuse, N.Y.: Syracuse University Press, 1999), Introduction; Part One; Part Two, pp. 79-82; Part Four, p. 196, and *passim*; Gershom Scholem, *Major Trends in Jewish Mysticism* (N.Y.: Schocken Books, 1967), pp. 1-39, 287-8; S. Giora Shoham, *Valhalla, Calvary & Aushwitz* (Cincinnati, Ohio: Bowman & Cody, and Tel Aviv, Ramot Publishing, 1995), pp. 59-61. Others, e.g., Moshe Idel, presenting a minority view, disagree that crises are the primary cause of mysticism, and that all mysticism is escapist; see, e.g., his *Messianic Mystics* (New Haven: Yale University Press, 1998), Introduction, Concluding Remarks, and pp. 146-7, 250-1, 260-1, 277. In fact, his evidence about his candidates demonstrates that their messianism was merely escapist experiences; even their occasional forays into the world were quixotic and suicidal attempts at immediate redemption and the end of history, like Shlomo Molkho's desire to see the pope, for no evident reason except martyrdom; ibid. and *passim*. Moreover, these were new, mystical, messianic, apocalyptic elements that were outside of the Judaism of the Bible and Rabbinic literature (ibid., p. 250). See also Allan Nadler, "Moshe Idel's Search for the Messiah," *Forward, March* 26, 1999, pp. 1, 11, 13, and the defense of Idel by David Ruderman in *Forward*, May 7, 1999, letter to the editor, p. 8. See also note 11.

Scholem, e.g., discusses how aspects of the mysticism that arose in Talmudic times influenced mystical responses in later periods of Jewish history, centuries later; see *Major Trends...*, *op.cit.*, pp. 80-118. Among other historians who accept the crises — mysticism connection in history, see, e.g., W.H. McNeill, *The Rise of the West* (N.Y.: Mentor Books, 1965), Chapter V, parts A-B, D; Fernand Braudel,

A History of Civilization, Richard Mayne, tr. (N.Y.: Penguin Books, 1993), pp. 177-85; and Robert Jay Lifton, *Aum Shinrikyo, Apocalyptic Violence and the New Global Terrorism* (N.Y.: Metropolitan Books, 1999), *passim*. While Joseph Dan believes that history is a "chaotic system," and that exact repetition is impossible, he agrees that a "system may include cycles and similarities;" see his *Mysticism, Op.cit.*, Volume I, Introduction, p. xii and Volume II, Chapter 2. In retrospect, these sources show that Ezekiel proved correct in a number of respects: Similar causes can cause similar effects, even in different times, places and cultures; indeed, such responses can themselves sometimes travel across time and space and cause similar effects in other places and nations.

14 See, e.g., McNeill, on the rise of Buddhism in the sixth century, B.C.E., *op. cit.* It is, of course, academic, whether Ezekiel actually knew or foresaw everything that happened in that era and region, or whether it was history that justified his concerns for his time and the future. Marcus Borg and Ray Riegert, "East Meets West," *Bible Review* (October, 1999):18, discuss a theory, dating back to a century ago, that equated the ancient Asian concept of an "angel messiah" of another world with Jesus, theorizing that the concept came to the Middle East with Jews returning from the Babylonian Exile in the sixth century B.C.E., and was later adopted by the Essenes, and applied to Jesus. While it was initially rejected because the Dead Sea scrolls had not been shown to contain any reference to Jesus or an "angel messiah," it has recently been elevated to a new status of possibility with the finding of the "angel scroll," containing an account of the travels through heaven of a man named Yesha, guided by an angel; see *The Jewish Week*, October 8, 1999, p. 3.

In the more individual field of suicide as a response to trauma, stress, and the breakdown of values and order, a recent impressive, scholarly work evaluates this response across time, age, gender, occupation and other variables, to develop a broad message about when suicide may occur, as the last act of people with manic-depressive illness, who conclude that life no longer offers them any other choice. See Kay Redfield Jamison, *Night Falls Fast* (N.Y.: Alfred Knopf, 1999) and the review by Alan Wolfe in *The Wall Street Journal*, October 13, 1999, page 28.

15 See, generally, Scholem, *Major Trends, op. cit.;* on mystical union with the Divine, see Moshe Idel, *Kabbalah: New Perspectives* (New Haven: Yale University Press, 1988), pp. 35-73. The desire to "see" God, including phallic aspects of that activity, is documented, e.g., in Elliot Wolfson's *Through a Speculum That Shines: Vision and Imagination in Medieval Jewish Mysticism* (Princeton: Princeton University Press, 1994). Some practices involving union were embodied in anthropomorphic ideas and practices in Zoharic Kabbalah involving eating experiences, which bear similarities to Christian doctrines of transubstantiation and the Eucharist. These experiences are described by Joel Hecker in his lecture, "The Blessing in the Belly: Eating Experiences in Zoharic Kabbalah," Thirteenth Annual Conference of the Association of Jewish Studies (1998), tape no. 181220-2.2, Audio Archives International, Inc., La Crescenta, CA 91214.

I believe that the mystical impulse dates back, in "mainstream" Jewish tradition, not to the *Merkavah* mysticism and *Heikhalot* literature in the aftermath of the destruction of the Second Temple (see Dan, *Jewish Mysticism, op.cit.,* note 11, Volume 1, Chapter 2), but to the bloody religious encounters between Christendom and Jewry beginning in 10th century Italy and reaching its terrifying crescendo with the mass martyrdom of German Jews during the First Crusade in 1096; see, e.g., Shmuel Shepkaru, "From After Death to Afterlife: Martyrdom and its Recompense," *AJS Review* (No. 1, 1999):1-44. Shepkaru's description of the suicides of fathers and mothers, and their murders of their children, in response to a seemingly triumphant Christianity in history, to escape to their new home with God in heaven, is the ultimate mystical experience. Martyrdom with this goal and expectation occurs, among eleventh century Rhineland Jewry, for the first time in Jewish history (ibid.), as Jews go from trauma and catastrophe to escapism and mystical union.

From 1096, the confluence of martyrdom, ascent to Heaven as the ultimate religious victory, and the direct relation between each individual and God, take on a "unique Ashkenazic, yet not exclusively Jewish" caste and become a major attribute of Ashkenazic literature and belief (ibid.). From the standpoint of the history of Jewish mysticism, it is noteworthy that the 1096 martyrs surely were aware of the anonymously written book of *Yosippon*, which appeared in 953 C.E. (ibid.), and was accepted and revered by medieval Jewry as the original account by Josephus of the fall of *Masada* in 73 C.E. *Yosippon* repeats, and thereby supports, from Josephus's original account in his *Wars of the Jews*, Eleazar's plea to his fellow Jews defending the fortress to kill their families and themselves and to heed *ancient mystical Indian philosophy* that death is more to be cherished than life, which will liberate their immortal souls to join God in the afterlife that is free of the world's miseries in a place of eternal purity. See Yosef Hayim Yerushalmi, *Zakhor* (Seattle: University of Washington Press, 1982), pp. 35-7; *Josephus — Complete Works*, William Whiston, tr. (Grand Rapids, Mich: Kregel Publications, 1981), pp. 601-3. See also, Shulamit Elitzur, "*Aqedat Yitzhak: Bivhi o besimha? Hashpa'* at *Masa'ei Hatzlav al Hasipur Hamiqrai,*" *Et Hada'at I* (1997), pp. 15-36; José Faur, *In the Shadow of History* (Albany, N.Y.: State University of New York Press, 1992), pp. 1-27.

16 For a nuanced presentation of this "middle course," and the inevitable but necessary risks that it entails, see Lichtenstein, "Torah and General Culture...," *op.cit.*, note 12. In a similar vein, see the remark of Harav Kook on the "over-spiritualization" of the Jews in *galut*, reported in Herbert Wiener, *91/2 Mystics — The Kabbalah Today* (N.Y.: Macmillan, 1992), p. 302.

17 On Abarbanel as statesman, royal advisor, financier, as well as Jewish scholar and community leader, see, e.g., Marc D. Angel, *Voices in Exile* (Hoboken: Ktav, 1991), p. 32; Howard M. Sachar, *Farewell España* (N.Y.: Alfred A. Knopf, 1999), pp. 68-73; Yitzhak Baer, *A History of the Jews of Christian Spain* (Phila.: Jewish Publication Society, 1978), Vol. 2, pp. 318 ff., 426, 433 ff. 442.

18 *Deuteronomy* 29:13. Guttmann, Judaism, *op.cit.*, note 11, Chapter 1, emphasizes two key points in Biblical Judaism: first, the primacy of man's individual moral responsibility and free will, based on a transcendent God's absolute freedom of will; and second, that "the moral activism of the Bible envisages the world as the scene of the realization of a Divine order, which is an order of moral will and moral life," without any room for magic or myth. Guttman notes that, in Jewish mysticism, God's transcendence is diluted or bridged, man's individuality is viewed as a barrier between God and man, to be annihilated; God's absolute freedom of will is absent; and myth and magic play important roles; see also generally, Scholem, *Major Trends...*, *op.cit.*, note 3, *passim*.

19 *Zachariah* 14:9

Hellenism versus Hebraism on the Inevitability of Tragedy: Studying the Cain and Joseph Stories

Recent disputes about the idea of "cycles of violence" have turned on the implication, based on the Greek world view, that the pattern of historical cycles is unbreakable, and thereby denies that any blame can be attached to any participating party. In Greek tragedy, catharsis is achieved through understanding the iron laws that underlie human fate. The Jewish worldview sees the cycles of human history differently, as opportunities to redirect the course of human events as part of the process of human redemption. Catharsis is not acceptance through understanding, but rather, heroic human effort to triumph over the self and the environment.[1]

A recent book on the German philosopher, Martin Heidegger, commented on the effect of his embrace of Nazism on his children as being like a "Greek tragedy," in that the sins of the father were visited on his son and daughter.[2] This short and simple view of tragedy is based on a cyclical view of history, that "no event is unique, nothing is enacted but once...; every event has been enacted, is enacted, and will be enacted perpetually; the same individuals, have appeared, appear [again], and will appear at every turn of the circle."[3] If all is cyclical, then the action and reaction tell the whole story — a story that keeps repeating itself.

Not so in Judaism, as I would like to show is demonstrated in the very first book of the Jewish Bible, *Genesis*. Themes, motifs, symbols, may repeat themselves — indeed, they often do — to alert us to the fact that a continuation of a long, unified process is going on. People are continually given opportunities to redeem themselves from past mistakes by the exercise of their moral free will. What is implicit in *Genesis* is, of course, made explicit over and over in the Prophets — the abiding reality of free will and its function in human life.

So here we have another aspect of the Greek-Hebrew dichotomy — destiny versus free will. As Cahill has shown (see note 1), free will is the basis of human progress and moral redemption; destiny is the basis of cyclical history and tragedy.

The key to a proper understanding of the *Genesis* tales is not segmented midrashic commentary on a word, phrase or sentence, as homiletically rewarding as that might be, but understanding episodes in their developing, evolving completeness. And the longer the "melodic line," or the "process," that can be shown to be encompassed, the more we have undoubtedly uncovered the redemptive process — opportunities won or lost — that has taken place under the veneer of isolated action.

Let me illustrate with two episodes from *Genesis*, one short and one long.

The first is the story of Cain and Abel. At first glance, the story is short and not at all complex. Cain, Adam's oldest son, works the soil and, in gratitude for his success, gives a share of the fruits of his toil as an offering to God. Abel, his younger brother, a shepherd, follows suit, and brings an offering from his flock — "from the firstlings....and from their choicest..." (*Gen.* 4:4).

God shows special regard toward Abel's offering, causing Cain to be "angry and crestfallen" (4:5). God questions his despondency in a fatherly way (4:6), assuring Cain that all will be well if he acts properly; but if he does not, he will fall prey to sin. Cain and Abel have an altercation of some kind, beginning with words and ending with Cain killing Abel. God punishes Cain by causing him to be forever a wanderer, unable to work

134

the land, deprived of the permanence in life that he previously had enjoyed, but assured that he will be protected from murder by others by a Divinely placed physical mark that will be visible to all (4:15). Cain fathers a son, who builds a city, and six generations of descendants ending in the era of Noah and the Great Flood. Cain is accidentally killed by his great-great-great grandson, Lamech.[4]

What happened here? Is there a complex moral thread that binds this all together? Or is it just a simple case of two victims of their character flaws, one too zealous, one too jealous, end of story — at best, a short Greek form of tragedy.

Let me try to unravel what I think occurred. Cain, for the first time in human history, brings a tribute offering, in which he recognizes God as the source of his successes in life, from the wheat and other grains and produce of the soil that he had worked. Note that Cain breaks new moral ground, having received no guidance from his father, Adam, who never — by word or deed — pays tribute or offers gratitude to God for his ability to gain a livelihood from the soil, or the ability to father a family, before or after his expulsion from the Garden of Eden.[5] Moreover, Jewish law as later enacted, regarding tribute offerings (Lev. 2:1), does not require that you give any tribute, nor — if you do — that it be the first or choicest of the fruits of your toil. Indeed, this offering (*minhah*) is described in *Leviticus* as characterized by its modesty. It is the thought that counts, and which is accorded Divine favor. It would appear, therefore, that Abel, in bringing his offering from the choicest and first-born of his flock, sought not only to emulate but to outdo his older brother, with the effect — and perhaps the purpose — of showing him up, demonstrating greater zealousness and piety, to impress his parents and, of course, God. God, for His own reasons, rewarded that act — perhaps because he had to if it was well intentioned, perhaps as a test of Cain's moral mettle — by heeding Abel's offering as something special.

This led to Cain suffering from depression. Abel made no attempt to comfort his brother, to ask why he was depressed. Abel is silent. But

God puts his arm around Cain, as it were, asking him, "Why are you depressed? (4:6) Things aren't that bad. You have done nothing wrong — indeed, your voluntary gift was a new and good thing in the world, — nor have I punished you in any way for it. Your brother followed your lead, but his offering was more impressive, that's all — and I had to recognize that. But your depression over this is a dangerous state; it can easily lead to your doing something wrong, to lashing out, out of frustration, out of a sense of worthlessness, loss of self-esteem. You need to look at the bright side of things, what is good in your life, and the opportunities that life presents for the future, and not dwell on hurts, real or imagined, of the past. If you improve and do well in this regard, your depression will be lifted from you."[6]

But Cain is in too deeply. He can't accept God's fatherly warning. The text tells us that he speaks to Abel (4:4), undoubtedly reproaching him for showing him up — making him look bad to his parents and to God: "And why, for what? I was the first to present God with a tribute offering from the fruits of my toil. You copied what I thought of first, and then tried to outdo me. Couldn't you have just done the same, as a good younger brother should, copying the good behavior of his older brother? Or perhaps you wanted to suggest to father that he should also make a tribute offering from 'the choicest, first-born of his flock' — which would be me, of course, leaving you alone to partake of father's affection and largesse." The altercation continues from their house out into the fields (4:8), perhaps even over a period of days. At this point the text becomes unclear about what happened next, but the Midrash tells us that the phrase "and [Cain] rose up" against Abel indicates that Abel was the stronger of the two and had Cain pinned to the ground; Cain, sensing danger to his life, said something like "I give up" or "have mercy," and when Abel loosened his grip on him Cain "rose up" from the ground[7] and, in self-defense — it seemed to him that he was in a fight for his life — killed Abel.

What punishment is appropriate here? And how will Cain react to it? It seems clear that Cain didn't know what "killing" someone meant; there had been no such thing as death in the world before. He took the offensive when he had the chance, so the Midrash tells us it was an unwitting killing[8] — we would call it an assault, probably in self-defense under the circumstances. But God's punishment is severe enough. Cain is exiled from his land, condemned to wander the world with the "mark of Cain" on his forehead for all to see, as a warning that he is under God's protection (*Gen.* 4:14–15) and, of course, marking Cain's moral fall.

Cain, so easily depressed, should certainly have gone into an even more serious depression at this juncture in his life, a depression that would prevent or abort all normal creative activity. Surely he would be too ashamed, embarrassed, to start a family now. But no, the very next words of the text tell us that Cain "rises up" again, as it were, but this time redemptively: "And Cain knew his wife, and she conceived..." (4:17). Because having children is shown as a mark of God's providence in *Genesis*, this prompt Divine response to Cain's determination to seize the opportunity of life is evidently a reward for Cain's penance; God's grace is upon him no less than the mark on his forehead, for all to see. Cain has shown the moral courage to face life, to live life, not to deprive his wife or himself of a family, nor to deprive his children of the opportunity for life even if it means having to face the challenge of a father marked for a previous serious transgression, and overcome it. Six generations of progeny followed. This is not cyclical, as in the Greek version of life, but "processive" as Cahill calls it,[9] and redemptive — and for all of us who witness it through the Biblical lens, it is instructive and inspiring, thought provoking and uplifting.

What would the story mean through the lens of the Greek cyclical worldview? How would the Greeks fill in the blanks? How would Cain and Abel play out as Greek tragedy? I think this story as Greek tragedy would add that Abel in fact asked his father whether it would be alright to make an offering to God from his flock like his brother did. How happy this made Adam, the admiring, doting father: "Look at that, Eve. So big and strong[10] and with such a big heart, such religious sensitivity, too."

But Abel is not done. "And, father, would it be alright to make the offering from the choicest, fattest, first-born of my flock? Would that be too ostentatious, wouldn't that make Cain look, well, less thankful to God, by comparison?" "No, my son, it's a beautiful thought, go for it." And the rest is, as they say, tragedy. From this double dose of goodness, by the doting parent and the eager-to-please, narcissistic son — whose very name, in Hebrew, means vanity — come inevitable, tragic death to the son, exile to his brother, and parents bereft of both children. In Greek tragedy, this is The End — curtain.

I can hear readers asking, "Well, isn't this tragedy, family tragedy, repeated in one form or another, that is, cyclically — in the Greek sense — throughout *Genesis*, with Sarah preferring Isaac, which culminates in the Binding of Isaac episode and Sarah's death when she learns about it;[11] Isaac preferring Esau, culminating in the destruction of his family after Jacob must steal the blessing intended for his brother and flee his threatening brother, his parents and his home; and Jacob preferring Joseph, which culminates in the entire family winding up in Egypt where they become enslaved?"

Yes, but this precisely my point. *Genesis* is not just the cyclical repetition of the same tragedy over and over again. In each case there are continuous opportunities for moral successes and failures. In each case there are openings for redemption, there is personal growth, there are processes not cycles because in each case the outcome is not destined, but subject to the free will of its participants. It is possible to break the cycle by understanding its causes — in *Genesis* it is unjustified preferences among family members — confronting them, and changing them by redemptive action.

And this leads me to my next illustration, the tale of Joseph. Follow the coat, because that is the symbol that calls our attention again and again to another turn in the plot, caused by free will, and the possibility of change, growth, progress, and redemption, the very opposite of cycle, of destiny, of human helplessness in the grip of larger forces, that are the hallmark of the Greek tragic worldview.

In skeletal outline, Jacob favors Joseph, son of the deceased Rachel, Jacob's true love, over his first-born and the other children of his other wife, Leah, whom Jacob was tricked into marrying by his uncle, Laban, because Leah was the eldest. Jacob's favoritism is symbolized by the coat of many colors that he gives to Joseph. The brothers resent Joseph's dreams of family domination and, when the opportunity arises, they sell him to a slave caravan that carries him to Egypt. The brothers drop a piece of Joseph's coat in animal blood and present it to Jacob as evidence of Joseph's death (*Gen.* 37:2–33).

Joseph, meanwhile, experiences a meteoric rise from a houseboy to Prime Minister of Egypt. This career was almost derailed when the wife of his first master continually sought to seduce him. His final resistance to her entreaties is marked by her pulling off his coat as he pulls away from her. She then runs into the street brandishing his coat and crying out, "Here is the proof that it was Joseph who tried to force himself on me, and he was forced to run out of the house coatless when he was about to be found out" (*Gen.* 39:1–20). Joseph's moral courage, in rejecting the "gift" of the wife's favors because of his good looks and charm (*Gen.* 39:6), in contrast to his earlier acceptance of the favoritism of Jacob over his brothers, becomes the beginning of Joseph's redemption. But, for now, this newfound moral strength lands him in jail, where his demonstration of dream-solving paves the way ultimately for his rapid rise to Prime Minister (40:7–41:48).

Eventually the brothers must go to Egypt for food because of a famine in Canaan. Joseph recognizes his brothers but they don't recognize him. He tricks them into bringing to Egypt Jacob's youngest child, Joseph's only brother, Benjamin, by their mother, Rachel, and then Joseph tricks them into thinking that Benjamin has stolen his special cup for which he must remain in Egypt, while the other brothers are free to go. At this point they rend their garments (44:13) — a sign of mourning over many things: the inevitable death of Jacob when they return without Benjamin; their own deaths, figurative and psychological, at being the instruments of their father's death and their own decimated moral and material condition without Jacob's presence; and Benjamin's inevitable living death, or worse, as a slave in Egypt. Finally, the rending of their garments symbolizes retribution for causing Jacob to rend his garments when he heard of Joseph's death. Their penance has begun, with the symbol — clothing — of their earlier betrayal of Joseph and their father, Jacob. Judah, the leader of the brothers, who guaranteed to Jacob that no harm would come to Rachel's other son (Gen. 43:8–9), pleads for Benjamin for the sake of their father. They offer to remain as slaves in lieu of Benjamin (Gen. 44:9, 44:16). Judah now implores Joseph to let Benjamin return for the sake of preserving Jacob's life. Joseph, sensing from Judah's words the precarious nature of his father's health, and remorseful over not letting his father know for so many years that he was alive, finally reveals himself, breaking down with emotion at the redemptive acts of Judah and his other brothers.

Clearly, these are no longer the brothers who were willing to sell Joseph into slavery because of their envy; they were now prepared to sell themselves into slavery for the sake of Joseph's brother and their father. The brothers are sent back with presents to bring Jacob back to Egypt to live during the coming expected years of famine. To each Joseph gave two sets of specially fine, elegant garments, but to Benjamin, his brother by their mother Rachel, he gave five times as many such garments.[12] This is the final appearance of the symbol of clothing in this long story — that Jacob would recognize as evidence that the torn, bloody coat that his sons had earlier shown to him was false evidence about Joseph's death, and these garments represented the truth about his life. Of course, the clothing would be a constant reminder to the brothers of how they had treated Joseph in the past.[13] But might it also suggest a repeat favoritism against them which — transmitted as a renewal of their earlier hostility to their progeny — might have contributed to their seceding from the tribes of Benjamin (and Judah) to form a separate Jewish state of Israel a few hundred years later? The potential for tragedy remains when the cause of trouble is not fully understood and, therefore, repeated.

Jacob did wrong by his sons in favoring Joseph, with the coat of many colors and his parental toleration of Joseph's dreams of family dominance. But he is redeemed by his willingness to send his other favorite, Benjamin, to save the family from the on-going famine in Canaan.

The brothers did wrong in carrying their resentment too far, selling Joseph into slavery, and representing to Jacob that Joseph was killed, waiving before his eyes a torn piece of Joseph's special coat. They are redeemed when they are willing to trade their lives to save Joseph's only full brother, Benjamin.

Judah, who had done wrong by proposing that the brothers sell Joseph into slavery, (Gen. 37:26), stands up as the guarantor of Benjamin's freedom so Benjamin can go to Egypt (43:8–10). This bond is later reflected in their progeny's bonding together as the Kingdom of Judah, from which the other ten tribes seceded.

Joseph did wrong in lording it over his family — his mother and father and especially his brothers (37:2–11) — as if his father's acts of favoritism were not provocative enough. The many-colored coat, which he evidently wore all the time,[14] was a constant reminder to his brothers of where they stood in Jacob's affections. Joseph's beauty and narcissism almost led to his demise. Joseph redeemed himself by his moral discipline in resisting the seduction efforts of his employer's wife, represented — once again — by his coat which she pulled off him as he ran from her into the street, and by forgiving his brothers.

Later, when Jacob is blessing Joseph's sons, Menasseh and Ephraim, Joseph insists that his father place his right hand over Menasseh, as the first born, and not switch his hands, as he was about to do, onto Ephraim. Jacob, as a grandfather, and speaking with the power of prophecy, prevails. We are left to contemplate whether the brothers are witnessing another act of favoritism by Jacob (Gen. 48:1–22).

This long story is not cyclical but progressive. Free will conquers destiny. A skeletal Greek version of this family's tribulations as tragedy might run something like this: Jacob favors Joseph. His half brothers are envious and plot to dispose of him, which they soon succeed in doing, representing to Jacob that Joseph is dead. The brothers, except the youngest, Benjamin — now Jacob's favorite — are forced to go down to Egypt for food during a severe famine in Canaan. Joseph, having succeeded — as he had dreamed — of reaching the pinnacle of power, fails to recognize his brothers and — suspecting them of being spies — has them killed. Jacob soon realizes that something has happened to them, and decides that he and Benjamin must go to Egypt to find them. Joseph recognizes his poor old father, and both — realizing what has happened — fall into each others arms, sobbing in tragic sorrow. Benjamin, wearing a new many-colored coat as his father's new favorite son, stands by, taking it all in. The End — curtain. There are no opportunities for redemption here. There is just the force of destiny, man as the plaything of the gods, with no free will, and no chance to rise above his past, and sanctify his life. The Talmudic Sages said, "Where a man who has repented his past stands, no one else can stand" — no matter how righteous.[15] There is no such idea in Greek tragedy. It is everywhere in *Genesis*, instructing us by its own special form of theater, in what makes mankind, each of us, special.

....
NOTES

1   See, e.g., Thomas Cahill, *The Gifts of the Jews* (New York: Doubleday/Anchor, 1998), pp. 5, 250-1; Joseph B. Soloveitchik, "Catharsis," *Tradition* (Spring, 1978):38-54.

2   Richard Wolin, *Heidegger's Children* (Princeton: Princeton University Press, 2001), reviewed by Damon Linker, "Philosophy and Tyranny," *First Things* (January, 2002):41.

3   Cahill, *The Gifts…, Op. cit.*, p. 5.

4   *Gen.* 4:17-24 and commentary of *Artscroll, Genesis* (Brooklyn, N.Y.: Mesorah Publications, 1995), *ad loc*. There is another Lamech, who fathered Noah, who was not of Cain's line but descended from Seth, the son of Adam and Eve. (I am grateful to Deane S. Berson of Cascade, CO., for calling this to the editor's [and my] attention.)

5   When Adam is expelled with Eve from the Garden of Eden, his punishment is to have to gain his bread "by the sweat of [his] brow" (*Gen.* 3:19), and not effortlessly as before, but God's role in the blessings of nature is no less important in the post-Eden world. Adam's lack of gratitude for, or any acknowledgement of,

God's beneficence in his life, from Creation to Eve to his children, stands in sharp contrast to the kabbalist idea that Adam, before his fall and expulsion from Eden, is a cosmic being who contains the whole world in himself, and "whose station is superior even to...the first of the angels;" see Gershom Scholem, *Major Trends in Jewish Mysticism* (N.Y.:Schocken, 1961), pp. 279-80. Lack of gratitude to God may truly be considered Adam's "original sin." There is a midrash on the *Akedah* that traces God's decision to test Abraham to Satan's apparently valid claim to God that Abraham was so busy celebrating with family and friends over the birth of Isaac, at the very old age of Abraham and Sarah, that he forgot to offer to God even a token show of gratitude for the Divine gift of Isaac's birth (Rashi at Gen.22:1). Surely the same can be said of Adam, and, in contrast, praise is surely due to Cain for being the first human to say "Thank you" with an offering of the fruit of his toil, to God; see Elie Wiesel, *Messengers of God* (New York: Random House, 1976), Chapter 5 ("The Sacrifice of Isaac: A Survivor's Story"), Pocket Book edition, pp. 104-7.

6   The usual interpretation of the first half of *Gen*. 4:7 is along the lines of "If you act correctly (or "do right") you will be forgiven" (or "there is uplift" in the sense of "your countenance or depression will be lifted"). But this does not follow very well from "Why are you depressed?" which ends the prior sentence, which implies that Cain has *no reason* to be depressed because he has done nothing wrong. If so, why the lecture, "If you act correctly in the future, etc." If he did nothing that needs correction — as, indeed, he did not — then why the warning about doing something wrong in the future? Second, the Hebrew word for "act correctly" or "do right" in the abbreviated form in which it appears in 4:7 (*tetiv*), can mean "[if you] do right in your outlook, in your attitude to life," which makes more sense, in context, as a Divine suggestion to Cain on how to alleviate his depression. Third, the end of *Gen*. 4:7, "and if you don't [act correctly], sin awaits at the door," makes no sense; if you sin, sin is no longer at the door — it is inside the house! Because this is recognized by one commentator as "one of the most difficult and obscure Biblical sentences," I believe I am on solid ground in offering my interpretation; see Umberto Cassuto, *A Commentary on the Book of Genesis: Part One — From Adam to Noah*, Israel Abrahams, tr. (Jerusalem: Magnes Press, 1998), p. 208, citing B. *Yoma* 52a-b.

7   *Ber. R*. 22:8, 17; *Artscroll Genesis, Op.cit.*, ad loc., p. 150.

8   *Ibid.*, at *Gen*. 4:12, p. 154; *Me'am Loez*, at *Genesis* 4:15.

9   Cahill, *The Gifts...*, *Op. cit.*, p. 251. Compare Cain's action to the decision of Moses' father and other Israelite husbands in Egypt, who divorced their wives in despair over Pharaoh's decree that all their newborn sons should be drowned in the Nile; see *Ex*. 2:1, Rashi *ad loc.*, and B. *Sotah* 12a. (They remarried at their wives seductive insistence!). Courage akin to Cain's is found among the Holocaust survivors who started new families after the war.

10 See note 7.

11 Rashi on *Gen*. 23:2.

12 *Gen*. 35:22 and *Artscroll Genesis, Op. cit.*, ad loc., p. 1980.

13 *Ibid.*, p. 1981. There is a midrash which states that Abraham was tested at the *Akedah* because he favored his son, Isaac, over his eldest son, Ishmael; Eli Wiesel, *Messengers of God* (New York: Random House, 1976), Chapter 5 ("The Sacrifice of Isaac: A Survivor's Story"), Pocket Book edition, pp. 104-7. It appears from this view that favoring one son over another is a mistake that, in fact, repeats it-

self throughout *Genesis*, always with unfortunate consequences; see discussion in Wiesel.

14 *ArtScroll, Genesis,* at *Gen.* 37:31, p. 1657.

15 B. *San.* 99a; B. *Ber.* 34b.

Genesis 9:12–17: "Look to the Rainbow" So Why Did the Sages Say "Don't Look?"

After the flood, God presents to the world, through Noah, the seven Noahide Laws,[1] and a Covenant of Peace, as Nachmanides describes it, not to destroy the world again, signified by the rainbow.[2] It is not clear whether the covenant is contingent on the world — somewhere at least — complying with the Noahide Laws or at least avoiding the level of corruption that preceded the flood.[3] But, in any case, when things look bad for the world, and there seems a likelihood or even a possibility that, because of human corruption, worldwide destruction is again a possibility, God says that the sign of the rainbow will be seen and, again, immediately thereafter — as if for emphasis — He repeats this thought by saying, "And I will cause you to see it [the rainbow] [and] remember the everlasting covenant between God and every living being...."[4]

There is no doubt that the Talmudic Sages had the power, the halakhic authority, to say "Sit and don't do it" (*shev v'al ta'aseh*) with regard to positive Biblical commandments. Therefore, even if looking to the rainbow for the consolation of God's Covenant of Peace is a commandment, as the double reference to looking at the rainbow perhaps might imply, the Sages could say, "Don't look." In fact, this is precisely what they did say. The Talmud joins looking at the rainbow with two other cases of looking at vessels of the Divine Glory — at Jewish rulers, and at the priests when they are blessing the Jewish people — as prohibited acts.[5]

Of course, God was fully aware that the rainbow had this special

Divine property or aspect to it when He twice called for the world to look at, to see, the rainbow and be reminded of its message, as God would remember.[6] What happened subsequently to cause the Sages to decree, "Don't look?"

I suggest that the answer lies in the text and the story that immediately follow. Immediately after Noah and his family leave the Ark and learn of God's Covenant of Peace, Noah becomes drunk and he becomes uncovered, i.e., his genital area, that part of himself that normally should be covered from others.[7]

The text continues that Ham, one of Noah's three sons, and the "father of Canaan," saw "his father's nakedness,"[8] and told his two brothers, Shem and Japheth. Their response was to go into Noah's tent and, out of respect for their father, they walked backward so as not to see their father in this state, and covered him with a garment. Not surprisingly, when Noah awoke and realized "what his younger son had done to him," he cursed his grandson, Canaan, son of Ham.[9] The Sages quite properly interpret the phrase "had done to him" to mean more than just seeing him, but, rather to refer to sexual abuse — that Ham sodomized and castrated Noah, preventing him from having a fourth son.[10]

Interestingly, the Sages say that it was just Shem who took the initiative in covering Noah — inferred from the singular form of "*he* took the garment" in *Gen.* 9:23 — and, therefore, his descendants, the Israelites, were rewarded with the Torah commandment of wearing fringes on the corners of their garments, which we recognize as the *tallit* (prayer shawl) or the smaller *tallit katan* worn under or over clothing.[11]

I suggest that the Sages saw, they intuited from their experience, a significant, psychosexual connection between the Divine blessing of mankind looking to the rainbow, the Divine Glory of mankind's Divine Parent, and the immorality of Noah's progeny, Ham and Canaan, immediately thereafter, in looking at the nakedness of their biological parent, and abusing him. In psychological terms, we may say that viewing the Divine Glory represented by the rainbow triggered in Ham an aspiration

146

to be God-like and to unite with God, the Divine Father. This brought him into conflict with his earthly, biological father, Noah, especially given his father's privileged relationship with God. The occasion of his father's nakedness gave him an opportunity to violate the taboo against viewing that aspect of his father that symbolized his power, privileges and the forbidden, an opportunity that Ham was unable to resist.[12] It was a short step from the forbidden viewing to the sexual abuse that ensued, to symbolically remove his father as an obstacle to his own aspiration toward the Divine. This psychological process of seeing, desiring, and acting out, may have been intensified if, as some commentators believe, Ham saw his father having sexual relations with his mother.[13] There is a kabbalistic view that the rainbow represented the Divine phallus, that brings to mind the perfect harmony and beauty of the sexual act performed by or with mystically-ascribed aspects of God (*sefirot*) viewed as a multi-faceted Godhead.[14] This would involve alternative scenarios in which Noah would, again, stand in the way of Ham's psychosexual desires.

I believe that another, psychoanalytic observation can be made concerning the story of Noah and his sons. It has been cogently argued that God's intervention at the *Akedah* to save Isaac — and, indeed, the idea of a Divine law-giver in Jewish tradition — serve to ameliorate the characteristic Oedipal conflict in Western Civilization between sons and fathers, by demonstrating that the father as well as the son are subject to a higher power and authority.[15] From this I would argue that the story of Noah and his sons, coming directly after God gives the Seven Noahide Laws to Noah and his family for the benefit of mankind, indicates two things: First, this encounter with the Divine moral authority did indeed ameliorate that father-son conflict; both Shem and Japheth display not the desire to destroy their father's power in a moment of great vulnerability, but — to the contrary — they show the highest respect and consideration to him. Second, there continues to be room for free will to operate; one son cannot resist the impulse to destroy his father's power and assume it for himself. The new condition of the world, under the revealed rule of a

Divine law-giver, has removed the almost iron inevitability of the son-father struggle so powerfully exemplified in Greek and Roman culture, but not totally. It has made possible a better relationship between father and son, provided each is willing to participate in it, but without guarantees. It provides an opportunity, an environment for a freely willed, mutually respectful relationship to exist. The rest is up to each son and father.

The forfeiture of the right to look upon the rainbow, as a sign of God's glory, was probably formally pronounced by God, many years after Noah, when Moses — who loved his people more than himself — [16] was terrified that God would remain endlessly angry at Israel because of its idolatrous sin of the Golden Calf. He felt compelled to ask God once more — as God had contemplated at the Rainbow Covenant — to see God's Glory, for assurance that God would no longer threaten, or even consider, the total destruction of the Jewish People. But God denied this request, saying: "No human being can look upon Me and live."[17] It was, of course, up to the Sages to determine whether this pronouncement was intended to apply to the rainbow.

They evidently thought that it did. And so the Sages decided that seeing the Divine Glory in the rainbow, in all of its sexual symbolism, is a blessing that mankind cannot afford, and, in light of God's pronouncement to Moses, should not and cannot be allowed to enjoy, because human beings can transfer their arousal and desire from close encounters with the Divinity to areas of their human relationships where such freedom must be curbed. The rainbow as a sign of God's Glory must be treated like Jewish rulers and like priests during their blessings — as vessels of the Divine Glory; we may not look at them, in order to maintain the sense of awe, fear and respect that they deserve.

Evidence of a similar point of view is found in the story in *Leviticus* 10:2 of Nadav and Avihu, the sons of Aaron, the High Priest. They died by a Divine fire "when they brought before God an alien fire that He had not commanded them." As God explains in *Leviticus* 10:3, "By those who are near Me shall I become sanctified...," meaning, according to Rabbi

Shlomo Riskin, "Come near to God, but not too near. Do not presume to take liberties with Divine encounters. Only God decides when, where, and the manner in which He is to be worshipped."[18]

Indeed, the very next section of *Leviticus*, after these tragic priestly deaths and the description of the Yom Kippur atonement service, deals with the prohibitions against sexual immorality — including, as the very first prohibition, "uncovering the nakedness of your father and mother,"[19] and, in the middle of this lengthy discourse, the reciprocal, ubiquitous Biblical prohibition against parents sacrificing their children to a god — any god.[20] The message, says Riskin, is clear: When we get too close to God, and think we know His will, soon every abomination may seem possible of being thought of as God's will, wherein man projects his own desires onto God. The remedy is never to get too close to God, never presume to know God's will, never to let love overcome fear, awe, respect, and the distance that signifies God's transcendence over man. Evidence of that same message may be found in *Deut.* 18:16–17, where Moses recounts how the Israelites refused to hear God's voice or "see" His fiery presence after the revelation of the Ten Commandments started, and God's response was: "They have done well in what they said." It would seem that this message runs counter to the Hasidic homily that the Israelites should not have withdrawn from their direct encounter with God at Mt. Sinai.[21]

It would seem that — for the Sages also — mystical experiences of God, including "seeing" aspects of the Godhead, or its male and female forms, e.g., the *Shekhinah*, must be strongly discouraged, and therefore must be considered to be in the direct line of fire, so to speak, of the Sages' prohibition against "seeing," "looking" or "staring" at the rainbow.[22] In this regard, perhaps, the Noahide origin of this prohibition that we have discussed in this paper may be the foundation of all three prohibitions discussed above — looking upon God's Glory in a rainbow, in a ruler, and in a priest in the midst of blessing Israel. By these prohibitions, like many others, the Sages sought for Israel to merit that blessing, and God's

149

Glory, in its midst.

As we all know, of course, Jewish history had the final say. The pressures of persecutions and expulsions in Europe, starting in the 11th century, caused the emergence of mysticism in Jewish tradition, and its core impulse to escape the troubles and traumas of evil in the real world, for the purity and peace of the Divine world, through mystical experiences of communion with God, and mystical ideas, images and visions of the Godhead, Creation and Redemption. By careful adherence to the ritual and ethical commandments, this new tradition became a pre-eminent part of mainstream Judaism, and has remained so to this day.[23]

....
NOTES

1   Their Biblical source is *Gen.* 9:1-7, as amplified in the Talmud, B. *San.* 56 a-b.

2   Nachmanides (Ramban), *Commentary on the Bible*, Charles B. Chavel, ed. and ann. (New York: Shilo, 1971), at *Gen.* 9:12. The covenant is that the world will never be destroyed again by *any* sort of catastrophe, not just by flood; see, e.g., the *Rif* (R. Isaac Alfasi) and Sforno on 9:11. The rainbow was chosen, according to one commentator, as the sign of God's new covenant because it is symbolic of God's Glory (Ezekiel 1:28); see *B'khor Shor* at *Gen.* 9:13. Ramban, on that verse, notes that the rainbow is inverted in the sky, symbolizing that no Divine aggression is aimed *at* the world, but *away* from it, which is the way warriors call for peace from their erstwhile opponents. Hirsch notes here that the rainbow is an arc connecting earth and heaven, and thereby symbolizes the eternal bond of peace between them; *The Pentateuch*, Samson Raphael Hirsch, tr. and ann. (Gateshead, England: Judaica Press, 1976), Vol. I, *Genesis*.

     It may be asked why God promised not to bring another catastrophe upon the world "because (sic) mankind's heart is directed to do only evil from his youth," a reason which seems to be illogical; indeed, that same reason, in virtually the same language, is given for God's earlier decision to *destroy* the world by the Flood (compare *Gen.* 6:5 and 8:21). I believe the answer lies in the word "only" ("to do only evil") contained in His reason for bringing the flood, which is missing from God's promise not to destroy the world again. The difference indicates that the new race of humanity, descended from Noah and his progeny, had the free will to do good, and gave every indication, by the acts Shem and Japheth, that it could do so. Thus, in contrast to the descendants of Adam — who is glorified in kabbalah, but who never showed gratitude to God for Eve, for his children, for the Garden of Eden, for the entirety of God's creations — the first thing that Noah did after emerging from the Ark was to bring a sacrificial offering of gratitude to God. It is no accident in my view that, immediately after that, God determines not to destroy the world again.

3   Sforno on *Gen.* 9:9, noting that the Covenant of Peace was contingent on murder — the cornerstone issue of the Noahide Laws — not becoming rampant again. But cf. *Hizkuni* on 9:11.

4   While many translate the Hebrew word in this text (*Gen.* 9:16), *u're'itiha*, to mean "I [God] shall see [the rainbow]," I believe the better translation, given the context and grammar of the entire sentence, is Abarbanel's "I will cause *you* [mankind] to see it." The commentators Sforno and *Ha' kitav v'Ha' kabbalah*, translate the word similarly. See also Radak on *Gen.* 9:14.

5   The classic illustration is in B. *R.H.* 29b, where the Sages prohibit blowing the shofar on *Rosh Hashanah* that falls on the Sabbath to prevent more serious violations, e.g., carrying the shofar on the Sabbath; see also B. *Yev.* 90b. The three prohibitions on viewing God's Glory are in B. *Hag.* 16a. On the rainbow as a reminder or symbol of God's image, see the Talmudic midrash, *Gen. R.* 35:3; and the commentary of *B'khor Shor*, on *Gen.* 9:13-14.

6   The commentators note that God does not forget anything, but the text here uses language that He will be reminded of His Covenant of Peace by the rainbow because the Bible speaks in human terms to humanity, to assure human understanding; see, e.g., Radak (R. David Kimhi, medieval Biblical commentator) on *Gen*: 9:15. Moreover, even if the rainbow cannot be seen for natural reasons, it is always seen by God; see Ibn Ezra and Abarbanel on 9:16.

7   *Gen.* 9:21. Rashi says, ad loc, that Noah uncovered himself, but Ralbag and *B'khor Shor* say that his grandson, Canaan, uncovered him, and the *Tur* says that Noah's son, Ham, did this and told his brothers, Shem and Japheth.

8   According to Rashi, at 9:22, citing rabbinic opinions, Canaan saw the nakedness of Noah, and told his father, Ham. The Hebrew word for nakedness here is *ervah*, which always connotes nakedness in the context of sexual immorality. Canaan and Ham are implicated in their callous disrespect for Noah in his defenseless, embarrassing, nakedness. Instead of modestly averting their eyes and covering Noah, and telling no one, they joyfully broadcast the situation publicly to the other brothers; Ramban and Sforno on *Gen.* 9:22. As we shall see below, sexual immorality was very much involved here; see text at note 10.

9   *Gen.* 9:24-5. It would appear from this that Canaan was first to see Noah uncovered; see notes 7 and 8. In the text of *Genesis*, Noah cursed Canaan, and blessed both Shem and Japheth for their respectful behavior: the descendants of Shem, as a follower of God, were to inherit the land of Canaan (Rashi at *Gen.* 9:26); and the descendants of Japheth would have extended boundaries (*Gen.* 9:26) and "dwell in the tents of Shem" (*Gen.* 9:27). The descendants of Canaan would be subject to the descendants of Shem and, according to Rabbenu Bahya, also to the descendants of Japheth; Ramban also allows for this interpretation. See *ArtScroll Genesis* (New York: Mesorah Publications, 1997), at *Gen.* 9:27. R. Samson Raphael Hirsch, in his commentary on the *Pentateuch* (ad loc.), sees Japheth blessed with the ability to create beauty (Greece — Hellenism) while Shem was blessed with the ability to create holiness (Israel — Hebraism), and the ideal is for the beauty of Japheth to be disciplined and guided by holiness, to "dwell in the tents of Shem."

10 B. *San.* 70a. The Sages Rav and Shmuel differ on whether Noah was sodomized or castrated. It is also not clear whether Noah was abused by Ham or Canaan. *Pirkei d'Rabbi Eliezier* and Ralbag say it was Canaan who castrated Noah; see discussion in *ArtScroll Genesis, Op. cit.* at *Gen.* 9:22-4. The Sages (B. *San.* 70a) seem to say that it was Ham, but the curse was placed on Canaan, Ham's fourth child (*Gen.* 10:7), because, in castrating Noah, Ham prevented Noah from having a fourth child. Ham was not the *youngest* of Noah's children, as the text describes him, but was *katan*, small, in the sense of "unfit," according to Rashi (9:24), based on the

fact that the Hebrew word for younger, *katan*, also means "small."

11 Rashi on *Gen.* 9:23. Japheth was also rewarded for joining Shem in this respectful act toward their father, in that his descendents, the Greeks, were given the privilege to be buried in the Land of Israel during the final war between Gog and Magog before the arrival of the Messiah; see Rabbenu Bahya Ben Asher (b. 1255) on *Gen.* 9:25. The privilege of covering the body with the *tallit* was the blessing given to Shem for respectfully covering his father's phallic nakedness, in contrast to the curse given to Ham, who defiled his father by gazing at his nakedness and then sodomizing and castrating him.

12 I acknowledge the assistance of the psychoanalyst, Robert Fiore, Ph.D., in developing this insight. On the importance of psychoanalytic input in interpreting and understanding certain behavior in sacred texts, see David Halperin, book review, in *AJS Rev.* (1996):153-6.

13 See discussion in *Artscroll Genesis, Op. cit.,* at *Gen.* 9:22, p. 302, noting that the phrase "Noah was uncovered in *his* tent" is spelled in Hebrew as *her* tent, referring to Noah's wife, and only Ham dared to disturb their marital intimacy.

14 Elliot R. Wolfson, *Through a Speculum That Shines* (Princeton: Princeton University Press, 1994), pp. 286, 334, 337-41, 361, 368-72, 386-7, 396; Moshe Idel, *Kabbalah: New Perspectives* (New Haven: Yale University Press, 1988), p. 227. There is also a kabbalistic interpretation of the rainbow as the sign of the covenant of circumcision; see the commentary of Nachmanides and Rabbenu Bahya ben Asher on *Gen.* 9:12ff.

15 S. Giora Shoham, *Valhalla, Calvary & Auschwitz* (Cincinnati: Bowman & Cody, 1995), pp. 110-118; Jose Faur, "De-authorization of the Law: Paul and the Oedipal Model," *Psychoanalysis and Religion,* Joseph H. Smith, ed. and Susan Handelman, assoc. ed. (Baltimore: John Hopkins University Press, 1990), pp. 227-9. Shoham also shows that this "Isaac Syndrome," as he describes it, can be carried to dangerous extremes; *Valhalla,* pp. 111-118.

16 *Ex.* 32:30-5.

17 *Ex.* 33: 18-23; cf. *Deut.* 34:10.

18 Shlomo Riskin, "Too Close for Comfort," *Jewish World* (Long Island), April 19, 2002, p. 7. It must be noted that Jewish mysticism, partly because of its strong emphasis on God's immanence, has always involved a strong element of the mystical union of man with God (*unio mystica*), at the initiation, in the place, and in the manner chosen by the mystic; see, e.g., Idel, *Kabbalah,* esp. chs. 3-5, and pp. 147-8, 151; and Wolfson, *...A Speculum..., Op. cit., passim.* The contrast with the extreme reluctance of prophets, in their encounters with God, to commune with God in any way, is striking. Although the mystical impulse for communion with God began as early as the second or third century, C.E., in the Land of Israel, with *Merkavah* mysticism and *Hekhalot* literature, it seems to have begun in mainstream Judaism with the impulse to see God "eye to eye," as it were, by the Rhineland martyrs during the First Crusade; see, e.g., Joseph Dan, *Jewish Mysticism* (Northvale, N.J.: Jason Aronson, Inc. 1998), Vol. I, chs. 2-3; Robert Chazan, *European Jewry and the First Crusade* (Berkeley: University of California Press, 1987), Appendix, esp. pp. 252, 254 and 281; and Jacob Katz, *Exclusiveness and Tolerance* (New York: Behrman House, 1961), p. 89, citing F.Y. Baer's article, "*Gezerot Tatnu,*" *Sefer Assaf* (Jerusalem, 1953), pp. 126-40. For a recent discussion see my paper in *The Edah Journal* 3.1, Tevet 5763 (2003).

19 *Lev.* 18:1-20, 22-30.

20 *Lev.* 18:21.

21 See Aryeh J. Wineman, "On *Ma'amad Har Sinai* in the Hasidic Homily," 33rd Annual Conference of the Association for Jewish Studies, Dec. 16-18, 2001, Audio Archives International, Inc., 3043 Foothill Blvd, Suite 2, La Crescenta, CA, tape no. 211216-3.13.

22 See, e.g., B. *Hag.* 11b, 14b, 16a; see generally, Ephraim Urbach, *The Sages* (Jerusalem: Magnes Press, 1979), pp. 184, 193-4, 212-13, 222-3, 417. See also note 18. For a recent study of the rise to prominence of the *Shekhinah*, as the female form of the Divine presence within the Godhead, in Jewish mystical thought, see Arthur Green, "*Shekhinah*, The Virgin Mary, and the Song of Songs: Reflections on a Kabbalistic Symbol in its Historical Context," *AJS Rev.* (2002):1-52.

23 See, generally, Gershom Scholem, *Major Trends in Jewish Mysticism* (New York: Schocken, 1961); Joseph Dan, *Jewish Mysticism* (Northvale, N.J.: Jason Aronson, Inc., 1998); David Berger, "Judaism and General Culture in Medieval and Early Modern Times," *Judaism's Encounter with Other Cultures*, Jacob J. Schacter, ed. (Northvale, N.J.: Jason Aronson, Inc., 1997), p. 87; Jacob Katz, *Exclusiveness and Tolerance, Op. cit*, and *idem., Tradition and Crisis* (New York: NYU Press, 1993), pp. 3, 24.

The Tower of Babel:
From Destruction to Dispersion

It is commonly thought that the Tower of Babel was a rebellion against God.[1] But if that was all there was to it, why wasn't it enough for God to simply destroy the tower? What does God creating a multiplicity of languages, and scattering the people across the face of the earth, have to do with it? And why is the Bible so mysterious in explaining the motives of the tower's builders? The text in *Gen.* 11:4 merely says, cryptically: "Come, let us build us a city, and a tower with its top in the heavens, and let us make a name for ourselves, lest we be dispersed across the whole earth."

As the Artscroll commentary summarizes the Midrash, "… [the deeds] of the generation of the Dispersion are veiled."[2]

The simple interpretation of the story, according to many commentators, is that the scheme of concentrating the population in one place was contrary to God's will that many nations multiply and inhabit all parts of the world, which was the Divine master plan of creation.[3] I believe this is the core of this story and its message, which I propose briefly to develop in the rest of this article.

Background Texts

Gen. 1:27–28 recounts that God created humanity in God's image, "male and female He created them," and blessed them: "Be fruitful and multiply, *fill the earth* and subdue it…" (emphasis added).

Gen. 9:1 and 9:7 contain a similar idea, in the form of a command-ment to Noah and his descendants (i.e., humanity) after the Flood: "And you…[shall] teem on the earth…" (9:7). The commentators deduce from this last phrase that God implanted in humanity, as a necessary ability to fulfill this command, a love of homeland wherever it may be.[4] Having now given mankind the seven Noahide Laws,[5] and commanded it to multiply and spread out across the face of the earth, God next — through the covenant of the rainbow — assures mankind that it will never face total destruction again by flood or any other catastrophe. It is safe, there-fore, to procreate, to spread out and populate the world, and develop a love and attachment for your homeland.[6]

The "Rebellion"

At this point, with a blueprint for morality and justice, the whole world before mankind to develop, and assurance of no further flood or other catastrophe to destroy all that mankind would build and create in the future, you would think that the rest of world history would be "smooth sailing." But, in fact, that is not what happened. Some 100 years after the flood, *before* the nations were separated in their respective lands across the earth, at a time when all the world's inhabitants still spoke one lan-guage, which is understood to be Hebrew,[7] a concerted, oppositional response developed to God's plan for mankind to disperse over the earth and form different communities, societies, nations, and cultures.[8] I be-lieve there were three elements in this opposition, or rebellion, against God's plan.

First, at its simplest level, there were skeptics who were fearful that, despite the "Rainbow Covenant," there might be another flood, and the best solution to that danger was for humanity to stay together in a large metropolis with access to tall buildings, of which the tower was the proto-type, with others as necessary to support the needs of a growing popula-tion. But to spread out into widely separated, thinly populated, societies would make mankind vulnerable to disaster if another flood or catastrophe should threaten. It is human nature, as we know from bitter experience, to plan the future based on the past. So a tower was the obvious answer to the next flood. The leader of this rebellion against God, in the form of distrust of His promises and rejection of His command to disperse over the earth, was Nimrod, whose name (in Hebrew) comes from the root *m, r, d,* meaning to rebel.[9]

Second, there was a more direct, confrontational argument against the Divine plan, not based on fear that someday humans might sin and God would decide that another flood or catastrophe was necessary, but rather, that being together would make for a better, more efficient world. Resources would be plentiful for all, activities would be more efficient, there would be less cultural clashes of all types, less fighting, and less wars — "the trains would run on time" argument, with everyone united. Language is culture, and one culture would be beneficial to all.

Third, there was the insidious aspect, perhaps intended, perhaps unintended, of this scenario. It inevitably would lead to conformity, dependence on a ruler to make decisions for all, absence of freedoms to do or think differently — the independence and freedom of thought and action that requires political mechanisms to resolve disputes and differences that are fundamentally inimical to dictatorial rule. This motive of dictatorial uniformity, of ideological control over society, was implicit in the statement, "Let us make a name" (*Gen.* 11:4) — exactly, one name, one form, one formula, one religion, one political party, one ruler. As one commentator astutely observes, the goal was to gain mastery over the entire human race.[10] The tower, of course, was not just a symbol of the power of the centralized ruler, the focal point for everyone's attention as the source of what to do and what not to do, what to think and what not to think, a seductive weapon to draw near, into this dictatorship over the masses, with one culture, one religion, one politics, one solution, for all. It was also a vehicle of observation and control over the masses from that central locus of power.

I suggest these three aspects of rebellion because they seem to me to be realistic forms of rebelling against God, rather than the simple notion, in some midrashic sources, that the rebellion was literally to build a structure that would allow man to ascend to heaven and wage war against God, and even take His place and dwell in heaven.[11]

God's Response

God's response was, therefore, far more sophisticated than simply destroying the tower as often as it would take to discourage that effort permanently. God was not interested in simply making a power statement, and rejecting the silly — when you think of it — attempt of mankind to wrest power from God. He was interested in making a statement as fundamental as how the world should operate and develop over history.

Language is culture, and by causing the physical dispersion that resulted from the sudden appearance of many languages that prevented completion of the tower,[12] He also achieved His primary goal, which was also of benefit to mankind — a multiplicity of cultures and nations, of ideas and activities, to conquer nature, disease, poverty, whatever would arise to afflict mankind. Variety breeds progress; uniformity breeds stagnation and decline. We know from biology what too much insularity and in-breeding breeds: disease which drives out health.

A second goal was to erase tyranny. We know from history what tyranny and too much political and social uniformity breeds: misery, the corruption of power, war, and, ultimately, decline from failure to be nourished by the cultures of other nations.[13] We know that institutions that seek universal power and control, to impose an ideology over the world, first doom the nations so subjected and subjugated, and end being destroyed themselves, from within and without. This was the theme of the political history of the 20th century. This was the character of Nimrod, who did not form or seek to influence nations, but to dominate and control, by might and power, all of humanity. Universalistic ideologies are inherently intolerant and aggressive in preserving what they consider the only truth and their sole power to determine it. Judaism, from its incep-

157

tion, tied its religion to its own nationhood and homeland, to avoid the hubris and the dangers in the view that there was only one way to find God. Western civilization separated Christianity from nationhood in the seventeenth century, to permit greater cultural variety tied to different ethnic and national interests, only after the religious wars that ensued after the Protestant Revolution had drained Europe to exhaustion. Islam never made the separation, although there is evidence that it may be slowly struggling now to do so.[14]

There is, I believe, a third reason why God caused mankind to divide into many languages, cultures and nations, and not just one. As *Genesis* recounts, God saw that, even after the Flood, most of mankind would be drawn to evil, as an inevitable aspect of the blessing of free will, without a model to show the way to the Divine message of ethical monotheism. This tendency, in fact, became immediately evident with the actions of Noah's son, Ham, and his grandson, Canaan, when they saw Noah drunk and naked, and failed to treat him in his condition with the proper respect.[15] Already, therefore, it was clear that there was little hope for such a model emerging from a humanity with one language and one culture; it would soon and inevitably decline in character to its lowest common moral denominator. Instead, God determined that through many nations there might be gradual progress, and that one nation would have to be assigned the task of carrying the message of ethical monotheism to the world — a nation that would agree to be subject to a far more detailed code of behavior than the seven Noahide Laws, a nation born of slavery and suffering that would assure that this code would be maintained, interpreted, applied, and lived, with justice and compassion. That nation, of course, was to be assigned the Divine language of Creation, Hebrew — the language that would signify, through the Torah, its historic destiny. All that was required was for God to find an individual from that Hebrew speaking group who would be worthy of becoming the father of the new nation of Israel, that would assume this burden. That person, as we know, was Abraham, who believed in a single, righteous Divine Creator, a person whom God trusted would pass on this message of ethical monotheism to his children.[16]

Imagine, on the other hand, the morally weak world of the Dispersion, and its progeny, entrusted with interpreting God's future code of human behavior, the Torah, with justice and compassion — a world full of scheming, aggression, and continued totalitarian leadership. As it is, the Israelites only gradually accepted their role — first, by their founder and father, Abraham, when he was told by God that his people would be born in slavery in order to learn to appreciate freedom,[17] again, at Sinai, when the nations of the world could not accept the burdens of God's new code, and Israel had to be forced to do so, by the demonstration and experience of God's power, and later, when they voluntarily re-affirmed their continued future adherence.[18] Indeed, soon after Sinai, the sin of the Golden Calf was so serious that God proposed to Moses to wipe Israel out and start a new nation from Moses. Only Moses' petition to God to maintain His faith in Israel as the carrier of the Divine message of ethical monotheism, through Israel's kings, prophets, and priests, caused that nation to survive.[19]

All of this was at stake when Nimrod and his popular supporters sought to make the world one nation, one language, and one culture, in perpetuity. The world owes God its unending gratitude that He rejected this misguided and dangerous idea.

Thus, God put the historical solution into motion by hastening the inevitable dispersion of the people to other places and climates, where they would have inevitably developed their own languages and cultures. When we think of the lengths to which totalitarian regimes have gone to keep people within their borders, from the Biblical period Egyptians to the 20th century East Germans, it was no small thing to force the issue in this way, to hasten the dispersion without the years of fear, oppression, and tragedy that would have been experienced by those seeking to get away from the monolithic rule envisaged for the "nation of the tower."

One of the most powerful statements ever written on the unique value of the freedom of the press, speech, and religion — of culture — for each nation, wherever it may reside, as the expression of the unique talents, abilities, ideas, and practices of that nation, was written by the Maharal, Rabbi Judah Loew of Prague in the 16th century, more than half a century before the far better known *Aeropagitica* of the great English poet, John Milton. Maharal argued that nothing comes from suppressing ideas that a ruler finds unpopular or objectionable; indeed, it is a sign of weakness, in suggesting that the received wisdoms of the ruler or the populace are too weak to withstand scrutiny. In this, Maharal was simply repeating, for a powerful, non-Jewish ruler — perhaps, in some ways like Nimrod, a few thousand years earlier — the classical rabbinic view of many cultures being allowed, even encouraged, to strive and thrive in God's creation, and make it a better place for themselves and, ultimately, for all of mankind.[20]

Moreover, Maharal's arguments for Jewish cultural autonomy, and its freedom, as a nation, from outside censorship and suppression, also imply that other nations can benefit thereby from Jewish culture, and the Jewish nation can benefit thereby from the cultural contributions of other nations.[21]

It is time — it is always time — for Jews to tap into their history; in the uniqueness of their origins they may find some lessons for their continued creative survival as a people and a nation.

NOTES

1. B. *Hullin* 89a; B. *Eruvin* 53a; B. *San.* 109a; Sforno at *Gen.* 11:4; Rashi at *Gen.* 10:8. These and other authorities name Nimrod as the person who organized the rebellion; however, in an interesting observation, the commentary of *Ha'amek Davar* on *Gen.* 10:9 states that Nimrod's strong leadership unintentionally reflected God's will because, without strong government, humanity cannot survive and thrive as a secure, civilized society. See generally the collection of authorities on *Gen.* 10:8-9 and 11:4 in *Genesis, Artscroll Tanach Series*, Meir Zlotowitz, tr. and comm. (Brooklyn, N.Y.: Mesorah Publications, 1977, 1999).

2. *Ibid.*, at *Gen.* 11:4.

3. *Ibid.* See also Radak, Ibn Ezra, *Kli Yakar*, and Cassuto, on *Gen.* 11:4.

4. See, e.g., Rashi, Abarbanel, and the commentary of Hirsch, *The Pentateuch*, Samson Raphael Hirsch, tr. and comm. (Gateshead, England: Judaica Press, 1976) at *Gen.* 9:7.

5. See *Pentateuch and Haftorahs*, J. H. Hertz, tr. and comm. (London: Soncino, 1938), at *Gen.* 9:7. The seven Noahide Laws — are: 1) the establishment of courts of justice; 2) the prohibition of blasphemy; 3) of idolatry; 4) of incest; 5) of bloodshed; 6) of robbery; 7) of eating flesh cut from a living animal — considered vital to the existence of human society.

6. *Gen.* 9:9-17.

7. Rashi and Ibn Ezra at *Gen.* 11:1; *Seder Olam*, ch. 26; and the *Malbim* at *Gen.* 11:7. By this dating, Abraham was alive, age 48, at the time of the events of the Tower! See Ibn Ezra and *Malbim* at 11:1 and 11:7. Cf. Artscroll *Genesis, Op. cit.* at *Gen.* 11:1 (that the Tower incident occurred 340 years after the flood). Current findings of comparative linguistics show conformance with the Biblical dispersion story; Nathan Aviezer, "The Spread of Languages and the Tower of Babel," *B.D.D.* 12 (Winter 2001):33-41; see also Isaac Mozeson, "Chattering Chimps or Babel's Babble?" *The International Jerusalem Post*, February 4, 2005, p. 25. "Scholars now believe that all of the 6,000 or so languages now spoken around the world probably descended from one language." See Nicholas Wade, "A Biological Dig for the Roots of Language," *New York Times*, March 16, 2004, pp. F1, 4.

8. *Gen.* 11:1-9. Within the framework of the Torah, and its recounting of Creation and the beginning of human history in *Genesis*, the world was created by Divine "word," as it were, which is Hebrew; man emerges as unique among the creatures of life by virtue of his ability to speak and his knowledge of language, presumably Hebrew, if we follow the various "naming" events in *Genesis* (e.g., Adam, Eve, the animals, Cain; see *Genesis*, Chapters 1-3 and 4:1). The emergence of languages as a unique human faculty is still considered as so remarkable a trait that evolution and natural selection cannot explain it, according to the prevailing view of Noam Chomsky. It is innate rather than learned, and arose all at once; see the recent discussion of current views, and recent research proposing possible alternative explanations, in Emily Eakin, "Before the Word, Perhaps the Wink?" *The New York Times*, May 18, 2002, pp. B7-8.

9. Sforno on *Gen.* 11:4. Nimrod was a mighty warrior who lay claim to Divinity, whose *modus operandi* was power and domination, even if it meant rebelling against God, i.e., God's plans for humanity; see, e.g. B. *Er.* 53a; B. *Hull.* 89a; *Me'am Lo'ez* on *Gen.* 10:8; and the following other authorities on that text: Rashi; Radak; Hirsch; and see also Ramban on *Gen.* 10:9, and the *Malbim* on *Gen.* 11:2.

10 See, e.g., Hizkuni, Rabbenu Bachya, *Malbim*, and Sforno, on 11:4; Cassuto at *Gen.* 10:1-32 (Introduction); and *Beis Halevi* (Spring Valley, N.Y.: Feldheim, 1990), p. 69. There was an emphasis on idolatry as the universal religion; B. *San.* 109a; Sforno and *Malbim* at *Gen.* 11:2,4.

11 See authorities discussed in the *Artscroll Genesis, Op. cit.,* on *Gen.* 11:4, at pp. 336-7, and especially Ibn Ezra at *Gen.* 11:3-4.

12 *Gen.* 11:7-9.

13 See, e.g., *Kli Yakar* on *Gen.* 11:4; the *Malbim* at *Gen.* 11:4-7. The decline of Islamic culture in the last five hundred years has been attributed in large part to a cultural hubris that prevented Islamic societies from being interested in, much less considering and adopting, ideas and practices of other cultures that were contributing new strength and achievement to other nations and civilizations during that period; see, e.g., Bernard Lewis, *What Went Wrong?* (New York: Oxford University Press, 2002). For a vivid illustration, in a fictional representation, of the concentration and the total subjugation of the masses, see the new release of a DVD film of Fritz Lang's movie epic, *Metropolis.*

14 See Ramban and Hirsch on *Gen.* 10:8; Sforno at *Gen.* 11:4, and Cassuto at *Gen.* 10:1-32 (Introduction). They argue that Nimrod did not found a nation but sought to control many nations with an ideology of aggression. On the contrast between Judaism, Christianity and Islam, see, e.g, Lewis, *What Went Wrong?, Op. cit., passim*; Gilles Kepel, Anthony F. Roberts, tr., *Jihad* (Cambridge: Belknap Press, 2002); and Robin Wright, "Mosque and State," *The New York Times* (Book Review), May 26, 2002, p. 10; Jonathan Israel, *European Jewry in the Age of Mercantilism, 1550-1750.* See, generally, on the contrast between revolutionary ideologies imposing equality and those creating freedom, Susan Dunn, *Sister Revolutions: French Lightning and American Light* (East Rutherford, N.J.: Farrer, Straus and Giroux, 1999); and, on the various historical paradigms for wars between nations, peoples and ideologies, Phillip Bobbit, *War, Peace and the Course of History* (N.Y.: Alfred A. Knopf, 2002).

15 *Gen.* 8:21, 9:21-7.

16 *Gen.* 18:19. On justice and compassion as the model for society, see *Zechariah* 7:8.

17 *Gen.* 15:1-21, esp. 6-21. There is no doubt that, in proclaiming the message to the world of ethical monotheism, Israel has also inevitably been subjected to persecution *on this account*, in the course of history, often being accused by its victimizers of conduct like their own. The Portuguese Nobel Laureate, Jose Saramago, recently claimed that the Jews want their persecutors to feel guilty in order to disarm them from criticizing Israel; see Paul Berman, "A Dark Cloud Rises, Something Has Changed," *Forward*, May 24, 2002, p. 9.

18 Rashi at *Ex.* 19:17, citing the midrash in B. *Shabb.* 88a. While the simple reading of the text is that the Israelites stood at the *bottom* of Mount Sinai, the literal meaning of the word *b'tahtit* is *under* it — implying that God threatened them with extinction if they did not accept the Ten Commandments and its amplification rendered through Moses, which they did, at *Ex.* 19:8. The second Covenant with Israel, whereby it renewed its acceptance of the Torah, after the sin of the Golden Calf and Moses' receipt of the second set of the Ten Commandments, is at *Ex.* 34:27-32. It was reaffirmed by Israel at the end of Moses' life, *Deut.* 26:16, 27:26, and *Deut.* 29-30, again in *Joshua* 24:1-28, and again after the downfall of Haman; see *Meggilat Ruth*, 9:27 and B. *Shabb.* 88a — for a total of five affirmations.

19 *Ex.* 32:7-14.

20 "Seventh Well," *Well of Exile (Be'er Hagolah*, Prague, 1598), chapter 2, and *passim*. This work is discussed in H.H. Ben Sasson, "The Middle Ages," *A History of the Jewish People*, H. H. Ben Sasson, ed. (Cambridge: Harvard University Press, 1976), pp. 715-6; Israel, *European Jewry...*, *op. cit.*, pp. 80-1.

21 Ben-Sasson's concluding remark that Maharal was calling for "greater tolerance in the outer world than he would agree to practice within Jewry" (ibid.) is not necessarily sound. Thus, while Maharal objected to Azariah de Rossi's path-breaking *Me'or Enayim*, and he forbade Jews to read or keep it in their homes, he did not object to David Gans' *Tzemah David*, which quoted de Rossi many times, including material that challenged traditionally accepted historical statements about Biblical and Second Temple chronologies; see Mordechai Breuer, "Modernism and Traditionalism in Sixteenth Century Jewish Historiography: A Study of David Gans' *Tzemah David*," *Jewish Thought in the Sixteenth Century*, Bernard Dov Cooperman, ed. (Cambridge: Harvard University Press, 1983), pp. 19-88, esp. p. 58. It is also possible that Maharal took a more liberal view around 1600 than he did in 1574 when de Rossi's book was published. See also Gil S. Perl, "'No Two Minds are Alike:' Tolerance and Pluralism in the Work of the *Neziv*," *The Torah U-Madda Journal* (2004): 74-98, especially the discussion of the Tower.

Rabbi Meir and His Wife, Beruriah: "Till Death Do Us Part"

The Sages of the Talmud transmitted what they called "the Bruriah Affair", a fascinating and disturbing story about the great Second Century Talmudic Sage, Rabbi Meir, who arranged for his wife, Beruriah, to be seduced by one of his students. Legend has it that his purpose was to prove to her, despite her feminist scoffing, the correctness of the Talmudic adage that women are temperamentally "light-headed."[1] She is said to have strongly resisted the seduction effort, but to have finally submitted. Discovering her husband's hand in the episode, she hanged herself in shame.[2]

What are we to make of this story? Is Meir the hero and Beruriah the villain? Is it the other way around? In fact, the story's problematic aspects defy comprehension. It takes two Talmudic heroes, and puts each in a terrible light. Why? Is there no other way to prove the alleged point of this story — And why the need to *prove* the point in the first place? There are countless adages in the Talmud that are posited and *not* proven, or balanced by counter-adages. Why must *personal* "dirty linen" be "washed," and then "hung out to dry" for all to see? Isn't that practice condemned by Jewish law and tradition as a form of *lashon hara* (speaking ill about another or even oneself, even if true)? The confessional memoir or biography has never been part of Jewish literature for this very reason. Finally, whatever R. Meir's agenda might have been, why did our Sages keep alive — as they must have, for the 800 years between the event and the

164

reporting of it by Rashi, the great Biblical and Talmudic commentator — a legend that maligns a woman who was a great scholar among men in her own right, and a woman of great piety as well?[3]

But apart from the gratuitous ugliness of the affair, there are additional, substantive questions about R. Meir's scheme. First, how could he have imagined that his pious, scholarly, demanding wife — of all people — would succumb to such a serious departure from her own, and her society's, moral structure? If he was proved wrong, didn't he risk *disproving* the adage he was trying to prove? How long did she have to resist before he would give in, and call off his student from this scheme; are we all expected to resist continued temptation indefinitely? Second, how could R. Meir have imagined that both his disciple *and* his wife would give in to the temptation that was arranged for them?

Third, and most importantly, wouldn't the moral turpitude of both prove that *men* as well as women are "light-headed," in the sense of being vulnerable to persuasion or temptation to improper behavior? Indeed, wouldn't their joint behavior prove that men, who take (or took!) the initiative in these matters, and are considered by the Talmud to be more easily sexually aroused than women,[4] are more "light-headed" than women? In brief, even if we accept what legend tells us about R. Meir's purpose, how would *this* scheme prove his point about women's *unique* vulnerability?

Finally, it is highly unlikely that anyone could know, or did know, first hand, what his purpose was: he certainly would not confide his alleged purpose to any of his colleagues, because — whatever his reason — there is a Biblical prohibition against "placing a trap before a blind person," what we would call today "entrapment." Nor would spreading the story materially advance his purpose of proving a point *to his wife.*

I believe that the motive element of this story was added later, that it is a misogynistic attempt to explain a terrible, seemingly inexplicable act of a great man. I reconstruct the sequence of the three segments of this legend as, first, the fact of Beruriah's behavior became a legend that lasted 800 years before Rashi wrote it down; second, that the behavior attributed to R. Meir in causing her fall is so incredible that it required the creation of some kind of test misguidedly designed for her by her husband; and therefore, that his purpose as it became attached to the legend was to prove a Talmudic adage about the (sexual) light-headedness of all women, through the behavior of a woman least likely to succumb. In fact, the legend was not about that at all.

I am prepared to accept that there is a basis in fact for the first two elements of the legend; something happened between Beruriah and the disciple, and R. Meir implicitly "confessed" to his role in that happening by his subsequent voluntary exile;[5] indeed, in his *post facto* remorse, he may well have confided his role to some of his colleagues. But the *motive* for what he did, it seems to me, cannot have been to make a point about women's "light-headedness" if only because his scheme implicates his student *and* his wife, that is, men and women alike. Then what motive did he have?

I believe that there was, in fact, a far more compelling point that R. Meir was trying to make — to his wife, to be sure, but also to all Jews for all time — growing out of his revolutionary experience in the second century C.E., during the Roman occupation of Palestine. The point at issue was the oft-repeated religious idea that "whatever happens is in God's hands," and specifically, the dangers of the misunderstanding and misuse of that idea as perceived by an activist like R. Meir.

Let us recall that, earlier, there was an episode in R. Meir's and Beruriah's life together when tragedy struck: their two children died prematurely, and Beruriah looked for a way to break the news to her husband. She decided to do so with an unanswerable legal parable: "What is the law," she asked him when he came home from the House of Study (*beit ha-medrash*), "if someone lends something to another person, and then comes for it to be returned?"

"Surely, the object must be returned," he answered. And, with that, she told him that their children had died.

I have heard and seen their story told on many occasions, and each time I find it difficult and troubling. "It is God's will," without more, is too glib a statement of Jewish theology. It tends to remove human will, the free will and responsibility for our actions, with which all persons are endowed, too easily. It is an outlook that too easily justifies passivity and inaction in the face of evil or danger. It is a slogan for the fearful, the willingly hopeless and helpless; those who would rather seek reasons for inaction than deal with the challenges, physical and moral, that continually beset us. It is a slogan that cannot be a force to improve the world, to bring about more righteousness and greater physical well being for mankind. It argues, emotionally and logically, that what is, must be, must have been Divinely willed — leaving little room for resistance, outrage, anger, dissatisfaction, forms of denial, questions, even prayer that a Divine decree be reversed or ameliorated. Yet, these are legitimate feelings and responses in the face of evil, tragedy and misfortune.[6]

Beruriah's approach to her children's death was, for R. Meir, too glib. It deprived him of the right to resist, to question, to doubt, if only for a short time, while he was an *onen* — that is, between the death of his children and their burial — that time when bereaved survivors are so overcome, so distraught, and often so un-accepting and questioning, that they are exempt from religious observances. Their minds are on their departed loved ones, surely. But their minds are often, and understandably, on the "why" of the tragedy. Theodicy, the suffering of the righteous and the innocent, is an issue that can never go away.[7] When all is well, who *needs* to deal with it? When tragedy strikes, who *can* deal with it? For many, what is there to say besides "All is in God's hands"?

But, for the bereaved, that does not satisfy: "I know it is in God's hands. If I didn't believe in God there would be no problem. But I do, and just because God is just and righteous, and what has happened is not, I need to understand why it happened. Job has taught that tragedy does not strike only the wicked; it can strike the righteous too — But why?"

167

As these kinds of thoughts course through the mind of a bereaved while his questions and his grief are at their most intense, how can one focus on words of praise and acts of homage to God? It is, at best, a time for silence, the silence of Aaron, the High Priest, when his two sons were suddenly and inexplicably consumed by fire.[8] So a mourner, at such times, is customarily exempt from most religious obligations.

But Beruriah took away her husband's right to actively resist, to question, intellectually and emotionally, what had happened. She reduced the untimely death of *their* children, his as well as hers, to a simple legal question of a borrower and lender of a chattel. R. Meir responded exactly as she intended, and had nothing else to say, or even feel. And, but for Beruriah's parable, he surely would have reacted; he was an activist in all things in his life.[9]

I suggest, therefore, that, at some point later in their relationship, circumstances contrived to stimulate in him a desire to prove — to all, and particularly to her — two things: first, how vulnerable we all are, and even she really was, despite her show of iron strength when their children died, a vulnerability that she had denied to him; and second, that the adage "Everything is in God's hands and must be accepted as Divine Will" is the road to the disaster of passivity — political, personal, religious and moral disaster — that undermines our free will and moral responsibility. R. Meir's goal was not to make his pious, scholarly wife feel cheap and "lightheaded", which she could never be, but to make her feel rage at injustice and shame at weakness — to feel something — anything but the helpless submission to God's will that makes every injustice inevitable and makes man feel morally powerless, as she had made R. Meir feel when he became a victim, with his children, of their untimely and undeserved death.

It was as if R. Meir was saying to Beruriah: "You may yield eventually and, if you do, you will realize that to resist evil, to fight for righteousness, for political, social and economic justice, to question and resist injustice no matter what its source, is our obligation, that flows from being born in

God's image, and the recipients of His Law. Any religious adage or idea that is used with the intent or effect of making man's struggle against evil and the blind malevolence of nature more difficult, or easier to avoid — no matter how well-intentioned and no matter how true in an *ultimate* theological and philosophical sense — takes away from our humanity and our Divine task in this world. The essence of Judaism is to ask questions, to promote justice, righteousness and well-being, and to search for answers and actions that will make sense to the "Four Sons" in every generation.[10]

I believe that there is evidence for my theory about what really motivated R. Meir to cause his wife to be tempted to seduction by his own disciple. R. Meir's teacher, the renowned Talmudic scholar, Elisha ben Abuyah, witnessed the tragic death of a young boy who fell to his death from a tree while engaged in performing two (of the four) Biblical commandments for which long life is expressly promised by Scripture.[11] The boy was climbing the tree to chase away the mother bird before taking her eggs (or her young), *and* he was doing so in respectful obedience to his parent. This tragedy pushed Elisha over the edge; he became an apostate. *Aher* (the "Other"), as he thereafter became known, was unable to accept this tragic death of an innocent, righteous, obedient, son; it broke his faith; it posed ultimate questions for which he could find no answers, although the Sages found in the Scriptural texts an answer to theodicy — promise of eternal life in the world to come.[12] For Elisha, however, life was a continuing battle — intellectual, emotional and physical — against injustice and evil, and the death of this boy became an abyss between him and God that he could not bridge. That boy's tragic death raised questions, doubts, anger, resistance, and, finally, total rebellion. Yet, despite this, and his inevitable excommunication (*herem*) by the Sages for his apostasy, his friend, disciple and colleague, R. Meir, continued to consort with him.[13]

R. Meir understood him and what he had gone through; he understood that, broken though Elisha now was in faith and spirit, his mind and heart were fighting for what was just, and against what was unjust, as best he could understand what those concepts meant, even if that caused him to cease believing in the very source of right and wrong, the very source of the idea of injustice, that had broken him. And the irony went further; for was not the broken promise of long life for that young boy, *God's* promise?

Deep down, R. Meir, too, had questions, and the right to those questions, about the death of that child, as he did about the death of his own children. This response was part of the essence of his humanity. Beruriah had taken away from him the opportunity to express this response, and that humanity, by reducing the death of his children to the cut-and-dried matter of the law governing a lender, a borrower, and the object of a loan.

At some point, R. Meir — his grief and doubts long bottled up within him, and the implications of his wife's easy reliance on "God's Will" wrestling with his religious, political, and personal activism — decided that he had to confront Beruriah, and her accepting, passivist ideology, in a dramatic way. He had to prove to her that life means — requires — response, the free will response, to tragedy and temptation alike. He would make her admit, at least to herself, and demonstrate to the world, that you can't walk away or hide from tragedy or temptation, from evil or misfortune, behind the slogan that "It is God's Will" — For there lies the slippery slope to error, and not true faith.

Ironically, R. Meir never did get to prove his point to the very person who most mattered to him. Shame overcame whatever lesson and enlightenment he intended for her. In his fight to prove that we must not easily succumb to injustice, he succumbed in much worse a way than Beruriah ever had. He shamed her forever, in the most heinous form, and in public — for how could such an affair be kept private? — which is equivalent to murder in Jewish law. True, she carried out her murder by her own hand, but it was surely her husband, R. Meir, who — far too lightly, if not "light-headedly" — caused her death.[14] Later, when the Talmud took written form (200–500 C.E.), the Sages confronted the problem of whether, and how, to deal with this tragic story. In the end, they compromised. Out of respect for R. Meir's greatness, they omitted this tragedy from the text of the Talmud; but, out of respect for moral truth, they perpetuated it as an oral tradition, despite the risks to accuracy in the process of transmission. We have the great medieval Biblical and Talmudic commentator, Rashi, to thank for bringing the story to the surface for all of us to ponder and to try to understand its complex, human, moral import.

....

NOTES

1 B. *Av. Z.* 18b and the Commentary of Rashi (1040-1105 C.E.) *ad loc.*; M. Herschel Levine, "Three Talmudic Tales of Seduction," *Judaism* (Fall, 1987):468-70. It is not clear from Rashi's language that Beruriah actually consummated the illicit affair, but she perhaps did reach the point where she consented to do so.

2 In a woman of Beruriah's piety, to reach the point of consent even without consummation could trigger a response of suicide. Rabbi Meir, in turn, is said to have gone into exile when he recognized his own guilt for the terrible consequences of his zealousness to prove a point. However, there is also evidence that his exile was the result of controversy regarding the religious leadership of Palestine; Levine, ibid., p. 468 and J. *Mo'ed Katan* 3:1.

3 *Encycl. Jud.*, s.v. Beruriah; B. *Pes.* 62b; *Tos. B.M.* 1:6; B. *Er.* 53b; B. *Ber.* 10a.

4 Judith Hauptman, *Rereading the Rabbis: A Woman's Voice* (Boulder, Colorado: Westview Press/Harper Collins, 1998), Chapter 2. Hauptman makes her case from numerous Talmudic sources. Whether R. Meir's student agreed to his teacher's plans, or succumbed to Beruriah's virtues on his own, he apparently fell into the affair more easily than the reluctant Beruriah.

5 Tal Ilan, "The Quest for the Historical Beruriah, Rachel, and Imma Shalom," *AJS Rev.* (1997):3-8. Scholars differ as to the historicity of the Beruriah stories in the Talmud as well as the seduction story alluded to by Rashi; ibid.

6 See, e.g., the story of the prophet Elisha and the Shunamite woman in 2 Kings 4. The contrasting legend of the death of R. Meir's children is told in *Yalkut Mishlei* 964.

7 Joel Wolowelsky, "A Talmudic Discussion of *Yissurim Shel Ahavah* (afflictions of [Divine] love)," *Judaism* (Fall, 1984):465-8.

8 *Lev.* 10:16-20.

9 J. *Mo'ed Katan* 3:1; B. *Hor.* 13b-14a; Levine, "...Tales of Seduction," *Op. cit.*, p. 468.

10 The Passover *Haggadah* makes reference to four basic types: the wise; the wicked; the simple; and those who are unable to inquire. On the need to be sensitive to the needs of each generation, see Shlomo Riskin, "A Woman's Touch," *The Jerusalem Post*, International Edition, May 2, 1998.

11 The four commandments are: giving respect and honor to one's parents (*Deut.* 5:16); the pursuit of justice (*Deut.* 16:10); sending away the mother bird before

taking her young or eggs (*Deut*. 22:6-7); and using just weights and measures (*Deut*. 25:15).

12 B. *Kidd*. 39b; B. *Hulin* 142a; *The Jewish Encyclopedia*, s.v., Elisha ben Abuyah; see generally Neil Gillman, *The Death of Death* (Woodstock, Vt.: Jewish Lights, 1997); see also the fine, intellectually stimulating novel by Milton Steinberg, *As a Driven Leaf* (N.Y.: Behrman House, 1939).

13 See citations in note 12; *Encyclopedia Judaica*, s.v. Meir; Ephraim E. Urbach, *The Sages*, Israel Abrahams, tr. (Jerusalem: Magnes Press, 1979), pp. 262, 465-6, 644.

14 One tradition has it that R. Meir's name was Mesha (*Encyl. Jud.*, s.v. Meir), an ironic reference to the Moabite king (ninth century, B.C.E.) who also sacrificed a beloved, his eldest son, in the belief that it was for God's Glory, and to prove his worthiness, and the unworthiness of his enemies — the Israelites, Judeans, and Edomites, who sought to put down Moab's rebellion against the kingdom of Israel.

3

History

The "Promise of Canaan" article reminds us that, at every step in our history, individual and national, we are presented with the choice to achieve or to delay the Divinely promised blessing of freedom in our own land.

The articles that follow for the rest of the book describe what became of our religion and nation when we abandoned God's plan for Israel, viz. *tikkun olam*,[1] thereby mutating from a confident, broad-based cultural model for the world to a fearful, suicidal, escapist religion that produced insular, deracinated, ascetic, non-activist religious communities — playthings of the gentile world at worst, or ignored by them at best.

Thus, in the face of persecution, loss of sovereignty, and exile we chose in our relationships with the non-Jewish world a mystically based path of withdrawal instead of struggle, hostility instead of interest (or even curiosity), insularity instead of achievement, helplessness and inactivity instead of self-realized efforts at national redemption worthy of God's help. When the Enlightenment came to the Western world, all we could achieve was to disintegrate into warring factions of beliefs and rituals. We mistakenly perceived our choice as either-or: to abandon religion or to abandon (or continue to ignore) advances in world culture, including our own among those who sought Jewish cultural renewal.

The Maimonidean Controversy of the thirteenth century, between rationalism and mysticism, continues to split world Jewry today. It is time to learn the lesson that the "either-or" model is an abandonment of Classical Biblical and Rabbinic Judaism. We need to return to a Jewish culture that is not afraid of engagement with the world but embraces engagement as essential to its *tikkun olam* mission lest we, God forbid, once more forfeit the opportunity that history has now presented with our own sovereign state of Israel and the freedoms we enjoy around the world. It can be done, and it must be done while retaining our Jewish religious and ethnic political identity.

"Religious Murders: Weeds in the Garden of Jewish Tradition?" shows how, after the destruction of the Temple in 70 C.E., misinterpretations of the Binding of Isaac story gradually entered Jewish memory — resulting in the misapplication of the *Akedah* at Masada in 73 C.E., where the last Jewish resistors in the rebellion against Rome committed suicide rather than surrender (the Sages showed their disapproval by silence about Masada in the Talmud); and the subsequent misapplication of the *Akedah* in the martyrdoms of German Jewry in 1096 during the First Crusade, in which parents killed themselves and their children rather than face forced conversion.

During the post-Destruction Talmudic Era (2nd–5th centuries, C.E.), new interpretations of the *Akedah* emphasized Abraham's greatness in being unreservedly and eagerly willing to sacrifice Isaac and thereby prove his loyalty to, and love of, God — instead of the *Akedah's* original message that Abraham went forward as God commanded *with faith* that God, in his righteousness, would never let the sacrifice of Isaac come to pass, because God abhors such immoral acts.[2]

During this period, with the rise and successful takeover by Christianity of religious leadership and political influence in the Roman Empire, there appeared — probably primarily among the priestly class — the anti-rabbinic *Hekhalot* and *Merkavah* literature and mysticism.[3]

After the problematic 1096 martyrdoms for which Abraham at the *Akedah* became the key rationale, as Christian pressures on Jews continued, doctrines regarding the *Shekhinah* as a Divine figure arose in 12th century Jewish theology, around the same time as Mary rose to prominence in Christian theology (see note in my Mysticism paper), to help explain the new, troubled condition of Jews in exile. In the 12th and 13th centuries, Jewish asceticism and mysticism arose among the German Pietists. Further mystical responses to historical trauma included the publication of mystical texts beginning with *Sefer Bahir* in the 12th century and the rise of kabbalah in Jewish thought beginning in the 13th century, especially with the publication of the *Zohar*, in response to the continued pressure on Ashkenazi Jewry in that century.[4]

The 13th century also witnessed the Maimonidean Controversy between kabbalists in Southern France and Northern Spain and rationalist, philosophic Maimonideans. The year 1492 saw the final destruction and exile of Spanish Jewry. By the end of 16th century the mythical Lurianic kabbalah, by now considered the best explanation of Jewish exile and suffering, had spread and become the preeminent touchstone of Jewish piety and religious thought.[5] The 17th century witnessed the mystical messianic rise and apostasy of Shabbetai Zvi and the Frankists after the Chmelnitzki massacres in Russia. The 18th century witnessed the rise of kabbalistic Hasidism and the periodic efforts of kabbalists, before and after, to eliminate from Jewish culture the study and practice of all aspects of what they believed to be non-sacred culture. They acted in opposition to other Orthodox views that sought to find a way to learn from new developments in world culture, including new ideas of many alienated Jews, who — with the advent of the Enlightenment in Europe — sought to introduce worthy elements of modernity into the narrow, often superstitious, insulated, and rigid parameters of Jewish education, experience and culture. These episodes in Jewish history created dangerous elements in Jewish tradition that to this day favor dismissing the pursuit of *tikkun olam* in this world, in favor of mythic understanding of Creation and the union of man with the Divine domain.

The "Court Jew" article argues that Jews, especially with the advent of Israeli sovereignty, must be careful to preserve their independence, loyalty and integrity when working with non-Jewish groups or entities. There will always be "Court Jews" seeking to understand and respond to this conundrum, who must find a way to be loyal both to their brethren and to the non-Jews who befriend them or rely on them, and to avoid the appearance of compromising the interests of either side. Historians today seem reluctant to discuss the Court Jew experience in the 18th century in the context of modern Jewish participation in local, national and world affairs. To be a Jew and to participate in the world has always been a difficult task, as so much of early modern literature attests (see chapter on Jewish literature below). But those who wish to participate need the guidance of experts on the past. They must seek it, and it should be provided to them by those with the expertise to do so.[6]

....

NOTES

1 See e.g., Shlomo Riskin, "United in Morality," *The International Jerusalem Post*, July 30, 2004, p. 31. The Jewish mission of *tikkun olam* is to spread the message of freedom, morality and peace (ibid.).

2 See B. *Ta'anit* 15a and J. *Ta'anit* 2:4 and commentaries thereon.

3 This mystical literature and practice was based on the Biblical description of Creation at the beginning of *Genesis*, and Ezekiel's vision (Chapter 1) of the throne-chariot. This mystical tradition was rediscovered and revived by the German Pietists in the 12th-13th centuries. See Dan, *Jewish Mysticism*, vol. 1 and vol. II, chapters 1, 2, and 20; Gershom Scholem, *Major Trends in Jewish Mysticism*, Second Lecture; and Rachel Elior, *The Three Temples*, (London: The Littman Library of Jewish Civilization, 2004). On historical trauma and the rise of ancient *Hekhalot* mysticism, see, e.g., Dan, *Jewish Mysticism*, Vol. 1, p. 107. See also, Elior, *The Three Temples*.

4 Some of these pressures are described in Ram Ben-Shalom, "The Ban Placed by the Community of Barcelona," *Revue des Etudes Juives* (July-December 2000): 401-3.

5 Yosef Hayim Yerushalmi, *Zakhor* (Seattle: University of Washington Press, 1982), pp. 73-4.

6 See interesting discussion in ibid., pp. 81-103.

The Promise of Canaan to Abraham's Seed

Many Jews are torn between a religious impulse or conviction that the Jewish People are entitled to all of the Promised Land (the land of Canaan in the Biblical period) as a matter of Divine promise (and therefore any compromise of this claim is prohibited) and an opposing impulse or concern, even conviction, that practical political considerations involving the State of Israel in the Middle East and the international community, as well as the importance of saving Jewish lives, require such a compromise. However, I believe that Jewish tradition, which is the basis for the religious impulse or conviction I have described, also provides the basis for mediating between these contending pulls. One must ask, first, for whose progeny was Canaan promised by God — Isaac's or Ishmael's? Was that promise unconditional and redeemable at any time? Were any of its conditions breached or unfulfilled, and — if so — does the Covenant remain as a guarantee to such progeny, or does history have a role in the eventual outcome?

Originally, God's promise of the land was to Abraham's progeny, without specifying whether through Sarah or some other wife (*Genesis* 15). Abraham and Sarah believed that the promise did not require a child born of Sarah, for they both agreed that, in light of her barrenness, he should take another wife, Hagar (*Genesis* 16:1–2), who bore Abraham's first son, Ishmael. One may already see here the concept of consequences from a breach of faith; for, if the promise was limited to Sarah's progeny, the decision to take Hagar brought Ishmael into the scene as a new claimant. Alternatively, the promise was not originally limited to Sarah's children, so — either way — we have two claimants. In this regard, it appears that in pressing Abraham to bear children with Hagar, Sarah and Abraham showed an absence of faith that she would be the mother of the son who would receive the bounty of God's promise, because it is only later that we are told that she was too old to bear children. (Genesis 18:11)

Ishmael's claim gains further support when God enters into the Covenant of Circumcision with Abraham and again promises him that his progeny will inherit the land of Canaan (Genesis 17:8). At this time, Ishmael is his only progeny; Isaac had not yet been born or even promised to him. Indeed, even when God promises a son to Sarah, Abraham — again showing a lack of faith — responds by expressing the hope that Ishmael may [continue to] live, presumably to carry on the line and inherit the land according to God's word (Genesis 17:18). Yet God allows Isaac to become a claimant to the land, by inferentially rebuking Abraham about Ishmael: "... and I will establish my covenant with him [the son of Sarah, Isaac] and with his progeny." It appears that God's earlier promise to Abraham that his circumcised progeny would inherit Canaan included his children that might *thereafter* be circumcised, i.e., Isaac, and not just Ishmael, who participated with Abraham in the first rites of circumcision. But something new is added at the end of Chapter 17 that further clarifies God's intent. First, Ishmael receives a new promise, to father "twelve princes" — who, presumably, will rule over *many* nations in *many* lands. This is more than, and different from, the original promise to Abraham that his seed would inherit *the* land of Canaan — *one* place, for *one* nation. Indeed, to underline this point, God now limits his promise, *briti* (My Covenant) (Genesis 17:7–9), of possession of Canaan, to Isaac. (Genesis 17:19–21)

But indications that the Covenant of the Land is meant for Isaac only may be found earlier, even in 17:8. There, God states that Abraham's progeny will inherit Canaan "as an everlasting possession, *and I will be their God."* What is the need for this final phrase? The medieval commentator, Rashi, says that as long as Abraham's progeny live in Canaan, God will rule over them, but if they live outside the Promised Land, they will have no covenantal relationship with God. By voluntarily living outside of the land, it is not only God's protection that will be lost but also His covenant of entitlement to the land. This rules out Ishmael's progeny, who are promised residency and rulership in many lands. But it also conditions the promise to Isaac's seed. If the Jewish people *can* live in the Promised Land, they *must,* or forfeit their Divine guarantee of possession later.

Another indication in 17:8 that the Land is promised only to Isaac is that Abraham's "seed" has already been defined in 15:13, i.e., the people who will spend 400 years of slavery in Egypt. This people, of course, is the Israelites and not Ishmael's descendants. The two ideas are connected. Exile enforced by slavery will not forfeit the Divine Covenant; living in a diaspora, when it is voluntary, will.

It is clear that the Israelites remained outside the land for far longer than they had to, and that far more so remained than had to. Opportunities were missed over and over again because some additional number of Jews, at some times in the thousands, at some times in the tens or hundreds of thousands, could have returned to the land but did not do so. This includes those who misguidedly took the defeat of the would-be messiah, Bar Kokhba (c. 135 C.E.), as a Divine sign that God did not want Jewish efforts to return to the land at any time, but at His time, and in His manner of choosing. It includes those who had no such compunction but failed to return to the land out of fear, inconvenience, and other reasons that did not amount to the enforced servitude of Egypt.

It appears that these failures allow the normal processes of history to intrude, to water down the Divine guarantee, so to speak, by historical factors that must be dealt with on that basis. So the Jewish claim to Canaan remains rooted in a Divine covenant but is now subject to some delay and difficulty from the normal causes of history because of a failure of all Jews to act with full faith in that promise.[2] Thus, the Sages considered that Abraham's treaty of peace with the Philistine king, Avimelekh, limiting Abraham's descendants' rights in the Promised Land, later caused a delay in the Israelite conquest of Jerusalem, where the Philistines had settled, from Joshua to David (Rashi and Radak on *Joshua* 15:63).

But what about the claim of the progeny of Ishmael? Their claims are even more flawed. First, they have steadfastly refused to recognize the claim of their brethren from Abraham their common father, and God's promise to their brethren. Second, we have seen that the Divine promise was limited to one nation in one land, committed to its possession, and fulfilling that promise as best they are able. In contrast, God predicted (or promised) that Ishmael, as he did in fact, would sire a nation in one sense, the Arab nation, but also a multiplicity of nations, with many lands and many sovereigns. In *Genesis* 16:10–12, God predicted that Ishmael would be a great nation, "and he will dwell in the face of all his brethren," which means that he will dwell in many lands. The Arab attempt to enforce a single sovereignty over the span of three continents, to form a single nation, as Islam sought for centuries after its birth, is in no way the same as the promise of the land of Canaan as the locus of a separate nation living by God's will. Ishmael's seed had a different Divine destiny from Isaac's.

There is a second infirmity in the Ishmaelite claim to be Abraham's progeny, promisees of the Land of Canaan. God's plan for Abraham's progeny was that they comprise a unique religious people, which — rooted in its own land and not just in a religious belief system — would have no incentive to impose its political or religious will on others but, rather, seek to spread ethical behavior based on belief in One God by example and persuasion. But commitment to a land and belief would be undermined by failure to observe one more condition: that Abraham's progeny not intermarry. That way lay dispersal of the people from their land and their religion.

Abraham recognized this condition against intermarriage without God ever having to tell him. Just as Abraham understood that Ishmael would necessarily intermarry in fulfilling God's promise that he would "dwell in the face of all his brethren" (*Genesis* 16:10–12), so did Abraham see that, to fulfill God's promise of building a nation through Isaac, Isaac had to marry within the family in order to carry out the Divine plan of one nation dwelling in one land, with One God, living by one law representing God's will.

So Eliezer, Abraham's servant, was sent back by Abraham to Abraham's family to find Isaac a wife there (*Genesis* 24:5–7), whereas Ishmael dwelt in the wilderness of Paran, outside the land of Canaan, and he took a wife from the land of Egypt, thus violating both conditions for the nation to whom Canaan was promised (*Genesis* 21:21). In contrast, Ishmael's children become princes of many nations, live in many lands outside the boundaries of Canaan, and dwell there and intermarry with their inhabitants (*Genesis* 25:16–18).

The same pattern of two brothers, one whose destiny is to carry on the Divine Promise of inheriting the land, and one who breached the conditions that might have entitled him to part of the Divine promise of the land, can be seen in the lives of Isaac's two children, Jacob and Esau.

Esau marries outside the family (*Genesis* 26:34–35, 36:2), two Hittites and one Canaanite, without any provocation or excuse on account of anything that Jacob may have done. Isaac is deeply distressed by this (*Genesis* 26:35), perhaps harboring the idea that Esau, whom he specially liked, might *qualify* for part of God's promise. In contrast, Jacob returns (at the urging of his mother) to the land of Isaac's and Abraham's family and marries within the family — Leah and Rachel, and their maid-servants, Bilhah and Zilpah, who, according to tradition, were also part of the family.

For those who are skeptical about my too easily writing off Esau's rights to the land and who point to Jacob's "stolen blessing" that rightfully belonged to Esau, it is clear from the text of that blessing (*Genesis* 27:27–28) that it contained no promise to Esau (really Jacob in disguise) that he

181

would inherit Canaan. Later (*Genesis* 28:1–4), when Jacob is about to flee Esau and seek a wife from Isaac's family, Isaac knowingly gives the blessing of the land to Jacob.

Finally, Esau voluntarily makes his home outside of Canaan, in Seir (*Genesis* 32:1), even while Jacob is away in hiding, thus violating the Divine requirement of commitment to living in the Promised Land. Jacob, meanwhile, returns to Canaan as soon as circumstances warrant, at God's command (*Genesis* 31:13), despite his continuing fear for his life and the lives of his wives and children at the hands of Esau.

The story of the rape of Dinah, on Jacob's way back to Canaan, is instructive on our question. Shekhem, a prince of the land of Canaan, rapes Dinah — but is so in love with her that his father offers Jacob's family the opportunity to live in peace with the Hivite people and intermarry with the Canaanites. They are even willing to undergo circumcision. A mighty tempting proposition: to live in the Promised Land; live there in peace, with fellow circumcised neighbors and family (to-be) members as "one nation" (*Gen.* 34:16). However, so strong is the prohibition against intermarriage, so at odds is this with God's plan for the Jewish people, that this most alluring offer to a small, fearful family on the run must be totally rejected. Unfortunately, it is rejected with misguided zeal, with a violence that cannot be condoned (*Genesis* 34:35–26, 31) and which threatens Jacob's entire family, as two of Jacob's sons murder the entire city while they are weak from the effects of their mass circumcision, done to please Jacob's family.

And so, in looking at the historical situation today, those who turn to the Bible for guidance will find that the Jewish people are fighting for the fulfillment of a Divine promise that was temporarily rejected by the Jewish People during their history by failures to seize opportunities for its fulfillment when they appeared. The price they are paying is to be forced to grapple with historical forces, in some degree, for what otherwise might have been more easily theirs, against an adversary that has evidently arisen through history, by God's will, to create that difficulty. In

Solomon's allegorical *Song of Songs,* we know what happened when the Lover (God) knocks on the door for His beloved, and she (Israel) finds it too inconvenient at the moment to admit Him (Chapter 5); the opportunity vanishes, and she must again resume her search in time and space for her Lover, hoping that another opportunity will come soon. For those who feel that the Jewish people are entitled to *all* of the Promised Land, now, I would suggest that God's promises are not negotiable checks cashable on the payee's demand. On the contrary, rejecting opportunities for payment when they are offered — even if only a small part of Israel is actually responsible — will certainly delay payment of the obligation or render payment more difficult.

Ironically, the current obstacle to the fulfillment of God's promise is the Ishmaelite people — our brethren — who might have qualified themselves for a partial share in the Divine promise but long ago abandoned it in favor of belonging to a nation of greater size, strength, power, and domain through the years of history, and who only now assert a separate, national claim to the Promised Land, which they for so long rejected. For them, too, there is a price that they will have to pay, a very large price, to God and history. May God bless both nations with good will to each other, and a peaceful life — together — in which God's ultimate plan, based on justice and compassion, will become manifest.

....

NOTES

1 God's promise may be forfeited by failure to act upon it (see, e.g., the Israelites' forfeiture of the prophet Elisha's promise that they would vanquish Mesha, king of Moab, in 2 *Kings 3)*; or by breaking implied or express conditions of God's promise. See the general discussion and collection of authorities in *ArtScroll Genesis* (Brooklyn: Mesorah publications, 1977), Vol. IV, on *Genesis 32:8,* 11. See also the Talmud, Tractate *Shabbat* 32a and *Berakhot* 4a; Rashi on *Genesis 32:11;* Nachmanides, *Commentary on the Torah,* Charles B. Chavel. ed. (New York: Shilo, 1971), on *Genesis* 15:7; Rabbeinu Nissim, *Commentary on the Torah,* at *Genesis* 15:2; *cf. Shabbat* 55a and *Berakhot* 7a; Maimonides, *Mishneh Torah, Hilkhot Yesodei Ha-Torah,* 10:4.

2 One man, Akhan, violated God's prohibition against taking spoils in the Israelite conquest of Ai in Canaan, under Joshua's leadership. All Israel was punished as a result, as God pronounced: "[All of] Israel has sinned." *(Joshua* 7:6-21).

Religious Murders:
Weeds in the Garden of Jewish Tradition?

Virtually all of the Jewish world has been dismayed by the recent killings by Jews of various people considered by them to be enemies of Judaism or of the Jewish people. These killings included the 1995 assassination of Prime Minister Rabin by Yigal Amir, the wanton shooting, in 1994, of Arab civilians by Baruch Goldstein, and the 1994 killing in New Jersey by Avi Kostner of his two children in order to prevent them from being raised as Christians by their mother. Moreover, these acts of violence have been particularly surprising to many Jews because the actors were known to be religious, observant Jews who were personally aware of the strong legal stand of Judaism against murder.

To counter any possible non-Jewish reaction that the killings were somehow sanctioned by Jewish law or tradition, a number of rabbis, scholars, and educators publicly and strongly condemned those killings as completely unjustified, being, rather, the acts of individuals acting completely outside the bounds of Jewish religious authority and tradition.[1]

One noted Orthodox halakhic authority cited a medieval commentary, *Daas Zekeinim* 9:4, as proving that Kostner's killings were prohibited "period, period, period."[2] One noted Jewish historian cited a midrash to the same effect.[3] Renowned educators were baffled at how any of these men could have picked up any idea in Jewish schools that the murders committed were justified. One noted Conservative halakhic authority similarly made clear that Kostner's action was completely unjustified.[4]

185

And a recent article in the highly respected Orthodox scholarly journal, *Tradition,* argues that the Jewish concept of *Tselem Elokim, i.e.,* that man is created in the image of God, under-girds and guides Jewish law in emphasizing that killing another human being is, as noted above, prohibited in virtually all cases. [5]

But the notion that these acts of violence were aberrations, and that there is nothing more that can be done in the realm of religious education to prevent such occurrences in the future, is difficult to accept. Indeed, one important Israeli educator has indicated that the national-religious camp has not yet purged itself of the possibility of future murders committed in God's name. Thus, even if it is true, as it probably was, that — ex *ante, before the fact* — we should not, and could not, have reasonably anticipated these killings, or killings like them, based on a *proper* understanding of Jewish law, tradition, and history, there is reason to be concerned *after the fact* about the adequacy of the analysis that has been made thus far of Jewish religious educational ideas and practices.

The need for such concern, and the kind of analysis that I propose in this article, has been dramatically increased by two subsequent Israeli polls that show strong backing for political assassination. In one of them, more than 25 percent of religious teenagers in Israel expressed support for the murder of Rabin, more than five times such support expressed by secular respondents.[6]

I am going to focus on a few sources — not primarily halakhic material, but nevertheless influential events, opinions, symbols in Jewish history — that lurk, to this day, in the Jewish past as possible sources of danger of future religious murders such as we have already witnessed and as polls thereafter portend, unless we begin to rethink, reevaluate, reinterpret, and re-teach what these sources mean and how they should be used. Each in its own way transmits the idea of embracing death as a fulfillment of God's Will. Such examination does not pose a danger of undermining the entire structure that supports the binding nature of Jewish tradition; religious Judaism has acted similarly in the past when it had to, e.g., change in attitude and practice regarding the education of women;[7] the problem of religious murder and its desecration of God's Name requires similar urgent attention today.

In the year 1096, the Crusaders, who were marching through Europe on their way to liberate Jerusalem from the "infidel" Muslims, came upon the Rhineland Jewish community in Mainz, Speyer, and Worms and determined to forcibly convert the other "infidels" who had denied the Christian faith over the years, the Jews. These communities tried to fight back, sometimes with the aid of Christian protectors, clergy and laity, sometimes without; ultimately *they* determined to trump the triumphalism of the Crusaders and to assert the supremacy of the Jewish faith, and their own loyalty to it, over that of their oppressor Crusader adversaries. So *they* killed their children and then themselves before they could be killed to avoid being forcibly converted. Not only were their actions chronicled by Jews a short time later in the most glowing terms and the martyrs described as "holy ones" *(kedoshim)*, but rabbis of great learning and status soon thereafter failed to challenge the propriety of the suicides and the murders as a sanctification of God's name. And, to enshrine permanently the actions of the martyrs as a model of faith for all time, the martyrdoms were embodied in Jewish liturgy, to be recited forever in penitential *piyyutim* (poetry).[8]

It seems to be generally agreed by most scholars that the suicides, and certainly the murders, were not supported by Jewish law as it existed at that time.[9] Indeed, the Chronicles of the martyrdoms cite no halakhic justification for either. Nor could the martyrs plead excusable suicide under Jewish law even as expanded by rabbinic *(Tosafist)* commentary shortly thereafter — out of fear of torture that would lead to conversion — because there is no indication that the Crusaders were interested in compelling conversion by torture; they wanted to capture live Jews and forcibly baptize them, thereby converting them, or kill them.[10] The chronicles make clear that the murders and the suicides were not done as a result of dementia or other form of mental derangement from fear, shame, or the other emotions that have excused suicide under Jewish law — as are recounted in various stories a thousand years earlier under Greek and Roman rule in the Land of Israel; to the contrary, the 1096 acts of martyrdom were deliberate, accompanied by blessings and other rituals signifying God's will.[11]

The martyrs could have resisted until death, as other Rhineland Jews did, or agreed to allow themselves to be dragged to the baptismal font, visibly resisting and protesting as they did so, only to return to Judaism later after the Crusaders moved on, or after moving on themselves to another city or town. But they chose not to do so and to abandon Jewish law in the process. For the martyrs perceived Christianity triumphant in the world, first over Judaism, and — by the time the Chronicles were written — over Islam, with the anticipated Crusader capture of Jerusalem. Jewry, innocent and faithful, had been displaced from its role as God's chosen people by its earthly enemy and oppressor. Jewish history seemed at an end. The only response left was to abandon life and history simultaneously — in addition, perhaps, to securing God's vengeance on the Christians, as Israel Yuval argues — to sanctify God's name in the world in an unprecedented way, one last time. To achieve this, they looked to Abraham at Moriah (the Akedah) as the model of spiritual perfection by his willingness to kill his beloved son, Isaac. Thus, they chose to kill their children and then themselves rather than serve as accomplices to their permanent degradation in history.[12] Without support of the law, the martyrs also relied on other non-halakhic but symbol-laden events in Jewish history for their actions: the martyrdom by murder and suicide at Masada; the destruction of the Temple; and other, passive martyrs of antiquity (e.g., Hannah and her seven sons, and Rabbi Akiva and his colleagues).

As to the Akedah, it contains no reference to Abraham actually killing Isaac, but its lesson, as generally taught, is that he was willing to kill Isaac and was rewarded for this passion to do God's Will. So, too, in 1096, it was (to the participants) clearly God's Will that their martyrdom take place; indeed, the martyrs were said by their chroniclers to have far exceeded Abraham in piety because they completed their acts and did so with many children.[13] Their *akedah* was the sacrifice and self-sacrifice of sacred persons like Isaac.

Masada was chronicled not only by Josephus, but — a thousand years later — by an anonymous Jewish author of the book of *Josippon,* which was well known and highly respected by European Jews in the 11th century. [14] It is noteworthy that the rationale offered in *Josippon* by Eleazar, the leader of the defenders of Masada, was the *Akedah,* portraying Abraham as giving Isaac true life through death, and the *Indian* philosophic ideal that one should abandon this world of evil and corruption in favor of the true life that exists after death.[15] While the 1096 chroniclers do not mention Masada, it may be reasonably assumed, from their high regard *of Josippon,* that the Rhineland martyrs considered Masada's earlier martyrs to be heroes and worthy of emulation.

The destruction *(hurban)* of the Second (and the First) Temple also was a sign, a metaphor for the martyrs of the Rhineland Community.[16] They viewed their martyrdom as the self-sacrifice of a sacred community, just as the Temple was the sacrifice of another sacred locus of God's presence.

The other martyrs of antiquity, like Rabbi Akiva, risked their lives and ultimately accepted death at the hands of their Greek and Roman persecutors; and the *laws* of religious martyrdom — codified in the Talmud (B. *Sanhedrin* 74a–b), and established *after* the *Akedah,* the Greek and Roman persecution, and the Temple destruction — specified that one should die *at the hands of the enemy* — *not by* one's *own hand,* and *not by* the murder of one Jew by another — rather than commit idolatry, bloodshed, or adultery. It is ironic that while Jewish law thus requires that bloodshed, the murder of others, is to be *resisted,* according to the Talmudic Sages, even unto death, that one should rather be killed than kill another, the 1096 martyrs turned this inside out and killed others — their own children, and then themselves — rather than allow themselves and their children to be killed or forcibly baptized by the Crusaders!

Yet their greatness in Jewish tradition lives on in recorded rabbinic praise and Jewish liturgy[17] — and has come back to haunt us to this very day, with another instance of a parent murdering his children, with Avi Kostner coming into court with books documenting what he viewed as similar precedent — citing behavior a thousand years ago.[18]

There is much work to be done, therefore, in the way we teach the 1096 martyrdom in Jewish tradition, liturgy, and history before we can say that it cannot plausibly be relied on, rightly or wrongly, by someone who finds himself in what he views as a similar circumstance.

Masada offers ironies of its own but is in no less need of reevaluation. For example, if the Jewish people view themselves as a "Light unto the Nations" (Isaiah 42:6), in carrying out their responsibility for witnessing to all nations the truth of the one God and His (one) moral law, what can we say, what justification can we offer, if the misguided, suicidal, religious cult of "Heaven's Gate" cited Masada as a precedent for violating a fundamental pillar of the Divinely revealed Noahide laws (*Gen.* 9:5), which apply to all humanity, and were later incorporated as a pillar of Jewish law at Sinai?[19] Shouldn't we have renounced the "martyrdoms" of Masada for the past two thousand years as totally outside of Jewish law and tradition and totally incompatible with the message of life that is represented by the *mikvah (pool* of ritual purification) that was used at Masada? How can we justify the swearing in of Jewish soldiers on Masada without agreeing that suicide is not just occasionally *excusable,* but generally *laudable,* as an act of religious heroism? Apart from the *mandatory* poison pill to be taken by, e.g., a spy, rather than suffer torture and reveal secrets to the enemy that will cause the deaths of others, which was not the situation at Masada, does Masada stand for victory — or defeat? The Israelis, to their credit, have recently downplayed the importance of Masada. Isn't it time that the suicides and murders atop that mountain — and the mystical, death-embracing rationale of Indian philosophy that Eleazar raised up as the "religious" banner — be denounced, fully and formally, in every Jewish school and from every Jewish pulpit, as *foreign* to Jewish ideas and practice?

And finally, we must return to what is a wellspring of all the death-embracing mystical behavior in Jewish history — in which the will of God is the "kiss of death" and the renouncing of life in the world for a greater, purely spiritual existence, beyond. I refer to the *akedah,* as it is taught, preached, and glorified, since time immemorial. Thus, Maimonides, despite his rationalism and his clear inability to explain the *akedah* rationally, asserts, in the *Guide for the Perplexed,* that Abraham proved his faith and love of God in the greatest way possible at Moriah, in his willingness to kill Isaac just because God asked this of him. [20] And this has been the message our children take home from school and our rabbis urge from the pulpit, as encouragement or consolation, week-in and week-out. "Be ashamed at how little you are asked to do for your people — look at Abraham," or "Be consoled at what you have sacrificed for your people — look at Abraham."

Maimonides' view has generally prevailed ever since, as part of the lachrymose history of the Jewish people, a history in which we highlight death more than life, defeats more than victories, and suffering more than happiness, as if these make us more spiritual and thus more pure and more worthy in the eyes of God.[21] But Maimonides' view is not the monolithic view of Classical, i.e., Biblical and Rabbinic Judaism. Let me cite some proofs.

A recent article by an Orthodox scholar categorically asserts that neither the rabbis nor we can allow the *akedah* to be understood as involving choice between killing Isaac or disobeying God (even though that was, in fact, the choice that Abraham had to make), because that understanding would necessarily create a halakhic issue, and Jewish law is clear that choosing to kill Isaac is absolutely prohibited; homiletic treatment of the story is all that Judaism allows. He suggests that the correct homiletic message of the *Akedah* is the need to balance uncritical obedience to God and man's assertion — in belief and action — of ethical values.[22] Interestingly, a similar approach to the *akedah* has recently

191

been endorsed from a psychoanalytical standpoint; however, it sees the overwhelming — though not universal — passivity and acceptance by European Jews of their fate during the Holocaust as reflecting God's Will as evidence of their conscious and subconscious reliance on the uncritical obedience and subservience message of the akedah, without the balance of Abraham as a defender of ethical values, fighting for justice at Moriah as he did at Sodom.[23]

The Talmudic Sages were evidently also concerned about the akedah transmitting a monolithic message requiring uncritical acceptance of what may be perceived as God's Will, without the balance of fighting for justice and ethical values. The Sages, seeking to eliminate such an understanding from our tradition, perhaps fearing its misuse in later times, state in a homiletical midrash that Abraham sought Divine permission to kill Isaac, or at least wound him, even after God told him not to even touch Isaac![24] The message is clear. If Abraham is understood to have the zealotry to kill his son at God's command to prove his perfect faith, he would also have the zealotry to kill or at least wound his son even after God's command that he not do so. This would certainly not make Abraham a rabbinic model for us, nor a righteous person worthy of Divine reward. But the Sages view Abraham as a spiritual model, craving his son's life, not his death. Thus, in another midrash, Abraham is pictured in agony over God's command that he sacrifice Isaac. In fact, the Sages tell us, in both the Babylonian Talmud and in the Jerusalem Talmud — thus earning for that view the highest, overriding respect in our tradition — that Abraham prayed to God that Isaac should be saved, not sacrificed.[25] And to make sure that this understanding was perpetuated in Judaism and Jewish history, the Sages established that, on fast days decreed in times of trouble, the people should assemble in the public square, and beseech God to answer Israel's, prayers "as He answered Abraham at Mount Moriah [to save Isaac]." That prayer was also incorporated in the penitential service of the High Holidays. And so we pray to this day.[26]

The rabbinic understanding of the akedah, therefore is twofold: (1)

Abraham was blessed because he proceeded with the sacrificial preparations with faith that God would ultimately answer his prayer and save
Isaac despite the Divine command to sacrifice him; similarly, the Jews
who were Divinely commanded to plunge into the Red Sea (*Ex.* 14:15)
did so *not* with a yearning for death by suicide because God commanded
it, but with faith that God would not let death prevail; (2) God does not
want or expect perfect faith if that means that man must murder his fellow man (or himself); better a less than perfect faith, and human respect
for life, for man created in God's image. The world that God created is
good, not evil (*Gen.* 1:1–31) and worthy of life dedicated to it in the sanctified manner that God's law prescribes.

But, despite the efforts of the Sages, the bare text of the *akedah* left its
message of the piety of uncritical subservience to the Will of God, without
the Sages' ethical leavening of man's responsibility to fight for human life.
Masada and the Martyrs of 1096 ensued, and their medieval and modern
progeny. [27] Each faced a new reality, tears in the expected order of life, individual and national Jewish trauma and catastrophe that compelled a response. In each case, that response — be it suicide, murder, or the willing
acceptance of death, based on a sense of hopelessness, helplessness, and
a yearning for the Divine — was felt to be the Will of God, even though
it was a response that enhanced death, not life, and carried the earlier
responses further than Jewish tradition ever contemplated or allowed. In
fact, as we shall see, the behavior of the 1096 martyrs, in particular, set
the stage for a millennium of Jewish mysticism by: (1) embracing death;
(2) basing their actions, not in Jewish law, but on an inner command of
their souls; (3) believing that life in this world is not considered to be of
value.[28]

And so, Amir, *et al.,* inherited certain traditions in Jewish history that
sanctioned and praised suicide, and even murder, where it seemed to
be the Will of God, because it was done for a holy purpose, without the
necessary balance that the Sages required of acting in accordance with
Jewish ethical and moral values embodied in Jewish law.

I believe, therefore, that Amir, *et al.,* may also have been influenced by the mystical ideas of the virtues of asceticism and even death present in so many aspects of Jewish education and discourse — from physical death through martyrdom, through spiritual death and union with God — embraced by mystical movements in Judaism over the last thousand years. In Classical Rabbinic Judaism, life was holy and pure, and death was evil and impure. But, faced with the trauma of the abyss between the glorious promise of its youth — Israel's Divine chosenness as a model of ethical monotheism — and the reality of an enduring exile without redemption and the emergence of persistent oppression and suffering, there emerged from the First Crusade, as part of mainstream Judaism and not just a suppressed, peripheral, minority view, the ideas of asceticism, obsession with the nature of the Godhead, and abandonment of the hostile, evil, material world for the world of death, physical or spiritual, and union with the Divine domain. In this new era of the trans-valuation of values, life now became evil and impure, and death the path to true life and spiritual purity.

The new, mystical outlook was manifested in succeeding centuries in many forms, from German Pietism, through kabbalah and Hasidism, and other ascetic, escapist, and messianic and apocalyptic movements. It was founded on a number of mystical ideas — theosophic, ecstatic, and theurgic — with potentially anarchic, rebellious, and antinomian implications (which were, to be sure, generally kept under control): (1) that God separated himself from the material world of Creation, and that evil was, simultaneously, a part of God and thus a part of the created world; (2) that during the cosmic catastrophe of Creation, Divine lights and sparks were scattered through the world, and that God was immanent in the world and not transcendent over and apart from it; (3) that this mythic God was knowable in anthropomorphic ways, having various aspects, genders, physical forms, and the need for sexual unions and even biological functions; (4) that man can acquire knowledge of God and commune and unite with Him, experiencing the "joy" of "annihilating the self" and mystically transcending the barrier of corporeal existence; (5) that man can and must battle and escape the evil of material existence by asceticism, poverty, rejection of activism in improving man's physical, economic, social, and political condition, and, instead, embrace the perfect life of martyrdom and the physical-spiritual bliss of mystical death through union with God, *unio mystica* — whenever man wants it and not just when God invites it — by means of prayer, ecstasy, and magic, providing a preparation for the perfect, ultimate, biological death of every person when their time comes; (6) that the true secrets of Torah, the "second" revelation of Judaism, can burst forth from the heart of every Jew who understands and practices the kabbalah — each moment brings its own novel understanding of God's Will; (7) that the shattered Divinity — see (2) above — depends on man's mystical behavior to restore the primordial, supernal perfection and harmony.

In sum, these ideas cause God to come closer to man physically and to resemble man more closely in His hypostases; in turn, they give man more direct access to God by physical union and to knowledge of His Will by personal revelation. Mysticism emphasizes the individual's personal, voluntary relationship with God rather than the covenantal, obligation relationship between God and the community of corporate Israel. As Scholem concludes in his book on kabbalistic symbolism, "It is mystical experience which conceives and gives birth to [religious] authority."[29]

As a result, while Jewish mysticism has made contributions to religious thought and practice directed to the preservation and enhancement of Jewish life in the face of persistent persecution, its mythic-theosophic outlook presents the danger of a few self-righteous zealots following the inclination of their own intellect, each becoming a law unto himself; social behavior that ignores and rebels against constituted authorities; the blurring of moral distinctions to achieve noble ends; and broader antinomian abuses, in which even death may become the object or the means of a zealous fervor to carry out God's Will. When coupled with the power to do so, such religious arrogance can become zealotry, and, in extreme form, political and religious anarchy.

Are these imaginary fears and dangers? I don't think so. Allan Nadler has shown that, some two centuries ago, outstanding Torah authorities expressed similar fears and dangers as the basis for their vehement opposition to Hasidism — not disagreeing with Jewish mystical ideas themselves, but with Hasidism's program of aggressively spreading these ideas among all, even the simplest, unlearned Jews. The *Mitnagdim,* as the opponents of Hasidism were called, insisted that Hasidism's mystical teachings — viewed essentially as a simplified, popularized form of kabbalah — should only be transmitted, if at all, to persons mature in years, and of demonstrated religious piety and scholarship.[30] Elisheva Carlebach has shown that the debate about whether and when kabbalah should be taught in Jewish schools goes back to the 16th century.[31] Isadore Twersky has shown that, in the 17th century, the eminent Talmudist, R. Yair Hayyim Bacharach, adopted the (later) *Mitnagdic* approach to kabbalah, because — lacking a continuous tradition like that governing halakhic development — kabbalah's open-endedness leads to the danger of erroneous ideas.[32]

Given the dangers involved, particularly in today's environment of Jewish power and empowerment, I believe that it is time once again for Jewish religious leaders to speak out against the premature and indiscriminate teaching and other dissemination of problematic mystical ideas and warn about the dangers involved. Nor can an exception be made for those who live in separate, ghettoized communities, because — in today's "global village" — no community can avoid the ethical and moral tests arising from its inevitable contact with others. As to the alleged benefits of mystical ideas in "outreach" programs addressed to those who do not accept Judaism as a religion of obedience to the commandments of a transcendent God but are searching for "meaning" in their lives through a voluntary, cultural approach: that argument was made, regarding Jews who were embracing the *Haskalah* (Jewish Enlightenment) some two hundred years ago, and it was rejected by the *Mitnagdim* (who were also opposed to the *Haskalah,* even then).[33]

In summary, the romantic, mystical *zeitgeist* of Jewish spirituality in the last thousand years, which is self-empowering in man's search for God's Will, provides the soil that can nourish an impulse to behavior contrary to Jewish law and ethical values by certain very vulnerable individuals who are traumatized by what they believe is a danger to cherished ideals. Our modern-day zealots, in their unfounded hubris and religious arrogance, do not pray that God save their victims, as Abraham did, nor do they ask wiser men for guidance, and the results are tragic, not only for their victims, but for the Jewish people.

Nor should we be unconcerned about the power and influence of zealots because they represent a minority view. Often, the nobility of zealots in their single-minded, idealistic fervor to destroy evil, even if in bizarre ways, produces a sense of guilt and even identification on the part of others — perhaps a majority of the community — who, despite discomfort or objections to the behavior produced by that zealotry, accept its apocalyptic, messianic worldview and the mystical, religious fervor of a minority. This is especially true in Israel, where the issues of national life and death burn hottest today. Indeed, the continued physical and psychological pressures on Israel's very existence seem already to have created self-destructive impulses on the left and the right, among intellectuals and non-intellectuals, within secular and religious elements of the population.[34] We have yet to fully accept Isaiah Berlin's deep understanding that the perfect society — like the perfect human — does not and cannot exist; that seeking to find it and impose it makes for zealotry, self-sacrifice, martyrdom, and — in extreme cases — violence against others in the name of illusory perfection; and that mutual tolerance, compromise, and humility, on the other hand, can literally save the world.[35]

Are there practical lessons to be learned here? I believe there are. We need to highlight in our understanding, teaching, and liturgy of the *akedah* the noble rabbinic conception of Abraham preparing for Isaac's sacrifice, while praying that God would save Isaac and, implicitly, expecting that his prayers would be answered; and God's rejection of human sacrifice — even to prove man's perfect faith. We need to highlight in our understanding, teaching, and liturgy of the Jewish martyrs of the Middle Ages — who murdered and committed suicide to resist forced conversion — a sense of empathy for, and not idealization of, the religious trauma they experienced; and their dilemma in choosing between a cathartic response to what appeared to be the sudden, permanent triumph of Christianity over Judaism, and their inability to find halakhic sanction for their death-embracing cry of despair, helplessness and hopelessness.

It is time, finally, to find the spiritual dimensions of Judaism else-where than in the problematic aspects of mysticism[36] and, as discussed above, to de-emphasize and re-evaluate those romantic, mystical myths, metaphors, and symbols that encourage or support any form of yearning for death, whether it be the spiritual, mystical "kiss of death" by God, or active death by the sword — one's own or that of the enemy. In Judaism, death is the source of defilement, of un-holiness. (Numbers 19:2) Let it remain so.

Nor can we allow Judaism to fossilize by demonizing the material world and modernity.[37] Making spiritual pursuits primary over working for a better life in the real world was rejected by the Talmudic Sages as the norm for most Jews. Thus, when Shimon bar Yohai, the traditional father of Jewish mysticism — after spending 12 years in a cave engaged in mys-tical experience and study — emerged and confronted Jewish farmers living under pagan Roman rule, busily plowing and sowing their fields, he chastised them: "You abandon life eternal for ephemeral life."[38] But pre-serving and improving life is not "ephemeral" or useless, and it is certainly not evil in a universe created by God; it is the very purpose of Creation. And so, God Himself responded to Shimon bar Yohai by crying out from Heaven: "Have you left your cave in order to destroy My world? Go back to your cave!"[39]

This must be the motto of Judaism in the modern world, if it is to survive and succeed.

....

NOTES

1 See, e.g., Marilyn Henry, "Father's Last Act," *The Jerusalem Post, 21* March 1997, p. 10; Miriam W. Jacobs, "Rabbinic Authorities re Kostner Case: Halacha Offers No Excuses For Murders," *Jewish Standard (New* Jersey), *21* March 1997, pp. 10, *30.*

2 Ibid.

3 *Toby Axelrod, "Evil Spirit," The Jewish Week, 21* March 1997, pp. 10-11.

4 David Feldman, quoted in Jacobs, *"Rabbinic Authorities...,* "Op. cit.

5 Eugene Korn, *"Tselem Elokim* and the Dialectic of Jewish Morality," *Tradition,* Winter 1997, *pp. 5-30.*

6 See "Some Religious Teens Back Rabin Assassination, Says Survey," *Jewish World* (Long Island), NY, 7-13 November 1997, *p. 2:* and Michal Yudelman, "Poll: 3,000 Justify Political Assassination," *The Jerusalem Post,* International Edition, week ending 8 November 1997, *pp. 1-2.* The educator's view is reported in "Beyond Fanaticism," *The Jerusalem Post,* International Edition, week ending 15 November 1997, p. 7.

7 Avraham Weiss, *Women at Prayer.* Hoboken, NJ: KTAV, 1990, chapter 5.

8 Haym Soloveitchik, "Religious Law and Change: The Medieval Ashkenazic Example," *AJS Review,* Fall 1987, pp. 205-222; Shalom Spiegel, *The Last Trial.* Philadelphia: The Jewish Publication Society, 1967, chapter 3; Jacob Katz, *Exclusiveness and Tolerance* (New York: Behrman House, 1959), chapter 7; *Kinot* for *Tisha B'Av,* Abraham Rosenfeld, translator (New York: Judaica Press, 1979), pp. 127, 133. 141, 169-170.

9 Soloveitchik, "Religious Law...," Op. cit.. pp. 209-210; Robert Chazan, *European Jewry and the First Crusade* (Berkeley: University of California Press, 1987), pp. 116-124.

10 Ibid., e.g. pp. 50-137, and the appendices; *Tosafot,* B. A.Z. 18a.

11 Chazan, *European Jewry...* pp. 123, 124; Soloveitchik. "Religious Law..," Op. cit., pp. 208-209.

12 Chazan, *European Jewry...,.* see note 10; Spiegel...., *Trial.* Op. cit., chapter 3; Katż, *Exclusiveness...,* Op. cit., p. 91; Israel Yuval, "Vengeance and Damnation, Blood and Defamation," *Zion,* 1993. No. 1, pp. 33-90, and responses thereto, especially of Mordecai Breuer and Ezra Fleischer, and Yuval's reply, *Zion,* 1994, Nos. 2-3, pp. 169-414. The martyrs cited not law but an inner command of their souls (Ibid., p. 303).

13 Spiegel (see note 8); Chazan. *European Jewry...,* Op. cit., p. 165. The martyrs cited traditions that Abraham had actually killed Isaac; ibid., pp. 158-159.

14 Ibid., p. 149; cf. p. 327, n. 33.

15 Josephus, *Wars of the Jews,* William Whiston, translator (Grand Rapids, Michigan: *Kregel,* 1981), book 7, chapter 8; *Sefer Yosippon,* D. Flusser, editor (Jerusalem. 1978-1980).

16 Chazan, *European Jewry ...,* Op. cit., p. 126.

17 See note 8; see also Fleischer. Op. cit., pp. 302-304.

18 Jane Calem Rosen. "Murdered with Love," *Jewish World,* 4-10 April 1997, p. 15.

19 *The New York Times,* 28 March 1997. p. A18.

20 *Guide to the Perplexed,* M. Friedlander, translator (New York: Dover, 1956),

p.160.

21 See. e.g., Harav Kook's remark about the over-spiritualization of Jews in the Diaspora; Herbert Wiener, *91/2 Mystics — The Kabbalah Today* (New York: Macmillan [Collier], 1992), p. 301. See also, Haym Soloveitchik, "Rupture and Reconstruction: The Transformation of Contemporary Orthodoxy," *Tradition,* Summer, 1994, pp. 64-130.

22 Korn, *"Tselem Elokim...,* "Op. cit. p. 24.

23 S. Giora Shoham, *Valhalla, Calvary & Auschwitz* (Cincinnati: Bowman & Cody, 1995), chapter 10.

24 *Lev. R.* 20:2; Spiegel, ...*Trial,* Op. cit., chapter 6.

25 Spiegel, ... *Trial,* Op. cit., pp. 45-49; B. *Ta'anit* 15a and J. *Ta'anit* 2:4 and commentaries thereon.

26 Ibid.; and, e.g., Phillip Birnbaum, *High Holiday Prayer Book.* New York: Hebrew Publishing Co., 1951, p. 563.

27 Reemphasizing the importance of ethical leavening is, I believe, what Korn is trying to do in his thoughtful, nuanced paper in *Tradition* (see note 5).

28 Ezra Fleischer, Op. cit., pp. 302-303. The mystical yearning for death — to escape this world for the non-corporeal world of spirituality, of Divinity — is a response to a perceived abyss between an ideal or desired reality and the imperfect reality of the real world; see Mortimer Ostow, *Ultimate Intimacy: The Psychodynamics of Jewish Mysticism* (London: Karnoc Books, 1995), *passim;* Allan Nadler, *The Faith of the Mithnagdim* (Baltimore: Johns Hopkins University Press, 1997), p. 105. See also generally Moshe Idel, *Kabbalah* (New Haven: Yale University Press, 1988); *idem., Hasidism* (Albany: SUNY Press, 1995), Introduction, Part 1, and Concluding Remarks. Gershom Scholem, in *Major Trends in Jewish Mysticism* (New York: Schocken, 1954), pp. 7-8, sees mysticism as an inevitable development in all religions; but cf. *idem., On the Kabbalah and its Symbolism* (New York: Schocken, 1965), p. 32: "Mysticism is a product of crises."

29 Ibid., chapters 2 and 3; *idem., Major Trends ...,* passim; *idem., The Messianic Idea in Judaism* (New York: Schocken, 1971), pp. 22-23, 62-77, 234-250, 292, 303; Ivan G. Marcus, *Piety and Society* (Leiden: E. J. Brill, 1981); Michael Fishbane, *The Kiss of God — Spiritual and Mystical Death in Judaism* (Seattle: University of Washington Press, 1994), pp. 13. 87-124; J. B. Soloveitchik, *Halakhic Man,* Lawrence Kaplan, translator (Philadelphia: The Jewish Publication Society, 1983), pp. 30-82; Shoham, *Valhalla ...,* Op.cit., p.117; *Ultimate Intimacy...,* Op. cit., *passim;* Joseph Dan., *Jewish Mysticism and Jewish Ethics* (Seattle: University of Washington Press, 1986), chapters 3, 4, 5.

30 Nadler, ... *Mithnagdim,* Op. cit., *passim.*

31 "Rabbinic Circles as Messianic Pathways in the Post-Expulsion Era," *Judaism,* Summer 1992, pp. 208-216.

32 "Law and Spiritualism in the Seventeenth Century: A Case Study in R. Yair Hayyim Bacharach, *Jewish Thought in the Seventeenth Century,* Isadore Twersky and Bernard Septimus, eds. (Cambridge: Harvard University Press, 1987), pp. 447-468.

33 Nadler, ... *Mithnagdim,* Op. cit., p. 37. On some current "outreach" programs, see, e.g., David Van Biema, "Pop Goes the Kabbalah," *Time,* 24 November 1997, pp. 92-94; on the special danger to religious authority from mystical teachings not preceded by full internalization of Rabbinic Judaism, see. e.g., Scholem, On *the*

Kabbalah ..., Op. cit., pp. 25-26.

34 Ostow, *Ultimate Intimacy ...*, Op. cit., p. 71; Serge Schmemann, "Israelis Turn Self-Critical As Mishap Kills Two," *The New York Times,* 18 July 1997, p. A9; Joseph Dan, "Why This Fierce Self-Mutilation?" *The Jerusalem Post,* 16 May 1997, p. 4; Aharon Megged, "The Israeli Suicide Drive," *The Jerusalem Post,* International Edition, week ending 2 July 1994. p 15; Hillel Halkin, "Israel Against Itself," *Commentary,* November 1994, pp. 33-39; Israeli polls cited in note 6.

35 Abba Eban, "Sir Isaiah Berlin: Man of Brilliance, Laughter and Faith," *The Jerusalem Post,* International Edition, week ending 15 November 1997, p. 6.

36 See, e.g., Ostow., *Ultimate Intimacy ...*, Op Cit., pp. 361-362.

37 For example, we should note mysticism's general antagonism to rationalism and scientific study in the Middle Ages and early modern period; see, e.g., Stephen Sharot, *Messianism, Mysticism and Magic* (Chapel Hill. NC: University of North Carolina Press, 1987), pp. 31, 69; Jacob Katz, *Out of the Ghetto* (New York: Schocken, 1978), pp. 34-36: Amos Funkenstein, *Perceptions of Jewish History* (Berkeley: University of California Press), pp. 216-217; cf. David B. Ruderman, *Jewish Thought and Scientific Discovery in Early Modern Europe* (New Haven: Yale University Press, 1995), pp. 370-372.

38 B. *Shabbat* 33b; Norman Lamm, "Adjusting Torah to the Real World," *The Jewish Week,* 6 June 1997, p. 28.

39 Ibid.

The Court Jew in the Modern World

I believe that the problems of the life and literature of Jews in the modern world since their European Emancipation about 200 years ago focus significantly on the dilemma faced by the "Court Jew," that elite group of wealthy Jews in the 17th and 18th centuries who served European rulers in exchange for the right to dwell outside the ghetto, move in non-Jewish society, and enjoy other special privileges — political, economic, cultural, and social — denied to their fellow Jews. This dilemma is how to live at "court," i.e., in positions of influence, power, and prestige in a non-Jewish society, contribute to it, and take from it, without risking loss of one's Jewish identity and commitment on the one hand, and the danger — physical and material — from the cross currents at court, on the other.[1]

The underlying element of this continuing dilemma is that, unique among religions and peoples in history, the Jewish people have traditionally defined themselves, in their source texts and in their consciousness, not just as a nation or just as a religion, but as a combination of both.

The "Court Jew" arose in the increasingly cultural, secularly-ruled Central Europe, filling a number of important needs of kings, emperors, dukes, and other rulers through contacts, capital, and expertise that had not yet developed in the Europe that emerged from the religious wars, plagues, and other calamitous events of the late Middle Ages. These needs included banking, army provisioning, and advice and implementation of tax policies to enhance the resources and powers of the new secular governments.

Successfully serving a Christian master sometimes led to difficulties created by elements of Christian society who were either disadvantaged by the Court Jew's proposals and activities on the ruler's behalf or were simply hostile to successful Jews; sometimes it led to criticism by the Jew's own people that he had not done enough in their behalf, or had prejudiced them, or had forgotten his Jewish identity, roots, and loyalty. The more intimately he became involved with the ruler's affairs, the greater the risk of such attacks. And, of course, there was always the risk of failure, and the punishment that an angry, frustrated ruler might direct at the Court Jew and his people because of it.

Jews in the courts of nations, embodying elements of the Court Jew, can be found much earlier in Jewish history, but with important differences. For example, Joseph, the Pharaoh's vizier, did not represent the Jewish people (i.e., his own family) except for a few years after they came to Egypt (yet I have no doubt that Thomas Mann had the dilemma of the Court Jew in mind when he wrote his novel, *Joseph* in *Egypt,* in the late 1930s); Esther became a Persian queen by royal command (though her dilemma in deciding whether to risk death to plead for her people, or her people's calumny if she did not, is powerfully drawn in the Scroll of Esther); Josephus did not represent the Jews in Rome's eyes or in the eyes of his own people (although he did in his own eyes, for which historians are thankful to this day); and Judah the Prince, the great Talmudist who compiled the *Mishnah* (c. 200 C.E.) only occasionally represented the Jewish people to the Roman government — he was not a Court Jew as a way of life. In general, we may say that prior to the Middle Ages, Jews representing their people in foreign courts operated as such only periodically, and at the fringe of non Jewish society, except the Jews of Spain.

While Jewish participation in foreign courts increased significantly in the Middle Ages — and in important ways we may consider them the first "Court Jews" — the viability of that role existed because Jewish identity in that period was simultaneously assumed by all Jews and thrust upon them. To be Jewish under Muslim or Christian rule involved hardship but no dilemma of identity. There was no way to "opt out" of the Jewish community and the beliefs and practices of its members, to become a secular citizen of a secular national state without a religious identity. One had to choose between Christianity, Islam, and Judaism.[2] In Christian lands, Jews had no particular cultural or even political or economic temptation to abandon their faith; most of the medieval period (except for the era and area impacted by the Renaissance) was the Dark Ages for Christian Europe. Moreover, before the rise of Protestantism in the 16th century, there was a strong religious duty, perceived by many Jews, not to embrace Catholic theology, because of such anthropomorphic doctrines as the virgin birth, the Trinity, and transubstantiation.

In Muslim lands, the vastly superior Muslim culture from the 10th to as late as the 12th century may have provided some temptation to Jews to acculturate and even assimilate, but Jews had no need to do so in order to benefit from that culture. *They* were tolerated as Jews (albeit with second-class status) and were able to — and did, in fact — appropriate and adapt those elements of Muslim culture that enriched Jewish life without compromise to Jewish religious or national identity.[3] A Jewish courtier, Hasdai Ibn Shaprut, high in the Caliph's councils, was given permission to take political steps to help Jews subject to persecution in other countries.[4] He even sought out the lost Ten Tribes, with a view toward the possibility of the reunification of the Jewish people as a political, geographic entity as it had existed before the Second Exile. Yet, even the Caliph had to be careful in his treatment of Hasdai, perhaps the first Court Jew, so as not to provoke the anger of his Muslim subjects.[5] Jewish poets could sing about Zion in poetry and liturgy, and work for their people and a foreign ruler without accusations of separatism or disloyalty.[6]

This so-called "Golden Age" of the Jews in Spain (from the 10th to the 12th centuries) was gradually lost with the Catholic reconquest of Spain from the Muslims. The Catholics engaged in the reconquest offered little reason or opportunity, culturally or otherwise, for the Jews to acculturate or assimilate.[7] Indeed, pressures on the Jews to convert were soon in coming, in contrast to Muslim toleration. While forced conversions under widespread physical duress began in earnest at the end of the 14th century, it soon became apparent to the Spanish people that the *conversos* (Jews who had converted under duress) were simply Jews who had assumed Christian appearances. The result was laws, applied in the 15th, 16th, and 17th centuries, based on the purity of blood concept *(limpieza de sangre)*, which discriminated economically and in other ways between "old" (i.e., real) Christians, and "new" (i.e., Jewish, not real) Christians.[8]

Nevertheless, the Christian rulers, especially during the early period of reconquest, from the 11th to the 12th centuries, needed the help of educated, wealthy, well-connected Jews to deal with the highly developed Muslim civilization that they encountered in the conquered Arab lands, and Court Jews are to be found already in this early period.[9] However, like the Court Jews in Muslim lands, they did not face the full force of the dilemmas that later Court Jews encountered in the early modern era.[10]

Over the years, especially from 1492 and continuing during the next few centuries, many *conversos* left Spain for Italy (Muslim), Turkey, and Northern Europe, where they returned to Judaism; often, however, it was a Judaism that stressed, as had their lives as *conversos*, the inner religious life of the Jew rather than external rituals, which, of course, in post-expulsion Spain, and especially under the Inquisition, would have meant torture on the rack, and even death on the cross.[11] This pattern positioned them to be specially able and willing to take advantage of the opportunity soon to be offered them of becoming integrated in non-Jewish secular states.

By the 16th century, the modern era in Christian Northern Europe had begun; culturally, modernity started with the Renaissance and culminated with the Enlightenment and modernity; economically and politically, it started with the rise of Protestantism with the ensuing religious wars between Protestant and Catholic domains culminating in the rise of the secular nation-state. These states grew in military and economic power and were, indeed, already competing for world hegemony after the discovery of the New World in 1492.[12] This growth was accompanied by the rise of Ashkenazic Jews in these lands along with the Sephardic Jews who had escaped from Spain and Portugal. Simultaneously, the power of Islam and Muslim nations began to wane by the end of the 17th century and, with it, the influence of Jews in Muslim lands, who shared the political and economic decline of their host nations.[13]

This early modern period ushered in the modern dilemma of Jews in *galut*, exemplified by the "Court Jews" of this period (1600–1800), whom we may fairly consider to be precursors of the emancipated Jews of the 18th and 19th centuries who followed them. In exchange for loyalty to the rulers of the lands in which they lived, the Court Jews were given an opportunity to participate in and enjoy the new culture, power, and wealth that non Jewish aristocrats and merchants enjoyed at the hands of their secular rulers.[14]

But they were never fully accepted by the Christian society in which they necessarily had to function and deal — the Ashkenazim less so than the Sephardim, who were more acculturated. Moreover, the Ashkenazim, now increasingly dominant demographically in Europe, were concerned about the loss of their tradition and identity, which they feared was inevitable with emancipation and acceptance in non Jewish society. Indeed, the experience of the Court Jews and their progeny (many of whom ultimately converted) provided ample grounds for such fears. Thus, it is not surprising that, when the Jews of Western Europe were offered emancipation, provided they give up their community autonomy and fully assimilated into non-Jewish society, the opportunity was embraced only reluctantly by many Ashkenazic Jews, who perceived the risk of trying to live as equals in Christian lands and enjoy the fruits of its culture, economy, political power, and the new freedom of its citizens.[15]

Nor is it surprising that, when Napoleon came to power, he convened (in 1807) a "Great Sanhedrin" of French rabbis to satisfy himself on whether French Jewry really intended to be fully integrated into French society as French citizens, politically and nationally, and to be Jewish only from a private, personal, faith-oriented religious standpoint.[16]

Nor is it surprising, finally, given the social failure of emancipation — the inability to change by law the general population's continuing hostility to Jews — that, for the wealthier and more talented Jews, the time eventually and inevitably came when some of them perceived that they would be able to demonstrate and enjoy their wealth and talents, by social acceptance and respect, only if they took the ultimate step of "voluntary" conversion — as in the case, for example, of Heinrich Heine — which occurred in Western Europe, especially in the late 18th and the 19th centuries. To be sure, there were exceptions to the tragic dilemma of the Court Jew. Mayer Amschel Rothschild succeeded in this role without succumbing to acculturation, but his case was rare and, it should be noted, he succeeded in preserving his Jewish identity only because, except for business, he never left the ghetto.[17] That was a price that the Jews could not have continued to pay without conceding that they were, indeed, a separate people, a distinct nation within the nations in which they lived and from whom they sought equality, and would necessarily seek protection.

Some of this history of the "Court Jew" was vividly portrayed in the 1996 exhibition on this subject at the Jewish Museum in New York, and in the fine novel by Lion Feuchtwanger, *Jew Suss*,[18] about the 18th-century Court Jew, Joseph Suss Oppenheimer. The Nazis, not surprisingly, made a propaganda film about Oppenheimer that depicted how he sought and used his power as a Court Jew to manipulate and control German rulers and German society to Jewish advantage and to take personal sexual advantage of German women and otherwise "contaminate" German society.

The great Israeli literary critic, Gershon Shaked, has demonstrated in German history and German Jewish literature a scenario of Jewish seduction by a Gentile culture representing universal human ideals, which is followed by assimilation with that world and then the abandonment of

207

one's own people and tradition for its narrowness and insularity, ending with rejection by the Gentile society whose culture was desperately sought. This rejection has been unconditional, as in the case of Germany, or conditional as in the case of France, England, Poland, and to a lesser degree the United States — that is, there could be acceptance only if the Jews made changes in their appearance, personality, means of livelihood, national identity, and loyalty, in public practices and rituals, such that they would cease — allegedly — to stand out as an offensive, separatist element in society, and, instead, live publicly by the civil religion, practices, and mores of the host majority.[19]

Thus, instead of respect and gratitude, the efforts of the "Court Jews" — who may serve as a metaphor for those Jews who sought to benefit, and benefit from, the scientific, cultural, economic, and political advances of Germany — were rewarded by rejection and vilification. The ultimate metaphor of the end of the Court Jews, and of emancipated European Jewry, is the notorious 18th-century etching showing Joseph Oppenheimer being hanged by a mob, in a cage, like an animal.[20]

Do the Western democracies offer a solution to the Court Jew dilemma? Do they offer such a solution as nations that — in theory, at least — are the sum of their immigrant parts, who can maintain their cultural and ethnic identities, under the protection of law, as long as they give allegiance to the secular moral values of the nation — freedom, tolerance, fairness, and equality of opportunity for all? Today's intermarriage statistics and other evidence of assimilation in the Western democracies readily indicate the price that is being paid for such success and acceptance. Whether it is an avoidable price remains to be seen.

Herman Wouk's novel, *Inside, Outside,* (Boston: Little, Brown' and Company, 1985) asserts essentially that, in America today, a Jew can be accepted in the inner sanctums of secular power without giving up any aspects of his Jewish identity, public or private, religious or national. From the perspective of those who gave European Jews their emancipation in the 18th and 19th centuries on condition that they live as Frenchmen (or

Englishmen, etc.) publicly, and as Jews privately, in the form of religious observance, Wouk would argue that, in America, there are no such conditions; one can live and succeed as a Jew both publicly and privately.

However, the Jonathan Pollard case — *despite his guilt* — gives us pause. In addition to the problematic circumstances surrounding his sentencing process and his unprecedented severe sentence, a Defense Department memo in 1996 pointed to the strong ethnic ties of American Jews to Israel as a factor facilitating aggressive Israeli theft of US military and industrial secrets. While repudiated by Secretary of Defense William Perry, it was never replaced. Many Jews are concerned about the "dual loyalty" issue this raised; they again became concerned in 1997 with the US Army probe of an American Jew who reportedly admitted to "inadvertently" sharing classified documents with Israel. While the generally tentative, defensive Jewish response to Pollard's sentence was undoubtedly due, in major part, to his guilt, I suggest that another factor was Jewish awareness of American sensitivity to the "dual loyalty" problem: one-third of Americans believe that American Jews are more loyal to Israel than to the United States, and an additional 20 percent say they don't know where Jewish loyalties lie.[21]

There is more recent evidence that America may not be willing, any more than other democracies, to live by the theory that one may have multiple national or ethnic allegiances and still be fully accepted as an American citizen equal to all others. Thus, a recent article in the *New York* Times notes that many ethnic groups in New York City are pressing to retain the citizenship of the land of their birth even after they become American citizens, and this has led to concerns about dual nationality and dual loyalty and influence in general, especially if it applies to large numbers of American citizens.

One Yale professor was concerned that in the event of war there might be dual or multiple claims on the individual to serve or not to serve. One leader of an immigration reform group criticized dual nationality as a sign of a reluctance to assimilate into America. Immigrants, he said, should have only one national allegiance, i.e., to the United States. "You ought to get on board or get out," because, "at some point you start looking like Rome, with an influx of alien hordes who never get on board."[22] Thus, America may not be that different, after all, from the European democracies that are periodically faced by strong popular resentment of the many immigrants coming from foreign countries, who allegedly not only threaten to take away jobs but also challenge the very ethnic-cultural identity of the existing population. America has certainly justified Wouk's optimism concerning American Jews being successful both as Americans and as Jews; however, once it becomes evident that there are many other groups in large numbers in America — Dominicans, Colombians, Mexicans, and others — who have strong ethnic national loyalties to a "homeland," it may develop that *all* such groups will come under increasing pressure, like European Jews in the 19th century, to "earn" their "emancipation," to choose — even in democratic countries — between an ethnic loyalty to a "homeland" and the enjoyment of full acceptance as citizens in their new countries of residence.[23] Not surprisingly, Jewish scholars have taken different views of how Jews should deal with success, influence, and power as a high profile but small minority — even in a country with as strong a civil rights tradition as the United States.[24]

It would seem at the very least, that as long as Jews live in Diaspora lands that demand *the fact and the appearance* of loyalty to the state, and as long as they wish to participate fully in the economic, political, cultural, and social life of those countries, they will face challenges no less daunting than those faced by their precursors, the Court Jews[25] — to contribute to the welfare of the nations to which they pledge loyalty as citizens, never to act in ways that would suggest they have any agenda contrary to the interests of their country, and to make every *effort* to demonstrate the complete congruence of the interests of their country and the country — be it Israel or any other — that continues to live in their thoughts, prayers, and traditions as a cultural and emotional homeland.[26]

NOTES

1   See Amotz Asa-El, "The Last Court Jew," *The Jerusalem Post*, 4 April 1997, p. 13; Gershon Shaked, *The Shadows Within* (Philadelphia: Jewish Publication Society, 1987), pp. 3-82.

2   Daniel J. Elazar, "Can Sephardic Judaism Be Reconstructed," *Judaism*, Summer 1992, p. 220.

3   Joseph Dan, "The Epic of a Millennium: Judeo-Spanish Culture's Confrontations," *Judaism*, Spring 1992, pp. 113-129; Eliyahu Ashtor, *The Jews of Moslem Spain* (Philadelphia: Jewish Publication Society, 1973, 1979, 1984), Vols. 1, 3.

4   Ibid.. Vol. 1, Chapter 5.

5   Ibid., pp. 139-162, 193-217.

6   Ibid., p. 253; *Selected Poems of Shmuel Hanagid* (Princeton: Princeton University Press, 1986).

7   Dan, "... Judeo-Spanish ... Confrontations," op. cit.; Yitzhak Baer, *A History of the Jews of Christian Spain* (Philadelphia: Jewish Publication Society, 1961), Introduction, Vol. 1, chapters 2, 3, 4, 6.

8   Chaim Potok, *Wanderings* (New York: Alfred A. Knopf, 1978), p. 321.

9   Baer,... *Jews of Christian Spain, op. cit.*, Chapter 1.

10 Lion Feuchtwanger, *Raquel, the Jewess of Toledo* (NewYork: Julian Messner, Inc., 1936) is a fine novel about how a Court Jew could find himself and his family at risk even in the early reconquest period, if his daughter became an object of a Christian ruler's desire.

11 Yosef Hayim Yerushalmi, *From Spanish Court to Italian Ghetto* (Seattle: University of Washington Press, 1981), Chapter 1; Yirmiyahu Yovel, *Spinoza and Other Heretics — The Marranos of Reason* (Princeton: Princeton University Press, 1989), chapters 1-3.

12 Jonathan I. Israel, *European Jewry in the Age of Mercantilism: 1550-1750* (New York: Oxford University Press, 1985), Chapters 1, 2 and 3.

13 H.J. Zimmels, *Ashkenazim and Sephardim* (London, Marla Publications, 1976), p. 76; *A History of the Jewish People*, H. H. Ben-Sasson, ed. (Cambridge: Harvard University Press, 1976), pp. 736-779.

14 Ibid.

15 Arthur Hertzberg, *The French Enlightenment and the Jews* (New York: Columbia University Press, 1968), pp. 8, 325-326; Jacob Katz, *Out of the Ghetto* (New York, Schocken, 1978), pp. 122,154-156. For new insights on court Jews as "port Jews," see, e.g., Lois Dubin, "Researching Port Jews and Port Jewries; Trieste and Beyond," and David Cesarani, "The Forgotten Port Jews of London: Court Jews Who Were Also Port Jews," in D. Cesarani, ed., *Port Jews in Cosmopolitan Maritime Trading Centers* (Portland, Or.; Frank Cass, 2002), pp. 1-11, 47, 57, 116-121. Cf. Jonathan Goldstein, "The Sorkin and Golub Theses and Their Applicability to South, Southeast and East Asian Port Jewry," ibid., pp. 179-196.

16 Ben Sasson, ...*Jewish People*, op. cit., pp. 761-763; *Transactions of the Parisian Sanhedrin* (New York: University Press of America, 1985).

17 Amos Elon, *Founder: A Portrait of the First Rothschild and His Time* (New York: Viking, 1996).

18 Carroll & Graf republished the original novel, *Power*, in 1984, first published by Viking Press in 1926. The exhibition is described by John Efron in "The Dangerous Art of Consorting With Europe's Kings — Exhibit Examines the History of Court

Jews," *Forward*, 6 September 1996, p. 13.

19 Gershon Shaked, *The Shadows Within*, op. cit., pp. 3-82; Todd Endelman, *The Jews of Georgian England, 1714-1830: Tradition and Change In Liberal Society* (Philadelphia: Jewish Publication Society, 1979); Harriet L. Parmet. "Jewish Life in Poland — Beginnings to the Eighteenth Century," *Jewish Spectator* (Winter 1996-1997): p. 33.

20 The etching was shown at the Jewish Museum "Court Jew" exhibition (see n. 18).

21 See, e.g. Edward Alexander, *The Jewish Wars* (Carbondale: Southern Illinois University Press, 1996), Chapters 9 and 12; Matthew Dorf, "The Detroit Question: Does 'Dual Loyalty' Stick," *Jewish World* (Long Island, New York), 28 February — 6 March 1997, pp. 3, 21. We may yet see "dual loyalty" fallout from the heavy representation of Jewish guests in the Clinton White House; see Matthew Dorf, "How Bigs Bunked in Abraham's Bed," *Forward*, 14 March 1997, pp. 1, 5; and *idem*, "Jews and the Lincoln Bedroom: A Quandary of Policy and Access," *The Jewish Standard*, 14 March 1997, pp. 15, 37.

22 Somini Sengupta, "Immigrants in New York Pressing Drive for Dual Nationality," *The New York Times*, 30 December 1996, pp. B-1, 4.

23 See, e.g., the discussion by Jonathan Mahler, "Don't Tell This to Mrs. Albright — Assimilation May Be Coming Back," *Forward*, 7 March 1997, pp. 1, 4; Peter D. Salins, *Assimilation American Style* (New York: Basic Books, 1996); and Georgie Anne Geyer, *Americans No More: The Death of Citizenship* (New York: Atlantic Monthly Press, 1996).

24 Compare, e.g., J. J. Goldberg, *Jewish Power: Inside the American Jewish Establishment* (Reading, MA: Addison Wesley, 1996), and Elliott Abrams, *Faith or Fear: How Jews Can Survive In a Christian America* (New York: Free Press, 1997). On recent court Jew issues and problems, see, e.g., Douglas Davis, "The Court Jew" in *The Jerusalem Post*, July 25, 2003, p. 16; Ami Eden, "Slips in the Lieberman Balancing Act," *Forward*, September 29, 2000, p. 6.

25 Even the most separatist Orthodox cannot avoid political dealings with neighbors and colleagues; see Joseph Berger. "Growing Pains for a Rural Hasidic Enclave," *The New York Times*, 13 January 1997, pp. A-1, B-5; Adam Dickter, "Junior Power Brokers," *The Jewish Week*, 10 January 1997, pp. 30-31. Supreme Court Justice Louis Brandeis defended American Zionists (and all immigrant groups) from any suspicion of dual loyalties in a 1915 address, "The Jewish Problem and How to Solve It," published in Hertzberg, *The Zionist Idea*, op. cit., pp. 517-523.

26 For recent studies related to the Court Jew issue, see Richard L. Cohen, "Jews and the State: The Historical Context," *Jews and the State: Dangerous Alliances and the Perils of Privilege*, Ezra Mendelsohn, ed., *Studies in Contemporary Jewry: An Annual* (New York: Oxford University Press/Harman Institute of Contemporary Jewry 2003), Vol. XIX, pp. 3-16, and *passim*. Cohen, and the volume generally, concentrate on the last 500 years, but he notes that the "tradition of Jewish alliances with the ruling authorities can be traced back to Hellenistic times," adding that "the [Talmudic] precept 'the law of the land is the law' originally formulated in the 3rd century became a guiding principle in medieval Jewish life." See also, Daniel J. Schroeter, *The Sultan's Jew* (Stanford: Stanford University Press, 2002); H. J. Zimmels, *Ashkenazim and Sephardim* (London: Marla Publications, 1976), pp. 44-5; and Joseph Hacker, "The Intellectual Activity of the Jews of the Ottoman Empire During the Sixteenth and Seventeenth Centuries," *Jewish Thought in the Seventeenth Century*, Isadore Twersky and Bernard Septimus, eds. (Cambridge: Harvard University Press, 1987), pp. 96, 106-7.

4

Jewish Mysticism

A s we have discussed above, Jewish mysticism and asceticism have, for the last thousand years, turned Jewry's eye from science, medicine, social science, and the humanities — opportunities and challenges essential to the Jewish mission of *tikkun olam* and its predicate, Jewish survival — by their focus on the Divine realm as their response to the historical catastrophes that have engulfed Jews in exile during the last thousand years.

One aspect of this mystical response has been the rise of Hasidism in the last three centuries, and — most recently — the problematic claims for the Lubavitcher Rebbe, after his recent death, to be the messiah and perhaps even an aspect or element of God. But these claims — in addition to being problematic relative to Jewish tradition, as David Berger has pointed out (see my essay on his recent book in this chapter) — look to a heaven-oriented, individual redemption and a magical, mythical, mystical focus in the Jewish world view, at the expense of work toward material and ethical progress in the world as well as in Jewish communities. "Saving Jewish souls" is not *tikkun olam*. It is trying to bring alienated Jews to a mystical, kabbalistic lifestyle and to mend what kabbalah describes as a broken Divinity (sic) (what we might call *"tikkun shamayim,"* "mending

Heaven") by mystical rites and concepts strange to Judaism.

As the eminent Jewish historian Yosef Hayim Yerushalmi has noted, "The extraordinary current interest in Hasidism totally ignores both its theoretical bases and the often sordid history of the movement."[1]

I have written on these topics, but much more needs to be written, by respected academic scholars, if Jewish historiography is to make the meaningful contributions to Jewish tradition and memory that Yerushalmi hopes for it.[2]

....

NOTES

1   Yosef Hayim Yerushalmi, *Zakhor* (Seattle: University of Washington Press, 1982), pp. 97-8.

2   Ibid, pp. 81-103. For a psychiatric review of mystical movements in history, see *Mysticism: Spiritual Quest or Psychic Disorder?* Committee for the Advancement of Psychiatry, Group for the Advancement of Psychiatry (New York: Mental Health Materials Center, Inc., 1976).

Jewish Mysticism:
Medieval Roots, Contemporary Dangers and Prospective Challenges

In this paper I would like to provide a preliminary examination of the role of certain problematic aspects of Jewish mysticism in mainstream Judaism. I will address, in particular, the following issues: Did mysticism arise within Talmudic culture or outside it, and in antagonism to it? If the latter, when did it appear as an accepted element of mainstream Judaism — and, in particular, Ashkenazi Judaism? Did it receive halakhic approval at that time, either before or after its practice in the Ashkenazi community? Were there problematic aspects to elements of this new mysticism that, while perhaps necessary, beneficial, and even inevitable during the medieval era, may no longer be so, and warrant reexamination and re-evaluation at this time?

Jewish mysticism, which I define below from Talmudic and other perspectives, arose almost two thousand years ago. It was an attempt to maintain a belief in a transcendent God in the face of the traumas of religious and political catastrophe that periodically confronted the Jewish people. Its principal elements were a desire to escape the reality of the abyss between Jewish chosenness and Jewish suffering, by a spiritual, psychological and intellectual understanding of God, along with a mystical ascent to and union with Him.[1]

Given the focus of this paper — the past and future role of mysticism in Jewish life — we need to consider the view of the Talmudic Sages (*Hazal*) on mysticism as a baseline for the discussion. In addition, we should consider the views of historians and psychoanalysts regarding the definition of mysticism and its causes and effects. *Hazal* sought to discourage mysticism, and, in the course of doing so, provide us with their views of what it is — at least in its objectionable aspects. There are three primary sources to consider, all in Chapter 2 of *Hagigah*. In the first, four Sages entered *pardes*, which Rashi and *Tosafot* interpret as a physical or spiritual ascent to heaven, and all but one were permanently and adversely affected. In the second, we find greater detail and amplification of *Hazal's* views. Except in certain limited cases, persons should not study or discuss matters relating to Creation; to Ezekiel's vision of the "Chariot," i.e., mystical ascent to heaven and what is seen and experienced there; and to sexual immorality. The Talmud also prohibits study of: "What is above; what is below; what came before [i.e., Creation], and what will come afterward [i.e., at the End of Days]." "What is above" seems to relate to the nature of God's being, i.e., theosophy. "What is below" seems to relate to God's governance of the world, including the problem of theodicy — how to account for a world where, despite God's providence, the good often suffer while the evil prosper — and the seeming contradiction between God's omniscience and human free will. In the third text, one is prohibited from "looking upon" (*lehistakel*) a rainbow, a Jewish ruler, and the priests as they bless the Jewish people — considered to be vessels of God's glory. In general, the Talmud covers what historians and psychoanalysts have generally agreed to be the core content of mysticism — the desire to ascend to heaven and achieve communion with God and to see and understand the world of the Godhead.[2]

Of particular significance, the Talmudic injunctions bear directly upon *hekhalot* and *merkavah* mysticism, the first major mystical movement in Jewish history, which emerged between the 2nd and 6th centuries. They relate directly to the rebellious aspects of that movement *vis a vis* Talmudic culture and its worldview, as follows: (1) *Hekhalot* mysticism incorporates the idea of a mystical leader publicizing the "Secret of the World," and, following from that, (2) it posits the ability of any person, with the proper mystical knowledge, to ascend to heaven and see God face to face. (3) It contemplates that this ascent can be at any time or place, at *man's initiative*. (4) *Hekhalot* literature contains a description of the celestial powers, or hypostases, the Divine pleroma. (5) God is conceived and described in its literature in bold, anthropomorphic terms (*shi`ur qomah*) consisting of gigantic physical dimensions. (6) This literature is anti-historical, describing pseudo-events as occurring in impossible time periods, in an un-Talmudic fashion. (7) It invents and employs a new, unique terminology. (8) It probably contemplates a separate demiurgic power separate from the Supreme God. (9) There is a dramatic descent, into the world, of the "Prince of Torah" (*Sar Torah*), an angelic being, at man's beckoning, to teach persons so desiring the entire Torah, both written and oral, virtually instantly. This negates, of course, the need for the entire ongoing Talmudic structure and halakhic process. Under any interpretation, these elements of *merkavah and hekhalot* mysticism clash directly with the Talmud's prohibitions. Not surprisingly, this fringe group had little influence on contemporary Talmudic culture and for centuries thereafter.

Elements of kabbalah, particularly as it arose in a formal way and in various forms in Catalonia in Northern Spain and in Provence — Languedoc in Southern France in the thirteenth century, thereafter in Safed, and later still in Europe generally, concluding with Hasidism in the eighteenth century, clearly depart in many similar ways from the Talmudic proscriptions and bear strong imprints of *hekhalot* mysticism after some 700 years of that mysticism lying dormant. Ecstatic and theosophic kabbalah include ascent to heaven; mythological and physical conceptions of God and Creation; unique terminology; secret teachings of the nature of the Divinity and how to achieve mystical ascent and union (*unio mystica*); new ways of approaching Biblical exegesis; and claims of unique access to religious truth by personal revelation. Historians recognize that

Jewish mysticism became dominant in Jewish piety and religious thought from the end of the sixteenth century until the present day.[3]

Not surprisingly, the historians who have dealt with the nature and history of mysticism have reached conclusions about working definitions basically similar to the Talmudic view. Gershom Scholem speaks of human, secret knowledge of God, and experiencing the Divinity through "seeing," noting that classical Judaism is "more widely removed from mysticism than any other form." He sees the cause of mysticism as the abyss between the perfection of God and the evil that man encounters in the world, which the mystic seeks to bridge by "hidden paths," which becomes his "main preoccupation." These elements describe the essence of theosophic and ecstatic kabbalah, and the mysticism prohibited by the Talmud, particularly as mysticism adds a "new interpretation of old values," which often "differs entirely from the old and transforms their meaning." Thus, the *secret* revelation at Sinai, which is the source of mystical belief, is the "real and decisive" revelation, the only religious truth. Finally, the mystic is aloof from history; he seeks ways of "escaping from history rather than...understanding it." Moshe Idel similarly speaks of mysticism as "knowing" and "understanding" God and His "position in the universe," as well as "contact with the Divine" through ecstatic and unitive experiences. Joseph Dan generally agrees with these definitions or descriptions but adds an important feature: The mystic, and mystical movements, claim that knowledge of God, and all related religious truth, "cannot be achieved by the usual avenues of knowledge, by sensual perception, and by logical generalization and analysis." Nor can it be communicated by language, but only indirectly by symbols. The real world reflects and describes in a hidden way what is going on within the Godhead. In brief, mystical knowledge of God is secret, unique, superior, and impenetrable to those who do not share the mystical vision of the world.[4]

The psychoanalytic view of Jewish mysticism is in broad agreement with the foregoing express and implied definitions and causes of mysticism. In that view, mysticism is man's aspiration to experience union with the Divine, thereby returning to the loving embrace of the [Divine] Parent in order to escape living in history in the real world of unbearable reality and evil. Mysticism thus stands in stark contrast with classical Judaism: In the latter, "the human — Divine boundary is [never] transgressed. We are encouraged to *imitate* God, but never to *identify* with Him."[5]

To conclude this introduction and overview, we may posit that Jewish mysticism arose in Judaism outside of Talmudic culture and was contrary — even rebellious — to it. Because many of its antithetical elements became, in various forms, part of Jewish mystical movements during the last thousand years, there is a dissonance between them and Talmudic culture that needs to be confronted. Only consistent adherence to rabbinic normative ritual requirements has kept such movements within mainstream Judaism. But it is the prerogative and duty of this generation to consider whether those dissonant elements, which arose as a response to the trauma of pressure, persecution and expulsion coming from a hostile Christian environment, continue to serve the health of Judaism, in its religious and national aspects, in the radically changed environment of the late twentieth and early twenty-first century.

The Talmudic scholars created a Judaism founded on law, study, and prayer, through which Jewish life was able to continue despite the loss of the Temple and its sacrificial ritual. They built on an underlying optimism about Jewish survival and the continuing meaningfulness of Jewish religious practice and the idea of working to improve the material world. Talmudic society was based on reason; it was focused on holiness (*qedushah*) and practical wisdom (*hokhma*) in dealing with the problems of life. It was organized as a meritocracy based on knowledge and societal support, respect for different ideas on all sides of an issue, and the preservation of those ideas as part of the legacy of each era for the future. *Hazal* taught that there is wisdom in non-Jewish society, but Torah only in Jewish society.[6] Whatever other messages may be implied, there is every indication that Jews should pursue both. The *hekhalot* mystics of the

Talmudic era were far more interested in the personal, spiritual solace of communion with God.

Jewish mysticism erupted within mainstream Judaism, according to most historians, in the thirteenth century, in the form of the kabbalah, in northern Spain and southern France. At its core was the experience of "feeling at one, united," with the Divine world. It took three forms: ecstatic, as physical or psychological ascent and union — a form of death and rebirth; theosophic, as ideas and images of God and Divine behavior; and practical, as attempts to translate the ascent and the ideas of God into practical power or magic, including the concept of theurgy, helping to restore harmony within the Godhead. It has been shown that mysticism is a response to historical trauma and catastrophe and to a pervasive and protracted unbearable reality; it reflects the desire to find relief and comfort thorough return to the parent memory and the parent figure. In the thirteenth century, it centered on a conception of a complex and dynamic structure of various powers or aspects of God, which came to be known as the ten *sefirot*. That structure became part of a mythology of God's transformation from a single, omnipotent, transcendent, unknowable, spiritual perfection, to a multi-faceted, flawed, knowable Creator maintaining an immanent presence in the visible, material world — a world dominated by the implacable evil faced by the Jewish people in the Ashkenazic world of Christian Europe.[7]

I would argue that the fundamental, governing impulse of this mainstream mysticism became part of Ashkenazic Jewry's spiritual and religious tradition earlier than the thirteenth century — as early as the end of the eleventh century, when Rhineland Jews became the victims of the new, populace-driven, fervent Christian violence of the First Crusade mobs passing through Germany en route to liberating Jerusalem and crushing the Moslem "infidels" who had conquered it centuries earlier. The response of German Jewry to the threat of mass, forced conversions at the Crusaders' hands was a new, radical form of mass martyrdom, in which husbands and wives killed their children, each other and themselves to sanctify God's name.[8]

This response constituted a turning point in the motivation for mainstream Jewish martyrdom. For the first time, Jewish martyrs sought not just to carry out the Talmudic law requiring passive martyrdom, i.e., *to be killed* at the hands of their persecutors rather than convert, but to *avoid* such martyrdom in favor of *self-destruction, and to escape life in the real world — where Christianity seemed to be emerging triumphant in history — and to find their religious reward in ascent to heaven where they and their families would live on in a spiritual world of purity and peace.* This element of ascent to God to escape the evils of life defines the essence of a new medieval "mystical" impulse, as described by the historian Yitzhak Baer, and its breakthrough in mainstream Judaism.[9] The martyrs' primary accompanying religious purpose was to demonstrate Judaism's continued authenticity and superiority as a religion, and Jewry's continued worthiness to be God's chosen people, despite His evident intention, as the martyrs understood it, to abandon them to history for a Divine purpose that they could not comprehend. Their goal, in this regard, seemed to be for God to bring about the end of history and the final redemption, all as a result of their zealous bravery.[10]

The problematic nature of their use of family murder and suicide as a new, radical response to religious persecution was evident. The Talmud prescribed martyrdom by the *passive* acceptance of death at the hands of Israel's religious persecutors, not by suicide or murder, which remained among the most serious religious transgressions under all circumstances.[11] The martyrs of 1096 daringly departed from the Talmud's martyrological formula.

At this point in Jewish history — or, more specifically, Ashkenazic history — it was unclear how this daring new martyrdom would be regarded. Would it be rejected as a dangerous violation of Talmudic prohibitions against suicide and murder; excused as a transgression committed under extreme duress; or halakhically accepted and elevated, despite the means taken, to an act of *qiddush Ha-Shem*, sanctification of God's name? In fact, the new martyrdom and its accompanying mystical impulse became accepted by popular will and by the *silence*, for the most part, of halakhists about what *actually occurred*. Let us examine the evidence.

Chronicles of the martyrdoms, written anonymously over some seven decades following the events of 1096,[12] used an aggadic approach to elevate the martyrdoms to halakhic acts of *qiddush Ha-Shem*. Piecing together Jewish historical precedents, symbols and ideas lauding those who were willing to sacrifice their lives rather than betray their faith — albeit virtually never by suicide and murder as did Rhineland Jewry — the Chronicles elevated the martyrdoms of 1096 to the highest level of religious faith.[13] The *Tosafists*, the leading rabbinic authorities during the following two centuries (1100–1300 C.E.), generally did not comment on these specific martyrdoms, nor on the Chronicles and the arguments that they offered, even though many *Tosafists*, as has recently been recognized, dealt with some esoteric ideas and practices.[14] In their halahkic commentaries on the Talmud and other writings, however, they generally followed the seminal opinion of Rabbenu Tam, written at the beginning of the *Tosafist* period (c. 1100–1170) as a comment on a Talmudic discussion of suicide, who daringly expanded the Talmudic prescriptions of martyrdom as a passive act. He asserted that Jews who feared that unbearable torture during a religious persecution would cause them to leave their faith, or commit other major halakhic transgressions, were permitted (and, in some versions of his commentary, required) to commit suicide pre-emptively.[15] A few *Tosafists* even permitted the murder of children in such circumstances.[16]

This rationale, so far as we can ascertain from the Chronicles, did not apply to, nor govern, the motives and actions of the 1096 martyrs. Fear of unbearable torture was *not* the reason for the martyrs' actions; defiance of their persecutors was. This gap between what the *Tosafists* permitted and what the martyrs did, in the face of the *Tosafists'* undoubted awareness of the content of the Chronicles of the martyrs' actions

222

and the community understanding of these actions that the Chronicles reflect, raises serious questions about the halakhic authenticity and legitimacy of the martyrdoms. I have not found this problem commented upon in my research. It is noteworthy in this regard that Rabbenu Tam, the leading *Tosafist*, who pioneered the *Tosafist* position in which the martyrdoms of 1096 were not mentioned, specifically lauded the *passive* martyrdom at Blois, France, around 1170, about the time when the last major chronicle of the 1096 events was being produced.[17] But while this may support the view that the *Tosafists'* silence about the permissibility of the 1096 martyrdoms may fairly be construed as disapproval, Haym Soloveitchick has provided the basis for the opposite conclusion, namely, that the *Tosafists* were strongly committed to the religious behavior of the German-Franco Jewish community of which they were a part — a self-image unique to the medieval Ashkenazic community. *Tosafist* silence in these circumstances may therefore be construed as tacit approval of the new martyrdoms — at least with respect to the suicides — based on an empathy and an identification with them, and a deep religious conviction, notwithstanding the absence of *formal* halakhic authorization, that the acts of martyrdom of a pious community could not and should not be challenged. Further support for this conclusion arises from the silent acquiescence of the *Tosafists* in the incorporation in the *qinot* liturgy for *Tish'a be-Av* of references to the active martyrdoms of 1096, and the explicit recommendation of suicide by an English *Tosafist* to the martyrs of York, England, in the twelfth century.[18]

Perplexing questions persist about the 1096 martyrdom. Knowing that the martyrs had probably violated even the now radically expanded law of martyrdom, why didn't the *Tosafists* say something to that effect? Did they think that it was too late to criticize the martyrs' actions because the martyrs were already dead? But didn't they have an obligation to provide clearer, more explicit halakhic guidance for future situations that might arise? They had other options as well: regretting that the law had probably been violated because of the absence of halakhic guidelines to guide the martyrs in this unforeseen situation; or excusing the martyrs' radical behavior as occurring under great duress. The gap between what the *Tosafists* approved and what the martyrs did remains a fact — and unremarked upon, until now.[19]

In any case, this new martyrological and mystical impulse, as Yitzhak Baer has described it, to flee the world and ascend to Heaven to commune with God so as to escape the pervasive evil in the real world, soon became an accepted element of mainstream Judaism, moving from Germany to France and Spain. It developed into a major element in Ashkenazi literature and belief, formalized first as kabbalah, and, during the last three centuries, as Hasidism, which together became the primary, long-lasting, mystical progeny of the 1096 suicides and murders over the ensuing centuries.[20] There is an evident connection — not fully documented in the scholarly literature — among the *aqedah* as it came to be understood after the destruction of the Temple (70 C.E.) in Jewish midrashic literature; Jewish martyrdom, which so strongly relies on it; and the strong support for martyrdom, especially in Ashkenazi communities, under the influence of kabbalah, throughout the ages, as exemplified by the poetry of the early kabbalist leaders, Nahmanides and R. Solomon b. Abraham (thirteenth century), glorifying the killing of children by their parents as acts of martyrdom.[21]

Out of the martyrs' experience emerged four facets of Ashkenazi mystical spirituality that strongly influenced its religious outlook for the entire second millennium.[22] *First*, a sense of despair over life in the world, and a yearning to escape its tribulations and misfortunes for the eternal bliss and purity of living in heaven and paradise, in a world of light, seeing God "eye to eye." *Second*, feelings of indifference, hostility, and fear toward the Christian world and a "frenzied vilification" of it, coupled with a sense of religious, moral and cultural superiority over it. *Third*, a desire to separate from that world, which seemed to offer nothing but suffering, immorality and ignorance. *Fourth*, the discovery of the religious rationale for radical, mystical acts of suicide and murder, not in a reasoned, logical deduction from existing halakhic sources, but from an axiomatic belief in what was required of them based on their deepest religious intuitions — what we might describe as an internally generated knowledge or even revelation. "Who I am" determined for them how to respond to this sudden, new, powerful, and seemingly successful Christian onslaught to destroy Jews and Judaism totally and finally. Their models were Daniel and his friends; Hannah and her seven sons; Rabbi Aqiva and Rabbi Hananiah ben Teradion; and, of course, Abraham at the *aqedah*. All of them faced new situations without clear-cut religious guidance, extended the religious "envelope" that they had acquired, and added a new dimension to the traditional conception of proving one's devotion to God to fit the special, new circumstances they faced. The heroic new character of Christianity and Judaism at the end of the eleventh century precipitated a new level of Christian persecution *of* the Jews and, in turn, a new level of radical response *by* the Jews, based not on existing law, but on a frenzied fervor of separation, vilification, escapism, and heavenly ascent, and on the elevation of internal revelation over reason as the source of religious understanding and truth. In these ways, the permanent victims of a new, popular, triumphant Christianity sought to become the permanent victors. Martyrdom and ascent to heaven turned what was experienced as final religious defeat in world history to the "ultimate validation of religious triumph" and life in the eternity of the Divine domain.[23]

In considering the question of whether this "new" mysticism — abandoning the material world for repose in the heavenly world — arose within the Talmudic tradition, specifically in *hekhalot* mysticism starting in the second or third century C.E., we find that it probably arose outside of it. *Hekhalot* elements that are *contra* that tradition include ascent to heaven by *human* initiative; the magical, instantaneous and complete acquisition of Torah knowledge from the *sar ha-torah* ("Prince of Torah"); and other mystical ideas that are so significant that the view of this mysticism as produced "by and for rabbinic authorities" is a highly problematic, probably minority, position.[24] Citing these and other factors, Joseph

Dan has demonstrated that *hekhalot* mysticism was, in fact, a *rebellious* position, radically different from rabbinic tradition, that grew outside of Talmudic circles, and this appears now to be the prevailing view.[25]

A related issue is whether the increase in the ascetic ideas and practices of the German pietists (*hasidei ashkenaz*), and the mystical elements among the pietists, *Tosafists* and kabbalists in the late twelfth and thirteenth centuries, should be seen *not* as a response to the Crusader pogroms and Christianity's apparent triumph in history over Judaism (and Islam),[26] but rather as an internal development in rabbinic Judaism from *hekhalot* roots. To the extent that this position rests on the assumption that those roots were embedded within Talmudic culture, it is, as shown above, an untenable and minority view. In addition, it begs the question: the new mysticism may have had 500-year-old or even older roots, but what was the *reason* pietism and mysticism emerged *when* and *how* they did? The evidence I have presented and the underlying chronology suggest that the cause was the trauma to Judaism that suddenly seemed to destroy Judaism's most cherished beliefs about its destiny. Why else was this alleged organic development of mysticism and asceticism so late in coming? As Dan has noted,[27] mysticism arose in Christianity and Islam within two centuries of their births, which suggests organic growth; in Judaism, it took more than fifteen centuries (from Sinai, around 1200 B.C.E., to the *hekhalot* literature of 200–500 C.E); and then it first arose *outside* of mainstream Judaism — which certainly suggests external causes. One is not likely to find such a causal attribution in mystical literature because, as Dan has noted, new religious ideas seek to portray themselves as having an organic continuity with ancient tradition rather than be seen as merely a psychological response to a transient historical event.[28] For mystics, their truths have no beginning that is subject to historical inquiry; their truths are eternal, and have been secretly transmitted only to them, through an elite in history whose identity is unknown. Similarly, kabbalah, in all its forms, does not attribute its ideas to historical events like persecution or expulsion, but to secret revelations going back to Sinai, which elevates them to the authority and sanctity of Torah. Nor should this come as a surprise, given the understandable desire to point to the most sacred and ancient roots of its truths.[29]

The evidence supports the powerful impact of external causes. From the facts uncovered by Chazan, Soloveitchick and Kanarfogel,[30] it appears that a milder form of asceticism and esotericism developed before the First Crusade in response to a milder Christian hostility at that earlier time, and a more radical Jewish response developed after it — and continued to do so in various forms in the face of new developments and an ever more pervasive, insistent and continuing Christian hostility to Jewry in its Diaspora environment.[31] Therefore, any attempt to discount outside influences as a cause of Jewish mysticism simultaneously ignores not only the psychological mechanism of mystical responses, but that sense of continuing threat and vulnerability created by a triumphant, powerful, zealous, and hostile Christianity during virtually all of the last thousand years. Moreover, looking for *immediate* cause and effect manifestations reflects a too rigid and fragmented understanding and expectation regarding the nature of mystical responses, and — in particular — the pervasive and continuing nature of Christian threats and pressures on Jewry, and the Jewish responses to it. Sometimes the impetus to a mystical or messianic response may even be an event that provides hope that an apocalyptic end to history is imminent.[32] But, that, too, is in no way inconsistent with the paradigm I have described. Psychoanalytic studies have shown that mysticism is a psychologically based response to a perceived threat to one's identity, presented by the abyss between the real and the ideal in the world, and can lie dormant for a prolonged period.[33]

Therefore, the new ascetic-mystical spirituality of Ashkenazi Jewry arose not as an inevitable organic development from within rabbinic culture, but as a result of on-going Christian persecution and pressure, and a resulting sense of vulnerability and hopelessness of any redemption through history. If so, the progeny of that historical trauma, represented in Jewish mystical movements and their many forms of escapist, separatist, anti-rationalist, esoteric, and ascent religiosity, which have engulfed Judaism in the last one thousand years, culminating in Hasidism for the past two hundred and fifty years, is subject to reexamination and question in the radically new situation of Jews and Judaism in the twenty-first century.[34] This is especially the case given that this venerable religiosity was a response to a continuing psychological state of Jewish hopelessness and helplessness in *galut* — understandable, to be sure — over the succeeding centuries in the face of a continually hostile and threatening Christian Europe, far beyond anything encountered by classical Biblical and Rabbinic Judaism theretofore. Therefore, today's scholars in today's environment have a right and even a duty to consider whether at least some of these ascetic and mystical ideas and practices, having arisen as responses to historical trauma, may no longer be relevant, and may perhaps even be dangerous to Judaism today.

In conducting this analysis, historians should inquire, among other things, into the parallel, and the reasons for it, between Judaism's response to the cultural advances of Christian civilization in the last five hundred years, and that of Islam. The latter is characterized by a persistent disdain for a culture seen as hostile and inferior to Islam's self-sufficiency and superiority, based on its doctrines of an esoteric tradition dating back to Abraham, and Ishmael as his successor; successive revelations culminating in the final revelation to Muhammad; the treasuries of Moslem learning in Arabic texts; and the Islamic "feeling of timelessness, that nothing really changes."[35] The Moslem world has certainly maintained the loyalty of its masses to Islamic religious traditions and to its clergy, who are its guardians and interpreters and enjoy concomitant religious and political power. But the price paid by Islam — in the form of the backwardness, destructive zealotry and resistance to all change in that society, and the rest of the civilized word's response to it — has been a heavy one to this very day.

Has the anti-rationalist, mystical strain in Judaism caused a similar response to advances in Western civilization, with similar consequences? How does that strain, with its separation from, and hostility to, the non-

Jewish world, allow for the fulfillment of God's command to Adam to "fill the land and conquer it" (*Gen.* 1:28)? How does it allow for sanctification of God's Name among non-Jewish nations and peoples in fulfillment of God's blessing to Abraham that the nations will bless his progeny through the achievements of Jews for the benefit of mankind, and make the Jewish people a model for mankind's children (*Gen.* 12:4 and Rashi *ad loc.*)? Is that not the highest form of *qiddush Ha-Shem*, sanctification of God's name, and certainly the most creative and desirable form of this precept? How does separation from, and hostility to, the world and its pursuits contribute to the fulfillment of the Jewish hope — which is a thematic high point of the High Holy Day liturgy — for the time when all of mankind will "blend into one brotherhood," and "peoples...in all parts of the world...will unite to worship God with one heart...and [God] will abolish the rule of tyranny on Earth"? How does it contribute to Isaiah's prophecy (*Isa.* 42:6) that Israel will be a "light unto the nations"? How does it contribute to the promise of the ancient *Aleinu* prayer that man's purpose is to help "repair the world to be a kingdom of Heaven"? Viewing Israel and Judaism as a people *and* a religion, both of which are tied to a "promised land," how can Israel produce engineers, scientists, financiers, economists, historians, soldiers — workers and experts in every field necessary for the health, safety and welfare of the nation — if the only way of life that is the ideal for all is one based on mysticism, kabbalah, Hasidism and their beliefs, practices, and goals?

In considering these and other contradictions between mysticism and classical Jewish ideals, it is noteworthy that Judaism has recently elicited powerful admiration even in Christian scholarship for pioneering the *opposite* idea — that progress in history, in the spiritual and material senses, far from being relegated to the dustbin of history by a flight to personal, mystical salvation, is both desirable and possible, as part of the Divine plan of creation. But that praise was directed at Classical Biblical and Rabbinic Judaism, and not to the escapist, separatist and culturally hostile mystical religiosity of the last one thousand years.[36]

Historians should perhaps also consider whether post-Zionism's one-sided and self-destructive questioning of the very legitimacy of the State of Israel from its inception, is, as the Israeli writer Aharon Megged has suggested, a suicidal impulse, which may be considered a secular form of Judaism's thousand-year mystical drive to spiritually annihilate the real world,[37] with all of its seemingly insoluble problems and inherent imperfections, and achieve a mystical union with an unidentified realm of absolute purity. Both positions thereby seek to escape from a perpetually hostile world in which one cannot achieve material solace *and* moral perfection.

In addition to addressing these kinds of questions, other problematic aspects of Jewish mysticism, many of which have been criticized by J.B. Soloveitchik and other scholars,[38] should be considered. These include, or subsume, an ideology of myth and magic including belief in evil as an independent power — for some, like the mystic Isaac Luria, part of the Godhead itself; the spiritual *hubris* of an ideology that assumes a mystic's unique access to God and to religious truth by revelation and union; a fragmented Divinity dependent on human acts of mystical ritual for the restoration of Divine harmony;[39] disengagement from worldly affairs that embody mankind's striving for dignity and freedom, including the self-empowerment of Jews in the diaspora and their achievement of independence in their homeland;[40] a hostile and fearful isolation from all forms of non-Jewish cultural achievement (*madda*), including science, history and the humanities;[41] religious stringencies and a lock-step uniformity in practice; dependence on religious leaders on all issues, from politics to dress codes; and an evident indifference not only to the non-Jewish world's activities, but to that world's opinion of Jews and Judaism. These have certainly contributed to the "massive" defections from traditional Judaism since the Enlightenment some two hundred years ago.[42] Are these aspects of the "sanctification of God's Name," or the opposite?

Lastly, and perhaps most importantly as a destructive element in Jewish history, is divisiveness. This element in Jewish mysticism has two aspects: separation from the established Jewish community; and attacks, usually in concert with other extreme elements, against moderate, even Orthodox, religious elements in Judaism who might successfully question mysticism's claims to an exclusive access to an ancient, secret truth, and who are perceived as a threat to mysticism's beliefs, practices, and power in the Jewish community. Separation from, and attacks on, the physical and cultural structures of Judaism are, indeed, based on mysticism's esoteric claim to religious authority that is beyond the scope of reason, coupled with its pessimism regarding the implacable evil that it sees in the material world, impelling it to escape the material realm and unite with the Divine world.[43]

This separation process can be found, with varying degrees of emphasis, in the emergence of the *hekhalot* mystics of the second and third centuries;[44] the pietists of Germany in the twelfth century[45] and even to some extent among *Tosafists* of that period;[46] the kabbalists of northern Spain and southern France at the end of the twelfth century;[47] and the Hasidic movement in Eastern Europe in the middle of the eighteenth century.[48] With regard to Hasidism, Dan writes:

> Modern Hasidism could be regarded as a model example of a mystical movement creating a schism within an existing religious structure, establishing its own institutions, dress codes, particular prayer book and customs, and style of ritual performance, as well as a mystical structure of leadership. The only unusual element in this picture…is that the establishment from which [Hasidism] separated was (and still is) led by a leadership that is [also!] motivated by kabbalistic theology and symbolism.[49]

Here Dan is noting the irony of Hasidism separating itself from an Orthodox establishment already imbued with kabbalistic ideas!

Attacks by these mystical movements against those who do not share their anti-rationalist worldview have occurred often and have succeeded in the last thousand years in keeping Ashkenazi Jewry in frequent, divisive turmoil, preventing the emergence of a successful, moderate, rationalist, Orthodox Judaism up until our own day.

1. In what became known as the Maimonidean Controversy (c. 1230), the new kabbalists of the late twelfth and early thirteenth centuries — presenting themselves as Talmudists and traditionalists but actually motivated by their secret tradition — penetrated, with the support of *Tosafists* and pietists, into southern France and northern Spain (Catalonia), looking for spiritual guidance to the ascetic and mystical traditions of the Franco-German communities, and attacking Maimonidean philosophy, rationalism, and the rabbinic tradition that had been centered in Andalusia. The goal of the anti-Maimonideans was to protect against the perceived threat of apostasy and the undermining of kabbalah and of Franco-German religious culture — though the latter, to be sure, was not monolithic. It was the kabbalists who were the decisive spiritual force in the challenge to Maimonides' philosophic works and to his rationalist supporters. The anti-Maimonideans were led by the kabbalists Solomon b. Abraham of Montpellier and Jonah Gerondi, supported by the kabbalist poet, Meshullam b. Solomon Dapiera. The results were catastrophic, including the burning by the Church of Maimonides' philosophic work, *The Guide for the Perplexed*. The controversy erupted again at the beginning of the fourteenth century, with the anti-Maimonideans now led by the mystically oriented Solomon ibn Adret (Rashba) (a disciple of Jonah Girondi) and by the anti-rationalist Asher b. Yehiel (Rosh) (a disciple of Meir b. Barukh of Rothenberg), after the Rosh had emigrated from Germany to Spain in 1302. It culminated in the two bans of Barcelona of 1305: the first forbade the study by persons under twenty-five years of age of "Greek" works of science (except for medicine) and metaphysics; the second limited the use of allegory in the interpretation of Scripture. The final result of the Controversy, according to Faur's analysis, was the undermining of the Sephardi community and its leaders and of their will to resist forced conversion under Christian pogroms and persecution,

and, finally, expulsion.[50]

Because of Nahmanides' stature, his role in this matter requires special comment. As Baer notes, "He identified himself unequivocally at the outset with the position taken by the zealots of Montpellier, but his tactics were different."[51] In his efforts to mediate the dispute, he sent a letter to the rabbis of northern France, the *Tosafists*, urging them to rescind the ban on Maimonides' philosophic works, to prevent a schism in the ranks of Jewry. "The Torah would be divided into two Torahs, and all Israel into two sects." This much was clearly an effort at mediation. But the letter also included elements that could only make the existing schism worse. Thus, he praised Maimonides for erecting "a Talmudic stronghold, a tower of strength to the Lord," but then he felt compelled to add "and a shrine for the ignorant masses, who breach the fences…," adding, to make his meaning clear, that Maimonides' writings were not for the pious Ashkenazi Jews of France and northern Spain, but for the wayward Jews of the southern lands, the Sephardim, who were, in Baer's words, "consumed by the sword of freethinking and apostasy." The subtle messages conveyed by Nahmanides are that Maimonides' words were good for good Jews, and that they were well intentioned in 1190 (when the *Guide for the Perplexed* was written, forty years earlier), but evidently ineffective, and perhaps worse. Finally, Nahmanides reveals his disapproval of Maimonidean rationalism and its adherents in language that could only deepen the schism between the two contending groups, whatever the final outcome of their bans and counterbans. His letter is inconsistent with the admirable intent of some scholars to portray Nahmanides, in Dan's words, as trying "not to take any side," to be "acceptable to both camps," to "hide his own ideological preferences," and to "preach unity to the quarreling radicals on the two sides." In Nahmanides' words:

> May, you, Sirs, be spared a pain such as ours;
> for the sons have strayed from the father's table, and
> have contaminated themselves with the food and
> wine of the Gentiles; they mingled among the nations

> and learned their ways...Men in the royal service
> have been permitted to study Greek sciences, to learn
> the art of healing and the science of measurement,
> and all the other sciences and their application, so
> that they may earn their livelihood in the courts and
> palaces of the kings.

Yitzhak Baer, quoting this, comments: "Nahmanides' intentions are clear. He hoped to free his people from the embrace of the outside world and the lure of its culture and royal favors..." — a culture which, in Maimonides' view, contained wisdom. Moreover, Nahmanides cannot condemn the "sons" in this way without implying some condemnation of the "father" and the spiritual food that he placed on his "table" before them, which must not have been strong or satisfying enough to prevent the "sons'" from straying.

It is, therefore, all too true that the Maimonidean controversy is with us still, with no little thanks to the great Jewish thinker and leader, Nahmanides, who — given his leadership abilities and stature — could have stamped out the schism started by R. Solomon b. Abraham and his fellow kabbalists by insisting that there is more than one way to live a life of Torah and to come close to God. But to say that, to press that fundamental *anti*-schismatic idea, he would have had to believe it. As a kabbalist, he did not. And we are still struggling with this dispute, and writing about it, to this day.

Ever since Baer's history of the Jews of Spain, it has been taken as a truism that Jewish apostasy in Spain was the result of secular acculturation caused by the values of Maimondean rationalism and philosophy. But a study of the history of the main body of Spanish exiles, who emigrated to the Ottoman Empire in 1492 at its invitation, suggests strongly that Baer was wrong. For some two centuries thereafter, Jewish history is marked by the many contributions of the exiled Spanish Jews to the life of the Empire, in trade, military organization and procurement, finance, and other professions. These are rationalist exiles who, if Baer had been correct, would have chosen conversion over exile!

2. Kabbalah had its next major impact on the moderate rationalism of Moses Isserles and Mordecai Jaffe in Poland, and of Judah Loew (Maharal) and David Gans in Prague. Under the influence of the European Renaissance and Reformation during the sixteenth and early seventeenth centuries, these scholars engaged the new scientific breakthroughs of the period, especially the astronomy of Copernicus, Brahe and Kepler. They represented a unique and promising Jewish openness to new ideas and discoveries, by non-Jewish and Jewish scholars, in science and religion. But this Jewish opening to the world quickly closed under the pressing and spreading influence of Lurianic kabbalah, as it rose to preeminence in Jewish piety and religious thought and imposed its own claim to exclusive truth about Creation and the cosmos. Kabbalists promoted a hidden truth revealed at Sinai as the deeper and authentic meaning of the revealed Torah, taught to and transmitted secretly by initiates over the centuries. They rejected science and philosophy, human reason and experience, as sources of truth, despite the warnings of the Sages about the spiritual peril in the study of mystical secrets. As Jacob Katz has noted, kabbalah "claimed to represent the deepest layer of metaphysical truth, accessible only through revelation...whether it was simultaneous with, prior to, or [subsequent] to the giving of the Law on Sinai...a scrupulously guarded tradition transmitted by means of a chosen elite..." Yet, such was its power over Jewish thought by the sixteenth century, that few if any questioned how this tradition and ideology could co-exist with the fact of more than a few instances of inconsistency between kabbalah and the Talmud.

Judaism and Jewry in the sixteenth century thus suffered the tragedy of losing what we may describe as Renaissance-influenced, syncretistic, rationalistic rabbinic figures like Maharal and Isserles, Ovadiah Sforno and Eliezer Ashkenazi, with their selective involvements with science, philosophy and kabbalah in a rationalistic framework. Also lost were philosophically and scientifically oriented, eclectic Renaissance kabbalists like

Yohanan Alemanno and Abraham Yagel. These misfortunes were compounded during the early seventeenth century by the loss of similar eclectic figures and their acquaintances, like Simone Luzzatto, Leone Modena, Joseph del Medigo, and Menashe ben Israel, who variously accepted, rejected and modified kabbalistic ideas philosophically and theologically, and who died shortly before the advent of Sabbateanism. The combination in these outstanding figures of philosophy, science, *halakhah*, and sometimes even kabbalistic ideas, portended something new in Judaism, reflecting in various ways Renaissance and Marrano rationalism and openness; they remind us in some ways of the multi-faceted thought of Rav Kook. Idel describes the tragedy of their untimely loss:[52]

> The passing of these figures, together with the banishment of rationalistic trends in Amsterdam and Hamburg, caused a void…a void which was filled immediately afterwards by Sabbatean frenzy. Only a century after their disappearance, Modena, del Medigo, and ben Israel became paragons of Jewish enlightenment.[52a]

Idel's idea applies in many ways today as well. The void that has taken place in Judaism through the absence of a successful, modern, vibrant Jewish enlightenment, represented so modestly today by Modern Orthodoxy and the *Torah u-Madda* movement, has been filled by a gradually escalating extremism, again making claims to exclusive access to truth and to unconditional supremacy, culminating in Habad messianism and — for some — even deification of their deceased leader, the Lubavitcher Rebbe.

3. Hasidism allied itself in the nineteenth century with its erstwhile antagonists, the Mitnagdim, who actually shared their belief in kabbalah (though not for the masses), against the emerging *Haskalah* movement, which sought a synthesis of traditional Judaism with elements of modernity. *Haskalah* lost out, and the result was another missed opportunity for a rabbinic Judaism leavened with compatible elements of the important

new thinking of the *Haskalah*. This occurred even though the *Haskalah* was beginning to emerge among the disciples of the Vilna Gaon — who, despite his acceptance of kabbalah, also accepted a role for reason and science in Judaism.[53]

4. Hasidism — which largely carried on the kabbalistic tradition — likewise allied itself in the nineteenth century with extremist followers of the Hungarian religious leader, Moses Sofer (*Hatam Sofer*). After his death, they united against even those elements of modernity that this very conservative, anti-*Haskalah* rabbi — like other rabbis of his time, e.g., Jacob Emden and Ya'ir Hayyim Bacharach — had accepted in his own lifetime. These extremists succeeded in their opposition to the eminent Orthodox religious leaders, Rabbi Esriel Hildesheimer and Moses (Maharam) Schick, after years of attacks on their moderate, somewhat modern views. And, at the end of the nineteenth century, Hasidism helped cause the failure of the incipient Zionist movement of the *hovevei tsiyyon*, even though it had the support of some of the greatest Orthodox rabbis.[54]

5. The first half of the twentieth century again witnessed aggressive attacks by Hasidism allied with other *haredi* elements in Orthodoxy against those Jewish groups that did not adhere to their ideology or program. Their zealousness, including charges of heresy against their opponents, succeeded in driving from public Jewish life, and from leadership of a developing Modern Orthodoxy, another esteemed and learned rabbi, Yehiel Jacob Weinberg, who stood for Zionism, the study of Hebrew, academic Jewish studies, secular studies, tolerance of non-Orthodox Jewish groups, and the use of reason in the understanding and application of Jewish law. Weinberg also stood against Judaism's long-standing hatred and contempt for other religions and cultures — which he feared was reciprocated — and against religious and Orthodox factionalism and strife.[55]

6. More recently, despite the stature of Rabbi Joseph B. Soloveitchik, z.ts.'l, during his lifetime, the Modern Orthodox and related *torah u-madda* movements have been under siege, suffering a leadership crisis. Within the last few years, the threat of further divisiveness has arisen from

the claims being made for the deceased Lubavitcher Rebbe as messiah and Divine — claims which relate directly to Hasidism's kabbalistically based pantheistic views, which were a factor in the Vilna Gaon's issuance of a ban on the new, mystical movement some two centuries ago.[56] In any case, the persistent attacks from the more aggressive, zealous Orthodox groups, with their predominantly Hasidic component, have largely succeeded in keeping the moderate Orthodox forces on the defensive. (A limited exception has been the increasing success of recent initiatives in Modern Orthodoxy, including a growing movement among Orthodox women, for a greater role for women in Judaism.)

Scholars should consider whether there is a consistent, centuries-old pattern here of mystical and other *haredi* Jews allying themselves against any perceived threat from more modern, tolerant and rationalist forms of Orthodoxy, and — if so — what elements of belief, doctrines, ideas, and values they may share that have contributed to this pattern of alliances over the years. For example, the possibility that this consistent opposition to Jewish rationalism derives from a jointly held theological idea: that, under the influence of kabbalistic mysticism and pietism, non-Hasidic and Hasidic *haredi* Judaism long ago agreed that the evil of the material world is inherent and insurmountable. The non-Hasidic *haredim* seek escape through asceticism, while Hasidic Jews seek escape through *devequt*, union with the Divine.[57] The one seeks to escape the evil of reality by self-denial, the other by transcending reality as an illusion. Neither has sought an active, creative and beneficent engagement with the world, and neither regards *madda* as a Divine gift to be perfected.

A hundred years ago, there was an important debate about Hasidism among historians and other intellectuals. They argued over who should shepherd Judaism from the restrictive life of the ghetto towards greater spiritual freedom and national autonomy.[58] While the "debate" had no winner, the real winner in Jewish life was Hasidism, which continues to thrive to this day, having permeated traditional Judaism in *galut* with its mystical outlook of separation from, and hostility toward, the Jewish

Enlightenment as well as other peoples and cultures, and its dangerous ideas of pantheism, escapism, and anti-rationalism.[59]

But there was something hopeful about that debate: its assumption was that there were elements of the ascetic and mystical Jewish way of life that may have served Jewry well in the past, but needed reexamination in the modern world. Let me cite one example.

Nahmanides, a physician and an early leader of kabbalah, stated: "One cannot…profess the faith of Moses unless he believes that all of the phenomena to which we are subject are miracles every one, *not caused by any natural law*" (emphasis added).[60] Thus, given the dominance of kabbalah in Jewish tradition since the sixteenth century, it is not surprising that, prior to Jewish Emancipation in the modern era, Jews could not possibly be expected, much less encouraged, to pursue science, technology, or even medicine. Not only was religious community support for such activity lacking; but, as a matter of principle, if there are no "laws" supporting these disciplines, only Divine miracles on which to rely, what is there to study?

I have left for final and separate consideration the complex — and, as will soon appear, related — issues of whether Jewish mysticism may be considered a form of idolatry, a matter that inevitably impinges on any Jewish embrace of mysticism. This challenge was made to kabbalah as far back as the thirteenth century;[61] it suggested that the idea of the ten *sefirot* (emanations, aspects or powers of God) was inconsistent with the Divine unity.[62]

Moshe Halbertal has elaborated four aspects or definitions of idolatry in Jewish tradition:[63] (1) betrayal and rebellion against God, whose omnipotence and status as exclusive leader and protector of Israel, mankind and the created universe is thereby negated; (2) metaphysical error, having an erroneous concept of God in mind during prayer — in particular, anthropomorphic conceptions or other projections of human qualities onto God, thereby also reducing or denying the Divine authority of God's commandments by blurring the abyss between the Commander and those who are commanded; (3) the view of God as comprising a multiplicity of aspects or powers or intermediaries that depend on man, and human actions, to become unified, thereby blurring the distinction between polytheism and monotheism;[64] and (4) worshiping God in a wrong or erroneous manner.

In kabbalah, the realms of evil in the world — known as *qelippot* ("husks") — are inhabited by destructive angels, or evil spirits, says the modern kabbalist, Adin Steinsaltz, who has written that there is so much evil in the world that these angels "appear to be *independent beings...,* *subjects of a sovereign realm of evil*" (emphasis added). This gnostic statement from Lurianic kabbalah[65], which postulates evil as an independent power and an aspect of the Divinity that emerged during the process of Creation as God sought to purify the Divine pleroma of evil, contains aspects of idolatry as described by Halbertal. It invites the kind of despair that can find solace solely in an escapist, mystical ideology and way of life. Shlomo Riskin has concisely expressed the crucial psychological connection between mysticism and idolatry: "Idolatry results from feeling impotent in a world controlled by external and irrational forces which we humans can, at best, 'bribe,' but can never work with in partnership."[66]

The worst fears of the Vilna Gaon and other Mitnagdim, in the wake of the then-recent Shabbtai Zevi episode of a false messiah engendering widespread Jewish apocalyptic excitement, have recently been again realized with the advent within Habad of messianic and Divinity claims for the deceased Lubavitcher Rebbe and associated practices in worship that raise the specter of idolatry.[67] The idea of a nation or people being redeemed through the death and (expected) return to life of a "messiah" before completion of his messianic mission is based on kabbalistic doctrines and has distinct and obvious parallels to Christian messianic doctrines.[68] In turn, these have roots in certain dangerous Jewish midrashic and liturgical texts dealing with the *aqedah*, in which Isaac was actually sacrificed and then returned to life by God to father the Jewish people.[69] The redemptive value of human death and union with God (or the universe) is part of Jewish — indeed, all — mystical thought.[70] Its potential to undermine the foundations of Jewish identity has now become readily apparent, as has its adverse effect on Judaism's role as a member of the larger family of nations.[71]

In sum, what I call the "culture of mysticism and asceticism" was an understandable and excusable response to a thousand-year-long, pervasively oppressive era of Christian triumphalism and the concomitant persecution of European Jewry. But it now is time to ask whether there have been enough changes — including the emergence of the State of Israel and significant alteration of Christian attitudes toward Jews and Judaism — to warrant a comprehensive, multi-discipline reconsideration of some elements of that response that may have weakened Judaism and Jewry over the past ten centuries. Indeed, the foregoing discussion suggests that such a reconsideration is long overdue. Certainly, the unquestioning verdict that the mystical response offers unmitigated and continuing benefit and enrichment to Jewry and Judaism, and the almost universal rabbinic adoption of that view — even among many Modern Orthodox Jews today — need to be reexamined. Indeed, perhaps the most important benefit from such a reexamination would be to help develop an authoritative and attractive intellectual presentation of a traditional Judaism that will fill the void that now exists — especially in Israel — between the *haredi* and secular societies, which threatens the future of Jewry as a nation and as a religion.[72]

A published symposium of outstanding historians, rabbis and other scholars, with an opportunity to respond to one another, addressing these issues would be an excellent beginning to a long overdue project. Considerable relevant published scholarship already exists, but much more analysis seems necessary to fully set out the relevant issues and evidence.[73]

One of the outcomes that I foresee from such a study is the development of a solid intellectual foundation for a form of Modern Orthodoxy as a viable counterweight to the beliefs and many of the practices of Hasidic and *haredi* Jewry today.[74] Rabbi Joseph B. Soloveitchik's worldview, as summarized recently by Eugene Korn, is that "the ideal Jew…shuns both withdrawal from humanity and assimilation to a universal identity."[75]

The view of Gershom Scholem, probably the greatest objective scholarly defender of Jewish mysticism, is that it is caused by terror, and fear of evil in the world which is viewed as coming from demonic forces, which Scholem considers "one of the most dangerous factors in the development of kabbalah." He concludes: "Anyone who concerns himself seriously with the thinking of the great kabbalists will be torn between feelings of admiration and revulsion."[76]

Like so many great scholars, Scholem presents both cases, but was unable, or unwilling, to make a decision. I believe that, at this point in our history, we — like the Talmudic Sages in somewhat similar circumstances — must do so.

Perhaps it is inevitable in our modern age that both types of Judaism, rationalist and anti-rationalist, this worldly and otherworldly, will exist. Yet it is doubtful that Judaism can thrive with the strife of such competing ideologies, each claiming superiority and primacy.[77] But, if there is such a need, or if — in any case — we cannot avoid such competition, the analysis and the debates that I propose will demonstrate also that this fragmented Jewish identity can only exist and thrive on the basis that each side recognizes and acknowledges Judaism's need for the other in order to fulfill their common destiny.

NOTES

1 See, e.g., Gershom Scholem, *Major Trends in Jewish Mysticism* (New York: Schocken, 1961), pp. 1-39; Mortimer Ostow, "Judaism and Psychoanalysis," in *Judaism and Psychoanalysis*, ed. Mortimer Ostow (New York: Ktav, 1982), pp. 4-41; *idem.*, "The Jewish Response to Crisis," in *Judaism and Psychoanalysis*, pp. 233-66; *idem.*, *Ultimate Intimacy* (London: Karnoc Books, 1995), pp. 3-44, 78, 127; Moshe Idel, *Kabbalah: New Perspectives* (New Haven: Yale University Press, 1988), pp. xviii, and 65 ff; Joseph Dan, *Jewish Mysticism* (Northvale, New Jersey: Jason Aronson, Inc., 1998), vol. I, Introduction and Chapters 2-3, vol. III, Introduction and Chapters 1-2, and vol. IV, pp. 152-7. The psychological and ahistorical "messianic" activities of certain mystics were so detached from realistic, historical considerations as to amount to suicidal, eschatological attempts to escape history, not influence it; see Moshe Idel, *Messianic Mystics* (New Haven: Yale University Press, 1998), *passim*; Dan, *Jewish Mysticism*, vol. I, Introduction and Chapters 1-3, and vol. III, pp. xxi-xxv. On the importance of psychoanalytic inputs, from a historian's standpoint, for the study of mysticism, see David Halperin, book review, *AJS Rev.* (1996): 153-7.

2 See *Hagigah* 11b, 14b, 16a; *Yerushalmi Hagigah* 77b; *Tosefta Hagigah* 2:3-4; and *Shir Ha-Shirim Rabbah* 1:4. See generally, Ephraim Urbach, *The Sages* (Jerusalem: Magnes Press, 1979), pp. 184, 193-4, 212-13, 222-3, 417; Eliezer Berkovits, *God, Man and History* (Jerusalem: Shalem Press, 2004), pp. 39-40; and authorities collected in the *Artscroll* edition of the Mishnah, *Seder Moed*, vol. IV (Brooklyn, New York: Mesorah, 1981), at *Hagigah*, Chapter 2.

3 Dan, *Jewish Mysticism*, vol. I, Introduction, and Chapters 2-3, and vol. III, Introduction and Chapters 1-2 and pp. 346-48, and vol. IV, pp. 76, 154; Michael D. Swartz, *Scholastic Magic* (Princeton: Princeton University Press, 1996), pp. 10-13, 218-21; David Berger, "Judaism and General Culture in Medieval and Early Modern Times," in *Judaism's Encounter With Other Cultures*, ed. Jacob J. Schacter (Northvale, New Jersey: Jason Aronson, Inc., 1997), p. 87; *ibid*, Jacob J. Schacter, Introduction, Gerald Blidstein, Chapter 1, and Berger, Chapter 2; Ostow, *Ultimate Intimacy*, pp. 37, 121-205. Rachel Elior, *The Three Temples* (Portland, Oregon: The Littman Library of Jewish Civilization, 2004), 254 ff., 264-5, concludes that *Hekahalot* literature and traditions were "blurred and repudiated by the [Talmudic] sages," citing *Hag.* 2:1, but notes that some Talmudic authorities attached sanctity to the *Hekhalot* priestly traditions, citing B. *Suk* 28a. See also Marvin A. Sweeney, "Pardes Revisited Once Again: Reassessment of the Rabbinic Legend," *Shofar* (Summer 2004):54-6. Dan pungently notes that the establishment from which Hasidism separated "was (and still is) led by a leadership that is motivated by kabbalistic theology and symbolism;" *Jewish Mysticism*, vol. III, p. 42.

4 Scholem, *Major Trends*, see note 1; *idem.*, *On the Mystical Shape of the Godhead* (New York: Schocken Books, 1991), p. 160 f., and discussion in Arthur Green, "Shekhinah, The Virgin Mary and the Song of Songs," *AJS Rev.* (April, 2002), pp. 20-1, which attributes the emergence of the *Shekhinah* in the twelfth century as a female divinity "perhaps as the result of the profound shock caused by the persecutions associated with the Crusades;" Idel, *Kabbalah*, see note 1; Dan, *Jewish Mysticism*, see note 1; Ostow, *Ultimate Intimacy*, p. 28. On the importance of "seeing" God in Jewish mysticism, see Elliot Wolfson, *Through a Speculum that Shines* (Princeton; Princeton University Press, 1994). The most plausible traumatic cause for *hekhalot* mysticism — aside from the destruction of the Temple — was the era of the Roman Hadrianic decrees and persecutions after the Bar Kokhba

rebellion (c. 130 C.E.); cf. Dan, *Jewish Mysticism*, vol. I, p. 107.

For the purpose of clarification of the complex issue of what parts of *hekha-lot* and *merkavah* literature are mystical in nature within a proper definition of "Jewish mysticism," Dan notes the following: cosmogony and cosmology, magic and angelology, homiletical exegesis, and hymns and prayers about the heavenly realms, are *not* mysticism. In contrast, ascent through the seven heavens to see God on His throne, God's measurements in physical dimensions, manuals on how to ascend to the Divine realms, personal revelations rather than careful, rabbinic exegesis and midrash as the source of truth — these are all mystical in nature; see, e.g., *Jewish Mysticism* , vol. I, p. 39.

5   Ostow, *Judaism and Psychoanalysis*, p. 35 and *idem.*, *Ultimate Intimacy*, see n. 1. In contrast, "the moral activism of the Bible envisages the world as the scene of the realization of the Divine order, which is an order of moral will and moral life" without any room for magic or myth; see Julius Guttmann, *Philosophies of Judaism*, tr. David Silverman (New York: Schocken, 1973), chapter 1, n. 11. Scholem had to choose between viewing kabbalah as rooted in ancient Judaism and thereafter secretly transmitted to the medieval period, and seeing it as a medieval phenomenon that reflected the tensions of Jewish thought and society in the High Middle Ages. At first, he chose the former, but eventually he realized that the latter view was correct; Dan, *Jewish Mysticism*, vol. IV, pp. 235-8. It appears that Idel may be making a similar error; *ibid.*; pp. 238-9. See also David Greenberg and Eliezer Witztum, *Sanity and Sanctity: Mental Health Work Among the Ultra-Orthodox in Jerusalem* (New Haven: Yale University Press, 2001); Edward L. Greenstein, "Some Developments in the Study of Language, and Some Implications for Interpreting Ancient Texts and Cultures," Shlomo Izre'el, ed., *Semitic Linguistics: The State of the Art at the Turn of the Twenty-First Century* (Winona Lake, Indiana: Eisenbrauns, 2002), pp. 457-60.

6   See *Num.* 10:31 (Rashi, ad loc.); *Sanhedrin* 17a and 17b; *Menahot* 65a; see also Maimonides, *Mishneh Torah, Hilkhot Sanhedrin* 2:1 and *Hilkhot Talmud Torah* 5:1 ff.; Judah Halevi, *Sefer ha-Kuzari* 2:64; Gerald J. Blidstein, "Rabbinic Judaism and General Culture: Normative Discussion and Attitudes," in *Judaism's Encounter With Other Cultures*, pp. 1-56. On Talmudic reason and the discouragement of mysticism, see, e.g., *Hagigah* 6a, 11b and 14b, and *Bava Metsi`a* 59b. See generally, Berkovits, *God, Man and History*, pp. 102-18; Hava Tirosh-Samuelson, *Happiness in Premodern Judaism* (Cincinnati: Hebrew Union Press, 2003); Yosef Yitzhak Lifshitz, "Foundations of a Jewish Economic Theory," *Azure* (Autumn 2004-5765):41-4. Also, it has been noted that the *Haskalah*, in "providing a response to the challenges posed to Judaism by the new science…, had its roots…in traditional rabbinic culture, and, particularly, in two internal sources of inspiration: first, the tradition of the moral and educational criticism of [Maharal of] Prague in the sixteenth century; and second, in the idealization of the Sephardic model (for example, the Jewish schools in Amsterdam)." These elements in Jewish tradition provided an "interpretation that legitimated change from within," similar to Christian theological enlightenment efforts "to renew religion and advance religious concepts that are consistent with reason and natural religion" (see citations below).

Both movements in the late 18th century failed because they fell victim to politicization, and lost their original objective of a religious and moderate enlightenment, becoming instead secular and radical movements. This occurred in two ways. First, "enlightened" Jews established links to the state via ties of the wealthy

Jewish elite in Berlin; and second, through internal conflicts between *maskilim* and Orthodox. See David J. Sorkin, *The Berlin Haskalah and German Religious Thought* (London: Valentine Mitchell, 2000). The *Haskalah* turned from intellectual concerns for the Jewish religion to political concerns about Jewish afflictions in Gentile society. Its success in the latter area led to its failure in the former; ibid. See also, Shmuel Feiner, reviewing Sorkin's book in *The Jewish Quarterly Review* (Winter 2004):204-8. Yet, it is quite clear that the roots of the Enlightenment lay, at least in part, in the impact of the Renaissance and the Reformation on Italian, as well as Central European and Dutch Jewry; see, e.g., David B. Ruderman's stimulating review of Adam Sutcliffe, *Judaism and Enlightenment* (Cambridge: Cambridge University Press, 2003), in *The Jewish Quarterly Review* (Summer 2004):523-6. See also "Rabbi Chaim Eisen," in *Learning in Jerusalem: Dialogues with Distinguished Teachers of Judaism*, ed. Shalom Freedman (Northvale, New Jersey: Jason Aronson, Inc., 1999); Shlomo Riskin, "The Wisdom of the Maccabees and the Greeks," *Jewish World*, December 6-12, 1996.

7   Mortimer Ostow, "Introduction" and "The Jewish Response to Crisis," and Jacob Arlow, "The Emergence of Mystical Leadership," in *Jewish Mystical Leaders and Leadership in the 13th Century*, eds. Moshe Idel and Mortimer Ostow (Northvale, New Jersey: Jason Aronson, Inc., 1998); Dan., *Jewish Mysticism*, vol. III, pp. 9-12, and vol. IV, p. 243; and Idel, *Kabbalah*, esp. chapters 4-6, 8. God's immanence was particularly emphasized in mystical movements emphasizing union (*unio mystica*) with God — see note 39. The roots of kabbalah go back to *hekhalot* mysticism and German pietism, with their ideas of God's immanent glory (*kavod*), ascent of the soul, a pleromatic Godhead pre-figuring the ten *sefirot*, and a secret tradition, including mystical concepts of prayer; see also Scholem, *Major Trends*, pp. 80-96, 112-13, 176-81; Dan, *Mysticism*, vol. III, p. 42; Idel, *Kabbalah*, pp. 88-96.

An important — but not necessarily controlling or defining — element of Jewish mysticism is "seeing" or visualizing God. However, such experiences were discouraged by the Sages, e.g., in the case of looking at a rainbow, a Jewish ruler, or priests in the act of blessing the people, which were all considered to be vessels of the Divine Glory; see, e.g., *Hagigah* 16a and Wolfson, *Speculum, passim*; but cf. Dan, *Jewish Mysticism*, vol. II, p. 63. For persecution as a motive for mystical experience leading to conversion, see Benjamin Gampel, "A Letter to a Wayward Teacher," David Biale, ed., *Cultures of the Jews* (New York: Schocken, 2002), pp. 425-6 (conversion as a means to "gaze" upon the Divine).

8   Arlow, "Mystical Leadership," p. 200; Robert Chazan, *European Jewry and the First Crusade* (Berkeley: University of California Press, 1987), Chapters III, IV, VII, and the Appendix; *idem., God, Humanity and History* (Berkeley: University of California Press, 2000); Shmuel Shepkaru, "To Die for God; Martyrs and Heaven in Hebrew and Latin Crusade Narratives," *Speculum* (April, 2002): 311-41. See also Shepkaru's work cited below, note 9, p. 36. (See further in Appendix 1.)

9   Shmuel Shepkaru, "From After Death to Afterlife: Martyrdom and its Recompense," *AJS Review* (1999):1-44; Y. Baer, "*Gezerot Tatnu*," *Sefer Assaf* [*festschrift* in honor of Simhah Assaf] (Jerusalem: Mosad ha-Rav Kook, 1953), pp. 126-40, which is noted, without disagreement, by Jacob Katz in *Exclusiveness and Tolerance* (New York: Behrman House, 1983), p. 89. To my knowledge, Baer is the only historian who has characterized the 1096 martyrdoms as a "mystical" experience, although Shepkaru provides important supporting analysis for this view in his article. Cf. Scholem, who allows for the idea that the mystical *Shekhinah* as part of the

245

Godhead arose because of the persecutions of the Crusades; see *On the Mystical Shape of the Godhead* (New York: Schocken Books, 1991), p. 160f.

10 Chazan, *First Crusade*, Appendix (Chronicles of the 1096 martyrdom). The Chronicles reflect, on this issue, the view of the chroniclers *and* the view that they ascribe to the martyrs; see, e.g., *ibid.*, p. 282 (the view of the martyrs) and pp. 237, 256, 262, 267, 271-4 (views of the authors of the Chronicles). The martyrs' expectation, as set forth in the Chronicles, that God would reverse what they perceived as the victory of Christianity over Judaism, certainly implies that they expected this to occur in the near future, whether or not specifically linked to the "messianic era;" See Israel J. Yuval, "The Lord Will Take Vengeance, Vengeance for His People," *Zion* (1994): 351-414; cf. Chazan, *God, Humanity and History*, pp. 151-172.

11 Haym Soloveitchik, "Religious Law and Change: The Medieval Ashkenazic Example," *AJS Review* (Fall, 1987):208.

12 Chazan, *First Crusade*, pp. 40-9, 280.

13 *Ibid.*, pp. 155-8 and the Appendix. As Jacob Katz concluded, ordinary Jews martyred themselves, in David Berger's paraphrase, "not because of familiarity with the niceties of their halakhic obligations, but because they had been reared on *stories* of heroic self-sacrifice." See Jacob Katz, *Exclusiveness and Tolerance* (New York: Behrman House, 1983), pp. 84-5; David Berger, "Jacob Katz on Jews and Christians in the Middle Ages," *The Pride of Jacob*, ed. Jay Harris (Jacob Katz Memorial Volume) (Cambridge: Harvard University Press, 2002), p. 45.

14 Ephraim Kanarfogel, *"Peering Through the Lattices"* (Detroit: Wayne State University Press, 2000), *passim*.

15 *Avodah Zarah* 18a; *Gittin* 57b; *Rash mi-Shantz* on *Avodah Zarah* 18a; *Da`at Zeqenim* on Gen. 9:5; *Perushei ha-Torah leBa`alei ha-Tosafot* on Gen. 9:5; *Tosafot Elhanan* on *Avodah Zarah* 18a; and *Hiddushei Ritva* on *Avodah Zarah* 18a, citing *Gilyonei Tosafot*, "Great Sages of France" and the "Old One" (presumably — and probably erroneously — Rabbenu Tam), for the proposition that murdering children to prevent conversion is also at least permitted; see also Soloveitchik, "Religious Law," p. 210, n. 8. Some opinions refer to other authorities that prohibit suicide (and murder). See also Dov I. Frimer, "Masada in Light of Halakhah," *Tradition* (1971): 27-43.Cf. Rabbi Meir ben Barukh of Rothenburg, *Teshuvot, Pesaqim u-Minhagim*, ed. I.Z. Cahana (Jerusalem: Mosad ha-Rav Kook, 1957-1962), II:54; writing at the end of the *Tosafist* period, c. 1300, he seems to make no reference to a need for fear of torture, or else it is assumed without evidence. There may have been a personal reason for the strong support which R. Tam received by contemporary and later *Tosafists*, as one who could — better than they — put himself in the shoes of the martyrs through his own experience. As H. H. Ben Sasson notes:

Nor should we regard as an empty legend…that Christian knights dragged [R. Tam] out and attempted to inflict the "wounds of Jesus" upon his flesh, in order to take vengeance upon the acknowledged leader of the Jews for the alleged transgression against their messiah ("The Middle Ages," *A History of the Jewish People*, ed. H. H. Ben Sasson [Cambridge: Harvard University Press, 1976], p. 527).

Rabbenu Tam's special treatment of martyrs where torture is involved is consistent with his rationalism; see Kanarfogel, *Peering*, pp. 166-175. An objection to his halakhic innovation is that the Sages were presumably aware that the earlier Maccabee martyrs faced "the most inhuman tortures" to force them to participate in heathen rituals and, nevertheless, made no provision in the laws of martyrdom for suicide (or murder) induced by fear of such torture; see Elias Bickerman, "The Maccabean Uprising: An Interpretation," in *The Jewish Expression*, Judah Goldin, ed. (New Haven: Yale University Press, 1976), pp. 67-68; and Josephus, Complete Works, tr., William Whiston (Grand Rapids, Michigan: Kregel Publications, 1981), p. 257 (from *Antiquities of the Jews*, Book XII, Ch. V).

16 See note 13. (See further, Appendix 2).

17 Yosef Hayim Yerushalmi, *Zakhor* (Seattle: University of Washington Press, 1982), p. 49; see also note 12. cf. Jeremy Cohen, *Sanctifying the Name of God: Jewish Martyrs and Jewish Memories of the First Crusade* (Philadelphia: University of Pennsylvania Press, 2004), p. 22.

Rabbenu Tam should have referenced the more recent 1096 martyrdoms (which took place around the time of his birth) in *A.Z.* 18a. Instead, he cited the thousand year earlier suicides of the Jewish youths being carried into captivity by the Romans — which is odd if he believed that the Crusade martyrdoms comported with his expanded view of suicide as a permitted form of martyrdom. The Jewish youths presumably feared being forced by Roman torture to engage in compliant homosexual prostitution for the pleasure of their masters; see Louis Compton, *Homosexuality and Civilization* (Cambridge: Harvard University Press, 2003). There is virtually no mention of torture as the reason for the martyrdom in the 1096 Chronicles. Indeed, unlike the situation faced by the youths — torture or submit — the 1096 martyrs had the option of being killed by the Crusader mobs, and chose suicide instead, which is not a choice that R. Tam endorsed. As for murdering their children to prevent them from being raised as Christians, that does not appear to be a choice endorsed by the Talmud, and never received a consensus endorsement by the *Tosafists*.

18 *Kinot for the Ninth of Av*, tr. and ann. Abraham Rosenfeld (New York: Judaica Press, 1979), pp. 138-42, 148-9, and especially 168-72. A Christian commentator traced the Jewish suicides in 1190 to an innate tendency going back to Masada; Barrie Dobson, "The Medieval York Jewry Reconsidered," *Jewish Culture and History* (Winter 2000):10. On the *Tosafist* empathy with the martyrs, see Soloveitchik, "Religious Law." For some reason, Soloveitchik and others believe that the *Tosafists* approved the 1096 martyrdoms, despite the absence of fear of torture as their motivation; see, e.g., his "Halakhah, Hermeneutics and Martyrdom in Medieval Ashkenaz," *JQR* (Winter 2004):77-108 and *JQR* (Spring 2004): 278-299. On the precedence given to *minhag* in Ashkenazi Judaism, see Israel Ta-Shma, *Minhag Ashkenaz ha-Qadmon* (Jerusalem: Magnes Press, 1994), pp. 86-7, 98. (See further Appendix 3).

19 I did refer to it very briefly in my review of David Berger's recent book on Habad messianism; see "Challenging the New Chabad Messianism," *Midstream* (December 2001): 30-35. Jeremy Cohen has made a persuasive case that fear was the last thing on the martyrs' minds. Rather, the 1096 Chronicles show a motivation to suffer a heroic voluntary death on the field of an epic battle with Christianity to prove the continuing chosenness of Israel. Cohen adds that the authors demonstrate a need to portray, subtly, certain weaknesses among the martyrs, e.g., doubt, uncertainty, and indecisiveness about their martyrdoms. But — having shown this — there is all the more reason to ask: Why is the weakness of fear not suggested, if it existed? If it did not, then the *Tosafist* requirement of fear of torture has not been met, and Cohen cannot say that the *Tosafists* approved of

what occurred: See, e.g., Cohen, *Sanctifying the Name...*, p. 130.

20 See note 9; Idel, "Nahmanides: Kabbalah, Halakhah and Spiritual Leadership," in Idel and Ostow, eds., *Jewish Mystical Leaders*, pp. 91-94; and Israel Ta-Shma, "Rabbi Jonah Gerondi: Spirituality and Leadership," *ibid.*, p. 177. The inclination toward kabbalah existed already from the thirteenth to the fifteenth centuries, even among mainstream rabbis who were not kabbalists; *ibid.* Kabbalah came to dominate Jewish piety and religious thought from the sixteenth century to the modern era; Berger, "Judaism and General Culture," p. 87 and *passim*; Scholem, *Major Trends*, p. 302; Jeremy Cohen, *Living Letters of the Law: Ideas of the Jew in Medieval Christianity* (Berkeley: University of California Press, 1999), arguing — *contra* Chazan — along with Funkenstein that there was a gradual but fundamental shift in 11th, 12th, and 13th century Christian polemics and attitudes toward the Jews, especially following "discovery" of Talmudic Judaism, from tolerated "witnesses" to intolerable heretics. See also, Ram Ben-Shalom, "Between Official and Private Disputes: The Case of Christian Spain and Provence in the Late Middle Ages," *AJS Rev.* (April 2003): 23-72; Robert Chazan, "Medieval Anti-Semitism" and Jeremy Cohen, "Robert Chazan's 'Medieval Anti-Semitism,'" *History and Hate*, David Berger, ed. (Philadelphia: Jewish Publication Society, 1986), pp. 49-72; Ben Sasson, "The Middle Ages," *Jewish People*, pp. 477-89.

The general difference between Sephardi and Ashkenazi attitudes in their view of life is summarized, in part, by H. J. Zimmels in *Ashkenazim and Sephardim* (London: Marla Publications, 1976), p. 247: "Most Sephardi rabbis and philosophers agreed that abstinence and self-affliction were not the means of approaching God." Moreover, active messianism seems to have been more of a Sephardi than Ashkenazi response to persecution, e.g., David Reubeni, Shlomo Molkho, and Shabbtai Zvi and the worldwide response to his movement. See, e.g., Matt Goldish, *The Sabbatean Prophets* (Cambridge: Harvard University Press, 2004), Ch. 2; Gerson D. Cohen, "Messianic Postures of Ashkenazim and Sephardim," *Studies in the Variety of Rabbinic Cultures* (Philadelphia: Jewish Publication Society, 1991); Scholem, *Major Trends*, p. 309; and *idem.*, *The Messianic Idea*, pp. 92-5; Stephen Sharot, *Messianism, Mysticism and Magic* (Chapel Hill, N.C.: University of North Carolina Press, 1982), pp. 80-91. Sharot notes that mystics seek "union or direct contact with God," without "visible or material change in the world," "in order to escape or withdraw from the world, and are likely to show indifference to its material conditions." In contrast, see David Ruderman, "Forward," *Renewing the Past, Reconfiguring Jewish Culture*, Ross Brann and Adam Sutcliffe, eds. (Philadelphia: University of Pennsylvania Press, 2003), pp. vii and viii on the linking of the Haskalah to the openness of "Golden Age" Spain; see also the editors' Introduction, that both periods elevated reason as a major principle of Jewish thought; ibid, p. 3.

The millenarian, including messianic, figures, work though history, are activist (or take a symbolic, revolutionist stance) toward the world, looking for *world* redemption rather than the mystic's goal of *personal* salvation; ibid, p. 13. In this regard, I believe that Moshe Idel's attempt to conflate mysticism and messianism, in terms of shared characteristics, fails to take into adequate account their more significant, different characteristics. Both may result from persecution or other traumatic events, but their means of alleviation and remedy are significantly different. See, e.g., Idel's *Messianic Mystics* (New Haven: Yale University Press, 1998), Preface, Introduction, especially p. 3, and Concluding Remarks. Idel is aware of the differences, but sees some virtue in emphasizing occasional commonalities.

As I note elsewhere, messianic figures are only mystics to the extent that their missions are suicidal, and express an intent to experience union with the Divine through some revolutionary historic, but hopeless, gesture. Cf. note 20.

Recent scholarship suggests that the difference between Ashkenazi and Sephardi culture in regard to participation in world affairs and cultures is due, in part, to the settlement of so many primarily Sephardi *conversos*, in the centuries after the Expulsion in 1492, in "port cities," e.g., Amsterdam, Bordeaux, Hamburg, London, Trieste, and across the Atlantic — especially where Protestants flourished with similar experiences of breaking away from their inherited (Catholic) tradition. For example, Brann and Sutcliffe see Amsterdam's Sephardi culture in the 17th century as a bridge to the Haskalah; *Renewing the Past...*, p. 4. These cities were highly mercantile in their practices and values and, therefore, relatively inclusive and tolerant in their outlook and practices regarding minorities in their midst. Indeed, their culture encouraged diversity based on a group's contributions to the community's economic welfare. This pragmatism attracted and allowed Jewish integration and acculturation in these societies. See, e.g., David Cesarani, "Port Jews: Concepts, Cases and Questions," *Port Jews in Cosmopolitan Maritime Trading Centers*, D. Cesarani, ed. (Portland, Or: Frank Cass, 2002), pp. 1-11, and ibid., *passim*; Lois C. Dubin, *The Port Jews of Habsburg Trieste: Absolutist Politics and Enlightenment Culture* (Stanford: Stanford University Press, 1999). See also, Yosef Kaplan, *An Alternative Path to Modernity: The Sephardi Diaspora in Western Europe* (Leidin: Brill, 2000), pp. 1-28. On the difference between Gentile acceptance of Sephardim and Ashkenazim during the European Enlightenment, see Arthur Hertzberg, *The French Enlightenment and the Jews* (New York: Columbia University Press, 1968), pp. 179-80, 222-8, 246, 270-87, 314-51. It is not surprising, therefore, that not only was the "Jewish Question" less of a problem for Sephardim in Europe, but also, that Jewish mysticism, kabbalah, and Hasidism did not generally thrive in these more mercantile societies, nor did they succeed there in their battles, along with their other *haredi* allies, against Haskalah-oriented Judaism in those port cities and Protestant lands.

21 See, e.g., Nahmanides' Hebrew poems, *"Me'ah Batim"* and *"Tefillah al Horvot Yerushalayim,"* *Kitvei Rabbi Moshe ben Nahman*, ed. Charles B. Chavel (Jerusalem: Mossad Harav Kook, 1963), vol. I. It is startling that Nahmanides closely paraphrases the language of Micah 5:7, *condemning* child sacrifice, in his poem "... *Horvot Yerushalayim*" praising martyrological fathers who kill their children! See also the comments of Ben Shalom (Appendix 3) in "Between Sepharad and Ashkenaz," p. 259; and the Hebrew poem *"Eloqim hayyim, atsim ve-nogesim"* on suicide as *qiddush ha-shem*, by the kabbalist, R. Solomon b. Abraham of Montepellier, in *Sefer Gezerot Ashkenaz ve-Tsorfat*, ed. A.M. Habermann (Jerusalem: Mossad Harav Kook, 1946). Cohen, *Sanctifying the Name...*, pp. 34-8: Shimon bar Yohai, the supposed author of the *Zohar* in kabbalistic thought, speaks of Isaac having actually shed his blood on the altar; Levinson, *The Death and Resurrection...*, p. 193.

See generally, Shalom Spiegel, *The Last Trial* (Woodstock, Vt.: Jewish Lights, 1993); Arnold Band, "Scholarship as Lamentation: Shalom Spiegel on the Binding of Isaac," *Jewish Social Studies*, n.s. (Fall, 1998 — Winter 1999): 80-90; Marc Saperstein and Nancy Berg, " 'Arab Chains' and 'Good Things of Sepharad': Aspects of Jewish Exile," *AJS Rev.* (November, 2002): 301-16. See, relatedly, Ivan G. Marcus, *Piety and Society* (Leiden: Brill, 1981), pp. 150-51; Norman Lamm, ed. and ann., *The Religious Thought of Hasidism*, (Hoboken: Ktav, 1999), pp.

63, 68-9, 73, 552-3; and Shulamit Elitzur, "*Aqedat yitzhak: bi-vekhi o be-simha? Hashpa`at masa`ei ha-tselav al ha-sippur ha-miqra'i*," Ets ha-Da`at I (1997), pp. 15-36, comparing the joy of Ashkenazim with the sadness of Sephardim at Jewish martyrdoms in their respective martyrological poetry.

See also, Jose Faur, "Two Models of Jewish Spirituality, *Shofar* (Spring 1992):5-46; *idem.*, "A Crisis of Categories: Kabbalah and the Rise of Apostasy in Spain" in *The Jews of Spain and the Expulsion of 1492*, ed. Moshe Lazar and Stephen Haliczer (Lancaster CA: Labyrinthos, 1997), pp. 41-64. Faur notes that those who participated in the mass conversions after the Disputation at Tortosa (1413-1414) were those simple people "more susceptible to mystical lore than to philosophy"; *ibid.*, p. 63; *idem, In the Shadow of History*, pp, 26, 44; Ben-Shalom, "...The Case of Christian Spain and Provence," op. cit., note 20, pp. 23-71. (See further Appendix 4). Given the dominant role of kabbalah in Jewish piety and religious thought since the sixteenth century (see note 3), I sometimes will cite a non-kabbalist or non-hasidic individual to make a point about the growing influence of mysticism in Jewish thought for the last thousand years, unless they are known to be anti-mystical in outlook.

22 See, e.g., the 1096 Chronicles (see note 10 above); Shepkaru, "Martyrdom," pp. 41-4; Cohen, *Sanctifying...*, pp. 34-7, but cf. p. 38. Jacob Katz., *Tradition and Crisis* (New York: NYU Press, 1993), pp. 3-30, 183-213; *idem., Exclusiveness and Tolerance*, chapters VII and XI; Dan, *Jewish Mysticism*; , vol. IV, Chapter 7, discussing mysticism and the views of Scholem, *Wissenschaft* scholars, and Eliezer Schweid; Israel Ta-Shma, *Ha-Nigleh she-ba-Nistar* (Tel Aviv: Ha-Kibbutz ha-Me'uhad, 2001); and David Berger, "Jacob Katz," and "Judaism and General Culture," p. 87. On the emphasis of classical Judaism on life over death as a religious value, see Avriel Bar-Levav, "We Are Where We Are Not: The Cemetery in Jewish Culture," *Jewish Studies* 41 (2002):21 See also note 20.

It is appropriate, notwithstanding differences between different forms of Jewish mysticism, to make comparisons and generalizations based on shared similarities; see, e.g., Moshe Idel, *Hasidism* (Albany: SUNY Press, 1995), pp. 225, 234.

23 See Chazan, *First Crusade*, Appendix; and Shepkaru, "Martyrdom," p. 41.

24 See note 3; but cf. Kanarfogel, *Peering*, pp. 253-4.

25 Dan, *Jewish Mysticism*, vol. I, Introduction and Chapters 1, 2 and 3; see also Jose Faur, *Homo Mysticus* (Syracuse: Syracuse University Press, 1999), p. 31. Idel tries to argue that *hekhalot* mysticism was not in conflict with Talmudic Judaism, but his evidence is unpersuasive in the face of Dan's analysis; see Idel, *Kabbalah*, p. 262.

Further, the Talmud does not support asceticism as a Jewish way of life; see Sara Epstein Weinstein, *Piety and Fanaticism: Rabbinic Criticism of Religious Stringency* (Northvale, N.J.: Jason Aronson, Inc., 1997).

It is noteworthy that Christian mysticism started about 200 C.E., about the same time as *Merkavah* mysticism and *Hekhalot* literature, seeking, in a monastic setting originally, the presence of God and union with Him. See, Bernard McGinn, *The Presence of God: A History of Western Christian Mysticism* (New York: Crossroad Publishing, 1994), Vol. II, pp. 180-240, 420. It is clear, therefore, that mysticism was inherent in Christianity from the beginning; *ibid.*, p. xi. Beginning around 1200, Christian intellectuals, especially monks, believed that to read the Biblical text correctly "one needed to first have mastered the seven liberal arts..." They therefore "looked to the past for scientific knowledge preserved in Jewish and

Islamic culture;" ibid., pp. 368-71.

26 See, e.g., Ivan Marcus, *Piety*; and Kanarfogel, *Peering, passim*.

27 Dan, *Jewish Mysticism*, vol. II, p. xi. See also Gershom Scholem, *The Messianic Idea in Judaism* (N.Y.: Schocken, 1971), p. 90. Jewish mysticism, which Scholem has described as a gnostic quest to deal with the abyss between a benign God and an evil world, has followed a path that is, in this regard (see note 1), similar to certain Christian mysticism. See, e.g., Scholem, *Major Trends*, pp. 5, 8, 73-4, 114-5; and the insightful literary and theological analysis of Jeremy Driscoll, in "The Witness of Czeslaw Milosz," *First Things* (November 2004):28-33, which I would recommend to all students of mysticism. While it appears unlikely in the short or even intermediate run that Islam can purge itself from the fanaticism that now engulfs most of its active adherents (and the silence of almost all of the rest), there are indications of the beginning of an active attempt to purge this fanaticism from Islam's current mainstream beliefs and practices; see, e.g., Jennifer Friedlin, "The Americanization of Islam?" *The Jerusalem Report*, November 29, 2004, pp. 29-30.

28 Ibid., vol. III, p. 44. See also Scholem, *Major Trends*, pp. 80-7, 104-5, and *idem.*, "...Shape of the Godhead," p. 160 (see note 4), and the discussion in Marcus, *Piety*, pp. 150-1. Because he can't find references in pietist literature to the anti-Jewish attacks of 1096 and the resulting martyrdom (p. 151), among other reasons, Marcus is reluctant to connect them to pietist asceticism and mysticism. Dan asserts that martyrdom is the model for ascetic renunciation of this-worldly pleasure, for viewing life as a trial and a preparation for the next world for those who merit it, as in martyrdom (*ibid.*). Marcus' response is unpersuasive. Besides Scholem and Dan, Joseph Hacker also sees 1096 as a turning point in Christian persecution of Jewry and in Jewish responses to it. Of course, pietistic sources don't suggest that Christian persecution was the cause of their pietism (*ibid.*); that would undermine pietism's *religious* foundation of having received an ancient, secret tradition (see Dan, *Jewish Mysticism*, vol. III, p. 42), and make pietism simply a psychological phenomenon, in response to exoteric pressure; *ibid.*, vol. II, p. 31. Idel seems to buy into some form of historical causality when he writes that "the tendency to systematize earlier kabbalistic ideas and traditions became a major part of the process of reconstructing the shattered socio-economic experience...a gradual passage from esotericism to exotericism;" *Kabbalah*, p. 256. Couldn't that causality have also operated with respect to those "earlier kabbalistic ideas and traditions"?

29 See, e.g., Dan, *Jewish Mysticism*, vol. III, p. 41, vol. IV, p. 14. Idel looks for explicit connections in testing Scholem's ideas, e.g. in *Kabbalah*, p. 265 ("Lurianic texts never mention the [Spanish] expulsion"). I suggest that such a search is in vain, and the test is invalid, as indicated above. Idel admits that "kabbalah preferred an understanding of cosmic processes to...historical ones" (*ibid.*, p. 155). His similar attempt to prove the antiquity of the Lurianic ideas of God's contraction (*tsimtsum*) and the "breaking of the vessels" (*shevirat ha-kelim*) during creation are, for Dan, "unconvincing"; *Jewish Mysticism* , *vol. IV*, p. 229, and, to the same effect, Scholem's attempt to trace *hekhalot* mysticism to Talmudic culture (*ibid.*, p. 231).

30 See Scholem, *Major Trends*, pp. 80-7, 104-5; Haym Soloveitchik, "Three Themes in *Sefer Hasidim*, *AJS Review* (1976): 311-57; Chazan, *First Crusade, Op. cit*, pp. 217-222; and Kanarfogel, *Peering, passim*. See also, Ram Ben-Shalom, "The Ban Placed by the Community of Barcelona on the Study of Philosophy and Allegorical

Preaching — A New Study," *Revue des Etudes juives* (July-December, 2000): 401-3, on Church pressure on Jews and Judaism in the 13th century, when formal kabbalah arose.

31 See, e.g., Nissim Rejwan, *Israel's Place in the Middle East* (Gainesville, Florida: University Press of Florida, 1998), pp. 81-100. A traumatic external cause may also induce a mystical effect that is not immediate, but survives, "underground" as it were, for a long period, emerging when circumstances are propitious; Ostow, *Ultimate Intimacy*, pp. 140-1, and particular case histories cited, *passim*.

32 Idel, *Messianic Mystics*, e.g., pp. 79-84, 97-100, 137, 144-52. A mystic who waits until the time seems propitious for a suicidal act, that will bring an apocalyptic and messianic end to history and the suffering of his people, still acts out of hopelessness and not — as Idel suggests — out of hope; compare *ibid.*, and Idel and Ostow, *Jewish Mystical Leaders*, p. 7. See also note 2.

33 See note 22; Dan, *Jewish Mysticism*, vol. I, pp. 69-70, and vol. II, pp. 350-5.

34 See, e.g., Scholem, *Major Trends*, *passim*. (See further Appendix 5). Recent scholarship makes the case that Diaspora Jews did not sense any problem in their decision not to make their residence in the Jewish state existing at the time, when this did not threaten their Jewish identity. They maintained this view even during times when they appropriated elements of Gentile culture to their own uses. They enjoyed life in their host countries, but Jerusalem remained their true home.. They maintained their identity as part of the Jewish people or nation, viewing themselves "as colonists" from the land of Israel, living abroad. See Erich S. Gruen, *Diaspora: Jews Amidst Greeks and Romans* (Cambridge: Harvard University Press, 2002); review by Allen Kerkeslager, *Shofar* (Fall 2004): 176-8.

35 Bernard Lewis, *The Muslim Discovery of Europe* (New York: W.W. Norton & Company, 1982), pp. 295-308. See also *idem.*, *What Went Wrong? Western Impact and Middle Eastern Response* (New York: Oxford University Press, 2002), *passim*; and Karen Elliot House's review, "Why Islam Fell From Grace," *Wall Street Journal*, January 11, 2002, pp. W1 and 10. Lewis argues that Islam's failure to match the Western world's rise in the last 300 years is because of three major factors: its continuing integration of church and state, religion and politics; its unwillingness, because of a religion-based hubris, to consider what might be of value in other cultures; and its propensity to blame others for its decline instead of examining its own culture for causes. In contrast, Western civilization has drawn its strength from its simultaneous embrace of Greek knowledge and Jewish holiness or morality; see also Jeffrey Hart, *Smiling Through the Cultural Catastrophe* (New Haven: Yale University Press, 2001). These books raise questions that require serious introspection by Jewish scholars, including not only rabbis but academic scholars as well. I see no reasons, based on the need for academic objectivity, for the latter to avoid these issues. To the contrary; we need their objectivity to address the questions.

36 See Thomas Cahill, *The Gifts of the Jews* (New York: Random House, 1998). Some of the other contradictions I have alluded to include the following: How are mystical separation and anti-rationalism consistent with the Talmudic dictum that there is wisdom in the non-Jewish world (*Sanhedrin* 17a and *Menahot* 65a; *Lam. Rabbah.* 2:13, 17)? How do they allow Jewry to carry out the Biblical injunction of destroying Amalek in every generation in which nations appear that deliberately attack and terrorize defenseless, innocent non-combatants (*Deut.* 25:17-19)? How do they allow Jewry to engage in *imitatio dei* (*Ex.* 34:6-7), by which Jews are commanded, *inter alia*, to be creative in improving the world

(*tiqqun olam*), as God did in the process of Creation? (See, e.g., Irving A. Agus, ed., *Responsa of the Tosafists* [New York: Talpiot-Yeshiva University, 1954], Responsum 12 — where the rationalist Rabbenu Tam [see n. 15] embraces *tiqqun olam*; and Walter Wurzburger, comparing kabbalistic and modern Orthodox views on *imitatio dei*, "Rav Soloveitchik as a Posek of Postmodern Orthodoxy," in *Engaging Modernity*, ed. Moshe Sokol [Northvale, New Jersey: Jason Aronson, Inc. 1997], p. 124, and "Confronting the Challenge of the Value of Modernity," *The Torah u-Madda Journal* [1989]:104-112). And, finally, how does the separatist, anti-rationalist worldview, with its core belief in an independent power of evil in the world, allow for the concept of man's free will to conquer evil by the use of his human faculties (*Deut.* 8:1-20, 11:26-8, 27:1-26, 28:1-69, 29:1-28, and 30:1-20)?

Contrast these obligations (recently discussed by Saul Berman, "How a Jew Faces Evil," *The Jerusalem Report*, January 28, 2002, p. 55) with Hasidism's approach to the Holocaust, which was essentially passive acceptance of this evil as God's will, a test of a mystic's faith, and an opportunity to experience communion with God (*devequt*); see Pesach Schindler, *Hasidic Responses to the Holocaust in Light of Hasidic Thought* (Hoboken: Ktav, 1990). Compare Israel Yuval, "Vengeance and Damnation, Blood and Defamation: From Jewish Martyrdom to Blood Libel Accusations," *Zion* (1993):33-90, and the various responses and Yuval's reply in *Zion* (1994):169-414, dealing with the attitude of despair over any future for Jewry that motivated the suicidal martyrs of 1096, with Cahill's *The Gifts of the Jews*, pp. 146, 156, 240, 249.

What shall Jewry say about the vision of redemption in Lurianic kabbalah that, when Israel "mends" the world, it does not mend the nations of the world nor bring them closer to holiness, "but rather extracts the holiness from them and thereby destroys their ability to exist…," so that this form of kabbalah, which is so prominent today in Jewish religious thought, rejects the idea that Israel serves to "elevate the rest of humanity"? See Gerald J. Blidstein, "*Tikkun Olam*," (citing I. Tishby's analysis, and a similar overall perspective in the work of Gershom Scholem), in David Shatz, Chaim I. Waxman, Nathan J. Diament, eds., *Tikkun Olam: Social Responsibility in Jewish Thought and Law* (Northvale, New Jersey: Jason Aronson, Inc., 1997), p. 49. How do Jews explain to the world the "central text of Habad Hasidism," *Tanya,* whose author, rabbi Shneur Zalman of Liadi, Habad's founder, maintained — according to Allan Nadler — that "Jewish and gentile souls are fundamentally different, the former 'Divine' and the latter 'animalistic.'" Nadler adds that this viewpoint has "gained ground in recent decades, particularly among charedi thinkers;" "Charedi Rabbis Rush to Disavow Anti-Gentile Book," *Forward*, December 19, 2003, pp. 1, 4. See also the alleged recent statements of a *haredi* rabbi which has caused widespread controversy in the Orthodox world; ibid., and Steven I. Weiss, "Ultra-Orthodox Officials Go to Bat for Anti-Gentile Book," *Forward*, January 16, 2004, pp. 1, 19; and, on a related issue, see Nacha Cattan, "Critics Slam Rabbi, Y.U., Over Article on Gentiles," *Forward*, ibid., p. 19. Contrast this with the classical view of Judaism's gifts to the world in Jonathan Sacks, *A Letter in the Scroll: Understanding Our Jewish Identity and Exploring the Legacy of the World's Oldest Religion* (New York: The Free Press, 2000).

37 "The Israel Suicide Drive," *The Jerusalem Post International Edition*, July 2, 1994, p. 15; see also, Yoram Hazony, *The Jewish State: The Struggle for Israel's Soul* (New York: Basic Books, 2000); and Yoram Hazony, Michal B. Oren, and Daniel Polisar, *The Quiet Revolution in the Teaching of Zionist History: A Comparative Study of Education Ministry Textbooks on the 20th Century* (Jerusalem: The Shalem Center,

2000), Research Report No. 1. Perhaps the common European Ashkenazic heritage of post-Zionist secularists and ultra-Orthodox mystics provides a causal linkage; see, e.g., Shepkaru, "From After Death," pp.41-4.

38 *Halakhic Man*, tr. Lawrence Kaplan (Philadelphia: Jewish Publication Society, 1983), pp. 30-82; Faur, *Homo Mysticus, passim.*

39 See, e.g., Idel, *Kabbalah*, pp. 130, 148, 151, 223-9, including highly charged ideas of sexual relations between the *sefirot* and between man and God; Guttmann, *Philosophies of Judaism*, Chapter 1; Dan, *Jewish Mysticism*, vol. II, pp. xviii, 208, vol. III, p. 331, and vol. IV, p. 196; Scholem, *Major Trends, passim*; Allan Nadler, *The Faith of the Mithnagdim* (Baltimore, Maryland: Johns Hopkins University Press, 1997); and see generally, Idel, *Kabbalah*, Chapters 3-6. The strong element of mystical union in kabbalah stresses God's immanence, with its pantheistic elements, in contrast to the importance of Divine transcendence in classical Biblical and Rabbinic Judaism; see, e.g., Arlow, "The Emergence of Mystical Leadership: A Multidisciplinary Analysis," in Idel and Ostow, eds., *Jewish Mystical Leaders* , p. 203. Mystical union with God "meant to Jews — at least to Jews living inside the Muslim civilization — nothing but blasphemy and self-deification;" S.D. Goitein, *Jews and Arabs* (New York: Schocken, 1974), pp. 153-4. On the issue of evil, see also note 65. In the *Zohar* (III 152a; see the *Sulam* edition [Jerusalem: Yeshivat Kol Yehudah, 1991], vol. 13, *parashat be-ha`alotekha*, nos. 57 ff.), only those who "stood on Mount Sinai" can penetrate to "the root principal of all, namely, the real Torah." I assume that this must refer to those who claim to have secretly received this secret meaning over the centuries between Sinai and the emergence of kabbalah, some 2500 years later. (See further Appendix 6). On the incomprehensibility of the Zohar (from which I would conclude that its content is in the eye of its readers), see Jacob Neusner, "Mystical and Maddening," *The Jerusalem Post*, March 19, 2004, *Up Front* magazine, p. 33, reviewing, *The Zohar*, Daniel C. Matt, tr. and comm. (Stanford: Stanford University Press, 2003).

40 See , e.g., Spiegel, Band and Elitzur, cited in note 21; Katz, *Out of the Ghetto* (New York: Schocken, 1978), pp. 161-2; Scholem, *The Messianic Idea in Judaism* (New York: Schocken, 1971), pp. 190-193 (but Tishby disagrees, *ibid.*); Ostow, *Ultimate Intimacy, passim*; and compare Jonathan Sacks, "Markets and Morals," *First Things* (August-September 2000): 23-8; Scholem, *Major Trends*, Ninth Lecture. See also notes 34 and 54. See also Eliezer Don-Yehiya, "Two Movements of Messianic Awakening and their Attitude Toward Halakhah, Nationalism and Democracy: The Cases of Habad and Gush Emunim," Moshe Sokol, ed., *Tolerance, Dissent and Democracy* (Northvale, N.J.: Jason Aronson, Inc. 2002), pp. 261-310, noting that Habad seeks to embrace and redeem individual Jews, not Jews as a nation; thus, it is against Zionism along with other forms of modern nationalism, and sees no messianic significance in the state of Israel (pp. 263-75).

41 See, generally, Faur, *Homo Mysticus*, pp. 1-19, 79-82, 126, and *idem.*, *In the Shadow of History*, pp. 1-25; Dan, *Jewish Mysticism*, vol. III, p. 42; J.J. Schacter, ed., *Judaism's Encounter with Other Cultures* (Northvale, New Jersey: Jason Aronson Inc., 1997), *passim*; Allan Nadler, "Rationalism, Romanticism, Rabbis and Rebbes," Inaugural Lecture of Director of Research (YIVO Institute for Jewish Research, 1992), *passim*; Blidstein, *"Tikkun Olam,"* pp. 48-50. The conflict between the rationalism of classical rabbinic Judaism compared to Jewish mystical movements is exemplified by Nahmanides' stated intention to "free his people from the embrace of the outside world and the lure of its culture...and favors..."; see Baer, *Jews in Christian Spain*, vol. I, p. 104. (See further Appendix 7). On kabbalistic misogyny,

see Sharon Faye Cohen, "Kabbalistic Physiology: Isaac the Blind, Nachmanides and Moses De Leon on Menstruation," *AJS Rev.* (Nov 2004): 317-40.

The close connection of asceticism, magic, mysticism, and obsessive sexuality with Lurianic kabbalah has recently been developed by Lawrence Fine, *Physician of the Soul, Healer of the Cosmos: Isaac Luria and his Kabbalistic Fellowship* (Stanford: Stanford University Press, 2003), and review by Allan Nadler, "The Other Preacher From the Galilee," *Forward*, March 19, 2004, pp. 1, 10.

42 Lawrence Kaplan, "*Daas Torah:* A Modern Conception of Rabbinic Authority," in *Rabbinic Authority and Personal Autonomy*, ed. Moshe Z. Sokol (Northvale, New Jersey: Jason Aronson, Inc., 1992), pp. 1-60; and Moshe Z. Sokol, "Personal Autonomy and Religious Authority," *ibid.*, p. 171. On the flight of Jews from Orthodox Judaism as soon as the opportunity to do so arose, see Haym Soloveitchik, "Rupture and Reconstruction: The Transformation of Contemporary Orthodoxy," *Tradition* (Summer 1994):64-130, at p. 70; and Jeffrey S. Gurock, "Twentieth Century American Orthodoxy's Era of Non-Observance," *The Torah U-Madda Journal* (2000):99.

The trend to stringencies can be traced from German pietism, to the *Zohar* (which elevates poverty), Lurianic kabbalah, Hasidism, the Musar movement, and the recent history of stringencies discussed by Haym Soloveitchik in "Rupture and Reconstruction," *passim*; Simcha Krauss, "Orthodoxy's Retreat From Modernity," *The Jewish Week*, December 14, 2001, p. 28. See also note 21. (See further Appendix 8).

43 Dan, *Jewish Mysticism*, vol. III, ch. 1, and vol. IV, ch. 4 (competition with non-Hasidic *haredi* groups); Scholem, *Major Trends* , pp. 2, 8, 19-20, 146-9; *Zohar* III 152a. Sometimes, the extreme application of the separatist impulse of Hasidism can cause self-inflicted harm, e.g., the harm to the gene pool from the prohibition by some sects of inter-sect marriages; see Erik Schechter, "Rising from the Ashes," *Jerusalem Report*, May 22, 2000, p. 28.

44 Dan, *Jewish Mysticism*, vol. I, pp. xvii-xxvii, and Chapter 1, esp. pp. 75 and 101.

45 *Ibid.*, vol. II, pp. 19-62, 315-27; Ivan Marcus, *Piety*, *passim*, esp. pp. 21-3, 117-18, 150-1; Scholem, *Major Trends*, pp. 80-118. See also, Judah the Pious (Yehudah he-Hasid), *Sefer Hasidim*, ed. Judah Wistinetzki (Frankfurt am Main: M.A. Wahrmann, 1924), sec. 1530.

46 Scholem, *Major Trends*, Third Lecture; Y. Baer, *Jews in Christian Spain*, vol. II, pp. 196-7; Ephraim Kanarfogel, *Peering*, *passim*.

47 Dan, *Jewish Mysticism*, vol. III, pp. 40-3.

48 *Ibid.*

49 *Ibid.*, p. 42.

50 Dan, *Jewish Mysticism*, vol. II, pp. 51-2, 179-200, 347-51, and vol. IV, p. 152; Gershom Scholem, *Origins of the Kabbalah*, ed. R. J. Zvi Werblowsky, tr. Allan Arkush (Princeton: Princeton University Press, 1990), pp. 404-8; Daniel Jeremy Silver, *Maimonidean Criticism and the Maimonidean Controversy* (Leiden: Brill, 1965), ch. 9 and p. 98. See also Ben-Sasson, *Jewish People*, pp. 543-544; Faur, "A Crisis of Categories, pp. 41-62, "Two Models," pp. 5-46, *In the Shadow of History*, pp. 14-18, and "Anti-Maimonidean Demons," *The Annual of Rabbinic Judaism* (2003). Yitzhak Baer claims that the ban on science and metaphysics excluded astronomy and Maimonides' works, including the *Guide*; *Jews in Christian Spain*, vol. 1, pp. 301-302. There is a debatable story that Jonah Girondi changed his

view about Maimonides' philosophic works in the early 1240s, after witnessing the burning of the Talmud in Paris in 1240, which he interpreted as punishment for the successful anti-Maimonidean incitement of the Inquisition to burn Maimonides' works about ten years earlier; see Ta-Shma, "Rabbi Jonah Girondi...," in Idel and Ostow, *Jewish Mystical Leaders*, p. 157. Ta-Shma makes much of the fact that Spanish rabbis continued to accept philosophy (as well as kabbalah) even after the Maimonidean Controversy, until the fifteenth century (*ibid.*, pp. 164-5, 175-6). But this is not nearly as important as the power and influence that kabbalah, and kabbalists, acquired through their activity in that controversy, to the point where they more than equaled the influence of Maimonidean rationalism and its supporters by the end of that period (*ibid.*). See generally, Bernard Septimus, *Hispano-Jewish Culture in Transition* (Cambridge: Harvard University Press, 1982), ch. 4. Cf. on this entire matter, Berger, "Judaism and General Culture," pp. 85-108; Moshe Idel, "Nahmanides: Halakhah, Kabbalah and Spiritual Leadership," in Idel and Ostow, *Jewish Mystical Leaders*, p. 90. Their view of Ramban's role is more favorable than the conclusion I draw from Baer's discussion (see text at note 51).

51 (The balance of the text discussion here, to paragraph "2." dealing with Moses Isserles and Mordecai Jaffe, is based on the citations in this note, except as otherwise stated.) See Baer, *Jews in Christian Spain*, vol. 1, pp. 96-110; Dan, *Jewish Mysticism*, vol. II, p. 181 and vol. III, p. 42; Joseph Hacker, "The Intellectual Activity of the Jews of the Ottoman Empire," *Jewish Thought in the Seventeenth Century*, ed. Isadore Twersky and Bernard Septimus (Cambridge: Harvard University Press, 1987), pp. 95-136; Ben-Sasson, *Jewish People*, pp. 632-3, 734-5; H. J. Zimmels, *Ashkenazim and Sephardim* (London: Marla Publications, 1976), pp. 44-5. See also, *contra* Baer, Berger, "Judaism and General Culture," p. 114: "There is little evidence for the outright Averroist-style skepticism that Yitzhak Baer blames for the apostasy of beleaguered Iberian Jews;" Faur, "Anti-Maimonidean Demons." See also, note 50.

52 Jacob Katz, "Post-Zoharic Relations Between Halakhah and Kabbalah," Bernard Dov Cooperman, ed., *Jewish Thought in the Sixteenth Century* (Cambridge: Harvard University Press, 1983), p. 292 and *passim*; Idel, "Differing Conceptions of Kabbalah in the Early 17th Century;" and Robert Bonfil, "Halakhah, Kabbalah and Society: Some Insights into Rabbi Menahem Azariah De Fano's Inner World," *Jewish Thought in the Seventeenth Century*, ed. Isadore Twersky and Bernard Septimus (Cambridge: Harvard University Press, 1987), pp. 42, 196. See also Katz, *Exclusiveness and Tolerance*, p. 136 (but cf. the scholarly debate on Katz's formulation in David Ruderman, *Jewish Thought and Scientific Discovery in Early Modern Europe* [New Haven: Yale University Press, 1995], pp. 60 ff.); *ibid.*, *passim*, esp. ch. 2; David Berger, "Judaism and General Culture," pp. 87, 123, 134-40; Shlomo Riskin, "Cloud of the Unknown," *Jewish World*, March 8-14, 2002, p. 7.

This opening, for a short time, of Judaism to new ideas and attitudes, is reflected in a number of studies; e.g., Yerushalmi, *Zakhor*, Chapter 3; Isadore Twersky, "Talmudists, Philosophers and Kabbalists: The Quest for Spirituality in the Sixteenth Century;" Robert Bonfil, "Some Reflections on the Place of Azariah de Rossi's *Me'or Enayim* in the Cultural Milieu of Italian Renaissance Jewry;" and Mordechai Breuer, "Modernism and Traditionalism in Sixteenth Century Jewish Historiography: A Study of David Gans' *Tzemach David*" — all of which appear in *Jewish Thought in the Sixteenth Century*, ed. Bernard Dov Cooperman

(Cambridge: Harvard University Press, 1982), pp. 23-88. (Note the reference to the connections between the cosmopolitan intelligentsia of Prague and the Cracow community of Isserles, *ibid.*, pp. 52-53). On Isserles and the propriety of studying the material world and its nature, see R. Moses Isserles, *She'eilot u-Teshuvot* (Amsterdam, 1711), #7, #4c, citing *Megillah* 16a. See also Ben-Sasson, "The Middle Ages," *Jewish People*, pp. 707-15. It is worth noting that, although they knew kabbalah, and used it in some of their writings, the eclectic rabbinic figures discussed above, e.g., Maharal and Menasseh Ben Israel, were generally not kabbalists; see, e.g., Dan, "Manasseh ben Israel: His Attitude Toward the *Zohar* and Lurianic Kabbalah," and "Gershom Scholem: Between History and Historiosophy," *Jewish Mysticism*, vol. IV, pp. 57-66, 160-61 . The roots of the early Haskalah "lay in traditional rabbinic culture and, particularly, in two internal sources of inspiration: first,…the moral and educational criticism of [the Maharal] of Prague…and second, in the idealization of the Sephardic model…;" David J. Sorkin, *The Berlin Haskalah and German Religious Thought* (London: Valentine Mitchell, 2000), p. 40. (See further Appendix 9). On Maharal's stress on the importance of science, see *Be'er Ha'Golah*, Chapter 2 (B. *Pes.* 54a); Yitzchak Adlerstein, "A Tradition That Embraces Looking to the Heavens," *Forward*, January 23, 2004, p. 7. As to Yohanan Alemanno, cf. Hava Tirosh Samuelson, *Happiness in Premodern Judaism* (Cincinnati: Hebrew Union College Press, 2003), pp. 420-1. Her comment seems relevant generally to all kabbalists who sought union with God (*unio mystica*), and probably to a *lesser* extent to the philosophic Alemanno.

As to Idel's idea about what might have been, and my elaboration of it, see his "Differing Concepts of Kabbalah in the Early 17th Century," *Jewish Thought in the Seventeenth Century*, pp. 150-2, 178, 196-7 (the papers by Alexander Altmann, Robert Bonfil, Joseph Dan, and David Ruderman, in that volume, are also relevant); *idem.*, "The Magical and Neoplatonic Interpretations of the Kabbalah in the Renaissance," *Essential Papers On Jewish Culture in Renaissance and Baroque Italy*, ed. David B. Ruderman (New York: NYU Press, 1992), pp. 107-69; *idem.*, "Major Currents in Italian Kabbalah between 1560 and 1660," *ibid.*, pp. 345-68; Ben-Sasson, *Jewish People*, pp. 707-15; Soloveitchik, "Rupture and Reconstruction" pp. 64-130.

Marvin Fox applied a kind of hybrid analysis, similar to my own in some respects, in concluding that Rav Kook was — a poet! See his "Rav Kook: Neither Philosopher Nor Kabbalist," *Rabbi Abraham Isaac Kook and Jewish Spirituality*, ed. David Shatz and Lawrence Kaplan (New York: NYU Press, 1995), pp. 78-87. See also, Judith Bleich, "Rabbinic Responses to Non-Observance in the Modern Era," J.J. Schacter, ed., *Jewish Tradition and the Non-Traditional Jew* (Northvale, N.J.: Jason Aronson, Inc., 1992), pp. 104-15 (Kook versus Hasidim and other *haredim* on the need for modern rabbinical seminaries); Shnayer Z. Leiman, "Rabbinic Openness to General Culture in the Early Modern Period in Western and Central Europe," *Judaism's Encounter*, pp. 150-1; David Shatz, "Rav Kook and Modern Orthodoxy," *Engaging Modernity*, pp. 97-115; Aviezer Ravitzky, "Hadash Min Ha-Torah," *ibid.*, p. 51; and Bezalel Naor, "Plumbing Rav Kook's Pantheism," *ibid.*, p. 88, contrasting Rav Kook and Hasidism on kabbalah and Modern Orthodoxy. Cook was a mystic not in the sense of the definitions, and the beliefs and activities discussed earlier in this paper, but as an instrumental idea, to help view Jewish history as a process that is part of the Divine potential in, and the holiness of, the universe. Jews must unite with the Jewish people, with the Land of Israel, and, ultimately with Torah, to realize this Divine plan. Zionism, secular Jews, even atheists, were — in rebelling against the "atrophy of Judaism" — instruments of the return to this new harmony. They were not simply "destructive forces" but a natural reaction to a *galut* Judaism that had become over-spiritualized, and had "lost its contact with nature, work, society, and culture, with the fullness of human experience." See Jonathan Sacks, *One People — Tradition, Modernity and Jewish Unity* (Oxford, U.K.: The Littman Library of Jewish Civilization, 1993), pp. 72-4. I would describe all of these medieval-early modern personalities, mentioned above in connection with Idel's idea, as rational-philosophical rather than mythical; they were inquiring, optimistic and open to new ideas, with varied interests, and not wedded even to Cordoverian kabbalah as their exclusive or even primary access to truth. In their embrace of the world, they hearken back to Immanuel of Rome (fourteenth century) and the great figures of Golden Age Spain; see, e.g., Berger, "Judaism and General Culture," p. 126.

52a It is difficult to call R. Joseph Karo a mystic. He did receive an angelic voice that he experienced solely as it forced itself through Karo's lips; Karo did not see the *maggid*, as he called the angel, nor did he hear his message. It just came mumbling out through his lips; Idel, *Kabbalah*, pp. 84-6. These communications were unsolicited by Karo in any way, in contrast to mystics, who *seek* union with the Divinity; see Idel, *Kabbalah*, p. 35. The *maggid* conveyed no mysteries of heaven. He encouraged, chided and instructed Karo on matters of how to live his life — including, sometimes, advice on halakhic matters, which left little if any trace in his halakhic writings, although Karo did use Zoharic halakhic material on occasion to support some halakhic conclusions, not repudiated in the Talmud. But Karo never sought mystical union or ascent to heaven, nor access to Divine secrets, and there is no evidence that he embraced any formal theosophy or even any formal theurgical ideology, although he struggled to reconcile the ten *sefirot* with God's thirteen attributes. His use of kabbalistic ideas was primarily in offering homiletical interpretations of the commandments. Of course, he certainly must have participated in many or some of the public mystical rites in Safed during his years there when the city was populated with many mystics involved in mystical meetings and discussions. In that regard, we are not aware that he was invited to Isaac Luria's meetings with his disciples, or sought to be. He is barely mentioned by Scholem, Dan or Idel.

Joseph Perl, the noted anti-hasidic *maskil,* noted that Isaac Alfasi, Maimonides *and Karo*, in their codifications of Jewish law, had cleansed Judaism of its mystical accretions; see Nancy Sinkoff, The *Maskil,* the Convert and the *Agunah, AJS Rev.* (November 2003):288.

The only evidence of a possible mystical connection is Karo's wish to die as a martyr, to be burnt as a sacrificial offering, as a *kiddush ha-Shem*. He recognized that this could not happen under Moslem rule at that time, but only in Christian lands, *from which he had fled*. The *maggid* first assured him that he would realize this wish, but later assured him that the Moslems would prevail over the Christians in their continuing struggle in this period. If — along with the evidence above — we reckon these angelic experiences as reflecting Karo's own subconscious creation, as his biographer, R. J. Zvi Werblowsky, notes (see below), I believe there is ample reason for my difficulty in considering Karo as a mystic, much less a mystic who undermines the general scholarly description of mystical thought, worldview and activity as I have presented it earlier in this paper. On the other hand, Karo certainly saw his primary mission, as did his *maggid*, to create a permanent halakhic guide for the Jewish people, on how they should live in this world at every occasion. Thus, we can hardly draw objections, from Karo's inspiring and productive life, concerning the problematic aspects of Jewish mysticism that I raise in my paper. See generally on Karo, R. J. Zvi Werblowsky, *Joseph Karo: Lawyer and Mystic* (Philadelphia: Jewish Publication Society, 1977), esp. pp. 19 ff., 21, 83, 150-60, 190, 255, 257; S. Schechter, "Safed in the Sixteenth Century," *The Jewish Expression*, Judah Goldin, ed. (New Haven: Yale University Press, 1976), pp. 258-311; and Jacob Katz, "Post-Zoharic Relations Between Halakhah and Kabbalah," *Jewish Thought in the Sixteenth Century*, pp. 301-4.

53 Dan, *Jewish Mysticism*, vol. III, p. 42; Nadler, *Mithnagdim*, Chapter 6; Raphael Mahler, *Hasidism and the Jewish Enlightenment* (Philadelphia: Jewish Publication Society, 1985), Chapter 2; Idel, *Hasidism*, pp. 34-35; David Fishman, "A Polish Rabbi Meets the Berlin Haskalah: The Case of R. Barukh Schick," *AJS Rev.* (1987):95-121; Jacob Katz, Introduction; Emanuel Etkes, "Immanent Factors and External Influences in the Development of the Haskalah Movement in Russia," in *Toward Modernity*, ed. Jacob Katz (New Brunswick, New Jersey: Transaction, 1987), pp. 1-32; Israel Bartal, "'The Heavenly City of Germany and Absolutism a la Mode d'Autriche: The Rise of the Haskalah in Galicia," *ibid.*, pp. 33-42; Emanuel Etkes, "The Gaon of Vilna and the Haskalah Movement: Image and Reality," in Joseph Dan, ed., *BINAH: Studies in Jewish Thought* (New York: Praeger, 1989), vol. 2, pp. 147 ff. See also *Renewing the Past...*, Brann and Sutcliffe, eds., *passim*.

Recent scholarship has begun to challenge the long-held view that the emancipation of Jews in Europe (c. 1650-1900 and not 1770-1870) bore responsibility for dissolution of a cohesive Jewish community and for the consequent centrifugal effects of assimilation; see, e.g., David Sorkin, "Port Jews and the Three Regions of Emancipation," *Port Jews*, David Cesarani, ed. (Portland, Or: Frank Cass, 2002), pp. 31-3. On the GRA's opposition to Hasidic Kabbalism and his relationship to the Haskalah, see discussion by Eliyahu Stern, "Modern Rabbinic Historiography and the Legacy of Elijah of Vilna: A Review Essay," *Modern Judaism* (February 2004): 85-90; and D. Eliach, *The Gaon: The Story of His Life and an Explanation of the Teachings of Our Teacher and Rabbi, the GRA* (Jerusalem: Moreshet Yeshivot, 2002), Vol. III.

54 Moshe Samet, "The Beginnings of Orthodoxy," *Modern Judaism* (October 1988): 249-70; Katz, *Exclusiveness and Tolerance*, 166-8; *idem.*, *Jewish Emancipation and Self-Emancipation* (Philadelphia: Jewish Publication Society, 1986), pp. 128, 162. See also Berger, "Judaism and General Culture," pp. 138-9; Perl, "No Two Minds...," note 53. Allan Nadler, discussing Hungarian Hasidic groups, alludes to their causing a bitter split in Hungarian Jewry in the nineteenth century; Eric Siblin, "Dancing to the Maple Leaf Rav," *The Jerusalem Report*, March 27, 2000, p. 46. See generally, Howard Lupovitch, "Between Orthodox Judaism and Neology: The Origins of the Status Quo Movement," *Jewish Social Studies*, n.s. (Winter, 2003): 122-53. On Emden's equivocal and ambiguous views on kabbalah, Hasidism and the *Zohar*, see Yehudah Friedlander, "The Struggle of the Mitnagdim and Maskilim against Hasidism: Rabbi Jacob Emden and Judah Leib Mieses," *New Perspectives on the Haskalah*, Shmuel Feiner and David Sorkin, eds. (London: Littman Library of Jewish Civilization, 2001), pp. 102-112.

55 Marc B. Shapiro, *Between the Yeshiva World and Modern Orthodoxy: The Life and Works of Rabbi Jehiel Jacob Weinberg, 1884-1966* (Portland, Oregon: Littman Library of Jewish Civilization, 2000); *idem.*, "Scholars and Friends: Rabbi Jehiel Jacob Weinberg and Professor Samuel Atlas," *The Tora u-Madda Journal* (1997):105-21; David Singer, "Rabbi Weinberg's Agony," *First Things* (2001):34-

41, a review essay of Shapiro's book.

56 Nadler, "Rabbis and Rebbes," p. 4; see also David Berger's recent book, *The Rebbe, the Messiah, and the Scandal of Orthodox Indifference* (Portland, Oregon: Littman Library of Jewish Civilization, 2001), and my review essay, "Challenging Lubavitch's New Messianic Claims," *Midstream* (December, 2001):30-5.

57 Nadler, *Mithnagdim*, Chapters 4-5.

58 *Idem.*, "Rabbis and Rebbes;" see also, Dan, "Gershom Scholem: Between Mysticism and Scholarship," *Jewish Mysticism*, vol. IV, pp. 225-58.

59 See, e.g., Kanarfogel, *Peering*, p. 208, commenting on David Ruderman's observation that the German pietists had a scientific awareness. See also Faur, *Homo Mysticus*, p. 126; and David Fromkin, *The Way of the World* (New York: Vintage Books, 2000), pp. 132-3, noting that the early seventeenth century marked the separation of science from kabbalah and other magic and esoteric activity and belief. The problematic nature of Ruderman's broader view on the compatibility of kabbalah and science is reflected historically in the challenges by kabbalists to the introduction of rationalistic elements into Judaism during the past five hundred years, discussed above, and reflected currently, for example, in the basic incompatibility between Modern Orthodoxy (and its embrace of *madda*, or secular knowledge) and kabbalah; see David Shatz, "Rav Kook and Modern Orthodoxy: the Ambiguities of 'Openness,'" in Sokol, ed., *Engaging Modernity*, pp. 97-98. As Faur observes: "Mythical ideology will affect and finally dominate and subvert scientific progress;" *Homo Mysticus*, p. 126. See also note 60.

The continuing attraction of Hasidism to modern Jews, secular as well as religious, whether of Ashkenazi or Oriental origin, seems to be attributable to the mystical leadership of the *zaddik* or the *rebbe* of a particular Hasidic group. Another cause may be their fascination with the idea of mystical connection with the Divine, the ideas of the "nothingness" and "death" that accompany that union, and its erotic, sexual aspects; see, e.g., Dan, *Jewish Mysticism*, vol. III, pp. 66-69, 126, and vol. IV, pp. 76-85. See also, Idel, *Kabbalah*, pp. 62-70, 130, 148, 151, 223-5; Wolfson, *Speculum, passim*; Eli Shai, *The Messiah of Incest: New and Uncensored History of the Sexual Element in Jewish Mystical History* (Tel Aviv: Yediot Aharonot, 2002) (Hebrew); and David Rosenberg, *Dreams of Being Eaten Alive: The Literary Core of the Kabbalah* (New York: Harmony, 2000).

60 See, e.g., Nahmanides on *Gen.* 17:1 and 46:15, *Exod.* 13:16, and *Lev.* 26:11; see also his statement at *Lev.* 18:4 that Jews should abandon affairs of the world for *yihud* (communing or uniting with God). See generally, Ta-Shma, "Rabbi Jonah Girondi," p. 176; Faur, "Two Models," and *idem.*, "A Crisis of Categories," pp. 41-64; cf. Dan, *Jewish Mysticism*, vol. III, pp. 411-13, arguing that Nahmanides used witchcraft and demonology only as symbols of the miraculous element in the world under God's continuing governance. This sounds apologetic to me, because the idea of the miraculous as part of God's providence can be argued without recourse to witchcraft and demonology as symbols or otherwise. In a similar apologetic vein is Septimus' attempt to show how Nahmanides, viewed in a certain way, embraced a concept of nature, while conceding that the kabbalist's "nature" is "quite different from its rationalistic counterpart;" Septimus, *Hispano-Jewish Culture*, p. 111. Rav Aharon Lichtenstein, "Torah and General Culture: Confluence or Conflict," in Schacter, ed., *Judaism's Encounter* , pp. 237-39, shows that Nahmanides' attitude to science and philosophy was, at best, ambivalent. He [Nachmanides] "took pains to *insist upon their problematic aspects as avenues to*

truth, and to note that recourse to them, while perhaps necessary in certain circumstances, reflected weakness rather than strength, *perhaps even with respect to the scientific and medical realms"* (emphasis added). Note the connection between mystical *yihud* and the same term used in 1096 as synonymous with martyrdom; see Katz, *Exclusiveness and Tolerance*, pp. 88-9. Regarding Nahmanides' view that the world operates only by Divine miracles, see Saul Berman's insightful address, "Patriotism, Zionism and the Hand of God in History," as reported by Abigail Klein Leichman, "Berman Urges Action, Shopping, Prayer," *The Jewish Standard*, April 19, 2002, p. 9, explaining Maimonides' view contrary to Nahmanides', and the benefits of Rambam's reconciliation of human free will and the laws of nature with God's omnipotent ability — rarely used and never apprehended in advance — to control all events in humanity's and nature's realms. (See further Appendix 10).

61 Moshe Halbertal and Avishai Margalit, *Idolatry*, tr. Naomi Goldblum (Cambridge: Harvard University Press, 1992), pp. 199-200; Faur, "Two Models," pp. 7-17 (Faur regards idolatry as an aspect of mystical anthropocentrism — see note 25); Dan, *Jewish Mysticism*, vol. III, pp. 114-16; Abraham P. Socher, "Of Divine Cunning and Prolonged Madness: Amos Funkenstein on Maimonides' Historical Reasoning," *Jewish Social Studies*, n.s. (Fall 1999): 6-29, esp. p. 20; Gershom Scholem, R.J. Zvi Werblowsky, ed., and Allan Arkush, tr., *Origins of the Kabbalah* (Philadelphia: Jewish Publication Society, 1987, 1990), pp. 54, 398-99; Faur, *Homo Mysticus*, pp. 4, 9-13, 94, 121; and *idem.*, *In the Shadow of History*, pp. 10, 46, 74, 112, 127. Kanarfogel touches on issues of idolatry in *Peering*, pp. 194-95.

62 Nahmanides, a founder of formal kabbalah, asserted that idolatry only exists in kabbalah when one prays to *one* of the ten *sefirot* in isolation from the Divinity as a whole; see Halbertal, *Idolatry*, pp. 194-95. On Nahmanides and trinitarian doctrines in kabbalah, see Faur, "Two Models," pp. 43-46, and "Anti-Maimonidean Demons," sec. V.

63 Halbertal and Margalit, *Idolatry*, pp. 236-41.

64 See, e.g., *ibid.*, pp. 194, 198. Pantheism, with all of its dangers to monotheistic belief and normative practices, is an aspect of mysticism; see Scholem, *Major Trends*, pp. 221-25, 347-48. See also Berkovits, *God, Man and Reason*, pp. 39-40 (re pantheism). Cf. Pinkas Halevi Horowitz, *Shnei Luhot ha-Brit* (Jerusalem, 1993), *Sha'ar Otiyot Aleph* (some kabbalists accept Maimonides' 13 principles of Jewish faith).

65 See his "Worlds, Angels and Men," *Jewish Spectator* (Fall, 2000):10. The issue between the kabbalist, Isaac Luria, whose ideas dominated Jewish ideology after the sixteenth century, and his contemporary in Safed, Moses Cordovero, on the Divine roots of evil, is discussed in Dan, *Jewish Mysticism*, vol. I, p. 21 and vol. III, Chapter 16. As Joseph Dan has summarized:

> The unique position of the *Zohar* in the history of Jewish thought...is that demonic phenomena are related to, and reveal, the powers of the *sitra ahra* — the other side or left side, namely the evil element within the Divine world. The *Zohar* and all the kabbalists who followed it, including in this field Lurianic kabbalah, regarded demons, witches and their deeds as part of the cosmic conflict between good and evil which is the worldly reflection of the mythological conflict between God and Satan. See "Menasseh ben Israel's *Nishmat Hayyim* and the Concept of Evil in Seventeenth Century

Jewish Thought," *Jewish Thought in the Seventeenth Century* (Cambridge: Harvard University Press, 1987), p. 71.

In the *Zohar*, evil is a potentiality within God, and is let loose in the world by Adam's sin in the Garden of Eden. This separates the feminine *Shekhinah* from the male aspect of the Godhead, and they can only be united by Jews studying the Torah and performing the commandments according to the secrets of kabbalah.

The Lurianic view of evil, as an independent power, is remarkably similar to the Christian view that Satan cannot be entirely defeated even by God. See also Tirosh-Samuelson, *Happiness in Pre-modern Judaism*, pp. 300-1, 322-5, on the similar treatment of evil in the *Zohar*. This view, as Joel Carmichael points out, "explains the necessity of the church," which replaced the originally anticipated (by Paul) Kingdom of God — which failed to materialize. See Joel Carmichael, "Mystical Anti-Semitism and Xenophobia," *Midstream* (April 1986):15-16. Cf. Idel, *Hasidism*, pp. 41-2, on the impact of Shabbetai Zevi on Lurianic kabbalah's primacy. While Buber sought to portray Hasidism as changing Lurianic kabbalah's anti-worldly approach, the better view of scholars is that he was incorrect; see Jerome Gellman, "Buber's Blunder," pp. 20-40. Buber's romanticized view, which has proved attractive to many, is discussed in Joseph Dan, "A Bow to Frumkinian Hasidism," *Modern Judaism* (May 1991):175-94.

Idel portrays kabbalah and its mythological components as part of an "inner process" in Jewish thought. This defies the historical record that it first erupted as *hekhalot* mysticism, *outside* of Talmudic culture (200-500 C.E.), and then again, around the thirteenth century, as kabbalah, seeking redemption by escape from history into prehistory, and preventing appropriate Jewish responses to contemporary challenges of history, based on a mythology that was contrary to the rationalism of classical rabbinic culture; see the discussion of opposing views in Moshe Idel, "Rabbinism Versus Kabbalism: On G. Scholem's Phenomenology of Judaism," *Modern Judaism* (October 1991):281 ff., esp. 290-5; Dan, *Jewish Mysticism*, vol. IV, ch. 7, pp. 149, 153, 177, 179, and *passim*; see also Elior, "Messianic Expectations and the Spiritualization of Religious Life in the Sixteenth Century," in *Essential Papers*, ed. Ruderman, pp. 289-91. (See further Appendix 11).

66 Dan, *Jewish Mysticism*, vol. I, p. 21; Shlomo Riskin, "God's Algebra," *The Jerusalem Post, International Edition*, March 16, 2001, p. 39.

67 Berger, *The Rebbe, passim*. The nature of the experience of *devequt* and *unio mystica* as envisioned by the leaders of Hasidism, with its notion of retrieving Divine knowledge of use to the community as a result of the hasid's ascent experience, and the powers required to achieve that level of spirituality, inevitably meant that the *zaddik* or *rebbe* would soon acquire unique status in this regard and, thereby, in all aspects of community life. Even non-Hasidic Jews accepted his special powers. The *zaddik* also inevitably superseded the rabbi of the community in his claim to greater authority because of what we might loosely call his "Divine connections;" see Dan, *Jewish Mysticism*, vol. IV, pp. 112-28; Katz, *Exclusiveness and Tolerance*, chs. 21-22. In a sense, the Rebbe — as he is now viewed as a quasi-deity by many in Habad — serves a function similar to the *shekhinah*, as an object of adoration and devotion, perhaps even worship, that is interposed between God and the male worshipper. This role of the *shekhinah* arose in the twelfth century in parallel with, and as a response to, the revival of Mary, the mother of Jesus, to an analogous position, interposed between Jesus and Christian worshippers, to both of which feminine figures the male worshipper could be devoted; Arthur Green,

"*Shekhinah*, The Virgin Mary, and the Song of Songs," *AJS Rev.* (April 2002):1-52. Of course, in the case of the Rebbe, this puts the male worshipper in a male-to-male relationship. It may be noted, however, that homoerotic relationships are not uncommon in kabbalah; Wolfson, *Speculum*, pp. 369-72, 396.

68 Berger, *The Rebbe*; see also my article cited in note 53; and Jon D. Levenson, *The Death and Resurrection of the Beloved Son* (New Haven: Yale University Press, 1993).

69 *Ibid*; and Shalom Spiegel, *The Last Trial* (Woodstock, Vermont: Jewish Lights, 1993), pp. 32-44. See also Jose Faur, "De-Authorization of the Law: Paul and the Oedipal Model," *Psychoanalysis and Religion*, Joseph H. Smith, ed. and Susan Handelman, assoc. ed. (Baltimore: Johns Hopkins University Press, 1990), pp. 222-244.

70 Dan, *Jewish Mysticism*, vol. III, pp. 33-46; Scholem, *Major Trends*, pp. 4, 15, 146, 249. See also Idel, *Kabbalah*, pp. xvi, 44-7, 56, 65-70; and Ostow, *Ultimate Intimacy*, p. 28.

71 According to I. Tishby and other scholars, the effect of mystical union is to extract holiness from other nations and destroy their viability and ability to exist; see Blidstein's discussion in *Tikkun Olam*, p. 49. See also note 36.

72 The current situation is described, e.g., in Seffi Rachlevsky, *Hamoro shel Mashiah* ("The Messiah's Donkey") (Tel Aviv, *Yediot Ahronot*, 1998); and Lauren Gelford, "Between the Divide," *The Jerusalem Post Magazine, The Jerusalem Post*, October 27, 2000, pp. 10-11, 13. A start in filling the void between Israel's *haredi* and secular extremes — apart from the Conservative and Reform movements, which are still struggling for a recognition of authenticity from secular Israelis — can be found in *The Torah U- Madda Journal*, which commenced publication in 1989 by Yeshiva University; The Orthodox Forum series of conference volumes, initiated by Dr. Norman Lamm, President of Yeshiva University, in 1989, and published by Jason Aronson, Inc. since that date; and the collection of papers edited by Jacob J. Schacter, *Judaism's Encounter with Other Cultures*, published by Jason Aronson, Inc. in 1997. These papers — generally favorable to Judaism's constructive encounter with other cultures — contain little discussion of the problematic aspects of pietism and mysticism in preventing and delegitimizing any integration of non-Jewish culture with Judaism; but cf. note 71.

73 See Appendix 12.

74 See Walter Wurzburger's view that Modern Orthodoxy offers the greatest promise for the future; "The Sea Change in American Orthodox Judaism: A Symposium," *Tradition* (Summer, 1998): 136-8. See also Lichtenstein, "Torah and General Culture, Confluence and Conflict," in Schacter, ed., *Judaism's Encounter*, pp. 220-92; and Soloveitchik, "Rupture and Reconstruction," p. 81. (See further Appendix 13).

75 "*Nitzhuni Banai*, A Review Essay of *Love and Terror in the God Encounter, The Theological Legacy of Rabbi Joseph B. Soloveitchik*, by David Hartman," *The Edah Journal* (2:1) *Tevet* 5762, p. 7. On Torah and *Madda* (Wisdom), tradition and modernity, as part of Jewish education in Modern Orthodoxy, see Seth Farber, *An American Orthodox Dreamer* (Brandeis University Press, 2003), discussing Soloveitchik's vision.

A recent survey indicates that Modern Orthodoxy constitutes 74% of Orthodox Jews in the New York area, where most Orthodox Jews in the United States live. The criteria for Modern Orthodox (in contrast to *haredi*) was the response to the question of how important the participants felt it was to give their children a college or university education. Only those who responded "very important" were classified as Modern Orthodox; see Gary Rosenblatt, "Modern Orthodox Outnumber Haredim Here," *The Jewish Week*, February 25, 2005, pp. 1, 16-17. See also the editorial, "An Opportunity in Religious Zionism," in *Ha'aretz*, February 27, 2005, p. B4, arguing that current divisions among Israelis on how far to compromise with the Palestinians reflect, in part, the influence on "educated, moderate, knitted kippa-wears," who were "silenced by a group of extremist rabbis who competed with each other in issuing uncompromising rulings, who turned their backs on modernity and human needs, and who nurtured mystical symbols and leaders." The cause or motive was a "messianic clinging to territory and the growing religious extremism in all areas of life," [which] diverted the National Religious Party from its former path "and pushed it to the margins of the extreme right."

76 Gershom Scholem, *On the Kabbalah and its Symbolism* (NY: Schocken, 1965), pp. 99-100; see also, ibid., pp. 88-98, 101-107 (kabbalah as a revolt against classical Biblical and Rabbinic Judaism, including its insistence on Divine transcendence and Divine unity and its rejection of mythical and pantheistic ideologies) and pp. 108-117 (kabbalah's view of evil as demonic forces originating in the Godhead at the time of Creation, and redemption as the union of God with the *Shekhinah* through the "secret magic of human acts" and not from human efforts in history to perfect the world nor even from the efforts of the messiah against the forces of evil on the battlefield).

77 See, e.g., Nadler, "Rabbis and Rebbes," pp. 21-2. Jose Faur — rather surprisingly, given his prior emphasis on the importance of a multi-dimensional Judaism — suggests the benefits of such a role specialization at the end of his penetrating paper, "One-Dimensional Jew, Zero-Dimensional Jew," in *The Annual of Rabbinic Judaism*, ed. Alan J. Avery-Peck, William Scott Green and Jacob Neusner (Leiden: Brill, 1999), p. 50 and n. 76. In such cases, I believe each group will inevitably strive to prove its superiority and assert its dominance.

....

APPENDICES

Appendix 1

The 1096 martyrs were undoubtedly aware of the anonymously written historical work, the book of *Yosippon*, which appeared *circa* 953 C.E., and was accepted and revered by medieval Jewry as the original account by Josephus of the fall of Masada in 73 C.E. *Yosippon* repeats, and thereby supports, from Josephus' original account, in his *Wars of the Jews*, Eleazar's plea to his fellow defenders of Masada to kill their families and themselves and heed the *ancient mystical Indian philosophy* that death is more to be cherished than life, and will liberate their immortal souls to join God in the afterlife that is free of the world's evil and miseries, in a place of eternal purity and peace. See, e.g., Yosef Hayim Yerushalami, *Zakhor* (Seattle: University of Washington Press, 1982), pp. 35-7; *Josephus, Complete Works*, tr. William Whiston (Grand Rapids, Michigan: Kregel Publications, 1981), pp. 601-3. The Talmud's negative attitude toward such martyrdom is evidenced by its silence about Masada. Family murders and suicides similar to those in Rhineland Germany took place in Spain in 1391, when Jews were faced with the choice of death or forced conversion to Christianity; see Yitzhak Baer, *A History of the Jews in Christian Spain* (Philadelphia: Jewish Publication Society, 1978), vol. II, pp. 72, 102, 105-7, 130. It is noteworthy that the Rhineland martyrs recognized that their martyrdom was unprecedented (see the Appendix in Chazan, *First Crusade*, pp. 232, 237); indeed, some Jews who insincerely converted to save their children (and their wives and themselves) were praised for their continued loyalty to God and received from the martyrs messages of consolation and hope that things would work out (*ibid.*, p. 229). This sounds like a recognition that martyrdom by suicide and murder was not required by *halakhah*, yet the martyrs recited a blessing before killing their families and themselves, with the formulaic words "Who commanded us" (*ibid.*, p. 230). All of this makes the martyrs' actions so much more problematic and helps explain why the approval of suicide by the *Tosafists* was so limited and conditional (see text at notes 15-16).

Appendix 2

In offering their own radical but limited expansion of the Talmudic doctrine of passive martyrdom where fear of unbearable torture is involved, R. Tam and the *Tosafists* who followed his lead were rejecting *aggadah*-based and other arguments that some historians have recently offered, eight hundred years after the fact, to support the 1096 martyrdoms from a halakhic standpoint. These arguments are based on material that — like the material in the Chronicles — was surely known to the *Tosafists* over the two-hundred-year period spanned by their rulings, in which they generally sanctioned suicide *only in the face of unbearable torture*. Indeed, under the circumstances, I don't understand the point of trying to develop such arguments long after the *Tosafists* spoke on the issue; see Berger, "Jacob Katz," pp. 47-8. Berger's own reliance on the response of R. Meir of Rothenburg (*ibid.*, p. 48) does not derogate from the fact that the prevailing view among *Tosafists* follows R. Tam's formulation requiring fear of unbearable torture. R. Meir relied on the prior acts of pious Jews (*ibid.*). There is only one notable case in the 1096 Chronicles of a mass suicide (or murder) done out of fear of torture; Chazan, *First Crusade*, p. 278. See also Shalom Spiegel, *The Last Trial* (Woodstock, VT: Jewish Lights, 1993), pp. 131-6.

Appendix 3

A similar pattern of *ex-post* approval of martyrological family murders and suicides occurred in Spain at the time of the 1391 Christian pogroms; see above, note 9 and Ram Ben-Shalom, "Sanctification of God's Name and Jewish Martyrdom in Aragon and Castile in 1391: Between Sepharad and Ashkenaz," *Tarbiz* (Tevet-Adar 2001): 227-77 [Hebrew]. Ben-Shalom attributes the change in the Sephardi attitude when faced with conversion or martyrdom — from conversion in 1148 (by the fanatical Moslem Almohades tribes) to martyrdom in 1391 (by Christian mobs) — to Jewish absorption of Christian theology and ideology in the interim, glorifying suffering and martyrdom at the hands of their enemies. See also, on the transfer of the *aqedah* sacrifice paradigm from Judaism to Christianity, when the latter looked for a model for the sacrifice of God's only begotten son, and then this paradigm's transfer back to Judaism, when it looked for a model for its suffering as God's chosen people, Lippman Bodoff, "The Binding of Isaac: Religious Paradoxes, Permutations and Problems," *Midstream* (November 2001): 25-28; Daniel Boyarin, *Dying for God* (Stanford: Stanford University Press, 1999).

Appendix 4

Ashkenazi rabbis of Germany and Northern France, under Christian rule, who came to Provence in Southern France, and Catalonia in Northern Spain, starting in the thirteenth century, joined with kabbalists there in encouraging martyrdom, in contrast to Sephardi rabbis of the Maimonidean, Andalusian, tradition, who discouraged it except where clearly required by Talmudic law, as Faur notes (in "Two Models" and "A Crisis of Categories"). See also, Berger, "Judaism and General Culture," p. 114; and Soloveitchik, "Religious Law," p. 208. In this regard, the Chronicles of the 1096 martyrdom repeatedly emphasize that their *method* was unprecedented; see, e.g., Chazan, *First Crusade*, pp. 232, 237, 256. Indeed, at one point the Chronicles state that whoever speaks ill of those who converted "insults the countenance of the Divine Presence"; *ibid.*, p. 294.

Appendix 5

Idel argues that kabbalah was a response to Maimonidean rationalism, but Hava Tirosh-Samuelson, who agrees with Idel, undermines this view in citing all the magical, theosophic, ecstatic, sexual, and other mystical ideas in the *Zohar* and other kabbalistic literature. If the alleged Maimonidean offense was "deviation from authentic Jewish tradition," why construct a completely new mystical, mythical system instead of pointing out from Talmudic sources exactly where Maimonides went wrong? See Idel, *Kabbalah*, p. 251 and Tirosh-Samuelson, *Happiness in Premodern Judaism*, pp. 291-342. The two causes identified by Dan — i.e., new approaches to prayer and to ethical conduct — as explaining the simultaneous emergence of pietism in Germany and kabbalah in southwest Europe as mainstream forms of Jewish mysticism in the twelfth and thirteenth centuries, reflect a single, common cause: viz., what Dan describes elsewhere (in the context of second-century *hekhalot* mysticism) as a "spiritual crisis" experienced by the Jewish community, here caused by the historical trauma of persecution and persistent pressure by a triumphalist Christian civilization beginning with the First Crusade in 1096. Prayer is a call for help, comfort and consolation from a loving parent, sought through union with God, *the* loving Parent, and the necessary new theosophic understanding of the dynamic process among the *sefirot* within the Godhead that made such union doctrinally possible. This new understanding and opportunity for union represent a rebirth or a utopia that is — to use another formulation by Dan — an "expression of one's attitude toward the [terrible] present and the [glorious] past." Relatedly, the new ethics focuses on God's closeness to the Jewish people through the revealed commandments; Jewry's ability through their strict observance to theurgically restore harmony and completeness to the Divine realm; and the need of Jews to withdraw from the inherent evil of the material world represented by man's body, by means of an ascetic ethic that conditions its followers for mystical union and its ultimate physical form experienced as martyrdom. See Dan, *Jewish Mysticism*, vol. I, p. 110, and vol. II, pp. 57-63; *idem.*, *Jewish Mysticism and Jewish Ethics*, chs. 3-5; Marcus, *Piety* , pp. 150-1, n. 57. Of course, the mystics do not see themselves as reacting to these historically conditioned causes and responses, since they have "a deep faith in the eternal truth of their revelations and ideas," as Dan notes in *Jewish Mysticism*, vol. I, p. 78, and Berger concurs in, e.g., "Judaism and General Culture," p. 87. See also note 28; but cf. Marcus, *Piety*, p. 151, n. 57.

See also, Jerome Gellman, "Buber's Blunder: Buber's Replies to Scholem and Schatz-Uffenheimer," *Modern Judaism* (February 2000):20-40; Walter S. Wurzburger, "Rav Soloveitchik as a *Posek* of Postmodern Orthodoxy," in *Engaging Modernity*, ed.

Moshe Z. Sokol (Northvale, New Jersey: Jason Aronson Inc., 1997), p. 124; Ostow, *Ultimate Intimacy*; Faur, *Homo Mysticus, passim*, and *idem, In the Shadow of History*, (Albany, New York: SUNY Press, 1992), Introduction, Chapter 1, and p. 88. Faur treats these and related aspects of mysticism, such as those discussed by J.B. Soloveitchik (see note 29), as "anthropocentric." On the Talmudic treatment of asceticism, see Sara Epstein Weinstein, *Piety and Fanaticism* (Northvale, New Jersey: Jason Aronson, Inc., 1997).

Appendix 6

Lurianic kabbalah, considered by its adherents as the only true meaning of the Torah, was viewed by them as the meta-text of the mythology and meaning secretly revealed at Sinai and transmitted secretly to an elite few over the centuries; see Shaul Magid, "Lurianic Exegesis and the Garden of Eden," *AJS Review* (1997):37-76; see also Bruce Rosenstock, "Abraham Miguel Cardoso's Messianism: A Reappraisal," *AJS Review* (1998): 63-104. This mythology postulates that evil existed *within the Godhead*, which sought to cleanse itself through the process of Creation. Thus, it thrives as a Divine power in the world even now; Dan, *Jewish Mysticism*, vol. I, p. 21. While theurgy in kabbalah, which postulates that man can restore the harmony that was lost within the Godhead during Creation, is hubristic on an external, formal, level, it bespeaks a radical pessimism, signifying — especially in its Lurianic formulation — that redemption can come about only if fallible human Jews can manage to mend the Divinity and overcome the Divine power of evil in the world by the mystical performance of ritual and ethical commandments.

Kabbalah, especially in its Lurianic form, also seriously undermines traditional Jewish belief in a flesh and blood messiah as necessary for the redemption of Israel and the world; Scholem, *Major Trends*, pp. 273-4, 308. From the First Crusade martyrs, through Nachmanides, to Hasidism, we find the theme in Jewish mysticism that martyrdom, and the world to come that it assures, are more important than working for and experiencing the messiah and the messianic age; see Marc Saperstein and Nancy E. Berg, " 'Arab Chains' and the 'Good Things of Sepharad,' " *AJS Rev.* (November 2002): 301-16. See also note 40. This inherently pessimistic view regarding the possibility of the coming of the messiah and Jewish redemption succeeded, according to Dan, because it best mirrored Israel's plight among the nations at that time (sixteenth century and thereafter), scattered, in exile, busy fighting off intractable evil; see, e.g., Dan, *Jewish Mysticism*, vol. III, pp. 329-48. If Jewish reality today no longer corresponds to this description, isn't a new "mirror" appropriate, and isn't it possible — even probable — that the old mirror is distorting Jewish reality and Jewry's wisest response to it?

Appendix 7

A specific example is the reaction of traditional Jewish communities in early modern Europe toward the Jewish practice of medicine. When Jewish doctors, newly accepted and trained in medicine, returned to their communities, they were often not welcomed, but treated as competitors of the "folk-healers and *rebbes*," and their new science frowned upon. Indeed, Rabbi Nachman of Bratzlav, the great-grandson of the Baal Shem Tov, founder of Hasidism, urged his followers to eschew medicines in favor of the "prayers of the *tsaddiq*" (the "righteous one") of the community. When the renowned *musar* (ethics) teacher, Rabbi Israel Salanter, learned that his son had "gone to Berlin to study medicine, he…observed *shiv`ah*, seven days of mourning." Many Jews saw these new Jewish doctors as "acculturated destroyers of the tradition," and the level of their religious observance was questioned. We may well surmise the influence that these doctors had on the best and the brightest young Jews with whom they subsequently came in contact, regarding traditional Judaism, and the resultant defections that ensued from what these young men came to see as superstitious and narrow-minded religion. See Michael Nevins, *The Jewish Doctor* (Northvale, New Jersey: Jason Aronson Inc., 1994), pp. 71-75; see also John M. Efron, "Images of the Jewish Body: Three Medical Views from the Jewish Enlightenment," *Bulletin of the History of Medicine* (1995):349-66. See also *Berakhot* 60a; and Isadore Twersky, *Introduction to the Code of Maimonides* (New Haven: Yale University Press, 1980), pp. 61-96, 356-514 (on the attitude of classical Judaism toward science and rationalism).

Appendix 8

It should be emphasized that there is little consequential difference between "Lithuanian" and other *haredi* Jewry regarding the absorption of Jewish mysticism and its dismal view of this world and its escapist theology; see Nadler, *Mithnagdim*, pp. 106-7. The Sephardi tradition is significantly different, perhaps because it developed in the tolerant and culturally rich and stimulating environment of medieval Islamic Spain, and — with the subsequent decline of Islam in the modern period — Sephardic Jewry did not have to face the challenges of modernity until their return to the State of Israel; see, e.g., Berger, "Judaism and General Culture," p. 137; Ostow, "Jewish Response," p. 245; remarks of Zvi Zohar on Sephardi ideals of inclusiveness and the integration of Jewish learning with knowledge of general world culture in *A Word from Jerusalem*, Shalom Hartman Institute (September, 2000):6. See also the recent discussion of the non-*haredi* aspects of Sephardi Jews in Israel, and the flexible and innovative quality of R. Ovadia Yosef's halakhic rulings as their religious leader, "following the norm among past Sephardi [including Mizrachi] rabbis, whose rulings tend to be more moderate than those of Ashkenazi rabbis." This is true notwithstanding the frequent failure of the media to properly understand and explain R. Yosef's *oral* statements; Zion Zohar, "Oriental Jewry Confronts Modernity: The Case of Rabbi Ovadia Yosef, " *Modern Judaism* (May 2004): 120-49. Rav Yosef, says Zohar, "caught between tradition and modernity, " seeks to remain engaged with both for the benefit of his followers, to meet that community's needs. He does this within his goal of restoring the past glory of Sephardi rabbis "leading back to Spain," to return to the time when "Sephardi Jews were the preeminent spiritual, religious and intellectual force in the Jewish world" (ibid., at 142-3). Cf. Michael Arnold, "Rabbis' Edict on Land Use Sprouts Furor," *Forward*, September 8, 2000, p. 3 (Sephardi Chief Rabbi "bow[s] to threats of excommunication from Lithuanian *haredi* or fervently Orthodox circles" regarding the rules for observing the sabbatical year [*shemitah*] in Israel). On mystical ascent as of Ashkenazi extraction or influence, see Idel, *Kabbalah*, pp. 96, 101-2, 260-5.

Appendix 9

David Ruderman notes the view among scholars that the decline, by the early seventeenth century, of the brief flowering of Jewish interest in science in the sixteenth century, from "openness to insularity" (except in Italy, which was always unique in its openness; see, e.g., Moshe Idel, "Major Currents in Italian kabbalah between 1560-1660," in *Essential Papers On Jewish Culture in Renaissance and Baroque Italy*, ed. David B. Ruderman [New York: NYU Press, 1992], pp. 345-72), was caused by the rise of Lurianic kabbalah to dominance in Jewish piety and religious thought by that time; see Ruderman, *Jewish Thought*, ch. 2; Dan, "Manasseh ben Israel" *Jewish Mysticism*, vol. III, pp. 64-6. That strain of kabbalah has continued, of course, in a somewhat changed form since the middle of the eighteenth century, in Hasidism, which — as Norman Lamm notes — has generally rejected "organized secular education," "rational investigation" and "scientific thinking"; see *ibid.*; and Lamm, ed., *Hasidism*, pp. 67-71. Ruderman argues against the view that Lurianic kabbalah is the cause of the seventeenth-century decline in Jewish interest in science. I believe his view is unpersuasive:

1. While Israel Ta-Shma, cited by Ruderman, questions the extent of Lurianic kabbalah's dominance in Europe, and is joined in this opinion by Moshe Idel, theirs seems to be, from Ruderman's discussion, a minority view; Ruderman, *Jewish Thought*, pp. 58-9; see also Shaul Magid's review of Lawrence Fine, *Physician of the Soul, Healer of the Cosmos: Isaac Luria and His Kabbalistic Fellowship* (2003), in *AJS Rev.* (November 2004):370-1. Moreover, the Idel and Ta-Shma view fails to take into account the impact on the masses caused by the mediative role of their rabbis teaching them Lurianic kabbalah; thus, they learned it from an intellectual elite, who were familiar with it. In this regard, if, as Idel states, non-Jewish European thinkers were also familiar with it "from the late fifteenth to the late nineteenth century," surely many Jews were, too; see Idel, *Kabbalah*, pp. 258-64.

2. Ta-Shma cites the broad cultural interests of two eighteenth century rabbis, Emden and Eybeshitz, but neither was a kabbalist; the former was strongly opposed to Lurianic kabbalah and its Sabbatean offspring, which he accused Eybeshitz of embracing, and the latter strongly denied any sympathies with this strain of kabbalah. In any case, neither was a supporter much less an enthusiast of science, accepting it only to a limited extent and for a limited purpose; see, e.g., Berger, "Judaism and General Culture," p. 139; cf. Jonathan Israel, *European Jewry in the Age of Mercantilism* (New York: Oxford University Press, 1989), p. 257.

3. While Ruderman is puzzled by the claim that Lurianic kabbalah produced "closure" while the previously adhered to Cordoverian kabbalah "sustained openness," one answer seems clear enough: the former — in contrast to the latter — postulated a pessimistic mythology in which evil was part of the Godhead; Dan, "No Evil Descends from Heaven," *Jewish Mysticism*, vol. III, pp. 329-348, 353. What point could there be in the human pursuit of scientific or any other form of progress in the world if evil was an inherent condition of God and His creation? Cordovero's optimistic approach, that man caused evil, and had the power to relieve, reduce and eradicate it by acting to achieve progress in the world, coincided with the temporary Jewish openness, hope, and relative freedom from persecution in the Renaissance-Reformation dominated sixteenth century; Luria's pessimistic departure from Cordoverian-Safedian kabbalah coincided with the Counter-Reformation and the general return of Jewish persecution, "when history developing all around them was proving...the rule of evil in this world," thereby providing to Jews the perception of "a harmony between its [new, Lurianic] symbols and the [new] Jewish reality... [by] destroying the harmony in the Divine worlds and postulating that evil did indeed descend from heaven" (*ibid.*, p. 348).

4. The factors cited by Ruderman in lieu of Lurianic kabbalah to explain the decline of budding rationalism by the early seventeenth century (*Jewish Thought*, p. 92), would

necessarily have had the *same* kind of impact on *non-Jewish* scientific interest and achievement, but we know that, in fact, this was not the case (*ibid.*, pp. 370-1).

5. Ruderman suggests that kabbalah should not be viewed as incompatible with scientific endeavors because some scientists, such as Newton, were sometimes interested in kabbalah; *Jewish Thought*, pp. 310-31 and *passim*. However, it is incorrect to reason from the interest of scientists in kabbalah or other spiritual ideas to the interest of kabbalists in science; science is an *open* system of thought, and scientists are therefore interested in any idea, from whatever source, that may help provide a clue or a key to solving a scientific problem that has proved unsolvable by accepted scientific knowledge. See, e.g., Carl Zimmer, *Soul Made Flesh: The Discovery of the Brain — and How It Changed The World* (New York: Free Press, 2004), and Adam Zernan, "How Mind Became Matter," *New York Times*, April 4, 2004, *Book Review*, p. 16. On Newton's limited interest in the esoteric, see Jose Faur, "Esoteric Knowledge and the Vulgar," *Trumah* (Winter 2002): 184-91 (published in Heidelberg). In contrast, kabbalah is a *closed* system of thought that claims to have an exclusive access to truth and the method of its ascertainment, which specifically excludes reason, logic, experience, or the senses, including scientific theories, hypotheses and experimentation; see, e.g., Scholem, *Major Trends*, p. 9; Idel, *Kabbalah*, p. 241; and Dan, *Jewish Mysticism*, Vol. III, pp. 1-46. Ruderman at one point seems to accept the distinction, referring to the "...coexistence of mystical and rational elements [is] among *scientific thinkers*" (my emphasis), and his citations support this view; Ruderman, *Jewish Thought*, p. 132. But he seems to assert the opposite elsewhere, ibid., pp. 10-11, 371-2, ignoring the completely closed nature of mystical thought and its systems.

One of the best, most nuanced discussions of the relationship of scientific thought and investigation with religious ideas and the acquisition of knowledge is developed by Matt Goldish in *The Sabbatean Prophets* (Cambridge: Harvard University Press, 2004), Chapter 1, and *passim*. He shows how the line of differentiation between scientific and religious thought gradually shifted in location and emphasis as science, partly motivated by religion, continued to develop from the 16th century onward. In no way did this history demonstrate that mysticism and science, and — more particularly — kabbalah and science were compatible activities for scientific minds and methods; ibid. Similarly, the history of Jewish messianism shows that Sephardim were more interested than Ashkenazim in the more practical, historical aspects of messianism (ibid., Ch. 2). Further, such messianism was more influential in circles of Sephardi and *converso* culture (ibid). Among kabbalists, messianism was not so much practical as it was escapist, part of the effort towards union with the Divine. Mysticism initially developed among Sephardi and Ashkenazi communities under Christian rule; among kabbalists, on either side, it was largely theological, mythological, magical, and escapist.

Appendix 10

Amos Funkenstein concludes that the absence of any significant Jewish participation in science, as it flowered in the early modern period, was significantly caused by "the absence of a sense of the relative autonomy of such [scientific] pursuits as legitimate or even God-willed," referring undoubtedly to the anti-rationalist, separatist, and mystical orientation of Jewish religious thought in this period. David Ruderman disagrees; see *Jewish Thought*, pp. 370-2. I think Ruderman's view that Jewish scientific achievement lagged because of discrimination is unpersuasive, especially in light of other evidence, including that in his book and in his article, "The Impact of Science on Jewish Culture and Society in Venice (with special reference to Jewish graduates of Padua's Medical School)," in *Essential Papers*, pp. 519-53; see also Dan, "No Evil," *Jewish Mysticism*, vol. III, pp. 329-348; Daniel Boorstin, *The Discoverers* (New York: Random House, 1983), pp. 294-420; Joseph Hoffman, "The Medicis and the Jewish Question," *The Jerusalem Post*, International Edition, October 22, 2004, pp. 24-5; and Ben-Sasson, *Jewish People*, pp. 670-90; cf. Jonathan Israel, *European Jewry in the Age of Mercantilism* (New York: Oxford University Press, 1989), pp. 254-7. My view is based on essentially uncontested facts, as shown in those sources:

1. There was an elite layer of broadly scientifically aware Jews during this period who studied, practiced and wrote in this field, including Tobias Cohen, David Nieto, and Joseph Delmedigo.

2. There was strong support for this activity in classical Jewish sources, including rabbinic and Sephardi rationalist — philosophical ideas, but not in kabbalistic or other mystical works.

3. Jewish professional activities were primarily in medicine and related fields, e.g., botany and zoology — but they were utilitarian activities like patient care, not experimentation geared to new scientific discoveries.

4. The major scientific discoveries in this period were in physical sciences, like mechanics, pneumatics and astronomy, by Christians.

5. Most of these discoveries came about as a result of experiments outside the universities; see, e.g., Kaplan, *An Alternative Path...*, op. cit., note 20, p. 15.

6. Most of these experiments and related activities were performed by the discoverers individually, with limited — usually their own — funds, performed as side, non-money-making activities or avocations to their normal, full-time economic activities, which ranged from teaching to commerce.

7. Secular studies were largely excluded from Jewish school curricula because of rabbinical and community opposition. This was true even during the Jewish Enlightenment, c. 1750-1880 — except, not surprisingly, in Italy, where such studies had long been included.

8. The scientifically informed Jewish elite (see "1." above) recognized that Jews were too poorly educated in science to be prepared for university level studies. However, there were some Jewish preparatory schools for entrance to university medical schools, with rabbinic and scientific curricula.

9. The Jewish community and its religious tradition during this period were opposed to scientific study and experimentation.

10. The universities, including the medical schools, sporadically accepted Jewish students in the fifteenth-sixteenth centuries, mainly in Italy and France, and increasingly thereafter throughout Europe, as part of the Enlightenment, and finally in England in the 19th century. The universities provided a broad education in various scientific fields, and the Jewish graduates brought this growing knowledge to their communities throughout Europe. On the other hand, most of the science that was taught in the universities was, for a long time, very ancient and very wrong, and was overturned by the new scientific discoveries. See also paragraph 5 above.

11. Jewish institutions, e.g., the Council of Four Lands, had taxing authority for projects deemed important to the community, but these did not generally include support for scientific studies or experiments. The Council did pass ordinances for the support of *yeshivot* and their students; H.H. Ben-Sasson, "The Medieval

Period," p. 683. However, some Jews did receive support from Christian governments and private persons, especially in the translation of scientific texts.

12. Scientific textbooks were widely available, from the sixteenth century on, within and outside the universities. But cf. Ram Ben-Shalom "Between Official and Private Disputes," p. 66.

13. Jewish thinkers who followed emerging scientific advances recognized that Jewish inferiority in scientific study, knowledge and activity was based on a prevailing and persisting cultural inferiority; there was no claim made that this inferiority was caused by externally imposed restrictions on Jewish opportunities.

14. Given the notable and influential personalities discussed by Ruderman, who were aware of, and knowledgeable in, science, and the many Jewish students who gained a broad background in science from their medical school studies (see "10." above), the question arises: Why were Jewish interest, study, experimentation, and discovery in science in early modern Europe so lacking, apart from the study and practice of medicine, if not because of internal, cultural factors?

15. There is also the evidence of the *modern* period, in which virtually all institutions involved in scientific activity have become open to interested and qualified Jewish students, and yet, kabbalistically oriented religious Jews (see, e.g., Berger, "Judaism and General Culture," pp. 87, 133-8) have continued their early-modern-period record of inconsequential scientific interest and achievement.

16. Scholars more and more believe that science arose "only once, in Europe and nowhere else, as a direct result of the researches of medieval Catholic scholastics;" David Klinghoffer, "Christians Should Thank the Jew," *The Jewish Week*, February 27, 2004, citing, e.g., the historian, Rodney Stark.

My reconciliation of these facts is represented by the following comments of Ruderman and Boorstin. As Ruderman observes:

> The contest between science and Jewish tradition had left its shattering mark on the cultural sensibilities of Jews like [Tobias] Cohen, [David] Nieto, [Joseph] Delmedigo, and many others in Padua and elsewhere. The results of the new scientific explosion were imposing, and they no longer could be explained away solely by appeals to the grandiose cultural achievement of an ancient past. The emerging sense of Jewish inferiority among such impressionable Jewish observers of enlightened Christian society would become a propensity for an increasing number of university-educated Jews in subsequent years (emphasis added). See Ruderman, "The Impact of Science," p. 539.

Boorstin covers the issue of mysticism's attitude toward science similarly, much as Faur does, as noted above (see note 59):

> "While Hindus and Buddhists sought ways out of history, Christianity and Islam sought ways into history. Instead of promising escape from experience, they sought meaning in experience... both rooted in [classical] Judaism...." *The Discoverers*, pp. 566-7.

On balance Funkenstein, and Ruderman's observations *here*, are correct.

Jewish thought was dominated by kabbalah from the 16th century on, and embraced the view strongly espoused by Nachmanides, that God alone — and not unchanging natural and scientific laws (created by God for humanity's discovery and control) nor free will — determines (which implies fatalism and determinism) what occurs each moment of history in nature as well as society. Therefore, we can see a relationship between Islam's and Judaism's acceptance of this atomistic view, and the decline or absence of achievements in these religions in mathematics and the physical sciences beginning, in the medieval period, with the Muslim philosopher al-Ghazzali. This explains as well why David Hume's brilliantly argued atomism failed to stem Christian scientific discovery; it never became part of Christian dogma. See the discussion in Alain Besançom, "What Kind of a Religion is Islam?" *Commentary* (May 2004):42-8; letter to the editor and response by David Berlinski and Alain Besançom, respectively, in *Commentary* (September 2004):13-15.

Appendix 11

Norman Lamm's recent book, defending Hasidism as not anti-intellectual, is an anomaly in terms of the author's motive — he seems to admire those who have little admiration for the *Torah u-Madda* program that Lamm has so strongly endorsed for so long. It is also unpersuasive in terms of any suggestion that Hasidism, and the kabbalah on which it is based, are, in any realistic sense, rational, notwithstanding that much mystical thought, including Hasidism, may be characterized as the fruit of "intellectual" activity; see Lamm, ed., *Hasidism, passim*. For example, Hasidism, with a radical innocence that leads to passivity in the face of evil, as evident from its response to the Holocaust (see note 36), sees all phenomena as being in states of "smallness" and "greatness," and evil is, therefore, illusory because it is just the good in a state of "smallness" that, with faith and confidence, can flower into goodness; *ibid.*, p. 483. This view hardly helps mankind, including the Jewish people, to know how to respond to the Bin Ladens, Stalins, Hitlers, and the other Amalek-like nations that arise in history to devour the weak, defenseless and innocent. It stands in stark contrast to the simpler and more understandable and useful conception of Biblical and Rabbinic Judaism of human free will, humanity's capacity to choose between good and evil, and mankind's responsibility to destroy evil, to punish it and eliminate it, wherever and whenever it appears. Hasidism also certainly seems at odds with Modern Orthodoxy and *Torah u-Madda* Judaism regarding the value of secular education, the status of Zionism and the State of Israel, the role of women, and in its attitudes towards non-Orthodox Jews, non-Jews, and non-Jewish culture; see, e.g., *ibid.*, pp. 67, 426, 513, 516, 530, 585-8; and Berger, *The Rebbe* , p. 7, n.2.

When we contrast Lamm's book on Hasidism with his subsequently published collection of earlier essays, *Seventy Faces: Articles of Faith* (Hoboken: Ktav, 2002) and his numerous previous books, we can readily see that Hasidic thought is an intellectual creation, but *obscurantist* in nature, and a search for a life of the spirit, while Lamm's Modern Orthodoxy, featured in his many books and essays, is an intellectual creation, *rationalist* in nature, and also in search of the life of the spirit. I say this notwithstanding Lamm's occasional attempts to bolster a rationalist argument with an incomprehensible kabbalistic idea, e.g., at p. 87: "In His absoluteness, the kabbalists taught, the world does not even exist for Him. In this respect, God is the 'Great Mystery' and man must forever despair of being able to understand Him." It seems to me that the kabbalists spent a lot of time and effort trying to do so, and did not despair of such effort. It is difficult to accept, therefore, Bernard Dov Cooperman's notion that — in analyzing Jewish intellectual history — it is "tendentious" to see an "interpretive grid" in the categories of philosophy and kabbalah that we may reasonably characterize as "rationalism *versus* obscurantism"; see Cooperman's "Afterward" in Katz,

Tradition and Crisis, pp. 250-1. The fact that Jewish mysticism and rationalism may share the same end, a life of the spirit, should not obscure the fact that they represent very different means to achieving it — nor should it obscure the possibility that those differences may now be more important than the common purpose they pursue.

Appendix 12

See e.g., the debate by early 20th century Jewish historians concerning Hasidim vs. Mitnagdim as "the spiritual forebears of the Jewish passage from the restrictive life of the ghetto towards greater spiritual freedom and national autonomy," discussed by Nadler in his monograph, "Rabbis and Rebbes." (The balanced presentation is marred by Nadler's attribution of the quality of "freedom and individualism" to the Izbitzer Rebbe's "expression of... religious determinism" based on Hasidism's view of Divine immanence, by which all of the human spirit must be Divine even when it sins; *ibid.*, pp. 5, 21-2). See also the various views on Jewish mysticism of Heinrich Graetz and other *Wissenschaft* scholars; Gershom Scholem; Eliezer Schweid; and Joseph Dan, in "Gershom Scholem," *Jewish Mysticism*, vol. IV, pp. 131-90. All seem to agree, however, even Scholem, that Jewish mysticism is an attempt to escape from the reality of life to a primordial past, through communion with God; that this involves abstaining from practical messianic or any other rational historical action or engagement in worldly affairs; and that this also involves an annulment of the world's value through achieving a sublime union with God. It is, indeed, for these reasons, that Graetz believed, as Schweid defends him, that Jewish mysticism:

> distorted man's ability to orient himself and to respond appro-
> priately to concrete reality... and to grapple with its problems...
> These philosophers and scholars [N. Krachmal, Zunz, Graetz,
> and Geiger] saw in kabbalah's domination of the thoughts,
> feelings, and responses of Jews regarding the reality that sur-
> rounded them a major stumbling block that needed to be
> overcome to save the nation from [further?] decline.

It is difficult, given Scholem's definition of Jewish mysticism (*ibid.*, p. 153), to agree with his view that kabbalah was the "core of the ongoing revolution that gave Judaism the power to survive in a hostile environment and prevented its spiritual fossilization and stagnation (*ibid.*, at p. 148); survival power, yes, but fossilization — once that survival power was no longer needed — perhaps was the price! Schweid, therefore, seems substantially correct in his approach to the problematic nature of mysticism in Jewish history. For a historical overview of the role of the Haskalah in the development of the current divisions in Orthodoxy, see Shmuel Feiner, "Towards a Historical Definition of Haskalah," *New Perspectives on the Haskalah*, pp. 184-219.

The "Postscript" by Yerushalmi in the 1996 edition of his *Zakhor* contains stimulating ideas touching on the separate realms of tradition and the search for historical truth, and how they feasibly might interact. See also, Seth Farber, "Jewish Orthodoxy as an Academic Discipline," *Le'Ela* (June 2000):35-40.

Appendix 13

For some indications that Modern Orthodoxy is in need of intellectual and institutional strengthening, see Moshe Sokolow, "Soloveitchik Lite," *The Jerusalem Report*, January 31, 2000, pp. 48-9. Lichtenstein adds the important recognition that encountering and engaging the world through *madda* entails statistical risks that some who are so engaged may sometimes, to some extent, falter religiously, but that the *Torah u-Madda* position can "still be sustained," depending, in each situation, on the over-all anticipated "balance of benefit and loss" ("Torah and General Culture," p. 286). Cf. Alan Brill, who, in his recent analysis of the *Torah u-Madda* concept, urges the importance of recognizing that Judaism and Torah are embedded in Jewish culture generally, and, as such, have always existed together with what only recently has been separated out as "*madda*."

> Openly opposed to Saadyah and Maharal, whose Judaisms were embedded in culture, R. Lichtenstein's essay, following nineteenth century thinking, assumes no tradition of Jewish culture except for the few texts he cites — without noting the irony — to justify the reading of modern Western secular culture.

See "Judaism and Culture: Beyond the Bifurcation of *Torah* and *Madda*," *The Edah Journal*, 4:1 (2004):7. On the issue of *madda*, see also *Yoma* 86a; *Yerushalmi Bava Metsi`a* 2:5; Maimonides, *Mishneh Torah, Hilkhot Yesodei HaTorah*, ch. 5; *Shulhan Arukh, Yoreh De`ah* 157. Lichtenstein's paper is, to my knowledge, the most comprehensive and nuanced single exposition of the *Torah u-Madda* position. It should be noted that he emphasizes the value of *madda* in enhancing Torah understanding and values; while he does not explicitly relate *madda* to *tiqqun olam* or *qiddush Ha-Shem* as I have discussed them, the connection seems implicit in his analysis. However, he does note that an absence of *madda* has sometimes led to a *hillul Ha-Shem* (p. 236).

In any case, the connection of *madda* to *qiddush Ha-Shem* was expressly made by Rabbi Esriel Hildesheimer at the end of the nineteenth century. There was a scholarly debate on whether Rabbi Hildesheimer considered *madda* as having "inherent worth" or just "practical value." Given that he expressly stated that Jewish excellence in secular studies and activities was a *qiddush ha-shem*, how could anyone possibly argue that such effort had no inherent worth? See Marc B. Shapiro, "Rabbi Esriel Hildesheimer's Program of *Torah U-Madda*," *The Torah U-Madda Journal* (2000): 82, 84. Rav Kook offers the strongest and simplest argument for secular activities, dispensing with kabbalistic ideas of mystical exegesis, sefirotic emanations, and the intricate structure of mystical ritual activity. For him, spirituality is the *result* of using the tools of modern culture to guide the historical, earthly process of redemption; it is not achieved by casting off corporeality or by the negation of the self; see Eliezer Schweid, "'Prophetic Mysticism in Twentieth Century Jewish Thought," *Modern Judaism* (May 1994):166-9.

Challenging Lubavitch's
New Messianic Claims:
A Review Essay of David Berger's
The Rebbe, the Messiah,
and the Scandal of Orthodox Indifference
(London: Littman Library Of Jewish Civilization, 2001)

Professor Berger has written a courageous and important book, and a very interesting one, on the claims to being Messiah and to Divinity on behalf of the Lubavitcher Rebbe, within the Lubavitcher movement (Habad), since the death of the Rebbe in 1994.

It is courageous because it is the first book of its kind, and is directed against an icon of Orthodoxy. It is important because it has something important to say to a number of different constituencies. To the non-Jewish reader, it spells out why Judaism has always rejected the claims for Jesus as Messiah. For Jewish readers generally, who support and admire the Lubavitcher Rebbe and the Lubavitcher movement for their work in developing and maintaining Judaism in places, and people, that have been neglected by other Orthodox Jews, Berger has issued a warning that the product that is now being sold by many Lubavitcher representatives and publications may be bad for their Jewish consumers' religious health — in particular, claims among significant elements of the movement, perhaps supported by some things that the Rebbe said while alive, that he is or may be the Messiah, and may even be Divine. These ideas, argues Berger very powerfully, are contrary to fundamental tenets of Judaism.

For Orthodox Jews, Berger adds two important additional messages: first, that — if he is right — there are concrete actions that they must take, according to the *halakhah* (Jewish law) by which they live, to de-legitimize Lubavitch, including the following: no admitted messianist should be recognized as an Orthodox rabbi in good standing and allowed to serve as such, e.g., as a synagogue rabbi or cantor, as a member of a rabbinical court, as a principal or teacher of Jewish studies in an Orthodox Yeshiva or day school. Messianist institutions, e.g., camps and schools, should not be supported or attended. The ritual slaughter of meat by messianists cannot be considered valid; and so on.

Berger's second message is to ask why other Orthodox leaders and institutions have been so reluctant to support his advocacy on these issues. This book should go a long way to convince them that there are issues here worthy of their concern.

But, precisely because of the importance of this book to these varied groups, I believe it is important in a review to call attention to certain weaknesses or reservations one might reasonably have as to some of its aspects.

Berger is greatly disturbed by the fact that attributing Messiah status to the Rebbe undermines a two thousand year old argument of Judaism against accepting the messianic status of Jesus — namely, that Judaism requires that the Messiah shall have, during his life, successfully fought the wars of the Lord for Israel; rebuilt the Temple in its place; and gathered the dispersed of Israel to their homeland, *while still alive*. Thus, for Berger, whatever status the Rebbe may have had as a *potential* Messiah while still alive, ended on his death before these accomplishments were fully achieved. The supporters of the Rebbe as Messiah argue that what remains to be done will be accomplished when the Rebbe "returns." They avoid the Christian idea or concept of a "second coming" by arguing that he never died, but is still alive. This, of course, inevitably leads to claims of Divinity, which are also being made in the Rebbe's behalf by

277

some elements in Habad.

Berger argues, correctly, that these claims for the Rebbe as Messiah, despite his death, undermine the argument that Jews have always been able to present to explain why they rejected Jesus as Messiah, i.e., that Jesus *died before* "his work" was completed, which — in Jewish law — is a test that the Messiah must pass. With the new claims now being made for the Rebbe, the issue is no longer, *whether* such a person can be the Messiah, but simply *which one* among the claimants is the true Messiah; either, in principal, can be. Indeed, one might add, so may others, past and present, qualify. This situation hardly gives Christians bent on converting Jews much leverage or support for *their* candidate. Indeed, it opens up the entire field! So one finds it difficult to see why Berger believes that Jews are now shorn of their ability to fight off those who want them to convert to Christianity: There are already too many candidates — even two is one too many!

This leads me to a further point. While Berger stresses — to the point of having a separate appendix devoted to it — the numerous and long-standing Jewish authorities who spell out the Jewish religious criteria for the true Messiah, he does not adequately emphasize and spell out *the common sense rationale for these criteria* — and, particularly, the criterion that the Messiah must accomplish his tasks *before he dies*. But this is a crucial element in persuading anyone about the legitimacy and correctness of the Jewish theological position, and rebutting the messianic claims of all prior candidates so far. The use of reason (*sevarah*) in rabbinic rulings is quite accepted and common in Jewish law. That is why many Jewish scholars, such as Maimonides, have devoted so much effort explaining the reasons for religious commands.

In this case, the idea that a person can claim the allegiance of an entire people, or the world, for centuries, that such person is the Messiah, before that person has demonstrated by his achievements in behalf of Israel and the world that he is, in fact, God's messenger for that purpose, not only requires a suspension of conviction — even if it is joined to a simple, unsupported faith — but requires Israel and the world to reject all other candidates *who may arise with equal or better credentials after that presumed Messiah's death.* There is absolutely no rational basis to expect any people to carry such an irrational burden of uncertainty for a period just short of eternity. And this is true whether the claim is based on a "second coming" or on the return to the world of an alleged Messiah who allegedly never died.

In either case, the required suspension of knowledge as to the claimed Messiah, or any others who might come along — before or after — with credentials as good or better, simply cannot stand. At the very least, it supports the reasonableness of the Jewish position until now that belief in Jesus as Messiah could not be entertained, much less required as a test for Jewry's right to live in peace and tranquility, without having to experience continued pressure, by force and other means, to consent to such a belief. Yet, this common sense argument in support of the Jewish religious position, as articulated by rabbis for two millennia, is not adequately made in Berger's book. I think it should be.

Another important omission relates to Berger's disappointment that Orthodox leaders and laity have lagged so far behind in supporting his arguments against Habad messianism. Berger lists seven different reasons, usually given by others, why he now believes that support for his view has been so slow in coming: 1) to avoid community strife; 2) Lubavitcher hasidim live an exemplary Orthodox life; 3) Orthodoxy is already "Balkanized," so it is used to different Orthodoxies; 4) Lubavitch is a *small* movement, intertwined with other Orthodox groups in many ways; 5) Lubavitch is a *very large*, successful movement, of international, global reach and influence; 6) the messianism in Lubavitch is a "transient insanity"; 7) "they do so many good things." Berger has no trouble dealing with each of these. The hardest one, obviously, is the last, and his response is clear and powerful: "And yet — if the emissary is a messianist, all this good turns to ashes." Good deeds that are part of a messianist mission "become instruments of a campaign to deform Judaism." So

279

Lubavitch's very "outreach" successes are now part of the problem; they "hurl me [Berger] into depression."

Berger mentions four other reasons for the lack of Orthodox support for his position, which he readily answers: 1) this messianic belief is not so terrible; 2) Hasidism would be threatened if hasidim were told not to believe what their Rebbe told them; 3) the fight against Habad will be difficult. "Why start a fight with Lubavitch if we will lose support from Lubavitch sympathizers?" 4) Beliefs change, religions evolve!

Berger seems to think that he has found the reasons for the lack of support of his challenge to Habad messianist ideas and practices, even as he answers them. I don't think he has. Let me explain why I think there is much more to be said about this situation. In a long essay called "Judaism and General Culture in Medieval and Early Modern Times," Berger wrote that "mysticism... [achieved] a pre-eminent position in Jewish piety and religious thought by the sixteenth and seventeenth centuries."[1] Berger is referring to kabbalah, particularly Lurianic kabbalah, which is the core of Hasidism, including Habad.[2] No less a figure of contemporary Orthodoxy than Norman Lamm, President for many years of Yeshiva University, recently wrote a book on the religious thought of Hasidism, praising it for its wisdom, "the *new ways of envisioning God*, the world, oneself. The exegesis, the theology and the impetus to inner renewal mutually enhance each other. *Ultimately, they are seen to be one and the same*" (my italics).[3] But the lurking problem is that "new way of envisioning God," as we shall see.

Indeed, even the *Mithnagdim*, the Orthodox who so strongly opposed Hasidism at its inception some three centuries ago, accepted and embraced kabbalah and were represented among its leading scholars, including the Vilna Gaon. They parted company with Hasidism in opposing its widespread dissemination of what *Mithnagdim* considered kabbalah's dangerous aspects. Yet, even here, such a notable *mithnagid* as R. Hayyim of Volozhin encouraged his disciples to study some form of kabbalah, in particular Lurianic kabbalah, every day.[4]

I have no doubt that the Orthodox for whose support Berger is long-ing are, generally speaking, believers in kabbalah. Believing in kabbalah, they believe in Hasidism and especially its most successful exponent, Habad. Indeed, I get the distinct impression that, but for the messianic and Divinity claims of the Lubavitch movement, Berger was and remains a great admirer of Lubavitch without reservation or qualification as to its kabbalistic content. So much so, that he is at great pains to tell us at the very beginning of his book how he criticized another Jewish historian in a book review for that historian's ridicule of a young Lubavitcher hasid in a synagogue in Spain, who was overweight, had his shirttail out, with food residue on his mouth, who was working to rekindle Jewish observance in Spain, despite the fact that the hasid seemed in his appearance to be violating one of the cardinal religious prohibitions in Judaism — i.e., that when a Torah scholar has even a stain on his clothing he is committing a desecration of God's name and is subject to death.[5]

This depth of identification with the hasid, Berger's "deep reservoirs of sympathy," suggests to me that, even as Berger was writing this book, there was a total embrace of all of Habad's principal elements except for the new messianic and Divinity claims being made for the Rebbe. I have no doubt that a similar embrace is shared by Orthodox Jews generally. So I am not surprised by their lethargy in following Berger in his challenge to Habad. Nor will Habad go away easily in this confrontation.

The upshot of all this is quite significant when we realize that kabbal-ah, and Lurianic kabbalah in particular, is identified as one of the key con-tributors to the last false Messiah in Jewish history, Shabbtai Zvi, in large part growing out of its radical "new way of envisioning God," as Norman Lamm correctly viewed it. We must remember that fear of claims for a false Messiah — it was not long since Shabbtai Zvi — was the key factor in the opposition of the *mithnagdim* to Hasidism.[6]

Moreover, the doctrine of God's immanence that is central to Hasidic thought, which postulates that God's presence is pervasive in the cre-ated, physical universe, blurs the distinction between the material world of man and the ineffable, spiritual, transcendent world of God; it was the basis for the Lurianic doctrine that the supporters of Shabbai Zvi used to explain how he could die and still be the Messiah: he didn't die, argued his supporters, he simply was transferred from the material domain of human perception to the Divine domain of God, from which he will return to lead the completion of the redemption.[7] As Idel has pointed out, the hasidic *tzaddik's unio mystica* (mystical union with God) is based on Divine immanence, which was the hasidic doctrine that was a key factor in the challenge of the Vilna Gaon and other *mithnagdim* to Hasidism.[8] From the Lurianic doctrine of immanence as adopted and understood by Hasidism, it is a short step to the hasidic doctrine of the *tzaddik's* (the Rebbe's) ability to achieve mystical union (*unio mystica*) with God, and — from there — to the Rebbe's Divine essence and status as Messiah, which completes the implications of the hasidic doctrine of immanence in terms of the Rebbe's relationship with God as part of the Divine unity. It is worth noting that the ecstatic, mystical ascent to God by the 13th century kabbalist, Abraham Abulafia, was the forerunner of the hasidic doctrine of *devekut* or union with God, and Abulafia considered himself to be the Messiah.[9]

The Rebbe, in hasidic thought, also has the power to annihilate the unclean and evil forces in the world that prevent the Messiah's arrival, an idea based on the Lurianic concept of *tikkun* (mending the Divinity by certain mystical acts of the righteous), but the *tzaddik* was prohibited from using this power because it would cause the immediate coming of the Messiah,[10] presumably because of the confusion this would cause in world Jewry in light of the then recent experience with the false Messiah, Shabbtai Zvi. Once again, it is a short step from the idea of the special ability of the *tzaddik* (the Rebbe) to bring on the Messiah's coming, and identifying the Rebbe himself as the Messiah who is bringing the redemption, especially with the Shabbtai Zvi experience so far in the past and the great difference between the Rebbe and Shabbtai Zvi in terms of their piety and accomplishments.

Here, then, are relevant kabbalistic sources, concepts and materials which Habad has at is disposal to meet Berger's challenge. While they are generally to be found in Berger's book, they are not presented in an organized fashion. While Habad also has not yet marshalled its arguments in the way I have described, it must be anticipated that they will do so if Berger's challenge begins to gather strong and effectual support. But let's be clear. These arguments have been stated or may readily be implied from Habad's responses already, as Berger indicates. For example, the answer to how the Rebbe can be the Messiah, if he died before his messianic tasks were completed, is that he didn't die; he is Divine, and simply moved to the Divine realm. Thus, the claim for the Rebbe's Divinity enhances the claim that he is the Messiah, by removing Berger's argument that he can't be the Messiah because he died before his work was completed. What is Divine, by definition, cannot die. Berger may not agree with the idea of a Divine — in some sense — Messiah, but he presents no conclusive array of sources on that point. Berger's opposition to the claims made for the Rebbe as "fully God," because they are like the Christian doctrine of Incarnation, may find wide acceptance among Jews. However, claims that the Rebbe has acquired some form or aspects of the Divine essence may find more ready acceptance among the Rebbe's admirers and Lubavitch's supporters, as long as the opposition to such claims is as complex in its formulation and presentation as appears in Berger's Appendix II.

There are other elements in Judaism, outside the mystical tradition, which the Rebbe's supporters may present to show that the Rebbe did not "die" despite his burial in 1994. There is the *aggadah* in the Talmud that the Messiah was born on the day that the Second Temple was destroyed, and remains alive in the earthly paradise and awaits the time of the redemption, sometimes appearing at the gates of Rome. Is it possible that this *aggadah* may be reconstituted and applied in some way — combined, perhaps, with the kabbalistic doctrine of *gilgul* (the transmigration of the soul to another human being to assist the fulfillment of a person's task in this world) — to support messianic claims for the Rebbe? Perhaps the Rebbe did not die but was "taken" by God, like Enoch, who "walked with God" and did not die a natural death, or like Elijah, the prophet, who also never died but was "taken" by God, with the accepted expectation in Jewish tradition of his future return, as reflected, e.g., in "Elijah's Chair" at circumcisions. The Talmud says that the last two thousand years of the history of the world is the age of the Messiah. We are now in the year 5765. Here too, Habad may find support for its messianic claims. It may be anticipated that Habad supporters of the Rebbe's Divinity will assert that angels also embody the Divine essence, and we know from Tanakh that they appear as human to humans, they return to their source as elements of the Divinity, and humans even bow down to them when they ascertain that they are Divine, as occurred with the parents of Samson. This, they will assert, can also be applied to the Rebbe, who, being Divine, could not die. Finally, they may point out — ironically, to be sure — that a number of great medieval Jewish philosophers, including R. Hasdai Crescas and R. Joseph Albo, asserted that, contrary to Maimonides, faith in the Messiah is not one of the foundational religious principles of Judaism,[11] so how can there be *undisputed* criteria about the Messiah as a challenge to the Rebbe?

One way or another, the supporters of the Rebbe as Messiah and Divine will find a way to plausibly present their claims to the Orthodox community. Why this sudden, dangerous, but insistent plunge by Habad into messianic waters, that have proved so treacherous in the past? The prevailing opinion is that messianism, like mysticism and apocalypticism, is a response to the trauma of some unbearable reality, which is reflected in a desire to escape to rebirth and the welcoming embrace and comfort of a parental figure.[12] It is difficult to find such a reality in the last two decades. I suggest, however, that the trauma in this case is the loss of the Rebbe's leadership, guidance, and charisma, and — with it — the threat to Habad's entire institutional network and way of life. If the trauma is the Rebbe's loss, then the solution and response could not be simpler or more obvious: the Rebbe did not die; he lives — indeed, he is the Messiah.

In sum, if most of Orthodox Jewry, for centuries, have embraced kabbalah and Hasidism, which is its current embodiment, as a fresh new source of Jewish spirituality, it will be very difficult to convincingly show them that the claims made for the Rebbe are clearly false and outside any legitimate boundaries of Orthodoxy. When those claims are alleged and shown to be organic to kabbalah and Hasidism in their derivation, it will be difficult to cause religious Jews to discard a belief in the Messiah based on such roots, especially when people are searching today for a sign that good will ultimately triumph over evil.

This brings us back to the importance of making the case — not made adequately in Berger's book, in my view — for the common sense correctness that underlies the halahkic pronouncements on which Berger relies. To paraphrase my earlier discussion, you cannot become class valedictorian by walking out of a half-finished final exam and assuring everyone that you will be back at some uncertain future time to correctly complete the rest of the exam. This reasoning can and should be applied to the rabbinic views cited by Berger in Appendix I about the Messiah having to complete his work before his "death," to mean not just death in some limited, technical sense, but any departure of the claimed Messiah from the world as a human being, visible to all as such, before he has completed his tasks.

Berger is encouraged by the support he sees in the resolution of the Rabbinical Council of America (RCA), the umbrella organization of the mainstream Orthodox rabbinate in the United States, which supports Berger's view on the messianic issue. I would not be so sanguine. After much prodding, they passed a resolution which, *without mentioning its connection to Habad, the Rebbe, or the messianic claim being made in his behalf*, simply refers to "disturbing developments that have recently arisen in the Jewish community," and recites *as an abstract halakhic proposition* that Judaism does not accept a Messiah who "will begin his Messianic mission only to experience death, burial and resurrection before completing it."[13] There is not only no explicit reference to the strong, official view within Habad for the challenged messianic position, but there isn't even a reference to Habad at all. The many Jews, including many Orthodox Jews, who are unaware of the existence and strength of the view in Habad regarding the Rebbe as Messiah, are not likely to make that connection merely from learning about the resolution in some way. As for those who are aware of its intent, the resolution is far too brief to persuasively negate the Habad arguments I have outlined, and the strong ties of such Jews to Habad, and their faith in Habad's religious correctness.

This is not the first time that a powerfully endorsed halakhic position failed to achieve an impact on the religious community in large part because that position failed to indicate to whom it might — indeed, should — apply. In 1096, many Jewish martyrs in Germany, who were facing forced conversion by Crusader mobs, chose to kill their wives, their children, and themselves before facing death at the hands of their Christian persecutors. The position generally adopted by the *Tosafists* in the following two centuries, following the precedent of Rabbenu Tam (d.1170), was that martyrdom by suicide (not murder) was permitted where one faced unbearable torture that would lead to certain serious transgressions, like conversion to Christianity. This formulation was generally *followed despite the fact that the chronicles of that martyrdom show that such fear was not the governing concern of the martyrs.*[14] We know from the subsequent history of Ashkenazi Jewry that the martyrs were never criticized or questioned for their radical acts, but were extolled in Jewish tradition thereafter as having sanctified God's Name for their behavior.[15]

In sum, this is an important, courageous, carefully and clearly argued, and generally persuasive book — enhanced, in this regard, by its memoir form, which draws the reader into Berger's legitimate agony as his awareness of the problematics of Habad messianism grows along with his equal despair that no one else seems to care. But, as I have shown, there are crucial areas left unexplored, that need to be explored, particularly by someone as expert in Jewish history and religion as Berger.

Perhaps the most regrettable omission from the book, if we are concerned about preventing future false messianic and Divinity claims — as we should be — is a discussion of what elements of kabbalah in general and Hasidism in particular have been conducive to this most recent manifestation of messianic and Divinity claims. Is it the emphasis on immanence? Is it the various notions of the *tzaddik's* (or Rebbe's) special power to experience union with the Divinity, partake of the Divine influx, and bring back to his community special, useful, magical knowledge?[16] Even the kabbalistic concept of the *sefirot* (Divine emanations and aspects), as applied in Habad belief, may be a causative factor.[17] And we have touched on other questions that may be asked in a similar vein. Whatever they are determined to be, it is these doctrines, ideas, concepts, and beliefs that should become the primary objects of a concerted Orthodox challenge. Once that challenge has been effectively communicated — and this may take some time as an educational process — then it will be far easier to challenge those groups that continue to include those elements as central to their beliefs and practices.

In the meantime, we are left with the following sequential thoughts. If kabbalah can produce two false Messiahs, Shabbtai Zvi and the Rebbe,[18] isn't it probable that it will produce a third and even fourth in the future? In which case we have two problems: the first, is, can we accept any messianic criterion that can produce more than one candidate? The second problem is kabbalah, and its current embodiment in Hasidism, that has in fact already done so. Berger has written a generally fine book on the first problem. It's time for another fine book, hopefully by Berger, on the second.

....

NOTES

1   *Judaism's Encounter With Other Cultures*, Jacob J. Schacter, ed. (Northvale, N.J.: Jason Aronson, Inc., 1997), p. 87.

2   Allan Nadler, *The Faith of the Mithnagdim* (Baltimore: The Johns Hopkins University Press, 1997), Ch. 2; Berger, *The Rebbe...*, *Op. cit.*, p. 124.

3   I am quoting from the review, by Nehemia Polen, of *The Religious Thought of Hasidism: Text and Commentary*, Norman Lamm, tr. and ed. (New York: KTAV/ Yeshiva University Press, 1999), in *Tradition* (Fall 2001): 80-3.

4   Nadler, *...Mithnagdim*, *Op. cit.* On the attitude of the Talmudic Sages discouraging mystical speculation, see *Hag.* 2:1 and B. *Hag.* 14b; also see generally Ephraim Urbach, *The Sages* (Jerusalem: Magnes Press, 1979), p. 193.

5   Berger, *The Rebbe...*, *Op. cit.*, p. 8. The authorities that seem to deal with the hasid's appearance include B. *Shabbat* 114a; Rambam, *Hilkhot De'ot* 5:9, and *Hilkhot Yesodei ha-Torah* 5:11.

6   See note 3; Nadler, *...Mithnagdim*, *Op. cit.*, p. 34. On the roots of Sabbateanism in Lurianic kabbalah, see Gershom Scholem, *Major Trends in Jewish Mysticism* (New York: Schocken, 1961), pp. 287-324.

7   Gershom Scholem, *Shabbetai Sevi* (Princeton: Princeton University Press, 1973), pp. 871-2, 918-9, 929; *idem.*, *Major Trends...*, *Op. cit.*, pp. 294-9. It seems that *Hasidim* and *Mithnagdim* generally shared a strong belief in God's immanence, although the Vilna Gaon was disturbed by the heretical danger of this Hasidic doctrine — it would appear, not without reason; see Nadler, *...Mithnagdim*, *Op. cit.*, Chapter 1. The fact is that immanence and transcendence — which is the core of classical Rabbinic Judaism — are basically inconsistent; see Scholem, *Major Trends...*, *Op. cit.*, p. 180; Julius Guttmann, *Philosophies of Judaism* (New York: Schocken, 1973), pp. 3-18. I use the term "immanence" to include "panentheism;" see David Novak, *The Election of Israel* (Cambridge: Cambridge University Press, 1995), pp. 16-17.

8   Moshe Idel, *Hasidism* (Albany: SUNY Press, 1995), pp. 18, 111-26; Nadler, *... Mithnagdim*, *Op. cit.*, pp. 11-28.

9   Idel, *Hasidism*, *Op.cit.*, p. 16. Habad Hasidism interpreted the Lurianic doctrine of God's contraction (*zim zum*) to permit creation of the material world as not really a contraction but an act of "concealment" of His presence in the universe "from human consciousness;" see Nadler, *...Mithnagdim*, *Op.cit.*, p. 13.

10 Gershom Scholem, *The Messianic Idea in Judaism* (New York: Schocken, 1971), pp. 184-202.

11 Scholem, *Major Trends...*, *Op. cit.*, pp. 280-4, but cf. Eli Muller, "Yosef Backtracks on Holocaust Slur," *The Jerusalem Post*, Internet Edition, August 7, 2000; *Gen.*5:24; 2 Kings 2:11-12; Mal. 3:23; Judges 13:8-24; Yitzhak Baer, *A History of the Jews in Christian Spain* (Philadelphia: Jewish Publication Society, 1978), Vol. 2, pp. 179, 210; B. *San.* 97, 98a; J. *Ber.*2:4. On Enoch, cf. B. *Hag.* 15a. By *gilgul* I mean various forms of metempsychosis detailed by Harris Lenowitz (see note 18, at pp. 67, 126, 150, 199-201). However, in support of Berger's position, the rabbis at the Disputation of Tortosa (1413-1414) asserted that there will be nothing Divine about the Messiah; and they rejected the view that the Messiah would die as part of his pangs and travail in the midst of his redemptive mission; ibid., pp. 188, 190, 192, 200. As is well known, the rabbis also there reiterated Nachmanides' earlier view at the Disputation of Barcelona (1263) that the Jews were not bound to ac-

cept the *aggadah* as binding in matters of belief; ibid., p. 195.

12 See, e.g., Mortimer Ostow, "Judaism and Psychoanalysis," and "The Jewish Response to Crisis," in *Judaism and Psychoanalysis*, Mortimer Ostow, ed. (New York: Ktav, 1982), pp. 1-44, 231-66. On the Disputation at Tortosa, see Baer, ...*Christian Spain*, *Op.cit.*, Ch. XI.

13 Berger, *The Rebbe...*, *Op. cit.*, p. 69.

14 See e.g., B. *Avodah Zara* 18a; Dov I. Frimer, "Masada — In Light of Halakhah," *Tradition* (1971):32-3. The chronicles are appendices in Robert Chazan, *European Jewry and the First Crusade* (Berkeley: University of California Press, 1987), where this martyrdom is discussed in detail. See also, Jacob Katz, *Exclusiveness and Tolerance* (New York: Behrman House, 1961), pp. 82-92; and Haym Soloveitchik, "Religious Law and Change," *AJS Review* (1987): 205-22.

15 See, e.g., the *Kinot for the Ninth of Av (Tisha b'Av)*, Abraham Rosenfeld, tr. and ann. (New York: Judaica Press, 1979), pp. 138-42, 148-9, 169. See generally, Jacob Katz, *Exclusiveness and Tolerance*, *Op. cit.*; and Soloveitchik, "Religious Law...," *Op. cit.*

16 See, e.g., Idel, *Hasidism*, *Op. cit.*, *passim*, especially Introduction and Concluding Remarks.

17 Berger, *The Rebbe...*, *Op. cit.*, p. 124.

18 There are others; see, generally, Harris Lenowitz, *Jewish Messiahs* (London-New York: Oxford University Press, 1998), *passim*.

5

Literature

The clash between creative artists and ultra-Orthodox Judaism is inevitable to the extent that the latter can rarely live up to its ideals of ethical and moral behavior. Moreover, it generally takes an outsider, someone who is familiar with the ideals and the existence of such inconsistent behavior, to bring such inconsistency to the attention of the Jewish world, and sometimes — inevitably — to the outside world. This, in turn, causes a rift within Judaism, of the kind we are seeing recently in charges against certain Jewish authors who have written about such inconsistencies.[1] The fact is that there has been very little great or important creative Jewish fiction written by religious Jews, for whom the exercise is a waste of time that should be devoted to prayer, mystical activity and study of sacred texts. Moreover, the best authors of Jewish fiction have been Jews alienated by mainstream religious Jewry's withdrawal from *tikkun olam* in the post-medieval world, in favor of *tikkun*, the mystical mending of the Divinity. This literature has sought for Jews to recognize ignorance and superstition within their own communities, to achieve a Jewish identity brave enough to participate in worldly ethical, aesthetic, political, economic, and scientific endeavors, and to lay foundations for the Jews' return to their national homeland.

I.B. Singer and his predecessors were interested in describing where Jews had gone wrong and might have gone right had they not carried as baggage an insular, isolated, superstitious cultural life with which made them vulnerable to temptations of every sort, in messianic, sexual, religious, and social activities and ideas.

S.Y. Agnon sought to explain how the declining, disappearing European Orthodox Jewish world could preserve its best aspects for a new Jewish people struggling to emerge as an independent, modern nation in the land of Israel.

Many find in the stories and novels of **Kafka** only universal themes of humanity caught in a mindless, merciless web of bureaucracy and existential chance, from which there is no escape. Others look for the Jewish element in these writings because Kafka's non-fiction — his letters and diaries in particular, and the story of his life — are so full of his tragic, unsuccessful search for a meaningful Jewish identity.

My essay on his letters to Felice Bauer illustrates why the search for Kafka's place in Jewish literature is rewarding. He provides an ironic example, nearly lost, of what Jewish and world literature have gained by his withdrawal from Judaism, and what Judaism and the world lost by Judaism's hostility to creative artists like Kafka, and their painful, yet powerful response.[2]

What this distorted struggle for an integrated, modern Jewish personality has produced, and failed to produce, because of the rigidity and hostility of Orthodoxy to the new Western culture of science, social science, humanities, and nationalism, can be seen in the recent selection by a group of scholars of the 100 greatest books of Jewish (fiction) literature (see my review, **"Firing Off a Jewish Canon,"** in this chapter).[3]

The struggle by Jews to achieve and maintain Jewish cultural identity, in the face of Judaism's cultural insularity, was not shared by Sephardi luminaries under medieval Islamic rule in Spain and is documented in various ways in the essays of this section on Jewish literature.[4] The essay on **Yehudah Halevi** demonstrates, indirectly, the kind of creative writing

— a combination of philosophy, history, and literary imagination — possible when Jews are living in an environment of self-respect, absence of oppression, openness between Jewish culture and its (early Islamic) host culture, where each maintains its cultural identity while borrowing from the other.[5]

....

NOTES

1 See, e.g., Letters to the Editor, *New York Times*, February 27, 2005, Book Review, p. 4; Daniel Schifrin, "The Superficial Reader," *The Jewish Week*, February 25, 2005, p. 58; Marvin Schick, "Fiction Posing as Fact," ibid. p. 15; letters to the editor by Binyamin L. Jolkovsky and Rabbi Avi Shafran, ibid., pp. 6-7; and Wendy Shalit, letter to editor, *The Jewish Week*, March 11, 2005, p. 6.

   An excellent example is the work of the great Yiddish novelist, Chaim Grade, who "explored the tensions of religiosity in the face of both secular seductions and personal and national adversity;" see Curt Leviant, Introductions to Grade's *The Agunah* and to *The Yeshiva*, about a Jewish soul — seeking ethical perfection — in torment, "powerfully affected by ...religion, doubt, and eros."

2 For a fine review of Kafka's life, I recommend Ernst Pawel's *The Nightmare of Reason* (New York: Vintage Books, 1985). On Kafka and other German Jewish writers, see Gershon Shaked, *The Shadows Within* (Philadelphia: Jewish Publication Society, 1987).

3 "The 100 Greatest Works of Jewish Literature," *Pakn Treger* (Fall 2001):5-48.

4 Eliyahu Ashtor, *The Jews of Moslem Spain* (Philadelphia: Jewish Publication Society, 1984), Vol. 3, pp. 3-58.

5 For an interesting analysis of Cynthia Ozick's view of what Jewish literature theoretically should comprise, see Hillel Halkin, "What is Cynthia Ozick About?" *Commentary* (January 2005):49-55. Her test is not easy to apply, as evident from some of the authors whose work she seems to exclude from this category. There is no doubt that, in Classical Judaism, *hokhmah* must have a moral or ethical purpose that will help humanity in a spiritual or material way. Ozick has provided such a test to remove Jewish fiction from the realm of idolatry. To her, all sacred Jewish texts necessarily contemplate interpretation, because to worship the literal words take away their life. It is Karaism, she believes, where the words are worshipped and not their meaning, which should be timeless; ibid.

   Franz Kafka, Isaac Babel, Joseph Roth, Henry Roth, Chaim Grade, the Singer Brothers, Abraham Cahan, Lion Feuchtwanger, Ludwig Lewisohn, S.Y. Agnon, Saul Bellow, Abraham Cahan, Bernard Malamud, I. Peretz, Sholem Aleikhem, Mendele Mokher Seforim, Elie Wiesel, Herman Wouk, and Primo Levi, to name only a few, all wrote at least some Jewish stories that one would be hard put to call Karaitic or idolatrous by Ozick's understanding. Cf. ibid, p. 54.

Firing Off A Jewish Canon:
A Review Essay of Ruth R. Wisse's
The Modern Jewish Canon:
A Journey Through Language and Culture
(New York: The Free Press, 2000)

Ruth Wisse has written a very important — and long overdue — book on great novels of Jewish literature, focusing on Jewish works of the last century. It is particularly timely because the National Yiddish Book Center recently invited a panel of judges to create a list of 100 of the most important Jewish books. Wisse's book will undoubtedly make an important contribution to that endeavor.[1]

The book is important, Wisse tells us, because teaching Jewish civilization is important — for its own sake and as a counterpoint to antisemitism, and .... learning about the Jews is more important for the future of humankind than learning about their [the Jews'] extinction. I think there is something at least as urgent today that needs to be added as a great virtue of this book: It will strengthen Jewish identity among many who are unaware of Jewish contributions to world literature, and Jewish culture.

The benefits of the political, social and economic freedom enjoyed by Jews in the last two centuries has inevitably produced acculturation and assimilation, including vast defections from Judaism — both as a religious and national or ethnic identity — identities that are worth preserving. Moreover, the problem has become significantly and increasingly acute even in Israel, where post-Zionist ideology is moving toward a conception of Israeli identity and the Israeli polity as embracing a secular democratic state that has no necessary connection to a concept of Jewish civilization and Jewish culture.

This problem, of course, has always been the problematic core — and uniqueness — of Judaism, which has been from its inception, both conceptually and practically, a religion and a polity or ethnic political community. So much so, that even Spinoza understood that Jewish ritual was an important part of a Jewish political identity. Unfortunately, he concluded — with a prescient, if flawed, analysis — that, in the diaspora, the rituals of Judaism were dispensable, without explaining how a Jewish return to their own land and nationhood could be achieved if Judaism became just a Unitarian style religion of universal moral values and behavior over a prolonged period in the diaspora.

Ruth Wisse now reminds her Jewish audience — which, I believe, is the primary audience for this book — that Judaism, as a civilization, has produced, in addition to its many contributions to economics, law, philosophy, music, and poetry, to name just some of the important aspects of Jewish civilization during the past 2000 years, a body of literature in its principal modern form, the novel, that ranks with the literature of other nations for its artistry and its message of life, of struggle and survival, and sometimes, of individual and national redemption in history.

For those who have lived without knowledge of this aspect of Jewish civilization, which, in fact, is almost as long as the history of the novel itself — or longer, if we consider the novels and other fictional works produced during the Inquisition's reign — Wisse sets before us a notable and representative sampling of Jewish culture — great novels of the last century — that is worthy of respect, of study, of appreciation, and of understanding. In this regard, she has made the beginning of a vital contribution to stemming the tide of continuing defections from Jewish identity, insofar as they are caused by an almost total ignorance of all of the vibrant aspects of Jewish civilization since the loss of Jewish nationhood 2000 years ago, and completion of the Talmud 1500 years ago. That void in Jewish self-knowledge easily becomes a void in Jewish self-respect and, ultimately Jewish identity and the benefits of its preservation.

In addition to noting this crucial objective in her book, that I believe Wisse should have explicitly emphasized, there is the related question of the causes of this problem, and the importance of Wisse's book, and similar efforts that will surely flow from it, in correcting or ameliorating those causes. Their root, I believe, is a terribly unfortunate bifurcation in Ashkenazi education (which is the focus of Wisse's book) between religious and secular studies, now called *Torah U-Madda* by those engaged in the battle of Modern Orthodoxy with its allegedly more observant opponents on this and other issues, e.g., Zionism. Secular studies were always considered much less important in Ashkenazi culture, in significant part because they were not seen as having "Jewish" content, and this in turn was reflected in the training and expertise of the teachers, and the much stronger emphasis in the classroom on religious studies at the expense of other subjects. When the Jewish Enlightenment movement in Europe (*Haskalah*) sought to include secular studies in the Ashkenazi curricula, they were fought by the religious element, both Hasidim *and* Mithnagdim, of Northern Europe. Italy had always made room for both in its curricula, especially after 1492 with the influx of Sephardi Jews, who had the benefit of a three hundred year tradition under Moslem rule of a high regard for the humanities, producing *Jewish* contributions to non-religious cultural forms like music, poetry, philosophy, and even history, as the noted historian, Yosef Hayim Yerushalmi, notes in *Zakhor*. The effects of the renaissance strengthened this tradition.

This bifurcation was extended in the United States from the elementary school level to the high school level, and then to the university level until the advent of Jewish studies programs, most notably with the study of Jewish history, and — more recently — Holocaust and Hebrew literature. In the 1980's, I did a survey of all the North American day schools to ascertain what Jewish novels they read in their afternoon, secular studies programs. Based on (the usual) 10% response, I easily concluded that there were practically none being taught, with a smattering of exceptions. Wisse's book implicitly points up the continuing need for Jewish educational institutions to include, and to train teachers to know enough to include, in their curricula, at least some of the important works of Jewish literature, and to require a general familiarity with a basic canon. For her book, after all, is — at bottom — suggesting a yardstick for an important element of *Jewish* literacy. The situation has greatly improved, at the high school and college level, but much remains to be done. I would add that developing a canon (or even a few canons!) Is just the beginning of the efforts, and the opportunities, that Wisse's book will lead to, and by no means the easiest. There will be a need for grants and other funding to prepare the teaching materials needed for teacher training and the facilitation of the process of introducing canon works into curricula by teachers at all levels. These materials, in turn, will provide opportunities to develop others for a variety of media and other instructional forms, including movie and TV script outlines, and adult education materials, which will then produce sources of new funding to keep the cycle going.

Thus, Ruth Wisse has broken the ice in many ways, for many purposes, that will gradually emerge, in recognizing the need for, and proposing and describing in admirable detail, an open canon of important modern Jewish novels printed in English — regardless of the language of the author or the original publication. The result is a book that should be an eye-opener for academics and laity alike, about works and authors that have stood the test of time.

Wisse should be congratulated also on not being so hampered by the problem of defining "Jewish literature" that she would omit discussion of wonderful novels by non-Jews on Jewish life. In this regard, I would point to her comments on George Eliot's *Daniel Deronda*, a great novel that played an important role in conditioning the English public to the virtues of Zionism, and to its acceptance of the Balfour Declaration not long thereafter.

Wisse is also to be commended for giving us more than just a list of great Jewish novels (I prepared such a list myself in the 1980's which was reviewed by academics, and was accepted by Ms. Fradle Freidenreich, Director of the Jewish Educational Service of North America [JESNA] at the time). Wisse has grouped her choices — or, more accurately, illustrations — of great Jewish novels in historical and thematic ways. This provides context and insight, and highlights her criterion for a modern "Jewish" novel as a "repository of modern Jewish experience." She applies this criterion broadly, and her groupings allow her to pass critical judgments on Jewish novels with regard to their contribution to the perpetuation of Jewish tradition and political identity, which are the key themes that govern her selections.

Some of Wisse's selections, and the period-theme with which they are associated, are: Sholem Aleichem, Franz Kafka, and Abraham Cahan (From Modern to Modernist Literature); Isaac Babel, Joseph Roth and Sholem Asch (Jewish Literature of War and Revolution); I. B. and I. J. Singer, Der Nister and S.Y. Agnon (Jewish Literature of the Thirties); Primo Levi, Elie Wiesel and Aharon Applefeld (Literature of the Holocaust); Arthur Koestler, Bernard Malamud, and Chaim Grade (Jewish Literature of Mid-Century); and Saul Bellow, Cynthia Ozick, A.B. Yehoshua, and Philip Roth (From Modernism to Postmodernism).

I was disappointed not to see the literature of the *Haskalah* treated in a separate chapter. That movement, in 19th and early 20th century Europe, sought to help Jews and Judaism partake of modernity without losing its Jewish identity — an issue that remains alive today in Israel no less than in the diaspora. Instead, Wisse treats some of the *Haskalah's* most important writers as aspects of the issue of Hebrew (now primarily Israeli) literature, and what that literature lacks by way of elements of the Jewish cultural tradition of the past. The *Haskalah* deserves more. Indeed, I suspect that, if separately treated, it would shed light on the current irony that there seem to be more "Jewish" elements in diaspora "Jewish"

297

literature than in Israeli literature. But that, it appears, will be a topic to be treated in another book — hopefully by Ms. Wisse and, I suspect, by others.

Sometimes, her criticism of a canon candidate, as lacking a loyalty to Jewish identity, is so trenchant that it might have a counter-productive result: if the work is so problematic, one might ask, why bother to read it? It is unfortunate that she did not treat her objections more explicitly as illustrations of the dilemma at the core of Jewish existence that I mentioned above — whether in the diaspora or in Israel as a political entity among the nations: If you are a member of a religion *and* a nation, and a small minority among other religions and nations, how do you control the forces that tend to fracture that combination in so many ways? Thus, e.g., the classic formulation: "If you are just a religion, why are you so separate, and if you are a nation, how can you be a part of us unless you share all of our (avowed) democratic values?" But, I would argue, how the Jew survives in the non-Jewish world — whether these "worlds" are defined religiously or ethnically and nationally — and the related problem of how a Jew deals with the developing non-Jewish culture, are the problems of virtually every major Jewish novel. This is a large statement about what I believe are the central problems of Jewish existence in the modern world of secular states, and it applies to Israel and Israelis no less than to Jews in the Diaspora. Israel, like Jews in the diaspora for centuries, even millennia, faces a continuing struggle to simultaneously survive *and* keep those differences that are its identity alive. The record of that struggle, everywhere, is the essence of Jewish literature. Therefore — writers who struggle with these problems should be read just because they have struggled with these problems, and their answers — whatever they are — need to be evaluated with understanding and even sympathy, and their work recommended for reading and study, precisely because of the dilemma that underlies them — even if we think, or Wisse thinks, that their answers are wrong.

I conclude by noting two omissions from Wisse's book: The first, a reviewer's prerogative, is to mention some of *my* favorites that she omitted. These include: Lion Feuchtwanger, who wrote wonderful novels about turning points in Jewish history; Jakob Wasserman, who struggled with his Jewish identity among Germans who hated him *because of it*; Michael Blankfort; Israel Zangwill; Jay Neugeboren's *The Stolen Jew*; Thomas Mann (a non-Jewish writer), for *Joseph and His Brothers*; Joseph Roth (who is barely mentioned and a far worthier choice than Philip Roth, given Ms. Wisse's own criteria for a writer of Jewish literature); Andre Schwartz-Bart; Moshe Shamir (whose novels, like *The King of Flesh and Blood* and *He Who Must Die*, deal brilliantly with historical Jewish personalities, viz., the Hasmonean King Alexander Yannai and King David); and Herman Wouk, (*Inside, Outside*; *Marjorie Morningstar*; *Winds of War*; *War and Remembrance*; and *The Caine Mutiny*).

The second omission is a bibliography — even just a representative sampling — acknowledging the importance of critical studies of Jewish literature published in the past, which — while not focused on a canon — provide a valuable foundation, with Wisse's book, for future work that will develop the contents and significance of the entire body of Jewish novels, short stories and plays that will comprise what will be an ever-developing canon of worthy works of Jewish fiction. These critical works include — and this is by no means a complete list — works by Daniel Walden, Louis Harap, my beloved teachers, Gershon Shaked and David Roskies; Leon Yudkin; Mark Shechner; Sol Liptzin; Lvov-Rogachevsky; Ephraim Sicher; David Paterson; Murray Baumgarten; Esther Fuchs; Alan L. Berger; Ellen Schiff; Max Nadel; Robert Alter; Arnold Band; Murray Black; Josephine Knopp; Harold Fisch; Azriel Eisenberg; Leslie Fiedler; Hana Wirth-Nesher, Jacob Kabakoff; Nechama Ashkenasy; David C. Jacobson; Kent State University *Studies in American Jewish Literature*; and the journals *Prooftexts* and *Yiddish*, to name just some among many. Any canon should, I believe, contain as complete a bibliography as possible not only of the body of literature that was deemed worthy of consideration, but of those whose efforts of cataloging and critiquing Jewish literature, past and present, provide the material that is so crucial to the first canon, and will connect one canon to the next.

On Sephardi literature, for those who might be interested, I recommend, for a start, Colbert Nepaulsing, *Apples of Gold in Filigrees of Silver: Jewish Writing in the Eye of the Spanish Inquisition*, as a taste of how far back courageous, life-embracing Jewish fiction goes. His analysis of Jewish novels as coded *samizdat* under relentless persecution, is eye opening and deeply moving.

With these small caveats, I recommend Ruth Wisse's new book as a required part of every Jewish library, and every Jewish Studies or Rabbinics program.

. . . .
NOTE

1   The list compiled by the panel can be found in the Center's magazine, *Pakn Treger*, in its special issue, Fall, 2001

Kabbalistic Feminism in Agnon's *Betrothed*

Introduction

The struggle to provide and maintain a Jewish identity as the core of Israeli culture, in the face of the chasm in Jewish life opened up by modernity between the self and reason at war with community and faith, is an underlying theme in much of Agnon's work. He simultaneously developed this theme and reflected it in his writing technique, by using modern literary approaches to character analysis and plot development, together with traditional Jewish symbols, allusions and subtexts. Nowhere is his concern about the importance of maintaining the Jewish core in Israeli life — indeed, in the lives of Jews everywhere, but even, perhaps, especially, in Israel — than in his two novellas, *Edo and Enam* (1950), and *Betrothed* (1943).[1]

Betrothed, written in the midst of the Holocaust, sought to provide some reassurance that, somehow, the bones of Jewish tradition would yet live — or, more precisely, magically come alive again in the *Yishuv*, in the newborn Jewish homeland of *Erez Yisrael*. The reassurance is conveyed in *Betrothed* through the mystical doctrines of kabbalah, that portray history as the pre-destined process of the liberation of the sparks of Divine holiness temporarily captured in a world of evil, and their ultimate reunification with the Godhead through a spiritually redeemed Israel (Jacob in the story) united with the *Shekhinah* (Shoshanah in the story). But Agnon adds a strong dramatic touch to his novelistic treatment, pitting the spiri-

tual, feminine *Shekhinah* of kabbalah against six secular, lovely, but lethal, spiritually debilitating young women of the *Yishuv*, in a cosmic battle
for the soul of Jacob. The latter, in context, is made into an anti-hero;
while ambitious and dedicated to his own professional advancement, he
remains passive, uninterested and even oblivious of the spiritual battle
around him.

Summary of the Story

As children, living in the European *galut*, Jacob and Shoshanah (before
Betrothed starts) had sworn eternal faithfulness to each other while playing together at the home of her parents, who had reached out to Jacob
when his mother died in his youth. Their betrothal is consummated in
a ceremony in which she cuts off a lock of her hair and his, and burns
the hair, and they both consume the ashes.[2] As the novella opens, Jacob
is a young man living in the Land of Israel. His *aliyah* was funded by
Shoshanah's wealthy father, Ehrlich, but started as an educational and
career opportunity rather than as an expression of any Zionist idealism by
either of them. Jacob has remained in the *Yishuv* as a teacher at a university, where he does research in the dead plant life of the Mediterranean,
an activity "remote from the interests of the Jewish settlements;" not surprisingly, his cultural interests run to Hellenism rather than Hebraism.[3]

He lives in a secular city, Jaffa, where each person is busy "pursuing
his own ends,"[4] and associates with a circle of six similar secular young
women; together, they become known as the "Seven Planets."[5] Oddly,
there is not even the hint of any sex or romance between Jacob and any
of them, despite their variety of origins, physique and personality. They
spend time together in the homes, streets, and beaches of Jaffa, on the
Mediterranean, under what seems like a remote, unseeing, star-filled sky
— bonded to nature, happy together in an innocent, almost childlike
way, in a cyclical, unchanging existence, with no evident goals, cares or
concerns. Jacob is passive to them, and to the land and its culture.

Suddenly, Jacob learns that Shoshanah and her father are coming to

Palestine for a brief visit, at the end of a long, worldwide trip that has taken them to many countries, before returning home to Vienna. Meeting Shoshanah for the first time as an adult, after many years, he immediately senses a permanent attachment to her — based more on their mutual childhood covenant than on any special feelings that she now engenders. But he feels undeserving of her, and unhappy, without knowing why.[6] Shoshanah seems jealous of his six girl friends[7] — particularly of Tamar, to whom Jacob has been most physically attracted (although Shoshanah had no evident way of knowing this) — and insists that Jacob repeat his childhood vow of faithfulness and marriage. But their future as a couple is clouded. First, there are her continued bouts of somnolence, interrupted only by a rewarding tour of the *Yishuv* — in which she is impressed by the rebuilding of the land and language of the Jewish people[8] while her father continues to view it as a place for the old, for retirement and death.[9] Second, Shoshanah's and Jacob's outlooks are fundamentally different. He values his freedom and his career, and looks at the world optimistically, as a place of opportunity. She sees herself as separated from the world, a world which humans have nothing "to be proud about."[10] Third, Jacob is offered an attractive new position in America, and he quickly decides that it's time to move on, even if this means leaving Palestine and Shoshanah.

At this point, Shoshanah falls into a virtual coma; her doctor's scientifically based prognosis is that she will die unless she returns promptly to Vienna for some unspecified treatment.[11] Jacob finds out about her illness and, this one time revealing a religious sensibility, prays: "Oh God,... save *me* in Your great mercy"[12] (emphasis added). Yet, he is determined to go do America. To deter him, Tamar attempts to seduce Jacob, but they are interrupted by the rest of the women, who succeed in moving the action, one last time, to the seashore, under the stars. They determine that one of them shall marry Jacob and go to America with him — the victor in a race that reverses the Greek practice; the girls will race for the man. The night and the rite capture the passive Jacob into seeming acquiescence at his coming captivity. Just when it appears that Tamar is about to win the race, Shoshanah appears and overtakes the pack, captures her human prize, and crowns herself with the garland of seaweed which the girls prepared for the victor.

Story Analysis

The battle of the contending forces of tradition and modernity in Jewish history is portrayed in *Betrothed* through the Jewish community in the Land of Israel, as it struggles to create a new homeland for the Jewish people. Agnon praises those who love the land and its people, who come to the land, work the land, and stay in the land — for whatever reason or motive. The Yemenite Jews have difficulty in reconciling Biblical texts with the world of reality, but — unlike Jacob — they continue to live and work in Israel, and to study Torah and obey its commandments. [13] The Russian Jews are enthusiastic and passionate to the point of incivility, and the *Sephardim* are unsociable and superior, but both are loyal to their People and their Land. Yet, while the return to the Promised Land has required the destruction of the passivity, the defeatism — indeed, even the traditional faith — of most of Diaspora Jewry, Agnon recognizes that there can be no justification for the return unless the new Israel, represented by Jacob, inherits the tradition of Jacob's ancestors — represented, as we shall see, by Shoshanah. Even her secular father, Ehrlich, is able to discern that she and Jacob are eternally tied together, as he says to Jacob after the latter has decided to leave Shoshanah and the Land of Israel:

> "Let me put it to you this way. Suppose I am holding on to some valuable object, which I am about to return to its *rightful* owner. Suddenly, the object slips from my hands before it has reached the owner and there we are, both left empty-handed; I who had it in my grasp and he who reached out to take it" (emphasis added).[14]

But that eternal bond, that alone can give a reborn Jewish people an identity, is threatened by secularism, on two fronts. First, is the battle for Jacob's loyalty to the Land, represented by the invitation from New York that he go there to become a full professor and occupy an academic chair that has been established in his honor. Second, is the looming battle for Jacob's spiritual and cultural loyalty between Shoshanah and the six maidens — indeed, between Shoshanah and the entire secular ambiance of the story, from Vienna to Jaffa, from her father to the "Seven Planets," from ancient sea to modern university. Both battles are ultimately a battle between Judaism and Hellenism, for Jacob's soul. Given his secular training and career, and a life that is not rooted in Jewish tradition, it seems inevitable to Agnon that secular Judaism means the death of Judaism and ultimately of the Jewish people.

Thus, Jacob's response to the call of New York to his career is single-minded and unreserved acceptance. His decision to leave, and Shoshanah's resultant sickness, produce another challenge, one last attempt by the six maidens to capture Jacob as a husband for one of them, if not for the land and its people. For them, the issue is who will go with Jacob to America. Looking out from the shore to a passing ship, too far to permit a perception of its direction, "to Jacob and his companions it made no difference where the ship was headed."[15] For them, as for Ehrlich, travel is the goal, to see the world; all places and cultures are equal. Leaving the Land of Israel is no different than coming to it, if there is no special meaning to *Erez Yisrael*.

We are now ready to understand Shoshanah, and her role in the battle for Jacob's soul, a battle between Past and Future, Religion and Nature, Spirituality and Science, Hebraism and Paganism, Jewish tradition and Greek and Roman culture, God and Nature, the three-century old Death of Religion and its rebirth. For Agnon, however, there is more to the tale than just that clash; at stake is the inevitability of its resolution, an inevitability that Agnon represents for us in the symbols that permeate *Betrothed*.

Jacob is seemingly a permanent part of a secular circle which Agnon describes, in the words of the Jaffa community, as the "Seven Planets."[16] These, in turn, represent the kabbalistic concept of the seven lower *sefirot*, or emanations of God, which represent the Divine in the material, observable universe, and guide its destiny. The three uppermost *sefirot* are *Keter* (the *ein sof* or eternal Godhead), and *Hakhmah* and *Binah* (wisdom and intelligence), the two forms of knowledge in their male and female aspects. Together they make up the three upper *sefirot* that man cannot even approach. But through Torah, and the kabbalistic understanding of its symbols and commandments, man may comprehend and achieve the essence of the seven lower *sefirot*: *Tiferet* (beauty or compassion) (Jacob and the People of Israel); *Hesed* (love) (Abraham); *Gevurah* (power) (Isaac); *Nezah* (endurance) (Moses); *Hod* (majesty) (Aaron); *Yesod* (foundation) (Joseph); and — the tenth and most mystical of the sefirot — *Malkhut* (kingdom) (David). The last *sefirah* is not limited, however, to David. Indeed, in Lurianic kabbalah it stands for the *Shekhinah*, the feminine, merciful aspect of God that must combine with *Tiferet* (Jacob) and ultimately with the Godhead itself, with *Keter*, in order for the world to operate in harmony and thereby be redeemed and returned to its original perfection, the perfect unity of God. Shoshanah, in Jewish tradition, is the *Shekhinah*. Thus, the history of the universe becomes, in kabbalah, a spiritual process of world redemption, in which the *Shekhinah* is the catalyst. Somehow, Shoshanah must become part of Jacob's circle of seven — and transform it by her presence and union with Jacob from seven secular "planets" to seven holy *sefirot*. Because of this Divine Plan, comprising the subtext of *Betrothed*, harmony will come, and redemption is inevitable.[17]

The Israeli critic, and my revered teacher, Gershon Shaked, has recognized the importance, for Agnon, of the miraculous in explaining Jewish history and its eternality. He argues that Agnon usually provides non-realistic, even miraculous escapes from the historical abysses and dead-ends faced by Jewish ideals and traditions, when his characters are confronted or mocked by the stubborn realities of modernity. Agnon generally provides

>...a miraculous and non-rational counter-plot, deriving from irrational realms .... These works do not end happily, with reconciliation, but rather with acknowledgement of the dead-end, the gap between the powers at odds with each other....

>According to the nature of things and logic, recent generations of Jewish society have reached a cul-de-sac, and each generation, everywhere, is threatened with devastation. One might possibly say that the final lesson of Agnon's view of history and society is that the society exists by virtue of miracles, and if we do not depend on miracles, we have nothing to depend on.[18]

Jewish tradition is rich in the symbolic importance of the *Shekhinah* and its metaphor, Shoshanah (or rose). The Midrash speaks of the *Shekhinah* as the Divine Presence, an aspect — and more particularly the feminine, daughter, sister, and bride, aspect — of the Godhead, to which (a male) Israel seeks to cleave. It also equates that term with *Knesset Yisrael*, the Jewish people in its ideal (feminine) form, which claims (a male) God as hers alone, as Shoshanah claimed Jacob when they were children. Their mutual oath in *Betrothed* is like a modern double ring ceremony; each is dedicated to the other — "*Dodi li, v'ani lo*," as we read in *Song of Songs*, the canonical love duet and love longings between God and Israel as they eternally search for each other in the streets of Jerusalem. The Midrash speaks of Israel, the *shoshanah* of God, as a "rose among the thorns," in that, like Agnon's Shoshanah, it withstood foreign cultures while in *galut*, preserving the purity of Jewish belief, of Jewish monotheism and spirituality.[19]

Agnon does not leave Shoshanah's status, as a player in a cosmic process, to our imagination or speculation. He does more than simply provide her with a name with traditional connotations. He endows her dramatically with redemptive qualities. She is a *galut* girl who, unlike Jacob, has not lost her Jewish pride and identity despite the past secular ambience of her family and country. Though a latecomer to the Holy Land, she knows where she belongs when she gets there.

The *Shekhinah* (Shoshanah) has been in *galut*, where our tradition tells us it went to accompany and preserve Israel in its wanderings among the nations (B. *Meg.* 29 a).[20] It has always sought to remain close to Israel, just as Shoshanah and Jacob, although having different parents, lived together in Vienna as part of one family. Shoshanah and the People of Israel were, from the beginning of exile, betrothed, as God took Israel for His bride on Mount Sinai. It was an oath taken to last until redemption, and the final unity of the People of Israel with the *Shekhinah*, in the Land of Israel.

But, as the *Zohar* represents, they have become separated, and, wandering from land to land, she is now tired, sleepy, although still able to withstand long voyages. Agnon's imagery reminds us of *Song of Songs*, where Shoshanah (there representing the Jewish People [2:1]), describes herself as "asleep, but my heart is awake" (5:2). She can endure separation and endless travel among the nations away from Jacob as long as she is not permanently rejected by him. She is prescient (recall her meeting with Tamar), suggesting powers that are more than mortal, the powers of spiritual insight. Indeed, when Jacob and Shoshanah first meet, as adults, in *Erez Yisrael*, Shoshanah speaks optimistically of "the resurrection of the dead," a concept which the secular Jacob emphatically rejects. [21] For Shoshanah, there is more to history than man's perception of reality; for Jacob, there is only reality, the lessons of science. Her response, as if sensing that there will soon come a time when resurrection of the dead will have to be a reality for both of them, is described in the following way by Agnon:[22]

> At that moment Shoshanah seemed to hover
> (*merahefet*) over those blue distances she had spoken
> of. Then, suddenly, she answered Jacob's gaze. She

took out her handkerchief, wiped her eyes, opened
them and looked at him with absolute love. After a
while she said, "I am going to close my eyes and you,
Jacob, are to kiss me on the eyelids." Jacob's own eyes
filled with tears. With the tears still there, he placed
his lips on her wet lashes.

Later, when Jacob is about to be enveloped in a pagan marriage rite
orchestrated by the six maidens, this kiss and its remembrance will save
him,[23] protecting him from an enveloping, consuming alien embrace.
We should note Agnon's use of the word *"merahefet,"* hovering, to describe Shoshanah's spirit, with its connotation of the Divine Spirit, from
the opening lines of *Genesis*.

Shoshanah is not close to her father,[24] who is secular; and Agnon
suggests that his love for her is less as a daughter than as an heirloom, a
treasured object of which one is proud, behind glass or in a portrait, but
which is not a part of one's active life. She remains aloof from foreign
cultures and uncontaminated by them. For Shoshanah, her childhood
oath with Jacob is a lasting one. She loves the Land of Israel, as we see
in her joy at her father's decision to settle in *Erez Yisrael*, and at the use
of the Hebrew language as the language of prayer and daily life by her
reborn People in a reborn Land. Shoshanah identifies Hebrew with the
siddur, the Jewish prayer book and its language of prayer, that brings man
in direct contact with God. Unlike Jacob, she believes in personal rebirth
— personal resurrection — one of Maimonides' thirteen fundamental
creeds of Judaism.

Jacob, like her father, shares neither her spirituality nor her faith.
Indeed, she is the only protagonist in the story with a belief in, and an attachment to, Jewish land, liturgy, ritual, history and theology. Neither her
father, nor Jacob, nor the "six maidens," show a loyalty to these values.
It is her full acceptance of Jewish tradition that differentiates her from
the others, that separates the *Shekhinah* from the other, opposite, forces
contending for Jacob's soul. These forces include the locus of the story

— multi-national, secular Jaffa, which Agnon points out was established by Japheth, father of Indo-European nations and cultures, and the Greek and Roman traditions and values of Western civilization. Jacob still clings to them; Shoshanah easily sheds them.[25]

To realistically portray Jacob as both Shoshanah's beloved and the object of her spiritual battle for him, Agnon insightfully makes Jacob merely a passive, easily diverted, symbol of Hellenism. His life represents not Eros and instinct, as in the case of the six maidens who surround him, but knowledge and science — not Dionysus but Apollo.[26] As we have seen, the key to the meaning of Shoshanah's relationship with Jacob is provided by the kabbalah and its imaging of the cosmic process of redemption. Significantly, for Agnon, it is Shoshanah who must pursue and capture the passive Jacob, who is incapable of overcoming his desire to pursue, alone, a secular scientific life — despite his instinctive understanding that without Shoshanah he is nothing.

At the beginning of the story, the *Shekhinah* and Israel have become separated; we recall her words in *Song of Songs*, "*ani yeshena, v'libi er,*" "I am asleep but my heart is awake," and we read about Shoshanah's initial intermittent dazedness, sleepiness, and her glazed, uninterested look as she waits unsuccessfully for Jacob to choose her over her spiritual adversaries, and bring redemption to the world.[27] She has been this way since he left her years ago to find his individual fulfillment.[28] Meanwhile, Jacob has been bound up in a life from which every element of Jewish tradition has been lost. But, soon after Shoshanah's arrival in Palestine, she has Jacob reaffirm his oath of loyalty to her, to the *Shekhinah*, which he does without hesitation or reservation, although, as his actions show, still without real love and total commitment.[29]

From that moment on, Shoshanah is alert, active, even enjoying material pleasures.[30] Yet, Shoshanah is still unhappy as she contemplates the future, knowing from her past European, Viennese experience that life even together with Jacob will be difficult in a hostile, warring world, in which evil is so powerful. Shoshanah's sadness is not a private death wish, but the real concern of someone who is aware of Jewish suffering, [31] fore-seeing that so much hardship is in store for them in the real world.

In contrast, Jacob is optimistic about the future, which he can see only as a vibrant young man, and not as a Jew threatened by the cultures that surround him. "Both of us are young enough, with all of our life before us." It is Jacob, the modern man of science and reason, who is unrealistically optimistic, who — caring only about himself — cannot accurately see where a world without spirituality is heading.[32] But Shoshanah, sensitive to Israel's tradition and history, despairs, because she is concerned that the future may not be "any better than the life that lies behind." [33] The depth of Agnon's own despair in the middle of the Holocaust is represented by the despair of the *Shekhinah* itself, even as it contemplates renewed spiritual union with Israel, in the Land of Israel.

Jacob, because of his estrangement from Judaism, now is twice tempted to betray Shoshanah. First, he accepts the offer to become a professor in a New York university, without thought or regret. Shoshanah presumably learns about Jacob's decision when the rest of Jaffa learns about it, as they do very quickly.[34] Only then does she succumb to a new kind of sleep, seemingly permanent and just short of death, an illness both real and metaphysical, as she is about to be abandoned again by Jacob.

But the lure of a new, voluntary *galut* in New York is not the only temptation facing Jacob. A far more serious test immediately awaits him, a test to which Shoshanah herself must respond, lest the Divine Plan for redemption go awry. For the six maidens now make one last effort to capture Jacob permanently, which is to say, to exclude the *Shekhinah* permanently from their community, and from ever marrying Jacob. It begins as Tamar comes to see him in his room for the first time [35] — Tamar, whom Shoshanah perceived as the true obstacle to her spiritually and physically uniting with Jacob and entering the "circle of seven," as Jewish tradition envisions, and thereby changing its essence from natural "planets" to spiritual *sefirot*. It is Tamar to whom Jacob has been most attracted physically and with whom he has most nearly formed a physical attachment. It is this

311

Tamar, whose name connotes a dark moral aspect in Jewish tradition,[36] who now appears, asking Jacob for advice on two strangely contrasting career paths, which now become understandable in their symbolism. The first alternative is for Tamar to go to Europe and become a doctor (a traditional and honorable career for a Jew) and thereby leave room for Shoshanah to join the circle of seven. The second, is for Tamar to remain in Israel and take up sculpturing (symbolic of graven images) and the beauty of form, a cultural symbol of Paganism and Hellenism, with their emphasis on strength and beauty. As we shall see, Tamar's appearance in Jacob's room, ostensibly for career advice, is a ruse for arousal. Tamar is out to become, and is about to become, the wife of Jacob — which will permanently exclude Shoshanah from the "planets," destroy the re-unification of the Divine *sefirot*, and bind Jacob forever to all that Tamar represents.

In short order, Tamar is joined by the other five girls, and there soon commences an unmistakably pagan, Greek rite under the stars, at the water's edge of Jaffa. They encircle and dance around Jacob, reminiscent of the psalmist's remark, *"sabuni gam sevavuni"* ("they encompassed me about"), in describing the encirclement of Israel by its enemies. Soon, the girls decide to emulate the Greeks and have a race, with the win-ner — the "mighty runner" — to be crowned by Jacob and given to him in marriage.[37] Jacob is described as in a state of being "carried be-yond himself'," as he had been all those other nights that he and the six maidens had walked by the sea under the stars feeling at one with the mighty beauty of nature around them — heaven and earth, land and sea — "which had become a single whole."[38]

But, adds Agnon, so that the reader keeps the invisible Divine role in mind, "this [unity of' nature] was contained in yet another greater whole that no eye could see."[39] Indeed, while Jacob now "put[s] Shoshanah en-tirely out of his mind" and is completely in the power of the maidens and the outcome of their rites, Agnon has not forgotten her: "Her memory formed a circle around his heart, like the golden lashes around her eyes as she slept,"[40] the lashes that she had earlier insisted that Jacob kiss, with evident prescience.[41]

The race commences, with the one who proves to be the most "mighty," not the one whom Jacob truly loves, to be his bride.[42] Here, Agnon presents a powerful irony. Jacob, who prides himself on his independence and freedom, has now become the object of capture and enslavement by those who symbolically represent precisely those values and virtues he has most sought in life. His enslavement will be symbolized by his being crowned by the victor with the very seaweed, the subject of his professional excellence, that symbolized that freedom and independence.[43] To compound the irony, his enslavement is about to be achieved by Tamar, who is about to win the race, and with it Jacob, and thereby change a destiny that, of course, cannot be changed, because for Agnon there is a "greater whole that no eye could see."[44] We know that Tamar wants to win the race and Jacob, because Agnon is careful to point out that she overtakes first Rachel and Leah, then Mira, Asnat and Raya, who had alternately taken the lead.[45] Indeed, it is now evident from this effort that winning Jacob was her objective when she came to his room, ostensibly to discuss career choices.

Shoshanah suddenly appears, in her white nightgown, "like a maiden suddenly alarmed in her sleep,"[46] alarmed because history is about to be irrevocably changed, because a destiny foretold in Jewish tradition is about to be permanently altered, nullified. She almost literally rises from the dead and wins Jacob's hand, crowned by the garland of seaweed prepared by her adversaries,[47] which recalls her garland when, as children, she and Jacob first vowed their eternal union. She triumphs not because such an outcome is rational, but because for Agnon she is an instrument — the crucial instrument — of God's Divine plan for Israel. Harmony has been restored to history through the Divine Plan as understood by kabbalah.

Agnon's imagery of a near-death Shoshanah saving Jacob, the assimilated Jew, from extinction, re-enacting a pre-ordained cosmic process,

313

points to an important message. Shoshanah can never be re-united with Jacob unless she pursues him, because the modern pull of acculturation makes him incapable of permanently identifying with and choosing either Shoshanah or her opposites. For him, as Gershon Shaked suggests,[48] they are all sisters, each other's and his, and so he cannot independently unite with any of them without help. But, Agnon inverts the kabbalistic tradition of the *Shekhinah* waiting for an impatient lover, the *ze'ir anpin*, to symbolize how difficult the process of redemption will be. In the modern world, man cannot rely on a kabbalistically foretold destiny; only a miracle, wrought by those who believe in miracles and embrace those who do not, will suffice.[49]

How Does It End?

Agnon never lets us be certain of what the verdict of history will be, which is to say, whether history and not God will really write the final text of his story. For, at the end of *Betrothed*, we are told that this is the end of the story "for the time being." On what does the outcome depend? That we are not told. In the end, perhaps, it is for each of us to answer that question, by our faith, or our actions, perhaps both. Is Israel safe, even within the Land of Israel, if its culture, indigenous or imported, is a secular culture without religious content?[50] For the hideous possibility of Israel permanently exiled in its own land, *Betrothed* provides the healing balm of the possibility of a faith that such a permanent separation is impossible between Jacob and his eternal, historic, covenanted companion, Shoshanah. Such an exile, resulting from the permanent incompatibility between the Shekhinah and Israel, would be contrary to God's plan in Jewish tradition, which provides the underlying text for this story.

There remains the question of whether there is a possibility, as some critics suggest, that the ending of *Betrothed* is a parody of Jewish tradition, a sick joke played at Jacob's expense. Is *Betrothed* a story of Thanatos,[51] symbolized by Shoshanah capturing Jacob in a final deathly embrace, or — as I have suggested — a symbolic tale of hope for a Judaism and

314

a Jewish people saved at the last minute from the deathly embrace of Hellenism and assimilation?

There does seem to be a sharp contrast, as Shaked suggests, between the *Shoshanat Ya'akov*, the Shoshanah of Jacob in the Jewish tradition (in the Purim poem established by the Great Assembly in the 5th Century, B.C.E.) who is *zahala ve'sameha*, happy and joyous, and the almost always sad, sleepy, and death-obsessed Shoshanah of Agnon's novella. Yet, it is difficult to support the view that Agnon is parodying the tradition — giving us a story ending in death and not life (or ignoring Jewish tradition altogether, as a minority suggest) — rather than employing it, as I argue, as a serious subtext for *Betrothed*. To adopt the parody view, one would have to believe that Agnon adopted in *Betrothed*, while the Holocaust was raging, the critique of traditional Judaism by the anti-Semite Nietzsche as the life-denying way of life, par excellence. One would have to believe that Agnon embraced in *Betrothed*, while Jewry's religious sages were being murdered, the anti-religious, secularist-nationalist views of such as A.D. Gordon, M.J. Berdiczewski and Ahad Ha'am. This is too radical a view for Agnon; it is not his way.[52] I believe, therefore, that Shoshanah is seriously and not ironically symbolized, and her sadness and death obsession are not meant to ridicule the *Shekhinah* of Jewish tradition but to reflect on its historic crisis and describe its ultimate redemption. But there are additional historical and textual reasons that may be adduced.

Betrothed was written in 1942–43, when Hitler still occupied most of European Russia and most of North Africa, and was close to seizing Palestine and the rest of the Middle East, when the Holocaust had become known as an actuality if not in its full dimensions of 6 million Jewish dead. Shoshanah has a right, as it were — without symbolizing Thanatos — in a work written to be read by readers living in the awesome eye of Hitler's racial devastation, to envy the dead and to foresee tragedy lying ahead for her and for Jacob. Yet, she seeks and obtains Jacob's commitment to marriage and a future life together, and looks forward to it; she praises the rebirth of Hebrew and the Jewish people in the *Yishuv*; and she literally jumps for joy when learning that she and her father will live in *Erez Yisrael*. These are not the indications of a person who craves death, but of a sensitive, aware, realistic person who spiritually and ideologically wants to live and achieve her destiny, even while — on a realistic and rational level — she recognizes how difficult Jewish life can be.

And there is the concluding personal observation by Agnon at the end of *Betrothed*, where he tells us that, because Shoshanah and Jacob were betrothed to one another through a solemn vow, he has titled the work *Sh'vuat Emunim*, the vow of those who are faithful (to God? to each other? to both?) and not, as "at first we had thought to call it, *'The Seven Maidens'*." The concept of covenant between Jacob and Shoshanah overcame the secular, ambivalent, ironic concept of seven maidens (i.e., the inappropriate combination of the *Shekhinah* with her spiritual antagonists). For, without Jacob, there is no special content to "seven maidens;" they would merely symbolize seven women fighting for the loyalty and love of a man. But, because of the childhood oath sworn by Jacob and Shoshanah, symbolizing the covenant at Sinai between Israel in its historic youth and God, the title — and the story's significance — had to be restated as the "Vow of the Faithful."[53]

The tale will, indeed, continue, as Agnon has noted, but the chasm between Jewish dreams and Jewish realities, and the modern chasm between what our minds believe and our souls perceive, will ultimately be bridged, as *Betrothed* reassures those with faith in Jewish destiny and redemption.

....

NOTES

1 As to *Edo and Enam*, see Cynthia Ozick, "Agnon's Antagonisms," *Commentary* (December 1988): 43-8. Recent treatments of Agnon as a modern traditionalist are Anne Golomb Hoffman, *Between Exile and Return: S.Y. Agnon and the Drama of Writing* (Albany: SUNY Press, 1991); *idem*, "Agnon for All Seasons: Recent Trends in Criticism," *Prooftexts* 11 (January 1991): 80-95; Gershon Shaked, Jeffrey M. Green, tr,. *Shmuel Yosef Agnon: A Revolutionary Traditionalist* (N.Y.: New York University Press, 1989). As Robert Alter writes in *Defenses of the Imagination* (Phila.: Jewish Publication Society, 1977), p. 170:

   "Yet Agnon could not, I think, have written at all without in some way using his work to sound the abysses of modern history, for modern history constituted a ruthlessly uncompromising challenge to the validity of the [Jewish] language, values and traditions from which he shaped his fiction."

2 Chapter 3, page 12 (format hereafter 3:12), and 24:104. References are to the chapter and page number of the English translation of *Betrothed* in *Two Tales by Agnon: Betrothed and Edo and Enam* (N.Y.: Schocken Books, 1966). This ceremony recalls many similar kabbalistic rituals to ward off future misfortune. See Stephen Sharot, *Messianism, Mysticism, and Magic — A Sociological Analysis of Jewish Religious Movements* (University of North Carolina Press, 1982), pp. 42-43. After they meet again, Jacob remembers how, just before the vow, she had plunged into her father's pond and emerged, covered with seaweed, and he realizes how this event may have determined his choice of career — and, Agnon intimates, the future events in his life. Interestingly, the garland of laurel wreath is both a Greek and Jewish tradition. In Judaism it represents not only victory and royalty but beauty, the bride, and the priesthood. See Eliezer ben Yehudah, *A Complete Dictionary of Current and Modern Hebrew* (N.Y.: Thomas Yoseloff, 1960), Vol. III, p. 2395, s.v. *kalil*; see also *Kinot for Tishah B'Av (klilat yofi)* and the *hoshanot* for *Succot (even shtiyah)*.

3 1:9; 5:21. Jacob is wont to thank the "gods" when things are going well, but rarely God as One. Compare 22:89, 28:120, and 29:121 with 23:97.

4 1:3-3; 26:114

5 5:22

6 7:30; "Without her, the whole world would be lost to him" (22:93). At one point, imagining that Shoshanah's father disapproves of him as a future son-in-law, Jacob uncharacteristically resolves to marry her by force, if necessary, as a symbol of his freedom (20:80-81).

7 19:69-70, 76; 21:83-4; 22:90-1, 94; 29:123.

8 22:87-8; For Shoshanah, the rebirth of the Hebrew language, "the language of the prayer book," is "wonderful."

9 Chs. 12-14, 21. For her father, steeped in secular universalism and cynicism, all people, places and cultures are the same, and none are worthy of special commitment. The land of Israel is a place for death and the object of charity, not for life and financial commitment looking toward historical rebirth and rejuvenation.

10 22:88, 92.

11 25:105, 106, 109.

12 25:12

13 12:46-47.

14 25:109.

15 31:130.

16 Agnon here alludes to a mixed symbol, connoting Hellenism and Jacob's potential liberation to Hebraism. In astronomy, the "Seven Sisters" is the term used to describe the Pleiades, a star field in the large constellation of Taurus; see Gilbert E. Satterthwaite, *Encyclopedia of Astronomy* (N.Y.: St. Martin's Press, 1971). Note how Jacob, in his passive relationship to the six maidens, becomes — symbolically — one of seven "sisters." In Jewish tradition, the Pleiades, known as *Kimah*, symbolize the seven pillars of Jewish wisdom, *hokhmah*. See *Proverbs* 9:1; *Amos* 5:8; *Job* 9:9 and 38:31 in the *Mikraot Gedolot* edition of *Tanakh* (N.Y.: MP Press, 1981). At the same time, the aspect of Paganism and Hellenism is also conveyed, because of the esteem paid by ancient cultures to the Pleiades. See the commentary in *Tanakh* (Tel Aviv: S. L. Gordon, 1956), at *Job* 9:9 and 38:31. Moreover, in his commentary on *Proverbs* 9:1, Abraham ibn Ezra suggests, in his often-used elliptical way in sensitive interpretive areas, that Wisdom's seven pillars may refer to secular or other forbidden knowledge.

17 Symbolically, Agnon refers to Shoshanah as a "sleeping daughter of a Queen" (15:56), referencing the kabbalistic idea of the symbolic significance of four *sefirot*, two from the upper *sefirot* and two from the lower *sefirot*, representing two sexually related pairs: [Beginning after the uppermost *sefirah*, the *ein sof*] Wisdom (*Hakhmah*), the Supernal Father, and Intelligence (*Binah*), the Supernal Mother; Compassion (or Beauty, *Tiferet*), representing Jacob, their son and the People of Israel; and the last of the lower *sefirot*, which is the tenth, Kingdom (*Malkhut*), their daughter. See Raphael Patai, *The Hebrew Goddess* (N.Y.: KTAV, 1967), pp. 162-78, 267; Sharot, *Op.cit.*, p. 32. In the sexual mythology of kabbalah, the estrangement between Jacob and Shoshanah in the real (lower) world both reflects and causes a similar estrangement between God's male and female aspects in the spiritual (upper) world. The metaphor for both is the destruction of God's bedchamber (as it were), the Temple. The observance of the Commandments, the union of Jacob or Israel with the *Shekhinah*, restores harmony among the family, the four aspects of the Godhead, and among the *sefirot* generally. See Sharot, *ibid.*, pp. 32-33. On the *sefirot* in kaballah generally, see Philip S. Berg, *Kabbalah for the Layman* (Jerusalem: Press of The Research Centre of Kabbalah, 1982); Gershom G. Scholem, *Major Trends in Jewish Mysticism* (Schocken Books, 1961), pp. 205-233; Barbara T. Stephens, "A Cry in the Wilderness: *Shekhinah* as Psychological Healer," *Journal of Psychology and Judaism*, Vol. 15, No. 1 (Spring 1991): 29:42.

18 "By Some Miracle: S. Y. Agnon — the Literary Representation of Social Dramas," appearing in *Modern Hebrew Literature* (Spring/Summer 1986): 11-16, reprinted in Shaked's book, *The Shadows Within: Essays on Modern Hebrew Literature* (Jewish Publication Society, 1987), pp. 134-44.

19 The Jewish mystical tradition ascribes to God and Israel both masculine and feminine aspects (Scholem, *Op.cit.*, pp. 229-30; Raphael Patai, *Op.cit., passim)*; both are used and intermixed in *Betrothed*. For example, while Agnon primarily uses the kabbalistic image of a male Jacob and female *Shekhinah*, he does not hesitate to describe her as jumping, dancing and running (3:13-14) in her youth, reminiscent of the similar qualities ascribed to God, represented as Israel's male lover in *Song of Songs* (ch.2). Similarly, Shoshanah, representing God in *Betrothed*, faces a sickness of love (when she is betrayed by Jacob's decision to go to New York) that

is reminiscent of the pangs of love, *holat ahavah*, experienced by the feminine Israel (Shoshanah) in her love of God (her male lover) in *Song of Songs*.

20 B. *Meg.* 29a

21 22:95.

22 Ibid.

23 31:128.

24 18:68.

25 Because God only dwells in the tents of Shem (*Gen.* 9:29), Jaffa — representing Japheth and not Shem (B. *Yoma* 96) — is depicted as inhospitable to the Jewish religious and spiritual essence of the *Shekhinah* (Patai, *Op.cit.*, p. 144).

26 26. 5:21. See Alan J. Mittleman, "Christianity in the Mirror of Jewish Thought," *First Things* (August-September 1992): 18, for an interesting analysis of these two approaches to religion as developed by Leo Baeck.

27 13:50.

28 32:92.

29 15:56-58.

30 22:86.

31 22:92. As noted in n. 49, some critics interpret Shoshanah as death.

32 *Ibid.*

33 *Ibid.*

34 23:97-99.

35 29:120.

36 19:76; One recalls Tamar and Judah and Tamar and Amnon, although the Midrash sought to justify Tamar's actions with Judah within the halakhic rules of Levirate marriage. It has been observed that Tamar, in Hebrew, means "substitute," which suggests, in *Betrothed*, the idea that she is the intended substitute for Shoshanah as Jacob's mate, until the miraculous, last-minute victory of Shoshanah. See, generally, Devora Steinmitz, *From Father to Son: Kinship, Conflict, and Continuity in Genesis* (Louisville, Ky.: John Knox Press 1991), p. 163. See also, Mordecai A. Friedman, "Tamar, A Symbol of Life: The 'Killer Wife' Superstition in the Bible and Jewish Tradition," *AJS Review*, Vol. XV, No. 1 (Spring 1990): 23-61.

37 31:132.

38 31:128-9; even here, however, Agnon conjures up a mixed image, in which there is also an ancient Hebrew element, the festival of prayer and thanksgiving in the pre-synagogue Biblical period at Pharos, which were offered — it appears from Philo — on the beach, true to the historic origin of such gatherings as non-sacrificial assemblies around deserted altars, near city gates; Salo W. Baron, *The Jewish Community* (Phila.: JPS, 1949), p. 86.

39 31:129.

40 31:128.

41 22:95.

42 31:128-32.

43 30:127; 31:135. Agnon here employs another ambivalent, mixed Greek and Hebrew symbol: the laurel wreath (see n. 2).

44 31:129.

45 32:137.

46 32: 138.

47 32: 139.

48 "Portrait of the Immigrant as a Young Neurotic," *Prooftexts* (January 1987): 41-52; *Shmuel Yosef Agnon: A Revolutionary Traditionalist, Op.cit.*, pp. 171-86.

49 The literary critics of *Betrothed* with whom I am familiar either (1) do not offer a rigorous analysis of Agnon's kabbalistic symbolism; (2) see Shoshanah as representing death rather than redemption; or (3) treat *Betrothed* as a psychological tale rather than a cultural allegory. See Dov Sadan, *On S. Y. Agnon* (Hebrew) (Tel Aviv, 1959), pp. 74-88; Robert Alter, *Defenses of the Imagination, Op. cit.*, pp. 187-98; Hayyim Nagid, "The Vow, the Moon, and the Crown: On Kabbalistic Symbolism in *Betrothed*," *La Merkhav* (*Masa* Section) (Hebrew), October 13, 1967; Dina Stern. "The Betrayal and Its Consequences: A Study of *Betrothed*" (Hebrew) (Tel Aviv. 1964); Arnold Band, *Nostalgia and Nightmare: A Study in the Fiction of S.Y. Agnon* (University of California Press, 1968), pp. 367-82; Naomi Tamir, "*Betrothed* — Four That Are One" (Hebrew), *Hasifrut* 3 (1972): 479-506; cf. 507-16; Baruch Hochman, *The Fiction of S.Y. Agnon* (Cornell University Press, 1979), pp. 4-5; Harold Fisch, *S.Y. Agnon* (N.Y.: Ungar, 1975), pp. 32-41; Gershon Shaked, *Shmuel Yosef Agnon ...*, *Op cit.*, pp. 178-85.

50 The continuing relevance of Agnon's concern in these two novellas is attested to by Eliezer Berkovits (who lived in Israel from 1975 until his recent death) in *Crisis and Faith* (N.Y.: Hebrew Publishing Co., 1975); see also his remarks quoted in *The Jerusalem Post, International Edition*, Week Ending July. 11, 1992, p. 8B.

   The problem of a secular, Jewishly empty culture in Israel does not necessarily imply that so-called "secular studies," both science and social science, from math to humanities, should be disregarded or discarded. Apart from the necessity of such education for a Jewish (or any other) nation to function — internally and in its international relationships — the concept of *Torah U'Madah* or *Torah Im Derekh Eretz* is a positive value for many traditional, committed Jews. See, e.g., *The Torah U' Madah Journal*, Vols. I (1989) and II (1990), published by Yeshiva University; and Mordechai Eliav, "Various Approaches to *Torah Im Derekh Eretz*: Ideal and Reality," *Tradition* (Winter, 1992): 99, 104-7.

51 See, e.g., Gershon Shaked, "Portrait of the Immigrant as a Neurotic," *Prooftexts* (January, 1987): 47.

52 As Dan Miron has noted:

   Agnon could not in any way have ...[debased] the religious order of the universe to the level of cultic order in the world of pagan myth ....Agnon did not dare to leave his readers mired in ethical stupefaction and religious doubt without any promise of a future solution.

   See, "Domesticating a Foreign Genre: Agnon's Transactions with the Novel," *Prooftexts* (January 1987): 10; cf. p. 11.

53 Current attempts to relate a Mother-goddess form of *Shekhinah* to nature, representing the engine of Creation, were rejected in Tanakh as idolatry; the concept seems to be referenced in Agnon's description of the six maidens and their nature rites under the stars (see p. 301); Meredith Price, "The Feminine Divine," *The Jerusalem Post, Up Front*, April 29, 2005, pp. 28-30.

Letters to Felice:
Kafka's Quest for Jewish Identity

Introduction

Because of the universal historic traumas of the past half century, scholars for many years treated Franz Kafka (1883–1924), like George
Orwell and *1984*, as a prophet of political oppression, and the psychic
abyss perceived to exist between God and the political institutions of
society on the one hand, and individual man on the other. His characters
were Everyman, and his messages universal.[1] More recently, however,
history has taught a new lesson — that people still crave ethnicity and
community, an identity that is drawn from the particular aspects of their
culture and history, and not from the allegedly universal experiences of an
abstract, depersonalized mankind or any of its putative classes. Not surprisingly, therefore, there has emerged a new awareness of Franz Kafka *as
a Jew,* and not just as a precursor and symbol of the tragedy that engulfed
the world after his death.

The absence, in any of his fiction, of any evident references to the
Jewish experience, or to Kafka's *own* life as a Jew, contributed to the early,
more abstract understanding of his work and its significance. However,
one must also consider Kafka's non-fiction, the greater part of his output,
in which he was far more explicit about matters relating to his Jewish
identity. This should not be surprising. In early 20th century Prague, Kafka
and his family were part of a Jewish community that was surrounded by

two warring anti-Semitic ethnic groups, the Czechs and the Germans, neither of which would accept Jews socially or culturally. The most comprehensive attempt to interpret Kafka's fiction from a Jewish standpoint is
the challenging recent book by Ritchie Robertson,[2] but the best, surely
most well rounded portrait of Kafka, which takes into some account the
Jewish aspects of his inner life and surroundings — and, to some extent,
of his literary output — is the biography by Ernst Pawel, *The Nightmare of
Reason.*[3] Still more of such analysis remains to be done.

It is the thesis of this paper that Kafka's correspondence with Felice
Bauer from 1912–1917, uniquely among his published works, documents
the development by Kafka of a strong Jewish identity. I further argue that
this developing identity was largely coincident with, and made possible
by, Felice's decision to terminate their first engagement, in the summer of
1914.[4] Close analysis of the letters suggests that, at the beginning of their
relationship, Kafka did, indeed, view himself as scholars of his work and
life have generally characterized him: alone and alienated in an environment of which he lacked understanding and over which he had no control; subject to the unknown laws and commands of unknown powers,
that he had violated in unknown ways; guilt-ridden about his perceived
physical and personal inadequacies; without roots or destiny; a secular
cipher in a maze of an abstract political and social reality; without race
or roots in space or time to provide him with an identity; without hope
for meaning or salvation, in a life seen as totally arbitrary. Kafka viewed
his art primarily as a refuge, a reason for living in a cave free from commands or commitments, rather than a calling to help humanity; a way to
escape from a world from which otherwise there is no escape. However,
after the first breakup of his relationship with Felice, he emerged fundamentally altered: he was willing to find fault and place blame on others
and not just on himself; he was able — but for the problems posed by
the World War (Pawel 332) — to produce productively as an artist; to develop emotional ties with women even if never to the point of marriage;
and — most importantly — he generally ceased writing about himself in

his nonfiction as powerless and infirm, without virtue or identity. Indeed, a contrary development occurred: freed from having to make the symbolic commitment to the demands and expectations of family, religion and people symbolized by a middle class marriage to Felice Bauer, he developed a powerful Jewish consciousness — no less powerful because he could only articulate that vision and press its value on others rather than be able to live such a life himself, almost until he died.

Ironically, Kafka considered his failure to marry Felice as conclusive evidence of his failure to develop as a normal human being. I suggest that this accounts for the strange abyss between his non-fiction and his fiction. In the former, Kafka was able to document and reveal his personal development as a man and a Jew, as well as a writer of fictional parables about others, with a clear sense of identity, strongly held ideas and values, and a firm sense of belonging through his interest in, and relationships with an extended family. This family included friends, colleagues, and the community of East European Jewish refugees with whom he came into contact as a result of World War I. But Kafka's personal development never came to be reflected in his fiction, in which he continued to express the lingering, painful memories of his early life and his guilt as a stunted failure, the perplexed, isolated, inadequate man that he confessed to Felice he was and would always be. What he thought he was, he expressed in his art. What he really was — or, more accurately, came to be — he expressed in his private papers, diaries, letters, and — most fully, I believe — in the *Letters to Felice*. In dramatically documenting the development of Kafka's personality and Jewish identity, the *Letters* — viewed in its entirety — represents what has been called Kafka's "longest novel, the only one he ever completed" (Pawel 280)[5] and the one that most reveals his true self.

II: The Story of Kafka's *Letters to Felice*

To summarize the story: Kafka is born (1883) into a middle class family. His father is a business man, with a controlling personality (202, 310–11,

524–26; Pawel 7, 72); his mother is loyal to his father, and unavailable to Kafka (57, 94, 133, 210, 261; Pawel 14–15), who is also deprived of siblings for five years (113). They observe the Jewish rituals in a mechanical and partial way (502–3), and wish for Kafka to live a similar life, following the pattern of semi-assimilated Jews in the hostile *galut* environment of Western Europe that conditioned conformance, crude selfishness, and a parvenu mentality rather than self-respect, and communal ethnicity and integrity (423; Pawel 31, 55–9, 151). The parents remain controlling, and Kafka remains dependent on them even as a young adult, reflecting their mutual desire that Kafka live with them or close to them and share his meals with them (57, 524–26; Pawel 169, 319), the weakness of Kafka's temperament, the strength of his father's, and the strong, though conflicted, emotional ties between parents and son (524–26; Pawel 54–60).

In 1912, to please his parents, Kafka ardently courts Felice Bauer, a middle class, educated, lively, religiously observant Jewish woman whom he has just met, who seems to meet his parents' requirements (5, 7, 11, 15–16, 160, 185–6, 270, 283, 310, 484; Pawel 266–7, 289, 303). To gain his independence from them, Kafka pursues the intellectual life of a writer (21, 27, 138, 357).[6] He professes to be ascetic (31),[7] a vegetarian, thin (152), unsocial (156, 276, 308, 460), unconcerned with clothes or dress (243), and conscious of being weak and in continuing bad health (20, 59, 66–7, 123–4, 174, 211, 260, 269–70, 295–6, 424), and he uses all of these as excuses to discourage Felice whenever she makes a positive response to his ardent letters of love. As if to confirm his independence, Kafka begins, via letters, to court Felice's best friend, Greta Bloch, who finds herself in the position of gradually responding to Kafka, while ostensibly carrying out Felice's request to ascertain whether Kafka loves Felice (323–4, 385, 394, 430; Pawel 304). In a "trial" of Kafka by Felice in 1914, after two years of Kafka's volatile courtship, Greta testifies against Kafka, as does Felice, and she breaks their engagement.[8]

The next three years, 1914–1917, involve an attempt by Kafka and Felice to find a compromise between his wish for solitude in the service of his art, and her wish for a bourgeois, married, urban Jewish life (440–1, 443, 453–63; Pawel 346–7). Their relationship follows a pattern of pursuit and rejection similar to that which led to Felice's termination of their engagement in 1914, but far more intermittently, and with little agitation and self-flagellation by Kafka.[9] Indeed, there is even a second engagement, which is broken like the first, but with far less pain and trauma to Kafka.

Of greater importance to him personally, is the satisfying week that he finally spends with Felice in Marienbad in 1916, in which their love is finally physically consummated. Here they experience mutual happiness for a fleeting moment in their relationship (473–7; Pawel 344–6).

The primary psychic focus of these three years (1914–1917), however, is not Kafka's quest for Felice but his quest for identity — specifically, his identity as a Jew — and to find a path of spiritual fulfillment.[10] The choice begins as one between organized religion and spirituality, a new form of the original choice between marriage and writing. Soon the choice becomes one between West European Judaism and East European Judaism, between enlightened, rational, intellectual Judaism and mystical, ethnic, community and people-oriented Judaism, between the *haskalah* (Enlightenment) of Western European Jews and the Hasidism of Eastern European Jews (185–6, 475, 482, 500–3; Pawel 337–8).

Ultimately, Kafka integrates the self-respect and people-hood of Zionism, Hasidism, and East European Judaism, into a spiritualized religion and a sense of community and nationality, of racial pride, self-help, sharing, and commitment. These come together for him in real life through the Jewish People's Home, established in 1916, in Prague, for Jewish refugee children from Galicia. Helping these children, providing for their education and welfare, becomes Kafka's passion, and the true realization for him of Judaism, Zionism, and spirituality (482–513).

Yet, Kafka remains tied to his past because he has never fully freed himself from his ties to his parents. His father remains for him all powerful and arbitrary — and so, for Kafka, God, too, is still controlling, all powerful, arbitrary, unjust, and without understandable meaning.[11] Thus, while Kafka's new freedom from Felice permits his spiritual development, his continued bondage to his father prevents him from translating his new insights into practice as part of his own life. Instead, he transmits these insights to Felice, with the same fervor as his earlier protestations of love, for her to adapt as her way of life. Through Felice and the Jewish Home, Kafka becomes a surrogate father to the children, and Felice's spiritual husband. The personal break between them in 1914 is finally resolved through the spiritual bond between them created by Felice's acceptance of Kafka's vision of Judaism, Zionism, and transcendent spirituality (500–13).

Kafka, the *galut* intellectual, can only remain on the outside looking in. He now knows the correct path for others, but is unable to make it part of his own life. Like his hero, Moses, he can bring his fellow Jews to the Promised Land, but he is unable to enter (502–3, 543–5).[12]

At the very end of his relationship with Felice, Kafka is afflicted with tuberculosis, and envisions this as the ultimate victory of what he perceives as his "evil" self — the German writer who wishes to live alone — over his "good" self — the Jew who wishes to marry, have children and live among, and as a part of, his own people (543–5).

III: The Letters from 1912 to 1914: Confessions of Inadequacy

Kafka's relationship with Felice is most insightfully reviewed in two parts: the first takes place from the summer of 1912 to the summer of 1914, concluding with the termination of his engagement to Felice in July of 1914. In that period, he alternatingly first pleads his case to Felice as an ardent, seriously intentioned suitor, and — when she indicates a favorable response — as ardently explains why she should not think of marrying him, because he is unworthy and will be unsatisfactory as a husband, lover, and father. This ambivalence is a metaphor of Kafka's early struggle with his identity as a Jew. Seeking to marry Felice is an attempt by Kafka to find a Jewish identity, and to effectuate a relationship with God and the

Jewish people through the normal Jewish bourgeois lifestyle of his time:

> Yet in ways that he had only just begun to probe, his Jewishness, or lack thereof, was close to the core of his conflict over Felice. Unmarried, he was neither a man nor a Jew — a non-Jew, non-German, non-Czech, none but his own naked self adrift in a cold and hostile world. At the same time, he was quite definitely more of a non-Jew than anything else. If he could but find the gate that would admit him, he too could rejoin the ancestral tribe, become part of humanity, sustained by faith and a sense of belonging that would at last make it possible to live and to die. The handwriting on the prison wall spelled out the choice as well as the price: Marry Felice, surrender your self-hood, and the gate will be flung open, the tribe will embrace, engulf, and swallow you; silence your anguish and your voice, and blind faith will supplant the clear-eyed vision of guilt.[13]

Yet, in fleeing from the prospect of such a marriage and the responsibilities of identity associated with it, Kafka also continuously gave voice to criticisms of himself and of Jewish customs that rise to the level of self-hate, and a source of a deep urge to deny his Jewish identity. This self-denigration and self-denial mirrors the insults and defects of a despised and caricatured Jewish people, with which Kafka was personally familiar (Pawel 60, 203–6).

Thus, we find him obsessed with the physiognomy of Jews, with hooked nose and apoplectic complexion (86), and the "Jewish" (sic) relationship of eyes to nose (223), and "Christian looking" younger women and men (111, 243).[14] He says to Felice, "You want a man, not a flabby worm" (211). He speaks of his general physical weakness and hypochondria, and his continuous exhaustion (123,260,269–70,308,425). He likes Felice's sister's eyes and nose structure because, although it is Jewish, "nevertheless (sic) she is strong and not easily crushed by misfortune" (223).[15] He expresses jealousy of Felice's German (non-Jewish) admirers who, in contrast to himself, are "healthy, well dressed and amusing" (243).

It is plain from the letters that Kafka's fear of a sexual relationship with Felice was, in part at least, based on fear of impotence (37, 233, 270–2; Pawel 285–6); like his other physical obsessions, this, too, reflected the anti-Semitic picture of the Jew as sickly and anti-instinctual.

Like its sexual aspects, the trappings of marriage are also rejected, as a bourgeois life style. Thus, Kafka rejects a synagogue service, and the massive, heavy furniture that Felice has picked, as symbols of enslavement, "stifling," (462–3) and a "tombstone" (462; Pawel 310, 312). In a tirade written just after Felice decided to break their engagement at her Berlin "trial" of Kafka in July 1914, [16] he writes: "I asked you to cancel the ceremonies in the synagogue; you didn't answer" (440). [I wanted] "an apartment higher up than the 4th floor, not in Prague, elsewhere," in other words far from people, society, and Felice's friends and the social obligations that they would impose. "I don't need a permanent home from whose bourgeois orderliness I propose to run this business [of marriage] — not only do I not need this kind of love, it actually frightens me" (44). He recollects with pleasure a literary passage, in a book that he and Felice had once enjoyed, that speaks of furniture as "frivolity," and suggests that the passage be "cut in stone" [like a commandment] and "placed above the furniture store" (484). Here we have Kafka's disgust with the Jewish middle class,[17] which is to say, with himself and his family, which — considering his views on sex and asceticism — suggests that there is at war here, within Kafka, a Christian versus Jewish view of life in terms of the ideal, which Kafka was always seeking.

Kafka's ambivalence about marriage, of course, also reflects a desire to be German, to be like those who hate him but who lack his infirmities, or what he sees in himself, through German rejection, as infirmities. This is spelled out in a remarkable passage in which Kafka describes the pleasure which he takes in recalling an experience earlier in his life with a friend, the physically large and strong son of a Jewish bookstore owner. Kafka sees his friend dusting off the Jewish prayer shawls in the store window, while near him are "obscene" (Jewish) books, and Kafka then follows his friend to the exclusive German club to which he — but not Kafka — belongs, recalling that his Jewish friend considered himself a German (203–4).

The Germans, in Kafka's recollection, accept not the intelligent, sensitive Jew (Kafka) but his friend, the gross, yet strong and healthy Jew, who, in a display of independence from his Jewish father, leaves behind the useless, unwanted, dusty prayer shawls and the "obscene" books to join his German friends in revelry, while Kafka stands outside admiring his friend's good luck, and wishing that he could be like him, accepted by the club.

Kafka's second relationship with Felice takes place between the summer of 1914 and October 1917. Relieved of an obligation to make good on his inner need to marry the symbolically bourgeois, Jewish Felice, Kafka is able overtly to pursue a more gradual and freely achieved quest for a Jewish identity[18] — through an evolving articulation of the religious, cultural, and national aspects of Judaism as he came to understand it. Thus, while it is true, as Arnold Band has noted, that Judaism, marriage and writing were Kafka's avenues of escape from the "unbearable emotional maze of his life," the truth is more complicated, as Kafka's *Letters to Felice* show. It appears that marriage was but the first of these avenues which he fully pursued, evidently because marriage would have provided the more symbolically meaningful achievement of relief from the psychic pressures that plagued him.[19] But Felice's termination of their engagement discharged Kafka, as it were, from any further responsibility to achieve an identity and Jewish connection through a bourgeois Jewish marriage, as the paucity of his letters to her thereafter indicates. As a result, Kafka became able to pursue his quest for self-respect and sense of belonging through his writing and an understanding, at least, of his Jewish identity. One may even plausibly conjecture that had Kafka lived longer than his forty-one years, the sense of worth and confidence that he gained from his literary achievements, and his increasingly strong Jewish identity, might finally have permitted him ultimately to marry successfully and to live, as well as to write about, Judaism — as we know from the plans that he began to make to go to Palestine in the last few years of his life.

IV: The Letters from 1914 to 1917: Quest for Identity

Kafka`s successful quest for identity as a Jew is played out in the psychic and spiritual drama depicted in his letters to Felice after that traumatic summer of 1914. Shortly after the end of their engagement, he portrays two selves that have been locked in combat within himself. The one, with perhaps only modest improvement or cultivation, might still assume the challenges and responsibilities of marriage, fatherhood, children, an apartment, rules and routine, and all that marriage and its commitments stand for. The other self is desperate for freedom and independence, creativity, and solitude, capable of suffering for a life devoted to writing and of "meanness" (438–40). Here is the first departure from Kafka's past rhetoric with Felice — an admission that to be the solitary writer involves a moral defect. And, in that same letter, after carefully explaining why he and Felice were each justifiably afraid of the other, there is another departure — the suggestion of the possibility, which neither had proposed before, of a compromise, a middle way between the extreme lifestyle of solitariness and freedom sought by Kafka the writer, and Felice's desire that he accept society and responsibility. Although he is unable to suggest a concrete plan of compromise (440–1; Pawel 346–7), this idea presages a new development in his philosophic outlook — the view that the good life requires some degree of commitment and action, and not just the solitary theorizing, or even creativity, of the artist.

We also see Kafka beginning a process of repentance, of recognizing that a wrong has been done to Felice, admitting it, and — partially at least — suggesting the possibility that the wrong will not be repeated.

Whatever merit there is to the high regard enjoyed by Kafka as a speaker for alienated man and a prophet of political developments long after his death, it seems that his novel, *The Trial*, written conemporaneously with most of the *Letters to Felice*, was, from the standpoint of Kafka's subconscious, an exorcism, a playing out of his recognition of the need for a real trial, on account of his arrogance and vanity in his relations with Felice, his invasion and conquest of her very psyche with no real intent ever to make good on his protestations of love in the way which he knew that Felice would want and expect.[20]

Most importantly, however, the final 100 pages of the *Letters*, that comprise Kafka's second relationship with Felice, focus on four Jewish themes: Zionism, Judaism and religion generally, East European, as compared to West European, Judaism, and — the point of synthesis for all of these commitment alternatives — the Jewish People's Home.

Kafka's relationship to Zionism at first seems neither clear nor constant (15–16, 84, 207–8, 239, 421, 423, 482, 501), but I believe that there is a pattern to his understanding of, and sympathy for, the movement, which changed over time in parallel with the advent of a new spirituality in his outlook brought about as a result of the First World War. Early in his correspondence with Felice, there is distinct ambivalence to Zionism. When he first meets her, he is impressed with her interest in the study of Hebrew, and they even discuss a trip to Palestine at their very first meeting![21] Yet, early on, he writes to her about a young man he met who is

> sensible, keen, active, amicable, but who has a degree of composure I find altogether disturbing...At that moment my indifference to him as a person or to any form of Zionism was immense and inexpressible...(207–8).

But, just a few months later, in April 1913, his advice to his East European friend, Lowy, who is having trouble making ends meet from his Yiddish Teater group, is: "Go to Palestine" (239). Here we have another clue as to how Kafka is going to resolve the terrible war within himself between commitment and contemplation, joining the Jewish people or living in spiritual, artistic isolation: he will urge it on others as the right path, but remain Hamlet-like as far as his own life goes. For now, his ambivalence continues. Thus, in a strange letter written in September of 1913, he writes about his feelings toward Zionism at a Zionist Congress: [I feel] "for the entire concept", but not "for the essential part" (317).

By August, 1915, he chides Felice about her attitude to

> …Zionism, with which you are not sufficiently familiar. Through the Jewish Home other forces, much nearer to my heart, are set in motion and take effect. Zionism, accessible to most Jews of today, at least in its outer fringes, is but an entrance to something far more important. What's the good of writing? You are silent (482).

Zionism has now become not an end, which evidently Kafka could never appreciate, but a means to a larger, transcendent goal, in which he could believe.

That same dichotomy permeated his view of Judaism and religion, a dichotomy between the institutional and the spiritual:

> How devout are you? You go to the synagogue; but I dare say you have not been recently. And what is it that sustains you, the idea of Judaism or of God? Are you aware, and this is the most important thing, of a continuous relationship between yourself and a reassuringly distant, if possibly infinite height or depth? He who feels this continuously has no need to roam about like a lost dog, mutely gazing around with imploring eyes; he never need yearn to slip into a grave as if it were a warm sleeping bag and life a cold winter night; and when climbing the stairs to his office he never need imagine that he is careening down the

well of the staircase, flickering in the uncertain light,
twisting from the speed of his fall, shaking his head
with impatience (185–6).

Yet, we must note that Kafka, unlike Heine, whom he disliked on
many counts, both personal and aesthetic, never thought of conversion
or any overt identification with Christianity. For Kafka, "Christianity is an
alien faith" (126).[22] Judaism, as a faith and as a religion, was obedience
to the Commandments, and Kafka is upset that Jews have neglected their
faith (151).

...(keeping the Commandments is not an outward thing; on the contrary, it is the very essence of
the Jewish faith) (502–3).

Elsewhere, Kafka draws a picture of his ambivalence to Judaism as
an ill-fitting garment, unwanted and rarely used, together with a strong
statement of his respect for Judaism, and despair at its lack of observance
by others:

At the very moment you read this letter I may be
driving to the synagogue — wearing my old tailcoat,
cracked patent-leather shoes, a top hat far too small
for me, and with an unusually pale face (because
nowadays I always take so long to get to sleep) in my
position as an usher sitting next to a pleasant, pretty,
elegant, and above all very considerate and modest
cousin — where the marriage will be solemnized with
that tremendous solemnity that upsets me every time.
Because the Jewish public in general, here at any rate,
have (sic) limited the religious ceremonies to wed-
dings and funerals, these two occasions have drawn
grimly close to each other, and one can virtually see
the reproachful glances of a withering faith (151).

The idea of spirituality as commitment to community begins, ironically, with Kafka comparing Judaism, to some disadvantage, with the

"ancient, heart stirring, expectant Germany of the last century," and the community and comradeship of German writers, editors and readers (158–9). Moreover, this admiration for Germans is coupled with self-hatred of his latent Jewish personality, that is, his internalized view of the German view of Jews. Thus, at the same time, he expresses self-consciousness for behaving in an "exaggerated conspicuous Jewish way at a Buber lecture" (on Hasidism or Zionism) (161). Yet, within a few years, his emerging idea of true spirituality — living together in a community of sharing and commitment — was to be transferred from Kafka's "writer" self and its limited community of editors and readers, to Kafka's "husband" or Jewish self, with the entire people of Israel as the community (412, 500).

Kafka's next step in his quest for spiritual identity is recognizing that one cannot prove God first and only then begin to embrace a formal religion. One "can prove the existence of God by one's own concept," but it "can be disproved by the absence of any such concept" (258). Thus, without faith, we make God up, and such a religion is inevitably weak. Ultimately, Kafka was unable to embrace either a Judaism of pure faith or a Judaism of practice and ritual (502–3), but here he was groping for the important idea, whether for him or for others, that deeds and rituals as part of a religious community must come first, before faith, and that only through them is a sustainable faith and community possible.

The concept of Judaism as a faith community was now beginning to be more attractive to Kafka conceptually, although accompanied by continuing regret that it was not for him. Thus, barely a year after asking Felice what Judaism means to her, religion or God, deed or creed, he writes in June 1914:

> Owing to circumstances and temperament [I am]
> excluded from every great soul-sustaining community
> on account of my non-Zionist (I admire Zionism and
> am nauseated by it), non-practicing Judaism (423).

Here we find, for the first time, the articulation of the idea of Judaism as a faith community, such as he had undoubtedly been hearing about from Martin Buber in the lectures that Kafka had attended (157–8, 161, 163–4). By "soul sustaining community," he is embracing the idea of people, structure, commitment, rules, the package which he had rejected when the issue for him was marriage. Yet, he regretfully acknowledges that such a life is not for him. [23] He was let down by the spiritual and religious inadequacy and hypocrisy of his father, and, without that legacy of childhood training in Judaism in an environment of love and integrity, it is too late now for him.

There was a fleeting moment later, in 1914, when a new opportunity for commitment to form a community opened up for Kafka: to be a soldier and fight for the Kaiser and for the Germany that part of him loved. Ironically, that odd opportunity failed to materialize because of his health,[24] the same problem which he earlier used with Felice to escape the commitment of marriage.

Two years later, as we recall, in the summer of 1916, Kafka and Felice spent a glorious week in Marienbad. All of his fears about sexual impotence disappeared. He remained there after she went back to Berlin, and here begins Kafka's final ascent to his vision of what it means to be a Jew. For, by now, the issue is no longer merely deed or creed. It is, even more, a battle between Judaism West European style, and Judaism East European style. Is real Judaism the rational, austere, cold, dignified, intellectual Judaism of Germany, always so alien to him, or the warm, social, exuberant, and mystical Judaism of Galicia? The letters enlighten us greatly, and trace the story. The week after Felice left him, Kafka writes enthusiastically about the Belzer Rebbe, then vacationing at Marienbad too:

> ...we were not even aware of the most distinguished visitor to Marienbad, a man in whom so many place their trust: the Rabbi from Belz, no doubt at present the chief representative of Hasidism. He has been here for 3 weeks. Last night for the first time

> I joined him and some 10 of his entourage on their
> evening walk. A great deal could be said about it, but
> I have just written about it at length to Max [Brod]
> who had informed me of the Rabbi's presence here
> (475).

One can trace a direct path from the Belzer Rebbe to East European Judaism, which, as we shall see, Kafka chose as the model for Felice in connection with her work at the Jewish People's Home.

It seems no accident, after this time with Felice and an inspiring evening walk with the Rebbe, that the next day Kafka reports on the gargantuan meals (with meat!) which he is eating, and that he is getting "fat" (475–7)! Suddenly, finally, a note of happiness, contentment, and spiritual ease creeps into the hitherto spare, severe, and demanding prose of Kafka's letters.

But there is one more step left. We have a life style, a leader with charisma; and we have Kafka now referring to life with Felice as a "blessed way of life" (477), thus almost closing the circle between his phobia of marriage and his achieving a Jewish Persona. What is still missing is a concrete opportunity for Felice to live the kind of Jewish life that Kafka has chosen as correct — thereby permitting Kafka, as we shall see, to live a life as a Jew vicariously, through her.

The East European way was not suddenly chosen by Kafka that night when he walked with the Rebbe, or as part of the afterglow of his (finally) consummated relationship with Felice. It goes back, and one senses that it goes back, to Kafka's own experience with, and reaction to, the players and the plays of the Yiddish theatre, which he described to Felice early in their relationship.[25] But this was, nevertheless, only theater, and not life. The opportunity to live a Jewish life in a real community was presented in 1916, with the establishment of the Jewish People's Home for the education of the children of Jewish refugees from Galicia.[26] And, for the last 75 pages of the Letters, Kafka proceeds to encourage, cajole, and press Felice at every opportunity to play an active role in the Home (482–513). It is more important than her job, her family, the theater, or even literature, and its essence — now the essence of Judaism for Kafka — is its all-embracing humanity:

> The main thing is the human element, only the human element ... your office, your family, literature, the theater, were able by their very nature to claim only part of what is best in you; ... here, [with the Home] however, lies the actual connecting link which in its turn will let everything else, including your family, etc., benefit by what is best in you (498).

Its importance lies less in the benefits which it confers on the children than on the spiritual benefits, the spiritual life, which it will provide to Felice:

> As far as I can see it is positively the only path, or threshold to it, that can lead to spiritual liberation. The helpers, moreover, will attain that goal earlier than those who are being helped. Beware of the arrogance of believing the opposite, this is most important (500).

The Home is the only important reality:

> Only the reality of the Home can teach you anything of importance — any reality, however small. Don't be prejudiced in favor or against, nor let the thought of me affect your open mind. You will see those in need of help, and opportunities of giving help judiciously, and in yourself the power to help — so help. It is very simple, yet more profound than any fundamental idea. Everything else you ask about will, if you go through with it, follow quite naturally from this one simple fact (500).

One can try to make the children into the Berlin version of West European Jews — "contemporary, educated" — but "with that not much would be achieved" (500). The ideal, rather, is East European Jewry, their values and way of life:

> If, for instance, I had to choose between the Berlin Home and another where the pupils were the Berlin helpers (dearest, even with you among them and with me, no doubt, at the head), and the helpers simple East European Jews from Kolomyja or Stanislawow, I would give unconditional preference to the latter Home — with a great sigh of relief and without a moment's hesitation. But I don't think this choice exists; no one has it; the quality corresponding to the value of the East European Jew is something that cannot be imparted in a Home; on this point even family education has recently been increasingly unsuccessful; these are things that cannot be imparted, but perhaps, and here lies the hope, they can be acquired, earned. And the helpers in the Home have, I imagine, a chance to acquire them (500) [27]

Ultimately, the Home becomes the source of Kafka's belief in Zionism. The connection of the Home with "Zionism (valid for me ...)" is that Zionism "gives the Home a youthful, vigorous method, youthful vigor generally, and that, where other means might fail, kindles national aspirations by invoking the ancient prodigious past" (501). Some day, he adds ambiguously, "you may realize that I am not a Zionist" (501), presumably because Kafka stresses its spiritual dimension, the opportunity it provides for people to live in a real community, helping each other as Felice is helping the Galician refugee children. There is even a place for Judaism in such a community, a Judaism that Felice can teach the children because she was once a practicing Jew, which Kafka cannot be, as much as he would like to be:

> On the whole it will be up to you to get them to trust you in other than religious matters and, where

the sharing of religious experience is needed, to let the dark complexity of Judaism, which contains so many impenetrable features, do its work. Nothing of course should be blurred in this way, as people are inclined to do here. In my opinion this would be entirely wrong. I wouldn't think of going to the synagogue. The synagogue is not a place one can sneak up to. One can do this today no more than one could as a child; I still remember how as a boy I almost suffocated from the terrible boredom and pointlessness of the hours in the synagogue; these were the rehearsals staged by hell for my later office life. Those who throng to the synagogue simply because they are Zionists seem to me like people trying to force their way into the synagogue under cover of the Ark of the Covenant, rather than entering calmly through the main door. But as far as I can see, it is quite different for you than it is for me. While I should have to tell the children (it is unwise, of course, to encourage such conversations, and on their own they would arise but rarely, for town-bred children have sufficient experience of the world and, if they are East European Jews, know how to protect themselves and at the same time to accept the other person) that owing to my origin, my education, disposition, and environment I have nothing tangible in common with their faith (keeping the Commandments is not an outward thing; on the contrary, it is the very essence of the Jewish faith) — thus, while I would somehow have to admit it to them (and I would do so candidly, for without candor everything would be quite pointless in this case), you on the other hand may not be altogether lacking in

339

tangible connections with the faith (502–3).

And so, at the very end of the story of the Letters, Kafka leaves to Felice his Jewish legacy. But it is for her to carry on, not for him, because of the permanent, debilitating flaw of his childhood. Here, in the Home, God, Kafka's father, Felice, Zionism, Jewry, and Kafka meet. It is the home and community that he always longed to be part of, to provide identity and meaning to his life. One may venture to suggest that he would probably have preferred to be an orphan in such a refugee shelter of East European Jews, rather than a biological child in an emotionally and religiously empty parental home, neglected by his mother and tyrannized by his father — as he had been as a child.

The Home also provides a remarkable fulfillment of Kafka's longings for marriage and fatherhood, both of which were frustrated by the permanent war between his two selves. Indeed, it finally fulfills the longing of his Jewish self for the marriage to Felice that could never occur. For Kafka's strong, continuing interest in every aspect of the education and welfare of the Jewish refugee children in the Home amounts to nothing less than his adoption of them as his own children and, in guiding Felice's care of them, Felice becomes their mother and ultimately, in Kafka's eyes, his spiritual wife:

It is almost as though the girls were my children
and had acquired a mother... (506).[28]

For him, the Home has provided a surrogate relationship with Felice no less strong than marriage. "I can think of no closer spiritual bond between us than that created by this work" (500).

Here, Kafka describes the spiritual bond between them created by the Home as superior to the normal love of a man for a woman, whereas — before the crucial breakup of their first engagement — the normal bond of love was expressed in almost identical fashion to be superior to the spiritual bond, created by "rabbinical blessing."[29] Thus, Kafka's spiritual union with Felice through the Home is now the surrogate for normal, sanctified, marital union, as well as for his parental home in which he was so unhappy.

In the end, the spiritual war within Kafka is finally resolved at both levels on which it was fought:, the level involving his inability to marry Felice, have children and a family, and the level involving his quest for identity — the battle between Kafka the German writer and Kafka the East European Jew. In both cases, the war was both won and lost. It was won in the sense that, as a result of his disengaging from the tormenting ambivalence of his personal, legal, social, and physical relationship with Felice, he was able to conceptualize and even experience spirituality, commitment, Zionism, and Jewish identity — via a surrogate Home which embraced them all. It was lost because, as a result of his continuing unresolved love-hate relationship with his father, and to a lesser extent with his mother, and the hypocrisy of the family's religious life, he was never able to translate his new vision of Judaism, Zionism, and spirituality into a permanent part of his own life, through a wife, children, and a family and community life (502–3, 524–5, 549–6).

But there is an epilogue to this drama, one of sadness and irony. For, in the last pages of the *Letters*, Kafka writes about blood gushing from his lungs, and the doctors' diagnosis of tuberculosis, and concludes that it can never be cured, because it is not a physical wound amenable to medical cure. [30] Rather, it is, in Kafka's diagnosis, a spiritual wound from a mortal blow struck by his solitary German writer self, whom Kafka calls his "evil" side, against his "good" side, the side of his self that still longs for marriage and family, the self that finally chose, at least for others, community, nationhood and commandments, and the self-respect of East European Jewry (543–6). Kafka's internal conflict has been nothing less than a war:

> As you know, there are two combatants at war
> within me. During the past few days I have had fewer
> doubts than ever that the better of the two belongs
> to you. By word and silence, and a combination of
> both, you have been kept informed about the prog-
> ress of the war for 5 years, and most of that time it has

caused you suffering.

...Of the two who are at war within me, or rather whose war I consist of... the one is good, the other evil... Until very recently, however, despite reverses, it was possible for me to imagine that the most improbable would happen (the most probable would be eternal war), which always seemed like the radiant goal, and I, grown pitiful and wretched over the years, would at last be allowed to have you.

Suddenly it appears that the loss of blood was too great. The blood shed by the good one (the one that now seems good to us) in order to win you, serves the evil one. Where the evil one on his own would probably or possibly not have found a decisive new weapon for his defense, the good one offers him just that. For, secretly, I don't believe this illness to be tuberculosis, at least not primarily tuberculosis, but rather a sign of my general bankruptcy ... The blood issues not from the lung, but from a decisive stab delivered by one of the combatants ...

And now I am going to tell you a secret ... I will never be well again. Simply because it is not the kind of tuberculosis that can be laid in a deckchair and nursed back to health, but a weapon that continues to be of supreme necessity as long as I remain alive. And both cannot remain alive (544–6).

In Kafka's eyes the battle was over: the writer had defeated the husband, and the German had defeated the Jew. Yet, while Kafka would die within seven years (1924) from his spiritual and physical wound, the real victor in the battle for Kafka's soul — as we know from the *Letters*, which Kafka never knew would survive [31] — was Kafka the Jew.

To be sure, the victory is to a deracinated, uprooted, diaspora Jew.

But Kafka finally achieves a posthumous victory of identity and commitment. The ultimate irony of his life is that while Kafka saw the battle as a lost one, the limited victory he in fact achieved in his quest for a Jewish identity may enable other Jews to understand their predicament more fully, and perhaps realize in their lives what Kafka could only understand and express in his art, but was unable to experience in his life.[32]

....

NOTES

1 " ... latter day intellectuals express a pronounced tendency to convert [Kafka, Gershom Scholem, and Walter Benjamin] into prophets of our postmodernist dilemmas;" Robert Alter, *Necessary Angels — Tradition and Modernity in Kafka, Benjamin, and Scholem* (Cambridge and Cincinnati: Harvard University Press and HUC Press, 1991), p. 89; cf. p. 53. See also, Elias Canetti, *Kafka's Other Trial* (N.Y.: Schocken, 1974); *The World of Franz Kafka*, J.P. Stern, ed. (London: Weidenfeld and Nicholson, 1980); Alfred Kazin, "Kafka," in *The Inmost Leaf: A Selection of Essays* (N.Y.: Harcourt, Brace, Jovanovich, 1979), pp. 142-48; Albert Camus, "Hope and the Absurd in the Work of Franz Kafka," in *The Myth of Sisyphus and Other Essays (N.Y.:* Alfred A. Knopf, 1955), pp. 124-38; Arthur A. Cohen, "Franz Kafka: Artist of the Incomplete," *Orim*, Vol. III, No. 2, Spring 1988. Earlier critics who emphasized the Jewish aspects of Kafka's work include Benjamin and Scholem, discussed in Alter's *Necessary Angels,* and Hannah Arendt, in "The Jew as Pariah, A Hidden Tradition," Part II in *Reconstructionist* (April 3, 1959): 8-14 (describing *The Castle* as a parable of the Jewish condition in exile).

2 *Franz Kafka — Politics, Judaism and Literature* (Oxford, 1985). See, also, Arnold Band, "The Margins of Assimilation," *Modern Judaism (May* 1988): 135-55; Gershon Shaked, *The Shadows Within* (Philadelphia: Jewish Publication Society, 1987), pp. 3-21, 65-6; Robert *Alter, Necessary Angels;* Jean Jofen, "Kafka and the Rebbe of Gur," *Modern Jewish Studies,* VII *(Yiddish,* Vol. VII, No. 4, 1990): 85-91.

3 *The Nightmare of Reason* (New York: Vintage, Random House, 1985). Citations to Pawel are generally included, where necessary, for additional support from other Kafka writings, of factual points and conclusions that are drawn from the *Letters to Felice.*

4 Editor's Note to *Letters to Felice* (New York: Schocken, 1973) on p. xxv. Page citations in the text and the following footnotes are to the Schocken edition, unless otherwise stated.

5 Pawel never explains why the *Letters* is a "novel." For the interesting view of the *Letters* as fiction, a "theatrical performance ... in which Kafka plays all the parts," see Pietro Citati, *Kafka* (N.Y.: Alfred A. Knopf, 1989), pp. 44-5; cf., p.4l.

6 See also Pawel, pp. 96, 99: "Most of those who started to write in German," he wrote to Max Brod in June of 1921, "wanted to get away from their Jewishness, usually with their fathers' vague consent (the vagueness of it was what made it outrageous). They wanted to get away, but their hind legs still stuck to the fathers' Jewishness, while the forelegs found no firm ground. And the resulting despair served as their inspiration."

7 Pawel, p. 209, sees Kafka's vegetarianism as a subconscious, compulsive ritual "that replicated the talismanic function of Jewish dietary law and served needs and goals far different from those of which he was consciously aware."

8 See n. 16.

9 The entire three-year period, from October, 1914, when the first engagement terminated, to October, 1917, when the letters ceased, is covered in only the last 100 pages of the 550 page book. Clearly, while Kafka's "pursuit," as it were, of Felice formally continued during this period, it was intermittent and relatively half-hearted, as compared to the flood of beseechments and self-denigration of the first 450 pages of his letters covering the first two years of their relationship (Canetti, Kafka's Other Trial, p. 78).

10 Interestingly, Kafka's expressions of self-hatred virtually cease in this period.

11 Letters, pp. 524-26, and see also pp. 63, 310; n. 18; Pawel, pp, 207, 272; Alter, pp. 106-120.

12 We know from Ritchie Robertson's book that Moses, like Napoleon, was a hero and leader with whom Kafka identified (pp. 120, 134, 139, 221, 247). As to Napoleon, see Robertson at, e.g., pp. 132-4; 216-17, and Pawel, p. 214. Kafka's interest in Napoleon is also documented in the Letters, pp. 134-172.

13 Pawel, p. 289, and see also pp. 303, 306, and Letters, pp. 272-80. Pawel has stressed that "Kafka's oft-cited note of January 8, 1914, 'What do I have in common with the Jews? I have hardly anything in common with myself,' must be read" in the context of Kafka's running argument with the note's addressee, Max Brod, regarding Brod's "increasingly dogmatic Zionism" (p. 308).

14 See, also, his remarks about shyness, and Jewish clothes and eating habits (Pawel at pp. 110, 163, 169).

15 Elsewhere he refers to himself as "the crooked Western Jew" (emphasis supplied) and "the crumbling Jew" (Pawel,. pp. 180-1).

16 Felice's decision to terminate her engagement to Kafka was made after a "trial" in which she was the plaintiff as well as the judge, with Kafka, of course, as defendant — a defendant who did little to defend himself from accusations that he had long made against himself. See Pawel, pp. 312-13. and Letters, pp. 436-41.

17 One cannot refrain from mentioning Kafka's humorous reference to Felice's "unerring eye for the average Jewish wedding present" (p. 489), a comically hostile remark against her bourgeois values. He harbored similar hostility to rabbinic marriage (p. 392). Alter notes the connection between Kafka's rebellion against his bourgeois origins and his father's complacent, superficial, assimilationism (Necessary Angels, pp. 31-32, 119).

18 The need to marry and displace his father and, thereby, become a middle class Western Jew like his father (Pawel, pp. 239, 363-64,369), was constantly frustrated by Kafka's guilt, impotence, and desire for solitude and independence, caused by "a mother lost to him, along with two rivals [his deceased younger brothers] killed by his own lethal fantasies" [wishing or imagining their death], and his "obsessive struggle against an omnipotent father" (Pawel, pp. 16-17, 63). See, also, Band, pp. 148-55. Pawel notes that, in 1911, Kafka was "beginning to confront the whole problem of Jewish identity or, more precisely, of his own identity in a non-Jewish and anti-Jewish world" (p. 228). Thus, Kafka's relationship with Felice, which began in 1912, can be seen as an inevitable and crucial stage in this process, in which she first becomes a metaphor for his quest and then, after his

release from the impossible burden of a commitment to marriage, becomes the means, the channel through which Kafka is finally able to develop that identity. It is not surprising, therefore, that, by the end of his life, Kafka was dreaming about going to Palestine, and studying Torah and Talmud with the last love of his life, Dora Diamant (Pawel, p. 436). Alter views Palestine and marriage as "unrealizable consummations" for Kafka (*Necessary* Angels, p. 42).

19 Arnold Band, p.150; *Letters*, pp. 272-80; Pawel, p. 270 (Kafka's first letter to Felice was "a first blow in the struggle for his liberation"), ibid., p. 275 (Kafka envisaged marriage as a "more or less normal existence which would somehow resolve his conflicts, assure his independence, and enable him to function effectively both as a husband and a writer. The illusion did not outlive the Spring."); and p. 288 ("His creative vein, however, began to give out."); see also, n. 13.

20 Indeed, on p. 275, he clearly recognizes that he has "tormented" her. See, also, Shaked, p. 66; Canetti, p. 81, makes little of Kafka's guilt. But, clearly, there is much more to *The Trial* than Kafka's sense of guilt from his treatment of Felice. Kafka, like Gershom Scholem and certain other West European German Jews, although uprooted by their upbringing from Jewish religion, nevertheless sought Jewish roots and identity. As a result of having to come to terms with rejection by the gentile world because of their Jewishness, these Jewish intellectuals were attracted to the proud and unselfconscious ethnicity, piety, and sense of community, including both its mysticism and Zionism, of East European Jewry. Arthur Hertzberg and Gershon Shaked thus understand Kafka's *The Trial* as asking two basic questions: "Why is this 'European' being persecuted even by the most enlightened of his society, a society he accepts and wishes to remain a part of?" and, "Of what is he guilty?" Both reach the conclusion that the Jews of Europe were fated to impersonal and baseless persecution; no matter how long and hard they tried to ascertain, confess and correct their real and imagined flaws, they could never attain social acceptance, because the European hatred of the Jew was too irrational and too deep (Arthur Hertzberg, *The French Enlightenment and the Jews* [Jewish Publication Society, 1968], p. 336; Shaked, pp. 1-11, 65-.6; cf, p. 31). Alter sees Kafka as caught in the no-man's-land between a discredited religious tradition and the inconvenience and worthlessness of modern secular culture (*Necessary Angels*, pp. 100-120).

It is worthwhile to contrast Kafka with Jewish writers like Stefan Zweig and Berthold Auerbach, who were comfortable and confident in their liberal, assimilated state, and others like Arnold Zweig, Joseph Roth and Jakob Wasserman, who internalized anti-Semitic hatred and tended to justify the victimization of the Jew in European societies; Shaked, pp. 23-7, 46-7, 62-8; Jeffrey L. Sammons, "Observations on Berthold Auerbach's Jewish Novels," *Orim*, Spring 1986, Vol. 1, No. 2. Nevertheless, even in the works of Roth and Wasserman one finds glimpses of a recognition that, ultimately, the rejected Jew can, and must, find salvation in the authentic expressions of the Judaism of East European Jewry (Shaked, pp. 34, 67).

21 *Letters*, pp. 5, 15-17, 85. Ten years earlier, in 1902, he had written mockingly of his friend Bergmann's Zionism (Pawel, p. 67).

22 Discussing the German word for mother — *Mutter* — Kafka said:

"*Mutter* to a Jew sounds particularly German; it unconsciously contains Christian chill along with Christian splendor. The Jewish woman referred to as *Mutter* therefore becomes not only comical but a stranger as well. I believe that only the memories of the ghetto are what still preserves the Jewish family..." (quoted in Pawel, p. 249).

23 Pawel, pp. 53-60, 98-100; see also, *Letters*, p. 502: " ... owing to my origin, *my education*, disposition, and environment, I have nothing tangible in common with their faith..."

24 *Letters*, pp. 449, 454, 458; Pawel, p. 326. Yet, he deprecated patriotic parades as "disgusting" (Pawel, p. 320).

25 *Letters*, pp. 25-6, 128, 179, 239, 249, 264, 267; see also Pawel, p. 239-42; Robertson, pp. 14-37; Alter, p. 38. Pawel's statement, p. 240, that Kafka was later to shed his romanticized 1911 view of the East European Yiddish Theater as representing traditional Judaism and community is contradicted by Kafka's later endorsement of East European Jewry as precisely the kind of faith community which is most authentically and worthily Jewish, as Pawel notes at pp. 335-6.

26 *Letters*, p. 477; Pawel, pp. 335-6: "To Kafka ... the Galician refugees were the living embodiment of Jewishness ... These masses possessed precisely what Western Jewry had long since lost — deep roots, a sense of belonging, and communal strength..."

27 The books that Kafka recommends include Sholem Asch's *Stories from the Bible*, Peretz's *Popular Tales*, and works of Sholem Aleikhem (pp. 509-12), although Kafka thought that the latter might be "too sarcastic and complex" (pp. 510-11).

28 See also, *Letters*, pp. 507-10, 519-22, 531-32, 536, 538.

29 *Letters*, p. 500; compare with p. 392. It remains to be noted that, in finally defining his Jewish identity in terms that embraced East European Judaism, Kafka achieved another form of triumph over the crippling effects of a dominating father — because his father looked down on East European Jews, as did most of Prague's Jews (Pawel, pp. 245-46). For the view that Kafka's identification with East European Jewry was a form of rebellion against his Westernized parents, see Michael A. Meyer, *Jewish Identity in the Modern World* (Seattle: University of Washington Press, 1990), pp. 30-2.

30 There is now substantial medical support for the view that the human body can succumb to a major, intense, emotional, or psychological conflict because of its impact on the immune system; J.R. Calabrese, M.A. Kling, and P.W. Gold, "Alterations in Immunocompetence During Stress, Bereavement, and Depression: Focus on Neuroendocrine Regulation," *The American Journal of Psychiatry*, Vol. 144, No. 9, September 1987.

31 Kafka gave instructions that his work should be destroyed after his death, but his good friend, Max Brod, defied that order, as did others like Felice Bauer who possessed parts of his literary legacy; "Kafka's True Will, an Introductory Essay," by Erich Heller, in *Letters to Felice*, pp. vii-ix; see also n. 4, above.

32 Contrast the unconscious nature of the motivations of Agnon's "hero," Jacob, in *Betrothed* with Kafka's very Jewish attempt at a *conscious* self-understanding of the frustrating factors affecting his behavior, to help reshape his life in a productive and bearable way, implicitly rejecting a Hellenistic or Freudian determinism; see, e.g., ...*Agnon*, pp. 171 ff. and Lee Siegel, "Freud and His Discontents," *The New York Times Book Review*, May 8, 2005, p. 29.

I.B. Singer and His Predecessors

I

Isaac Bashevis Singer has achieved what certainly may be regarded as one of the highest honors to which any writer can aspire, the Nobel Prize in literature. One would think that such an award would either represent or create a consensus about the nature of his achievement. In fact, this has not been the case. Jewish opinion continues to be divided over whether Singer has been uniquely mischaracterizing *shtetl* life, with his tales of sex, demons, and debasement, in order to pander to current popular literary fads and tastes (a charge somewhat like that made by many about Philip Roth), or whether he is a Yiddish writer who is very much like the fathers of Yiddish literature — Mendele, Peretz and Sholom Aleikhem — or whether, perhaps, he falls into some third category. A close reading of his works and those of his predecessors will suggest that the truth is more complex. Singer's work provides both continuity and contrast with the past.

Mendele, the father of modern Yiddish literature, was primarily a *maskil* (a representative of the Jewish Enlightenment) who wrote works of imaginative satire, designed to hold up a mirror to the Jews of the *shtetl* and their self-destructive qualities. Jews are quarrelsome, disunited, hair-splitting, divorced from action, from sexuality, and from nature, perpetually allowing themselves to be kicked and trod upon, without respect for, or interest in, modern education, even as they cling to their traditional

347

superstitions of demons and magic rituals regarding what causes evil in the world, and, most particularly, the evils suffered by the Jewish people. They are full of talk, daydreams, glorious pride in their martyrs, fantasies and hopes of magical relief from their troubles, and redemption by a Messiah. They are powerless, led by leaders who bow and scrape, like beggars, before others, and — what is worse — are uninterested in power, the importance of self-help, of raising themselves up by education and new, productive economic activity. Characteristically, the *shtetl* male is not a model of achievement but a *luftmensch,* the powerless and incompetent husband, constantly ridiculed by a wife who is buried in economic and sexual frustration.

In one of his representative works, *The Mare,* Mendele tells the picaresque tale of the narrator, a *luftmensch* Jew, and a mare as they discuss the Jewish condition that each represents — each an aspect of the Jewish psyche. The crucial message of the story is simply that Jews can't merely demand humane treatment, they can't achieve success by dreams, and they can't wish away anti-Semitism. At the end, a drunken Ashmedai, the Devil and King of the Demons in Jewish tradition, and who, in the story, represents the evil power that seems eternally to control Jewish fate and is blamed for all the evil that befalls Israel, is used to mock Jewish intellectual poverty. "Where should I let you off?" he asks the airborne *luftmensch.* "Tell me where you live. I found you up in the air, after all." The Jew cannot answer, but dumbly looks "toward the east." And, then, Mendele has Ashmedai instruct the narrator on how to lead his people, through the Devil's "Ten Commandments": 1. Put yourself before the community. 2. Feed people rituals, piety, so they can't think about how really to solve their problems. 3. Pretend to be compassionate. 4. Make alliance with the strong, e.g., the tax collector. 5. Make continuing religious demands on the people. 6. Lull people with fairytales. 7. Don't respond to complaints; join the people in complaining. 8. Belittle your opponents. 9. Backbite your opponents. 10. Use "home" remedies; encourage the people in their superstitions.

The narrator resists, and is hurled to earth by Ashmedai for his defiance. He awakes from his dream in his room, his mother by his side. He had failed his university exams in history and literature, and his mother had brought him home where he had been in a coma. Forget these "stories," she advises, "just get married. It's the way of the world. It's customary and traditional for us Jews." Nothing has been accomplished, and nothing will be accomplished in the *shtetl,* says Mendele.

Indeed, even when a Jew is smart enough to see the need to get out of the *shtetl* and actually go "to the East," to Palestine, as occurs in Mendele's *The Travels and Adventures of Benjamin the Third,* he has no idea of where he is, where he is going, nor how to get there. In a highly amusing exchange with his friend, Senderel, who agrees to join him in the trip, Benjamin asks where they will get money for food and clothing for their trip and Senderel answers that they'll beg: "What do all other Jews do? ... It's an ancient Jewish custom: merely a free loan!" This unfinished book is a series of one mishap after another, all because the hero and his friend are incompetent simpletons. You can take the Jew out of the *shtetl* but you can't take the *shtetl* out of the Jew. The solution is not more dreams, even Zionist dreams, but, first must come the reeducation and self-improvement of the Jewish people in the ways of the modern world.

In *Benjamin,* too, we find devils and demons being blamed as part of *shtetl* superstition for all the bad things that happen to Jews, and even, ironically, when something good is happening, like Benjamin's trip, that does not conform with *shtetl* ways. Thus: Most of the people, however — and the women were of the number — waxed eloquent: "Benjamin must be in cahoots with *Them* ... with the Powers of Darkness. He must be hand in hand with the Evil One."

And when they share their plans with skeptical Jews on the way, the reaction is that Benjamin must be more than an ordinary mortal: "Who knows, perhaps Benjamin is a reincarnation of someone else." If it's not the Devil, it's another soul that must be to blame.

Thus, Mendele remains the liberal, modernist *maskil.* He depicts shtetl Jews as superstitiously blaming the Devil for Jewish troubles. The Devil is also used by Mendele as an active character in his stories, both to embody the real devil of Czarist Russia and the forces of reaction, as well as to mock and satirize the ways in which Jews are their own worst enemies. His agenda is social, educational, political, religious, psychological. Get with it, he is saying, leave the past, leave the shtetl outlook, customs, rituals, and culture, because they chain you to a past from which there can be no redemption.

II

With Sholom Aleikhem we come to a much different point of view. He considered Mendele his cultural father and, in the beginning, he, too, was a maskil in his critical approach to shtetl life. However, Sholom Aleikhem eventually turned away from such ridicule, when he saw that the Gentile world would continue to reject and persecute Jews no matter how they might speak, dress, or think, and that Jews had to create their own new cultural identity out of their own past. An important transitional story in this development is The Haunted Tailor, which recounts the inter-family and inter-shtetl turmoil that results from a flawed society and family structure of ignorance, superstition, sexual frustration, and disunity. The poor hero, a tailor sent by his shrewish wife to another town to buy a goat, buys one that mysteriously gives milk only in the seller's house but not when the tailor brings it home. In the end, the resultant buffeting which the tailor suffers causes him to break down physically and mentally and, indeed, as the story ends, to turn virtually into a goat himself, with the two towns at the brink of bloodshed in defending the "honor" of their respective citizens. Here, the elements of ridicule are still strong.

We also see in The Haunted Tailor the beginning of the use of Satan as tempter: "All at once ... out of no place, Satan the tempter whispered into his ear: Listen to me, Shimon-Eli, you fool, why are you standing here, singing on an empty stomach," and persuades him to cut short his prayers and go to his relative's inn for food and drink. But, after this story, Sholom Aleikhem treated the *shtetl* with sympathy, tenderness, and affection for its warm community feeling, the humor despite adversity, the loyalty to Jewish traditions, the perseverance in the face of adversity. His reaction to the new anti-Semitism of the 1880s was to embrace his people with love.

What we have here is the transition to a new, romanticized view of the *shtetl* as a place of innocent, childlike, nostalgic folk life, a secularized, non-halakhic, idyllic view of a past that the author knew was unreal, but which he created for the purpose of giving Jews a cultural identity. With such an agenda, Satan ceases to have the function that he played in Mendele as a vehicle of bitter satire regarding Jewish inadequacies and illusions. Instead, Satan becomes a humorous aspect of the many folkways and beliefs that keep people going, like the folk beliefs of every other culture. The innocent rituals and symbols help give people a shared past, an identity, a mode of easy communication, and a practical way of getting through the inevitable difficulties of life that all people encounter.

Sholom Aleikhem's most popular creation was Tevya the Milkman, a figure larger than life, designed to entertain the Jewish people and give them some pride in an idealized, though difficult, past that stands for Jewish values divorced from halakhah and messianism, a culture that was Jewish even while it was secularized. Sholom Aleikhem's literary technique is to treat sympathetically the cultural shell of traditional small town Jewish life, while cutting out its theological inner workings. One could cite Scripture, as Tevya so artfully did, without necessarily living it in all its detailed rigor. This shell was necessary because it was the only way that Sholom Aleikhem could transmit his subtle, secularized message. In contrast with Peretz, as we shall see, Sholom Aleikhem identified himself with traditional *shtetl* life, even as he subtly distanced himself from it by his humor and his stance as narrator, observing as an outsider. If Germans and other peoples could have a national identity based on their idealized folk pasts, he said, why not the Jewish people?

When, however, Sholom Aleikhem tried to move beyond the *shtetl*, as he did in his novel, *In the Storm,* he created uninteresting, cardboard figures representing the new trends among Jewish youth, Zionists, Socialists, and Bundists, those who looked to find a way out of the past and into a new Jewish future of some kind, and those who believed that the only solution was to change society and abandon class, cultural and even national differences and boundaries.

III

Peretz was a liberal, secular humanist who did not identify himself with the *shtetl,* but looked at it from the outside. His people are not from a folk past but a mythic one. There is neither bitter ridicule, nor even a tender, sympathetic, nostalgic, backward look at the foibles of a simple people. Rather, using a much sketchier portrayal of personalities and places than did Sholom Aleikhem, Peretz created heroic fables of a people who are moral heroes. Moreover, their heroism is not because of their devotion to halakhah, or because of other-worldly saintliness. Rather, it is because they embody, in their *shtetl* garb, modern moral values that go beyond Jewish tradition and halakhah and are often even in conflict with it. Even when they succumb to temptation, the Devil, now portrayed as the tempter, the evil inclination, must struggle mightily, and when they fall it is not a matter of moral disgrace.

For Peretz, the Jewish heroes were Biblical personalities, men of great universal moral strength, with something to teach the modern world. Our men and our women, as Peretz argued in *What Our Literature Needs* and as he portrayed them in his stories, must become live heroes and not dead saints. We must get out of the *shtetl* and deal with the experiences and cultures of other Jews and other peoples throughout the world.

Peretz, like Sholom Aleikhem, used the Hasidic world as his literary prop, as the frame and the packaging for his broad, worldly, modern moral messages. Those messages were almost always upbeat, stressing what Jews could accomplish when faced with moral challenges. Thus, his works are serious, intellectual, almost abstract in their spare use of color and detail. For Peretz, a good. Jew was a liberal, modern thinking European.

There are four stories that I think dramatically illustrate Peretz's viewpoint. In the classic *If Not Higher,* the skeptical Litvak seeks to ascertain the basis for the adulation of the Hasidic rebbe of Nemirov by his disciples. On the night of *selihot* , when the penitential prayers are said before *Rosh Hashanah*, he follows the rebbe into a forest, where he sees him, disguised as a peasant, chopping wood and delivering it to a widow's cottage, which he cheers and warms with a good fire. To the claim of the rebbe's disciples that their master ascends to heaven during *selihot,* the no-longer skeptical Litvak answers: "If not higher." The virtue of the rebbe is not halakhic or even traditional saintliness; it is *this-worldly* ethics. The rebbe is not a man of God but a moral hero of the kind that each of us can become. There is a level of goodness that is beyond heaven. The ability to reach heaven may, indeed, be limited to the saintly rebbe, but the ability to reach "even higher" is one that we each can attain.

In *Devotion Without End,* Miriam, a lovely young bride, disguises herself as her husband in order to cheat the Angel of Death, in the form of Achnai, the snake, which is destined to kill her husband, Hanania, on the eighth day of their marriage. She successfully fools the Angel of Death and, when her soul reaches heaven, she is mistaken for Hanania. There she is asked, in accordance with Jewish tradition: "Did you study the Torah each day?" to which she replies: "Lord of the Universe, have you ever directed the daughters of Israel to study your Torah?" At this point, tumult breaks out in the heavenly court; the heavenly decree has been thwarted because Hanania has been saved by Miriam's sacrifice. Miriam's soul is allowed to return to her body since it was not she who was supposed to die, whereupon she is restored to life, and she and Hanania live happily ever after.

Peretz here glorifies the love of a Jewish bride which reaches self-sacrifice, even though her actions are contrary to halakhah and the Divine decree, and are performed by someone who is not even instructed in Torah — although, Peretz may be implying, she should have been! Hers is the moral grandeur of the hero in Dickens' A Tale of Two Cities.

In A Pinch of Snuff, Satan is allowed to try to bring down the rabbi of Helm. The rabbi resists bribery and seduction, but Satan finally fools him into a technical violation of the laws of T'hum Shabbat, the boundary beyond which a person may not travel on the Sabbath. First, Satan moves the tree that the rabbi had marked as the boundary. Then, while the rabbi innocently reaches for his snuff box that had been blown away from his reach by Satan, the latter replaces the tree in its original place. "The rabbi looked up ... the sun had set. The stars were out. For a pinch of snuff he had violated the Sabbath." Here, it is Satan himself who is parodied. All that work, and so little to show for it. The rabbi's entrapment may be viewed as a sin (unintentional, to be sure) in the eyes of Heaven, and as an accomplishment by Satan (the youthful devil, who achieved this success, "waited for the ovation to let up"), but for Peretz the hero is the rabbi, and the moral victory in this encounter is his, despite the technical violation of halakhah.

And, finally, there is the classic Bontsha the Silent, the paradigm of the simple man, the archetypal Jew, whose life contained little good but, also, little evil, whose only desire, passion if you will, even when the Heavenly court offers him anything he desires as a reward for his simple life, is a hot roll with fresh butter every morning for breakfast!

Peretz here makes two points. First, man is not only not evil and, in fact, capable of moral courage, but even his desires are modest and, withal, rarely fulfilled. Second, the passive acceptance of injustice in this world is not a virtue, and it cannot be remedied even in a promised world to come. There must be justice here, or there is no justice. For Peretz, ultimately, it is unacceptable for the Jewish people to remain the crippled, overly spiritualized chosen people of their post-Biblical tradition. The suffering of Jewish martyrs, such as that described in his story, Three Gifts, is beautiful, but useless. Jews must strive to become the normal, healthy, natural human beings of their classical past, and join the rest of humanity

in trying to achieve a better world through a return to the physical courage and moral heroism of their Biblical ancestors, the men and women,
young and old, who made myth into a reality.

IV

Among Singer's other major predecessors we need mention — briefly
because of space limitations — only S. Anski, Itzik Manger, "Der Nister,"
and two of Singer's earlier contemporaries, his brother, I.J. Singer, and
Chaim Grade. Anski, like Sholom Aleikhem, sought to locate and create a new cultural identity for a secularist, non-Zionist, non-traditionalist
Jewish people. He based it on folk materials, which he literally went out
and searched for from town to town in an ethnographic expedition, as
one would collect other artifacts. His exotic play, *The Dybbuk,* is based on
folk memories going back to Chmelnicki's pogrom in 1648, but, in his romantic, expressionist drama, the wills of the two young lovers overcome
both society and religion. There is little moral criticism or challenge in his
work, but, rather, the intrigue of the strange, a folkish obsession with the
boundary between the living and the dead, and the plot tension associated with society's attempt to thwart romantic love — all suffused with
folk traditions, symbols, and practices.

Itzik Manger resembles Sholom Aleikhem in elevating the common
Jew, the tailor, of the *shtetl,* as his folk hero, and seeking, through his imaginative reworking of Biblical tales, to create a Jewish folklore, which — he
emphasized in his essay, *Folklore and Literature* — is essential if the Jewish people are to have a living literature. His work goes beyond Sholom
Aleikhem in his satiric and irreverent treatment of the Jewish "establishment," including the religious and political heroes of the past and the
present, but he always does so with imagination and good humor.

"Der Nister" embraced the new symbolism, primitivism, and abstractionism of the early 20th century, which eliminates the identifying characteristics of a particular culture, blurring time and space, mixing symbols
and metaphors, and the cultures and religions which they represent, in

355

jarring incongruities, in favor of emphasizing the common experiences and needs of mankind. It stresses clever technique and calls attention to the artist rather than to the subject, in an elitist rebellion against realism. Yet, its obscurity does not prevent "Der Nister," as in his great story, *Under a Fence: A Review,* from making strong points about the transition from a narrow, obsolete religious past to a secularized, modern, materialist present, in which the hero-scholar leaves his abandoned and rejected academic tower for a circus, at the direction of a Mephistophelian dustman who claims his soul under the guise of being his new protector. In the process, the scholar debases himself through his love for a circus beauty, and causes serious injury to his daughter who joins the circus with him. But "Der Nister"'s work does not deal with Jewish culture at the human level, the daily moral problems that people face, and how they meet them. It is much more analytical, historical, and even determinist, in its vision and sweep, and, ultimately, more successful in saving the soul of the artist than the soul of his people or of mankind. Indeed, anticipating his later *The Family Mashber,* this story portrays mankind at a cul-de-sac, stuck in an endless war between the equally morally objectionable polarities of life — art and materialism versus religion and tradition, Hellenism against Hebraism — leaving the sensitive man, or Jew, lying drunk under a fence with no place to go. Ironically, "Der Nister" was killed by the new socialist society that was heralded as mankind's new savior.

In addition to the *shtetl* literature of satire and idealization, fantasy, and expressionist abstractionism already mentioned, we must refer to the brief flowering of the *post-maskilic* Yiddish novel of social realism in the four decades beginning in the *1930s,* exemplified by "Der Nister" in *The Family Mashber* (a style forced on him by Communist cultural ideology), I.J. Singer, in such works as *Yoshe Kalb* and *The Brothers Ashkenazi,* and Chaim Grade, in such works as *The Yeshiva, The Agunah,* and the novellas in *Rabbis and Wives.* All wrote in a *verismo* style, showing the darker underside — the conflicts within, and among, Jews of every class and religious outlook — of the oppressive, tightly-knit Jewish communities of

Eastern Europe, and depicting the shattering impact of economic, social and intellectual change on Jewish religion, family structure, and community life.

V

In I.B. Singer's works, we shall find a literature that draws on the literary attitudes and materials of all of his predecessors, albeit with an emphasis on the bizarre and the melodramatic rather than on folk quaintness or social and psychological realism. His work is overwhelmingly shaped by his moral sensibility and his pessimism about man's capacity to cope with the moral challenges of life, depicted in the daily struggles of individual Jews, grappling with their humanity and its weaknesses, in every environment and era. In this regard, despite his close identification with the ghetto life of the past and the similarity of the subject matter of much of his work with that of his *maskilic* predecessors, which is so integral to the very language of his work, Singer emerges as a writer of universal modern significance. For him, the problem is not the need to change the superstitious, Eastern European *shtetl* Jew into a modern, Westernized, secular citizen of each country, but the universal condition of man, at every moment vulnerable to his or her passions and lusts — in Freudian terms, the dominance of man's ego and id.

Singer can best be understood as a teller of moral tales. In some, epitomized by such works as *The Slave, Short Friday, Shosha,* and *The Spinoza of Market Street,* he portrays man as he can be at his noblest — loyal, persevering, loving, patient, sensitive, devout, meeting the challenges of life with physical and moral heroism. More characteristically, however, his tales involve the successful temptation of a vulnerable human being by some embodied Satanic representative. The latter is often the narrator, to emphasize the kabbalistic idea of evil's reality and almost limitless power. Even the morality of good people is questioned, as in the story *Alone,* where the demonic woman who has failed to seduce the hero taunts him by questioning if he would have spoken of God's omniscience and resisted her had she been beautiful. Whether it is pride, lust, envy, greed, or vanity, all of the moral weaknesses of modern man plague men and women alike in such stories as *The Mirror,* where the narcissistic, beautiful, and lovely wife, Zirel, succumbs to become Ashmodeus' whore, and *Zeidlus the Pope,* where a Yeshiva boy dies at the Devil's hand and learns, too late, that there is a God, having succumbed through vanity to the Devil's suggestion that his learning will be fully appreciated only if he abandons the Jewish people and succeeds in becoming the Pope. Like Peretz, Singer believes that Jewish literature must deal with the moral challenges of man's life, but he differs in his view of man's moral strength and the power of evil, reflecting the difference in the reality of 1900 as compared to the middle of this century. Thus, for Peretz, there is always hope, and his stories are optimistic models of what man at his moral best can achieve. For Singer, having lived long enough to see not only the mega-evil of Communism and Nazism, but the daily evil growing worse every day on the streets of New York, life is more often the story of man's moral failures. Evil has achieved such power in the world that man's free will has almost — but not quite — been nullified. Singer's pessimism is extreme. S.Y. Agnon, who lived through much of the same terrible time frame as Singer, portrayed his Jewish characters more subtly, more understandingly, less cynically and less despairing of their vulnerabilities and motivations. Perhaps witnessing, as a Zionist, the growth of the *Yishuv* (the Jewish settlement in Palestine) provided Agnon with a balance of hope that Singer lacked.

It is useful to compare Agnon's story *And the Crooked Shall Be Made Straight* with Singer's *The Unseen.* In Agnon, the hero, Menashe Hayyim, by mutual agreement with his presumably barren wife, goes off to travel for a time and collect money so that they can get back on their feet after a series of financial mishaps. Because he is unable to avoid squandering the money that he collects, Menashe Hayyim stays away long beyond the time when he is expected to return, and, when he is, erroneously, reported dead, his wife remarries and has children. When he does return, he chooses not to reveal himself, preferring to live in a cemetery — thereby, symbolically, legitimizing his widow's remarriage and ensuring her happy new family life. In Singer's story, *The Unseen,* a similar idea is played out, not as a portrayal of moral courage and heroism that rises, to paraphrase Peretz, "even higher" than the law, but, rather, as the debasement of two Jews even on the holiest night of the year, the eve of Yom Kippur. A divorced wife, feeling compassion for her now poor and ailing former husband — and lonely while her present husband is away, as he generally is — finally shares with her first husband the love that they were unable to find while they were married. For Singer, man is corrupted and debased by his desires for himself, while, for Agnon, man is elevated and ennobled by his compassion for others. In each story there is an adulterous relationship, but in one it is noble and results from selflessness, while in the other it is base and results from selfishness. Each of these masters sees man with different motivations.

Another Singer work that may be compared to Agnon's story is his novel, *Enemies, A Love Story.* There, four Holocaust survivors, a man and the three women to whom he becomes simultaneously married (only in part, unwittingly), cling to each other out of passions born from love, gratitude and tradition, as survivors cling to the wreckage of a ship that has gone down. As a result, they bring new emotional havoc to their lives, because no one of them is able fully to rise above passion to the ethical imperatives of duty and compassion.

Singer's use of the Devil and demons in his stories symbolizes the difference between his outlook and those of his predecessors like Mendele and Sholom Aleikhem. They use the Devil and demons sociologically, as a symbol of the superstitious beliefs of the *shtetl.* Singer, as he has said, uses them for their symbolic power and because he believes in their reality. In a word, they represent for him the tremendous, almost dualistic, gnostic power in the world, as bitterly told in the story, *The Last Demon,* in which the demon/narrator bemoans his fate as the last of his group. With the destruction of the Jews and the universal debasement of man, there is no more work for him. Yet, he concludes, as long as one Jewish book, or even a Jewish letter, remains, he will always have a worthy and powerful adversary.

Many critics contend that, since the innocent and pure optimism of such early works as *The Slave,* Singer has for a long time ceased to write with the hope, much less about the reality, of a humanity that is capable of rising to its moral challenges. While much of his work supports such a view, a later novel, *King of the Fields, is* dramatic evidence to the contrary. There, Singer portrays men and women who are able to achieve a semblance of humane sensibility even in a primitive, pagan, society of constant violence and savagery. This novel also portrays a well-developed idea in Singer's earlier work, in such novels as *Satan in Goray* — the crucial difference between societies that are based on man-made "religions," of nature and power, the secular "isms" of modern man seeking meaning and purpose in a world without God, in which man or a Messiah of man's imagination and creation is at the center, contrasted with religion based on the Jewish concept of a Divine moral authority in the universe Who is apart from, and above, nature, and Who demands allegiance and obedience from all of mankind.

There are other works of Singer to be noted that are perhaps more sophisticated and restrained in the hope they hold out for a "kinder, gentler" humanity. In *The Seance,* two elderly people, she an eccentric medium, he a former philosopher who now believes in nothing, not even in her, whom he recognizes as a fake, both adrift and alone in the world, each searching desperately for the warmth if not the love of companionship, provide each other with a reason to live. As she affirms at the end of the story: "There is no death. We live forever, we love forever." And, in the haunting story, *The Cafeteria,* Singer describes the intermittent friendship between the narrator, Singer himself, and the lonely, brave, romantic Esther, who cannot find honesty or love in the world. Indeed, she insists that she has seen Hitler himself in the cafeteria, among us — perhaps even, in some way, a part of us. Yet, when the narrator learns of her

360

suicide, he laments: "She could have got a better bargain even in this world."

The ultimate strength of Singer lies in his ability to portray man's lust for life, together with the artist's vision of life as a continuing moral challenge which is, all too often, a daunting and overwhelming one. His target is not — as it is for Mendele — Jewish superstition, and his goal, unlike Sholom Aleikhem's and Anski's, is not molding folk artifacts into a cultural identity. His realistic technique is far from the self-conscious abstractions of "Der Nister" (before *The Family Mashber)* and the spare, intellectual, Hasidic stories of moral challenge and victory of Peretz. His goal, consistently realized, is to portray modern man, largely through East European Jewish life, in his unequal struggle to overcome the evil that — for Singer, in such works as *The Family Moscat, The Last Demon,* and *Satan in Goray* — man himself has set loose in the world by his abandonment of God and his worship of Messianic and Utopian ideologies — secular or religious — that seek to eliminate the need and opportunity for individual moral choice. In almost always portraying his characters in personal rather than political or social tensions, Singer reveals his animus toward secular humanism and all the ideological "isms" that it has spawned, which simultaneously suppress human individuality and enshrine man — with all his selfish passions — as his own God.

There is a seeming inconsistency between Singer's recognition of the overwhelming power of evil, and his continuing respect for Judaism, its moral and ritual precepts, in such works as *The Penitent* and *Shosha*. But, for Singer, religion — and, particularly, Judaism — is the only "ism" which provides any hope that man may overcome his passions, precisely because it is not created solely out of man's own debasement. As Yasha, the hero in *The Magician of Lublin,* finally recognizes: "A religion was like an army — to operate it required discipline. An abstract faith inevitably led to sin." But religion must struggle with doubt and lust, and man's free will to make moral decisions, and the outcome is not guaranteed. As he remarks in the "Author's Note" at the end of *The Penitent:*

361

> The powers that assail us are often cleverer than every one of our possible defenses; it is a battle that lasts from the cradle to the grave. All our devices are temporary, and valid only for one specific attack, not for the entire moral war.... Resistance and humility, faith and doubt, despair and hope, can dwell in our spirit simultaneously. Actually, a total solution would void the greatest gift that God has bestowed on mankind — free choice.

In this regard, it is noteworthy that, for Singer, the Holocaust is not a new watershed but merely a new context for the eternal challenge of each person's moral responsibility — and, for some, the opportunity for new temptations and new rationalizations. The challenge facing the hero, a multi-wived Holocaust survivor, in *Enemies, A Love Story,* is not much different than that facing the *shtetl* Jews of *Satan in Goray* three centuries earlier. In this regard, Singer is like Manger, for whom the denizens of Heaven are subject to the same weaknesses and foibles as the residents of Earth; time and place make no difference in man's behavior. We will always be morally tested, says Singer, and the Divine commandments of religion are thus literally eternal as man's only reliable guide in making moral choices.

For Singer, therefore, like for Cynthia Ozick, the Jewish artist has a moral mission, as a secular prophet whose calling is to remain the adversary of man's weaknesses and passions even until the Last Demon has been abolished. Yet, one is tempted to ask: What lies in store for Jewish fiction literature in the Diaspora after Singer? Is it possible that Jewish writers rooted in Jewish tradition will pass from the scene before the Last Demon? In his important essay, "The Problems of Yiddish Prose in America",[1] Singer has already indicated that writers in Yiddish cannot survive in a culture that does not speak the Yiddish language; a living language must be spoken. It is, indeed, because of this that Singer uses East European Jewry as his metaphor for modern society — it is their culture that he and Yiddish "know" best. Irving Howe has expressed the equally troublesome view that, with the successful acculturation of the American Jew, there can be no more significant Jewish American literature, because its essence has been Jewish alienation which, in this country, is rapidly disappearing.[2] But, if writers of the past are soon to pass, and writers of the present are increasingly without a constituency for whom they have a message, what, if anything, is next? To this, Singer surely provides an important answer: there will always be a Jewish literature as long as there is a Jewish people who will be morally challenged in their lives, as all of humanity is destined always to be challenged. The specific issues facing Jews will be different, and the contexts too, of course — be it women's role in Judaism, the nature of Jewish identity and loyalty in the Diaspora, questions of bio-ethics, or issues of class and politics. The packaging is endless and limitless, but a moral agenda will always remain. Asking Singer what remains to comprise the "stuff" of a Diaspora Jewish literature is like asking Englishmen or Italians what remains to comprise the "stuff" of their respective national literatures. The answer surely includes the moral struggles of each people in its particular environment.

Moreover, the issues need not be only the personal, moral challenges faced by each individual in his daily life. There has been, and continues to be, a good deal of important Jewish literature about other subjects. Yet, most of this creative writing goes largely unstudied, unread, and unrecognized, as part of the Jewish literary tradition. Based on a survey that I conducted a number of years ago, it appears, sadly, that the curricula of virtually all of our Jewish studies programs in universities, seminaries, and day schools, contain but a limited number of the high quality, and often classic, works of Jewish fiction by such writers as Asch, Babel, Broch, "Der Nister," Disraeli(!), Feuchtwanger, Grade, Heym, Jabotinsky(!), P. Levi, Joseph Roth, Scliar, Wasserman, and Zweig, and American writers like Blankfort, Burnshaw, A. Cohen, Lewisohn, Morgenstern, Neugeboren, Nissenson, Steinberg, Wouk, Yezierska, and Zeldis, all of which deal with a myriad of Jewish problems and experiences that might interest and enrich Jewish students, who too often must struggle with fiction that does not touch their identity and concerns as Jews.[3]

I believe that we need to take three important steps to help develop further this universal Jewish literature. First, we need methodological work that will begin to articulate the bases and criteria for a modern, creative development and renewal of a Jewish literary history that already exists, and has existed, often without being aware of itself beyond the limited horizons of each society in which it grew.

Second, Jewish literary scholars, critics and publishers, wherever they are found, need periodically to come together and maintain the kind of information network that will rapidly inform them about the works of Jewish writers (and perhaps, also, works by non-Jewish writers on Jewish history and life, whether a history work by a Paul Johnson or novels like *Daniel Deronda* by George Eliot and the *Joseph* trilogy by Thomas Mann) from around the world. Summaries and critical evaluations of these works should be exchanged as they become available, and summaries and evaluations commissioned where they are not reasonably forthcoming in the press and literary establishments of each country. Third, we must find ways to translate these works into the principal languages with which Jews are familiar, to permit the most effective dissemination of such works among Jewish people everywhere.

By expanding the horizons of Jewish literature in this way, we will simultaneously encourage writers all over the world to think in terms of a single Jewish people, its history, its destiny, its challenges, and its achievements.

In these ways we can give Isaac Bashevis Singer a literary continuity as he passes on the tradition of challenging the moral fiber of our people, as have so many of his illustrious predecessors throughout world history.

NOTES

1 This essay was published in 1943, and was first translated and appeared in English in *Prooftexts, Vol.* 9, No. 1 (January 1989): 5-12.

2 "On Jewish American Writing," *Tel Aviv Review, Vol.* 2, Fall 1989/Winter 1990: 343-8.

3 For Jewish drama and dramatists, a good place to start is Ellen Schiff's insightful book, *From Stereotype to Metaphor* (Albany: SUNY Press, 1982). For a recent compilation of the 100 best works of modern Jewish literature, see *Pakn Treger* (Fall 2001):6-40.

Der Nister's *"Under A Fence:* A Review"

I

At the turn of the 19th century, Jewish intellectuals had reached the end of the line regarding the utility of the century-old *haskalah* program. It failed because Jewish rationalists who sought to solve the problems of anti-Semitism and alienation had come to a cultural cul-de-sac; they had gone too far to return to a life according to the tradition and its religious underpinnings that they had intellectually rejected, yet they could not gain acceptance by Gentile society even by modernizing their thought, dress, speech, education, occupation, and political outlook to match that of their hosts in the Diaspora. Indeed, by the end of the century this lack of acceptance turned into new, violent hostility beginning in 1882 and on into the 20th century.

For some, the response was Zionism. Others, like Ansky and Sholom Aleikhem, sought to create a new Jewish culture, without faith, using materials from Jewish life in the past. A third solution was more radical in terms of Jewish identity, consisting of pressing for changes in the society that had rejected their desire to become like the Gentiles. For them, the solution was socialism, the Bund, even political revolution. Thus, a tremendous pent-up creative energy was released with the overthrow of the Czarist regime, producing for a short while a burst of experimentation in all art forms — until Soviet authorities demanded the more restricted forms of socialist realism. An outstanding example of this artistic energy is the story "Under a Fence: A Review," written in the late 1920s by *Der Nister*,[1] the pen name of the Russian Yiddish writer, Pinhas Kahanovitch, who sought to explore the new, expressionist form of writing before he was forced into the more realistic mode of his great novel, *The Family Mashber.*

His goal was to reduce man's experience and identity to a common denominator by the use of abstract symbols, and by scrambling and blurring reality's concrete symbols, even those of people, time, and place, in order to undermine the "fences" that separate mankind, whether political, cultural, or religious. What is reenacted in form is everyman, anyman, anywhere, anyplace. The location and time of scenes are deliberately blurred. Scenes shift magically, surrealistically, by the author's pen. The line between dream and reality is similarly blurred, as if to suggest that even this distinction does not matter. Yet, as this story demonstrates, *Der Nister* — like Kafka — was unable to embrace fully the expressionist movement's glorification of a new man — freed from tradition, yet with boundless love and humility, a composite of Christ, Marx, Nietzsche, Darwin, and Freud. Indeed, he remained ambivalent even about his Jewish identity, even as he sought to drown it in the faceless abstractions of his story.

II

"Under a Fence: A Review" takes the form of a story within a story, or a dream within a dream — this is never clear until the end — of a scholar who is in love with Lili, a circus lady, who spurns his love in favor of one of the circus strongmen. The scholar is the last of a long line of scholars that formerly resided in a tower. Alone and abandoned there, he is enticed by an apparition in the form of a dustman to leave the tower and join the circus. The rite of passage, as it were, is a fantasy scene in which the scholar is required to burn a straw effigy of his wife, and the scholar's straw daughter is saved, and magically turned into a human being by the dustman. In a mock trial of the scholars, initiated by the dustman for the benefit of the circus audience, they are found guilty of being "useless garbage" and condemned to death by burning, as was the scholar's wife. The former chief scholar of the tower, Medardus, then holds his own trial and condemns the hero for forsaking his tradition and for allowing his daughter to become a performer with him in the circus — as a result of which she has sustained a serious injury, plotted by Lili, who is jealous of the daughter's beauty and talent. The scholar awakens at this point, lying under a fence, evidently having dreamed this story of his life after he became drunk when Lili rejected his love.

III

Suffusing the entire story is *Der Nister's* cynicism at the two intellectual forces that have confronted Jewish history, the scholarship of Judaism and the idle, useless games of Hellenistic and Roman culture, with their emphasis on strength and beauty symbolized by the tower and the circus. The broader theme may be the transition in Russia and perhaps the world from the Judeo-Christian religious tradition to the Socialist-Communist materialist outlook, or the polarities of God and Religion versus Art and Idolatry, and how these polarities of man's existence continue to debase man as long as they are not in harmony.

The traditional past is mocked along with the materialistic present. Throughout the story it is the scholar who is the victim, the *shlimazel*, who fails himself and others, who pratfalls even as he makes the heroic gesture, a fool and a failure. In the end, he is mocked, rejected, and punished by his past and his future, by what he left and what he sought. He has reviewed his life without finding in it any hope, lying drunk all night under a fence — a fence that separates his past and future, his roots and his ambitions, neither of which provide any hope or hospitality. He is lying at the margin, at a border, between two destinies, unable to be part of either.

Lili's plans to maim or perhaps even kill the scholar's daughter calls to mind two symbols in Jewish literature: one is Lilith, the demon first

368

wife of Adam, symbol of sexuality and thus part of the circus culture, a baby killer in East European Jewish mythology, who succeeds because of, or despite, the father-scholar's attempts to ward her off by loving her. The second symbol is the daughter, all purity and dignity, the *Shekhinah* in exile who, in a symbolic inversion, instead of protecting the scholar from the circus influence, is sold into bondage to that life and becomes so good at it as to make Lilith herself jealous. *Der Nister* even mocks the Lilith myth in which she kills children because of their purity; here she attacks the daughter for outdoing her in circus artistry and beauty!

There is the suggestion of a Freudian relationship between the professor and his daughter. Thus, the professor burns the straw incarnation of his wife and saves the straw incarnation of his daughter, symbolically carrying her beneath his belt, from which she springs as his own flesh and blood almost literally from his loins. Throughout, the professor's love for his daughter is reflected in descriptions of her physical attractiveness and dexterity. The professor is inevitably drawn toward Lili, a woman with whom he can only have a relationship of shame and rejection, as self-imposed punishment for his obliteration of his wife and his repressed desire for his daughter that his superego will not let him fulfill. Significantly, he is accused in the story of being a "lecher" not because of his relationship with Lili but for allowing his beautiful daughter to exhibit herself and perform in the circus.

The scholar is portrayed as having no ideas of his own as to how to live when he leaves his past. As the dustman later boasts, the scholar had to rely on him because he was never trained in how to live and contribute and get along in a world of people and nature, outside of the scholarly tower that he and his fellow scholars and his teachers inhabited for so long.

The tower, the world of scholarship, of Jewish tradition, is portrayed as one in which there is now nothing left but sawdust and straw, a ship that all have abandoned including the captain. It is a male-oriented and male-dominated world, where cultural hegemony is patrilineal. The head of the scholars' academy, Medardus, is the thinly disguised Metatron, the highest angel in kabbalah, the keeper of the Divine secret, and — in the Zohar — the heavenly archetypal man. Intellectual nourishment is supposed to be transmitted by a father, but there is nothing left to be transmitted. Thus, in the tower it is the scholar as father, rather than his wife as mother, who has the breasts, but their child can receive nothing from them because they are dry. The future offered by the dustman, who stands for the professor's present empty reality as well as his hope for the future, is the world of the circus, the only possible salvation for useless people.

The professor understands that the circus is a dangerous place. "Your life is cheap. You are there only to gratify others. Your soul hangs by a thread, and your life is unimportant." One recalls the chapter in Kafka's *Amerika* of "The Nature Theater of Oklahoma," where the hero finds a home, status, and acceptance — but only if he is content to live without hope of change, without dignity and identity, with no more importance than a dancing elephant entertaining a bored mob that is incapable of thought, happy only when stimulated by the comic or risky acts of others, that give the latter importance by stressing the degradation and humiliation of others.

In a significant scene, *Der Nister* rejects the world of scholarship and tradition as the people bury the rejected, obsolete chief scholar, Medardus, in the earth and the sea in a mass open air burial site, under a wide blue sky. Nature buries scholarship in an open air ceremony. The burial is a pagan rite, a ritual of spiritual and cultural liberation, as birds symbolizing nature and freedom not only emerge from the professor's head, eyes, and limbs, giving him relief and happiness, but become the reincarnated form of Medardus himself.

Der Nister's rejection of his own Jewish tradition is symbolized dramatically when the scholar is "liberated" by the dustman from the tower. Like the *hometz* of the Passover liberation ritual, the object of a ritual burning, his "useless" straw wife is burned as a symbol of the rejected tradition of the now "redeemed" professor. His redemptive path to the circus has been found, in another ironic twist, in what the dustman characterizes as a holy book of prophecy, the last and only book remaining in the tower. Recalling King Josiah and the lost book of *Deuteronomy*, the dustman reads to the people how the professor's new life in the circus has been foretold in this lost document. Here, *Der Nister* mocks both Judaism and Christianity, which use the prophets as vehicles for validating their religious and spiritual lives. The people are told how the prophetic book requires the redeemed professor to adhere only to the circus, to study it day and night because its details and secrets must be learned gradually, and to love that circus life with all his heart and soul and might, and we sense *Der Nister* making a twisted, mocking use of the *Shma* imagery, the way Berlioz turns the theme of his beloved into a witch in the last movement of his *Fantastique Symphony*.

The dustman represents man's Faustian faculty of reasoning, questioning, and unrest, and the dark side of that faculty which is Mephistopheles, who mocks what is best in man by holding it up to a mirror that seems eternally capable of convincing even the wisest man that what is good is evil, and what is evil is good. Thus, he easily persuades the scholar that he is a fool who has ceased to have anything meaningful to live by or transmit to others, a personality without spiritual resources, living in a past that has literally and spiritually turned to dust.

But *Der Nister*, living under the new spiritual and cultural tyranny of Soviet Communism, brilliantly turns the dustman into a second force, one that not only "redeems" from a "dead" past, but which then assumes the role of a new master, imposing an equally dead future. As the narrator leaves the abandoned, crumbling, empty tower of tradition and scholarship with rites of freedom, he is led by his "redeemer" to a new form of enslavement, that of materialism and slavery of the senses, managed and controlled by the very dustman who saved him. The faculty of reason that saves can enslave; Christ can turn into Dostoyevsky's Grand Inquisitor and Marx can turn into Lenin and later into Stalin. Thus, the dustman refuses to let the professor experience real freedom; he is too naive, too uneducated. He needs to be guided by those with more knowledge and sophistication — and to formally renounce his past. Indeed, in the circus "trial" of the scholars, Der Nister uncannily anticipates the Soviet show trials of the 1930s, which were designed to insure that the state's new slaves would never be tempted to abandon their new Eden.

In the scholars' trial before Medardus, the professor confesses that he betrayed his teacher, adding the explanation that he had no choice because the tower community disintegrated; it was abandoned, and all its scholars, himself included, had no preparation for the outside world and had to follow wherever the dustman would tell them to go. Der Nister, like the Haskalah Enlightenment, inverts the Jewish mission of tikkun olam (moral elevation of the world) into Jewish ignorance and helplessness in taking care of itself, much less shouldering the burden of leading the way to righteousness for the rest of the world.

The professor's teacher, Medardus, as chief judge, makes a strange case for Jewish tradition: first, he tells the hero, even if you are the last Jew you shouldn't abandon your faith; second, tempters like the dustman are not real but are products born in the minds of "sick scholars," i.e., those not loyal to (Jewish) tradition; and third — and here Der Nister mocks both Christian asceticism and the family fragmentation of Hasidism — the professor should never have believed the dustman's first trick, showing the professor as part of a closely knit family of father, wife, and daughter, because he should have known that good scholars can have no wives and no children!

In the end, not surprisingly, the professor wakes up drunk, dirty, ashamed, unable to comfort his daughter who is crying for him in his grief and debasement. For Der Nister, Jewish history is over. The Jewish faith community is abandoned and exists no more. The hero, the remnant of a community of faith and tradition, will condemn himself for his new circus life, as Medardus and his scholar colleagues continue to condemn him. Yet, he will pursue Lili anyway, at risk to himself and his loving, pure, daughter, alienated from his past and future, no good to his child, who stands as the spiritual proxy for his wife — the *Shekhinah* whom he has rejected for Lili. So much for Jewish past and future in *galut*.

Thus, while *Der Nister* has redeemed his art, he has not redeemed his Jewish soul. He remains a hidden Jew, a cultural Marrano masquerading as an artist like all the other artists in the circus of *galut* culture and society, lying drunk under the fence that continues to separate Jews from their past and their future.

"Under a Fence: A Review" stands as one more monument to the loss caused by the later Soviet intolerance of artistic innovation, and reminds us of what is possible when such innovation is allowed to flourish. Whether a distinctive Jewish literature can continue to flourish *anywhere* in *galut*, given the impact of modernity on Jewish history, is another subject.

NOTE

1 *Ashes Out of Hope: Fiction by Soviet-Yiddish Writers*, Irving Howe & Eliezer Greenberg eds. (NY: Schocken, 1977).

Was Yehudah Halevi Racist?

The Philosophy of Rabbi Yehudah Halevi, as developed in his classic Kuzari,[1] has never achieved the standing and respect among secular scholars that it has among religious Jews. One cause, I believe, is Halevi's attribution of racial superiority to the Jewish people with regard to their spiritual and religious qualities.[2] This difference is evident by comparing the traditional form of sanctity accorded to Kuzari in the form of rabbinic commentary, most notably the commentaries Kol Yehudah and Ozar Nehmad,[3] with the discomfort of scholars like Heinemann and Baron toward Halevi's racial views.[4] Scholars like Husik, who take a more neutral stance on Halevi's views, provide little by way of explanation, much less justification, for Halevi's racial views.[4] Thus, Husik observes:

> God and the Jewish religion are not simply facts to be known and understood like the laws of science. They are living entities to be acquainted with, to be devoted to, to love. Hence, quite a different way of approach is necessary. And not everyone has access to this way. The method of acquaintance is open only to those who by birth and tradition belong to the family of the prophets, who had a personal knowledge of God, and to the land of Palestine where God revealed himself."[5]

Note how Husik fails to explain the connection between Halevi's view that the Jewish people were chosen by God to receive God's commandments through the revelation at Mount Sinai,[6] and the racial idea that only those who are Jews *by birth* have the capacity for prophecy.[7]

Thus, argues Halevi, even converts to Judaism do not achieve that capacity through conversion.[8] Here, of course, Halevi is *contra* to Maimonides and other halakhists, as far back as the Talmud. Maimonides concludes that converts can affirm that God has "sanctified us" and "commanded us" in the various blessings no less than any natural born Jew, and they have the right to consider themselves as having stood at Mount Sinai and personally heard and received the commandments of the Torah.[9]

Given our modern sensitivities to any philosophy that may be described as racist in character, whether the thrust of such racism is the inferiority of others or the superiority of the claimant, the credibility of all of *Kuzari* is in jeopardy among all but the most devout Jews unless some sense can be made of its racial claims. Unfortunately, no such attempt has been made on a comprehensive basis (at least to the author's knowledge) in any of the literature on Halevi.[10] One writer has even observed that Halevi did not seriously entertain the notion of Jewish biological superiority.[11] The power of the argumentation in *Kuzari* in so many areas other than that involving Halevi's racial claims demands, at the very least, that such an attempt be made.

This means, simply, that before we cavalierly apply the modern terminology of "racist" or "racism" to any of Halevi's thought, given the automatic response that such characterizations are bound to invoke, we need first to understand exactly what Halevi believed, why he believed it, and then to compare it to the beliefs of other religions. Then we can evaluate its acceptability and determine the extent, nature and circumstances of any "racist" views. There is, surely, a difference between apologetics and understanding.

Halevi makes his case for Judaism by resorting to the story of the conversion to Judaism of the king of the Khazars, and then of his people, in the Caucasus in the eighth century. In brief, as is well known, the king sought to determine the true religion by asking, first a philosopher and, then, representatives of the two major faiths to defend their views. Unsatisfied, he finally sent for a representative of the Jews despite their low condition, which indicated that theirs was not the true religion.

The rabbi showed the king that philosophers never agree among themselves and have never become important religious leaders. Moreover, Islam and Christianity both accept the basic texts and tenets of Judaism. These facts already suggest that the latter is the true faith. Halevi's principal argument is not based on reason, however, but on history. The rabbi in *Kuzari* traces the genealogical history of the Jewish people, culminating in the revelation to them of the Torah by God at Mount Sinai. The chosenness of the Jews for revelation cannot be challenged because it was publicly seen and transmitted without dissent by so many thousands of people, in contrast to the more private experiences and revelations of the major contending faiths. This genuine and indisputable historical tradition of the Jewish faith provides the surest foundation for truth.

Our first observation about Halevi's approach to the superiority of the Jewish people is historical. His primary reason for writing *Kuzari* was to prevent Jews from weakening in their faith, faced as they were with the ascendancy of Islam and Christianity and their own degradation. This is evident in the description that Halevi gave to his book: "A Defense of the Humiliated Faith." *Kuzari* was addressed to Jews, not to the world, and sought to give them the self-respect that, he understood, was increasingly in jeopardy.[12] Halevi wrote in an age in which each of the major world religions seemed in control of its own destiny and claimed the unique truth and superiority of its faith. Each made Judaism and Jews the object of political oppression and religious disrespect. While Islam and Christianity were engaged in mortal combat, Halevi despaired of any hope that his people could find support or salvation in the camps of *Kedar* or *Seir,* East or West. Because of his pride as a Jew, he developed an understanding of his religion and his people's destiny that sought to turn the tables on history, and restore to his people and their faith the special status that they had once enjoyed when Judaism was the only monotheistic religion in the world.

This leads to the second important observation about Halevi's philosophical views. For him, as the rabbi continually emphasizes in *Kuzari*, historically, reason and speculation have never been, and inherently can never be, the way to religious truth.[13] As the moral philosopher Alasdair MacIntyre has pointed out, even the philosophers of the 18th Century Enlightenment never succeeded in their great ambition to establish a unified understanding and standard of what is "good" and "just."[14] If, *contra* to Maimonides, religious truth and unity with God cannot be achieved by man through the development of his reasoning powers, it follows that these can he achieved only through prophecy — a status of grace accorded to man by God and a status that must be biological — and, to the extent that it is characteristic of a group, racial-inherited rather than acquired by human intellectual effort. This, for Halevi, is a matter of both logic and history, and is the reason why he spent so much time tracing the lineage of the Jewish people from Adam to Moses, through the prophets of Israel who appeared in each generation. It was to the Jewish people, having become, uniquely, a nation capable of prophecy, that God revealed himself and his Torah at Sinai.[15]

For Halevi, therefore, the inability of even converts to Judaism to achieve the level of prophecy is not a matter of xenophobia but a matter of sound reasoning and experience. If individuals or groups could become spiritually equal to the Jewish people through an act of will and intellect, the true religion would have developed naturally, without the need for God's revelation. This is precisely the claim of the philosophers and precisely where history has proven them wrong.[16] Halevi would certainly have been delighted to augment Jewish ranks and power through converts and not to discourage them by offering them an inferior spiritual status. But the nature of his argument in defense of Judaism through revelation compelled a different result. God's plan was twofold: to bring His Will to the world as quickly as possible — that is, by revelation — to

377

a people that had developed the special quality of prophecy, the worthiness to receive God's revelation and commands in a direct relationship with Him. This message was then to be disseminated among the nations by the great moral leaders of the world whose task, like that of the Khazar king, is to inspire and persuade others to follow God's revealed commands.[17]

The third observation to be made about Halevi's claim of Jewish racial superiority is that it does not mean, as history demonstrates, freedom from suffering and oppression in this world. On the contrary, other nations are accorded the privilege of experiencing material, cultural and political success and decline, based on the normal factors at work in history. Only the Jews experience fortune and misfortune based on the moral quality of their life. Israel is merely promised that it will never be totally destroyed, that it will survive, even as a remnant, to carry on its spiritual mission to the world of revealing and bearing witness to God's existence and His commands as revealed in the Torah.[18]

The fourth observation is that Halevi does not claim the superiority of natural born Jews over converts or Gentiles, apart from prophecy, which is the ultimate of many levels of spirituality, involving man's direct relationship with God. Apart from the potential for prophecy, to which few born Jews ever succeeded, in any case, born Jews have no superiority in any characteristic or quality, including morality, intellect, or in the economic, military or cultural sphere.[19] Thus, for Halevi, all people can aspire to live in purity and righteousness and to find closeness to God in this world and the next. Moreover, given the demise, during the First Exile, *before the advent of Christianity and Islam,* of even this very limited gift of prophecy until the Messiah, when all the world will achieve a unity under God,[20] the superiority of born Jews can be viewed as designed, not so much to demonstrate the present superiority of the Jewish people over other peoples, but to restore their pride through an understanding of their historic glory as the one people of the ancient world worthy of God's single — and eternal — public communication of His moral will to mankind.[21]

It should be recalled that Halevi wrote in an era in which Christians and Muslims alike not only preached the superiority of their religion, but, based on that superiority, justified the imposition of varieties of indignities on members of other religions. By contrast, Christians and Muslims are not deemed by Halevi as rejectors of God, or as infidels who are not entitled to equality in life and liberty because they do not adopt the one true faith. They are considered as people who remain to be educated in the full covenant of God, but who, nevertheless, can, and should, seek to lead lives on the highest plane of morality and purity, and will receive their heavenly reward for doing so. It is Judaism's sister religions, however, that historically preached a superiority that extended far beyond Halevi's claims for born Jews — a select, Divinely selected few in any case — to attain prophecy. For these religions, failure to accept their creed and live by their religious precepts warranted subjugation, scorn and abasement in this life and no share in life hereafter. Apart from their theology, they practiced oppression and brutality against non-believers.[22]

The fifth and final observation relates to the modern idea of individual equality. The principal argument against Halevi's racial view is that other religions permit, indeed encourage, individuals of other faiths, or of no faith, to join their ranks and achieve, in theory at least, full equality with their new co-religionists. Indeed, as we have seen, this is the view of most Jewish halakhists regarding Judaism. It is primarily Halevi who would deny even to converts the ability to achieve prophecy and union with the Divine Influence. The modern stress on individual equality and reason simply cannot accept Halevi's refusal to accord equality to converts or even comprehend a reason for his refusal to do so. Surely, it may be argued, nothing in Halevi's *Kuzari* absolutely compelled him to take a position against the complete spiritual equality of converts. Indeed, one may reasonably so characterize the views of the many rabbis who otherwise admired the *Kuzari* but shared Maimonides' position on the full equality of converts with born Jews.

I believe there are halakhic, historical, and philosophical dimensions to this problem that are worthy of consideration. Halakhically, one must recognize that Halevi is not the first or only rabbi to recognize differences between born Jews and converts. There are recognized differences in such areas as inheritance in the Holy Land, bequests, and convert disqualification to be king, or marry a priest (Note the occasional *benefits* of the distinction between a convert and a born Jew, e.g., a proselyte has the status of a legitimate Israelite even if his father is a *mamzer*). Historically, we may note first that Christian nations never accorded equality to Jewish converts as a matter of fact, even if the Church did so as a matter of religious doctrine. This is evident, for example, from the statutes on the purity of blood in Spain in the medieval period, and the persistent anti-Semitism, culminating in the Nazi, regime, whether Jews converted to Christianity or not during the modern period in Western Europe. Second, Halevi lived at a time when the "privilege" of converting was not an aspect of the inherent spiritual equality of all persons, as some may perceive it today, but as an aspect of the superiority of the new religion of the convert over that of his or her prior inferior religious status. This is why the normal manner of conversion to Islam and Christianity through most of world history, until modern times, has been by some form of coercion. There is no sense of dignity or equality accorded to a person who is compelled to abandon his faith. Thus, it is reasonable to conclude that Halevi did not perceive the issue of the status of converts to Judaism in the same light as moderns do, and it is even reasonable to speculate that he might well have treated this subject differently had he been writing today.[23]

From the philosophical standpoint, it is important to note that, for Halevi, Judaism is not just a religion to which one may, in concept, adhere by affirmation to accept and practice its doctrines and precepts. It was, for him, a quality of people-hood, nationhood, to which he was committed in belief and action, as we know from his philosophy of the holiness of the Land of Israel, his inspiring nationalistic poetry, and his selfless act of lonely *aliyah* to Palestine.[24] The concept of the Jews as a people, a once independent nation, is far more consistent with the idea that there may be inherent limitations on how fully a convert can ever cleave to, and become part of, such a group, than a concept of the Jews as merely a faith community whose identity is, by hypothesis, simply and solely based on sharing that community's religious beliefs. To this day, the right to become a naturalized citizen is a privilege not a right, natural or constitutional, even in America; only a *natural born* American, for example, may qualify for the presidency. Very few Americans would characterize this as a racist doctrine. To characterize as racist Halevi's view that converts cannot qualify to prophecy, particularly when there are no more prophets, and there will be no more prophets until the advent of the Messiah, seems, at the very least, wrong-headed.

Moreover, while Halevi is clear about the disqualification of converts to achieve prophecy, there is an interesting question as to whether Halevi believed that the progeny of converts were similarly disqualified.[25] If they are not disqualified, Halevi's alleged "racism" affects only one generation, which hardly makes Halevi into the kind of racist to which our modern sensitivities so severely object.

From a logical standpoint, it would seem that Halevi must surely treat converts and their progeny in the same manner. If, as he maintains, the Jewish people had reached a certain status of spirituality through a biological process separating them from the Gentile world continuing over centuries, the progeny of converts would not seem to be in a position ever to hurdle that gulf any more than converts can. But, if we pursue the logic a bit further, it becomes apparent that the progeny of a convert who marries a born Jew, for example, already has closed at least some of the biological gap.[26] To pursue a modern analogy, the son of a naturalized American is qualified to become president, and no one claims this to be illogical or unreasonable. Clearly, Halevi's view cannot be definitely ascertained by reasoning alone.

Given Halevi's stature and his general care in spelling out his views in *Kuzari*, it seems appropriate to make an analysis of the text to discern his intent. If we turn to the words of the text of *Kuzari* itself, the issue seems still to be unclear.[27] Halevi says that a convert and his progeny may approach God very closely (but) those who become Jews do not take equal rank with born Israelites, who are specially privileged to attain to prophecy, while the former can only achieve something by learning from them, and can only become pious and learned, but never prophets.

From this one may argue that a descendant of two converts or even of just a Jewish mother who is a convert, being *"born"* a Jew, may achieve prophecy, and even more so the descendant of a male convert who marries a "born" Jew. Indeed, the progeny of every convert married to a "born" Jew is biologically at least partly a "born" Jew, and each succeeding generation is more so. As discussed earlier, however,[28] the varying renderings of I, 115 in the available translations of Kuzari, regarding who may be fit to attain the Divine Influence, provide an additional element of confusion as to the intent of this section.

However, the ability of such progeny to achieve the level of prophecy is certainly a reasonable and, probably, better understanding of the text, for the following extra-textual reasons. First, the halakhah prohibits publicizing that one is a convert — in part, I suggest, to assure that his or her progeny have a seamless identity with the Jewish people.

Second, it seems highly likely that Halevi, accepting the Jewish idea of the Messiah coming from the family of David, would reject any idea that the progeny of a convert cannot attain to prophecy, because both King David, a prophet, and (through him) the Messiah, derive from the marriage of Boaz to the convert Ruth.[29]

A final indication of Halevi's attitude toward converts and their progeny comes at the very end of Kuzari.[30] The rabbi, having told the Khazar king that he wishes to go to Jerusalem, is asked by him: "What can be sought in Palestine nowadays since the Divine reflex is absent from it, whilst, with a pure mind and desire, one can approach God in any place?" The rabbi answers that this still is the only way for a *born Jew* to live a pure spiritual life:

382

> The visible Shekhinah has, indeed, disappeared
> because it does not reveal itself except to a prophet
> or a favored community, and *in a distinguished place.*
> As regards the invisible and spiritual Shekhinah, it is
> with every *born Israelite* of virtuous life, pure heart,
> and upright mind before the Lord of Israel (empha-
> sis added) . . . No function can be perfect (except in
> Palestine); heart and soul are only perfectly pure and
> immaculate *in the place which is believed to be spe-
> cially selected by God.* (emphasis added)

I believe, that from this concluding section of *Kuzari*, we can draw a number of conclusions related to the issue of the spiritual level achievable by a convert's progeny. First, most converts are not likely to identify with the Land of Israel as their land, nor to consider leaving their homeland, their family and their social and economic status in the Diaspora. The Khazar king, like Halevi's paradigmatic convert, *by his question and his actions* as recited in the text, evidences no desire to live in the Land of Israel. Even after Halevi's answer, he prefers to remain and live as a king outside of Palestine rather than to renounce that privilege for a life as an ordinary Jew in the Land of Israel where — partly from observing the positive commandments relating to living in the Holy Land — his progeny could aspire to "live a pure spiritual life."[31] Second, converts cannot be prophets because they generally do not aspire to live in Palestine — the only place where prophecy is possible.[32] Third, Halevi assuredly did not mean to exclude the generational progeny of a convert when he spoke of "every born Israelite" returning to Palestine to reside with the invisible *Shekhinah;* such progeny do not share the converts' natural psychological reluctance to leave their homeland, as Ruth's sister-in-law, Orpah, and the Khazar king. Finally, Halevi's goal was to *maximize* and not minimize the number of returnees to the Holy Land. It follows that Halevi considered a convert's progeny as "born" Jews in terms of the gift of prophecy as well.

In summary, we have seen that (1) there were special historical circumstances for Halevi's desire to restore the pride of the Jewish people in their spiritual heritage; *Kuzari* was addressed to his own people to redress their despair at being an oppressed nation as well as a despised faith; (2) there was a logical basis for Halevi's view of the special spiritual quality of the Jewish people, because his proof of the truth of Judaism was based on God's revelation of the Torah to the Jewish people alone, based on their prophetic capacity rather than on Judaism's provability as a philosophic truth which all persons and nations could equally accept; (3) Halevi's unequal treatment of converts as compared to born Jews in terms of their ability to achieve prophecy was in a historical context in which conversions were not designed to recognize the spiritual equality of the converts but, rather, the spiritual inferiority of their *prior* religious status; (4) while other religions do grant theoretical equality to converts, that equality was virtually never adhered to as a matter of practice; (5) Halevi's doctrine of the inequality of converts is limited to the particular matter of prophecy, and not to any other matter of morality or intellect, or any other of man's cultural achievements, and this gift was given to very few born Jews, in any event, and was given and withdrawn prior to the advent of any other monotheistic religion. In the days of the Messiah — which all monotheistic religions would help bring about — all men will unite spiritually under God on an equal basis; (6) conversion to Judaism was viewed by Halevi as more than just conversion to a faith or an ideology to which individuals could aspire by an act of intellect; it was adherence to a nation, a people, where facts of birth and genealogy continue to be relevant to this day; and, finally, (7) although the textual evidence is not crystal clear, particularly in light of conflicting Hebrew translations of *Kuzari*, the better view seems to be that, for Halevi, the incapacity of converts for prophecy was limited to them and did not pass to their progeny. At worst, he did not consider the "pass on" question and, in either case, his attitude would hardly be characteristic of modern racists who emphasize the permanence of racial inferiority. The totality of these factors precludes any simple, invidious characterization of Halevi's *Kuzari* as racist in any

384

modern sense of that term.

I suggest, therefore, that, for Halevi, the special access of the Jewish people to the Almighty at Sinai, an event never repeated, based on a capability no longer operative, was part of his proof of the special quality of Judaism, and the special ancestry of the Jewish people that privileged them to experience revelation. It was designed by Halevi to give his suffering people pride in their past, their spiritual heritage, and the special qualities that merited their heritage as an act of God's grace, and to encourage them through that pride not to feel inferior to the other religions then regnant about them, nor to succumb to religious despair. Ultimately, his message was for Jews to take heart and, following his own example, begin the long spiritual and political journey home, as a nation, back to their homeland, where Jews could once more live in freedom and independence among the other nations of the world.

....
NOTES

1   *The Kuzari* (Schocken 1964). In this paper, references to *Kuzari* are to this edition, translated by Hartwig Hirschfeld, with an Introduction by Henry Slonimsky.

2   The paradigmatic statement of that claim is Halevi's view in *Kuzari*, 1, 115, that even converts to Judaism cannot aspire to prophecy, this being reserved to "born Israelites." The full text of this crucial paragraph reads as follows, with some important deviations among the extant translations, noted in footnote 10:

> Now we do not allow any one who embraces our religion theoretically by means of a word alone to take equal rank with ourselves, but demand actual self-sacrifice, purity, knowledge, circumcision, and numerous religious ceremonies. The convert must adopt our mode of life entirely. We must bear in mind that the rite of circumcision is a Divine symbol, ordained by God to indicate that our desires should be curbed, and discretion used, so that what we engender may be fitted to receive the Divine Influence. God allows him who treads this path as well as his progeny, to approach Him very closely. Those, however, who become Jews do not take equal rank with born Israelites, who are specially privileged to attain to prophecy, whilst the former can only achieve something by learning from them, and can only become pious and learned, but never prophets.

3   The commentaries of R. Yehudah Moscato *(Kol Yehudah)* and R. Yisroel Halevi *(Ozar Nehmad)* may be found, e.g., in *The Book of the Kuzari* (Hebrew), tr. by R. Yehudah ibn Tibbon (Warsaw, Poland; Jerusalem, Israel 1975).

4   Isaak Heinemann, Introduction to "Yehudah Halevi: Kuzari" in *Three Jewish Philosophers* (New York: Atheneum, 1981), p. 24, and Salo W. Baron, "Yehudah Halevi: An Answer to an Historic Challenge," *Jewish Social Studies III* (1941): 264-72.

5   Isaac Husik, *A History of Medieval Jewish Philosophy* (Meridian Books and Jewish Publication Society, 1958-60), p. 152.

6   I, 11, 25, 95, 100; II, 56; Husik, *Op. cit.*, pp. 156-8.

7   The uniqueness of Jews and Judaism, according to Halevi, rests in the ability of certain Jews (in the past) to attain to the level of prophecy, and in the capacity of the Jewish people — as a nation and individually — to come under, or attain connection with, the Divine Influence *("Inyan ha-Eloki")* (I, 4; II, 12; III, 1 and *passim)*. Individuals who attain the latter spiritual level are called "pious," which is just below the level of prophecy (III, 11, 17, 20)

8   *Kol Yehudah* and *Ozar Nehmad* comment on *1, 115* that the converted Edomite prophet, Obadiah, was a special case, and note that an exception does not negate the (Halevi) rule. Balaam was the last of a special group of *heathen* prophets; Louis Ginzberg, *The Legends of the Jews,* Vol. III (Jewish Publication Society, 1968), pp. 855-6.

9   H. H. Ben-Sasson, ed., *A History of the Jewish People* (Harvard University Press, 1976). Part V, pp. 585-7; Isadore Twersky, *Introduction to the Code of Maimonides* (Yale University Press, 1980), pp. 485-6. However, the king and certain other community officials had to be born Jews. (Tractate *Sota,* 41b *[Tosafot]* and *Yevamot,* 45b*)*.

10 Guttmann makes an attempt to do so but is incomplete and problematic in certain respects; Julius Guttmann, *Philosophies of Judaism* (New York, 1964), pp. 126-7; see also *Kuzari,* I, 111. For example, Guttmann states that converts can come under the Divine Influence (p. 127). This view is problematic, depending on the translation that one adopts of I, 115. Some read that converts may perhaps be successful in receiving the Divine Influence, which may imply that their progeny may be "born Israelites" who may attain prophecy; others read that it is the *progeny* of converts who may be successful in reaching that (and *only* that) spiritual level, which implies that they are not "born Israelites" and cannot reach the higher level of prophecy, at least for some undisclosed number of generations into the future. The *Kol Yehudah* in the Warsaw edition interprets 1, 115 to mean that the convert's *progeny* may achieve the level of the pious. As to the generational limits of the disqualification of a convert's progeny, see n.26, *infra.*

11 Heinemann, *Op. cit.*, p. 24.

12 See also Husik, pp. 152-6; H.H. Ben-Sasson, *op. cit.,* pp. 535-6.

13 I, 1-4, 13, 63-5; IV, 3.

14 Alasdair MacIntyre, *Whose Justice? Which Rationality?* (University of Notre Dame Press, 1988); see also the review by Richard John Neuhaus in *Commentary* (June, 1988): 64-8.

15 1, 79 and *passim.*

16 See n. 13, in particular the rabbi's cogent and concise statement in 1, 13.

17 I, 100-103. While the Midrash recounts that God offered the Torah to *all* of the nations, their rejection of the Torah may be evidence that in fact they were not worthy of prophecy. Arguably, the offer was made knowing that it would be rejected, so that the other nations could not later challenge the chosenness of the Jewish people by claiming that they, too, would have accepted the Torah had it been offered to them.

18 I, 109; II, 32-44, IV, 3. See also other sources on the doctrine of special Jewish providence, collected in Frank Talmadge, "R. David Kimhi as Polemicist," *Hebrew*

Union College Annual XXXVIII (1968), p. 231, n. 94.

19 I, 115.

20 1, 87; III, 41, 65, 67; IV, 23.

21 Ben Sasson, *Op. cit.*, pp. 535-6.

22 Compare I, 111; III, 11; and IV, 23 with H. H. Ben-Sasson, *Op. cit.*, Ch. 27; Druck, *Op. cit.*, pp. 60-2; David Berger, ed. *History of Hate* (Jewish Publication Society, 1986), *passim.*; and Bernard Lewis, *The Muslim Discovery of Europe* (W. W. Norton & Company, 1982), pp. 171-84. For Halevi, Christianity and Islam help prepare the world for true monotheism, acceptance of the Noahide Laws, and the advent of the Messiah (IV, 23). By contrast, according to R. David Kimhi, a leading anti-Christian polemicist (as incorporated in his Torah commentaries), the Jewish people must behave on a high moral level not only toward fellow Jews but toward Gentiles as well (Talmadge, *Op. cit.*, p. 225). See also *Numbers* 15:16, *Deuteronomy* 10:19, and *Deuteronomy Rabba* 3:3 for numerous Biblical and midrashic injunctions against discriminating or oppressing non-Jews.

23 For example, he might well have clarified his views on the capacity of the progeny of converts to attain prophecy, and he might have limited the disabilities of converts and their progeny to the extent that he considered essential to the rest of his philosophy. Note, e.g., in III, 11, Halevi's ambiguous statement that "observant" Jews may make the ritual affirmation associated with bringing the "first fruits" to the Temple even though the full text would literally exclude the possibility of their affirmation by converts or their progeny (See the discussion of this point in Twersky, *Op. cit.*, p. 485). Indeed, Halevi might well have concluded that while Israel was the only *people* that had such capacity, *individuals* of other nations could — by their special qualities, either learned or inherited — at least achieve the Divine Influence, if not prophecy.

24 I, 16; II, 14; III, 1; IV, 23; V, 23-28. S. D. Goitein, "The Biography of Rabbi Judah Halevi in the Light of the Genizah Documents," *Proceedings of the American Academy for Jewish Research 28* (1959), pp. 28 ff.; see also Ross Brann, "Judah Halevi: The Compunctious Poet," *Prooftexts* , (May 1987) which discusses whether Halevi really did renounce the learning and manners of his earlier life in Spain when he set out for Palestine and a life of religious devotion.

25 See, in particular, I, 115.

26 I, 115. The reference to "purity of lineage" in I, 95, where Halevi traces how the Jewish people reached their exalted spiritual capacity, suggests that the extent of a progeny's ability to attain to prophecy or come under the Divine Influence may depend on the extent of such a person's ancestral mix of born Jews and converts. See also Arthur Hyman in his introduction to *Essays in Medieval Jewish and Islamic Philosophy* (KTAV, 1977), discussing the lack of clarity in Halevi's treatment of the Divine Influence. To that same effect see Hartwig Hirschfeld, Introduction, *The Kuzari* (London: M. L. Cailingold, 1951).

26 See n. 2.

27 See n. 10.

28 III, 19; IV, 23.

29 V, 23. Some may view this argument as conclusive on the issue.

30 Earlier, the king had indicated the same lack of interest in *aliyah,* even after he had converted to Judaism at the end of Part I. See, e.g., II, 23 ("*thy law*"; "*thou fallest short*") and III, 11 (the "observant Jew" can live a happy life "even in exile").

Presumably, Halevi is not suggesting that there is no halakhic requirement that a convert make *aliyah,* in light of the contrary Biblical paradigms of Abraham and Ruth, but merely that such an act would be unusual and, perhaps, should not be deemed a condition of conversion.

31 Prophecy comes through the *Shekhinah* (Divine Presence), which is operative only in the Land of Israel, or — if outside — for its sake (I, 95; II, 14, 50; III, 22). See also the detailed comments on II, 14 and the concept "for its sake" *by Ozar Nehmad* and *Kol Yehudah,* referred to in n. 3. The *Shekhinah* is apparently the name that Halevi gives to the Divine Influence in the Land of Israel (I, 95; II, 14).

6

Science

There can be no doubt that Jews cannot live in isolation from the world's scientific, religious and legal issues, nor from their political ramifications. Devotees of other religions seek a fair opportunity for their children to learn about scientific views as debated by respected scientists in the field. As the Jewish voice among Christian nations, how should we respond to scientific and constitutional questions? Should we automatically reject the views of Christian "fundamentalists"? What view should Jews take in their own private schools? In any case, should Jews go public on these issues, even where their interests as Jews may not be threatened?

It is a fact (see my essay **"Science and Religion"**) that most scientists continue to believe in a *"personal* God."[1] I emphasize "personal," because that describes more than a pre-Creation clockmaker; rather, it describes a God who is involved, in unknown ways, in human affairs.

Besides the scientists, most people in the United States undoubtedly believe in a personal God. Most such people believe that the universe was created, at a single point in time, by what is called the "Big Bang." Indeed, if we look for a scientific consensus on any issue being discussed in this chapter, it is that Aristotle was incorrect about the eternal nature of the universe. Rather, it came into existence at a point in time. And this is believed despite the questions that this concept has always raised, e.g.: From what matter, if any, was the universe made? How did *that* come into being? Into what is the universe expanding? And so on. In any case, the *fact* of the "Bang," by scientific consensus, now overrides the as yet many unanswered questions about it.

It is equally true that, more recently, it is not only religious people (sometimes generically called "fundamentalists") who question or reject the materialistic explanation of the origin and development of earth's species. There are also many respected scientists who now believe that there are holes in the theory of evolution — too many scientists and too many significant holes to permit evolution to be accepted as a consensus scientific view (as it once was) in the same way that creation of the universe by a "Big Bang" now is.

Moreover, at least one reputable scientist has a *scientific* explanation that harmonizes the six days of Biblical creation and species development with scientifically accepted measurements of time, except that he uses a different physical perspective in his calculation.[2]

It has long been said that an omnipotent Divinity and a Divinely revealed, historically true Bible were impossible because science has shown that nature's laws are immutable. But science has now shown that those laws are probabilities, not certainties; they operate *almost* always, but not always. This means that there is now a scientifically acceptable definition of miracles when there is a departure — unusual, unexpected and unpredictable — from the normal course of the laws of matter and nature. "Quantum mechanics," as this probability science is known, provides a hole in what used to be the certainty of scientific laws, through which Divine intervention is possible.[3] It would be comforting to know that educational systems are not afraid to discuss these issues in the classroom. Despite Einstein's famous remark that "God does not play dice with the universe," it is hard to see how Divine intervention in the normal course of nature in order to achieve a Divine objective constitutes "playing dice," a game in which the players cannot begin to predict the outcome, and generally lose their shirts!

How should Jews react to competing Separation of Church and State claims on these matters? The first amendment "carries water" on each "shoulder:" The government can't fund or establish religion, and the government can't prevent freedom of religion, both beliefs and rites. But if a public school wants to teach that a previous scientific consensus is wrong (and that what used to be only a religious viewpoint, right now, at least, explains the evidence better), isn't this a free speech issue for the students? When they express views or ask questions about these issues, how should the teacher answer? The essays in this chapter deal with some of these issues.[4]

. . . .
NOTES

1 Ibid, note 11.

2 See Gerald L. Schroeder, *Genesis and the Big Bang* (New York: Bantam, 1992); Charles H. Townes, "Our Special Universe," *The Wall Street Journal*, March 11, 2005, p. A10. This Nobel Prize physicist has been arguing that science and religion are alike more than they are different, and will eventually merge. He believes that searching for order in the universe and purpose are not the same, but are not far apart; see "The Convergence of Science and Religion," *Think* (an IBM journal) (1966); Dennis Overbye, "Physicist to Get Templeton Prize for Progress in Spiritual Matters," *New York Times*, March 10, 2005, p. A20.

3 See, e.g., Brian Greene, "One Hundred Years of Uncertainty," *The New York Times*, April 8, 2005, p. A27; and *idem.*, *The Fabric of the Cosmos* (New York: Vintage [Random House], 2005), esp. pp. 79-95, 178-180, 201-16, 437-9.

4 It is unfortunate that it is Christian and not Jewish — much less Orthodox Jewish — scholars who have been in the vanguard of urging that evolution is not a factually proven theory in light of our current scientific knowledge. In contrast, we sometimes find ultra-Orthodox rabbis fighting even other ultra-Orthodox Jews who have scientific expertise, on scientific issues like the age of the world, and treating their differences as an issue of heresy instead of a search for truth. See Alex Mindlin, "Religion and Natural History Clash Among the Ultra-Orthodox," *The New York Times*, March 22, 2005, p. F3; Tamar Rotem, "The Rabbi Who Wrestles with Crocodiles," *Ha'aretz*, April 15, 2005, p. B6.

Science And Religion:
Are They Still Separate Worlds?

Imagine being told by someone that the universe was created at a point in time, from nothing, in a vacuum of empty space, and that this creation was outside the laws of nature and, therefore, cannot be explained by scientists in scientific terms.

You would immediately conclude that the source of this information was a right-wing religious person or group, pushing religious belief as truth or fact, and probably advocating that this kind of purely religious belief masquerading as scientific fact should be taught in the public schools as part of respectable science.

In fact, these statements represent a current, respected scientific view of creation of the universe. Among cosmologists and physicists, that event has a technical, scientific name: It is a "naked singularity": "singularity," because it is not subject to any laws of physics or other laws of nature known to science; and "naked," because — unlike singularities that scientists believe take place in the hidden confines of the black holes in the universe (points of energy, of infinite density, of dead stars, where the laws of time, space and causality do not exist) — the singularity of creation is observable by man.[1]

The implications of this current scientific view are obviously significant and will emerge further as we examine this view in some greater detail.

The vacuum of empty space does not contain even an atom of matter. However, it does contain particles of "virtual matter," particles (and their waves and antiparticle partners) that materialize and disappear for the tiniest fractions of a second, and never become real matter. If such a pair of "virtual" particles appear near a black hole, one particle may be sucked into it, and the other may escape. If it does, the escaping particle is transformed into a particle of real matter, taking some of the black hole's energy with it.

About 15 billion years ago, after one such an encounter, a fluctuation in the vacuum of space somehow, in a way scientists cannot explain, resulted in a titanic transformation of the escaping virtual particle into our own real — not just virtual — infant universe, a transformation which scientists now call the "Big Bang."

Also, for reasons that scientists cannot explain, the new, infant universe settled into the lowest possible energy state, assuring it of a stable existence, since — at any higher energy level — the new universe would long since have been destroyed by one of the cosmic rays that continually bombard it.

Scientists have come to terms with the "singularities" that take place within black holes. Besides being essential to explain observed, measured aspects of the universe, and being logical consequences of Einstein's general theory of relativity, these "singularities" provide scientists with the consolation of being hidden from scientific observation. Thus, while these phenomena are not subject to known laws of science, their existence is, in every sense, academic. However, if a "singularity" were to become "naked," i.e., visible, detectable, measurable, unshielded, as it were, by the black hole's normal ability to seal off everything that goes on within it, even its own light, then it would be an affront to the idea of the existence of universal laws of nature, which defines the nature of scientific activity itself.

Dr. Stephen Hawking has said that nature "abhors" naked singularities, and that — while theoretically possible — there is no generic way in which they can occur according to the known laws of physics.[2] What this means is that the creation of the universe was a *unique* "naked singularity;" we cannot and should not expect to find any scientific rules for any other events, in the past or in the future, in which the laws of nature — of time, space, and causality itself, the essence of nature and its scientific understanding — are suspended and do not operate. Nevertheless, some of Dr. Hawking's colleagues believe, or, more accurately, have faith, that other singularities will be found, and that scientists will eventually develop a new scientific theory, one that would be, indeed, revolutionary, which will explain all singularities, and at least "naked" ones, in a scientific way.[3] Of course, as at present, even such future scientific explanations would not necessarily undermine or negate a religious dimension regarding the physical phenomena involved.

Creation is not the only area where scientists are suggesting that something other than scientific causality may be required to explain the evidence of scientific inquiry. In recent years, respectable scientists, both Christian and Jewish, have written quite boldly to challenge the view, that has long prevailed, that science has nothing to say about theology and religion respecting the latters' traditional beliefs about creation, and the emergence of plant, animal and human life. These scientists have concluded that there are rational bases to believe that there is evidence of purpose in the creation of the universe and the emergence and development of its inhabitants. They have shown that science fails adequately to explain what occurred, i.e., science proves that there is no acceptable scientific explanation. Indeed, crucial elements of this cosmological, chemical, paleontological, biological, and archeological evidence point away from a natural cause, one explained by known scientific theory, in favor of existence by intelligent design or purpose.[4]

For example, many respected scientists are impressed with the appearance of life on earth almost as soon as it could host life, instead of the developmental interval that would be expected; at the discontinuities in the emergence of various species, e.g., the sudden emergence, in the early Cambrian period (some 600 million years ago), of myriad species without any fossil evidence of prior evolutionary development; at the parameters of the laws of nature that came into being with the universe that are precisely those necessary to sustain life — which, absent purpose and design, must be described as, statistically, unbelievably lucky accidents and coincidences; at the existence of only one genetic code for all forms of life, and the virtual impossibility of its random development; at the irreducible complexity in the biochemistry of the cell; and, on a more fundamental level, the increase in complexity and order in nature for which neo-Darwinism provides no grounds of expectation.[5]

In brief, at the macro and micro level, in the field and in the laboratory, in fossils and molecules, conventional laws of science leave many questions without answers, for many scientists, except intelligent design — by a designer. Indeed, the issue of the existence of a designer is now considered sufficiently scientifically respectable that a front page article in *The New York Times* highlighted that the National Association of Biology Teachers has recently amended its platform to allow for the possibility of a designer at the helm of evolution. "The diversity of life on earth," the platform now states, "is the outcome of evolution: an unpredictable and natural process" — but that process is no longer described as "unsupervised" and "impersonal."[6]

This is not to say that many scientists do not continue to believe that natural explanations exist (a *scientific* position) or will be found (a *faith* position); indeed, some even believe that non-natural explanations should not be considered or entertained (a *materialist philosophic* position) to explain creation and the emergence of life and its various species. It is to say, however, that the debate is now a scientific one, in large measure, between respected scientists and scientific evidence and argument on both sides.

In these circumstances, some scientists have even opted to believe in extra-terrestrial intervention, without any evidence for such intervention, solely to solve the problem of the absence of an adequate scientific theory to explain the scientific evidence. Not surprisingly, given this impetus, such intervention proposals create new scientific problems of credibility.[7] On the other hand, scientists — and others — who accept the idea of intelligent design in the universe will have to deal with the presently expected death of our sun in about 5 billion years, and the resultant transformation of the earth to a "cold, lifeless cinder, if there is anything left."[8]

Since scientists are a lot more familiar with traditional religious beliefs concerning creation and evolution of the species than religious professionals are with the latest scientific findings and writings in the many disciplines — from mathematics to cosmology — that impact on these religious beliefs, it is not surprising that these new writings emanate primarily from scientists rather than from representatives of the various religions.

Somewhat more surprising, at least in theory, is the failure of the discipline of philosophy to play a major part in the dissemination of these new scientific developments.

As the noted astronomer, Dr. Owen Gingerich, summarizes, after the scientific revolution of the sixteenth and seventeenth centuries, philosophers were divided between deists, those who put God outside the universe, having set it in motion according to physical laws, and theists, who continued to view God as maintaining an active role in the world. But after Darwin's evolutionary theory, with its inherent denial of design, became the reigning philosophy of intellectuals, the choice became one between atheism and theism. "Science remained a neutral way of explaining things, neither anti-God nor atheistic."[9] Religion and science occupied separate domains in thought, social discourse, and the law. However, given recent scientific thought and the accumulating evidence, science and religion, as they relate to statements about the issues of creation and life, cannot any longer be considered entirely separate domains. Scientific inquiry, evidence, and rational hypotheses to explain that evidence, can no longer be considered to have no relevance to what have traditionally been pigeon-holed as solely religious questions.

Paradoxically, for those who still believe that materialist explanations exist for all phenomena, faith is required that such explanations will be found in the future. For those who believe that the universe is subject to Divine design and purpose, it is a matter of logic that the universe could not exist in a way, i.e., subject to such scientific laws and physical values, as would conflict with this Divine role; for them, materialist explanations will never provide all the answers. And for many scientists today, this is becoming increasingly true; as the astronomer Owen Gingerich has noted, "I am not prepared to concede that arguments from design are necessarily contra-scientific in their nature."[10]

Interestingly, a recent survey of scientists, updating an earlier one in 1916, has found that, then as now, about 40 percent of the responding biologists, physicists and mathematicians continue to believe in a personal God.[11] Thus, there is no basis to fear that acknowledging that life was designed by an intelligent agent will discourage the search for scientific, natural explanations for the universe and events within it, nor is there any basis for the claim that maintaining a belief in intelligent design *and* scientific inquiry is irrational and, in some way, unscientific.[12]

In any case, an important implication flowing from the increasingly common ground for inquiry and discussion about creation and life between science and religion, has to do with the right of students to learn, and the responsibility of public schools to teach, what scientists are doing and thinking concerning these issues in light of their inquiries and the evidence. I will have more to say on this point shortly.

A related implication is that, unless jurists, lawyers, civil rights groups, parents, educators, theologians, and philosophers begin to study and gain a reasonable, working, up-to-date knowledge in the new scientific activity an debate relevant to their work, we are doomed to continue to consider church-state separation and educational policy questions based on traditional notions of the inherent separation of science and religion, even while science is beginning to propose and discuss ideas that support traditional religious views regarding issues like creation and the emergence of life on earth. As a result, our children are likely, as a general matter, to be deprived of comprehensive instruction in what science has to say about these matters. Moreover, if such material is not part of the school curriculum, there is little likelihood that students will have the ability, interest or incentive to inquire about such scientific developments on their own.

Indeed, since students would clearly be entitled to accurate answers to such questions if they were to ask them, doesn't it make sense that such material should be included in the curriculum in the first place, and that teachers should be required to maintain an up-to-date general knowledge of scientific debate that impacts on traditional scientific explanations and understandings on the creation of the universe and the existence of the earth's plant and animal species?

Yet, proposing the teaching of these new developments is likely to be regarded as a strategy of religious extremists to teach religion in the public schools instead of (sic) science. We are dealing here with a longstanding view, noted above, that science not only approaches certain issues, like creation and the emergence of the earth's species, differently from religion, i.e., based on evidence, not faith, which is still true, but reaches conclusions clearly opposed to religion's views on these issues, which is no longer uniformly true. The Scopes "monkey trial" in the 1920's remains the most vivid event in United States history exemplifying the faith-science conflict, and the assumed total irrelevance of the Bible to real events of the universe's development. Historically, to protect the right of the faithful to believe contrary to the (*always provisional*) findings of science; to protect the right of those who trust science for their answers; and to avoid teaching religious views in public, tax-supported schools to those who enjoy the right not to accept (or be subjected to) such religious views — it has been accepted that schools should not teach material that may tend to give aid, comfort and support to religious doctrines.[13]

But, as I have shown, it is no longer true that science's findings on the issues of creation and earth's species development are categorically and universally considered by scientists to be in conflict with traditional religious, i.e., Biblical, tenets on these issues. Many scientists believe that there are no credible scientific theories to explain these matters, and that scientific knowledge and reasonable inferences from it comport closely, in the case of creation and the appearance of the various species, with religion's understanding of these events.[14] It appears, e.g., that creation was a process not subject to human scientific laws.[15] Shouldn't that be taught in all public schools, along with its implications for the reasonable-ness of the idea that the *cause* of this scientifically unexplainable event may also rationally be considered to be unexplainable by any scientific laws? Why shouldn't students be taught, in addition to what they have been taught until now about the origin of the universe and life, that there is scientific evidence that points to the involvement of intelligent design, which some scientists are now prepared to say implies a designer? Thus, the biologist Michael J. Behe concludes that — while biochemistry books do not have to explicitly says that "God did it" — the "reluctance of science to embrace the conclusion of intelligent design that its long hard labors have made manifest has no justifiable foundation."[16]

If this sounds to some students like a scientific definition or restate-ment of the concepts of "miracle" and "God," that is a rational conclusion from scientific evidence, which they should be entitled to draw. What will the biologists be allowed to say when they are asked in school class-rooms — as they inevitably will be — why the words "unsupervised" and "impersonal" have been deleted from the description of evolution in their charter? Is there any valid constitutional reason why they can-not answer, or even initiate the idea, that "there is credible, substantial scientific evidence that the origin and development of life's species was *not* "unsupervised" and "impersonal?" Where, if anywhere, should a line be drawn in teaching this material in the public schools? I submit that as long as the intent is to teach science, and to allow classroom discussion of reasonable conclusions that individuals may wish to draw from such scientific developments, such a teaching approach is legal, and desirable from an educational standpoint.

I do not believe that the current *Lemon* test of the U.S. Supreme Court[17] would stand in the way of teaching scientific material that may cause some students to adopt, or more firmly to adhere to or accept, religious points of view on issues with which such scientific material deals. Indeed, to *prohibit* the teaching of such nonsectarian, scientific material, which is inherently religiously neutral in content, provided it is taught without a specific intent to instill religious views in students but only to fully cover the relevant scientific material, or for a government supported school to refuse to teach such material, would itself constitute a violation of the freedom of speech and religion provisions of the First Amendment, if a reason for such prohibition or refusal was to discourage religious beliefs that might take root, or be strengthened, as a result of exposure to such scientific evidence and opinion.

The situation might be different if this material was taught by religious representatives, e.g., priests and rabbis with an interest in slanting the material in content or emphasis. But apart from that kind of an exception, if the *bona fides* of the secular purpose of teaching this material cannot reasonably be questioned, there should be no problem in meeting the *Lemon* case requirements of a proper secular purpose and the avoidance of improper church-state entanglements in the classroom. True, that case also requires that the activity not provide substantial support for any religion or religious beliefs. But if it is proper to teach children to read English even though this information or skill can be used to read the Bible, the teaching of science should also be permitted as a secular subject, even if the material may reasonably be appropriated by a student to provide support for a religious belief. Where the material is inherently neutral, any such effect should be deemed incidental and not legally relevant.[18]

One final point. Education today is structured in a "Catch-22" mode from the standpoint of capturing for our children in the classroom the benefits of recent developments in science. Parents, and most educational professionals, have not been trained to be alert to such scientific developments, and have little knowledge or interest in them. Teachers of science have been trained in the existence of religious and scientific beliefs as two domains of thought. The same is true of those who teach the teachers; how much interest can they have in new scientific developments that impact on what have been considered to be "religious" issues unless they are religious themselves? The "Catch-22" problem here is twofold: First, who will see the need to add this new scientific material to the curriculum? Second, if no one really cares about these new developments, and therefore there is no intent to prevent the teaching of this material, there may be nothing illegal about its continued absence from public school curricula! But that does not detract one bit from the harm being caused to the students who are not receiving the most comprehensive, up-to-date education in science that is possible. Where do we cut into this circle of lack of awareness or lack of interest, or both, that affects teachers, students, and parents?

I suggest, and hope, that a first step, to which this article makes a small contribution, is for interested scientists to work with educators, especially in the sciences and law, to increase *general* awareness of the problem. This should help begin the necessary correction in teacher training and instruction, teacher-parent interest and awareness, and — ultimately — student benefit, at all levels of the education process.

....

NOTES

1   The discussion that follows is based on three articles that appeared in *The New York Times* (NYT): Malcolm W. Browne, "Physicists Confirm Power of Nothing, Measuring Force of Universal Flux," NYT, 1/21/97, pp. C1,6; *idem.*, "A Bet on a Cosmic Scale, and a Concession, Sort Of," NYT, 2/12/97, pp. A1,22; George Johnson, "What a Physicist Finds Obscene," NYT, 2/16/97, p.E4. Scientists are closing in on another piece of the creation puzzle, the age of the universe and its rate of expansion. It is hoped by scientists that the latter will be low enough to explain the formation of clusters of galaxies in space from the smooth, uniform universe that existed right after the Big Bang. Scientists are also working on two other pieces of the puzzle, the average density or mass of cosmic matter and what is called the anti-gravity force (if it exists), which will determine if the universe is in equilibrium between collapse and eternal expansion. See John Noble Wilford, "Scientists, Once Starry-Eyed, Get Clearer View of the Universe," NYT, 4/7/97, pp. A1 and B8; *idem.*, "New Data Suggest Universe Will Expand Forever," NYT, 1/9/98, pp. A1, 17.

2   Browne, "A Bet...," *Op. cit.*, p. A22.

3   See articles cited in note 1. Interestingly, Hawking's discomfort with the entire notion of "naked singularities" (see Browne's article in note 1), has caused him to deal with the scientific incomprehensibility of Creation in a curious way — that is, that the universe is not here because of a deliberate, *super*natural design or purpose, but rather that the universe *must* be this way *because* we are here. It just is. But this leads, paradoxically, to the same logical conclusion as the notion of singularities, i.e., that, absent any scientific explanation, the logical inference may be drawn of purpose and design in the creation of the universe. See discussions of Owen Gingerich, "Dare a Scientist Believe in Design?" (Chapter 1) and Russell Stannard, "God's Purpose In and Beyond Time" (Chapter 3), in *Evidence of Purpose — Scientists Discover the Creator*, John Marks Templeton, ed. (N.Y.: Continuum, 1994), citing Stephen Hawking, *A Brief History of Time* (N.Y.: Bantam, 1988), p.125. See also David Berlinski, "Was There a Big Bang?" *Commentary* (February 1998):38. A striking new theory offers a *scientific* explanation for the origin of the universe, and concludes that the underlying elegance and simplicity of its structure, from the smallest particle to the universe as a whole, points to a "design that was extremely unlikely to have come about by chance." See Ernest J. Sternglass, *Before the Big Bang* (N.Y.: Four Walls and Eight Windows, 1997), p. 221 and generally, Chapter 15).

4   See, e.g., *Evidence of Purpose, Op. cit.*; John Polkinghorne, *The Faith of a Physicist* (Princeton: Princeton Univ. Press, 1994); Gerald L. Schroeder, *Genesis and the Big Bang* (N.Y.: Bantam, 1992); Michael J. Behe, *Darwin's Black Box*, (New York: The Free Press, 1996).

5   Ibid.; Schroeder, *Genesis...*, *Op.cit.*, pp. 98-146, 162-5; *Evidence of Purpose, Op. cit.,; passim*; Polkinghorne, *...Faith of a Physicist..., Op. cit.*, p. 17.

6   Schroeder, *Genesis..., Op.cit.*, p. 114; Behe, *Darwin's Black Box, Op.cit.*, p. 251. The recent change of view by the biology teachers group, and its scientific background, are discussed by Laurie Goodstein in "New Light for Creationism," NYT, Week in Review, December 21, 1997, pp. 1, 4.

7   Schroeder, *Genesis..., Op.cit.*, pp. 114, 127, 139-41, 157-9; Paul Davies, "The Unreasonable Effectiveness of Science" (Chapter 3), in *Evidence of Purpose, Op.cit.*, pp. 52-3; Behe, *Darwin's Black Box, Op.cit.*, p. 248.

8 On the sun's future, see John Noble Wilford, "The Spectacular Shudders of Dying Stars," NYT, 12/23/97, pp. 1, 6.

9 Gingerich, "Dare a Scientist..." in *Evidence of Purpose*, *Op.cit.*, p. 29.

10 Ibid., p.31.

11 Natalie Angier, "Survey of Scientists Finds a Stability of Faith in God," NYT, 4/3/97, p. A14; "Faith and Reason," *Bible Review* (December 1997): 21. See also the recent survey data of scientists showing that "about 40 percent...said not just that they believed in God, but in a God who communicates with people, and to whom one may pray 'in expectation of receiving an answer;'" Cornelia Dean, "Evolution Takes a Back Seat in U.S. Classes," *The New York Times*, February 1, 2005, p. F6.

Many medical doctors are also religious. A recent survey showed that 74% of doctors believe that medical miracles have occurred in the past, and about the same percentage believe that they can occur in the present. More than half claim to have personally seen patient healings that they consider miraculous. Interestingly, Christian doctors are more open to interpreting medically unexplained healings as miracles than Jewish doctors. See Richard John Neuhaus, "The Public Square," *First Things* (March 2005):67.

12 Behe, *Darwin's Black Box*, *Op.cit.*, pp. 241, 251-2.

13 The decision of the United States Supreme Court in the Louisiana "Creation Science" case is an example, in which a law designed and framed to teach scientific evidence, relating to issues of creation and evolution, was found to be unconstitutional without a full trial, because the Court was persuaded that *some* of the sponsoring legislators intended the law to allow the teaching of *Genesis* as if it were science, and that the law would be so understood and implemented; see *Edwards v. Aguillard*, 482 U.S. 578 (1987). My concern that this decision was thwarting a legitimate statutory educational objective was noted in "Secular Humanism and Creation Science in Public Schools," *Jewish Spectator* (Winter 1989):38-41.

14 These inferences do not necessarily negate Darwin's adaptive-mutation approach to explain changes that occur within various species *after* they appear on the scene, for which there is far more evidence than for the all-embracing theory that every species, including each of its complex, specialized organs, developed from a prior species based on adaptations to the environment by mutation to achieve survival benefits. The fossil evidence and its time frame simply do not support any such theory with anything approaching a scientific level of confidence. See, e.g., Schroeder, *Genesis....*, *Op.cit.*, pp.105-114, 128-41. A conference of cosmologists and astrophysicists, in the Spring of 1997, discussed how contemporary cosmology might be compatible with various religions; see Margaret Wertheim, "God is also a Cosmologist," *The New York Times*, 6/8/97, p. E16.

15 See, e.g., sources in n.1.

16 Behe, *Darwin's Black Box*, *Op.cit.*, p. 251.

17 *Lemon v. Kurtzman*, 403 U.S. 602 (1971). The *Lemon* test requires that, for a government activity to be permitted, it must have a secular purpose, provide no substantial support for religion, and it must not involve undue entanglement of the government with religion.

18 See, e.g., John Noble Wilford, "Spectacular Fossils Record Early Riot of Creation," *The New York Times*, April 23, 1991, pp. C1, 10. See also p. 414, note 2.

Secular Humanism and Creation Science in the Public Schools

Recent decisions[1] by the Federal courts involving claims by Christian Fundamentalist parents, under the Freedom of Religion provision of the First Amendment to the Constitution, have sanctioned the use of public school curricula that the parents believe teach ideas in the field of ethics, morality and science that are inimical to their religious beliefs. The courts in these cases have invoked legal doctrines and determinations that threaten the rights to religious freedom of all religious groups. Yet, religious denominations across a very broad spectrum have either not participated in these cases, as in the case of Catholic groups (despite the serious decline in enrollment at Roman Catholic schools in the last two decades), or generally supported these judicial outcomes, as in the case of mainline, non-Evangelical Protestant groups and Jewish civil rights and defense organizations. Even those organizations representing Orthodox constituencies generally failed to take a stand. Much of the media coverage treats these cases as Fundamentalist attempts to impose their narrow religious beliefs on the public schools. The truth about what these cases are really about is more complex.

For many years, the primary concern of religious groups has been to safeguard their children from pressures to introduce religious doctrines and practices into the public schools that conflict with or undermine their beliefs. They also sought to protect their right to create and use private parochial schools in preference to using the public schools. They were largely successful. Indeed, the courts ruled that *any* religious instruction was unconstitutional because it violates the constitutional right to believe or *not* to believe.

However, the First Amendment also prohibits state (and federal) governments from *interfering with* as well as *establishing* a religion. The recent cases raise the vexing question of whether the wall of separation has been built so high that it now has become a form of anti-religious state action. Both the courts and pro-separationist groups for many years argued that today's victim will not be the last, but only the first. That approach does not seem to have prevailed in the recent cases involving the Christian Right. As a result, dangerous precedents for all religious groups have been set. The focus of this analysis is on the recent Tennessee, Alabama and Louisiana cases involving secular humanism and creation science, because of their importance to all parents, and the widespread publicity and comment they received.

In the Tennessee case, parents objected to a variety of teaching materials, including portions of the *Diary of Anne Frank,* and texts incorporating the ideas of pacifism, feminism, and secular humanism, which conflicted with their children's religious beliefs. While some of their concerns were exaggerated or debatable, their basic objections were not fanciful. They did not seek to have the school texts changed but only permission to remove their children from class when the objectionable material was being taught, as a legitimate exercise of their freedom of religion. There was actual experience with that approach indicating that it did not affect the quality of the children's education.

Philosophically, the parents objected to secular humanism instruction generally, because of the cumulative impact of pedagogic materials that they allege teach a "man is the measure" philosophy, which substitutes man for God and reduces a person's choice of religion, and decisions about right and wrong, to an individual's or a society's preferences at the moment.

The media generally ignored the moral relativism aspect of the

Tennessee case. Much of the media, for example, expressed concern over textbook censorship, in particular what was viewed as an attack by Christian Fundamentalists on the widely revered *Diary of Anne Frank,* and fear of a nationwide offensive by them to introduce Christianity into the public schools. Anne Frank's ideas of Jewish destiny and man's inherent goodness are easy to defend. What is harder to deal with is whether a child can maintain his or her religious beliefs and can effectively learn about values in daily living if morality is taught solely as a matter of individualistic preference, without normative content or character. In addition, forcing children to learn Anne Frank's idea that all religions are the same was, for the objecting parents, not an example of religious tolerance but of religious intolerance.

Most interested religious organizations displayed a lack of interest in the effect of secular humanism on moral instruction and religious beliefs. They, too, were concerned about any wide-ranging censorship of educational texts, and about a nationwide Fundamentalist offensive in the schools. Jewish organizations in particular were also concerned about the threat posed by the Tennessee case to the right of parents to keep their children out of public schools in order to teach them sectarian religious ideas and practices, a right which Jews, as well as Catholics, have always regarded as precious.

When the case was appealed, these organizations did not defend the Christian parents' legitimate concern, affecting *all* religious groups, to protect their children from anti-religious teachings in the public school. Instead, they generally remained silent, relying on the appeals court to affirm the trial court's decision in favor of the parents, evidently hoping thereby to avoid having to openly support Christian Right views. One major Jewish organization actually opposed the parents' right to withdraw their children from class. Unfortunately, that decision was reversed by a Federal Court of Appeals, which ruled that students can be required to remain in class for instruction with materials that offend their religious beliefs, as long as the instruction is not overtly anti-religious or coercive. As applied, these requirements seem more stringent than those that would be used to test the constitutionality of instruction *favoring religious* beliefs. In any case, requiring students to study textbooks that teach only the secular humanist view that moral values are made by man alone, contrary to their religious beliefs, would appear to constitute instruction that is expressly anti-religious and coercive. The court's decision to the contrary erroneously implies that states can compel the use of such textbooks in religious schools. Finally, in refusing to excuse students from classroom study which they find in good faith to be religiously objectionable, the decision bespeaks an anti-religious purpose analogous to an employer's refusal to reasonably accommodate the religious practices of an employee.

In any case, requiring students to study textbooks that teach only the secular humanist view that moral values are made by man alone, contrary to their religious beliefs, would appear to constitute instruction that is expressly anti-religious and coercive.

Early in 1988, the Supreme Court refused to grant a petition to review the Court of Appeals decision in the Tennessee case. Shortly thereafter, the Supreme Court affirmed the right of the Federal Government to develop portions of a national forest considered sacred by certain Indian tribes, on the ground that a legitimate government activity does not have to accommodate to personal religious beliefs unless there is a direct attempt to coerce or penalize such beliefs. This decision has been called by the American Jewish Congress, which supported the Indian position, one of the worst church-state decisions in the last twenty-five years. Yet, this case presented essentially the same issue as that raised by the parents in Tennessee. Thus, the lack of interest in the Tennessee case demonstrated by virtually all religious groups may well have been a major factor in the court's disposition of both cases, and its current broad reading of government power to interfere with religious beliefs and practices.

The Alabama case has produced a similarly dangerous result in a case that also raised the secular humanism issue, but in a different procedural framework. There, instead of pulling their children from class, as in Tennessee, the parents argued, and the trial court agreed, that secular humanism is itself a religion that unconstitutionally inhibits and is hostile to theistic faiths. Virtually all the Jewish and mainline Protestant organizations taking part in the appeal not only condemned the decision but failed to indicate any understanding of the parents' concerns that the overall approach and impact of the Alabama curriculum's secular humanist philosophy — whether or not it is technically a "religion" — is anti-religious. Unlike the trial court, they were unimpressed by the startling approach of Alabama textbooks that teach morality as a branch of "Home Economics." Nor did they evidence concern that the children were being taught that the criteria for deciding moral questions was the same as for *buying a pair of shoes!* While the trial court's broadside banning of 44 textbooks may have been extreme, these organizations did not suggest a more balanced approach that would have recognized and partially remedied the parents' concerns without ravaging the entire curriculum.

Once again the trial court's decision was reversed by a Federal Court of Appeals, in another opinion that threatens the religious rights under the First Amendment of parents of all faiths. While agreeing that "the state may not establish a religion of secularism in the sense of affirmatively opposing or showing hostility to religion," the Court of Appeals permitted the use of all of Alabama's secular humanist textbooks because they do not "*explicitly* state that the validity of a moral choice is to be decided by a student" (emphasis added), although the Court recognized that the texts may *implicitly* have so stated, as the trial court had found.

While it has long been accepted that public school teaching about the existence of God as a matter of religious belief is an unconstitutional interference with the religious freedom of students who do not share a belief in a Deity, it is now clear from the evidence in the secular humanism cases that teaching children to make moral choices solely as a matter of personal preference is an equally unacceptable interference with the religious freedom of students who believe that many moral issues have normative and not just subjective content, based on the commands of a Deity. Yet, neither the courts that have been upholding secular humanism curricula in the public schools, nor those who have enthusiastically embraced their decisions, have seen fit even to articulate this dilemma, much less begin to grapple with developing constitutionally permissible compromise approaches. One such approach might take the form of teaching, *as a matter of history and sociology and not religious dogma,* how the moral and ethical values of our society originated among men and women who believed them to be religiously ordained, and how they are still accepted by a society that generally continues to share those beliefs. The Supreme Court's 2005 "Ten Commandments decisions" may signal such a view; 125 S. Ct. 2722 and 125 S. Ct. 2854. Such an approach would provide a clear-cut sanction for the teaching of such public documents as the Declaration of Independence, Lincoln's Gettysburg Address and Second Inaugural, and similar documents which have stressed the religious, God-based nature of the ideals and moral values of our society.

It would be convenient, to be sure, if there was a nonreligious yet persuasive way to establish what is "good" and "just," to justify society's moral code. It is widely accepted that all philosophic attempts to do so, as noble as many have been, have failed. No such justification has been or can be offered that does not ultimately reduce to subjectivism.

If students are tested on their studies of morality and ethics and their answers substitute their own religious beliefs for the secular humanism approach they were taught, can they be given a failing grade on that account, or is this prohibited government coercion and interference regarding their religion? If they are given a passing grade in such circumstances, is this prohibited government support of religion? These are some of the paradoxes created by public school texts and curricula that establish man as the sole source of his own value system, with no recognition to the possibility of religious belief as the basis for society's norms of conduct, and the historical role of such belief in the creation of such norms in society.

The issue of God and Creation is equally complex. In the Louisiana case the Supreme Court found an unconstitutional religious purpose in a state law that prohibits public schools from teaching evolution, allegedly unless "creation science" in the form of the religious doctrine of creation is taught as well. Its decision was based primarily on the remarks of a few legislators when the law was introduced that they wanted to put more of the Biblical account of creation into the curriculum. The court, without any trial to ascertain how Louisiana school officials intended to interpret the law and administer it, refused to believe that they would adhere to its explicit requirements that creation science could only be taught based on "scientific evidences for creation and inferences from such evidences" as part of a program "to encourage the teaching of all scientific theories about the origins of humankind." Although the court pointedly indicated it would uphold a law that truly provided such a program, it made no attempt to fashion a decree that would have required Louisiana officials to strictly adhere to such requirements for scientific evidences and inferences. Nor did the religious organizations in the case propose either a trial or a decree as a way to uphold the law based on enforceable legal assurances that these requirements would be strictly followed. Instead, they generally pressed for a finding of unconstitutionality, disregarding or denying the possibility that advances in science and mathematics might have something useful to contribute to our understanding of the creation of the universe and our planet, and the origin and development of its species.

Is it any less constitutional if a Creator is not the only rational explanation but is taught as one of a number of rational explanations which many scientists as well as religious authorities now offer?

Certainly in light of Dr. Arno Penzias's Nobel Prize for his discoveries supporting the "Big Bang" theory of creation, and the other accumulating advances in science, many scientists infer a Creator as the most likely explanation for the universe's origin and the awesome scientific beauty of its development. The noted science writer and reporter James Gleick recently wrote that some scientists increasingly see evidence of design in physics and mathematics that cannot be explained away, and that science may be "reaching a level of knowledge that will confirm God." If scientists ever generally agreed that a Creator was the most rational explanation of the history of the universe, as they did about the once theological issue of heliocentrism, teaching of that explanation would surely not be unconstitutional. Is it any less constitutional if a Creator is not the only rational explanation but is taught as one of a number of rational explanations which many scientists as well as religious authorities now offer? Recent initiatives in Texas and California by creationists to assure the teaching of creation theory — at least in a form for which there is some scientific evidence — indicate that this issue will not go away. Indeed, a "new" Supreme Court may, a few years from now, cause strict "separationists" to rue their unwillingness to consider a more balanced approach to meeting the needs of religious families, those who believe, with some justification, that teaching evolution as the *only* explanation of creation is not only bad science, but directly contradicts and thereby interferes with their religious beliefs in violation of the Constitution.

The quest for a high wall of separation between Church and State has been motivated largely by fear that anything less might lead to the introduction of unacceptable religious beliefs and practices in the schools, and undermine the social equality that was a fundamental goal of every immigrant group. In a time when religious-based values prevailed throughout *society*, when crime was an isolated, fringe phenomenon in society, and the family was a secure, healthy institution supplementing the "three Rs" of school instruction with religious and moral training, the "high wall" between Church and State in the public schools generally did not betray hostility or constitute a threat to parent and student religious beliefs.

These factors have virtually disappeared. Congress has been at work for a long time studying how to help restore a semblance of healthy family life. Religion is not taken seriously by many philosophers and college educated people as a defensible intellectual system. Moral subjectivity reigns in every area of criminal behavior, from Wall Street to Drug Alley.

411

With the breakdown of the societal structures that formerly disciplined social conduct and assured a modicum of civilized behavior in our streets, offices and homes, many citizens now look to the schools to teach morality or — at least — to not undermine it. They are looking for some way in which morality can be presented with the most intellectual and emotional effectiveness, that is, as a religiously based value of a nation born of religious values and still dedicated to them. To be sure, there are limits to the extent these views can or should be accommodated in public schools under our constitutional form of government. What these people see, however, are textbooks and curricula that appear to persistently undermine religious beliefs and values, implicitly and explicitly, at the very moment when they are most endangered, and parents struggle to support them.

Under a constitutional system in which it is legally permissible to teach that the morality of decisions relating to honesty, respect for parents, drug use, or sexual habits are matters of individual choice, and legally permissible to teach ideas contrary to student religious beliefs if the instruction is "merely" persuasive and implicit but not coercive and explicit, and when the religious motives of some legislators for teaching good scientific theories about creation and evolution disqualify such theories from the curricula, it is not surprising that parents with religious beliefs are looking in their frustration to find any and every way to protect their children. A recent poll by the Williamsburg Charter Foundation showed that only twelve percent of the ministers, fourteen percent of the priests, a plurality of thirty-two percent of the rabbis, and fifty-five percent of the academics, believed that secular humanism has a "good impact" on the country. *About seventy percent believe that public schools should teach both evolution and the Bible's account of the creation of life on earth, including a majority of every group polled except for academics.*

Frustrated parents will look for ways around the recent court decisions and the attitude they reflect, which can embrace everything from parent attempts to take over school boards and introduce new curricu-

412

la more consonant with their own beliefs, withdrawal of students from public schools, distribution of religious materials on school premises, pressures for voluntary meetings of religious groups on school premises, constitutional amendments for public school meditation or prayer, new versions of Louisiana's "creation science" law, and pressures on or for candidates for public office to assure government sympathy and not hostility to religion.[2] One may legitimately wonder whether these backlash effects may not be a lot worse for consistent advocates of Church and State separation and opponents of Christian Fundamentalists than any benefits they may have gained from the recent decisions favorable to their cause.

In my opinion, the various religious communities must reconsider their traditional position on the educational issues raised by the court decisions I have discussed. They must become sensitive to the constitutional, educational and political aspects of these issues and strive to find an imaginative middle course between two equally objectionable practices: those that are essentially anti-religious in their impact and those that primarily advance sectarian religious beliefs. In such a course lies the best hope for preserving a living Constitution that will continue to address the needs and protect the rights of all citizens in the face of continuing scientific, sociological and political change.[3]

....

NOTES

1   These decisions date back to the late 1980s but had a lengthy impact. As predicted below, however, the situation has dramatically changed because religious people have taken over curricula decisions from secularists and those believing in a so-called "high wall" of Church — State separation. See, e.g., Cornelia Dean, "Evolution Takes a Back Seat in U.S. Classes," *New York Times*, February 1, 2005, p. F6.

2   As this book goes to press, it is clear that evidence for a non-materialist design purpose as an explanation for Creation and development of life has grown significantly, as has support for such explanations among many respected scientists. For example, if — as most scientists believe — the universe at Creation was so small that the probability and randomness of quantum mechanics were operating, then it is a *scientific* fact that the probability of Creation as we know it was immeasurably small. Therefore, some external intervention was almost surely necessary for Creation to occur, which some may call, or attribute to, God. See, e.g., discussion in Dennis Overbye, "Remembrance of Things Future: The Mystery of Time," *The New York Times*, June 28, 2005, pp. F1, 14.

    At the same time, local school boards are increasingly making sure that evolution is not taught as proven, consensus-based scientific fact, but only a theory, with important weaknesses, leaving room for a rational, scientifically based acceptance, at least for now, of non-materialist explanations, that are more consistent with, although not necessarily congruent with, various religious beliefs, explanations and descriptions, of creation of the world, the universe, and its living species. See, e.g., Jodi Wilgoren, "In Kansas, Darwinism Goes on Trial Once More," *The New York Times*, May 6, 2005, p. A18.

3   For a disturbing article on the issues and outcomes in some past Church-State cases, see David Brooks, "Mr. Bush, Pick a Genius," *The New York Times*, July 14, 2005, p. A25.

7

Music

Jewish music has always been the primary artistic expression of the Jewish people. Because of the Second Commandment against "graven images", the plastic arts — including painting and sculpture — have been prohibited in any form that would represent God. The result was a focus on music, song and — until the destruction of the Second Temple — instruments. In addition, music coupled with liturgy in Temple and synagogue rites is most suited to represent or reflect textual ideas and emotions.

From the time of the Levites, who sang the liturgy in Temple times, Jewish music has drawn on the music of many cultures, peoples and areas, including all the lands to which Jews have dispersed, for more than two thousand years.[1]

As a result, Jewish liturgical music has three important characteristics: it has great variety; it has been subject to continuing change with the movements of the Jewish people in exile; and Jewish music as it exists and may develop in the future — as it has in the past — must gain the acceptance of the Jewish community for which it is intended to be sung and heard. This helps explain why a large part of Jewish music has been led and created by lay people in contact with the music of local host populations. Such leadership cannot be elitist except to a limited extent.

Today, Jewish music includes varieties of Sephardi and Ashkenazi music — including French, German, Italian, Polish, Hungarian, Romanian, Russian, Iraqi, Syrian, Turkish, and other music in folk and classical forms.

Jewish music also varies in its emotions and ideas: gratitude, requests, sorrow, penitence, joy, and so on. It can be a waltz, a march, an unmetered chant, with sobbing, with clapping, with dancing, or just concentration. The music usually needs to fit a liturgy or text, in a choral or solo presentation.

Such vocal music intended to be sung or heard by the community, especially in a liturgical setting, survives only with congregational interest and support. Trying out new music is risky and needs congregational acquiescence. This places a special obligation on the prayer leader, whether a professional or lay person, to cultivate the utmost musical knowledge and taste and keep the music fresh and interesting so as to appeal to the variety of musical exposures and educations of the congregants.

Today this means a broad knowledge of Classical music, Hasidic music, Ashkenazi and Sephardi melodies and chant modes (scale forms), fitting folk song and other secular music, and even the music of other faiths going back to Gregorian chants and composers like Claudio Monteverdi — religious music that is closest to the years when the Levites sang in the Second Temple.[2]

The following essays discuss the approach we should take toward music in the synagogue and, indirectly, the kind of musical experience and education I encourage for congregants and leaders, to heighten creativity and religious experience during prayer.

There is much to learn, and much to experience — even by the most learned — where music sheds its special light on the meanings and emotions contained in our liturgy. As with science, Biblical exegesis, Jewish literature and history, we can raise our intellectual and religious experience of synagogue music by opening ourselves to greater understanding of the discipline involved — not only of liturgical texts, but also the music that may be used to accompany it. While complex choral music is generally incompatible with strong congregational participation in Jewish services, it is worth occasional hearing to improve our musical appreciation ability, and — quite often — such music can be simplified by an experienced *hazzan* for use in congregational singing. What we do not want is a situation described by Werner,[3] where rabbis so discourage innovations in synagogue music that, eventually, the basic tradition itself gets lost "and what remains are just weeds smothering noble plants." With a cooperative relationship between rabbi, congregation and *hazzan*, it should be possible to expand congregational musical horizons and enhance the experience of prayer, over the years, in many ways.

....
NOTES

1 See, generally, Eric Werner, *A Voice Still Heard* (University Park: Pennsylvania State University Press, 1976), pp. 8, 19, 22, 34, 47, 56-9, 6, 82, 93, 100, 120, 140-6, 151 and *passim*; and A.Z. Idelsohn, *Jewish Music in its Historical Development* (N.Y. Schocken, 1967) pp. 3-24, 61, 110-126, 132, and *passim*. There are two organizations — The Institute for Jewish and Community Research and *b'khol lashon* — that are dedicated to exploring the music and other aspects of the cultures of "Jews of Color" from all over the world; see Debra Nussbaum Cohen, "The Color of Inclusion," *The Jewish Week*, February 25, 2005, pp. 26-7. The Yemenite Jews claim that "the trope and cadence of their *Shabbat* prayers are the same as they were in First Temple times;" ibid.

2 Idelsohn, *Jewish Music*, pp. 17-18, 20, 56, 61, 111, 131; 357 ff. and 379 ff.; and Werner, *A Voice…*, pp. 213, 238, 323.

3 Ibid., p. 236; see also pp. 288-9.

Innovation In Synagogue Music

Recent interest in the development of synagogue music, as reflected in the quality of cantorial vocalism, cantor association conferences, publications on synagogue music,[1] public interest in the cantorial art, and programs to encourage the renewal of forgotten Jewish synagogue music and the creation of new music for the liturgy,[2] have raised again an issue that has received much treatment among cantors and scholars in the past and which has significant implications for the future development of synagogue music. That issue concerns the source of synagogue music. Must it be derived from Semitic and Oriental or Middle-Eastern music presumably sung by the Israelites in Palestine prior to their Exile?[3] Or, as more recently formulated by a leading cantorial scholar, may new synagogue music idioms be introduced to enrich the traditional musical *nusah,* that is, the traditional musical modes that are associated with specific parts of the liturgy, and certain High Holy Day melodies known as *"mi-Sinai"* tunes, developed sometime before 1450?[4]

While this article deals with the canon of music used in Ashkenazi synagogues, I would argue that the issue applies in theory to Sephardi music as well. For a variety of historical and cultural reasons related to their surrounding cultures over the years and the relative stability of their own culture, Sephardi music has been relatively less subject to fission, differentiation and change over the years. With its virtually complete relocation to Israel, there is no reason to believe that this situation will change.[5]

I believe that as a matter of history and halakhah, Jewish music has developed and should continue to be permitted to develop to meet the spiritual needs of the Jewish people, without being subject to any geographical, ethnic or time-bound formula as a test of authenticity. Indeed, neither halakhah nor history has ever imposed a test of authenticity. To the extent that we have been induced in recent decades to search for and define an "authentic" Jewish musical idiom, Ashkenazi culture has been thwarted in the development of idioms, melodies and compositions that might have by now been accepted as part of its synagogue musical tradition, and has dismissed or ignored entire musical cultures, such as the treasures of Sephardi and 19th-century German synagogue music.

We must strive to introduce fresh musical elements into our synagogue services in the form of a serious, coherent body of music that speaks succinctly and directly to the modern congregations of 20th and 21st-century Jews. We are looking for inspiration, transcendence, and a sense of community in the synagogue. Unless the music of the liturgy provides it, the void will be filled with cheap, vulgar, faddish or otherwise inappropriate music — for which, ironically, there is ample halakhic support.[6] While a limited and discriminating use of some secular melodies may have a place in the synagogue, such melodies are too often the rule rather than the exception.

Unfortunately, those who criticize these melodies have offered little but chants based on our 500-year-old musical *nusah* as an alternative, as any cantor searching for a moving and modern melody for the *kedushah* prayers on *Shabbat* can testify. It is one thing to urge that there is a need to re-educate our lay people in the traditional motifs and melodies which constitute the core of our musical tradition, and to treat that tradition respectfully. It is quite another to argue that the musical *nusah* of our liturgy is a closed canon, and that we therefore can never add to its musical idioms and melodies of the early 15th century (which is when Maharil, cited as the original halakhic authority for this closed canon doctrine, lived).

Moreover, synagogue music, like other aspects of Jewish culture, did not cease to develop at some particular date, and most particularly not in 1450. Sephardic, German and Eastern European Jewry all took their own musical paths, reflecting the history and creativity of their communities and the differing impacts of the foreign cultures surrounding them. But, I would argue, Jewish musical development would have occurred even if we had never been exiled from our land. As the cultures of other nations have developed, so would have Jewish culture and Jewish music in its own land. Of course, with Jewry's dispersion to many lands, and its later expulsions from and immigration to many lands, it was inevitable that Jewish culture and Jewish music maintained, mutated and synthesized aspects of its own culture and that of the nations of *galut* in many different forms. Moreover, just as Jewish history and music did not stop in 1450, the art of music and musical composition among the nations did not stop in 1450. Indeed, one can argue that the art of musical composition only began to divorce itself from the umbilical cord of religious music around that time.

Thus, the musical sensibilities and sensitivities of the Jewish people in *galut* could not and did not stop in 1450. And, perhaps most important, the sensitivity of the Jewish soul, and the worthiness of the people of Israel to pray and sing before God, did not begin to deteriorate in 1450.[8] Indeed, to the extent we seek to reflect the heights and depths of Jewish experience as a nation in our communal prayers, the period from 1492 on has surely witnessed these in as great or greater a measure than the period in which the traditional music of our liturgy was created, viz. 900–1450 C.E. There have been new movements in Jewish music, like that of Hasidism of the 18th century and the varieties of 19th-century German synagogue music, born of new needs and new musical culture. The 2000-year-old Semitic content and the 500-year-old chants and *"mi-Sinai"* tunes of our traditional synagogue music cannot be legislated as the end of Jewish musical creativity and the only test of authentic Jewish music in the synagogue or anywhere else. If there has been a relatively unchanging quality to Jewish music for centuries, I submit it was because of respect for tradition, the undoubted excellence of the traditional (pre-1450) musical *nusah,* and the fact that time largely stood still for Ashkenazi Jewry musically in the *galut,* as it did for the Western world by and large until the Enlightenment.

Continued innovation in synagogue music helps remove routine from the prayer services and can add to our *kavanah* (sincerity and intent of emotion). Using new musical idioms[9] that were not (and could not have been) composed in the medieval or pre-medieval period appeals to modern Orthodox Jews who are comfortable functioning within the contemporary culture, and encourages compositions by sensitive Jews who are trained in modern idioms. New expressions can bring new or deeper meaning to an ancient text, thus bringing out the eternal aspects of our liturgy.

It has been argued that because of Maharil's ruling, and the ancient modal character of Jewish prayer music, any innovation in the classical musical *nusah* and *"mi-Sinai"* tunes must be based on the three basic sources of synagogue music: the *te'amim* (music used to ritually chant Biblical texts in the synagogue), the traditional (pre-1450) *nusah* modes, and the *"mi-Sinai"* tunes.[10] But the evidence fails to support this view. Maharil wrote in (about) 1400 that a cantor or *sheliah tsibbur* should not change the custom or tunes of the place against the wishes of the *manhigim,* the leaders of the community, who presumably represented *da'at kahal,* the view of the community.[11] This view is brought down by Rema in his glosses to the *Shulhan Arukh;* Rema uses the same words except that he changes *"makom* (place)" to *"ir* (town or city)." In the late 1600's this ruling, still formulated as *"minhag ha-ir,"* is brought down by Abraham Gumbiner (the *Magen Avraham)* with the reason added *"she-mevalbel da' at ha-kahal* (the change will confuse the sense of the congregation)."[12] This same prohibition and its reason are finally repeated close to our own day by the *Mishna Berura.*[13] The Vilna Gaon refers to a concern for *"mahloket,"* and seems to view Maharil's ruling as an issue of local custom generally rather than as just an aspect of traditional liturgy and music.[14]

However, these texts (and Maharil's story illustrating the seriousness of the prohibition by noting the death of the daughter of the *rabbi-hazzan* who defied the wishes of a congregation's leaders) are addressed to the rabbi and the *hazzan* and not to the community. If the community wants to try a new *piyyut* or new melody, there is nothing in any of these texts that says it may not do so. Indeed, what is prohibited according to Maharil is for a cantor or a rabbi to defy a local community's wishes and sing or recite a melody or a *piyyut* — even one sung or recited elsewhere — which the community's leaders do not wish to be sung or said.

Moreover, there is nothing in these texts that freezes the musical canon of our prayer to the particular modes, motifs or tunes of any particular years. *Orah Hayyim* and other texts mentioned above do not prohibit a cantor from trying out new melodies for any part of the service, as long as he is not acting contrary to the wishes of the congregation. These texts certainly do not support the view that changes in *nusah* must be based on the modes incorporated in our music prior to 1450, and they do not support the rule that *"mi-Sinai"* tunes dating up to 1450 are the only ones that can be sung to High Holy Day texts. Indeed, accepted *nusah* modes (e.g., *mi sheberakh* and certain *"mi-Sinai"* tunes) came *after* the Maharil, and differ in basic respects from prior Jewish music.[15]

If the preceding is correct, it follows that a congregation is free to add to or modify the musical *nusah,* as long as the new music does not violate any other halakhic restrictions, e.g., music used for the religious services of other faiths, which is precisely how some of our traditional *nusah* and other synagogue melodies gradually developed.[16]

Indeed, changes have been made by the *hazzanim* of Eastern Europe even in the basic *nusah* of the High Holy Days, down to the 18th century or even later. These changes, moreover, incorporated musical scales and modes that were based on local musical idioms that were different from what the closed canon advocates argue are the basic elements of synagogue music which have controlled — and are perpetually required to control — synagogue music innovation. Thus, we find that cantors in Eastern Europe introduced Ukrainian (Ukrainian-Dorian) music (called the *mi she-berakh* mode) that now dramatically punctuates the music of *Rosh Hashanah*, notably at such points in the liturgy as *Ve-al ha-Medinot* and *Ha-Ben Yakir Li.*[17]

The concern that changes in *nusah* must be based on canonic guidelines as a test of legitimacy fails to recognize that there were no such guidelines when the so-called "authentic" or "legitimate" *nusah* developed. They did not exist to determine the acceptability of the 18th-century changes in *nusah* for *Ve-al ha-Medinot,* or for the Tatar *ahavah rabba* mode, gradually adopted for the synagogue in many countries in the 17th century, which Idelsohn assures us was not related to the other earlier, allegedly authentic Jewish modes derived from *te'amim*. What makes that mode acceptable today, according to Idelsohn, is not its musical genealogy, but that "it nestled itself in the fertile soil of the receptive Jewish soul."[18] That must be the ultimate guideline, as it always has been, for "authentic" musical *nusah*. Indeed, if a community is not free to add to the *nusah* it has been using, it is not clear why it should be free to introduce a new melody for any other part of the service that has been sung in a particular way for a long period. Yet the history of synagogue music is replete with new music introduced over the years and accepted by different communities all over the world.[19]

Indeed, one may reasonably conclude from our history that congregations have implicitly never excluded the possibility that some *piyyut* might come along that would merit inclusion in the service. Therefore, one cannot say that any community or congregation, in not chanting a *piyyut* or a melody in the past, meant to permanently bar itself from adopting one which might be composed or commend itself in the future — one which it decided would beautify its services with greater spirituality and holiness, just as Maharil's ruling has never been interpreted to exclude the *ahavah rabba* mode that German communities first heard and adopted two centuries after his death. Moreover, if we are worthy to compose new music

423

for *U-Netaneh Tokef,* for which there are no *"mi-Sinai"* tunes, surely we are equally worthy to compose new music for other prayers.

The "closed canon" approach, with its emphasis on modes instead of set melodies or compositions, resolves the tension between creativity and tradition in favor of the latter. Most innovations in the arts and sciences consist, for extended periods, of improvements on an existing body of culture rather than radical change. But periodically there are breakthroughs that hurdle the human propensity to cling to the traditional, and thus do art and science progress.

One can, perhaps, ask how far the concept of *minhag avoteinu be-yadeinu* (the custom of our fathers is in our hands and is not to be changed) applies to freezing a particular melody or *nusah*. Our halakhic literature shows at the very least a divided character and orientation on the ability of a congregation to change its *minhag* voluntarily. Perhaps the most generic and most analogous cases were those involving massive congregational and community adoption of the Sephardic pronunciation and liturgy for prayer, beginning with the rise of Hasidism and its use of the Sephardi liturgy. Indeed, even rabbis who accepted the idea of *minhag avoteinu be-yadeinu* and *al titosh torat imekha* (do not forsake your mother's teachings) were among those who permitted congregations to change to Sephardi pronunciation and liturgy.[20] Moreover, those who opposed changes in Ashkenazi liturgy generally did not expressly oppose changes in pronunciation, and their prohibition of changes in liturgy generally were for reasons that do not seem to have any application to changing or adopting new melodies.[21]

Some Jewish musicologists seem to hold views that may limit innovation in synagogue music, to the extent they evaluate the worth and "genuine" quality of *nusah* and prayer melodies, in part at least, by age, and whether they are of "Semitic," "Jewish-Semitic" or "Oriental-Semitic" origin, or whether in their "very nature" they please the "Jewish spirit" or are based (in part at least) on "traditional" or "Jewish motives."[22] The latter definitions are, of course, entirely circular. As to the Semitic and Oriental requirements, it is not at all clear how much of our musical *nusah* of that origin was originally Jewish, and how much derives from the culture of the surrounding peoples of the Middle East. In any event, neither age nor Middle East origin makes a melody superior. What does is its strength in conveying the emotions and meaning of our prayers — in a word, its acceptance by the "Jewish soul" — as Idelsohn elsewhere suggests[23] — not its source or its age.

The overwhelming, tragic aspects of the Diaspora notwithstanding, it has nevertheless benefited Israel and the entire world in that it allowed each to contribute the best of its knowledge and culture to the other. Indeed, Israel was also a carrier of the cultures of others to all parts of the world where it was dispersed. In many ways we are a mixture of peoples from countries all over the world. We should be suspicious of arguments that ascribe cultural superiority or authenticity to aspects of Jewish culture on the basis of "purity," age, or origin. Any such philosophy of musical superiority or inferiority is dangerous and must be rejected.[24]

For those who question the possibility of being deeply religiously moved by a synagogue service that departs from so-called authentic *nusah*, I would cite the Friday night service recently composed by Abraham Kaplan.[25] One cannot listen to this service without being persuaded by its "rightness" as music for Friday night, even though it is not written in the traditional modes for that service. It beautifully portrays the tender, awakening soul of a Jew on a Friday night, it perfectly reflects the meaning of the words of the liturgy as well as its feeling, and the worshiper's glowing feeling of holiness, joy and excitement on the first service of the *Shabbat*. It is entitled to become a permanent part of our musical *nusah*. More importantly, our congregations are entitled to the opportunity to experience the music and decide for themselves.

In conclusion, let me suggest some guidelines to *hazzanim* for the introduction of new music into the synagogue services:

1. The criterion for changes in the modes or melodies of liturgical texts for which a traditional musical *nusah* exists should be the very difficult

one of whether this new music seems to have the special qualities to make it a permanent and regular fixture in the service. Of course, the more ingrained the melody or mode that is being changed, and the greater its importance in the service, the more careful with change one should be. A session with the congregation to go over new music is a worthwhile idea where a significant innovation is contemplated.

2. New material should be introduced in small doses. The cantor should try not to make a whole *kedushah* new, or a whole service new, unless it is unavoidable, as in the case of a special concert service devoted to a composer or to a new work.

3. The music should return from new to traditional musical *nusah* whenever possible. People feel less anxious if they periodically "come home" musically.

4. Music that is not being accepted should not be pressed. If, after three or four hearings at the most, there is no solid congregational response, it is likely that the problem is more than just unfamiliarity. Reintroduction after a decent interval is possible.

5. Music that is associated with the worship services of other faiths should be avoided, and a similar attempt should be made regarding the songs of the "wicked." There is, for example, some halakhic soundness in the Israeli rejection of Wagner and his music because of *him* and what he stands for; yet even this can be pressed too far.

6. After new melodies are introduced, there should be some agreement as to when and where that new melody will be used, and how it should be used. Indiscriminate use cheapens any melody and mocks the text of the prayer. There are times when uses of melodies from one holiday in the prayers of another makes sense, but those occasions are rare. (For example, a quotation from the music of the *Avodah* of *Yom Kippur* may be used in the section of the prayer for rain on *Shemini Atzeret* that concerns Aaron.)

7. In general, the law permits secular music like love songs and classical music, Jewish folk music, and Jewish music composed for holy texts

like *Song of Songs*.[26] However, cantors should be careful to avoid confusion, distraction and divisiveness in their choice of melodies. Thus,
care should be taken in the use of secular music in the synagogue
service. It must, of course, be appropriate musically and fit the text
and surrounding material. Beyond that, such music should, first, be
limited generally to a source that is not well known and which has
no association that takes away from its ability to enhance the text of
the prayer. Second, the cantor should try to keep the quotation short,
particularly where it will become recognizable if extended. Third, he
should beware of classical music that was written or used as religious
music. Fourth, where the prayer will be enhanced by the knowledge
and connotation of the outside source, a recognizable quotation may
be appropriate. For example, a number of *hazzanim* use the music
from *"Yerushalayim shel zahav"* in the last section of *kedushah* for
Shaharit on *Shabbat*. Similarly, one may use a short but recognizable
quotation from it in the repetition of the *amidah* for *musaf* on the High
Holy Days, where the cantor chants the phrase, *"Ve-lirushalayim, ir
kodshekha."*[27]

The problems of *hazzanut* are solvable by the same method that has
kept Judaism alive: education. Our composers, like our cantors, need to
be trained in all aspects of Jewish musical tradition. Our cantors need
training in classical music, musical composition, and improvisation to assure taste in music selection and variety in musical rendition.[28] The congregation must be continually trained formally and informally by cantors
(including *ba'alei tefillah*) who themselves are constantly stretching and
refining their musical taste.[29] Such a cooperative relationship will assure
that we maintain our traditions while being open to the careful introduction of new music, and that we develop the discrimination to take hold of
the worthy and reject the unworthy. Without such education, openness
and good taste, *hazzanut* will return to the excesses of the past — either,
at one extreme, where "anything goes," or, at the other extreme, where
an increasingly distant and professional elite[30] sings uninteresting and ul-

timately irrelevant music to an unhearing, uninterested and uninvolved congregation.[31]

....

NOTES

1   Among the scholarly publications in the United States are *The Journal of Jewish Music and Liturgy* published by the Belz School of Jewish Music in conjunction with the Cantorial Council of America; *The Journal of Synagogue Music* published by the Cantors Assembly; *Musica Judaica* (and a very expanded *Newsletter)* published by the American Society for Jewish Music (ASJM); the *Bulletin of the Jewish Liturgical Music Society of America;* and, in Israel, *Orbis Musicae,* published by Tel Aviv University's Department of Musicology.

2   Note, for example, the important new records being produced by the *Beit ha-Tefutsot* (Diaspora) Museum in Tel Aviv, Israel, documenting historically important cantorial music; the tapes being produced by the Park Avenue Synagogue of its concert services of new and classical cantorial compositions; the records of newly commissioned synagogue service music at Congregation Beth Abraham of Dayton, Ohio; and similar ventures where adequate funding has been available. Abraham Kaplan, Jerome Kopmar, Shalom Kalib, and Ralph Schlossberg are among a larger number of Jewish composers writing beautiful and inspiring new music for the liturgy. The recent completion by Cantor Jacob Lefkowitz of the CCA of his musical setting to the Psalms ("A Song in Every Psalm") is a noteworthy recent example of a non-liturgical composition which is nevertheless of great potential use in the liturgy. See my review of this work in this book.

3   See, e.g., Abraham Wolf Binder, *Studies in Jewish Music* (Bloch Publishing Company, 1971), pp. 83, 94-95, 107, 230-35, 282-88.

4   A mode is a combination of short musical phrases within a scale based on the ancient Oriental practice, in contrast to the more encompassing structural arc and regular meter of a melody or tune, based on the more recent Western practice. The modes constitute the musical building blocks and connective tissue for the rendering of the prayers by the Cantor; Abraham Zvi Idelsohn, *Jewish Music in its Historical Development* (Schocken 1967), p. 24; Eric Werner, *A Voice Still Heard: The Sacred Songs of the Ashkenazi Jews* (Pennsylvania State University Press, 1976), pp. 18-19; Macy Nulman, *Concepts of Jewish Music* (Cantorial Council of America 1975), p. 73.

   Nulman, pp. 5, 72-3, 78, citing R. Jacob Levi Mollin — called Maharil (1365-1427) — and *Orah Hayyim* 619, maintains that new synagogue music must be based on the traditional *nusah.* See also Idelsohn, p. 178. Werner includes in his definition of *nusah* certain seasonal motifs, like the *Maoz Tsur* melody sung on Hanukkah, despite the often idiosyncratic rather than regularized use of these motifs with the liturgy. The *"mi-Sinai"* tunes are melodies composed primarily for the High Holy Days (and for *"Tal"* and *"Geshem"* on Passover and *Shemini Atseret*) in southwestern Germany from the 11th to the 15th centuries. References in this paper to the year 1450 are based on Cantor Macy Nulman's use of the period 900-1450 C.E. for the development of Jewish liturgical modal "chants" and *"mi-Sinai"* tunes, although the modes, in general, are older than the *"mi-Sinai"* tunes. Nulman, pp. 72-73; Werner, p. 61; Idelsohn, pp. 136-7, 144, 147. Werner suggests that the *"mi-Sinai"* tunes developed until 1550; Werner p. 32.

5   See Werner, p. 29, for a somewhat overstated but essentially valid contrast of the extent of variety and change in the Ashkenazi and Sephardi synagogue traditions. One must also distinguish between the musical tradition and *nusah* of East European and West European Ashkenazi Jewry. While the differences between Ashkenazi and Sephardi Jewry were primarily based on cultural separation, those between the two Ashkenazi branches were also caused by cultural antagonism and hostility, particularly after the Enlightenment. See, e.g., Werner, pp. 2, 5-9, for East European criticisms of the great 19th-century German cantor-composer Salomon Sulzer. For a recent scholarly picture of the repulsion and attraction by German Jews for their East European brethren, see Shulamit Volkov, "The Dynamics of Dissimilation: Ostjuden and German Jews," *The Jewish Response to German Culture,* J. Reinharz. and W. Schatzberg, eds. (University Press of New England 1985), pp. 195-216. In part because of attitudes deplored in this article, ". . . the pure Western Ashkenazic style is slowly fading away, yielding to a mixed tradition in which the Polish element is stronger;" Werner, p. 146.

6   See, e.g., Rabbi Ovadia Yosef, *Yehaveh Da'at, Vol.* 11, no. 5 and *Yabia Omer, Vol. VI,* no. 7. Rav Yosef, citing many authorities, is generally lenient with respect to love songs, Jewish or non-Jewish, although he prohibits love songs and probably other music that bring to mind the secular lyrics of the music and thus distract from the *siddur* liturgy. The authorities cited by Rav Yosef generally permit, with the caveat just noted, Jewish and non-Jewish secular music. There is *contra* authority that takes a much stricter approach to the use of non-Jewish music. See Y. Y. Hahn Neuerlingen in *Yosef Omets,* para. 602, which seems to be followed by Nulman, *op. cit.,* pp. 73-6. There is authority prohibiting all love songs on the theory that the melody inevitably suggests the lyrics in such cases (Rabbi Eliezer Yehuda Waldenberg, *Tsits Eliezer, Vol.* XIII, no. 12). Finally, there is the interesting view of the hasidic master, Rabbi Nahman of Bratzlav, who prohibits the melodies of a *rasha* ("wicked" person, undefined), except for use by those engaged in the study of Talmud in the evenings, who presumably are able thereby to nullify any insidious effects from such music *(Likkutei Moharan,* Ch. 3, Part 1). Rav Yosef in *Yabia Omer* cites authorities that prohibit music used in the religious services of other faiths. Music for Conservative and Reform services would seem *not* to fall in this category, although I have heard certain Orthodox cantors express a concern that it might. However, Rav Yosef cites interesting authority *contra,* which not only permitted but encouraged the adapting of certain church music to the High Holy Day liturgy where it conveyed a quality of submissiveness. See Rabbi Yisrael Moshe Hazzan in "Krakh Shel Romi," no. 1, p. 46.

7   See Nulman, p. 76. See also the interview with Cantor Bernard Beer, Director of Yeshiva University's Belz School of Jewish Music, in *The Commentator* (Yeshiva University's student newspaper), October 1, 1987, p. 6.

8   David Hartman, *A Living Covenant* (Free Press 1985), chapters VI and VII. See also my article on Hartman's views, "Fear and Awe: May Man Bring Song to Prayer?" in this chapter.

9   As with secular music, new modes of musical expression do not replace traditional music, but become part of the tradition. In the context of music generally, the point has recently been made that certain types of musical idioms are inherently capable of effectively communicating only certain types of ideas and emotions, and that to restrict musical idioms to any one category restricts the ability of the composer to broaden the scope of his musical message to meet the interests of his listeners. Neil M. Ribe, "Atonal Music and its Limits," *Commentary,* November 1987.

10 Nulman, pp. 5, 72-3, 76, 78, 146; Idelsohn, pp. 110-11, 176-83, 199-214. See also Werner, pp. 14-17, 32, 46-50, 60, 203-4, 217-18, 241, 294. They suggest that *nusah* historically and traditionally was based on improvisations on modes rather than "set" melodies or tunes. Indeed, Werner suggests that the Jewish antipathy to "set tunes," harmony and notation may be associated with "the antipathy of most Semitic nations to painting and sculpture"! Werner, pp. 17, 50. However, the view of scholar Max Wohlberg is that Jewish prayer music in the Temple included melody, "the pleasant tune, the melodic chant," and children's voices were added to those of the Levites in unison to achieve "sweetness." See his "Toward a New Congregational Chant," *Community and Culture-Essays in Jewish Studies, In Honor of the Ninetieth Anniversary of Gratz College, 1895-1985* (Seth Press, Philadelphia 1987), p. 245. In any case, melodies do not have to be pressed between bar lines and sung in strict meter if the liturgy requires such freedom; indeed, most *"mi-Sinai* tunes were not composed metrically; Werner, p. 32. Most importantly, there is no evidence that the Levites considered their music a closed canon, or that they would have rejected more modern forms of melody, composition or harmony had music advanced that far while the Temple stood. Moreover, the prophetic and rabbinic desire that Israel pray "as if with one mouth," i.e., in unison, seems to connote "set" tunes or melodies and perhaps even meter and not (solely) the improvisational surprises of creative modal chant. See Werner, pp. 15-17; Idelsohn, p. 21. The desire of modern congregations to sing therefore suggests the need for balance between unison singing, modal chant, and choral works of "art" music in and among our synagogues; Werner, pp. 236-7.

11 See, e.g., *Sefer Maharil* (Jerusalem), *Hilkhot Yom Kippur,* p. 47, beginning with *"Sheliah Tsibbur. ..."*; Rema's gloss to *Shulhan Arukh, Orah Hayyim* 619:1.

12 Ibid.; *Mogen Avraham,* n. 7.

13 *Mishnah Berura,* n. 7.

14 Ibid., *Be'ur ha-Gra.* That these rulings are found in sections dealing with the liturgy on *Yom Kippur* raises the very intriguing question of whether they were ever intended to apply to other holidays, or *Shabbat.* Significantly, the prohibition in Maharil is not contained in the immediately preceding sections dealing with the prayers on *Rosh Hashanah* and *Shabbat,* and similarly in Rema. Except for the view of the Vilna Gaon, the issue seems far from being free of doubt.

15 See Werner, pp. 32, 58; Nulman, pp. 5, 173-4; Idelsohn, pp. 185, 198-200. The *ahavah rabba* mode, which Cantor Nulman suggests is part of the canon that Maharil fixed as permanent, did not become part of the musical *nusah* until the 17th century (Idelsohn, p. 147). While it was used in certain Eastern European countries as early as the 13th century (Idelsohn, p. 87), it was certainly a change of Ashkenazi *nusah* and *minhag,* and was unknown to Maharil!

16 Abraham Milgram, *Jewish Worship* (Jewish Publication Society, 1971), p. 373.

17 Idelsohn, p. 185. Quite clearly this musical idiom, known as the *mi she-berakh* mode, came centuries after Maharil, and differs in many basic features from traditional *nusah*. Most importantly, when it was introduced by the *hazzanim* in Eastern Europe, *they* were changing the traditional *nusah* in order to make the liturgy more moving and meaningful for the congregation. Wide acceptance in recent centuries by Ashkenazi Jewry certainly justifies the innovation. But where would we be if the objection had been made that this innovation was not traditional *nusah* and was, on that account, prohibited as a departure from literally centuries, if not millennia or more, of *minhag?*

18 Idelsohn, pp. 84, 87, 147, 192-5 and Werner, pp. 56-8. Cf. Nulman, p. 174.

19 One commentary on *Orah Hayyim* by David Oppenheim (1664-1736), *Nish'al David, Vol.* I, pp. 3-6, observing that the Levites in the Temple were forbidden to make alterations in their musical instruments *(Arakhin* 10b), states that the same applies to synagogue melodies handed down by tradition. See Louis Jacobs, *A Tree of Life* (Oxford University Press 1984), p. 234. But this begs key questions: *who is* forbidden, *when* (if ever) does or did the "tradition" close, *why* should it ever close, if it ever did, *who* (if anyone) closed it, and isn't there a way to keep it open? Oppenheim may merely be summarizing Maharil.

20 *Responsa of Hatam Sofer, Likkutim* to *Hoshen Mishpat,* nos. 54-57, (discussed in Jacobs, pp. 229-30) ruled against the (then) new Reform practices in their synagogues (e.g., leaving out significant portions of the prayers and using musical instruments in the synagogue). He maintained that the texts of the traditional liturgy and the prohibition on playing musical instruments in the synagogue, having been formally promulgated by our sages centuries earlier during the formative period of the Talmud, constitute rabbinic decrees *(takkanot)* that subsequent sages — even sitting as a court — cannot abrogate unless greater in learning and number, and that the original reason for the decree still exists. Thus, the *Hatam Sofer's* views on Reform practices (notwithstanding occasional references to "the customs of our fathers and their fathers") do not seem to limit the right of a synagogue community to change melodies or *piyyutim* that do not have the legal status of *takkanot* established in Talmudic times. Z. H. Chajes, writing slightly later, clearly bases his attack on Reform on their disregard of rabbinic decrees stemming from the authors of the Talmud. See Jacobs, pp. 230-32 and footnotes thereto, citing Z. H. Chajes, *Minhat Kena'ot,* in *Kol Sifrey Maharats Hayyot,* Vol. 2, pp. 975-1036.

Also of interest is the vague reference by R. Dr. H. J. Zimmels, in *Ashkenazim and Sephardim* (Marla Publishing, London 1976), p. 114, to a reported quarrel "from the beginning of the eighteenth century," which arose in Ferrara, Italy, "about an attempt made there to exchange the Sephardi melody of the priestly blessing for the Ashkenazi melody," citing opinions by Mordecai Zahalon, R. Jacob Olmo and R. Phinchas Hai Anav in books written in 1715. Zimmels does not indicate the extent of community support for the change, and how the problem was resolved. It would seem that the matter was one on which learned men differed.

21 See Zimmels, Chapters 2 and 5, and particularly Part III of Chapter 5, pp. 308-332. *Hatam Sofer* argued against changing to Sephardi liturgy in his *Responsa, Orah Hayyim,* nos. 15, 16, 197.

22 See, e.g., Rabinovitch, p. 133 ("...all the cantor's improvisations must be within the scope of the traditional modes, modes which look back to remotest [sic] time"); Binder, pp. 83, 94-5, 107, 230-35, 282-88; Idelsohn, pp. 24, 89, 175-78. But cf. p. 87, where Idelsohn refers to Tatar music that "nestled itself in the fertile soil of the receptive Jewish soul," and the similarly broad view expressed at p. 194: "Of far deeper significance is the truth that genuine music is the offspring of profound emotion: of exaltation, pain, or joy," a test which surely has no chronological or geographic bounds.

23 See footnotes 22 and 29. Werner is critical of Idelsohn's subjectivity and circular approach in unfavorably comparing Western with Eastern Ashkenazi music. Werner, pp. 25, 144-5. I venture the view that advocacy of modal and East European music including folk songs and dances in preference to the Westernized melodies and art music of the German tradition are really variations of the argu-

ment that only Oriental music provides the basis for an authentically "Jewish" synagogue music. Werner, pp. 134, 219; Nulman, pp. 72-7; Idelsohn, pp. 176-7, 183, 211-4, 232-3.

24 See, e.g., Idelsohn, pp. 136, 177. As Max Wohlberg has noted, wherever the Jewish people lived, "they could not escape some influence of local custom and native music" (Wohlberg. pp. 244-6). At the 1987 Conference on Jewish Musical Traditions (sponsored by the ASJ M and the Jewish Theological Seminary), Cantor Abraham Lubin criticized Idelsohn for challenging the authenticity of the Germanic music of the 19th-century composer-cantor Salomon Sulzer on the ground that Idelsohn failed to understand what Sulzer was trying to accomplish. I would go further and argue that the very foundation of Idelsohn's position is unacceptable; no person or group has the right to decide what kind of music is authentically Jewish. That is a judgment to be made by the Jewish people in all their wisdom and with all their variety. It is, ultimately, a judgment that has been made and will continue to be made by history.

Ascribing superiority to particular strains in Jewish culture still persists among some. See, e.g., the remarks of Israeli sociologist Jeff Halper that "Judaism is an Eastern religious and cultural system" and that an "authentic" Jewish culture must "reflect the East much more than the West" (*Congress Monthly,* March/April 1986 [Special Issue], p. 15). Fortunately, his views were forcefully rebutted by Israeli author Amnon Shamosh (p. 39).

25 Available on tape through the Park Avenue Synagogue in New York.

26 See n.6.

27 It is not the assimilation of foreign matter that is problematic but the purpose and technique involved. Gradual, graceful and subtle use to enhance prayer by musical expressiveness has produced important, indigenous music that Jews have made their own, whereas the desire to copy, popularize, and entertain produces music that will always be viewed as "alien" even by the cantors and congregants who are singing it. Werner is not totally clear on how to make this distinction. Compare chapters 6-7 and p. 218 with pp. 117, 125, 188, 236, 241-2 and 323.

28 Salomone de Rossi and Sulzer were so trained, which was important to their ability to compose and arrange Jewish synagogue music for their day with taste and dignity. Werner, pp. 125, 187, 203-4, 211, 218, 224. Sulzer sought to restore tradition and aesthetics to Viennese synagogue music and to keep the musically intelligent younger generation from being driven out of the synagogue by rediscovering the "old national melodies and modes," which had to be "collected and arranged according to the rules of art. Yet new compositions were also indispensable...." Werner, p. 212.

29 Idelsohn, pp. 192-5, 213; Werner, pp. 122, 131, 172, 188.

30 There is an elitist view of the cantor as always having the principal role, with the congregation subordinate, which harks back to that of R. Yehuda Halevi, who described the music in the Temple as the exclusive domain of a priestly aristocracy uniquely able to devote full time to the study and performance of music. See R. Yehuda Halevi's *The Kuzari* (Schocken, 1964), p. 123. In fact, the cantor's role is largely culturally determined, which in turn may affect the nature of the music used for the liturgy. Obviously the role of the congregation in Sephardi services is greater than in Ashkenazi services, and largely replaces the choir in Sephardi congregations. Similarly, the wealthy and highly musically cultured German congregations of the 19th century looked for a joint cantor and choir role that was vastly

different from that which one would encounter in a small, relatively poor Eastern European synagogue, or a modern American or Sephardi synagogue, without a choir.

31 Wohlberg has observed that Ashkenazi services tend to have less congregational singing than otherwise might be feasible because the cantor in many communities evolved into a "vocally endowed artist and musician who continually sought to enlarge the area of his musical efforts" (Wohlberg, pp. 246-8). This view is strongly controverted by many American cantors, who recognize and attempt to satisfy congregational needs to sing. On the congregational and cantorial roles in synagogue music, see my article "Music for the Jewish Liturgy: Art for Whose Sake," in this chapter.

Music For Jewish Liturgy:
Art For Whose Sake?

The nature and role of Jewish music in the synagogue and the related issue of the respective roles of cantor and congregation in chanting that music have not been consistent or free from dispute. Our tradition does not shed light on the extent to which the people assembled in the Temple joined the Levites in their songs, and there is no indication of the extent to which the music sung in the Temple was continually augmented by new compositions — and, if so, who composed them. The long history of the Diaspora provides a pattern of varied practices on these matters, with little normative guidance from the various Jewish halakhic sources.

For example, the cantor, described as the *shliah zibbur* (representative of the congregation) should have a pleasant voice, among other attributes of age, character, religious practices, and marital status. He was admonished not to tax the congregation in his singing or to prolong the service unreasonably (*tirha d'zibbura*). There was also the fourteenth century ruling of Rabbi Jacob Molin (*Maharil*) that one must not change the customs of a synagogue in any matter, even in regard to the introduction of melodies to which the people are not accustomed. As a practical matter, this ruling left the cantor free to introduce new music where there was no established custom or where a congregational openness to musical innovation existed. The ruling was designed to protect the traditional structure of synagogue music (*nusah*), and it has succeeded.

One can easily agree to these parameters of the cantor's responsibility without beginning to agree on other, fundamental issues of his role versus that of the congregation in synagogue singing that are beginning to divide cantor and rabbi, cantor and congregation.

Indeed, with the increase in women cantorial graduates and the longer term growth trend in graduates from the major cantorial schools of all persuasions, we can expect the debates to continue and the problem to widen. These are far less acute in synagogues that do not depend on a regular professional cantor (*hazzan tmidi*) to lead the services but, rather, utilize the volunteered services of competent but non-professionally trained laity. However, the problem exists to some extent there, too, as will be evident from an analysis of its dimensions.

On the one hand, we have a cantorial tradition that goes back to the Middle Ages. It flowered in Europe over the last two centuries, was transferred earlier in this century to the United States, England and South Africa (there is not much professional cantoring yet in Israel) and, after about two decades of relative decline, is enjoying a rejuvenation today. This is particularly true in Reform and Conservative synagogues as they move to increased ritual observance. This tradition embraced the idea that the cantor was expected to have a quality voice, to be trained in musicianship, and to sing significant, often complex compositions composed by him or by others, enriching the text by vocal embellishments and word repetitions, often augmented by a choir. The congregation served more as audience than as an active participant. Exceptions were the older Southern and Western congregations in Europe, whose congregational singing dated to medieval times and was a continuation of the Oriental, Italian and Spanish-Portuguese service.[1] With the growth of the cantorial tradition, the compositions for the liturgy became increasingly elaborate and, indeed, independent works of art in their own right, often absorbing the modes of harmony, structure and melody to be found in the surrounding secular culture, but not always sufficiently tied to the meaning of the liturgical text.

The best of these compositions had many virtues. They were written to assure proper pronunciation and phrasing of the Hebrew words and text, and to focus on the meaning of the liturgy and its significance. Indeed, the distinctive musical rendition of particular parts of the liturgy which vary by holiday and between holidays and weekdays probably developed from cantorial innovations of special expressiveness, beauty and power that gradually became accepted, between the eighth and thirteenth centuries, as permanent elements of the service.[2] Cantorial music moved and enlightened, engendering not just heightened awareness and understanding, but the special mood — of joy and sorrow, triumph and despair, inspiration and even catharsis — to match the occasion and the text. It provided a channel whereby the worshipper felt connected ultimately, not just to the prayer book and its liturgy, but to his fellow man, and sometimes — where truly inspired or moved — even to the Divinity, and sensed the Almighty's majesty and power, his care and love of the Jewish people and mankind.

At the worst, these compositions and cantorial renditions became the incarnation of art for art's sake. They were opportunities to show off compositional flair and vocal dexterity, interposing complexity and diversion and, ultimately, a barrier between worshipper and text. The result was congregational impatience and boredom. Services either took too long, or required the perfunctory performance of major parts to allow time for ambitious and sometimes uninteresting compositions. The question that begged to be asked was: For whose sake is the music? The Almighty's? The congregation's? The composer's? The cantor's?

It should be noted that the cantorial tradition did not take strong root in Sephardi services. The classicism of Sephardi culture deemphasized the florid, emotional aspects of *hazzanut,* and encouraged congregational chanting rather than solo singing. Moreover, by discouraging the rococo-like *piyyutim* (poetry) of Ashkenazi culture, Sephardim limited opportunities for the cantor to exhibit musical creativity. The result, Millgram points out, has been the relatively "monotonous rendition" of the services which is not palatable to most Ashkenazi Jews.[3]

436

There has also been a fairly distinct Hasidic style of individual congregant prayer and expression which was originally loud, chaotic, and lusty. Today it is more organized, focused around the often beautiful, haunting and original compositions of the *rebbe* or the sect's regular composers, such as those of the Modzitz Hasidim. The classic Hasidic style was thus distinct both from the relatively rapid, inartistic *davening* led by a *ba'al tefilah* (non-professional leader of the service) characteristic of non-affluent Ashkenazi Jewry, and from the cantorial tradition that could be found in the relatively larger, more affluent congregations.

A countertrend to the cantorial tradition developed in non-Hasidic congregations about fifty years ago. It sought to fill the vacuum between the short, democratic but perfunctory service of the traditional synagogue, in which the services were often just an unavoidable break between the learning of Torah, and the musically adventurous but elitist cantorial tradition. This countertrend, as paradigmatically embodied in the Young Israel movement, was part of a much broader attempt to make the synagogue a more democratic institution in Jewish life. Its purpose was to attract the young, Americanized, second and third generations to Judaism and away from assimilation, by giving everyone a greater say in the synagogue in every way. This trend strove to eliminate favoring the wealthy with synagogue honors, whether of ritual or leadership. It sought to encourage sermons by members of the congregation as well as the rabbi, sermons in English, shorter services, the leadership of the services by all members of Jewish musical and Hebrew language ability, and — a crucial change from tradition — congregational singing.

Congregational singing necessarily put a premium on easy to recognize, relatively simple melodies that could be sung week in, week out. Indeed, their familiarity was considered their strength. At its best, this approach involved the congregation in a way that a professional cantor and choir never could. It produced an interest in, and identification with, the liturgy. It gave youngsters, who are notoriously impatient when inactive, a role in the services that provided an outlet for their energy, and a vital reason to return every week to the synagogue.

At its worst, it resulted in its own musical dynamic that tended to split music from liturgy. The goal was the pretty, singable tune, whether or not it fit the meaning and significance of the text and the day in the Jewish calendar. Since familiarity was crucial, music new to the congregation was feared and avoided. Congregations were "led" in prayer by musical cues, calling forth mass, automatic musical responses. Indeed, during the persecutions of Jews in Europe in the fifteenth and sixteenth centuries, congregations succeeded in pressuring cantors to sing popular tunes of the marketplace on Sabbaths and holidays, to help them forget their dire condition during the rest of the week.[4] As in later years, even until now, this appears to be a case where the cantors and traditional modes of song are not satisfying to the people. When this happens, change is inevitable. It is ironic that current cantorial complaints against congregational singing based on folk songs, love songs, and other non-liturgical sources echo complaints against the excesses of cantors by rabbis and congregations centuries ago.[5]

The increasing separation of music and meaning was less of a problem at the inception of this populist trend in synagogue music, when the laity was largely unaware of the meaning of the Hebrew text, and synagogue democratization to counter assimilation was paramount. More recently, the growing knowledge and sophistication of the laity in music and liturgy has made the populist approach increasingly obsolete. Again, the question inevitably to be asked is: For whose sake are these melodies being sung? The cantor's? The congregation's? The liturgy's? The Almighty's?

At present, the cantorial tradition has increasingly been taken over by the Conservative and Reform movements, where classically — given the societal status of their congregants — the goal of democratization has had less of a priority. The move to the populist tradition, and away from the cantorial, has taken its firmest hold in Orthodox synagogues.

This divergence between the cantorial/Conservative and congregational/Orthodox approaches to synagogue music was paralleled by a similar divergence in Europe in the nineteenth century. The wealthier, more upwardly mobile, and more conservative Jewish bourgeoisie-entrepreneurs-intelligentsia in Europe emphasized order, reason, dignity, and the absorption of the best of the secular culture around them. The poorer working classes and small shopkeepers emphasized (and needed) emotion, excitement and spontaneity, mass participation, a certain amount of the chaotic element in the service, and loyalty to Jewish tradition to the exclusion of the secular culture around them. Later in its history, however, much of the Hasidic movement — for example, the Ger movement — moved away from emphasis on unbridled joy in religious song to the Mitnagdic conservatism and emphasis on ritual observance and Torah study. "Anything new is forbidden by the Torah," was a saying of the Hungarian rabbi, *Hatam Sofer,* that was popular with the Ger Hasidim. Their attitude against changes in dress and the reading of new, secular literature undoubtedly applied to innovation in synagogue music as well.[6]

Emerging changes of a sociological nature are also having an impact on both the cantorial and congregational traditions. There is a new emphasis on "learning" (Talmud study and commentaries thereon) and de-emphasis of aesthetically experienced communal prayer among the current Orthodox generation. The result is a movement back to the centuries-old tradition of short, unmusical services. The formula is more important than the feeling. Decorum is absent. The *hazzan is* discouraged from word repetition even where it enhances the text, and prayer is viewed as an unavoidable interlude between long stretches of "learning." This approach has been strengthened by synagogue music which is perceived as irrelevant, boring or worse.

The ritualistic attitude to prayer has some theological support in certain views of the *Tosafot,* the *Tur* and the *Shulhan Arukh,* the nineteenth century code, *Hayyei Adam,* and the philosophies of prayer of Rabbi J. B. Soloveitchik and the Israeli philosopher, Yeshayahu Leibowitz. Their views seem to question whether man can still personally pray with proper devotion, as he did in rabbinic times. Indeed, for Soloveitchik, the highest if not the only legitimate form of prayer is based on man's terror and unworthiness before God. Thus, the justification for prayer today is duty, paralleling the binding of Isaac and the Temple sacrifices, leaving little room for spontaneity, novelty, melody, or self-expression in worship. A broader view of prayer, as embracing the personal and creative expression before God of man's deepest feelings, longings and needs, is held by the Talmud, by Maimonides, and, most currently, by the Israeli philosopher, David Hartman.[7] Interestingly, one is less likely to find the anti-aesthetic attitude in Israel, perhaps because a more fully rounded and less guilt-ridden Jewish life can flourish there, with less of the traditional *galut* fear concerning the continuity of religious practices.

But it is not just the Orthodox who are changing. Among Conservative and, increasingly, even Reform congregations, trends to greater observance and ethnicity have caused a major increase in synagogue attendance and a heightened desire to participate in song during the service. There is a new urge to identify with their service, their liturgy, their people and — as it were — with their God. Such desire for aesthetic, musical self-expression produces a new sense of communion with their fellow congregants, the rabbi, and the cantor and the choir, too, who were previously viewed as remote symbols of a Judaism that was respected but rarely fully practiced.

Thus, the Conservative (and Reform) congregations increasingly want more singing, the very Orthodox want less, and both are unhappy with their past musical traditions. In this period of transition, as the roles of the cantor and the congregation evolve, a debate has begun between those who want the synagogue service to be a forum for congregational singing, and those, led by professional cantors, who view congregational singing as a threat not just to the cantorial profession and the jobs that it provides, but to the beautiful musical tradition of the liturgy.[8] In a word, as generations and their priorities change, the choice that seems to arise is one between elitist artistry and populist philistinism. I say "seems to arise" because, as I will seek to argue, I think this choice is neither the only one nor the most desirable one.[9]

I suggest that before one can develop a concept of the proper role for cantor and congregation, there is a need to recognize a variety of concepts that are not mutually exclusive. There are solo and congregational singing, virtuoso and lyrical singing, modern and traditional music, familiar and unfamiliar music, great music and ordinary music, music that heightens the emotions and underlines the themes of the liturgy, and music that inspires the fellowship of a congregation joined in song. There are prayers and places and occasions for each of these in particular synagogues, at particular points in the liturgy, for the particular tastes of the Jews who make up a particular *zibbur,* or congregation.

The people of Israel in prayer deserve better than the false dichotomy of art versus mass singing. A *shaharit* or *musaf* service on a *Shabbat* or *Yom Tov,* or a High Holiday, must always seek to inspire, to guide, to teach, and to explain what is going on in the liturgy, through music. This must be done without creating *tirha d'zibbura,* a burden on the congregation. To achieve these objectives, there is a need for good *nusah* and good music throughout, whether by cantor or congregation, that is right for the mood and theme of the day. Think of the challenge in this regard of the *Shabbat* between *Yom Ha'Shoah* and Independence Day and *Yom Yerushalayim.* There is a need for new music that *will become* familiar, and for the careful introduction of new modes and modern compositional ideas. There is even the need for changes in *nusah,* where they do not depart significantly from the accepted tonality and feeling of the basic *nusah.*

Finally, I suggest that it is time for a new, post-Holocaust approach to the music of prayer, that stresses neither the virtuoso cries of the oppressed of our past nor the trivial "pop-art" of fad tunes of the present, but, rather, a lyrical and sophisticated rendering of the kaleidoscope of themes and emotions in our liturgy. Such music, by modern composers like Ralph Schlossberg, Abraham Kaplan and Jerome Kopmar, together with many of the masterpieces of the past and the best of music in the popular idiom, will bring a new interest and excitement to our prayers and help us transcend a world that is, indeed, "too much with us."

No hazzan is more important than his zibbur, to whom he owes his ultimate obligation, allegiance and authority. Zibbur and hazzan have gone through much together in our history, beginning with the songs of the Levites and the classical Sephardi collaboration of hazzan and congregation, through the melodies of Hasidic "rebbes," the heartfelt renditions of hazzanim of our golden age, the classical compositions for the synagogue liturgy of the last century, the Biblically oriented and nation building music of the people of Israel, be it songs of love, longing, triumph or despair, and the new, modern compositions of many talented composers now writing synagogue music. The creative tension between cantor and congregation must continue to combine the familiar with the new, to provide davening, prayer experiences, which are ever fresh and not routine, as in the rabbinic injunction al t'hi tfilatkha keva (do not let your prayers be routine). This can only be accomplished, as in the case of learning, as we increase, together with our teachers and our cantors, the variety and sophistication of the methods that we use to render and explicate the text, whether of Torah or of liturgy. The lesson for hazzan and zibbur alike surely is: by continued mutual openness and receptivity one to the other, to continue to guide and inspire each other and to thrive as a harmonious unity rather than as adversaries.

NOTES

1 A. Z. Idelsohn, *Jewish Music in its Historical Development* (Schocken Books, 1967), p. 281.

2 Abraham Millgram, *Jewish Worship* (Jewish Publication Society, 1971), pp. 513-30.

3 Millgram, p. 526.

4 Idelsohn, p. 178.

5 Millgram, p. 528.

6 Raphael Mahler, *Hasidism and the Jewish Enlightenment* (Jewish Publication Society, 1985), pp. 55, 64-7, 313-14.

7 David Hartman, *A Living Covenant* (The Free Press, 1985), chapters 6 and 7. There also may be a relationship between intensive Talmud study and asceticism and, ultimately, spiritual purification. This phenomenon goes back at least to the 13th century in Provence, France, when cadres of students were selected for seven years of intensive, isolated and ascetic Talmud study. See I. Twersky, *Rabad of Posquieres* (Jewish Publication Society, 1980), pp. 25-27.

8 The *piyyutim,* in particular, with their rhythmic regularity, seem ideally suited for congregational singing and are surely unsuitable for the virtuoso improvisations of *hazzanut.* This is not to deny the important role of the cantor in finding, commissioning and selecting appropriate music for these sections of the liturgy.

9 An interesting article in Dennis Prager's newsletter, *Ultimate Issues,* highlights this dispute ("When Rabbis and Cantors Become Doctors and Artists," *Ultimate Issues* [Spring 1985]: 12). In it, the editor notes the complaint of a cantor at the pervasive congregational rejection of great music for the synagogue as performed by professional cantors (and choirs). He then develops his own credo that synagogues are for congregational singing of familiar melodies, while the great music of which the cantor writes is for the concert hall. I think an "either-or" approach will tend to be rejected by a significant portion of the congregation.

Fear And Awe:
May Man Bring Song To Prayer?

The *siddur* insists that man, being insignificant before God, should pray with fear and trembling before Him. Each morning, we immediately thank God for restoring our soul to what otherwise would be a dead body. The opening prayer in the liturgy, *ma tovu*, expressly calls on Jews to pray to God "in fear of Thee," *beyiratekha*.

Almost immediately thereafter, when saying *Asher Yatsar*, we again point out man's insignificance. God made us with orifices and vessels, the malfunction of any one of which would cause us to be unable to even stand before God. Within minutes we recognize again that we live by virtue of the soul, the *neshamah*, that God has given to each of us, that He may recall at any moment, and which He will ultimately take back from us. Here again we acknowledge God's eternity and man's mortality. This prayer is quickly followed by the story of the *Akedah* which, in context, is designed to suggest that man, even one as pure as Isaac, has no standing to be other than a *korban*, a sacrifice — indeed, a *korban olah*, if you will, a total sacrifice. The message is spelled out for us immediately after the *Akedah* in the formulation that each person (named "Adam," which stands for man at his most basic, imperfect and universal) should acknowledge that he or she is nothing and deserving of nothing, and hence can say nothing before God. *Ma nomar le'fanekha?* "What can we say before you, our God and God of our fathers?"

Thus, our liturgy commands recognition of the idea that we must approach God in prayer with awe, with fear and trembling, based on a recognition of human inconsequence. The question, however, remains: having entered God's sanctuary and presence with this feeling of awe, and having approached the Almighty with this overwhelming sense of our poverty of character and deed before God's perfection, is there anything else we may be allowed to feel and express in our prayers?

In his recent book, *A Living Covenant,*[1] Israeli philosopher Rabbi David Hartman questions certain writings of Rabbi Joseph B. Soloveitchik that appear to answer this question negatively, and deals similarly with the views of the deceased Israeli philosopher, Yeshayahu Leibowitz, who argues that one is not required to bring any devotional feelings to the act of prayer, but merely *kavanah latset,* the intention to discharge an obligation to God, as one must intellectually intend, for example, in taking the *lulav* and *etrog,* the "four species," on *Succot* (the holiday of Tabernacles).[2] Hartman disagrees with both and, based on Talmudic and other sources, emphasizes the importance of man's freedom and responsibility. He argues for feeling and spontaneity in prayer, and even novelty (within the prescribed liturgical structure), all of which would reflect man's sense of dignity and adequacy. His conclusion is: "Rather than self-negation and self-effacement, prayer reflects the worshiper's confident mood of being fully accepted by God as a total person."[3]

Essentially, Hartman relies on Rabbinic authorities in the Talmud and on Rambam, while conceding that the more ritualistic approaches of Rabbi Soloveitchik and Leibowitz are supported by later medieval and modern authorities.[4] Hartman may be overly generous in conceding that the ritualistic view has predominated since the days of Rambam. In fact, what is more likely to be true is that it has been the predominant Ashkenazi view.[5]

I suggest that Hartman may really not be so far from Rabbi Soloveitchik's position, because prayer is a process that inherently requires awe *and* adequacy, and inevitably reflects a continuing tension between them. The very act of seeking God implies adequacy and wor-

445

thiness; yet the very acts of petition and praise imply God's greatness and our impotence.

In this regard, I would like to offer some items of evidence on the issue, in the hope that it may stimulate further expressions of view on the questions Hartman has raised, which are so timely and challenging today to Jews of every persuasion. My approach is a simple one: if we are interested in how to pray, I believe we should look first in the liturgy itself for guidance.

First, and most obviously, is the prayer we recite right after admitting that man is no different from animals, "for all is vanity," that is, all of creation, including man, is as nothing compared to God. "But," we say at that point in our morning liturgy, "we are Your people," the "children of Your covenant ... the assembly of Jacob. . . out of Your love for whom . . . You have called us Israel and *Jeshurun*.[6] *Therefore, we are required* to give praise and thanks ...to Your name. How fortunate and how happy we are, how good is our lot and pleasant our allotment in life," and "how fortunate and happy we are" to say the *Shema* each day, twice a day, evening and morning.

Suddenly, with this crucial *aval*, "But," we turn our unworthiness to the most sublime worthiness, and our despair at being no different from animals to the pride of being uniquely called upon to give praise and thanks to God. The form this praise takes appears after the brief learning interlude preceding the *kaddish de-rabbanan: mizmor, shir;* "melody, song!" From this point on, the liturgy is literally filled with references to song, culminating with the *az yashir,* "Then, Moses and the children of Israel sang this song to God."

Song is the ability to reach back into one's experiences, feelings and thoughts and express emotions and ideas in a unique blend of concentrated meaning and beauty. Prayer through song is an act that goes beyond fear and trembling, beyond self-effacement and unworthiness. It represents art as well as holiness, man's ability to add a personal, aesthetic dimension to enhance and deepen the sacred, using the powers and skills God has given him. Was this not the purpose and function of the singing and playing of the Levites in the Temple?

Man sings to God when Moses and the Children of Israel sing and when David sings, that is to say, man sings when the gulf between God and man is at its greatest, either because of His manifest greatness or our own manifest weakness. The flower of faith flourishes in either soil, and therefore our liturgy stresses the connection: "And they (the Israelites) believed in God and in Moses his servant. *Then* sang Moses and the Children of Israel this song to God, and they sang, 'I will sing unto the Lord *for (i.e., because)* He has triumphed in strength....'" Precisely, that is, when the Israelites should have felt most insignificant, self-effacing and unworthy in the face of the manifest gap between their helplessness and the Almighty's strength, that was the time when the people sang.

Midrash Rabbah on *Exodus* 23 recounts how only Israel sang before God, and how Israel, inspired by its faith in God, brought God into the world through its song.

1. Rabbi Berakhya said in the name of Rabbi Abahu: "Although Thou art eternal, from the beginning of time, Your seat was not established and You were not known in the world until Your children sang before You (at the Red Sea)."

2. ". . . and with the merit of their (the Israelites') faith, the holy spirit rested upon them and they sang."

3. "From the day the Almighty created the world until the Israelites stood at the Red Sea, no one sang before God except for the Israelites (at the Red Sea)... 'For this I have been waiting.'"

Can there be more cogent proof that faith brings about the special ability to sing to God, that Israel's song brings God into the world, and that God waits anxiously to hear Israel in prayers of song?

We have two similar statements in tractate *Hullin,* 91b: "Israel is more precious to God than the angels because Israel sings every hour, whereas the angels sing once a day, or some say once a week, or some say once a month, or some say once a year." Further, we are told, "the angels may not sing above until Israel sings below." Again, we see that Israel is expected to sing, is praised for its song, and loved for its song, by the Almighty.

Truly, the numerous references to Israel in song throughout our liturgy and in our classic Talmudic texts provide us with more than just historical information. They are there to provide a model for Jews throughout history, in their prayers and in their lives. The message of song is self-expression, joy, even in sorrow and despair. It means, and requires, a sense of confidence and worthiness, the ability to give back to God something more than He gave us, through our own efforts, using the powers and resources He has provided to us. Jews without song would have despaired and abandoned their faith a long time ago.

As far back as the story of Cain and Abel we have learned the importance of offering the best of our resources and talents when we express our feelings and thoughts in prayer. This is part of what we mean when we talk about bringing poetry and music to prayer. Certainly this presents dangers. We can become so caught up in creating the beauty of our offerings that we forget their content and purpose. Yet, Judaism rejects the joyless, self-negating, ascetic approach to life despite the safety that asceticism provides to us from temptation, pride and sin, because asceticism rejects the very purpose of our creation and God's express wish in *Genesis* that we conquer the universe. The Temple itself, in all its beauty, going back to the tradition of its designer under God's direction, Bezalel, created a constant temptation that one would think of that beauty and not of one's sin or God's glory during times of sacrifice or prayer. Yet, our beautiful Temple, and the music and the instruments used by the Levites in prayer, reflect the Almighty's wish, as it were, for beauty in our services as a handmaiden of religious expression. The test for man in prayer at all times is to avoid aesthetics for their own sake, and any involvement in aesthetics that detracts from sincere devotion and sincere intentions, *kavanah,* in prayer.

I do not suggest that there are not times when we should feel inadequate and unworthy. But we never should feel so unworthy that we are incapable of prayer. Our physical, emotional and intellectual resources must be summoned and controlled to present even the most desperate cry for help. What I am suggesting here is that, psychologically, man in prayer is never so bereft of freedom and control that he is unable to add elements of dignity and beauty to his service to God, even when they are petitions — perhaps especially at such times. A worthy cantor, *sheliah tsibbur,* should always be alert to his role as well as his text. This means an awareness of volume and articulation, accent and phrasing, *nusah* and melody, that give our prayers dignity, character and moving power.

Prayer is, in important aspects, a substitute for and a parallel to the sacrifices brought in the Temple. But sin offerings and *olot* totally consumed, symbolically, in place of man on the altar, representing man's unworthiness before God, were not the only sacrifices brought. There were also the sacrifices of *todah* and *shelamim,* which were expressions of gratitude and wholeness, in which man felt happy in his lot and thankful to God. In such cases, man was even allowed to partake of his own sacrifice, in recognition of the fact that he was a partner with God in carrying out God's plan in this world, a role which implied, surely to some extent, a sense of adequacy, dignity and worth.

It may be argued that while we were once worthy to so approach God, we are no longer. Hartman does, indeed, refer to rabbis who have argued this view.[8] But, as noted above, the text of our liturgy which was composed by our sages seems plainly to require praise and song. *Lefikhakh anahnu hayyavim lehodot* requires a sense not just of adequacy but of closeness, a feeling of belonging to a people whom God has loved and in whom He has rejoiced, *she-ahavta oto* and *she-samahta bo.*

But I think we can go a step further, and here I would like to introduce an idea of my late Talmudic teacher, Rabbi Bunimovitz, z"l, of Yeshiva Etz Chaim of Boro Park, regarding the seemingly internally contradictory aspects of the Sabbath prayer, "The Soul of Every Living Thing," *nishmat kol hai.* In brief, the part beginning *ilu pinu* plainly asserts that if all of man's powers of expression were magnified beyond plausibility, humanity would still not be able adequately to praise God for His greatness and all He has done for us. The gap, in brief, between God's majesty and humanity's smallness can never be bridged. Yet, the very next sentence, in seemingly one of the most dramatic non-sequiturs in our liturgy, says: "Therefore (sic?) the limbs that You have differentiated for us, the spirit and breath You have placed in our nostrils, and the tongue which You have placed in our mouths, *they will* praise and bless You!" What is there in the second formulation that allows us, indeed requires us, to stand up and praise God despite the overwhelming and persuasive statement of the first formulation that we have no ability to praise God adequately, and presumably therefore no right to attempt to do so?

Rabbi Bunimovitz answered that in the second formulation it is not *man's* powers and abilities that address God but the powers and abilities *that God gave to man: she-pillagta banu, she-nafahta be-appeinu,* and *asher samta be'finu.* We have the right, in fact the duty, to address God because *we do so with the resources that He has provided to us,* because surely those resources, those attributes and capabilities — whatever else we may use them for — have no higher or greater God-given purpose than to address the Almighty in petition and praise. We are not without standing; we are not praying without right. We may be poor in deeds and learning, in wealth and power, but we offer and we utilize the abilities that God has provided to us as resources for prayer. We wish it could be more, but You, our God, have given us whatever You wished us to have, and this gives us the right to approach You with that, and only that, to clothe us, to guide us, to enable us to address You.

If a beggar were to come to a king's palace and the king instructed his servants, "Tell the beggar to put on these clothes and stand before me," has the beggar any choice but to wear the clothes he has been given and to appear? Does he have the right to say, "These clothes are inadequate for a presence before the king; therefore I have no right or duty to appear"?

To the extent that these concepts are the basis of our *present* liturgy, our worthiness to address God with feeling and song did not cease some time in the past; it exists to this day.

The prayer a*shrei*, recited three times daily, offers evidence not only on the variety of emotions and renditions of prayer, but on the importance of sincerity — the matching of feeling to word. Thus, the sentences beginning with the letters *dalet, heh, vav, zayin, yud,* and *kaf* present a spectrum of different kinds of feeling in prayer. Of particular importance is the sentence beginning with *karov,* in which we say that prayers offered to God *be-emet,* with sincerity of thought and emotion, are described as prayers that God will answer. This is the very opposite of ritualism.

A little later, in Psalm 149, "*Hallelujah,* sing unto the Lord a new song, His praises are sung in the midst of His devout followers, *hasidim,*" a model service is characterized, with *simha, gilah,* and *zimrah* — all forms of joy — and instruments which were designed to reflect different feelings and emotions.[9] "The glories of God are in their throats," the Psalm continues, clearly referring to song, to artistic vocal expression.

Two more texts in the liturgy make the point in a clear, slightly more sophisticated way, and begin to bridge the tension between awe and song in prayer. First, *yishtabbah* tells us that it is fitting for Israel to address God with song and melody, *shir* and *zimrah,* as well as with praises and other encomia.

Second, we see from the prayer *et Shem ha-Melekh* that the angels, whom we are to emulate in prayer, praise God with an interesting combination of attitude and emotion, with *nahat ruah* and *yirah.* The former concept embraces freedom and ease, spontaneity and feeling, appropriate to the liturgy they utter. But the latter concept embraces the awe and the fear that we each must feel in the presence of the Almighty, accessible though He is to us.

Here, indeed, is where the entire liturgy prior to *Shema* and the *Amidah* has been leading. It has been pointing from the very beginning of the service to the need for feeling both awe and ardor, contriteness and confidence, inadequacy and inspiration, just as the angels pray with *yirah* and *nahat ruah*.

We know that Rabbi Soloveitchik (the "*Rav*") understands and advocates feeling and ardor, and the sense of adequacy necessary to present our prayers before God with dignity and a beauty of expression that serves the thoughts, ideas and emotions of our prayers. We know this from works of the *Rav* which Hartman himself cites. [10] The tension between the different aspects of prayer developed in the *Rav's* writings reflects a theme in many of them. I refer to the inherent duality of man's nature and man's task, which is to be a being of nature and of spirit, of science and of belief, to be creative but disciplined, confident and submissive, to be God-like and God fearing.[11]

One can find this tension, this dual strain of confidence, adequacy and freedom on the one hand, and inwardness, inadequacy and submissiveness on the other, not only in our liturgy but throughout our history. Indeed, one can speculate that, in ways not yet fully explicated, the contrast between classical Sephardi and classical Ashkenazi culture is to a significant degree a reflection of this duality and tension in Jewish history and culture.[12]

Hartman has done a valuable service both in exploring the problems of the ritualistic approach to prayer that results from placing primary emphasis on man's unworthiness, and in exploring the glories of man's unique ability to sing before the Lord with a sense of dignity, freedom and responsibility, with the innovation and creativity in word and song that this allows. But he has perhaps failed to adequately recognize the two strains that are necessary to prayer both in his own thinking and in his presentation of the *Rav's* views.

In my own view, the real problem is the way we understand and live with this duality. There is, to be sure, an element of trust in man in the optimistic approach of the one strain, and an element of mistrust of man in the pessimistic approach of the other. As we have remarked, the *Rav's* philosophical writings display a very keen awareness and appreciation of the dual nature of man, and the need for both creativity and discipline in his life.[13] But the inner conflict between these paradigms necessarily requires an attempt at synthesis and reconciliation, guided by the principles of our tradition. To ignore the need for such synthesis and reconciliation is to invite extremism on the right and the left, and the disunity that results when the views of our Sages are not fully understood or fairly represented. What is needed is an express recognition that both elements are important, both man as creator and man as humble servant, and that we must, in all aspects of our lives, continue the effort to harmonize them and keep them in fruitful balance. Even more, we need mutual toleration for the balance we each strike within the broad boundaries of Jewish law.

By understanding that there are polarities and, thus, extremes to be avoided, lies the best hope, I believe, for the continued spiritual development of our people, so many of whom yearn to identify spiritually with our traditions and the continuity of our history.

....

NOTES

1 *The Free Press*, 1985, pp. 131-179.

2 *Op. cit., p.* 163.

3 *Op. cit., p.* 179.

4 *Op. cit., pp.* 171-73.

5 Hartman cites *Tosafot,* the *Tur, Shulhan Arukh,* and the early nineteenth-century code, *Hayyei Adam (pp.* 171-2). While the *Shulhan Arukh* is by the great Sephardi Rabbi Joseph Karo, there is room for further discussion. Rabbi Dr. H. J. Zimmels, in his *Ashkenazim and Sephardim* (Marla Publications, London, 1976) points out that the Sephardim generally looked for the reasons of the commandments, whereas the Ashkenazim considered them as "royal decrees," for which reason was not necessary (pp. 249-50). Jacob Elbaum's article "Ethical Literature in Poland," in *Jewish Thought in the Sixteenth Century,* B. D. Cooperman, ed. (Harvard Univ. Press, 1983), pp. 157-59, suggests that there was a strongly kabbalistic influence in the idea that all Jewish ritual has mysteries, and that all the commandments, in all their minute detail, should be carried out even if their reasons are unknown to us, and real *kavanah* is not possible. Elbaum notes *Rema's* lament that "even householders who cannot distinguish between their right and their left and walk in darkness, who are incapable of explaining a Torah portion with Rashi's commentary, nevertheless are quick to study kabbalah." Elbaum adds (p. 165) that this argument recurs in other authors. The Hasidic movement, which in part was a reaction to the systematic and sophisticated Lurianic kabbalah, certainly relied heavily on

kavanah, and indeed on joy, often unbounded, in its approach to prayer. The rabbis of Italy during the 15th-18th centuries stressed the importance of educating children to understand the meaning and purpose of the prayers. See Simcha Assaf, *Sources in the History of Jewish Education* (Devir, Tel Aviv 1931), Introduction to Vols. I and II. Maharal also emphasized the importance of understanding the meaning and purpose of *mitzvot.* See Seymour Fox, "The Moral Philosophy of MaHaRaL," appearing in Cooperman, *op. cit.,* at pp. 167, 173.

6   One is entitled to ask: Why do we remind God at this point that He called Jacob by another name, *Jeshurun* — a name so rarely found in either scripture or the liturgy? It has been translated and defined by the Septuagint (the third century, B.C.E. rabbinic translation of the five books of Moses, the Pentateuch, into Greek); by R. David Kimhi and R. Abraham ibn Ezra; and by R. Obadiah Sforno, as beloved, upright, and clear-sighted, respectively. This already indicates that the meaning is not clear and there is room for more than one interpretation. In the context of our issue, I suggest that *Jeshurun* also stands for Israel's ability and its right, because of its uprightness — its *unique* ability and right according to *Midrash Rabbah* on *Exodus* 23 — to sing before God. *Jeshurun* may thus come from *shira,* song, as well as *yashar,* or upright. As Moses and the Children of Israel sang (and that song, not insignificantly, is a major part of every day's liturgy) so may we sing. Our liturgy seems to say, "You gave us that right when You gave us that name" of *Jeshurun.* Names in Jewish history, from the very first chapters in *Genesis,* are fraught with significance for the people who bear them.

7   *Exodus* 14:31-15:1.

8   See Hartman, pp. 171-3.

9   See R. Abraham Portaleone, *Shiltei ha-Gibborim.*

10 See Hartman, pp. 133-9.

11 As Rabbi Soloveitchik eloquently writes in *Halakhic Man* (Jewish Publication Society, 1983), halakhah — fashioning it and observing it — is man's role as God's partner in completing Creation, and to this end man must not, cannot, feel inadequate in his halakhic activities (pp. 99-101). Man, created in God's image, also incorporates "the most terrible chaos and void," and must choose whether to be "noble or degenerate"; through Halakhah, man "creates himself' (p. 109). For man, in his role as creator, creation means "spontaneity, actuality, action, renewal, aspiration, and daring" (p. 131). "The goal of self-creation is individuality, autonomy, uniqueness, and freedom" (p. 135).

12 Two interesting and contrasting sources in this regard are Moses Shulvass, *Between the Rhine and the Bosporus* (College of Jewish Studies Press, Chicago, 1964), and Zimmels, *Ashkenazim and Sephardim,* pp. 5-7, 13-15, 19-20, 35-50, 61-68, 124-137, 164, 185. See Chapters 7-9, pp. 190-240, for Zimmels's analysis of the reasons for Sephardi and Ashkenazi differences in world and cultural outlook. Their differences were paralleled to some degree, in certain periods, by differences in certain moral standards and ritual practices (pp. 250-255). Shulvass asserts that Ashkenazi Jewry saved Italian Jewry from the danger of extinction by assimilation, by imparting to it the character of an ethnically composite Jewish community (p. 183). While his view may be overstated, it seems clear that each aspect of this duality of approach has its dangers. The strain of individual adequacy, confidence, reason, and art can lead to a breakdown in religious belief and practice, whereas the strains of inadequacy, pessimism, duty, asceticism, and inwardness can lead to narrowness and to divorce from human concerns and cultural achievements.

Rabbi Marc D. Angel, in his book, *The Rhythms of Jewish Living — A Sephardic Approach* (Sepher-Hermon Press, New York, 1986), discusses Ashkenazi strictness and Sephardi leniency in the halakhah, and some of the historic reasons for this difference (pp. 76-8).

13 See, e.g., Hartman's discussion, p. 133.

A Song in Every Psalm:
A Review of Cantor Jacob Lefkowitz's
Musical Settings to *Psalms*

Those of us who attend synagogue services on a fairly regular basis, or who are somewhat familiar with Jewish music as it appears in synagogues, on records, in concert halls (where it rarely appears), and as it is taught to Jewish boys and girls in Hebrew schools, are by now familiar with the fact that Jewish music today generally falls into a set number of stereotypes. There is "Klezmer" and hasidic music, Israeli dance, love, and pioneer music, the old, weeping style cantorial music, heavy, formal and overblown compositions, and works in modem idioms. Except where the music and its performance are of special artistry, it rarely moves us and rarely instructs us. It is too often either boring or cold, with a lack of the warmth and interest that are necessary to join music and people together the way Jews and Jewish music have been fused as one virtually throughout our history.

This modem alienation of our people from part of its Jewish soul — which Jewish music has always sought to prevent — is partly the fault of the fast moving, fragmented, and overly stimulated era in which we live, and, to a large degree, of the music itself and the way it is performed. What used to be meaningful has become trite and sentimental, or irrelevant to the sophisticated, eclectic tastes of modem Jews.

There are, however, composers like Shlomo Carlbach, z"l, Ralph

Schlossberg, Abraham Kaplan, Jerome Kopmar, and a few others, who have created music we can treasure, because it is linked in its warmth with our past but speaks in a lean, modem way, and with a technique of composition that addresses the mind as it inspires the heart.

In this select company one must include Cantor Jacob Lefkowitz. His music eschews heaviness and effects for their own sake. It is steeped in tradition, but completely subservient to the text, which it serves with a lyricism that communicates with direct, pulsating impact the *meaning* of the text and its emotional force.

I believe that his musical setting of the Psalms, "A Song in Every Psalm," even on the basis of the few times I have heard it, may deservedly be considered a classic of Jewish music. The poetry of the Psalms has fittingly been ascribed to King David, because it is the poetry of kings. It embraces, as David did in his life, the full spectrum of experience, emotion, and thought, from defeat to triumph, from despair and petition to praise and joy. And the Psalms are never without dignity, never without strength, never without the joy and confidence that King David feels about his life and its worth, and the power and compassion of his Father and King.

Jacob Lefkowitz's music is worthy in every respect of King David's Psalms. He has captured their soaring optimism of faith and joy in his wondrous new work. Playing my tape again recently I was startled not only at how fresh each short piece sounded on rehearing and how singable each piece is, but how difficult it was to single out any one for special praise because each is so distinctive. Among my favorites are the lively march for Psalm 3 with its pressing, bursting "*kuma, kuma, kuma*" (rise up, rise up, rise up); the wonderfully frenzied music in Psalm 10 (Arise, O Lord! O God!); the moving Psalm 15 ("Lord, who may abide in Your sanctuary") with its traditional but lean cantorial style — lyrical, with deft modern touches — and so true to the text (as each piece is), as the music gives each of the attributes of the righteous man its own distinctive musical phrase; the brilliant, exciting and tuneful "patter" style song for Psalm 28 ("Deliver Your people"), punctuated with declamations and syncopations that propel and underscore the text with such deft musicality; the unspeakably beautiful and tender rendering of the famous Psalm 34, "Who is the man who is eager for life … guard your tongue from evil"; the heartbreaking music for Psalm 78 ("But He, being merciful") that brings us back, with a few deft strokes, to the highest level of cantorial singing as rendered by Yossele Rosenblatt at his compositional best; the almost swaggering and so aptly confident Psalm 79, where David cries out "Help us, O God ... for the sake of the glory of Your name" — that is, for *Your sake!* — with that special joy of hasidic music at its best that reflects a Jew's joy as he stands before God in prayer; the gentle, wondrous quality of gratitude of Psalm 85 ("Faithfulness and truth have embraced"), with its idyllic American flavor, describing God's bounty to man; the classical marching mode used to describe the elemental forces of nature in Psalm 93 (The Lord is King, He is robed in grandeur"); the tuneful, lively, syncopated Psalm 133 ("*Hinay ma tov u'ma na'im*") and its contrasting middle section that transports us instantly to an evening campfire in Israel under a peaceful sky; and the lively march of Psalm 150 with its urgent, pressing "Halleluyah ("give praise to the Lord") in a syncopated, accented, form that culminates in a short triumphant code.[1]

Merely to traverse the scope of this music is to suggest in the barest and most inadequate way the treat that awaits all those who will be privileged to listen to this music. And here I want to make two final points.

First, as Cantor Macy Nullman has written in his important work, *Concepts of Jewish Music and Prayer* (Hallmark Press 1985), the composition of new Jewish music for the synagogue, if it is to be meaningful and attractive to modern listeners, requires "experience in hearing and performing authentic synagogue song, technical training, historical knowledge, a sense of style, and (the right) blend of all these elements" (at p. 77). In an article in this chapter, I wrote that "it is time for a new, post-Holocaust approach to the music of prayer, that stresses neither the virtuoso cries of the oppressed of our past nor the trivial 'pop-art' of fad tunes of our present, but, rather, *a lyrical and sophisticated* rendering of

458

the kaleidoscope of themes and emotions in our liturgy." The modern Jew at worship not only needs, but longs for the moral dimension of art, and the artistic dimension of worship. He craves music anchored in the past in its passion and its compassion, but looking forward with optimism and a sense of dignity. I believe Cantor Jacob Lefkowitz has written a major work that fulfills all these hopes and aspirations for new Jewish music.

My second point is of a more pressing nature, but one that must be made if wonderful music like Jacob Lefkowitz's *Psalms* is to have a life and a future among our people — and, indeed, because of its universal artistic nature, hopefully among an even wider sphere of listeners. I refer to the necessity that artists perform this work, and that we — the collective Jewish people from whose life and history it has been taken and which it so eloquently represents in its many hues and shapes — that we bring this music into our lives, our homes, our synagogues, and schools, in records, tapes, and live performances, in whatever reproduction forms we favor. Only in this way will all of us be able to experience this kind of music and make it a permanent part of our culture, as it deserves to be.

....
NOTE

1   The settings of the Psalms are included in The Complete Manuscripts of Jacob Lefkowitz, a 4-volume set, and 39 of the Psalms are available in a 2-cassette set — both available for purchase from Cantor David Lefkowitz, Cantor of the Park Avenue Synagogue in New York City.

Author's Bibliography

Midstream, January/February, 2005, p. 33 "Preparing for the Akedah"

Midstream, February/March, 2003, p. 28 "*Gen.* 9:12–17: 'Look to the Rainbow' — So Why Did the Sages Say 'Don't Look?'"

Midstream, January, 2003, p. 28. "The Tower of Babel: From Destruction to Dispersion"

The Edah Journal, 3:1, Tevet 5763 (2003), on line at www.edah.org "Jewish Mysticism: Medieval Roots, Contemporary Dangers and Prospective Challenges"

Midstream, September/October, 2002, p. 33. "Hellenism vs. Hebraism on the Inevitability of Tragedy: Studying the Cain and Joseph Stories"

Midstream, January 2002, p. 22. "Thoughts on Reading the *Akedah* Again"

Midstream, December, 2001, p. 30. "Challenging Lubavitch's New Messianic Claims," Review Essay of David Berger's *The Rebbe, The Messiah, and the Scandal of Orthodox Indifference*

Midstream, November, 2001, p. 25. "The Binding of Isaac: Religious Paradoxes, Permutations and Problems"

Shofar, Fall, 2001, p. 130. "Firing Off a Jewish Canon," Review Essay of Ruth Wisse's *The Modern Jewish Canon: A Journey Through Language and Culture* (New York: Free Press, 2000)

Jewish Bible Quarterly, October–December, 2000, p. 251. "The Tragedy of Jephthah"

Abraham & Family: New Insights into the Patriarchal Narratives, Hershel Shanks, ed. (Washington, D.C.: Biblical Archeology Society, 2000), p. 13. "Who's Testing Whom: Was Abraham Really Ready to Kill His Son?"

BDD, Journal of Torah and Scholarship, Winter, 1999. "Ezekiel 20:25–6: Did God Ever Command the Sacrifice of Israel's First Born Sons?"

Midstream, July/August, 1999, p. 13. "Rabbi Meir and His Wife, Beruriah — 'Till Death Do Us Part'"

Midstream, February/March, 1999, p. 10. "The Message of the Prophet Elisha"

Midstream, September/October, 1998, p. 9. "Science and Religion: Still Separate Worlds?"

Midstream, January, 1998, p. 9. "Religious Murders: Weeds in the Garden of Jewish Tradition?"

Midstream, October, 1997, p. 6. "The Court Jew in the Modern World"

Midstream, June/July, 1997, p. 17. "The Promise of Canaan to Abraham's Seed"

JUDAISM, Fall, 1993, p. 422. "Kabbalistic Feminism in Agnon's *Betrothed*"

Bible Review, October, 1993, p. 53. "God Tests Abraham, Abraham Tests God"

JUDAISM, Winter (January) 1993, p. 71. "The Real Test of the *Akedah*: Blind Obedience Versus Moral Choice"

JUDAISM, Summer, 1991, p. 263. "*Letters to Felice* — Kafka's Quest for Jewish Identity"

Yiddish, Vol. 8, No. 1 (1991), p. 75. "Der Nister's 'Under a Fence: A Review'"

JUDAISM, Summer, 1990, p. 306. "I. B. Singer and His Predecessors"

JEWISH SPECTATOR, Winter, 1989, p. 38. "Secular Humanism and Creation Science in the Public Schools"

JUDAISM, Spring, 1989, p. 174. "Was Yehudah Halevi Racist?"

Tradition, Summer, 1988, p. 90. "Innovation in Synagogue Music"

JUDAISM, Winter, 1987, p. 97. "Music for Jewish Liturgy: Art for Whose Sake?"

Tradition, Summer, 1987, p. 62. "Fear and Awe: May Man Bring Song to Prayer?"

Journal of Synagogue Music, July, 1987, p. 17. "Music for Jewish Liturgy: Art for Whose Sake?"

"A Song in Every Psalm" (Music Review), Ibid., p. 52

The Jewish Standard (N.J.), May 24, 1985, p. 19. "On Giving Jewish Music Serious Attention"

Author's Biography

Since retiring in 1986 as Assistant General Counsel of AT&T Technologies, Inc. (now Lucent), the author has pursued graduate work in Jewish Studies at the Jewish Theological Seminary, Yeshiva University and Columbia University (1986–1990), building on his pre-law school background of fifteen years' study of Jewish texts — Tanakh, Talmud, History, and Literature — through his college years, at Yeshiva Etz Chaim of Boro Park, Talmudical Academy and Teachers Institute of Yeshiva College, and private Talmud study.

During 1990–1994 he served as Assistant, later Associate Editor of *Judaism*, and since his retirement from the law he has published more than thirty articles in numerous journals of Jewish Thought, including *Tradition, Midstream, Judaism, The Edah Journal, Bible Review, Jewish Bible Quarterly, B.D.D. A Journal of Torah and Scholarship* (Bar-Ilan University, Israel), *Jewish Spectator, Yiddish,* and the *Journal of Synagogue Music.*

The author has served in numerous leadership synagogue positions during the past fifty years, at the Young Israel of West Hempstead, New York, and Congregation Ahavat Achim of Fairlawn, New Jersey. These included service as President and other officer positions, trustee, various committee chairmanships and memberships, and serving as *ba'al musaf* on the High Holidays during 1960–2000. His published work has been praised by rabbinic and academic scholars, across denominations and study areas, as an important contribution to current issues in Jewish life and thought.

"Mr. Lippman Bodoff is a writer on Jewish themes who consistently raises interesting questions and thought provoking answers. I have no doubt that his essays will be of great interest to those wishing to learn and think more about Judaism, it's spirituality and sacred texts."

— *Rabbi Professor Jonathan Sacks*
Chief Rabbi of England and the Commonwealth

"In this volume, an impressive number of Bodoff's published essays demonstrate the author's mastery of the diverse sources of Jewish learning, from the most ancient through the most contemporary.

I have no doubt that the current volume will prove worthy of the reader's time and attention, and widen the circle of Mr. Bodoff's admirers."

— *Norman Lamm*
Chancellor and Past President, Yeshiva University;
Author, *Contemporary Orthodox Judaism's Response to Modernity*

"Your essay [on 'Was Yehudah Halevi Racist?'] is a masterpiece. I have already recommended it to the rabbi of my synagogue."

— *Emanuel Rackman*
Chancellor, Bar-Ilan University